HPCR MANUAL ON INTERNATIONAL LAW APPLICABLE TO AIR AND MISSILE WARFARE

The *HPCR Manual on International Law Applicable to Air and Missile Warfare* provides the most up-to-date restatement of existing international law applicable to the conduct of air and missile warfare. The *HPCR Manual* and its associated rule-by-rule Commentary are the results of a six-year endeavor led by the Program on Humanitarian Policy and Conflict Research (HPCR) at Harvard University, during which it convened an international group of renowned legal experts and practitioners to reflect on the current legal framework regulating air and missile warfare from various sources of international law. Through the publication of the *HPCR Manual* and its associated Commentary, HPCR hopes that legal advisors and military officers will benefit from an in-depth presentation – and interpretation – of international law applicable to military operations involving air and missile warfare. As a result, it is expected that a greater clarity of the law will enhance the protection of civilians in armed conflict.

The Program on Humanitarian Policy and Conflict Research (HPCR) at Harvard University is a research and policy center focusing on international humanitarian law and the protection of civilians in situations of armed conflict. The Program was established in 2000 as a collaborative effort between the Swiss government, the United Nations, and Harvard University. HPCR aims to provide legal and policy expertise in the development of cogent tools and methods to enhance the capabilities of professionals and agencies engaged in the implementation and monitoring of international humanitarian law.

HPCR

MANUAL ON INTERNATIONAL LAW APPLICABLE TO AIR AND MISSILE WARFARE

Produced By
The Program on Humanitarian Policy and Conflict Research at Harvard University

CAMBRIDGE
UNIVERSITY PRESS

CAMBRIDGE
UNIVERSITY PRESS

32 Avenue of the Americas, New York NY 10013-2473, USA

Cambridge University Press is part of the University of Cambridge.

It furthers the University's mission by disseminating knowledge in the pursuit of education, learning, and research at the highest international levels of excellence.

www.cambridge.org
Information on this title: www.cambridge.org/9781107625686

First published 2013
Reprinted 2013

A catalog record for this publication is available from the British Library.

Library of Congress Cataloging in Publication data
HPCR Manual on international law applicable to air and missile warfare / Program on Humanitarian Policy and Conflict Research at Harvard University.
pages cm
Includes bibliographical references and index.
ISBN 978-1-107-03419-8 (hardback : alk. paper) – ISBN 978-1-107-62568-6 (pbk. : alk. paper)
1. Air warfare (International law) 2. Humanitarian law. I. Harvard School of Public Health. Program on Humanitarian Policy and Conflict Research. II. Title: Manual on international law applicable to air and missile warfare.
KZ6680.H68 2013
341.6´3–dc23 2013001697

ISBN 978-1-107-03419-8 Hardback
ISBN 978-1-107-62568-6 Paperback

CONTENTS

FOREWORD

It is my pleasure and honor to present the *HPCR Manual on International Law Applicable to Air and Missile Warfare* and its *Commentary*. The *HPCR Manual* provides the most up-to-date restatement of existing international law applicable to air and missile warfare, as elaborated by an international Group of Experts. As an authoritative restatement, the *HPCR Manual* contributes to the practical understanding of this important international legal framework.

The *HPCR Manual* and its *Commentary* are the results of a six-year-long endeavor led by the Program on Humanitarian Policy and Conflict Research at Harvard University (HPCR), during which it convened an international Group of Experts to reflect on the existing rules of international law applicable to air and missile warfare. This Group of Experts, under the guidance of HPCR Senior Academic Advisor, Professor Dr. Yoram Dinstein, has conducted, since 2004, a methodical and comprehensive reflection on international legal rules applicable to air and missile warfare, drawing from various sources of international law. The Black-Letter Rules of the *HPCR Manual* were adopted by consensus by the Group of Experts in Bern, Switzerland, on 15 May 2009. The *Commentary* on the Black-Letter Rules was drafted by selected experts from the original group, under the supervision of Professor Dinstein and HPCR Project Coordinator, Bruno Demeyere. While the *HPCR Manual* restates current applicable law, the *Commentary* clarifies the prominent legal interpretations and indicates differing perspectives.

We would like, first and foremost, to acknowledge the remarkable role of Professor Yoram Dinstein throughout this process. His internationally recognized expertise and analytical engagement have been instrumental in maintaining the momentum and authority of this initiative over the years. Members of the Group of Experts (please see Appendix I for the full list) have individually made important contributions to each step of the process by studying a particular area of the law of air operations and by providing comments on the overall exercise. We would like to recognize, particularly, the members of the Drafting Committee (please see Appendix IV), who have invested countless hours in summarizing the various interpretations of the Black-Letter Rules discussed among the experts. HPCR Project Coordinator Bruno Demeyere managed this process in an adept and diligent manner that was much appreciated by his colleagues.

As ever, this project would not have been possible without the substantial financial support and generosity of its donors, primarily the Swiss Federal Department of Foreign Affairs. In addition, several governments supported the convening of the Group of Experts in their various meetings, as well as regional consultations, namely Australia, Belgium, Canada, Germany, the Netherlands, and Norway. The International Society for Military Law and the Law of War also facilitated consultations with military experts at regular intervals during the project. Words of gratitude are also in order for the Fritz Thyssen Foundation and the Max Planck Institute for Comparative Public Law and International Law for their support in hosting of the Group of Experts meetings. Finally, a word of special thanks goes to Barbara Fontana, from the Political Division IV of the Swiss Federal Department of Foreign Affairs, who kept a watchful and constructive eye on this process since its inception.

Through the publication of the *HPCR Manual* and its *Commentary*, HPCR hopes that legal advisors and military officers will benefit from an in-depth presentation – and interpretation – of international law applicable to air and missile warfare. As a result, it is expected that a greater clarity of the law will enhance the protection of civilians in armed conflict.

Claude Bruderlein
Director, Program on Humanitarian Policy
and Conflict Research

INTRODUCTION

A. The Background of the Project

Following a series of informal consultations with scholars and governmental experts, the Program on Humanitarian Policy and Conflict Research at Harvard University (HPCR) launched in 2004 a multi-annual project, with a view to restating the existing law of air and missile warfare. This initiative, based on the work of renowned international legal experts, culminated in the formulation of the present *HPCR Manual on International Law Applicable to Air and Missile Warfare* (hereinafter: the *HPCR Manual*).

Some 80 years earlier, in 1923, the famous Rules of Air Warfare were informally drafted at The Hague by a Commission of Jurists (established in 1922 by the Washington Conference on the Limitation of Armament). The Hague Rules, albeit not binding, have had considerable impact on the development of the customary law of armed conflict. Still, much has happened in the intervening 80 years in air warfare, which was in its infancy when the Hague Rules were drawn up. Air power has become a central component of the military arsenal of States and plays a critical role in modern warfare. As for missiles, they were not even conceived in 1923. The exponential changes brought about in air and missile technology in the last few decades have transformed the face of the modern battlefield, revolutionized military strategy, and created a series of distinct challenges to the protection of civilians in time of armed conflict.

Over the course of the recent decades, the challenge of applying existing law to the use of aircraft and missiles in time of hostilities has amply demonstrated that there are bones of contention regarding the scope and content of the international legal rules pertaining to air and missile warfare. More recently, the use of Unmanned Aerial Vehicles – frequently referred to as "drones" – has brought even greater attention to the need for a clear understanding of the applicable legal framework.

Although, since the drafting of the 1923 Rules of Air Warfare, a number of international treaties have been adopted in response to developments in modern warfare (in particular, the four 1949 Geneva Conventions for the Protection of War Victims and the two Additional Protocols of 1977, as well as diverse conventions regarding cultural property, biological weapons, chemical weapons, etc.), it must be taken into account that (i) these instruments, although containing rules relevant to air and missile warfare, do not address a number of important aspects of air and missile operations; and (ii) while the Geneva Conventions are universal in their scope of application, other instruments (especially AP/I) are not binding on all States: non-Contracting States (primarily the United States) explicitly contest some of their rules. It is for that reason that the Commentary on the *HPCR Manual* has endeavored to identify US practices and positions which are consistent with the rules of AP/I.

It is important to bear in mind that the current daunting challenges to the law of air and missile warfare are not derived merely from the rapid pace of development of new technologies. There is also an urgent need to confront new methods of warfare (however gruesome), introduced by international terrorism. At least since 11 September 2001, the law of armed conflict has been forced to consider, e.g., the use of a hijacked civilian airliner as a weapon (*cf.* Rule 63 (b) of this Manual).

The lack of a contemporary methodical restatement of the law regulating air and missile warfare has become particularly glaring in light of the successful effort to restate the law applicable to sea warfare, culminating in the *San Remo Manual on International Law Applicable to Armed Conflicts at Sea* (published by the International Institute of Humanitarian Law in 1995). Most of the rules of the *San Remo Manual*, while non-binding, have gained over time extended support from leading maritime powers. The *San Remo Manual* covers – to some extent – aerial elements of naval warfare, which are mentioned in the Commentary on the *HPCR Manual*. But, naturally, this was not the main thrust of the San Remo text.

The present project uses the *San Remo Manual* as a model. Like the *San Remo Manual*, the *HPCR Manual* must not be confused with a draft treaty, prepared as the groundwork for a future diplomatic conference. The goal is rather to present a methodical restatement of existing international law on air and missile warfare, based on the general practice of States accepted as law (*opinio juris*) and treaties in force. No attempt has been made to be innovative or to propose new norms (*lex ferenda*), however desirable this may appear to be: the sole aim of this project has been to systematically capture in the text existing rules of international law (*lex lata*). Since the authors of the *HPCR Manual* have no power to legislate, it is freely acknowledged that the emerging restatement must be evaluated not on the basis of logic, expediency, or policy considerations. The only test is whether the text of the *HPCR Manual* is an accurate mirror-image of existing international law. For its part, existing international law is presented with no attempt to conceal any blemishes or inadequacies.

All too frequently, due to the immense proliferation of international law – and the inability of any single expert to be familiar in detail with all its divergent branches – there is a growing tendency of overspecialization in the field. In the preparation of the *HPCR Manual*, it was deemed indispensable to tie together separate strands of the law, going beyond the strict law of armed conflict to incorporate norms of air law (the Chicago Convention of 1944 and its subsequent annexes), maritime law (the 1982 UN Convention on the Law of the Sea), etc., insofar as they are relevant to air and missile operations.

B. The Process

The genesis of the present project was in the first Informal High-Level Expert Meeting on Current Challenges to International Humanitarian Law (so-called Alabama 1 meeting), co-organized by HPCR and the Swiss Federal Department of Foreign Affairs in January 2003. A key recommendation of government representatives at the meeting focused on the importance of addressing potential gaps in the present law of armed conflict applicable to high-tech warfare. The theme of air and missile warfare was identified as a high-priority area for the restatement of existing international law. HPCR emerged as the facilitator of this new project (directed by Professor Yoram Dinstein as Program Advisor).

Following consultations with key governments and representatives of the International Committee of the Red Cross (ICRC), HPCR convened a Group of Experts, which ultimately grew to approximately 30 qualified international scholars and practitioners, including selected experts from government circles (military and civilian) and from the ICRC, all of them participating in the project in their purely personal capacity (the names of all the experts appear in Appendix I, A). Government representatives of donor countries (a roster that grew over the years to include Switzerland, Germany, Norway, Belgium, Sweden, Australia, and Canada) were also invited in their official capacity to observe the deliberations of the Group of Experts (see Appendix I, B). It ought to be made clear that the views expressed in the *HPCR Manual* do not necessarily reflect those of the governments or institutions for which some of the experts participating in the project are working.

The first meeting of the Group of Experts took place at Harvard University in January 2004, and it came up with a Plan of Action: more than 20 topics were selected and assigned to individual experts, with a view to the preparation of research papers (roughly matching the various Sections of the emerging *HPCR Manual*). It is hoped that the principal research papers will ultimately be published in a revised form: they lie at the root of the *HPCR Manual* and explain many of the decisions taken by the Group of Experts.

The Group of Experts met several times, in order to examine the research papers and debate legal issues. After thorough examination of the papers, the Group of Experts drew up a first version of the *HPCR Manual* (consisting of Black-letter Rules) in Brussels in March 2006. A final text of the Black-letter Rules of the *HPCR Manual* was adopted by the Group of Experts in Bern on 15 May 2009. A list of all sessions of the Group of Experts is produced in Appendix II.

From the onset of the project, it was perceived that – if the *HPCR Manual* is to have any impact in the world of reality – it cannot be finalized without prior consultations with governments. While HPCR did not seek the endorsement of governments for the Manual, it believes that their views as to the applicable law are indispensable to the elaboration of both the Black-Letter Rules and the Commentary. The first consultation took place when the Brussels draft Manual was presented to representatives from approximately 25 States at the Third Informal High-Level Expert Meeting on Current Challenges to International Humanitarian Law (so-called Alabama 3 meeting), held in Montreux, Switzerland, in May 2006. Participating government representatives provided many critical comments and observations. These were subsequently reviewed by the Group of Experts, leading to a considerable revision of the *HPCR Manual*.

The *HPCR Manual* (in a number of updated versions) was also submitted to a series of regional and bilateral informal meetings with State representatives (for a complete list of meetings, and States taking part in these consultations, see Appendix III). In all, most of the leading States in the sphere of air and missile warfare have been consulted. Although participation of States in any of the consultation meetings does not imply official endorsement of the specific formulation of any given Black-letter Rule of the *HPCR Manual*, it is hoped that the final text of the *HPCR Manual* will be put to actual use by their respective armed forces.

C. The Purpose of the *HPCR Manual* and Its Commentary

The *HPCR Manual* does not have a binding force, but hopefully it will serve as a valuable resource for armed forces in the development of rules of engagement, the writing of domestic military manuals, the preparation of training courses, and – above all – the actual conduct of armed forces in combat operations. In the first place, the goal is to provide armed services' lawyers – who advise military commanders, draft legal texts, and plan legal modules of military training – with a pragmatic and cogent text, assisting them in carrying out their crucial tasks. But, moreover, it is hoped that military commanders in the field will find in the *HPCR Manual* a practical tool that will make decision making easier in a real-time operational environment and that they will consult it when the need arises. In the final analysis, the possibility to consult the *HPCR Manual* ought to make the officers concerned (including, but not exclusively, individual members of aircrews) more confident of themselves at a time when decisions have to be made rapidly. If something goes wrong in a military operation, there is a regrettable tendency to appraise what happened on the basis of hindsight criteria. The objective of the *HPCR Manual* is to be of help to those who plan, approve, or execute air or missile operations before rather than after the event.

Surely, the *HPCR Manual* is designed for operational use not only by air forces but also by other segments of the armed forces in time of armed conflict, as well as by those organizations and entities mandated to monitor and report on the implementation of international law by the parties to armed conflicts. In particular, when it comes to targeting and precautions, knowledge and understanding of the law of air and missile warfare is of crucial importance not only to the commanders, air staffs, and aircrews of the attacking air powers but also to all those engaged in the protection of populations. Needless to say, it is hoped that the *HPCR Manual* will be used extensively in training and instruction courses (not only in wartime but also in peacetime), so as to familiarize prospective users with the patterns of behavior expected of them.

(i) *The Black-Letter Rules of the* HPCR Manual

The Black-letter Rules of the *HPCR Manual* are the product of the collaborative effort of the Group of Experts as a whole. In large parts, the Black-letter Rules reflect the overall consensus of the Group of Experts as to the state of the most salient elements of the existing law of international armed conflict (also known as International Humanitarian Law) bearing on air and missile warfare in 2009. Obviously, international law is not static. In time, the *HPCR Manual* may have to be revised to reflect future changes in the law.

Consensus for the purposes of the drafting of the Black-letter Rules of the *HPCR Manual* was understood to mean that no more than two participants in the Group of Experts had reservations about the language in which the Black-letter Rules are couched (caveats were then inserted in the Commentary). Whenever three or more participants in the Group of Experts objected to a given text, it was changed to meet such objections or bridge over conflicting views. In the rare instances in which compromise formulas proved beyond the reach of the Group of Experts, it was agreed to follow in the text the majority view but to give in the Commentary full exposure to the dissenting opinions.

The *HPCR Manual* is divided into 24 Sections of varying lengths, depending on the "density" of State practice and the consequent number of norms that have been consolidated in each sphere. Many Sections are divided into sub-sections of General Rules (applicable in armed conflicts across the board, including air or missile warfare) and specific Rules that are geared to air or missile operations.

It was debated in the Group of Experts whether or not to open the *HPCR Manual* with a Section enumerating the basic principles underlying the law of armed conflict. As a minimum, there are three such cardinal principles (listed by the International Court of Justice in its 1996 Advisory Opinion on the *Legality of the Threat or Use of Nuclear Weapons*, paras. 78 and 88), namely, (i) distinction (between combatants and non-combatants and between military objectives and civilian objects); (ii) the prohibition to cause unnecessary suffering to combatants; and (iii) neutrality (the prohibition of incursion by belligerent forces into neutral territory). There are other principles which may be deemed "basic," such as the Martens Clause and the limitation on the right of Belligerent Parties to choose methods or means of warfare. Ultimately, the Group of Experts decided not to include such a general Section in the *HPCR Manual*. However, most of the basic principles are, of course, incorporated in the relevant text (see, especially, Rules 2 (c), 4, and 5).

(ii) The Accompanying Commentary

Each Black-letter Rule of the *HPCR Manual* is accompanied by a Commentary that is intended to provide user-friendly explanations for both legal advisers and those who plan, approve, or execute air or missile operations on both sides of the armed conflict. The format of the Commentary is tailor-made to the requirements of the "ops" officer. Legal cites are kept to a minimum and the Commentary itself is often encapsulated in terse "bullet point" style. The rationale is that there is usually no real need to go through a legal disquisition in order to figure out what must or must not be done.

Since the success of the *HPCR Manual* is essentially contingent on its responsiveness to the needs of both legal advisers and "ops" officers in terms of clarity and relevance to realistic scenarios, the Group of Experts expressed preference for an easily accessible and comprehensible Commentary. The Commentary was formulated by a select Drafting Committee (the list of members and meetings of the Drafting Committee appears in Appendix IV). The Group of Experts as a whole frequently determined what the Commentary on specific Black-letter Rules ought to include. All participants also had an opportunity to see an earlier version of the Commentary and to critique it. Still, for obvious practical purposes, it was impossible to seek a line-by-line approval of a rather lengthy text by the entire Group of Experts. Hence, whereas the Black-letter Rules of the *HPCR Manual* reflect the views of the members of the Group of Experts, the Commentary must be seen as the sole responsibility of HPCR.

The specific goals of the Commentary are as follows:

a) Expound underlying premises in the Black-letter Rules and shed light on points that may require greater clarity.
b) Elaborate ideas mentioned *en passant* in the text, and explain decisions taken by the Group of Experts.
c) Cite treaties (a Table of Treaties cited in the Commentary appears in Appendix V) and other official instruments (such as recent military manuals), as well as relevant case law, in support of the text. There are no references to academic writings in the Commentary, it being understood that the views of scholars will be presented in full in the published research papers underpinning the *HPCR Manual*.
d) Address controversial issues not covered by the Black-letter Rules themselves.
e) Give full expression to differing positions that emerged in the deliberations of the Group of Experts about the substance of the law. The Commentary points out where compromise solutions have been worked out in order to reconcile divergent approaches.

f) Add to some Black-letter Rules an extrapolation that had originally been included in the black-letter language but was later relegated by the Group of Experts to the Commentary, as a mode of building a consensus for the black-letter phraseology (objections to the wording were often withdrawn on the understanding that a sentence or paragraph – the text of which was agreed upon – will appear in the Commentary rather than in the Black-letter Rule).
g) Indicate whether the Black-letter Rule is also applicable in non-international armed conflicts (see *infra* E of this Introduction).

D. Themes Excluded from the Manual

From the very inception of the project, it was understood that the *HPCR Manual* is designed for operational use in the conduct of hostilities (*jus in bello*). Hence, it does not cover issues of:

a) *Jus ad bellum*, especially questions of aggression, armed attack, and self-defense. A basic principle of the *jus in bello* is that it applies equally to all Belligerent Parties, irrespective of their respective standing pursuant to the *jus ad bellum*. In this context, it ought to be stressed that the *HPCR Manual* has been written without prejudice to binding decisions, adopted by the UN Security Council under Chapter VII of the UN Charter.
b) Individual penal accountability under international criminal law. In other words, the *HPCR Manual* deals with the substance of the law of armed conflict and not with its penal repercussions in terms of prosecution for war crimes (or any other crimes).
c) Implementation and enforcement of the law in the relations between States. Thus, in particular, belligerent reprisals are not dealt with.
d) There was discussion of human rights law without agreement. Most members of the Group of Experts believe that it has only minimal bearing on air and missile warfare in international armed conflicts because the law of armed conflict is *lex specialis*.

Moreover, although the original (2006) draft *HPCR Manual* dealt with issues of military operations in outer space, it was agreed to delete these Black-letter Rules from the text, in response to the vigorous recommendation of most government representatives in the Montreux meeting ("Alabama 3"). While the Group of Experts recognized the growing importance of outer space as far as reconnaissance or missile operations are concerned, it decided to abide by the view prevalent in Montreux, leaving the subject for a separate study in the future.

E. Scope of the Manual

In the Plan of Action session, the Group of Experts resolved not to address the subject matter of non-international armed conflicts. The decision met with harsh criticism in Montreux and the Group of Experts gave the matter further reflection. While accepting the Montreux desire to bring non-international armed conflicts within the framework of the *HPCR Manual*, it was impossible to ignore serious terminological difficulties implicit in the disparity between the Parties to the conflict. Terms such as "Belligerent Parties," "enemy," "Neutral," and even "combatants" are overtly inappropriate for usage in non-international armed conflicts. Instead of employing imprecise generic terms for both types of armed conflict, the Group of Experts arrived at the conclusion that it would be better to confine the Black-letter Rules to international armed conflicts, yet in the Commentary on every Black-letter Rule to indicate clearly whether it is specifically applicable also to non-international armed conflicts. Where this is not the case, the Commentary explains whether the Black-letter Rule is totally irrelevant to non-international armed conflicts or is applicable to them in a different fashion.

F. Terminology

As far as possible, the *HPCR Manual* uses consistent terminology throughout the Black-letter Rules. Where necessary, it is advisable to consult Rule 1 (Definitions) as a guide for the meaning of expressions employed elsewhere in the text. Definitions apart, certain linguistic usages may require an explanation:

a) The Group of Experts decided to avoid in the Black-letter Rules some popular terms that are apt to cause confusion (e.g., "dual-use facilities" and "information warfare").
b) Whenever the word "presumption" appears in the text, it is understood that the presumption is rebuttable.
c) The *HPCR Manual* generally avoids use of the term "shall," inasmuch as the Group of Experts wished to emphasize that the present Manual is a restatement of existing law and is not – by itself – the source of binding legal norms. Hence, when mandatory language (indicating

the existence of an international legal obligation) is called for, the expressions used are either "must" or "have (has) to." When the Group of Experts wanted to denote that a certain conduct is desirable albeit not obligatory, this is connoted by the words "ought to." The phrase "should" has been reserved to convey the message that there was a certain disagreement on the subject within the Group of Experts: some participants thinking that an obligation does exist and others denying it. In the absence of a consensus, it was felt best to signify through the word "should" that the existence of an obligation is cast in doubt.

d) The Commentary uses extensively abbreviations for names of treaties (e.g., GC/I), courts (e.g., ICJ), and common expressions (e.g., POW). A list of all abbreviations is appended herewith (Appendix VI).

BLACK-LETTER RULES OF THE HPCR MANUAL ON INTERNATIONAL LAW APPLICABLE TO AIR AND MISSILE WARFARE

Adopted by the Group of Experts in Bern, Switzerland, on 15 May 2009.

Section A: Definitions

1. For the purposes of this Manual –

(a) "Air" or "airspace" means the air up to the highest altitude at which an aircraft can fly and below the lowest possible perigee of an earth satellite in orbit. Under international law, airspace is classified as either national airspace (that over the land, internal waters, archipelagic waters, and territorial seas of any State) or international airspace (that over contiguous zones, exclusive economic zones, the high seas, and territory not subject to the sovereignty of any State).

(b) "Air or missile operations" mean military operations in armed conflict involving the use of aircraft or missiles of all types; whether in offence or defence; and whether or not over the territory of one of the Belligerent Parties.

(c) "Air or missile combat operations" mean air or missile operations designed to injure, kill, destroy, damage, capture or neutralize targets, the support of such operations, or active defence against them.

(d) "Aircraft" means any vehicle – whether manned or unmanned – that can derive support in the atmosphere from the reactions of the air (other than the reactions of the air against the earth's surface), including vehicles with either fixed or rotary wings.

(e) "Attack" means an act of violence, whether in offence or in defence.

(f) "Belligerent Party" means a State Party to an international armed conflict.

(g) "Cartel aircraft" means an aircraft granted safe conduct by agreement between the Belligerent Parties for the purpose of performing a specific function, such as the transport of prisoners of war or parlementaires.

(h) "Civilian aircraft" means any aircraft other than military or other State aircraft.

(i) "Civilian airliner" means a civilian aircraft identifiable as such and engaged in carrying civilian passengers in scheduled or non-scheduled service.

(j) "Civilian objects" mean all objects which are not military objectives, as defined in Rule 1 (y).

(k) "Civil defence" means the performance of some or all of the humanitarian tasks mentioned below, intended to protect the civilian population against the dangers, and to help it to recover from the immediate effects, of hostilities or disasters and also to provide the conditions necessary for its survival. These tasks are: (i) warning; (ii) evacuation; (iii) management of shelters; (iv) management of blackout measures; (v) rescue; (vi) medical services, including first aid, and religious assistance; (vii) fire-fighting; (viii) detection and marking of danger areas; (ix) decontamination and similar protective measures; (x) provision of emergency accommodation and supplies; (xi) emergency assistance in the restoration and maintenance of order in distressed areas; (xii) emergency repair of indispensable public utilities; (xiii) emergency disposal of the dead; (xiv) assistance in the preservation of objects essential for survival; (xv) complementary activities necessary to carry out any of the tasks mentioned above, including, but not limited to, planning and organization.

(l) "Collateral damage" means incidental loss of civilian life, injury to civilians and damage to civilian objects or other protected objects or a combination thereof, caused by an attack on a lawful target.

(m) "Computer network attack" means operations to manipulate, disrupt, deny, degrade, or destroy information resident in computers and computer networks, or the computer network itself, or to gain control over the computer or computer network.

(n) "Contraband" means goods which are ultimately destined for territory under the control of an enemy Belligerent Party and which are susceptible for use in international armed conflict.

(o) "Cultural property" means, irrespective of origin or ownership:
(i) Movable or immovable property of great importance to the cultural heritage of every people, such as monuments of architecture, art or history, whether religious or secular; archaeological sites; groups of buildings which, as a whole, are of historical or artistic interest; works of art; manuscripts, books and other objects of artistic, historical or archaeological interest; as well as scientific collections and important collections of books or archives or of reproductions of the property defined above;

(ii) Buildings whose main and effective purpose is to preserve or exhibit the movable cultural property defined in sub-paragraph (i) such as museums, large libraries and depositories of archives, and refuges intended to shelter, in the event of armed conflict, the movable cultural property defined in sub-paragraph (i);

(iii) Centres containing a large amount of cultural property as defined in sub-paragraphs (i) and (ii).

(p) "Electronic warfare" means any military action involving the use of electromagnetic and directed energy to control the electromagnetic spectrum or to attack the enemy.

(q) "Feasible" means that which is practicable or practically possible, taking into account all circumstances prevailing at the time, including humanitarian and military considerations.

(r) "International armed conflict" means an armed conflict between two or more States.

(s) "Law of international armed conflict" means all the principles and rules of treaty and customary international law binding on a State and governing armed conflict between States; the term "law of international armed conflict" is synonymous with "international humanitarian law relating to international armed conflict".

(t) "Means of warfare" mean weapons, weapon systems or platforms employed for the purposes of attack.

(u) "Medical aircraft" means any aircraft permanently or temporarily assigned – by the competent authorities of a Belligerent Party – exclusively to aerial transportation or treatment of wounded, sick, or shipwrecked persons, and/or the transport of medical personnel and medical equipment or supplies.

(v) "Methods of warfare" mean attacks and other activities designed to adversely affect the enemy's military operations or military capacity, as distinct from the means of warfare used during military operations, such as weapons. In military terms, methods of warfare consist of the various general categories of operations, such as bombing, as well as the specific tactics used for attack, such as high altitude bombing.

(w) "Military advantage" means those benefits of a military nature that result from an attack. They relate to the attack considered as whole and not merely to isolated or particular parts of the attack.

(x) "Military aircraft" means any aircraft (i) operated by the armed forces of a State; (ii) bearing the military markings of that State; (iii) commanded by a member of the armed forces; and (iv) controlled, manned or preprogrammed by a crew subject to regular armed forces discipline.

(y) "Military objectives", as far as objects are concerned, are those objects which by their nature, location, purpose or use, make an effective contribution to military action and whose total or partial destruction, capture or neutralization, in the circumstances ruling at the time, offers a definite military advantage.

(z) "Missiles" mean self-propelled unmanned weapons – launched from aircraft, warships or land-based launchers – that are either guided or ballistic.

(aa) "Neutral" means a State not a Belligerent Party in an international armed conflict.

(bb) "Precision guided weapons" mean weapons that can be directed against a target using either external guidance or a guidance system of their own.

(cc) "State aircraft" means any aircraft owned or used by a State serving exclusively non-commercial government functions.

(dd) "Unmanned Aerial Vehicle (UAV)" means an unmanned aircraft of any size which does not carry a weapon and which cannot control a weapon.

(ee) "Unmanned Combat Aerial Vehicle (UCAV)" means an unmanned military aircraft of any size which carries and launches a weapon, or which can use on-board technology to direct such a weapon to a target.

(ff) "Weapon" means a means of warfare used in combat operations, including a gun, missile, bomb or other munitions, that is capable of causing either (i) injury to, or death of, persons; or (ii) damage to, or destruction of, objects.

Section B:
General Framework

2. (a) The objective of this Manual is to produce a restatement of existing law applicable to air or missile operations in international armed conflict. This is without prejudice to the possible application of some of the Rules in this Manual to non-international armed conflicts (for details, see the Commentary).

(b) Nothing in this Manual affects existing obligations of States under treaties to which they are Contracting Parties.

(c) In cases not covered by this Manual, civilians and combatants remain under the protection and authority of the principles of international law derived from established custom, from the principles of humanity and from the dictates of public conscience.

3. (a) Subject to binding decisions adopted by the Security Council under Chapter VII of the Charter of the United Nations, the Rules reflected in this Manual also apply to all air or missile operations conducted by United Nations forces when in situations of armed conflict they are engaged therein as combatants, to the extent and for the duration of their engagement.

(b) The Rules reflected in this Manual also apply to armed conflicts involving any other international governmental organization, global or regional.

4. The fundamental principle is that, in any armed conflict, the right of the Belligerent Parties to choose methods or means of warfare is not unlimited.

Section C:
Weapons

5. Weapons used in air and missile warfare must comply with:

(a) The basic principle of distinction between civilians and combatants and between civilian objects and military objectives.

Consequently, it is prohibited to conduct air or missile combat operations which employ weapons that (i) cannot be directed at a specific lawful target and therefore are of a nature to strike lawful targets and civilians or civilian objects without distinction; or

(ii) the effects of which cannot be limited as required by the law of international armed conflict and which therefore are of a nature to strike lawful targets and civilians or civilian objects without distinction;

(b) The prohibition of unnecessary suffering or superfluous injury.

Consequently, it is prohibited to conduct air or missile combat operations which employ weapons that are calculated, or of a nature, to cause unnecessary suffering or superfluous injury to combatants.

6. Specific weapons are prohibited in air or missile combat operations. These include:

(a) Biological, including bacteriological, weapons.

(b) Chemical weapons.

(c) Laser weapons specifically designed, as their sole combat function or as one of their combat functions, to cause permanent blindness to unenhanced vision, that is to the naked eye or to the eye with corrective eyesight devices.

(d) Poison, poisoned substances and poisoned weapons.

(e) Small arms projectiles calculated, or of a nature, to cause explosion on impact with or within the human body.

(f) Weapons the primary effect of which is to injure by fragments which in the human body escape detection by x-ray.

7. The use of any weapon not expressly mentioned under this Section of the Manual is subject to the general rules and principles of customary and treaty law of international armed conflict (in particular the principle of distinction and the prohibition of unnecessary suffering), as well as to any other treaty law applicable for Contracting Parties.

8. There is no specific obligation on Belligerent Parties to use precision guided weapons. There may however be situations in which the prohibition of indiscriminate attacks, or the obligation to avoid – or, -in any event, minimize – collateral damage, cannot be fulfilled without using precision guided weapons.

9. States are obligated to assess the legality of weapons before fielding them in order to determine whether their employment would, in some or all circumstances, be prohibited.

Section D: Attacks

I. General rules

10. (a) In accordance with the basic principle of distinction, attacks must be confined to lawful targets.

(b) Lawful targets are:
(i) Combatants;

(ii) Military objectives (as defined in Rules 1 (y) and 22);

(iii) Civilians directly participating in hostilities (see section F of this Manual).

11. Attacks directed against civilians or civilian objects are prohibited.

12. (a) In case of doubt as to whether a person is a civilian, that person shall be considered a civilian.

(b) In case of doubt as to whether an object which is ordinarily dedicated to civilian purposes is being used for military purposes, it may only be attacked if, based on all the information reasonably available to the commander at the time, there are reasonable grounds to believe that it has become and remains a military objective.

13. (a) Indiscriminate attacks are prohibited.

(b) Indiscriminate attacks are those that cannot be or are not directed against lawful targets (as defined in Rule 10 (b)) or the effects of which cannot be limited as required by the law of international armed conflict, and which therefore are of a nature to strike lawful targets and civilians or civilian objects without distinction.

(c) Attacks must not treat as a single lawful target a number of clearly separated and distinct lawful targets located in a city, town, village or area containing a similar concentration of civilians or civilian objects.

14. An attack that may be expected to cause collateral damage which would be excessive in relation to the concrete and direct military advantage anticipated is prohibited.

15. (a) It is prohibited to order that there shall be no survivors in combat operations, to threaten an adversary therewith, or to conduct hostilities on that basis.

(b) Persons who are *hors de combat* – either because they have clearly expressed an intention to surrender or as a result of sickness, wounds or shipwreck – must not be attacked, provided that they abstain from any hostile act and no attempt is made to evade capture.

16. (a) At all times, and particularly after an engagement, Belligerent Parties must, without delay, take all possible measures to search for and collect the wounded, sick and shipwrecked, to protect them against pillage and ill-treatment, and to search for the dead and prevent their being despoiled.

(b) The wounded, sick and shipwrecked must receive, to the fullest extent practicable and with the least possible delay, the medical care and attention required by their condition. No distinction may be made among them founded on any grounds other than medical ones.

II. Specifics of air or missile operations

17. (a) Only military aircraft, including UCAVs, are entitled to engage in attacks.

(b) The same Rule applies to the exercise of other belligerent rights, such as interception.

18. Acts or threats of violence in the course of air or missile operations cannot be pursued for the sole or primary purpose of spreading terror among the civilian population.

19. Belligerent Parties conducting, or subject to, air or missile operations:

(a) Must take all possible measures to search for and collect the wounded, sick and shipwrecked, ensure their adequate care, permit their removal, exchange and transport, and search for the dead;

(b) Must, whenever circumstances permit, arrange cease-fires, if necessary through a neutral intermediary, to facilitate the activities described in paragraph (a);

(c) Ought to accept the assistance of impartial humanitarian organizations and facilitate their work in favour of the wounded and other victims of air or missile attacks.

20. Air or missile attacks must be conducted in accordance with those feasible precautions required under Section G of this Manual designed to avoid – or, in any event, minimize – collateral damage.

21. The application of the general Rules prohibiting attacks directed against civilians or civilian objects, as well as indiscriminate attacks, is confined to air or missile attacks that entail violent effects, namely, acts resulting in death, injury, damage or destruction.

Section E:
Military Objectives

I. General rules

22. In the definition of objects as military objectives (see Rule 1 (y)), the following criteria apply:

(a) The "nature" of an object symbolizes its fundamental character. Examples of military objectives by nature include military aircraft (including military UAV/UCAVs); military vehicles (other than medical transport); missiles and other weapons; military equipment; military fortifications, facilities and depots; warships; ministries of defence and armaments factories.

(b) Application of the "location" criterion can result in specific areas of land such as a mountain pass, a bridgehead or jungle trail becoming military objectives.

(c) The "purpose" of an object – although not military by nature – is concerned with the intended future use of an object.

(d) The "use" of an object relates to its present function, with the result that a civilian object can become a military objective due to its use by armed forces.

23. Objects which may qualify as military objectives through the definition in Rules 1 (y) and 22 (a) include, but are not limited to, factories,

lines and means of communications (such as airfields, railway lines, roads, bridges and tunnels); energy producing facilities; oil storage depots; transmission facilities and equipment.

24. The connection between a military objective and military action may be direct or indirect.

II. Specifics of air or missile operations

25. Aircraft may be the object of attack only if they constitute military objectives.

26. All enemy military aircraft constitute military objectives, unless protected under Section L of this Manual, or as otherwise agreed by the Belligerent Parties under Section N (V).

27. Without prejudice to Sections I, J and L of this Manual, the following activities may render any other enemy aircraft a military objective:

(a) Engaging in hostile actions in support of the enemy, e.g. intercepting or attacking other aircraft; attacking persons or objects on land or sea; being used as a means of attack; engaging in electronic warfare; or providing targeting information to enemy forces.

(b) Facilitating the military actions of the enemy's armed forces, e.g., transporting troops, carrying military materials, or refuelling military aircraft.

(c) Being incorporated into or assisting the enemy's intelligence gathering system, e.g., engaging in reconnaissance, early warning, surveillance or command, control and communications missions.

(d) Refusing to comply with the orders of military authorities, including instructions for landing, inspection and possible capture, or clearly resisting interception.

(e) Otherwise making an effective contribution to military action.

Section F:
Direct Participation in Hostilities

28. Civilians lose their protection from attack if and for such time as they take a direct part in hostilities.

29. Subject to the circumstances ruling at the time, the following activities are examples of what may constitute taking a direct part in hostilities:

(a) Defending of military objectives against enemy attacks.

(b) Issuing orders and directives to forces engaged in hostilities; making decisions on operational/tactical deployments; and participating in targeting decision-making.

(c) Engaging in electronic warfare or computer network attacks targeting military objectives, combatants or civilians directly participating in hostilities, or which is intended to cause death or injury to civilians or damage to or destruction of civilian objects.

(d) Participation in target acquisition.

(e) Engaging in mission planning of an air or missile attack.

(f) Operating or controlling weapon systems or weapons in air or missile combat operations, including remote control of UAVs and UCAVs.

(g) Employing military communications networks and facilities to support specific air or missile combat operations.

(h) Refueling, be it on the ground or in the air, of a military aircraft which is about to engage in, or which is engaged in, air or missile combat operations.

(i) Loading ordnance or mission-essential equipment onto a military aircraft which is about to engage in, or which is engaged in, air or missile combat operations.

(j) Servicing or repairing of a military aircraft which is about to engage in, or which is engaged in, air or missile combat operations.

(k) Loading mission control data to military aircraft/missile software systems.

(l) Combat training of aircrews, air technicians and others for specific requirements of a particular air or missile combat operation.

Section G:
Precautions in Attacks

I. General rules

30. Constant care must be taken to spare the civilian population, civilians and civilian objects.

31. All feasible precautions must be taken to spare all persons and objects entitled to specific protection under Sections K, L, M and N of this Manual.

32. Constant care includes in particular the following precautions:

(a) Doing everything feasible to verify, based on information reasonably available, that a target is a lawful target and does not benefit from specific protection;

(b) Doing everything feasible to choose means and methods of warfare with a view to avoiding – or, in any event, minimizing – collateral damage; and

(c) Doing everything feasible to determine whether the collateral damage to be expected from the attack will be excessive in relation to the concrete and direct military advantage anticipated.

33. When a choice is possible between several military objectives for obtaining a similar military advantage, the objective to be selected must be the one where the attack may be expected to cause the least danger to civilian lives and to civilian objects, or to other protected persons and objects.

II. Specifics of air or missile operations

34. Constant care must be taken by all those involved in planning, ordering and executing air or missile combat operations to spare the civilian population, civilians and civilian objects.

35. In carrying out air or missile combat operations, an attack must be cancelled or suspended if it becomes apparent:

(a) That the target is not a lawful target; or

(b) That the target is and remains entitled to specific protection in accordance with Sections K, L, M and N of this Manual; or

(c) That the expected collateral damage is excessive in relation to the concrete and direct military advantage anticipated.

36. In order to avoid the release of dangerous forces and consequent severe losses among the civilian population, particular care must be taken if works and installations containing dangerous forces, namely dams, dykes and nuclear electrical generating stations (as well as installations located in their vicinity) are attacked.

37. When the attack of a lawful target by air or missile combat operations may result in death or injury to civilians, effective advance warnings must be issued to the civilian population, unless circumstances do not permit. This may be done, for instance, through dropping leaflets or broadcasting the warnings. Such warnings ought to be as specific as circumstances permit.

38. Effective advance warnings must also be given before attacking persons and objects entitled to specific protection under Section K, L and N (I and II), as provided for in these Sections, as well as under Section J.

39. The obligation to take feasible precautions in attack applies equally to UAV/UCAV operations.

III. Specifics of attacks directed at aircraft in the air

40. Before an aircraft is attacked in the air, all feasible precautions must be taken to verify that it constitutes a military objective. Verification ought to use the best means available under the prevailing circumstances, having regard to the immediacy of any potential threat. Factors relevant to verification may include:

(a) Visual identification.

(b) Responses to oral warnings over radio.

(c) Infrared signature.

(d) Radar signature.

(e) Electronic signature.

(f) Identification modes and codes.

(g) Number and formation of aircraft.

(h) Altitude, speed, track, profile and other flight characteristics.

(i) Pre-flight and in-flight air traffic control information regarding possible flights.

41. Belligerent Parties and Neutrals providing air traffic control service ought to establish procedures whereby military commanders – including commanders of military aircraft – are informed on a continuous basis of designated routes assigned to, and flight plans filed by, civilian aircraft in the area of hostilities (including information on communication channels, identification modes and codes, destination, passengers and cargo).

Section H:
Precautions by the Belligerent Party Subject to Attack

42. Belligerent Parties subject to air or missile attacks must, to the maximum extent feasible, avoid locating military objectives within or near densely populated areas, hospitals, cultural property, places of worship, prisoner of war camps, and other facilities which are entitled to specific protection as per Sections K, L and N (II).

43. Belligerent Parties subject to air or missile attacks must, to the maximum extent feasible, endeavour to remove the civilian population, individual civilians and other protected persons and objects under their control from the vicinity of military objectives.

44. Belligerent Parties subject to air or missile attacks must, to the maximum extent feasible, take necessary precautions to protect the civilian population, individual civilians and civilian objects under their control against the dangers resulting from military operations.

45. Belligerent Parties actually or potentially subject to air or missile operations must not use the presence or movements of the civilian population or individual civilians to render certain points or areas immune from air or missile operations, in particular they must not attempt to shield lawful targets from attacks or to shield, favour or impede military operations. Belligerent Parties must not direct the movement of the civilian population or individual civilians in order to attempt to shield lawful targets from attacks or to shield military operations.

46. Both the Belligerent Party launching an air or missile attack and the Belligerent Party subject to such an attack have obligations to take

precautions. Nevertheless, the latter's failure to take precautionary measures does not relieve the Belligerent Party launching an air or missile attack of its obligation to take feasible precautions.

Section I:
Protection of Civilian Aircraft

I. General rules

47. (a) Civilian aircraft, whether enemy or neutral, are civilian objects and as such are entitled to protection from attack.

(b) Civilian aircraft can be the object of attack only if they constitute military objectives.

48. (a) All enemy civilian and State aircraft other than military aircraft may be intercepted, inspected or diverted in accordance with Section U.

(b) Neutral civilian aircraft may be intercepted, inspected or diverted in accordance with Section U.

II. Enemy civilian aircraft

49. Enemy civilian aircraft are liable to capture as prize in accordance with Rule 134.

50. Subject to the specific protection of Sections K and L of this Manual, enemy civilian aircraft are liable to attack if engaged in any of the activities set forth in Rule 27.

III. Neutral civilian aircraft

51. Neutral civilian aircraft are liable to capture as prize if engaged in any of the activities enumerated in Rule 140 and if the requirements of Rule 142 are met.

52. Neutral civilian aircraft may not be attacked unless they are engaged in any of the activities enumerated in Rule 174.

IV. Safety in flight

53. (a) In order to enhance their safety whenever in the vicinity of hostilities, civilian aircraft must file with the relevant air

traffic control service required flight plans, which will include information as regards, e.g., registration, destination, passengers, cargo, identification codes and modes (including updates en route).

(b) Civilian aircraft ought not to deviate from a designated air traffic service route or flight plan without air traffic control clearance unless unforeseen conditions arise, e.g., safety or distress, in which case appropriate notification ought to be made immediately.

54. Civilian aircraft ought to avoid areas of potentially hazardous military operations. In the vicinity of hostilities, civilian aircraft must comply with instructions from the military forces regarding their heading and altitude.

55. Whenever feasible, a Notice to Airmen (NOTAM) ought to be issued by Belligerent Parties, providing information on military operations hazardous to civilian or other protected aircraft and which are taking place in given areas including on the activation of temporary airspace restrictions. A NOTAM ought to include information on the following:

(a) Frequencies upon which the aircraft ought to maintain a continuous listening watch.

(b) Continuous operation of civilian weather-avoidance radar and identification modes and codes.

(c) Altitude, course and speed restrictions.

(d) Procedures to respond to radio contact by the military forces and to establish two-way communications.

(e) Possible action by the military forces if the NOTAM is not complied with and if the civilian or other protected aircraft is perceived by those military forces to be a threat.

56. If a civilian or other protected aircraft enters an area of potentially hazardous military activity, it must comply with a relevant NOTAM.

57. In the absence of a NOTAM (and, whenever feasible, in case of non-compliance with a NOTAM) military forces concerned ought to use all available means to warn the civilian or other protected

aircraft – through radio communication or any other established procedures – before taking any action against it.

Section J:
Protection of Particular Types of Aircraft

I. Civilian airliners

58. Civilian airliners are civilian objects which are entitled to particular care in terms of precautions.

59. In case of doubt, civilian airliners – either in flight or on the ground in a civilian airport – are presumed not to be making an effective contribution to military action.

60. While civilian airliners (whether enemy or neutral) ought to avoid entering a no-fly or an "exclusion zone", or the immediate vicinity of hostilities, they do not lose their protection merely because they enter such areas.

61. Any civilian airliner suspected on reasonable grounds of carrying contraband or otherwise being engaged in activities inconsistent with its status is subject to inspection by a Belligerent Party in an airfield that is safe for this type of aircraft and reasonably accessible.

62. Enemy civilian airliners may be captured as prize but only on condition that all passengers and crews are safely deplaned and the papers of the aircraft are preserved.

63. Subject to Rule 68, activities such as any of the following may render a civilian airliner a military objective:

(a) Being on the ground in a military airfield of the enemy in circumstances which make that aircraft a military objective.

(b) Engaging in hostile actions in support of the enemy, e.g. intercepting or attacking other aircraft; attacking persons or objects on land or sea; being used as a means of attack; engaging in electronic warfare; or providing targeting information to enemy forces.

(c) Facilitating the military actions of the enemy's armed forces, e.g. transporting troops, carrying military materials, or refuelling military aircraft.

(d) Being incorporated into or assisting the enemy's intelligence gathering system, e.g., engaging in reconnaissance, early warning, surveillance or command, control and communications missions.

(e) Refusing to comply with the orders of military authorities, including instructions for landing, inspection and possible capture, or clearly resisting interception.

(f) Otherwise making an effective contribution to military action.

II. Aircraft granted safe conduct

64. Aircraft granted safe conduct by agreement between the Belligerent Parties – such as cartel aircraft – are entitled to specific protection from attack.

65. (a) Aircraft granted safe conduct lose their specific protection from attack in any one of the following instances:

(i) They do not comply with the details of the agreement, including availability for inspection and identification.

(ii) They intentionally hamper the movements of combatants and are not innocently employed in their agreed upon role.

(b) Loss of specific protection will only take place if the circumstances of non-compliance are sufficiently grave that the aircraft has become or may reasonably be assumed to be a military objective.

66. In case of doubt whether an aircraft granted safe conduct qualifies as a military objective as per Rule 27, it will be presumed not to qualify as such.

67. Aircraft granted safe conduct are exempt from capture as prize, provided that they:

(a) Are innocently employed in their normal role;

(b) Immediately submit to interception and identification when required;

(c) Do not intentionally hamper the movement of combatants and obey orders to divert from their track when required; and

(d) Are not acting in breach of a prior agreement.

III. Provisions common to civilian airliners and aircraft granted safe conduct

68. Civilian airliners and aircraft granted safe conduct may only be attacked if they have lost their protection as per Rules 63 and 65 and if the following cumulative conditions are fulfilled:

(a) Diversion for landing, inspection, and possible capture, is not feasible;

(b) No other method is available for exercising military control;

(c) The circumstances leading to the loss of protection are sufficiently grave to justify an attack; and

(d) The expected collateral damage will not be excessive in relation to the military advantage anticipated and all feasible precautions have been taken (see Section G of this Manual).

69. Any decision to attack a civilian airliner or an aircraft granted safe conduct pursuant to Rule 68 ought to be taken by an appropriate level of command.

70. In case of loss of protection pursuant to this Section, a warning must be issued – whenever circumstances permit – to the civilian airliner or the aircraft granted safe conduct in flight before any action is taken against it.

Section K: Specific Protection of Medical and Religious Personnel, Medical Units and Transports

71. Subject to Rule 74, medical and religious personnel, fixed or mobile medical units (including hospitals) and medical transports by air, land, at sea or on other waters must be respected and protected at all times, and must not be the object of attack.

72. (a) Medical and religious personnel ought to wear a water-resistant armlet bearing a distinctive emblem provided by the law of international armed conflict (the Red Cross, Red Crescent or the Red Crystal). Medical units and medical transports ought to be clearly marked with the same emblem to indicate their status as such; when appropriate, other means of identification may be employed.

(b) As far as possible, the distinctive emblem ought to be made of materials which make it recognizable by technical means of detection used in air or missile operations.

(c) The distinctive emblem and other means of identification are intended only to facilitate identification and do not, of themselves, confer protected status.

(d) The failure of medical and religious personnel, medical units and medical transports to display the distinctive emblem does not deprive them of their protected status.

73. A Belligerent Party may inform the enemy of the position of its medical units. The absence of such notification does not exempt any of the Belligerent Parties from the obligations contained in Rule 71.

74. (a) The protection to which medical and religious personnel, medical units or medical transports are entitled does not cease unless they commit or are used to commit, outside their humanitarian function, acts harmful to the enemy.

(b) For medical units or medical transports, protection may cease only after a warning has been given setting a reasonable time-limit, and after such warning has remained unheeded.

(c) The following must not be considered as acts harmful to the enemy:

(i) that the personnel of a medical unit are equipped with light individual weapons for their own defence or for that of the wounded, sick or shipwrecked in their charge.

(ii) that a medical unit is guarded by sentries or by an escort.

(iii) that portable arms and ammunition taken from the wounded and sick, and not yet handed to the proper service, are found in the medical unit.

(iv) that members of the armed forces or other combatants are in the medical unit for medical or other authorized reasons, consistent with the mission of the medical unit.

(d) Medical units must not be used to shield lawful targets from attack.

Section L:
Specific Protection of Medical Aircraft

75. A medical aircraft is entitled to specific protection from attack, subject to the Rules of this Section of the Manual.

76. (a) A medical aircraft must be clearly marked with a distinctive emblem as provided by the law of international armed conflict, i.e., the Red Cross, the Red Crescent or the Red Crystal, together with its national colours, on its lower, upper and lateral surfaces.

(b) A medical aircraft ought to use additional means of identification where appropriate.

(c) A temporary medical aircraft which cannot – either for lack of time or because of its characteristics – be marked with the distinctive emblem, ought to use the most effective means of identification available.

(d) Means of identification are intended only to facilitate identification and do not, of themselves, confer protected status.

77. In and over areas controlled by friendly forces, the specific protection of medical aircraft of a Belligerent Party is not dependent on the consent of the enemy.

78. (a) In and over areas physically controlled by the enemy, as well as in and over those parts of the contact zone which are physically controlled by friendly forces or the physical control of which is not clearly established, the protection of medical aircraft can be fully effective only by virtue of prior consent obtained from the enemy. Although, in the absence of such consent, medical aircraft in the contact zone operate at their own risk, they must nevertheless be respected once they have been identified as such.

(b) The consent of the enemy as per paragraph (a) has to be sought in advance (or immediately prior to the commencement of the operation of a medical aircraft) by a Belligerent Party employing a medical aircraft. The request for consent ought to be accompanied by a detailed flight plan (as set forth in the International Civil Aviation Organization Flight Plan form).

(c) When given, consent must be express. Consent for activities consistent with the aircraft's medical status, e.g., evacuation of

the wounded, sick or shipwrecked, and transportation of medical personnel or material, ought not to be refused, unless on reasonable grounds.

79. Any conditions of consent obtained from the enemy for the protection of a medical aircraft must be adhered to strictly.

80. (a) While flying over an area covered in Rule 78 (a), medical aircraft may be ordered to land or to alight on water to permit inspection. Medical aircraft must obey any such order.

(b) If inspection reveals that the medical aircraft has been engaged in activities consistent with its medical status, it must be authorized to continue its flight without delay.

(c) However, if the medical aircraft has engaged in activities inconsistent with its medical status, or if it has flown without or in breach of a prior agreement, then it may be seized. Its occupants must then be treated in accordance with the relevant rules of the law of international armed conflict.

(d) Any aircraft seized which had been assigned as a permanent medical aircraft may be used thereafter only as a medical aircraft.

81. A medical aircraft must not possess or employ equipment to collect or transmit intelligence harmful to the enemy. It may, however, be equipped with encrypted communications equipment intended solely for navigation, identification and communication consistent with the execution of its humanitarian mission.

82. A medical aircraft may be equipped with deflective means of defence (such as chaff or flares) and carry light individual weapons necessary to protect the aircraft, the medical personnel and the wounded, sick or shipwrecked on board. Carrying of the individual weapons of the wounded, sick or shipwrecked during their evacuation does not entail loss of protection.

83. Subject to Rule 74, a medical aircraft loses its specific protection from attack if it is engaged in acts harmful to the enemy.

84. Except by prior agreement with a Neutral, a belligerent medical aircraft must not fly over or land in the territory of that Neutral, unless it is exercising the right of transit passage through straits used for international navigation or the right of archipelagic sea lanes passage.

85. (a) Should a belligerent medical aircraft, in the absence of a prior agreement with the Neutral or in deviation from the terms of an agreement, enter the neutral airspace, either through navigational error or because of an emergency affecting the safety of the flight, it must make every effort to give notice and to identify itself. Once the aircraft is recognized as a medical aircraft by the Neutral, it must not be attacked but may be required to land for inspection. Once it has been inspected, and if it is determined in fact to be a medical aircraft, it must be allowed to resume its flight.

(b) If the inspection reveals that the aircraft is not a medical aircraft, it may be seized. Any combatants on board will be interned by the Neutral in accordance with Rule 170 (c).

86. (a) Search-and-rescue aircraft used to recover military personnel, even if they are not military aircraft, are not entitled to protection.

(b) Medical aircraft must not be used to search for the wounded, sick and shipwrecked within areas of combat operations, unless pursuant to prior consent of the enemy. If medical aircraft nevertheless operate for such purposes they do so at their own risk.

87. Without prejudice to the status of medical personnel under the relevant provisions of the law of international armed conflict, members of the crew of medical aircraft must not be captured by the enemy and must be allowed to carry out their mission.

Section M: Specific Protection of the Natural Environment

I. General rule

88. The destruction of the natural environment carried out wantonly is prohibited.

II. Specifics of air or missile operations

89. When planning and conducting air or missile operations, due regard ought to be given to the natural environment.

Section N: Specific Protection of Other Persons and Objects

I. Civil defence

90. (a) Specific protection must be provided to civil defence organizations and their personnel, whether civilian or military. They must be entitled to perform their civil defence tasks except in the case of imperative military necessity.

(b) Specific protection must also be provided to buildings and materiel used for civil defence purposes and to shelters provided for the civilian population. Objects used for civil defence purposes may not be destroyed or diverted from their proper use except by the Belligerent Party to which they belong.

91. Belligerent Parties have to endeavour to ensure that – while exclusively devoted to the performance of civil defence tasks – their civil defence organizations, personnel, buildings and materials, as well as shelters provided to the civilian population, are identified as such by the recognized international distinctive sign for civil defence and any other appropriate means of identification.

92. The protection to which civilian civil defence organizations, their personnel, buildings, shelters and materiel are entitled does not cease unless they commit or are used to commit, outside their proper tasks, acts harmful to the enemy. Protection may, however, cease only after a warning has been given setting, whenever appropriate, a reasonable time-limit, and after such warning has remained unheeded.

II. Cultural property

(i) Use of cultural property

93. (a) Belligerent Parties must refrain from any use of cultural property and its immediate surroundings, or of the appliances in use for its protection, for purposes which are likely to expose it to destruction or damage.

(b) Cultural property or its immediate surroundings may only be used for military purposes in cases where military necessity imperatively so requires. Such decision can only be implemented after the emblems identifying the object in question as cultural property have been removed.

94. Belligerent Parties ought to facilitate the identification and protection of cultural property under their control, by marking it with the internationally recognized emblem and by providing the enemy with timely and adequate information about its location. However, the absence of such measures does not deprive cultural property of its protection under the law of international armed conflict.

(ii) Attacks against cultural property

95. (a) Subject to paragraph (b) and to Rule 96, Belligerent Parties must refrain from any act of hostility directed against cultural property.

(b) Cultural property, or its immediate surroundings, may only be attacked in cases where military necessity imperatively so requires.

(c) In attacking, through air or missile attacks, military objectives in the immediate surroundings of cultural property, the Belligerent Parties must take feasible precautions to avoid damage to the cultural property (see Section G of this Manual).

96. Whenever cultural property has become a military objective, the decision to attack the object must be taken by an appropriate level of command, and with due consideration of its special character as cultural property. An effective advance warning should be given whenever circumstances permit and an attack should only be conducted if the warning remains unheeded.

III. Objects indispensable to the survival of the civilian population

97. (a) Starvation of civilians as a method of warfare is prohibited.

(b) It is prohibited to attack, destroy, remove, or render useless objects indispensable to the survival of the civilian population, such as foodstuffs, agricultural areas for the production of foodstuffs, crops, livestock, drinking water installations and supplies and irrigation works, for the specific purpose of denying the civilian population their use.

(c) The prohibitions in paragraph (b) do not apply to such of the objects covered by it as are used by the enemy:

(i) as sustenance solely for the members of its armed forces; or

(ii) if not as sustenance, then in direct support of military action, provided, however, that in no event can actions against these objects be taken which may be expected to leave the civilian population with such inadequate food or water as to cause its starvation or force its movement.

IV. UN personnel

98. (a) UN personnel must be respected and protected.

(b) Directing attacks against UN personnel is prohibited, as long as they are entitled to the protection given to civilians.

(c) Directing attacks against material, installations, units and vehicles of the UN is prohibited, unless they constitute military objectives.

V. Protection by special agreement

99. Belligerent Parties may agree at any time to protect persons or objects not otherwise covered by this Manual.

Section O:
Humanitarian Aid

I. General rules

100. (a) If the civilian population of any territory under the control of a Belligerent Party is not adequately provided with food, medical supplies, clothing, bedding, means of shelter or other supplies essential to its survival, relief actions which are humanitarian and impartial in character – and conducted without adverse distinction – should be undertaken, subject to agreement of the Parties concerned. Such agreement cannot be withheld in occupied territories.

(b) Relief actions may be undertaken either by States or by impartial humanitarian organizations such as the International Committee of the Red Cross.

101. The Parties concerned must allow and facilitate rapid and unimpeded passage of relief consignments, equipment and personnel in accordance with Rule 100, subject to technical arrangements including search.

102. (a) Humanitarian relief personnel, acting within the prescribed parameters of their mission, must be respected and protected. The protection extends to humanitarian transports, installations and goods.

(b) Each Belligerent Party in receipt of relief consignments must, to the fullest extent practicable, assist the relief personnel referred to in paragraph (a) in carrying out their relief mission. Only in case of imperative military necessity may the activities of the relief personnel be limited or their movements temporarily restricted.

II. Specifics of air or missile operations

103. Whenever circumstances permit, Belligerent Parties conducting air or missile operations ought to suspend air or missile attacks in order to permit the distribution of humanitarian assistance.

104. "Technical arrangements" as used in Rule 101 may include such matters as:

(a) Establishment of air corridors or air routes.

(b) Organization of air drops.

(c) Agreement on flight details (i.e. timing, route, landing).

(d) Search of relief supplies.

Section P: "Exclusion Zones" and No-Fly Zones

I. General rules

105. (a) A Belligerent Party is not absolved of its obligations under the law of international armed conflict by establishing "exclusion zones" or no-fly zones.

(b) Zones designated for unrestricted air or missile attacks are prohibited.

106. Nothing in this Section of the Manual ought to be deemed as derogating from the right of a Belligerent Party:

(a) to control civil aviation in the immediate vicinity of hostilities; or

(b) to take appropriate measures of force protection in the form of, e.g., the establishment of warning zones.

II. "Exclusion zones" in international airspace

107. Should a Belligerent Party establish an "exclusion zone" in international airspace:

(a) The same rules of the law of international armed conflict will apply both inside and outside the "exclusion zone".

(b) The extent, location and duration of the "exclusion zone" and the measures imposed must not exceed what is reasonably required by military necessity.

(c) The commencement, duration, location and extent of the "exclusion zone", as well as the restrictions imposed, must be appropriately notified to all concerned.

(d) The establishment of an "exclusion zone" must neither encompass nor completely bar access to the airspace of Neutrals.

(e) Due regard must be given to the lawful use by Neutrals of their Exclusive Economic Zones and continental shelf, in particular artificial islands, installations, structures and safety zones.

III. No-fly zones in belligerent airspace

108. A Belligerent Party may establish and enforce a no-fly zone in its own or in enemy national airspace.

109. The commencement, duration, location and extent of the no-fly zones must be appropriately notified to all concerned.

110. Subject to the Rules set out in Sections D and G of this Manual, aircraft entering a no-fly zone without specific permission are liable to be attacked.

Section Q:
Deception, Ruses of War and Perfidy

I. General rules

111. (a) It is prohibited to kill or injure an adversary by resort to perfidy. Acts inviting the confidence of an adversary to lead him to believe that he is entitled to, or is obliged to accord, protection under the rules of the law of international armed conflict, with the intent to betray that confidence, constitute perfidy.

(b) The following acts are examples of perfidy as per paragraph (a): feigning of civilian, neutral or other protected status.

112. Without prejudice to the rules of naval warfare, the following acts are prohibited at all times irrespective of whether or not they are perfidious:

(a) Improper use of the distinctive emblem of the Red Cross, Red Crescent or Red Crystal, or of other protective emblems, signs or signals provided for by the law of international armed conflict.

(b) Improper use of the flag of truce.

(c) Improper use by a Belligerent Party of the flags or military emblems, insignia or uniforms of the enemy.

(d) Use by a Belligerent Party of the flags or military emblems, insignia or uniforms of Neutrals.

(e) Use by a Belligerent Party of the distinctive emblem of the United Nations, except as authorized by that Organization.

113. Ruses of war are permitted. Such ruses are acts which are intended to mislead an adversary or to induce him to act recklessly but which infringe no rule of the law of international armed conflict and which do not meet the definition of perfidy in Rule 111 (a).

II. Specifics of air or missile operations

114. In air or missile combat operations, the following acts are examples of perfidy (subject to the definition in Rule 111 (a)):

(a) The feigning of the status of a protected medical aircraft, in particular by the use of the distinctive emblem or other means of identification reserved for medical aircraft.

(b) The feigning of the status of a civilian aircraft.

(c) The feigning of the status of a neutral aircraft.

(d) The feigning of another protected status.

(e) The feigning of surrender.

115. Irrespective of whether or not they are perfidious, in air or missile combat operations, the following acts are prohibited at all times:

(a) Improper use by aircraft of distress codes, signals or frequencies.

(b) Use of any aircraft other than a military aircraft as a means of attack.

116. In air or missile combat operations, the following are examples of lawful ruses of war:

(a) Mock operations.

(b) Disinformation.

(c) False military codes and false electronic, optical or acoustic means to deceive the enemy (provided that they do not consist of distress signals, do not include protected codes, and do not convey the wrong impression of surrender).

(d) Use of decoys and dummy-construction of aircraft and hangars.

(e) Use of camouflage.

117. Aircrews conducting combat operations on land or on water – outside their aircraft – must distinguish themselves from the civilian population, as required by the law of international armed conflict.

Section R: Espionage

I. *General rules*

118. Espionage consists of activities by spies. A spy is any person who, acting clandestinely or on false pretences, obtains or endeavours to obtain information of military value in territory controlled by the enemy, with the intention of communicating it to the opposing Party.

119. Acts of espionage are not prohibited under the law of international armed conflict.

120. A member of the armed forces of a Belligerent Party who gathers or attempts to gather information in a territory controlled by the enemy is not considered a spy if, while so acting, he is in the uniform of his armed forces.

121. A member of the armed forces of a Belligerent Party who falls into the power of the enemy while engaging in espionage does not have the

right to prisoner of war status and may be prosecuted for his acts before domestic courts.

122. A member of the armed forces of a Belligerent Party who, having been engaged in espionage rejoins his own forces but is subsequently captured by the enemy, may no longer be prosecuted for his previous acts of espionage.

II. Specifics of air or missile operations

123. Military aircraft on missions to gather, intercept or otherwise gain information are not to be regarded as carrying out acts of espionage.

124. The use of civilian aircraft and State aircraft other than military aircraft of a Belligerent Party, flying outside the airspace of or controlled by the enemy – in order to gather, intercept or otherwise gain information – is not to be regarded as espionage, although the aircraft may be attacked at such time as it is carrying out its information-gathering mission.

Section S:
Surrender

I. General rules

125. Enemy personnel may offer to surrender themselves (and the military equipment under their control) to a Belligerent Party.

126. It is prohibited to deny quarter to those manifesting the intent to surrender.

127. Surrender is contingent on three cumulative conditions:

(a) The intention to surrender is communicated in a clear manner to the enemy.

(b) Those offering to surrender must not engage in any further hostile acts.

(c) No attempt is made to evade capture.

II. Specifics of air or missile operations

128. Aircrews of a military aircraft wishing to surrender ought to do everything feasible to express clearly their intention to do so. In

particular, they ought to communicate their intention on a common radio channel such as a distress frequency.

129. A Belligerent Party may insist on the surrender by an enemy military aircraft being effected in a prescribed mode, reasonable in the circumstances. Failure to follow any such instructions may render the aircraft and the aircrew liable to attack.

130. Aircrews of military aircraft wishing to surrender may, in certain circumstances, have to parachute from the aircraft in order to communicate their intentions. The provisions of this Section of the Manual are without prejudice to the issue of surrender of aircrews having descended by parachute from an aircraft in distress (see Section T of this Manual).

131. Subject to Rule 87, surrendering combatants, as well as captured civilians accompanying the armed forces (such as civilian members of military aircraft crews) and crews of civilian aircraft of the Belligerent Parties who do not benefit from a more favorable treatment, are entitled to prisoner of war status.

Section T:
Parachutists from an Aircraft in Distress

132 (a) No person descending by parachute from an aircraft in distress may be made the object of attack during his descent.

(b) Upon landing in a territory controlled by the enemy, a person who descended by parachute from an aircraft in distress is entitled to be given an opportunity to surrender prior to being made the object of attack, unless it is apparent that he is engaging in a hostile act.

133 This Section does not apply to airborne troops.

Section U:
Contraband, Interception, Inspection and Capture

I. Enemy aircraft and goods on board such aircraft

134. Enemy civilian aircraft and goods on board may be captured as prize on the ground or – when flying outside neutral airspace – be intercepted and ordered to proceed to a reasonably accessible belligerent airfield that is safe for the type of aircraft involved. Prior exercise of inspection is not required.

135. As an exceptional measure, captured enemy civilian aircraft and goods on board may be destroyed when military circumstances preclude taking the aircraft for prize adjudication, provided that all persons on board have first been placed in safety and documents relating to the prize have been preserved.

136. (a) Enemy military, law-enforcement and customs aircraft are booty of war. Prize procedures do not apply to captured enemy military aircraft and other State aircraft, inasmuch as their ownership immediately passes to the captor government by virtue of capture.

(b) If a military aircraft becomes disabled or experiences technical problems that require it to land in enemy territory, the aircraft may be seized and destroyed or converted for use by the enemy.

(c) Captured aircrews of military aircraft covered under this Rule are prisoners of war.

II. Neutral civilian aircraft

137. (a) Belligerent Parties are entitled to intercept neutral civilian aircraft outside neutral airspace, provided that due regard is given to the safety of civil aviation.

(b) If, after interception, reasonable grounds for suspecting that a neutral civilian aircraft is subject to capture exist, it may be ordered to proceed for inspection at a reasonably accessible belligerent airfield that is safe for the type of aircraft involved.

(c) As an alternative to capture as prize, a neutral civilian aircraft may consent to be diverted from its declared destination.

138. In order to avoid the need for interception, Belligerent Parties are allowed to establish reasonable measures for the inspection of the cargo of neutral civilian aircraft and the certification that an aircraft is not carrying contraband.

139. The fact that a neutral civilian aircraft has submitted to such measures of supervision as the inspection of its cargo and grant of certificates of non-contraband cargo by one Belligerent Party is not an act of unneutral service with regard to the opposing Belligerent Party.

140. Neutral civilian aircraft are subject to capture as prize outside neutral airspace, if it is determined as a result of inspection or by other means that any one of the following conditions is fulfilled:

(a) They are carrying contraband.

(b) They are on a flight especially undertaken to transport individual passengers who are members of the enemy's armed forces.

(c) They are operating directly under enemy control, orders, charter, employment or direction.

(d) They present irregular or fraudulent documents, lack necessary documents, or destroy, deface or conceal documents.

(e) They are violating regulations established by a Belligerent Party within the immediate area of military operations.

(f) They are engaged in breach of an aerial blockade (see Section V of this Manual).

141. Goods on board neutral civilian aircraft outside neutral airspace are subject to capture as prize in any one of the following cases:

(a) They constitute contraband.

(b) The neutral civilian aircraft is engaged in activities rendering it a military objective under Rule 174.

142. The capture of neutral civilian aircraft and of goods on board can be exercised only in the cases provided for in Rules 140 and 141 and is subject to prize adjudication.

III. Safeguards

143. In all circumstances of capture of a civilian aircraft – whether neutral or enemy – the safety of passengers and crew on board must be provided for. Documents and papers relating to the aircraft must be safeguarded.

IV. Determination of enemy character

144. The fact that a civilian aircraft bears the marks of an enemy Belligerent Party is conclusive evidence of its enemy character. Enemy

character of a civilian aircraft can also be determined by registration, ownership, charter or other appropriate criteria.

145. For the purposes of capture and prize, a civilian aircraft bearing no marks is presumed to have enemy character.

146. (a) If the commander of a military aircraft suspects that a civilian aircraft with neutral marks in fact has enemy character, the commander is entitled to exercise the right of interception and, if circumstances require, the right to divert for the purpose of inspection.

(b) If it is established, after inspection, that the civilian aircraft with neutral marks does not have enemy character, it must be allowed to proceed without delay.

Section V: Aerial Blockade

147. An aerial blockade is a belligerent operation to prevent aircraft (including UAVs/UCAVs) from entering or exiting specified airfields or coastal areas belonging to, occupied by, or under the control of the enemy.

148. (a) An aerial blockade must be declared by a Belligerent Party and notified to all States.

(b) The declaration must specify the commencement, duration, location, and extent of the aerial blockade and the period in which neutral aircraft may leave the blockaded area.

(c) Whenever feasible, a Notice to Airmen (NOTAM) about the establishment of the aerial blockade ought to be issued by the Blockading Party in accordance with Rule 55.

149. (a) The cessation, temporary lifting, re-establishment, extension or other alteration of an aerial blockade must be declared and notified to all States.

(b) Whenever feasible, a Notice to Airmen (NOTAM) about any changes under paragraph (a) ought to be issued by the Blockading Party in accordance with Rule 55.

150. An aerial blockade must not bar access to the airspace of Neutrals.

151. An aerial blockade must be effective. The question whether such a blockade is effective is a question of fact.

152. The force maintaining the aerial blockade may be deployed at a distance determined by military requirements.

153. (a) An aerial blockade may be enforced and maintained by a combination of lawful means of warfare, provided that this combination does not result in acts inconsistent with the law of international armed conflict.

(b) Aircraft in distress must be allowed to enter the blockaded area when necessary.

154. To the extent that an aerial blockade is maintained and enforced exclusively by military aircraft, the condition of effectiveness (Rule 151) requires a sufficient degree of air superiority.

155. An aerial blockade must be enforced impartially as regards the aircraft of all States.

156. For an aerial blockade to be considered effective under Rule 151, it is required that civilian aircraft believed on reasonable grounds to be breaching, or attempting to breach, an aerial blockade, be forced to land, inspected, captured or diverted. If civilian aircraft clearly resist interception, an order to land and capture, they are at risk of attack after prior warning. As for civilian airliners, Section J applies.

157. The establishment or maintenance of an aerial blockade is prohibited in any one of the following cases:

(a) Its sole or primary purpose is to starve the civilian population or to deny that population other objects essential for its survival.

(b) The suffering of the civilian population is, or may be expected to be, excessive in relation to the concrete and direct military advantage anticipated from the aerial blockade.

158. Subject to Rule 100, if the civilian population of the blockaded area is inadequately provided with food or other objects essential for its survival, the Blockading Party must provide for free passage of such foodstuffs or other essential supplies, for example by establishing a humanitarian air corridor, subject to the following conditions:

(a) The Blockading Party retains the right to prescribe the technical arrangements, including inspection, under which such passage is permitted.

(b) The distribution of such supplies may be made subject to the condition that it will be carried out under the local supervision of a Protecting Power or a humanitarian organization which offers guarantees of impartiality, such as the International Committee of the Red Cross.

159. The Blockading Party must allow the passage of medical supplies for the civilian population or for the wounded and sick members of armed forces, subject to the right to prescribe technical arrangements, including inspection, under which such passage is permitted.

Section W: Combined Operations

160. A combined operation is an operation in which two or more States participate on the same side of an international armed conflict, either as members of a permanent alliance or an *ad hoc* coalition.

161. A State may not invoke its participation in combined operations as justification for its failure to perform its obligations under the law of international armed conflict.

162. The legal obligations of a State participating in combined operations do not change when its armed forces are operating in a multinational force under the command or control of a military commander of a different nationality.

163. A State's obligations under the law of international armed conflict do not change when its air or missile forces are operating from the territory of a co-belligerent, including when its air or missile forces are operating from the territory of a co-belligerent that has different obligations under the law of international armed conflict.

164. A State may participate in combined operations with States that do not share its obligations under the law of international armed conflict although those other States might engage in activities prohibited for the first State.

Section X: Neutrality

I. Scope of application

165. Where the Security Council takes binding preventive or enforcement measures under Chapter VII of the Charter of the United Nations – including the authorization of the use of force by a particular State or group of States – no State may rely upon the law of neutrality to justify conduct which would be incompatible with its obligations under the Charter of the United Nations.

II. General rules

166. Hostilities between Belligerent Parties must not be conducted within neutral territory.

167. (a) Belligerent Parties are prohibited in neutral territory to conduct any hostile actions, establish bases of operations or use such territory as a sanctuary. Furthermore, neutral territory must not be used by Belligerent Parties for the movement of troops or supplies, including overflights by military aircraft or missiles, or for operation of military communication systems.

(b) However, when Belligerent Parties use for military purposes a public, internationally and openly accessible network such as the Internet, the fact that part of this infrastructure is situated within the jurisdiction of a Neutral does not constitute a violation of neutrality.

168. (a) A Neutral must not allow any of the acts referred to in Rule 167 (a) to occur within its territory and must use all the means available to it to prevent or terminate them.

(b) If the use of the neutral territory or airspace by a Belligerent Party constitutes a serious violation, the opposing Belligerent Party may, in the absence of any feasible and timely alternative, use such force as is necessary to terminate the violation of neutrality.

169. The fact that a Neutral resists, even by force, attempts to violate its neutrality cannot be regarded as a hostile act. However, the use of force by the Neutral must not exceed the degree required to repel the incursion and maintain its neutrality.

III. Specifics of air or missile operations

170. (a) Any incursion or transit by a belligerent military aircraft (including a UAV/UCAV) or missile into or through neutral airspace is prohibited. This is without prejudice to the right of transit passage through straits used for international navigation or archipelagic sea lanes passage.

(b) A Neutral must exercise surveillance, to the extent that the means at its disposal allow, to enable it to prevent the violation of its neutrality by belligerent forces.

(c) In the event a belligerent military aircraft enters neutral airspace (other than straits used for international navigation or archipelagic sea lanes), the Neutral must use all the means at its disposal to prevent or terminate that violation. If captured, the aircraft and their crews must be interned for the duration of the armed conflict.

171. Belligerent Parties must not commit any of the following acts:

(a) Attack on or capture of persons or objects located in neutral airspace.

(b) Use of neutral territory or airspace as a base of operations – for attack, targeting, or intelligence purposes – against enemy targets in the air, on land or on water outside that territory.

(c) Conducting interception, inspection, diversion or capture of vessels or aircraft in neutral territory.

(d) Any other activity involving the use of military force or contributing to the war-fighting effort, including transmission of data or combat search-and-rescue operations in neutral territory.

172. (a) Belligerent military aircraft may not enter the airspace of Neutrals, except that:

(i) Belligerent military aircraft in distress may be permitted to enter neutral airspace and to land in neutral territory under such safeguards as the Neutral may wish to impose. The Neutral is obligated to require such aircraft to land and to intern the aircraft and their crews.

(ii) The airspace above neutral international straits and archipelagic sea lanes remains open at all times to belligerent aircraft, including armed military aircraft engaged in transit or archipelagic sea lanes passage.

(iii) The Neutral may permit belligerent military aircraft to enter for purposes of capitulation.

(b) Neutrals must use the means at their disposal to require capitulating belligerent military aircraft to land within their territory, and must intern the aircraft and their crews for the duration of the international armed conflict. Should such an aircraft commit hostile acts, or should it fail to follow the instructions to land, it may be attacked without further notice.

173. A Neutral is not bound to prevent the private export or transit on behalf of a Belligerent Party of aircraft, parts of aircraft, or material, supplies or munitions for aircraft. However, a Neutral is bound to use the means at its disposal:

(a) To prevent the departure from its jurisdiction of an aircraft in a condition to make a hostile attack against a Belligerent Party, if there is reason to believe that such aircraft is destined for such use.

(b) To prevent the departure from its jurisdiction of the crews of military aircraft, as well as passengers and crews of civilian aircraft, who are members of the armed forces of a Belligerent Party.

174. Without prejudice to Sections J and V of this Manual, the following activities may render a neutral civilian aircraft a military objective:

(a) It is believed on reasonable grounds to be carrying contraband, and, after prior warning or interception, it intentionally and clearly refuses to divert from its destination, or intentionally and clearly refuses to proceed for inspection to a belligerent airfield that is safe for the type of aircraft involved and reasonably accessible.

(b) Engaging in hostile actions in support of the enemy, e.g., intercepting or attacking other aircraft; attacking persons or objects on land or sea; being used as a means of attack; engaging in electronic warfare; or providing targeting information to enemy forces.

(c) Facilitating the military actions of the enemy's armed forces, e.g., transporting troops, carrying military materials, or refuelling military aircraft.

(d) Being incorporated into or assisting the enemy's intelligence gathering system, e.g., engaging in reconnaissance, early warning, surveillance or command, control and communications missions.

(e) Refusing to comply with the orders of military authorities, including instructions for landing, inspection and possible capture, or it clearly resists interception.

(f) Otherwise making an effective contribution to military action.

175. The fact that a civilian aircraft bears the marks of a Neutral is *prima facie* evidence of its neutral character.

Commentary to the HPCR Manual on International Law Applicable to Air and Missile Warfare

Elaborated by the Drafting Committee of the Group of Experts under the supervision of Professor Yoram Dinstein.

Section A

Definitions

1. For the purposes of this Manual –

1. The definitions in this Section of the Manual were drafted by the Group of Experts. When they reflect a treaty text, the Commentary will quote that source, or at least cite it.

2. Definitions have to be read in the context of the Black-letter Rules appearing in the substantive Sections of this Manual. Generally speaking, it is in that context that the question whether the definition is applicable to non-international armed conflicts has to be addressed. Clearly, some definitions – e.g., Neutral (see Rule 1 (aa)) – have no bearing upon non-international armed conflict (this will be so indicated in the respective Commentary on the relevant substantive Black-letter Rules).

3. On the other hand, it is necessary to take into account provisions such as Art. 2 (6) of the 1996 Amended Protocol II to the CCW[1] and Art. 1 (f) of the Second Protocol to the 1954 Hague Convention.[2] Both the 1996 Amended Protocol II to the CCW[3] and the Second Protocol

[1] Art. 2 (6) of the 1996 Amended Protocol II to the CCW: "'Military objective' means, so far as objects are concerned, any object which by its nature, location, purpose or use makes an effective contribution to military action and whose total or partial destruction, capture or neutralization, in the circumstances ruling at the time, offers a definite military advantage."

[2] Art. 1 (f) of the Second Protocol to the 1954 Hague Convention: "'military objective' means an object which by its nature, location, purpose, or use makes an effective contribution to military action and whose total or partial destruction, capture or neutralisation, in the circumstances ruling at the time, offers a definite military advantage."

[3] Art. 1 (1) and Art. 1 (2) of the 2001 Amendment to the CCW, as adopted by the Second Review Conference of the CCW: "(1) This Convention and its annexed Protocols shall apply in the situations referred to in Article 2 common to the Geneva Conventions of 12 August 1949 for the Protection of War Victims, including any situation described in paragraph 4 of Article I of Additional Protocol I to these Conventions. (2) This Convention

to the 1954 Hague Convention[4] now apply both in international and non-international armed conflict.

(a) **"Air" or "airspace" means the air up to the highest altitude at which an aircraft can fly and below the lowest possible perigee of an earth satellite in orbit. Under international law, airspace is classified as either national airspace (that over the land, internal waters, archipelagic waters, and territorial seas of any State) or international airspace (that over contiguous zones, exclusive economic zones, the high seas, and territory not subject to the sovereignty of any State).**

1. Every State has sovereignty over the airspace above its land and water territory.[5]

2. Until the advent of the first artificial satellites in 1957, it was widely assumed that national airspace had no upper limit. However, once artificial satellites were launched into orbit around Earth, it soon became obvious that the area in which they travel does not come within any national airspace.

3. Satellites in low Earth orbit have to travel at minimal speeds of about 8 km (5 miles) per second in order not to slip out of their orbit due to the force of gravity. Even very thin air will heat up and slow down a satellite due to friction. The atmosphere will cause such objects traveling below an altitude of approximately 100 km (about 328.000 feet) for any prolonged time to lose speed, fall down and burn up in the process. The lowest point of the orbit ("perigee") of an artificial satellite will therefore have to be above that altitude.

4. Aircraft, deriving their support in the atmosphere from the reactions of the air (see Rule 1 (d)), have not been able to reach – in sustained flight – altitudes where satellites travel. Jet planes have great difficulties

and its annexed Protocols shall also apply, in addition to situations referred to in paragraph 1 of this Article, to situations referred to in Article 3 common to the Geneva Conventions of 12 August 1949. This Convention and its annexed Protocols shall not apply to situations of internal disturbances and tensions, such as riots, isolated and sporadic acts of violence, and other acts of a similar nature, as not being armed conflicts."

4 Art. 22 (1) of the Second Protocol to the 1954 Hague Convention: "This Protocol shall apply in the event of an armed conflict not of an international character, occurring within the territory of one of the Parties."

5 Art. 1 of the Chicago Convention ("Sovereignty"): "The contracting States recognize that every State has complete and exclusive sovereignty over the airspace above its territory."

exceeding 25 km (about 82.000 feet), while balloons can reach approximately 35 km (about 115.000 feet).[6]

5. Because of the decreasing density of the air, winged aircraft have to travel at ever-higher speeds in order to reach higher altitudes. At an altitude of approximately 100 km, a winged aircraft has to travel at about 8 km/sec. This is equal to orbital velocity, which means that the centrifugal force would prevent it from falling down, thus making the concept of winged flight meaningless. While this altitude of approximately 100 km is commonly accepted as distinguishing between aeronautical and astronautical flights, it has not gained universal approval for purposes of international law.

6. Ballistic missiles and aircraft that for a limited period of time follow a ballistic trajectory can, in principle, reach any altitude, including the region between the "highest altitude at which an aircraft can fly" under present technology and "below the lowest possible perigee of an earth satellite in orbit". It is not settled whether they would violate the airspace of any foreign State because of overflight at such intermediate altitude. Similar problems may arise if future technology makes it possible for some vehicle to hover or fly at such intermediate altitude, or to travel at orbital velocity at such altitude without slowing down and burning due to friction.

7. For the purposes of Rule 1 (a), national territory encompasses land, internal waters, archipelagic waters and the territorial sea under the sovereignty of a given State.[7] As far as the territorial sea is concerned, it must be observed that the right of innocent passage – to which all foreign ships are entitled[8] – does not extend to the airspace above the water.

8. As regards international straits[9] and archipelagic sea lanes,[10] aircraft of all States enjoy the right of transit passage.

[6] At the time of writing, the world altitude record for air-breathing jet propelled aircraft in controlled horizontal flight is 25.929 meters. Air balloons have reached 34.688 meters.

[7] Art. 2 of the Chicago Convention ("Territory"): "For the purposes of this Convention the territory of a State shall be deemed to be the land areas and territorial waters adjacent thereto under the sovereignty, suzerainty, protection or mandate of such State."

[8] Art. 17 of UNCLOS ("Right of innocent passage"): "Subject to this Convention, ships of all States, whether coastal or land-locked, enjoy the right of innocent passage through the territorial sea."

[9] Art. 38 of UNCLOS, see fn. 446.

[10] Art. 53 of UNCLOS, see fn. 447.

9. National military manuals treat this subject in different ways and do not therefore throw much light on the question of the highest altitude of the national airspace.[11]

10. "Territory not subject to the sovereignty of any State" refers to some parts of Antarctica.[12] In theory, it also refers to the possibility of new emerging islands in the high seas.

(b) "Air or missile operations" mean military operations in armed conflict involving the use of aircraft or missiles of all types; whether in offence or defence; and whether or not over the territory of one of the Belligerent Parties.

1. "Air or missile operations" is the generic phrase in this Manual referring to any military airborne activities. This includes attack and interception by all types of aircraft or missiles.

2. The term "air or missile operations" covers not only the phase when the aircraft or the missile is in flight, but also activities directly connected to the actual use of the aircraft or missile such as deployment, launching, guidance or retrieval. Such activities can take place in the air, on the ground or from a vessel. They can also take place before, during or after the flight phase of the aircraft or missile.

[11] Para. 217 of the German ZDv: "The dividing line between the airspace of the national territory of a state and outer space shall be drawn where, due to existing physical conditions, the density of the air is small enough to permit the employment of satellites. According to the present state of the art, the minimum flight altitude of satellites ranges between 80 and 110 km above ground level."

Para. 12.13 of the UK Manual ("Vertical extent of airspace"): "Views differ as to the precise vertical and horizontal extent of airspace. For practical purposes, it can be said that the upper limit to a state's rights in airspace is above the highest altitude at which an aircraft can fly and below the lowest possible perigee of an earth satellite in orbit. The result is that anything in orbit or beyond can safely be regarded as in outer space."

Para. 1.10 of the NWP ("Outer space"): "The upper limit or airspace subject to national jurisdiction has not been authoritatively defined by international law. International practice has established that airspace terminates at some point below the point at which artificial satellites can be placed in orbit without free-falling to earth."

[12] Para. 2 of Art. IV of the Antarctic Treaty: "No acts or activities taking place while the present Treaty is in force shall constitute a basis for asserting, supporting or denying a claim to territorial sovereignty in Antarctica or create any rights of sovereignty in Antarctica. No new claim, or enlargement of an existing claim, to territorial sovereignty in Antarctica shall be asserted while the present Treaty is in force."

3. The phrase "military operations" means (i) operations involving actual or potential use of force against an enemy; and (ii) operations in direct support of the aforementioned operations.

4. The words "in armed conflict" clarify that the military operations referred to in this Manual must take place in such context and not in connection with incidents that do not reach the legal threshold of armed conflict (see Section B). Operations for law-enforcement purposes are therefore not included, notwithstanding any use of force in their course. Such operations are normally conducted by police units, which are not considered combatants, unless incorporated into the armed forces.[13] Similar considerations apply to the coast guard.

5. When the armed forces undertake operations in support of civil society that are not related to actual – or potential – use of force against an enemy in times of armed conflict, such operations are not considered "military" in the sense of this Manual, although they could be qualified as "military" under national law.

6. The phrase "air and missile warfare", as used in the title of this Manual, adverts to air or missile operations that are specifically related to hostilities. In addition to air or missile combat operations (see Rule 1(c)), air or missile operations include surveillance, weather, reconnaissance, search-and-rescue, transport and other operations that may not be directly related to ongoing hostilities.

7. The inclusion of operations "whether in offence or defence" is intended to highlight the fact that an operation's tactical or operational character has no bearing on the law of international armed conflict applicable to it. Thus, for instance, there is no distinction in the terminology of this Manual between an offensive attack and a defensive counter-attack. For the definition of "attack", see Rule 1 (e).

8. Subject to the relevant rights of Neutrals (see Section X), Rule 1 (b) emphasizes that air or missile operations may take place anywhere. This includes: (i) the airspace above the national territory of all Belligerent Parties; (ii) the airspace above the high seas and above territory not subject to the sovereignty of any State; and (iii) the airspace above the contiguous

13 Art. 43 (3) of AP/I: "Whenever a Party to a conflict incorporates a paramilitary or armed law enforcement agency into its armed forces it shall so notify the other Parties to the conflict."

zones or the EEZ of all States (including Neutrals). The concepts of the EEZ and the continental shelf refer to the exploitation of natural resources. For the purposes of air or missile operations, these zones and areas are international waters and the air above them is international airspace. See also Rule 107 (e) and paragraph 3 of the Commentary on Rule 166.

(c) "Air or missile combat operations" mean air or missile operations designed to injure, kill, destroy, damage, capture or neutralize targets, the support of such operations, or active defence against them.

1. Air combat operations include attacks by aircraft on other aircraft and on surface targets (on land or at sea).

2. Missile combat operations include attacks on aircraft, surface targets (on land or at sea) or on other missiles by missiles from land or sea based platforms, as well as surface-to-surface missile strikes.

3. Air or missile combat operations are not confined to those aircraft or missiles conducting an "attack" (see Rule 1 (e)). Air combat operations typically include multiple elements, e.g., refueling; jamming of enemy radars; suppression of enemy defences by attacking enemy radar stations and anti-aircraft artillery or missile sites; use of airborne warning and control systems; bombing; fighter escort and fighter sweeps preceding bomber attacks. Operations integral to ground or naval combat against the enemy, such as dropping an airborne force or using airborne platforms to control attacks on enemy naval vessels, are likewise included in the scope of the term.

4. The targets of air or missile combat operations can be persons or objects. Rule 10 (b) explains which targets may lawfully be attacked.

(d) "Aircraft" means any vehicle – whether manned or unmanned – that can derive support in the atmosphere from the reactions of the air (other than the reactions of the air against the earth's surface), including vehicles with either fixed or rotary wings.

1. As used in this Manual, the term aircraft is used in its broadest sense, extending to airplanes (fixed-wing aircraft), helicopters (rotary-wing aircraft) and even balloons, blimps and dirigibles. The definition of aircraft is not limited in terms of function (e.g., combat, transport, refuelling, etc.), status (e.g., military, civilian, etc.), or size (e.g., from large transport

aircraft to small drones). Likewise, the definition of aircraft extends to all unmanned aerial vehicles, whether unarmed (UAV) or armed (UCAV), and whether remotely piloted or operating autonomously.

2. Aircraft which are lighter than air, like balloons or blimps, are aerostats. Simply put, aerostats float on the air. A powered, steerable aerostat is a dirigible. By contrast, "heavier-than-air" aircraft are aerodynes. In simplest terms, an aerodyne achieves lift by forcing air downward through contact with the aircraft's surface, especially a fixed-wing aircraft or a rotary-wing aircraft.

3. Aircraft may be unpowered (e.g., a glider), powered by propellers, rocket-powered, or powered by one or more jet engines. Jet engines take in air (usually through a turbine driven compressor), burn fuel and achieve thrust by expelling the exhaust.

4. In that the essence of an aircraft is reaction with the air, missiles do not qualify as aircraft because they, except cruise missiles at the time of cruising, do not derive their support from reaction with the air (see Rule 1 (z)).

(e) "Attack" means an act of violence, whether in offence or in defence.

1. This definition is based on Art. 49 (1) of AP/I.[14] The qualifier "against the adversary," which appears in Art. 49 (1) of AP/I, is omitted here to avoid confusion. An attack need not be directed against the enemy's military forces or assets for the Rules reflected in this Manual to apply. Most importantly, an "attack" qualifies as such even if it is directed – unlawfully – against civilians, civilian objects or Neutrals (see, inter alia, Rule 11 and Section X). In other words, the term "attack" is employed in Rule 1 (e) only to describe the physical acts which so qualify, without reference to their lawfulness.

2. The definition of "attack" is strictly a matter of the law of international armed conflict; it has nothing to do with the *jus ad bellum* concept of an "armed attack" appearing in Art. 51 of the UN Charter.[15] This means

[14] Art. 49 (1) of AP/I: "'Attacks' means acts of violence against the adversary, whether in offence or in defence."

[15] Art. 51 of the UN Charter: "Nothing in the present Charter shall impair the inherent right of individual or collective self-defence if an armed attack occurs against a Member of the United Nations, until the Security Council has taken measures necessary to maintain

that the Rules of this Manual apply to acts of violence in armed conflict regardless of whether such acts amount to an armed attack against a State in the sense of *jus ad bellum*.

3. The phrase "in defence" is used in its operational sense; it is not meant to refer to the *jus ad bellum* concept of "self-defence" as used in Art. 51 of the UN Charter.

4. As indicated in paragraph 7 of the Commentary on Rule 1 (b), "[a]ttack" does not necessarily imply conduct of an offensive nature against the enemy. That is, offensive and defensive operations are not distinguished from one another. For the purposes of this Manual, an attack is any military act of a violent nature. The term is narrower than the phrase "military operation", which may consist of one or more attacks, or none at all.

5. "Attack", as defined in Rule 1 (e), does not include intelligence gathering, propaganda, or any other military activities which do not result (or were intended, see the following paragraph) in death, injury, damage or destruction of persons or objects.

6. The term "attack" includes both operations that actually result in violent effects, and those which were intended to but failed. For instance, an aircraft which intends to bomb a target but is unsuccessful because its weapon system fails to release due to mechanical failure, has nevertheless conducted an attack. Similarly, enemy defences may effectively foil an attack and therefore an attack may not be completed; an incomplete attack, still counts as an attack.

7. The definition of "attacks" also covers "non-kinetic" attacks (i.e., attacks that do not involve the physical transfer of energy, such as certain CNAs; see Rule 1(m)) that result in death, injury, damage or destruction of persons or objects. Admittedly, whether "non-kinetic" operations rise to the level of an "attack" in the context of the law of international armed conflict is a controversial issue. There was agreement among the

international peace and security. Measures taken by Members in the exercise of this right of self-defence shall be immediately reported to the Security Council and shall not in any way affect the authority and responsibility of the Security Council under the present Charter to take at any time such action as it deems necessary in order to maintain or restore international peace and security." See also D of the Introduction as regards the exclusion of *jus ad bellum* issues from the scope of this Manual.

Group of Experts that the term "attack" does not encompass CNAs that result in an inconvenience (such as temporary denial of internet access).

(f) "Belligerent Party" means a State Party to an international armed conflict.

1. For the purposes of this Manual, a "Belligerent Party" is always a State.

2. An "international armed conflict" is an armed conflict between two or more States (see Rule 1 (r)).

3. For Contracting Parties to AP/I, according to Art. 1 (4) thereof, the phrase international armed conflict includes "armed conflicts in which peoples are fighting against colonial domination and alien occupation and against racist régimes in the exercise of their right of self-determination, as enshrined in the Charter of the United Nations and the Declaration on Principles of International Law concerning Friendly Relations and Co-operation among States in accordance with the Charter of the United Nations". Hence, Contracting Parties to AP/I, the term "Belligerent Party" extends to an authority representing a people engaged in a conflict of the type dealt with in Art. 1 (4) of AP/I. This is not accepted by non-Contracting Parties to AP/I.

4. Armed conflicts between the regular armed forces of a State and opposing non-State organized armed groups, or between non-State organized armed groups, are non-international armed conflicts (see the Commentary on Rule 2 (a), especially paragraphs 5, 6 and 7 thereof).

5. International law has not produced a universally-accepted term to refer to States engaged in an international armed conflict. For instance, whereas the 1907 Hague Convention (IV) uses the term "belligerents", AP/I adopts the phraseology "Party to the conflict". The semantic distinctions, however, are not substantive in nature. In view of the rather loose use of terms for describing those entities that, under the law of international armed conflict, qualify as Parties to an international armed conflict, the Group of Experts decided to adopt throughout the text of this Manual the expression "Belligerent Party", and to do so consistently in all contexts.

6. All belligerent rights reflected in this Manual are vested in Belligerent Parties as defined here, i.e., States engaged in an international armed conflict.

(g) "Cartel aircraft" means an aircraft granted safe conduct by agreement between the Belligerent Parties for the purpose of performing a specific function, such as the transport of prisoners of war or parlementaires.

1. The term "cartel" means an agreement between Belligerent Parties. Such an agreement is therefore constitutive for the special status of cartel aircraft. The agreement ought to be as specific as possible, spelling out the function which a cartel aircraft is supposed to perform, thus rendering it under certain conditions immune from attack and from capture as prize (for more details, see Section J (II) and Section J (III)).

2. In accordance with a well-established State practice in naval warfare, "cartel aircraft" may be commissioned for the carriage of exchanged POWs or for the carriage of "parlementaires". A "parlementaire" is a person who has been authorized by one of the Belligerent Parties to enter into communication with the enemy.[16]

3. It is now generally understood that Belligerent Parties are free to agree on any function a "cartel aircraft" is to serve. The phrase "such as" is used in Rule 1 (g) in light of the current practice whereby Belligerent Parties – in accordance with Art. 109 to Art. 117 of GC/III – have to endeavour to make arrangements for the repatriation or transport to Neutrals of certain categories of wounded and sick POWs. Other examples of functions for which cartel aircraft could be used may include the transportation of civilian detainees or of cultural property.

4. Any aircraft, whether designated or defined as military (see Rule 1 (x)), civilian (see Rule 1 (h)), medical (see Rule 1 (u)) or State (see Rule 1 (cc)), may become a "cartel aircraft" by agreement between the Belligerent Parties.

5. Cartel aircraft may lose their specific protection from attack in the circumstances set forth in Rule 65. Therefore, it is important that they scrupulously comply with the details of the agreement between the Belligerent Parties, and that they do not act in a manner inconsistent therewith. Moreover, they are subject to inspection by the opposing Belligerent

[16] Art. 32 of the 1907 Hague Regulations, see fn. 600.

Party, which is entitled to verify whether the "cartel aircraft" is in compliance with the details of the agreement.

(h) "Civilian aircraft" means any aircraft other than military or other State aircraft.

1. This definition is based on Art. 3 of the Chicago Convention, although that text refers to "civil aircraft".[17] The Group of Experts was divided on the correctness of using the adjective "civilian". A considerable number of members of the Group of Experts would have preferred the use of the adjective "civil" because that is the term used in treaty law and in national military manuals. The majority of the Group of Experts, however, favoured the use of the adjective "civilian" in order to emphasize that such aircraft are civilian objects (see Rule 1 (j)).

2. The Chicago Convention, as well as the SRM/ACS[18] and the definitions contained in State national military manuals,[19] all have in common that they are phrased in the negative. Accordingly, civilian aircraft are neither military aircraft nor any other State aircraft. For the definition of State aircraft, see Rule 1 (cc).

3. According to Art. 17 of the Chicago Convention, "[a]ircraft have the nationality of the State in which they are registered". Art. 18 of that same Convention provides that "[a]n aircraft cannot be validly registered in more than one State, but its registration may be changed from one State to another." Every aircraft engaged in international air navigation must "bear its appropriate nationality and registration marks" (Art. 20 of the Chicago Convention).

4. Civilian aircraft, whether of enemy or neutral nationality, are civilian objects and, thus, protected against direct (Rule 11) or indiscriminate

[17] Art. 3 of the Chicago Convention: "(a) This Convention shall be applicable only to civil aircraft, and shall not be applicable to State aircraft. (b) Aircraft used in military, customs and police services shall be deemed to be State aircraft."

[18] Para. 13 (l) of the SRM/ACS: "'Civil aircraft' means an aircraft other than a military, auxiliary, or State aircraft such as a customs or police aircraft, that is engaged in commercial or private service."

[19] Para. 12.6 of the UK Manual: "'Civil aircraft' means an aircraft that is not a military, auxiliary, or other State aircraft (such as a customs or police aircraft) and that is engaged in commercial or private service. (Definition adapted from the *San Remo Manual*)."

Para. 1009 of the German ZDv: "'Civilian aircraft' are all aircraft other than military aircraft as described in Section 1007 and State aircraft as described in Section 1008, serving the exclusively civilian transport of passengers or cargo."

(Rule 13) attack unless they are rendered military objectives (see, respectively, Rule 27 and Rule 174). Despite such protection from attack, civilian aircraft – in the course of an international armed conflict – are liable to interception and inspection (Section U). Enemy civilian aircraft are liable to capture as prize (Rule 134). Neutral civilian aircraft are liable to capture as prize outside neutral airspace only in the conditions enumerated in Rule 140.

5. For more details on the protection of civilian aircraft, see Section I.

(i) "Civilian airliner" means a civilian aircraft identifiable as such and engaged in carrying civilian passengers in scheduled or non-scheduled service.

1. While no treaty recognizes a separate category of "civilian airliners"[20] the unique standing of civilian airliners is acknowledged in the SRM/ACS[21] and various military manuals (UK Manual[22] and NWP[23]).

[20] The special protection of "civil aircraft" under Art. 3 *bis* of the Chicago Convention does not apply in situations of armed conflict. Art. 3 *bis* of the Chicago Convention reads: "(a) The Contracting States recognize that every State must refrain from resorting to the use of weapons against civil aircraft in flight and that, in case of interception, the lives of persons on board and the safety of aircraft must not be endangered. This provision shall not be interpreted as modifying in any way the rights and obligations of States set forth in the Charter of the United Nations."

[21] Para. 13 (m) of the SRM/ACS: "'Civil airliner' means a civil aircraft that is clearly marked and engaged in carrying civilian passengers in scheduled or non-scheduled services along Air Traffic Service routes."

[22] Para. 12.7 of the UK Manual: "'Civil airliner' means a civil aircraft that is clearly marked and engaged in carrying civilian passengers in scheduled or non-scheduled services along air traffic service routes."

[23] Para. 8.6.3. of NWP ("Enemy Vessels and Aircraft Exempt from Destruction or Capture") of NWP at subpara. 6: "Certain classes of enemy vessels and aircraft are exempt under the law of naval warfare from capture or destruction provided they are innocently employed in their exempt category. These specially protected vessels and aircraft must not take part in the hostilities, must not hamper the movement of combatants, must submit to identification and inspection procedures, and may be ordered out of harm's way. These specifically exempt vessels and aircraft include: . . . (6) Civilian passenger vessels at sea and civil airliners in flight are subject to capture but are exempt from destruction. Although enemy lines of communication are generally legitimate military targets in modern warfare, civilian passenger vessels at sea, and civil airliners in flight, are exempt from destruction, unless at the time of the encounter they are being utilized by the enemy for a military purpose (e.g., transporting troops or military cargo) or refuse to respond to the directions of the intercepting warship or military aircraft. Such passenger vessels in port and airliners on the ground are not protected from destruction."

2. The Group of Experts was divided on whether civilian airliners are a special category benefiting from specific protection beyond that due to the general protection accorded to civilian aircraft. The compromise was to recognize that civilian airliners are entitled to particular care in terms of precautions (see Section J (I) and Section J (III), especially Rule 58).

3. Civilian airliners benefit from particular care in terms of precautions in view of their world-wide employment in carrying civilian passengers in international air navigation, and in view of the vast risks to innocent passengers in areas of armed conflict.

4. Since "civilian airliners" are but a subcategory of "civilian aircraft", they must comply with the rules on registration and marking set forth in the Chicago Convention (see paragraph 3 of the Commentary on Rule 1 (h)).

5. The phrase "engaged in carrying civilian passengers" means that the civilian passengers must actually be on board the aircraft, whether in flight or while the aircraft is on the ground. Aircraft with no civilian passengers on board are "civilian aircraft", as dealt with in Rule (h) and in Section I. On the other hand, the mere fact that some passengers are members of the enemy's armed forces, does not prejudice the status of a civilian airliner. That does not mean that a civilian airliner may never be attacked (see Section J (I) and Section J (III)).

6. "Civilian airliners" will usually be identifiable as such because Belligerent Parties, as well as Neutrals, provide regular air traffic services within their respective flight information region (FIR) in accordance with ICAO regulations and procedures. Their status as civilian airliner, however, does not depend on whether the flight in question is scheduled. Similarly, it is immaterial whether the flight takes place along Air Traffic Service-routes. Since the object and purpose of the category of "civilian airliner" is to protect civilian passengers, civilian airliners having strayed from their Air Traffic Service-routes – e.g., in a situation of distress – are still entitled to particular care in terms of precautions.

(j) "Civilian objects" mean all objects which are not military objectives, as defined in Rule 1 (y).

1. This definition is based on Art. 52 (1) of AP/I, which defines civilian objects in the negative as "all objects which are not military objectives" as

defined in Art. 52 (2) of AP/I.[24] For the definition of military objectives, see Rule 1 (y) and Section E.

2. The civilian character of an object can be lost through location, purpose or use. For instance, a mountain pass is a civilian object but loses its character once it becomes militarily important by virtue of its location (see Rule 22 (b)). Similarly, a residence is a civilian object, but becomes a military objective if used to billet troops (see Rule 22 (d)). Finally, a civilian ocean liner being fitted for intended future use as a military troop transport qualifies as a military objective by purpose (see Rule 22 (c)).

(k) "Civil defence" means the performance of some or all of the humanitarian tasks mentioned below, intended to protect the civilian population against the dangers, and to help it to recover from the immediate effects, of hostilities or disasters and also to provide the conditions necessary for its survival. These tasks are: (i) warning; (ii) evacuation; (iii) management of shelters; (iv) management of blackout measures; (v) rescue; (vi) medical services, including first aid, and religious assistance; (vii) fire-fighting; (viii) detection and marking of danger areas; (ix) decontamination and similar protective measures; (x) provision of emergency accommodation and supplies; (xi) emergency assistance in the restoration and maintenance of order in distressed areas; (xii) emergency repair of indispensable public utilities; (xiii) emergency disposal of the dead; (xiv) assistance in the preservation of objects essential for survival; (xv) complementary activities necessary to carry out any of the tasks mentioned above, including, but not limited to, planning and organization.

1. This definition is almost identical to the definition of civil defence in Art. 61 (a) of AP/I. For the substantive provisions applicable to civil defence, see Section N (I).

2. In contrast to the broader meaning of "civil defence" which may include non-military measures relating to national defence (measures such as maintaining of law and order, safeguarding the position of public authorities, psychological defence, etc.), "civil defence" as defined in Rule 1(k) is limited to an exhaustive list of fifteen humanitarian activities aiming

[24] Art. 52 (2) of AP/I, see fn. 73.

towards: (a) protecting the civilian population against the effects of hostilities or disasters; (b) helping the civilian population to recover from the immediate effects of hostilities or disasters; and/or (c) providing the conditions necessary for the survival of the civilian population.

3. The activities listed in Rule 1 (k) fall under the definition of civil defence and thus are specifically protected only if their exercise is intended to protect the civilian population or civilian objects. The tasks need to be humanitarian and may not be considered as a contribution to the war effort. Fire-fighting, for example, is a protected civil defence activity only when rescuing civilians or when preventing damage to civilian objects. Personnel fire-fighting on a military airfield would generally not be protected under Rule 1 (k). However, if the fire on a military objective endangers the life of civilians or threatens civilian objects in the vicinity, the fire-fighting would be considered as a civil defence activity if it is done in view of protecting these civilians and civilian objects (see also paragraph 6 of the Commentary on Rule 10 (b) (i)).

4. Civil defence activities relate to effects of hostilities but also to those of a disaster, whether it be a natural disaster or a disaster caused by technical malfunction (e.g., a gas leak in a chemical plant). However, the law of international armed conflict would apply to civil defence activities performed in the context of a disaster and – totally unrelated to hostilities – only if these activities are performed in the territory of a State involved in an international armed conflict.

(l) "Collateral damage" means incidental loss of civilian life, injury to civilians and damage to civilian objects or other protected objects or a combination thereof, caused by an attack on a lawful target.

1. The concept of collateral damage lies at the heart of the principle of proportionality, which prohibits an attack that may be expected to cause collateral damage which would be excessive in relation to the concrete and direct military advantage anticipated to result from the attack (see Rule 14). The definition is drawn from the principle as set forth in Art. 51 (5) (b) of AP/I,[25] Art. 57 (2) (a) (iii) of AP/I[26] and Art. 57 (2) (b) of AP/I.[27]

[25] Art. 51 (5) (b) of AP/I, see fn. 188.
[26] Art. 57 (2) (a) (iii) of AP/I, see fn. 259.
[27] Art. 57 (2) (b) of AP/I, see fn. 259.

2. There are two categories of collateral damage referred to in Art. 57 of AP/I. One is that of incidental loss or injury to civilians and the other is that of damage to civilian objects. Strictly speaking, collateral damage relates only to the subcategory of damage to civilian objects. However, as used in this Manual, the term collateral damage extends also to the subcategory of incidental loss – or injury to – civilians.

3. Two factors underlie the term. First, the loss/injury or damage must be incidental. For instance, civilians or civilian objects that are intentionally or indiscriminately (and unlawfully – see, respectively, Rule 11 and Rule 13) attacked do not constitute collateral damage. Secondly, the death of, or injury to, combatants or civilians directly participating in hostilities does not constitute collateral damage. Similarly, damage to, or destruction of, military objectives (including civilian objects which have become military objectives through location, purpose or use) does not constitute collateral damage. Combatants, military objectives and civilians directly participating in hostilities are lawful targets (see Rule 10 (b)).

4. In the context of the law of international armed conflict, harm to civilians and civilian objects that the attacker did not expect is not collateral damage included in proportionality calculations, so long as the lack of expectation of harm was reasonable in the circumstances (see the Commentary on Rule 14). The key question with regard to such harm is whether there is compliance with the requirement to take feasible precautions in attack (see Section G).

5. Collateral damage does not include inconvenience, irritation, stress, fear or other intangible effects on the civilian population.

(m) "Computer network attack" means operations to manipulate, disrupt, deny, degrade, or destroy information resident in computers and computer networks, or the computer network itself, or to gain control over the computer or computer network.

1. Computer network attack (CNA) is a form of "information operations". In their broad meaning, information operations are defined as "[t]he integrated employment of the core capabilities of electronic warfare, computer network operations, psychological operations, military deception, and operations security, in concert with specified supporting and related capabilities, to influence, disrupt, corrupt or usurp

adversarial human and automated decision making while protecting our own."[28]

2. The essence of CNA is that a data stream is relied on to execute the operation against the targeted system. Thus, the means and methods used set CNA apart from other forms of information operations. CNA operations vary widely. They include, for instance, gaining access to a computer system so as to acquire complete or partial control over it; transmitting viruses to destroy or alter data; using logic bombs that sit idle in a system until triggered on the occasion of a particular occurrence or at a set time; inserting worms that reproduce themselves upon entry to a system thereby overloading the network; employing sniffers to monitor and/or seize data; securing entry into a system in order to manipulate data, for instance by altering, deleting, or adding to it, and simply penetrating a system to observe data resident therein.

3. A CNA can be directed against an individual computer, specific computers within a network, or an entire computer network.

4. The term "attack" in "computer network attack" is not meant to necessarily imply that all such operations constitute an attack as that term is used elsewhere in this Manual (see definition of "attack" as set forth in Rule 1 (e)). Some CNA operations may rise to the level of an attack as defined in Rule 1 (e), whereas others will not (see paragraph 7 of the Commentary on Rule 1 (e)).

(n) "Contraband" means goods which are ultimately destined for territory under the control of an enemy Belligerent Party and which are susceptible for use in international armed conflict.

1. This definition is based on Para. 148 of the SRM/ACS[29], as well as on Para. 7.4.1. of NWP[30] and on Para. 12.8 of the UK Manual.[31]

[28] DoD Dictionary of Military Terms, at 260–261.

[29] Para. 148 of the SRM/ACS: "Contraband is defined as goods which are ultimately destined for territory under the control of the enemy and which may be susceptible for use in armed conflict."

[30] Para. 7.4.1 of NWP: "Contraband consists of goods destined for the enemy of a belligerent and that may be susceptible to use in armed conflict."

[31] Para. 12.8 of the UK Manual: "'Contraband' means goods which are ultimately destined for territory under the control of the enemy and which may be susceptible for use in armed conflict."

2. The construct of contraband is only relevant to (i) neutral cargo; and (ii) neutral aircraft. As far as enemy cargo on board enemy aircraft is concerned, it is always susceptible to capture as prize (see Section U (I)).

3. Two cumulative elements are necessary for goods to qualify as "contraband": (i) they must be susceptible for use in international armed conflict; and (ii) they must be ultimately destined for enemy, or enemy controlled, territory.

4. In traditional practice, there were two categories of contraband.[32] Absolute contraband referred to goods that, by nature, were obviously destined for use during the hostilities (see Art. 22 of the London Declaration). Conditional contraband, by contrast, were goods that could serve either peaceful or military purposes (see Art. 24 of the London Declaration). Belligerent Parties were entitled to issue contraband lists upon commencement of hostilities, in order to place Neutrals on notice of those goods it considered to be absolute (see Art. 23 of the London Declaration) or conditional (see Art. 25 of the London Declaration) contraband, as well as those expressly considered to not be contraband ("free goods", see Arts. 27 to 29 of the London Declaration). During WWII and in post-WWII State practice, the traditional distinction between absolute and conditional contraband has eroded. In view of that practice, the Group of Experts decided that this distinction has become obsolete.

5. Goods "susceptible for use in international armed conflict", *inter alia*, comprise weapons, munitions, all other means of warfare, as well as items destined for use by the enemy's armed forces, such as uniforms, foodstuffs, or fuel. Belligerent Parties may publish contraband lists at the initiation of hostilities to notify Neutrals of the type of goods considered to be contraband, as well as those not considered to be contraband at all. The precise nature of a Belligerent Party's contraband list may vary according to the circumstances of the conflict[33] because it is impossible to define in advance which goods will be "susceptible for use in international armed conflict". It is a matter of dispute whether there is an obligation for Belligerent Parties to publish contraband lists. In any event, weapons and munitions qualify as contraband even if they are not included in such a

[32] The London Declaration was signed but not ratified. Most of its provisions, however, are regarded as reflective of customary international law. The Declaration is outdated as regards the distinction between absolute and relative contraband.

[33] Para. 7.4.1 of NWP: "The precise nature of a belligerent's contraband list may vary according to the circumstances of the conflict."

list. Foodstuffs or other supplies essential for the survival of the civilian population, and medical supplies for the civilian population or for the wounded and sick members of the armed forces, may not be declared contraband.[34]

6. The second element, i.e., that the goods must be "ultimately destined" for enemy, or enemy controlled, territory has two important implications. The first implication is that the doctrine of continuous voyage applies to all goods lawfully considered contraband. Hence, goods that, according to the cargo documents, are ostensibly bound for neutral territory, qualify as contraband if there are reasonable grounds for assuming that they will be carried from neutral to enemy, or enemy controlled, territory.

7. The second implication is that the concept of contraband is not applicable to enemy exports on neutral civilian aircraft. The only lawful method of warfare by which enemy exports on board neutral aircraft (or vessels) may be prevented is, in the view of the majority of the Group of Experts, an aerial (or naval) blockade. For aerial blockade, see Section V.

8. Rule 1 (n) is without prejudice to the powers of the UN Security Council under Chapter VII of the UN Charter. Hence, an embargo decided upon by the UN Security Council may apply to goods that are not "susceptible for use in international armed conflict".

(o) "Cultural property" means, irrespective of origin or ownership:

1. The substance of this Rule is almost identical to Art. 1 of the 1954 Hague Convention, which offers the most comprehensive definition of cultural property. Most other treaties only refer to components of the definition, such as (i) "buildings dedicated to religion, art, science, or charitable

[34] Arts. 27–29 of the London Declaration. See, e.g., also subparagraphs (1) and (2) of Para. 7.4.1.1 of NWP ("Exemptions to Contraband – Free Goods"): "Certain goods are exempt from capture as contraband even though destined for enemy territory. Among these items are free goods such as: (1) Articles intended exclusively for the treatment of wounded and sick members of the armed forces and for prevention of disease. (2) Medical and hospital stores, religious objects, clothing, bedding, essential foodstuffs, and means of shelter for the civilian population in general, and women and children in particular, provided there is not serious reason to believe that such goods will be diverted to other purpose, or that a definite military advantage would accrue to the enemy by their substitution for enemy goods that would thereby become available for military purposes."

purposes, historic monuments";[35] (ii) "historic monuments, museums, scientific, artistic, educational and cultural institutions";[36] or (iii) "historic monuments, works of art or places of worship which constitute the cultural or spiritual heritage of peoples".[37]

2. The list of examples contained in (i) and (ii) of Rule 1 (o) is not intended to be exhaustive, as indicated by the term "such as".

(i) Movable or immovable property of great importance to the cultural heritage of every people, such as monuments of architecture, art or history, whether religious or secular; archaeological sites; groups of buildings which, as a whole, are of historical or artistic interest; works of art; manuscripts, books and other objects of artistic, historical or archaeological interest; as well as scientific collections and important collections of books or archives or of reproductions of the property defined above;

1. The definition of Rule 1 (o) (i) covers all cultural property of great importance to the cultural heritage of every people. The phrase "the cultural heritage of every people" in the 1954 Hague Convention has led to differing interpretations. One line of approach is that the phrase refers to the cultural heritage of all peoples jointly, whereas another school of thought adheres to the view that the cultural heritage of each people (severally) must be respected.

[35] Art. 27 of the 1907 Hague Regulations: "In sieges and bombardments all necessary steps must be taken to spare, as far as possible, buildings dedicated to religion, art, science, or charitable purposes, historic monuments, hospitals, and places where the sick and wounded are collected, provided they are not being used at the time for military purposes. It is the duty of the besieged to indicate the presence of such buildings or places by distinctive and visible signs, which shall be notified to the enemy beforehand."

[36] Art. 1 of the Roerich Pact: "The historic monuments, museums, scientific, artistic, educational and cultural institutions shall be considered as neutral and as such respected and protected by belligerents. The same respect and protection shall be due to the personnel of the institutions mentioned above. The same respect and protection shall be accorded to the historic monuments, museums, scientific, artistic, educational and cultural institutions in time of peace as well as in war."

[37] Art. 53 (a) of AP/I: "Without prejudice to the provisions of the Hague Convention for the Protection of Cultural Property in the Event of Armed Conflict of 14 May 1954, and of other relevant international instruments, it is prohibited: (a) to commit any acts of hostility directed against the historic monuments, works of art or places of worship which constitute the cultural or spiritual heritage of peoples."

2. Cultural property may be movable or immovable; religious or secular. The definition also covers buildings and centres containing such cultural property.

(ii) Buildings whose main and effective purpose is to preserve or exhibit the movable cultural property defined in sub-paragraph (i) such as museums, large libraries and depositories of archives, and refuges intended to shelter, in the event of armed conflict, the movable cultural property defined in sub-paragraph (i);

This part of the definition relates to museums, libraries and archives. What counts here is not the nature of the buildings as such (which may have no historical or "artistic" interest, as per Rule 1 (o) (i)), but relates to the movable cultural property which is preserved in these buildings.

(iii) Centres containing a large amount of cultural property as defined in sub-paragraphs (i) and (ii).

Centres containing a large amount of cultural property may consist of entire towns (like Venice or Bruges) that encompass cultural property. The definition extends even to those parts of the town which do not qualify *per se* as cultural property under Rule 1 (o) (i) and Rule 1 (o) (ii).

(p) "Electronic warfare" means any military action involving the use of electromagnetic and directed energy to control the electromagnetic spectrum or to attack the enemy.

1. Electronic warfare (EW) is currently used extensively as a method of warfare. Yet, it is not specifically regulated or even mentioned in treaty law.

2. The use of "electromagnetic, directed energy, or anti-radiation weapons to attack personnel, facilities, or equipment with the intent of degrading, neutralizing, or destroying enemy combat capabilities" or to "preven[t] or reduc[e] an enemy's use of the electromagnetic spectrum"[38] constitutes electronic attack, the form of EW most relevant to this Manual.

3. Electromagnetic jamming and Suppression of Enemy Air Defences (SEAD) are common forms of electronic attack. In the former,

[38] United States Air Force, Electronic Warfare, Air Force Doctrine Document (AFDD) 2–5.1, 5 November 5, 2002, at page 7. Directed energy refers to technologies involving the creation of beams of electromagnetic energy or atomic or subatomic parts.

electromagnetic energy is radiated, reradiated, or reflected in order to impede the enemy's use of the electromagnetic spectrum. Typical targets include radar controlled weapons, intelligence networks, and command and control systems. SEAD comprises aerial operations that neutralize, destroy, or temporarily degrade elements of the enemy's ground-based integrated air defence system. These include early warning, ground-control intercept, and target acquisition radars; surface to air missiles; and anti-aircraft artillery. Many SEAD missions are performed using anti-radiation missiles that home in on energy emitted by the target.[39]

4. Although not deployed in the general inventory of any State's armed forces, a number of States have, or have had, research programs on electromagnetic bombs. Reports exist of limited use on the battlefield. An electromagnetic bomb disrupts and disables electronics by creating an electromagnetic pulse (EMP) upon detonation that causes current and voltage surges. Integrated circuits, transistors, inductors, and electronic motors are especially vulnerable to the effects of EMP.

5. As used in this Manual, EW encompasses all actions conducted against the enemy in the context of an international armed conflict, whether by the armed forces or even by non-military forces such as intelligence agencies. By contrast, EW unrelated to the armed conflict, such as that employed for strictly law-enforcement purposes, is not covered by this Manual.

(q) "Feasible" means that which is practicable or practically possible, taking into account all circumstances prevailing at the time, including humanitarian and military considerations.

1. This definition is based upon declarations made by States at the time of ratification of AP/I, where the concept "feasible" appears, e.g., in Arts. 41, 56, 57, 58, 78 and 86. A similar definition is given in the second sentence of Art. 3 (10) of the 1996 Amended Protocol II to the CCW.[40]

[39] *Ibid.*, at page 8.

[40] Art. 3 of the 1996 Amended Protocol II to the CCW: "(10) All feasible precautions shall be taken to protect civilians from the effects of weapons to which this Article applies. Feasible precautions are those precautions which are practicable or practically possible taking into account all circumstances ruling at the time, including humanitarian and military considerations. These circumstances include, but are not limited to: (a) the short- and long-term effects of mines upon the local civilian population for the duration of the

2. The term "feasible" appears in several Rules of this Manual and could have different practical meaning when the context is different. For instance, with regard to verification as to whether an aircraft in the air constitutes a military objective (see Rule 40), what is feasible may depend on the availability of technical means for observation and detection. This is supported by the ICRC Commentary on AP/I.[41] With regard to the removal of the civilian population from the vicinity of military objectives (see Rule 43), the feasibility may depend on the availability of means of transportation and alternative housing.

3. The feasibility of a particular course of action will depend on which information or which means are in fact available to military commanders at the relevant time and place. The mere fact that such information or such means exist somewhere is irrelevant for determining feasibility. Thus, Austria, when ratifying AP/I declared that Art. 57 (2) of AP/I "will be applied on the understanding that, with respect to any decision taken by a military commander, the information actually available at the time of the decision is determinative."

4. The term "at the time" is to emphasize that any judgment on feasibility is to be taken at the time in which attacks are decided upon or executed. This is a clear rejection of any hindsight analysis. For instance, Australia (among others), upon ratification of AP/I, in relation to Arts. 51–58 thereof, declared that "military commanders and others responsible for planning, deciding upon or executing attacks, necessarily have to reach their decisions on the basis of their assessment of the information from all sources, which is available to them at the relevant time." In other words, options that become apparent after the battle has been fought are not relevant if they were not apparent at the critical moment. See also paragraph 8 of the Commentary on Rule 12 (a) and paragraph 5 of the Commentary on Rule 14.

5. As made clear in the last part of this definition, feasibility is to be determined by taking into account both humanitarian and military considerations. Military commanders may, therefore, take into account

minefield; (b) possible measures to protect the civilians (for example, fencing, signs, warning and monitoring); (c) the availability and feasibility of using alternatives; and (d) the short- and long-term military requirements for a minefield."

[41] Para. 2198 and Para. 2199 of the ICRC Commentary on AP/I pertaining to the use of the words "everything feasible" in Art. 57 (2) (a) (i) of AP/I.

the circumstances relevant to the success of an attack or of the overall military operation, including the survival of military aircraft and their crews. However, the factoring in of such military considerations may not result in a neglect of humanitarian obligations under the law of international armed conflict. This means that, whereas a particular course of action may be considered non-feasible due to military considerations (such as excessive risks to aircraft and their crews), some risks have to be accepted in light of humanitarian considerations.

6. In the final analysis, the determination of feasibility under the law of international armed conflict remains "a matter of common sense and good faith".[42] There are currently no absolute standards applicable to any judgment on feasibility.

(r) "International armed conflict" means an armed conflict between two or more States.

1. In the past, treaties such as the 1899 and 1907 Hague Conventions used the term "war". More recently, the common phrase is "international armed conflict". A prime example is AP/I. The main reason for the use of the phrase "international armed conflict" is that its meaning is wider, and includes not only "wars" (whether or not declared), but also situations "short of war". What counts is that two or more States are engaged in hostilities with each other. The law of international armed conflict will then apply irrespective of the appellation "war".

2. It is not necessary that the use of armed force by one State meets with the armed resistance by the other State. Neither does the existence of an international armed conflict depend upon the duration or the intensity of the hostilities.

3. According to the second paragraph of common Art. 2 of the 1949 Geneva Conventions, these treaties "shall also apply to all cases of partial or total occupation of the territory of a High Contracting Party, even if the said occupation meets with no armed resistance." For instance, during WWII, German forces were met with no opposition when they invaded Denmark.

4. The degree of involvement of a foreign State with an insurgent armed group – triggering an armed conflict with the central government – is

[42] *Ibid.*, Para. 2198.

controversial. The ICJ[43] and ICTY[44] have taken different positions on the subject. Conversely, the armed conflict will not lose its non-international character if foreign armed forces, at the request of the government engaged in a non-international armed conflict, assist the government forces.

5. An international armed conflict may take place side by side with a non-international armed conflict (e.g., Afghanistan in 2001). This, however, does not mean that the international and the non-international armed conflict necessarily merge. Moreover, an armed conflict may commence as a non-international armed conflict but may evolve into an international armed conflict (e.g., the armed conflict in Bosnia-Herzegovina after Bosnia's independence in 1992).

6. Whether an international armed conflict has come into existence is a question of fact. Hence, the existence of such a conflict is not conditioned

[43] ICJ, Case concerning Military and Paramilitary Activities in and against Nicaragua (Nicaragua v. United States of America), Merits, Judgment of 27 June 1986, in ICJ Reports 1986, p. 14, at para. 115: ". . . United States participation, even if preponderant or decisive, in the financing, organizing, training, supplying and equipping of the *contras*, the selection of its military or paramilitary targets, and the planning of the whole of its operation, is still insufficient in itself, . . . for the purpose of attributing to the United States the acts committed by the *contras* in the course of their military or paramilitary operations in Nicaragua. All the forms of United States participation mentioned above, and even the general control by the respondent State over a force with a high degree or dependency on it, would not in themselves mean, without further evidence, that the United States directed or enforced the perpetration of the acts contrary to human rights and humanitarian law alleged by the applicant State. Such acts could well be committed by members of the *contras* without the control of the United States. For this conduct to give rise to legal responsibility of the United States, it would in principle have to be proved that that State had effective control of the military or paramilitary operations in the course of which the alleged violations were committed." (underlining added) The ICJ confirmed this jurisprudence (explicitly referring to, and rejecting, the ICTY standard as quoted in the following footnote) in ICJ, Case concerning the Application of the Convention on the Prevention and Punishment of the Crime of Genocide, Bosnia and Herzegovina v. Serbia and Montenegro, Judgment of 26 February 2007, in paras. 396–415.

[44] ICTY, Prosecutor v. Dusko Tadic, Case No. IT-94-1-A, Judgement of the Appeals Chamber of 15 July 1999, at para. 145: "In the light of the above discussion, the following conclusion may be safely reached. In the case at issue, given that the Bosnian Serb armed forces constituted a "military organization", the control of the FRY authorities over these armed forces required by international law for considering the armed conflict to be international was *overall control* going beyond the mere financing and equipping of such forces and involving also participation in the planning and supervision of military operations. By contrast, international rules do not require that such control should extend to the issuance of specific orders or instructions relating to single military actions, whether or not such actions were contrary to international humanitarian law." (underlining added)

on any formal recognition of either (i) a "state of war"; or of (ii) the enemy as a "State"; or of (iii) the enemy as a "government".

> (s) **"Law of international armed conflict" means all the principles and rules of treaty and customary international law binding on a State and governing armed conflict between States; the term "law of international armed conflict" is synonymous with "international humanitarian law relating to international armed conflict".**

1. The law of international armed conflict applies to all situations of international armed conflict as defined in Rule 1 (r). The law of international armed conflict must be clearly distinguished from the law regulating the legality of the resort to armed force by States ("*jus ad bellum*").

2. As far as the law of international armed conflict is concerned, it was common in the past to distinguish between "Hague law" (the law governing the conduct of hostilities) and "Geneva law" (the law aimed at the protection of victims of armed conflict). Today, there is general agreement that "these two branches of the law applicable in armed conflict have become so closely interrelated that they are considered to have gradually formed one single complex system, known today as international humanitarian law".[45]

3. Different terms are used to describe the law of international armed conflict, such as "international humanitarian law", "*jus in bello*", "law of war", "law of armed conflict". The Group of Experts was, however, in agreement that this is a semantic rather than a substantive issue. Therefore, they agreed to use both terms synonymously. However, in order to clearly distinguish between international and non-international armed conflicts it was decided to use the terms "law of international armed conflict' and "international humanitarian law relating to international armed conflict".

4. While treaties are binding only upon Contracting Parties, customary international law is binding on all States, except for those States that – from the very outset of the evolution of a specific customary rule – qualify as persistent objectors.

[45] ICJ, Nuclear Weapons Advisory Opinion, at page 256.

(t) "Means of warfare" mean weapons, weapon systems or platforms employed for the purposes of attack.

1. Although this definition is not set forth in treaty law, the Group of Experts considered it a useful and accurate reflection of common usage. In the law of international armed conflict context, means of warfare include those objects used to conduct attacks. They are the instruments used to cause, in the course of an armed conflict, (i) the death of, or injury to, individuals; or (ii) damage to, or destruction of, objects.

2. In aerial warfare, means of warfare include weapons, such as bombs, missiles and rockets, and the aircraft executing an attack. Means of warfare include other objects upon which the attacking aircraft directly relies to carry out the attack. For instance, aircraft which provide targeting data and other essential information to an aircraft actually engaging the target, qualify as means of warfare. In some cases, an aircraft can itself serve as a weapon, as was the case of the Japanese aircraft used for kamikaze attacks during WWII and civilian aircraft used to conduct a suicide attack. As the 2001 terrorist attacks against the Twin Towers in New York City show, hijacked civilian airliners may also be used as a means of warfare in flagrant violation of the law of international armed conflict.

3. The entire weapon system also constitutes a means of warfare. For instance, an aircraft used to conduct an attack together with associated systems integral to the execution of the attack constitute a means of warfare. Similarly, a ground based target designator used to guide a weapon to its target qualifies as a component part of a means of warfare. So too would aircraft employing electronic warfare systems or a UCAV. See also the definition of "weapon" in Rule 1 (ff).

4. The term "means of warfare" applies only in the context of an attack. Military equipment not designed or used to injure or kill the enemy or damage, or destroy objects does not qualify as a means of warfare. For instance, a transport or refuelling aircraft is not a means of warfare even though it contributes directly to military operations.

5. Means of warfare include non-kinetic systems, such as those used in EW and CNAs. The means would include the computer and computer code used to execute the attack, together with all associated equipment.

6. Means of warfare are distinguished from methods of warfare (see Rule 1 (v)).

(u) "Medical aircraft" means any aircraft permanently or temporarily assigned – by the competent authorities of a Belligerent Party – exclusively to aerial transportation or treatment of wounded, sick, or shipwrecked persons, and/or the transport of medical personnel and medical equipment or supplies.

1. Rule 1 (u) is based on the first paragraph of Art. 39 of GC/II[46] and on Arts. 8 (f), (g) and (j) of AP/I.[47]

2. A medical aircraft is defined by its function, i.e., the aerial transport of wounded, sick, or shipwrecked persons, and/or the aerial transport of medical personnel and medical equipment or medical supplies. The definition ought to be interpreted as also including the transportation of religious personnel.

3. In contrast to AP/I, this definition foresees the provision of medical treatment in a medical aircraft. The rationale behind this enlarged definition stems from an enhanced capacity to conduct such activities: armed forces are today often equipped with air ambulances providing not only the efficient evacuation of sick and wounded from the battlefield but which are also able to provide medical care *en route* (Medivac).

4. Any aircraft may become a medical aircraft, depending on its assignment. Hence, a military aircraft (see Rule 1 (x)) may become a medical aircraft, in which case it no longer constitutes a lawful target (unless engaged in acts harmful to the enemy) (see Rule 26 and Section L).

5. Search-and-rescue aircraft do not qualify as a medical aircraft nor must they be used to search for the wounded, sick and shipwrecked within areas

[46] First paragraph of Art. 39 of GC/II: "Medical aircraft, that is to say, aircraft exclusively employed for the removal of the wounded, sick and shipwrecked, and for the transport of medical personnel and equipment, may not be the object of attack, but shall be respected by the Parties to the conflict, while flying at heights, at times and on routes specifically agreed upon between the Parties to the conflict concerned."

[47] Art. 8 of AP/I: "(f) "'medical transportation' means the conveyance by land, water or air of the wounded, sick, shipwrecked, medical personnel, religious personnel, medical equipment or medical supplies protected by the Conventions and by this Protocol; (g) "medical transports" means any means of transportation, whether military or civilian, permanent or temporary, assigned exclusively to medical transportation and under the control of a competent authority of a Party to the conflict; (j) "medical aircraft" means any medical transports by air."

of combat operations, unless pursuant to prior consent of the enemy (for details, see Rule 86).

6. The terms "wounded", "sick", "shipwrecked" and "medical personnel" need to be interpreted in accordance with the 1949 Geneva Conventions and Art. 8 of AP/I 1977.[48] On the definition of wounded, sick and shipwrecked, see the Commentary on Rule 16. For further explanation on the definition of medical and religious personnel, see the Commentary on Rule 71.

7. A medical aircraft needs to be "exclusively" assigned to one of the tasks mentioned. It must therefore only contain categories of persons, medical equipment or medical supplies that fall under its definition as long as it is assigned to this purpose. For example, an aircraft carrying only medical and religious personnel or an air transportable hospital would qualify as a medical aircraft. If the aircraft, in addition, carries able combatants and/or items which do not qualify as medical equipment or supplies, it does not fall under the definition of medical aircraft.

8. The assignment of an aircraft to exclusive medical purposes has to be done by a competent authority of the Belligerent Party. Following the assignment, the aircraft becomes a medical aircraft, subject to specific protection as defined in Section L. Art. 8 (g) of AP/I[49] insists not only on assignment to the function of a medical aircraft, but also on control by the Belligerent Party. If the aircraft is either a military aircraft or any other State aircraft, full control by the Belligerent Party is implicit both at the time of the assignment and during its operation as a medical aircraft thereafter. If the medical aircraft is a civilian aircraft, the Belligerent Party incurs full responsibility to ensure that the aircraft will operate in keeping with the law of international armed conflict and in particular will not be abused, e.g., with regard to the display of the protective emblem (see Rule 72).

9. A medical aircraft may either be "permanently" or "temporarily" assigned to medical transportation or treatment. To be considered "permanent", medical aircraft must be (Art. 8 (k) of AP/I)[50] "assigned

[48] See fns. 229–230, 394.

[49] See fn. 47.

[50] Art. 8 (k) of AP/I: "'permanent medical personnel', 'permanent medical units' and 'permanent medical transports' mean those assigned exclusively to medical purposes for an indeterminate period. 'Temporary medical personnel', 'temporary medical units' and 'temporary medical transports' mean those devoted exclusively to medical purposes for limited periods during the whole of such periods. Unless otherwise specified, the terms

exclusively to medical purposes for an indeterminate period", whereas "temporary" medical aircraft are defined based on their assignment or use during a limited period of time. A medical aircraft's mission ends when it has been given a new assignment or use not related to medical purposes. Occasionally, the same aircraft is used as a matter of routine flying wounded and sick on one segment of its flight, and armed personnel and equipment on another segment. During that segment of the flight in which the aircraft is carrying wounded and sick, it is considered a medical aircraft notwithstanding the temporary nature of the assignment.

(v) "Methods of warfare" mean attacks and other activities designed to adversely affect the enemy's military operations or military capacity, as distinct from the means of warfare used during military operations, such as weapons. In military terms, methods of warfare consist of the various general categories of operations, such as bombing, as well as the specific tactics used for attack, such as high altitude bombing.

1. Although this definition does not appear in any treaty, the Group of Experts considered it a useful and accurate reflection of common usage. In the law of international armed conflict context, "methods of warfare" refers to how attacks and other hostile actions are conducted, rather than to the instruments with which they are conducted, which are "means of warfare". An example: an aircraft and its weaponry are the means of warfare used to conduct an aerial bombing campaign, which is a method of warfare.

2. Bombing campaign, missile attack, rocket attack, strafing, and conducting EW are specific methods of air warfare. The term can equally be understood in the sense of categories of operations, such as counter-air operations, SEAD, air interdiction, electronic warfare, and close air support of ground operations. Furthermore, "methods of warfare" also refer to broad categories of military operations of particular relevance to the application of the law of international armed conflict. Examples include starvation (see Rule 97), aerial blockade (see Section V), and establishment of a no-fly zone (see Section P). Finally, in its narrowest sense, methods of warfare can refer to specific tactics and tactical procedures.

'medical personnel', 'medical units' and 'medical transports' cover both permanent and temporary categories."

Release of a weapon at a particular altitude, angle of attack, and beyond visual range engagement are examples of methods of warfare in this sense.

3. Methods of warfare are a subcategory of military operations. Many military operations, such as resupply, transportation of troops and communications do not constitute methods of warfare unless they adversely affect the enemy's military operations or military capacity.

4. There is an on-going debate as to whether the use of riot control agents constitutes a method of warfare as that term is used in the CWC.[51] The definition set forth in Rule 1 (v) is for the purposes of this Manual only and is not meant to suggest any particular resolution of the riot control agent issue (see paragraph 9 of the Commentary on Rule 2 (a) and paragraph 4 of the Commentary on Rule 6 (b)).

(w) "Military advantage" means those benefits of a military nature that result from an attack. They relate to the attack considered as whole and not merely to isolated or particular parts of the attack.

1. The term military advantage is first found in Art. 24 (1) of the HRAW.[52] Today, it is also a crucial element of the definition of military objective (see Art. 52 (2) of AP/I,[53] as further reflected in Rule 1 (y) as well as in Section E of this Manual). Further, the concept of military advantage is central to the principle of proportionality (see Art. 51 (5) (b)[54] and Art. 57 of AP/I,[55] as further reflected in Rule 14 of this Manual), as well as to the requirement to take feasible precautions in attack (see Section G). As detailed in Rule 14, the expected collateral damage may not be excessive relative to the anticipated "concrete and direct military advantage".

2. Military advantage is determined at the time of planning or executing an attack. Anticipation of a military advantage is one of the constituent elements that can make an attack on an object lawful. The actual results of an attack are irrelevant to the reasonableness of the assessment of the military advantage at the time when the attack was planned or executed.

[51] Art. I (5) of CWC: "Each State Party undertakes not to use riot control agents as a method of warfare."

[52] Art. 24 (1) of the HRAW, see fn. 72.

[53] Art. 52 (2) of AP/I, see fn. 73.

[54] Art. 51 (5) (b) of AP/I, see fn. 188.

[55] In Art. 57 of AP/I (see fn. 259), the concept "military advantage" appears in Art. 57 (2) (a) (iii), Art. 57 (2) (b) and Art. 57 (3).

See also paragraph 4 of the Commentary on Rule 1 (q), paragraph 8 of the Commentary on Rule 12 (a) and paragraph 5 of the Commentary on Rule 14.

3. It has been suggested that "a military advantage can only consist in ground gained and in annihilating or weakening the enemy armed forces."[56] A better approach is to understand military advantage as any consequence of an attack which directly enhances friendly military operations or hinders those of the enemy. This could, e.g., be an attack that reduces the mobility of the enemy forces without actually weakening them, such as the blocking of an important line of communication. However, no military advantage can accrue from attacks directed against civilians or civilian objects, unless they have become lawful targets (see Rule 10). See also paragraph 10 of the Commentary to Rule 14.

4. Military advantage refers only to advantage which is directly related to military operations and does not refer to other forms of advantage which may in some way relate to the conflict more generally. Military advantage does not refer to advantage which is solely political, psychological, economic, financial, social, or moral in nature. Thus, forcing a change in the negotiating position of the enemy only by affecting civilian morale does not qualify as military advantage.

5. The concept of military advantage has to be understood contextually. For instance, attacking an apartment building occupied by civilians yields no military advantage, whereas attacking the same apartment building when used for billeting of troops would result in military advantage. Thus, the term is intricately tied to the qualification of an object as a military objective by nature, location, purpose or use. For the definition of military objective, see Rule 1 (y) and Section E.

6. Military advantage is generally[57] understood as referring to advantage accruing from an attack as a whole, and not only from isolated or particular parts of the attack.[58] For instance, attacks against specific

[56] Para. 2218 of the ICRC Commentary on AP/I.

[57] Upon ratification of AP/I, the United Kingdom has given the following understanding to Art. 51 and Art. 57 of AP/I: "In the view of the United Kingdom, the military advantage anticipated from an attack is intended to refer to the advantage anticipated from the attack considered as a whole and not only from isolated or particular parts of the attack." Similar understandings have been given by a number of States, e.g., by Canada.

[58] See also the Rome Statute of the ICC in Art. 8 (2) (b) (iv) that employs the term "overall" for the following war crime in an international armed conflict: "[i]ntentionally launching

military objectives may constitute part of a broader ruse strategy designed to convince the enemy that operations are likely to be focused on an area other than the actual location of a planned main attack (see Section Q, in particular Rule 116 (a)). The military advantage in such a case would include not only that resulting from destruction of the specific targets attacked, but also the advantage gained by causing the enemy to misdirect its defences away from the area of main attack. See also paragraph 7 of the Commentary on Rule 1 (y), paragraph 11 of the Commentary on Rule 14 and paragraph 3 of the Commentary on Rule 33.

7. On the concept of "military advantage" in the context of the principle of proportionality, see paragraphs 9–13 of the Commentary on Rule 14.

(x) "Military aircraft" means any aircraft (i) operated by the armed forces of a State; (ii) bearing the military markings of that State; (iii) commanded by a member of the armed forces; and (iv) controlled, manned or preprogrammed by a crew subject to regular armed forces discipline.

1. This definition is based on Art. 3[59] and 14 of the HRAW[60] that are generally considered as reflecting customary international law. The definition has been adopted (although with a slightly different wording) in the SRM/ACS[61] as well as in various national military manuals.[62]

an attack in the knowledge that such attack will cause incidental loss of life or injury to civilians or damage to civilian objects or widespread, long-term and severe damage to the natural environment which would be clearly excessive in relation to the concrete and direct overall military advantage anticipated."

[59] Art. 3 of the HRAW: "A military aircraft shall bear an external mark indicating its nationality and military character."

[60] Art. 14 of the HRAW: "A military aircraft shall be under the command of a person duly commissioned or enlisted in the military service of the state; the crew must be exclusively military."

[61] Para. 13 (j) of the SRM/ACS: "'Military aircraft' means an aircraft operated by commissioned units of the armed forces of a State having the military marks of that State, commanded by a member of the armed forces and manned by a crew subject to regular armed forces discipline."

[62] Para. 12.10 of the UK Manual: "'Military aircraft' means an aircraft operated by commissioned units of the armed forces of a state having the military marks of that state, commanded by a member of the armed forces, and manned by a crew subject to regular armed forces discipline."

Para. 2.4.1 of NWP: "Military aircraft include all aircraft operated by commissioned units of the armed forces of a nation bearing the military markings of that nation, commanded by a member of the armed forces, and manned by a crew subject to regular armed forces discipline, as well as unmanned aerial vehicles (see paragraph 2.4.4)".

2. The definition stipulates the characteristics an aircraft must have in order to be, and to qualify for the entitlements of, a military aircraft (see Rule 17). Aircraft lacking one or more of these characteristics may nevertheless be military objectives (see Rule 1 (y) and Rule 22).

3. A military aircraft must be "operated by the armed forces of a State". It is not necessary that it is operated by commissioned units of the armed forces of a State. Nor must the aircraft belong to the armed forces.[63] Today, ownership is not determinative because aircraft may remain the property of a private entity (as is the case, e.g., when the aircraft have been leased). The term "armed forces" is not limited to the air forces and comprises all services of the armed forces of a State.

4. A military aircraft must be "commanded by a member of the armed forces". Under Art. 14 of the HRAW,[64] the aircraft must be "under the command of a person duly commissioned or enlisted in the military service of the State." The term "command" as used in Rule 1 (x) refers to the individual aboard the aircraft (or controlling it remotely) who exercises authority over that aircraft. It is to be distinguished from the more general "command" over a military unit or organization.

5. If a military aircraft is manned by a crew, the members of the crew must be "subject to regular armed forces discipline". The members of the crew of military aircraft who are combatants must be accorded POW-status when captured. It follows from Art. 4 (A) (4) of GC/III that the crew of military aircraft may also comprise civilian members (who are entitled to POW-status when captured).[65] The presence of such civilian crew members who are entitled to POW-status on board military aircraft does not alter the aircraft's legal status. It ought not to be assumed that the entire crew of a military aircraft must consist of members of the armed forces.

6. The requirement of a crew under military discipline does not mean that all military aircraft must be manned by a crew. Today, UAVs as well as UCAVs also qualify as military aircraft, if the persons remotely controlling them are subject to regular armed forces discipline. The same holds true

[63] Para. 1007 of the German ZDv: "'Military aircraft' are all aircraft belonging to the armed forces of a state and bearing external marks distinguishing such aircraft of their nationality. The commanding soldier must be a member of the armed forces, and the crew must be subject to military discipline. Military aircraft need not be armed."

[64] Art. 14 of the HRAW, see fn. 60.

[65] Art. 4 (A) (4) of GC/III, see fn. 650.

for autonomously operating UAVs, provided that their programming has been executed by individuals subject to regular armed forces control.

7. Every military aircraft (unless specifically protected under Section L, Section J (II), or Section N (V)) qualifies as a military objective by nature (see Rule 1 (y) and Rule 22 (a)) because, by its nature, a military aircraft effectively contributes to the enemy's military action and its destruction, capture or neutralization will always constitute a definite military advantage.

8. By definition, aircraft operated by non-State organized armed groups (whatever the nature of the armed conflict) cannot qualify as military aircraft, although they may be military objectives.

9. An aircraft need not be specially designed or built for the performance of strictly military purposes. Hence, as recognized by Art. 9 of the HRAW,[66] any State aircraft or a civilian aircraft may be converted into a military aircraft. But, in order to qualify as a military aircraft, a converted aircraft must meet all of the conditions of the definition of Rule 1 (x).

10. The conditions enumerated in the definition of a military aircraft, do not require the aircraft to be armed.

11. The obligation of "bearing the military markings of that State" is based upon Art. 3 of the HRAW.[67] There is no necessity of two marks, one for the nationality and one for the military character. In some air forces, the same marking indicates both nationality and military character.[68] In order to be clearly distinguishable from other State aircraft, especially from police or customs aircraft, the marking of a military aircraft must

[66] Art. 9 of the HRAW: "A belligerent non-military aircraft, whether public or private, may be converted into a military aircraft, provided that the conversion is effected within the jurisdiction of the belligerent state to which the aircraft belongs and not on the high seas."

[67] Art. 3 of the HRAW, see fn. 59.

According to Art. 7 of the HRAW the "external marks . . . shall be so affixed that they cannot be altered in flight. They shall be as large as practicable and shall be visible from above, from below and from each side."

[68] Para. 12.10.4 of the UK Manual: "Military aircraft can include, for example, transport, reconnaissance, and meteorological aircraft of the armed forces of a particular state whether or not they are used in a direct combatant role. These aircraft must bear external markings indicating clearly their nationality and military character. In most air forces, the same marking indicates both nationality and military character, for example, the Royal Air Force roundel. Additional markings to indicate an international grouping such as NATO are permissible but modifications of this nature adopted by any state must be promptly notified to all other states. . . . "

indicate that the aircraft is employed for military purposes. Ordinarily, military aircraft appear in a special military register. Sometimes, however, they are identified as military in a civil register.[69] The requirement of markings indicating their nationality is to ascertain that a military aircraft has the nationality of only one State. A military aircraft may not possess more than one nationality (*cf.* paragraph 3 of the Commentary on Rule 1 (h)). This, however, is without prejudice to the right of bearing additional markings indicating an international grouping, such as NATO, provided that modifications of that nature are promptly notified to all other States.[70]

12. No aircraft other than a military aircraft of a Belligerent Party is entitled to bear the military markings of that State (see Rule 112 (c)).

13. Since only military aircraft fulfilling the aforementioned conditions are "entitled to exercise belligerent rights",[71] a military aircraft not properly marked as such is prohibited from engaging in attacks, interception or any other military operation entailing the exercise of belligerent rights, though it may carry out other security functions as assigned. Other aircraft, including State aircraft, are prohibited from exercising belligerent rights (see Rule 17).

14. The crux of the requirement is the marking itself. It is now common for States to use subdued or otherwise low-visibility markings on military aircraft (see also paragraphs 5 and 6 of the Commentary on Rule 114 (b) and the Commentary on Rule 116 (e)). The absence of official objection to this widespread practice seems to indicate that, generally, States do not consider this practice to be unlawful.

[69] EUROCONTROL, Decision of the Provisional Council Session of 12 July 2001, Principle 1: "Aircraft on a military register, or identified as such within a civil register, shall be considered to be used in military service and hence qualify as State aircraft; Civil registered aircraft used in military, customs and police service shall qualify as State aircraft; Civil registered aircraft used by a State for other than military, customs and police service shall not qualify as State aircraft." This decision is available via <www.eurocontrol.int/mil/public/standard_page/stateac.html>

[70] For the text of Para. 12.10.4 of the UK Manual, see fn. 68. The UK Manual refers, in support of that assertion, to Art. 8 of the HRAW, which reads: "The external marks, prescribed by the rules in force in each state, shall be notified promptly to all other Powers. Modifications adopted in time of peace of the rules prescribing external marks shall be notified to all other Powers before they are brought into force. Modifications of such rules adopted at the outbreak of war or during hostilities shall be notified by each Power as soon as possible to all other Powers and at latest when they are communicated to its own fighting forces."

[71] Art. 13 of the HRAW, see fn. 219.

15. Aircraft operated by private companies or other private contractors are civilian. Once a military aircraft is operated or commanded by such companies or contractors, it loses its status as a military aircraft and may no longer engage in attacks in international armed conflicts, though it may carry out security functions as assigned.

(y) **"Military objectives", as far as objects are concerned, are those objects which by their nature, location, purpose or use, make an effective contribution to military action and whose total or partial destruction, capture or neutralization, in the circumstances ruling at the time, offers a definite military advantage.**

1. The first use of the term "military objective" is found in Art. 24 (1) of the HRAW.[72] The seminal definition of "military objective" appears in Art. 52 (2) of AP/I,[73] upon which the definition in this Manual is based. This definition is considered to be reflective of customary international law, although there are differing interpretations of the definition in practice (see, e.g., the Commentary on Rule 24).

2. The definition is framed in terms of objects. Combatants and civilians who directly participate in hostilities are also lawful targets (see Rule 10 (b)). However, although these two categories are sometimes referred to as military objectives,[74] for the purposes of this Manual, military objectives are limited to objects.

3. The definition sets forth two separate yardsticks: (i) that the object makes an effective contribution to military action of the enemy; and (ii) that its destruction, capture or neutralization yields a definite military advantage to an attacker. In practical terms, compliance with the first criterion will generally result in the advantage required of the second. See also paragraph 4 of the Commentary in the *chapeau* on Rule 22.

[72] Art. 24 (1) of the HRAW: "Aerial bombardment is legitimate only when directed at a military objective, that is to say, an object of which the destruction or injury would constitute a distinct military advantage to the belligerent."

[73] Art. 52 (2) of AP/I: "Attacks shall be limited strictly to military objectives. Insofar as objects are concerned, military objectives are limited to those objects which by their nature, location, purpose or use make an effective contribution to military action and whose total or partial destruction, capture or neutralization, in the circumstances ruling at the time, offers a definite military advantage."

[74] See Para. 2017 of the ICRC Commentary on AP/I: "It should be noted that the definition is limited to objects but it is clear that members of the armed forces are military objectives."

4. The term "effective" merely means that there must in fact be a contribution to the enemy's military action. There is no requirement that the contribution be significant.

5. The four criteria – nature, location, purpose or use – are defined in Rule 22.

6. It is generally understood that the military advantage anticipated from an attack is intended to refer to the advantage anticipated from the attack considered as a whole and not only from isolated or particular parts of the attack (see paragraph 6 of the Commentary on Rule 1 (w), paragraph 11 of the Commentary on Rule 14 and paragraph 3 of the Commentary on Rule 33).

7. By the definition, the destruction, capture[75] or neutralization must offer a "definite military advantage" in the circumstances ruling at the time. The term "definite" is employed to exclude advantage which is merely potential, speculative or indeterminate.[76]

8. It is a matter of dispute whether the definition includes objects which indirectly yet effectively support military operations. There was, however, agreement in the Group of Experts that objects which directly support military operations, come within the boundaries of this definition. Yet, the NWP interprets the definition more broadly to include "war-sustaining" objects, explaining the phrase by reference to "[e]conomic objects of the enemy that indirectly but effectively support and sustain the enemy's war-fighting capability." See the Commentary on Rule 24 and Para. 8.2.5 of NWP.[77]

(z) "Missiles" mean self-propelled unmanned weapons– launched from aircraft, warships or land-based launchers – that are either guided or ballistic.

1. A missile is a self-propelled weapon launched through the air by an aircraft, a warship, or a ground-based missile launch platform. Missiles

[75] The notion of "capture" here is to be distinguished from the notion of "capture as prize" under Section U of this Manual.

[76] Para. 2024 of the ICRC Commentary on AP/I: "Finally, destruction, capture or neutralization must offer a 'definite military advantage' in the circumstances ruling at the time. In other words, it is not legitimate to launch an attack which only offers potential or indeterminate advantages. Those ordering or executing the attack must have sufficient information available to take this requirement into account; in case of doubt, the safety of the civilian population, which is the aim of the Protocol, must be taken into consideration."

[77] Para. 8.2.5 of NWP, see fn. 236.

are powered by either rocket or jet engines. Rocket powered engines employ liquid or solid fuels. The former typically characterize only larger surface-to-surface missiles while the latter are characteristic of air-to-air and air-to-ground missiles. Cruise missiles are typically powered by jet engines. Missiles are to be distinguished from munitions propelled by external force, such as a mortar or artillery shell.

2. Many missiles are guided. Guidance may be based on the use of radiated energy, such as homing in on the infra-red signature of the target or laser designation that allows the missile to track to the target. Laser designation of the target can be from the aircraft itself or other aircraft or ground forces. TV cameras that use either visible light or infrared pictures may also be used to guide the missile to the target. The missile may be guided to the target by a human operator or by a computer. Some missiles use satellite system data to guide to the target, as in the case of Global Positioning Satellite (GPS) data. Missiles may also contain an inertial navigation system (INS) to provide guidance. To improve accuracy, some missiles employ multiple forms of guidance.

3. Ballistic missiles follow a ballistic trajectory following a launch stage, that is, their path is determined by the laws of physics, specifically the law of gravity. Because the trajectory is ballistic, such missiles are typically used in surface-to-surface warfare, that is, launched from the ground or sea against land targets.

4. Missile variants include those designed for surface (including water)-to-surface, surface-to-air, air-to-surface and air-to-air attacks.

5. The term missile is not identical with rocket. "Rocket" merely refers to a type of object which employs a propellant to create thrust by expelling exhaust and therefore moving the rocket forward. Some missiles are rocket propelled. However, the term rocket is not limited to missiles. For instance, some satellites use rockets for maneuvering purposes.

(aa) "Neutral" means a State not a Belligerent Party in an international armed conflict.

1. This definition is in line with the definition of neutrality traditionally used in international law and as recognized in military manuals[78] as well

[78] Third subparagraph of Para. 7.1 of the NWP: "[a] neutral nation is defined as a nation that, consistent with international law, either has proclaimed its neutrality or has otherwise assumed neutral status with respect to an ongoing conflict."

as in the SRM/ACS.[79] Accordingly, for the purpose of this Manual, the status of a State as "Neutral" does not depend upon a declaration of neutrality nor is it to be judged in light of the various positions taken by States on the applicability of the traditional law of neutrality under the 1907 Hague Convention (V) and the 1907 Hague Convention (XIII).

2. Some members of the Group of Experts have taken the view that, under the UN Charter, States may unilaterally determine which Belligerent Party is, in their view, the aggressor and on that basis discriminate against it by assuming a posture of qualified neutrality, which enables them to depart from the traditional law of neutrality while not entering the armed conflict on behalf of the victim of aggression. The majority of the Group of Experts was not prepared to recognize an intermediate status of either "qualified neutrality" or of "non-belligerency", unless there was an authoritative determination by the UN Security Council under Chapter VII of the UN Charter.

3. The majority of the Group of Experts took the position that the law of neutrality becomes inapplicable if the UN Security Council has either (i) identified one or more Belligerent Parties as responsible for an unlawful resort to armed force in breach of Art. 2 (4) of the UN Charter;[80] or (ii) if the UN Security Council has taken preventive or enforcement measures under Chapter VII of the UN Charter against that Belligerent Party or Parties (see Rule 165).

(bb) "Precision guided weapons" mean weapons that can be directed against a target using either external guidance or a guidance system of their own.

1. A precision guided weapon is a weapon (as defined in Rule 1 (ff)) "that uses a seeker to detect electromagnetic energy reflected from a target or reference point and, through processing, provides guidance commands to a control system that guides the weapon to the target."[81] However,

Para. 12.11 of the UK Manual: "'Neutral' has traditionally meant any state not party to the conflict."

Para. 13.5 (m) of the UK Manual: "'neutral' means any state not party to the conflict. Commanders should follow instructions issued by the Ministry of Defence."

[79] Para. 13 (d) of the SRM/ACS: "'neutral' means any State not party to the conflict."

[80] Art. 2 (4) of the UN Charter: "All Members shall refrain in their international relations from the threat or use of force against the territorial integrity or political independence of any state, or in any other manner inconsistent with the Purposes of the United Nations."

[81] DoD Dictionary of Military Terms, 12 April 2001, at pages 423–424.

other systems may be used to enhance the precision of the weapon. In common usage, the term would encompass any weapon (and its incorporated munitions) that employs a guidance system to strike a target accurately.

2. Precision is sometimes wrongly characterized as a weapon's capacity to strike the precise point at which it is aimed (known as the "aimpoint"). In fact, this ability is correctly labelled "accuracy". It is measured in terms of circular error probable, the radius of a circle within which one-half of weapons launched will fall. Precision is a broader concept. It encompasses the ability to locate and identify a target, strike it accurately in a timely fashion, and determine whether desired effects have been achieved or restrike is needed. Robust command, control, communications, computers, intelligence, surveillance, and reconnaissance can be as determinative of precision as the weapon employed. Thus, when considering precision, it is more useful to think in terms of weapon systems, for the accuracy of a weapon in a particular attack may depend as much on the capabilities of the platform from which it is launched as on the technical parameters of the weapon itself.

3. Multiple forms of guidance are used in precision guided weapons (see Rule 1 (z) regarding the definition of missiles). The guidance may be internal (that is, contained within the precision guided weapon), or external (as in cases where the aircraft dropping the precision guided weapon provides guidance to target). Examples of guidance include laser guidance, radar guidance, infrared and infrared imaging guidance, electro-optical (TV) guidance, satellite data guidance, and inertial navigation guidance.

4. Modern weapons have different degrees of autonomy. Some weapons rely on a signal (radar, laser or other) from an aircraft or some other source operated by a human being in order to home in on the target. Other weapons rely on satellite-based GPS (Global Positioning Satellite) signals. Still other weapons have inbuilt capabilities that guide them to a target in the air or on the surface without external input. When an air-delivered guided weapon is independent of any signal from the launching aircraft, it has a "fire-and-forget" capability.

5. Numerous other terms are commonly used to refer to precision guided weapons. They include "smart" weapons, brilliant weapons, and PGMs ("precision guided munitions").

(cc) "State aircraft" means any aircraft owned or used by a State serving exclusively non-commercial government functions.

1. This definition is based on Art. 2,[82] Art. 4[83] and Art. 5[84] of the HRAW. Art. 2 thereof starts from the premise that "public aircraft" are either "military aircraft" or "non-military aircraft exclusively employed in the public service". Accordingly, the decisive criterion for an aircraft to qualify as a "State aircraft" is its employment for public service, not ownership.

2. The Group of Experts preferred the commonly used expression "State aircraft" over either the term "public aircraft" or the alternative term "auxiliary aircraft", used in some military manuals.[85]

3. The HRAW distinguish between (Art. 4) "public non-military aircraft employed for customs or police purposes" and (Art. 5) "public non-military aircraft other than those employed for customs and police purposes". According to Art. 5 of the HRAW, the latter are "treated on the same footing as private aircraft" and, according to Art. 32 HRAW,[86] are not subject to confiscation without prize proceeding, i.e., they do not constitute booty of war (see Rule 136 (a), which prefers the more comprehensive term "law-enforcement" over the term "police").

4. It is generally accepted that the approach to this subject which has been taken by the HRAW is still valid today. Military manuals explicitly refer to police and customs aircraft.[87] Moreover, the limitation of the category of "State aircraft" to those performing military, police or customs services

[82] Art. 2 of the HRAW: "The following shall be deemed to be public aircraft: (a) Military aircraft; (b) Non-military aircraft exclusively employed in the public service. All other aircraft shall be deemed to be private aircraft."

[83] Art. 4 of the HRAW: "A public non-military aircraft employed for customs or police purposes shall carry papers evidencing the fact that it is exclusively employed in the public service. Such an aircraft shall bear an external mark indicating its nationality and its public non-military character."

[84] Art. 5 of the HRAW: "Public non-military aircraft other than those employed for customs or police purposes shall in time of war bear the same external marks, and for the purposes of these Rules shall be treated on the same footing, as private aircraft."

[85] Para. 13 (k) of the SRM/ACS: "'Auxiliary aircraft' means an aircraft, other than a military aircraft, that is owned by or under the exclusive control of the armed forces of a State and used for the time being on government non-commercial service."

Para. 12.5 of the UK Manual: "'Auxiliary aircraft' means an aircraft, other than a military aircraft, that is owned by or under the exclusive control of the armed forces of a state and used for the time being on government non-commercial service."

[86] Art. 32 of the HRAW: "Enemy public aircraft, other than those treated on the same footing as private aircraft, shall be subject to confiscation without prize proceedings."

[87] E.g., Para. 12.6.1 of the UK Manual: "The Chicago Convention distinguishes between civil aircraft and State aircraft. The Convention applies only to civil aircraft. . . . aircraft used

has been recognized in Art. 3 (b) of the Chicago Convention,[88] within the framework of EUROCONTROL[89] and by national legislation.[90]

5. A police or customs aircraft, according to Art. 4 of the HRAW, "shall carry papers evidencing the fact that it is exclusively employed in the public service. Such an aircraft shall bear an external mark indicating its nationality and its public non-military character."

6. All "State aircraft" enjoy sovereign immunity in peacetime. During an international armed conflict, this immunity continues to be applicable only insofar as neutral State aircraft are concerned. As regards the State aircraft of the Belligerent Parties, sovereign immunity is inapplicable. A distinction is made, however, between military, law-enforcement and customs aircraft which can be seized as booty of war (see Rule 136 (a)) and other State aircraft, which can only be captured as prize following prize adjudication. See Rule 136 (a) and paragraph 3 of the Commentary on that Rule.

7. "State aircraft" other than military aircraft are not entitled to exercise belligerent rights (Rule 17).[91] They are not military objectives by nature (see Rule 22 (a) and Rule 23) and, thus, not liable to be attacked automatically as such. However, if enemy State aircraft engage in activities rendering them a military objective they may qualify as a military objective (see Rule 27).

(dd) "Unmanned Aerial Vehicle (UAV)" means an unmanned aircraft of any size which does not carry a weapon and which cannot control a weapon.

1. Unmanned aerial vehicles (UAV) do not carry human operators. They are operated remotely or fly autonomously based on pre-programmed

in military, customs and police services are deemed to be State aircraft under Art. 3(b) of the Chicago Convention."

Para. 1008 of the German ZDv: "'State aircraft' are all aircraft belonging to or used by the state and serving exclusively state functions (e.g. in customs or police service)."

[88] Art. 3 (b) of the Chicago Convention: "Aircraft used in military, customs and police services shall be deemed to be State aircraft."

[89] EUROCONTROL, Decision of the Provisional Council Session of 12 July 2001, Principle 1, see fn. 69.

[90] E.g., Section 3 of the Commonwealth Civil Aviation Act 1988 defines "State aircraft" as "(a) aircraft of any part of the Defence Force (including any aircraft that is commanded by a member of that Force in the course of duties as such a member) . . . ; and (b) aircraft used in the military, customs or police services of a foreign country." Available via <www.austlii.edu.au/au/legis/cth/consol_act/caa1988154/s3.html>

[91] Art. 13 of the HRAW, see fn. 219.

flight paths or other systems designed to allow them to operate autonomously. UAVs are a category of aircraft, for they use aerodynamic forces to provide vehicle lift and are designed for sustained, level flight. Missiles do not qualify as unmanned aerial vehicles (see Rule 1(z)). In particular, although they resemble UAVs, cruise missiles do not qualify as UAVs, because – as weapons – they constitute weapons themselves.

2. There is a very wide range of different types of UAVs. Some are very large, resembling an aircraft, whereas others are man-portable, usable by tactical forces. UAVs may be reusable, taking off and landing as manned aircraft do, or they can be expendable, that is, used for a single flight. There are both fixed-wing and rotary-wing (helicopter) variants. Many are capable of flight for extended periods, sometimes days, although others are capable of only short flights. UAVs may be jet powered or powered by a piston engine (propeller).

3. A UAV is not necessarily a military aircraft. It may constitute a State aircraft other than military aircraft, and it may also be a civilian aircraft. See the requirements of the respective definitions (for military aircraft, see Rule 1 (x); for State aircraft, see Rule 1 (cc); for civilian aircraft, see Rule 1 (h)).

4. The military roles of UAVs vary. They include both military and civilian functions. Examples of UAV usage include: reconnaissance and surveillance, transport of equipment and supplies (such as medical supplies for troops in the field), search and rescue, remote sensing (e.g., infrared, chemical and biological sensing), firefighting, meteorology (e.g., use in hurricanes), or for scientific research. UAVs can also be used to support an attack without becoming UCAVs (see Rule 1 (ee)).

5. UAV are employed for a number of reasons. For example, the use of manned aircraft may carry great risks due to enemy defences; manned aircraft are unavailable or cannot respond in a timely fashion; or alternative means of sensing (such as satellite imaging) are unavailable or untimely.

6. In military usage, UAVs are typically employed in environments where the use of manned aircraft would be dangerous, when manned aircraft are unavailable, for stealth purposes or owing to their extended loiter time. Man-portable UAVs are especially useful in providing reconnaissance for small, tactical engagements by ground units. A common use of UAVs is reconnaissance and surveillance, often in support of aerial or ground attack by other aircraft or ground troops. The unique characteristics of

UAVs allow them to operate in remote areas, survey and monitor the target area, often in real-time, for the presence of civilians or civilian objects, track potential mobile targets such as individuals and vehicles, and provide targeting information to forces tasked with attacking a target.

7. Their modest size and the noise signature relative to manned aircraft may make them useful in tracking individual combatants and military vehicles without alerting them to the fact that they are being observed. Further, the ability of UAVs to loiter often allows them to monitor the target area to assess the presence of civilians at the time of attack.

8. In the designation UAV, the letter "U" sometimes stands for "uninhabited" rather than "unmanned". Occasionally, the designation UAV is substituted by UAS, standing for unmanned aircraft system.

(ee) "Unmanned Combat Aerial Vehicle (UCAV)" means an unmanned military aircraft of any size which carries and launches a weapon, or which can use on-board technology to direct such a weapon to a target.

1. Unmanned Combat Aerial vehicles (UCAV) are armed UAVs (see Rule 1 (dd)) that may be used to attack targets. The UCAV may be remotely controlled and piloted. The various weapons that UCAVs carry can be controlled either (i) remotely; or (ii) by on-board systems. UCAVs often incorporate infra-red or TV sensors, or a sensor-suite consisting of multiple sensors.

2. Very few States currently field UCAVs. However, extensive use by the US, particularly in Afghanistan, has made their impact on the future battlefield clear-cut.

(ff) "Weapon" means a means of warfare used in combat operations, including a gun, missile, bomb or other munitions, that is capable of causing either (i) injury to, or death of, persons; or (ii) damage to, or destruction of, objects.

1. The essence of a weapon is that it is an object used to cause (i) death of, or injury to, persons; or (ii) damage to, or destruction, of objects. However, such death, injury, damage or destruction need not result from physical impact – e.g., the penetration of a bullet or even the blast effects of a bomb – since the force used does not need to be kinetic. In particular, CNA hardware, software and codes are weapons that can cause such effects through transmission of data streams. As an example, a CNA

(see Rule 1 (m)) on an air traffic control system can result in aircraft crashes so that the equipment and computer codes employed would qualify as weapons (or more precisely, a weapon system).

2. Weapons often constitute part of a weapon system (see paragraph 2 of the Commentary on Rule 1 (t)). A weapon system consists of one or more weapons with all related equipment, materials, services, and means of delivery and deployment (if applicable) required for self-sufficiency. A military aircraft armed with missiles and bombs (weapons) is a weapons system that includes, *inter alia*, the weapons, aircraft, and any systems commanding and controlling the aircraft or providing it data. Similarly, a warship armed with offensive and/or defensive weapons, such as those providing air defence capabilities, will be a weapon system. It must always be borne in mind that some weapon systems, like warships and military aircraft, are manned and/or operated by personnel.

3. "Means of warfare" is a broader concept than weapon, for it extends also to platforms and equipment which make possible an attack. For the definition of means of warfare, see Rule 1(t). As an example, AWACS carry no weapons, but are means of warfare used to facilitate, direct and control air-to-air combat. Similarly, the unarmed Joint Surveillance Target Attack Radar System is an airborne battle management, command and control, intelligence, surveillance and reconnaissance platform designed to provide, in part, information used in attacks conducted against ground forces, either from the air or ground.

4. By contrast, munitions (or ammunition) is a narrower concept than "weapon" and refers to the object that actually causes the injury, death, damage or destruction. Some weapons are munitions in themselves, as in the case of a bomb or missile which is carried aboard an aircraft. However, the term weapon also includes the integral equipment directly necessary to cause the force which launches the ammunition or munitions. Thus, anti-aircraft artillery (a weapon which is not a munition) fire anti-aircraft shells (munitions which are also weapons). For the purpose of this Manual, the term weapon includes munitions.

5. While it is true that almost any object can constitute a weapon in particular circumstances (for instance, a hijacked civilian airliner used to mount a suicide attack), as used in this Manual, the term weapon refers to those objects which are designed to be used as a means of attack.

Section B

General Framework

2. (a) The objective of this Manual is to produce a restatement of existing law applicable to air or missile operations in international armed conflict. This is without prejudice to the possible application of some of the Rules in this Manual to non-international armed conflicts (for details, see the Commentary).

1. This Manual is intended to be a restatement of existing international law applicable to air and missile warfare. The Rules incorporated in this Manual are drawn from treaties and customary international law. This Manual and the Rules incorporated in it do not by themselves create or develop legal obligations. Additionally, this Manual does not purport to reflect the entire spectrum of existing obligations that each State has to comply with pursuant to treaties to which it is a Contracting Party – subject to any reservations, understandings and declarations made – and to customary international law.

2. The reference in the text to "existing law" is intended to convey the message that this Manual is a restatement of the *lex lata*. No attempt has been made to introduce into the existing law innovations – desirable as they may appear to be – based on *lex ferenda*.

3. The term "applicable" – as it appears here and in other Rules of this Manual (as well as the semantic derivatives "applies" etc.) – is of course linked to the existing law. It is not this Manual *per se* that is applicable to States but the existing law reflected in the Rules.

4. The range of application of the Rules of this Manual is restricted to international armed conflicts, i.e., whenever there is resort to armed force between two or more States (see Rule 1 (r)). Yet, as explained in part E of the Introduction, this Commentary will indicate – on a

Section-by-Section or Rule-by-Rule basis – whether the same or similar Rules are also applicable in non-international armed conflicts.

5. Non-international armed conflicts are armed confrontations occurring between governmental armed forces and the armed forces of one or more non-State organized armed groups, or between such groups, arising within the territory of a State. The armed confrontation must reach a minimum level of intensity and the parties involved in the conflict must show a minimum of organization. While a conflict of a non-international character may spill over to the territory of another State, this does not alter its legal qualification.

6. Non-international armed conflicts are governed by Common Art. 3 of the 1949 Geneva Conventions[92] and by AP/II. Various other treaties also relate in part to such conflicts, and there is a growing body of customary international law related to them.

7. Non-international armed conflicts require a certain threshold, which differs in Common Art. 3 to the Geneva Conventions (referring merely to an "armed conflict not of an international character") and in Art. 1 (1) of AP/II (referring to an armed conflict between the armed forces of a State and "dissident armed forces or other organized armed groups which, under responsible command, exercise such control over a part

[92] Art. 3 common to the Geneva Conventions: "In the case of armed conflict not of an international character occurring in the territory of one of the High Contracting Parties, each Party to the conflict shall be bound to apply, as a minimum, the following provisions: (1) Persons taking no active part in the hostilities, including members of armed forces who have laid down their arms and those placed *hors de combat* by sickness, wounds, detention, or any other cause, shall in all circumstances be treated humanely, without any adverse distinction founded on race, colour, religion or faith, sex, birth or wealth, or any other similar criteria. To this end, the following acts are and shall remain prohibited at any time and in any place whatsoever with respect to the above-mentioned persons: (a) violence to life and person, in particular murder of all kinds, mutilation, cruel treatment and torture; (b) taking of hostages; (c) outrages upon personal dignity, in particular humiliating and degrading treatment; (d) the passing of sentences and the carrying out of executions without previous judgment pronounced by a regularly constituted court, affording all the judicial guarantees which are recognized as indispensable by civilized peoples. (2) The wounded and sick shall be collected and cared for.

An impartial humanitarian body, such as the International Committee of the Red Cross, may offer its services to the Parties to the conflict. The Parties to the conflict should further endeavour to bring into force, by means of special agreements, all or part of the other provisions of the present Convention. The application of the preceding provisions shall not affect the legal status of the Parties to the conflict."

of its territory as to enable them to carry out sustained and concerted military operations and to implement this Protocol").

8. As will be shown in various parts of the Commentary on this Manual, many of its Rules apply to any armed conflict above the threshold mentioned in the previous paragraph, regardless of whether it is international or non-international in character. However, below the threshold required for applying the law of non-international armed conflict, violence within a State – i.e., internal disturbances and tensions, such as the occurrence of riots and the taking of forcible means to control them – is a matter for law-enforcement, and is not subject to the application of this Manual. This is in keeping with Art. 1 (2) of AP/II.[93]

9. This Manual deals exclusively with armed conflicts. It follows that its prohibitions of certain weapons – as listed in Section C – are inapplicable to riot control situations. A prime example is the use of tear gas, unlawful in hostilities – when used as a method of warfare – but not banned in the course of riot control. See also paragraph 4 of the Commentary on Rule 1 (v) and paragraph 4 of the Commentary on Rule 6 (b).

10. Should a foreign State intervene militarily in a non-international armed conflict, it is necessary to distinguish between two opposing scenarios. If the military intervention by the foreign State is at the request and on behalf of the central government, the armed conflict remains non-international. Conversely, if the military intervention by the foreign State is against the central government, the legal situation is transformed. The armed conflict that develops between the two governments is international in character. All the same, this does not necessarily affect the non-international armed conflict (between the central government and any non-State organized armed group), which may continue to exist as before. See the Commentary on Rule 1 (r).

11. When a single State (like the former Yugoslavia) dissolves into several sovereign States, this may denote that a hitherto non-international armed conflict between several components of the mother country becomes – practically overnight – an inter-State armed conflict between the newly established States. While the transition is easy to explain in legal terms, it is liable to create many problems on the ground (as attested in the

[93] Art. 1 (2) of AP/II: "This Protocol shall not apply to situations of internal disturbances and tensions, such as riots, isolated and sporadic acts of violence and other acts of a similar nature, as not being armed conflicts."

Tadić case of the ICTY, where the majority of the Trial Chamber took one position as regards the nature of the armed conflict in the former Yugoslavia and the Appeals Chamber[94] overruled it).

(b) Nothing in this Manual affects existing obligations of States under treaties to which they are Contracting Parties.

1. This Manual seeks to reflect existing international law applicable to air and missile warfare, insofar as it is binding on all States. The Rules expressed in this Manual are of general applicability in all international armed conflicts.

2. If a treaty is universal in its scope of application (that is, every single State is a Contracting Party), its provisions will bind the entire international community. Still, at the present time, the only treaties that are truly universal are the 1949 Geneva Conventions. As far as other treaties are concerned, they create legal regimes applicable only among Contracting Parties. Within these regimes, States may assume treaty obligations that go beyond the confines of the customary law governing the rest of the international community, as reflected in this Manual.

3. Many provisions of non-universal treaties may, however, codify or generate customary international law. To the extent that such is the case, the treaty *per se* will still be binding only on Contracting Parties, but the substance of the provisions declaratory of customary international law will be considered as an expression of general law.

(c) In cases not covered by this Manual, civilians and combatants remain under the protection and authority of the principles of international law derived from established custom, from the principles of humanity and from the dictates of public conscience.

1. The text of this Rule is based on the famous "Martens Clause" (named after the Russian diplomat who initiated its adoption in the 1899

[94] ICTY, Prosecutor v. Dusko Tadic, Judgment, Appeals Chamber, 15 July 1999, IT-94-1-A, Para. 84: "It is indisputable that an armed conflict is international if it takes place between two or more States. In addition, in case of an internal armed conflict breaking out on the territory of a State, it may become international (or, depending upon the circumstances, be international in character alongside an internal armed conflict) if (i) another State intervenes in that conflict through its troops, or alternatively if (ii) some of the participants in the internal armed conflict act on behalf of that other State."

and 1907 Hague Regulations[95]). For recent expressions of the "Martens Clause", see Art. 1 (2) of AP/I,[96] as well as in the fifth paragraph of the Preamble to the CCW.[97] The Martens Clause has equally been mentioned in the ICJ Nuclear Weapons Advisory Opinion[98] and by the ICTY.[99]

2. The value added by the phrase "principles of humanity and from the dictates of public conscience" is not entirely clear in practice. The fulcrum of Rule 2 (c) is the reference to customary international law. Every codification of the law – whether binding or non-binding (like the present Manual) – is finite in its scope, and there can be no pretence to cover every aspect and dimension of the law of international armed conflict. Should a problem not covered by this Manual arise, the matter may be settled by custom as it exists beyond the framework reflected of the text.

3. Moreover, this Manual intends to reflect customary international law as it exists at the moment of its publication (2010). While written texts are theoretically frozen, the practice of States continues to evolve. The growth of customary international law never stops, and custom that may

95 Eighth paragraph of the Preamble to the 1907 Hague Regulations: "Until a more complete code of the laws of war has been issued, the high contracting parties deem it expedient to declare that, in cases not included in the Regulations adopted by them, the inhabitants and the belligerents remain under the protection and the rule of the principles of the law of nations, as they result from the usages established among civilized peoples, from the laws of humanity, and the dictates of the public conscience." The 1899 Hague Regulations, Preamble, para. 8, is identical.

96 Art. 1 (2) of AP/I: "In cases not covered by this Protocol or by other international agreements, civilians and combatants remain under the protection and authority of the principles of international law derived from established custom, from the principles of humanity and from the dictates of public conscience."

97 Fifth paragraph of the Preamble to the CCW: "Confirming their determination that in cases not covered by this Convention and its annexed Protocols or by other international agreements, the civilian population and the combatants shall at all times remain under the protection and authority of the principles of international law derived from established custom, from the principles of humanity and from the dictates of public conscience."

98 ICJ, Nuclear Weapons Advisory Opinion: After referring to the "cardinal principles in the texts constituting the fabric of humanitarian law", the Court stated as follows (at 257): "The Court would likewise refer, in relation to these principles, to the Martens Clause, which was first included in the Hague Convention II with Respect to the Laws and Customs of War on Land of 1899 and which has proved to be an effective means of addressing the rapid evolution of military technology. A modern version of that clause is to be found in Article 1, paragraph 2, of Additional Protocol I of 1977."

99 As an example of the ICTY case law, one can refer to Prosecutor v. Zoran Kupreski et al., Trial Chamber, Judgment, IT-95-16-T, 14 January 2000, paras. 525 to 527.

be discovered in the years ahead may fill any gap in the law reflected in the Manual.

4. The same principle applies in non-international armed conflicts. See the fourth paragraph of the Preamble to AP/II.[100]

3. (a) Subject to binding decisions adopted by the Security Council under Chapter VII of the Charter of the United Nations, the Rules reflected in this Manual also apply to all air or missile operations conducted by United Nations forces when in situations of armed conflict they are engaged therein as combatants, to the extent and for the duration of their engagement.

1. It used to be debated whether UN forces – tasked (deliberately) with, or embroiled (by circumstance) in, combat missions in situations of armed conflict – can be subject to the application of the law of international armed conflict (to the extent and for the duration of their engagement).

2. This question has now been resolved: irrefutably, the answer is in the affirmative. Any doubts that may have existed with respect to this issue have been put to rest in a landmark 1999 UN Secretary General's Bulletin.[101]

3. Rule 3 (a) reflects a basic *jus in bello* principle as regards the equal application of the law between Belligerent Parties, regardless of their respective standing under the *jus ad bellum.*

4. The scope of applicability of the law of international armed conflict to UN forces is dependent on two conditions: (i) there must exist an international armed conflict in which the UN forces are engaged as combatants; and (ii) there is no binding Security Council decision – adopted under Chapter VII of the UN Charter – which lays down mandatory rules to the contrary on specific matters.

5. Some members of the Group of Experts were of the view that the UN Security Council does not have the right to adopt a binding decision which would override any rule of the law of international armed conflict.

[100] Fourth paragraph of the Preamble to AP/II: "Recalling that, in cases not covered by the law in force, the human person remains under the protection of the principles of humanity and the dictates of the public conscience."

[101] Secretary General's Bulletin: Observance by United Nations Forces of International Humanitarian Law, 6 August 1999, UN Doc. ST/SGB/1999/13, in 38 *I.L.M.* 1656.

However, the prevailing opinion among the members of the Group of Experts was that, in view of the combined effect of Art. 25[102] and Art. 103 of the UN Charter,[103] the UN Security Council has the authority to do so. Of course, the UN Security Council is not expected to use that authority lightly. There is also an unresolved issue as to whether the UN Security Council has the power to override peremptory norms of international law ("*jus cogens*").

6. In any event, any binding Security Council decision diverging from the law of international armed conflict will have to be explicit and specific. Moreover, it can only apply to UN forces whose military operations are mandated (rather than merely "authorized") by the UN Security Council and where the troops are subject to direct UN command.

7. Rule 3 (a) applies also if the UN force is engaged in combat operations in a non-international armed conflict.

8. By itself, the mere fact that a UN force operates in a particular country does not turn a non-international armed conflict into an international armed conflict.

(b) The Rules reflected in this Manual also apply to armed conflicts involving any other international governmental organization, global or regional.

1. In recent years, international governmental organizations other than the UN (primarily NATO) have become engaged in combat in international armed conflicts. Plainly, the law of international armed conflicts applies to forces of such organizations as well.

2. Of course, all military forces engaged in an armed conflict operating under the banner of an international governmental organization consist of national contingents, and these are bound by the obligations imposed on their respective State by the law of international armed conflict (whether customary law or treaty law). No organ of any international governmental organization (other than the UN Security Council) has the power to detract from these obligations in any way.

102 Art. 25 of the UN Charter: "The Members of the United Nations agree to accept and carry out the decisions of the Security Council in accordance with the present Charter."

103 Art. 103 of the UN Charter: "In the event of a conflict between the obligations of the Members of the United Nations under the present Charter and their obligations under any other international agreement, their obligations under the present Charter shall prevail."

3. For combined operations, see Section W.

4. Rule 3 (b) applies also if the international governmental organization's force is engaged in combat in a non-international armed conflict.

4. The fundamental principle is that, in any armed conflict, the right of the Belligerent Parties to choose methods or means of warfare is not unlimited.

1. This basic Rule is based on Art. 22 of the 1907 Hague Regulations[104] and on Art. 35 (1) of AP/I.[105] All the Rules in this Manual lead back to this fundamental principle.

2. The main direct consequence of Rule 4 is the fundamental principle that military necessity does not justify any exception from any Rule in the Manual, unless such an exception is expressly stated in the Rule (see, e.g., Rule 95 (b)).

3. There is no difference in this respect between international and non-international armed conflict.

[104] Art. 22 of the 1907 Hague Regulations: "The right of belligerents to adopt means of injuring the enemy is not unlimited." Wording identical in the 1899 Hague Regulations.

[105] Art. 35 (1) of AP/I: "In any armed conflict, the right of the Parties to the conflict to choose methods or means of warfare is not unlimited."

Section C

Weapons

1. With the exception of Rule 9, which relates to the legal review of weapons, this Section applies equally in both international and non-international armed conflict.

2. The use of weapons in warfare, including in air and missile warfare, is restricted by both treaty law and customary international law. The former binds only States Party to the relevant instruments, whereas the latter binds all States. In some cases, the treaty law codifies a norm of customary international law. Section C sets forth Rules based in customary international law; treaty law may impose greater limitations for the armed forces of Contracting Parties to particular treaties.

3. A basic distinction exists between weapons that are unlawful by nature – because they are incapable of compliance with either the customary international law principle of distinction or that of unnecessary suffering (see Rule 5) – and weapons which are not *per se* unlawful, but are used unlawfully in violation of the provisions governing attacks (see section D). Disagreement exists over whether certain weapons are unlawful by nature, that is (in and of themselves), as distinct from their unlawful use in a particular context, for instance because they are expected to cause excessive collateral damage compared to the anticipated military advantage in the attendant circumstances (see Rule 14). Examples of weapons which have generated such controversy include cluster munitions; anti-personnel land mines; and depleted uranium munitions (see Commentary on Rule 7).

4. Even though, clearly, weapons may now or in the future be excluded merely on the basis of the general principles of distinction (including the prohibition against indiscriminate attacks (see Rule 13)) or unnecessary suffering, as expressed in customary international law, it must be admitted that, in practice – in the absence of specific treaty law applicable to the matter – some States may contest that such is the case.

5. Weapons used in air and missile warfare must comply with:

(a) The basic principle of distinction between civilians and combatants and between civilian objects and military objectives.

Consequently, it is prohibited to conduct air or missile combat operations which employ weapons that (i) cannot be directed at a specific lawful target and therefore are of a nature to strike lawful targets and civilians or civilian objects without distinction; or (ii) the effects of which cannot be limited as required by the law of international armed conflict and which therefore are of a nature to strike lawful targets and civilians or civilian objects without distinction;

1. The ICJ has recognized the principle of distinction as one of the two "cardinal principles contained in the texts constituting the fabric of humanitarian law." Based on this principle, the ICJ has noted that "States . . . must consequently never use weapons that are incapable of distinguishing between civilian and military targets."[106]

2. The principle of distinction in targeting requires that the weapon be capable of being directed against a specific military objective. "Capable of being directed" does not require terminal guidance to the target, or use of the most precise weapon under all circumstances. It prohibits "blind weapons" which cannot, with any reasonable assurance, be directed against a lawful target. Indiscriminate weapons are those that are likely to hit civilians and combatants, or civilian objects and military objectives, without distinction. An example is the uncontrolled balloon-borne bombs launched by Imperial Japan against the West Coast of the US and Canada during WWII.

3. The assessment of what "cannot be directed" may change over time with advances in technology. In other words: technological developments, and the wider availability of systems with increased precision, may shift general understandings as to when a weapon is incapable of being directed. In particular, improvements in the accuracy of weapons may heighten expectations of the general public as to precision, thereby causing the assessment of "cannot be directed" to evolve over time. It ought to be noted in this regard that, despite such expectations, most air forces at the present time do not field a robust precision attack capability.

4. Rule 5 (a) also prohibits use of weapons that have uncontrollable effects likely to harm protected persons and objects. In other words,

[106] ICJ, Nuclear Weapons Advisory Opinion, at page 257.

the consequences of using such a weapon cannot be controlled by the attacker. For instance, contagious biological weapons (as distinct from non-contagious ones) are prohibited on this basis because, once released, the biological contagions may not be restricted to combatants and can uncontrollably spread to civilians.[107]

5. In contrast to the Rules governing the principle of proportionality and the requirement to take feasible precautions in attack (see, respectively, Rule 14 and Section G), Rule 5 (a) does not expressly deal with the expectations of the attacker. It is possible that an attacker may not know that the effects of a particular attack would strike combatants and civilians, or military objectives and civilian objects, without distinction. Rule 5 (a) does not prohibit the use of a weapon if such effects are not reasonably in the contemplation of the attacker. On the other hand, if an attacker ought to have reasonably anticipated that the weapon would strike combatants and civilians, or military objectives and civilian objects without distinction, its use would be unlawful.

6. It is important to distinguish Rule 5 (a) from that prohibiting indiscriminate attacks (see Rule 13). Weapons that are capable of discriminate use – and hence in compliance with Rule 5 (a) – may be used indiscriminately in violation of Rule 13. For instance, State practice demonstrates that unguided bombs are not as such indiscriminate by nature. In many circumstances, they can be delivered against enemy combatants with little harm to civilians or civilian objects. An example would be the use of unguided bombs against troop formations in uninhabited areas. Additionally, unguided bombs can be fairly accurate depending on their methods of delivery. However, the release of unguided bombs over an area inhabited by civilians, without any effort to direct them against military objectives in that area, is an indiscriminate (and therefore unlawful) use of an otherwise discriminate weapon (see Rule 13).

(b) The prohibition of unnecessary suffering or superfluous injury.

Consequently, it is prohibited to conduct air or missile combat operations which employ weapons that are calculated, or of a nature, to cause unnecessary suffering or superfluous injury to combatants.

1. Although warfare necessarily involves the killing and disabling of combatants, the classical law of international armed conflict has prohibited

[107] Biological weapons have been prohibited in treaty law, specifically in the 1925 Gas Protocol and in the BWC (see Rule 6 (a)).

weapons that cause them suffering which is unnecessary, or injury which is superfluous. An example of a weapon prohibited on this basis is a glass filled projectile, for treatment of such wounds would be unnecessarily complicated and the disabling effect of the weapon could as easily be achieved using metal fragments.

2. The fourth operative paragraph of the 1868 St. Petersburg Declaration prohibited weapons that "uselessly aggravate the suffering of disabled men, or render their death inevitable."[108] The authentic French version of Art. 23 (e) of both the 1899 and the 1907 Hague Regulations uses the expression "maux superflus".[109] However, the non-binding English translation of this clause rendered the same expression once as "superfluous injury" (1899 version)[110] and a second time as "unnecessary suffering" (1907 version).[111] Art. 35 (2) of AP/I combines the two into "superfluous injury or unnecessary suffering," while leaving intact the French expression "maux superflus".[112] The expression "superfluous injury or unnecessary suffering" has also been used in the Preamble of the CCW[113] as well as in the Preamble of the 1997 Ottawa Convention.[114] This Manual applies this modern phraseology, it being understood that the semantic alterations do not affect substance, i.e., both expressions "superfluous injury" and "unnecessary suffering" – captured in French by the expression "maux superflus" – convey the same idea.

[108] Fourth operative paragraph of the 1868 St. Petersburg Declaration: "That this object would be exceeded by the employment of arms which uselessly aggravate the sufferings of disabled men, or render their death inevitable."

[109] Art. 23 of both the 1899 and the 1907 Hague Regulations: "Outre les prohibitions établies par des conventions spéciales, il est notamment interdit: . . . (e) d'employer des armes, des projectiles ou des matières propres à causer des maux superflus."

[110] Art. 23 in the 1899 Hague Regulations: "Besides the prohibitions provided by special Conventions, it is especially prohibited . . . (e) To employ arms, projectiles, or material of a nature to cause superfluous injury."

[111] Art. 23 in the 1907 Hague Regulations: "In addition to the prohibitions provided by special Conventions, it is especially forbidden . . . (e) To employ arms, projectiles, or material calculated to cause unnecessary suffering."

[112] Art. 35 (2) of AP/I: "It is prohibited to employ weapons, projectiles and material and methods of warfare of a nature to cause superfluous injury or unnecessary suffering."

[113] Third paragraph of the Preamble to the CCW: "Basing themselves on the principle of international law that the right of the parties to an armed conflict to choose methods or means of warfare is not unlimited, and on the principle that prohibits the employment in armed conflicts of weapons, projectiles and material and methods of warfare of a nature to cause superfluous injury or unnecessary suffering."

[114] Eleventh paragraph of the Preamble of the 1997 Ottawa Convention: "Basing themselves on the principle of international humanitarian law that the right of the parties to an armed

3. The 1868 St. Petersburg Declaration prohibited weapons that "uselessly aggravate the suffering", implying that it is the objective nature of the weapon, not the subjective intent of the design, that renders the weapon unlawful. Art. 23 (e) of the 1899 Hague Regulations refers to weapons "of a nature to cause" tracking the 1868 St. Petersburg Declaration approach. By contrast, the non-binding English version of the 1907 Hague Regulations used, in Art. 23 (e) thereof, the phrase "calculated to cause". Although this may suggest that the intent of the weapon design was the determinative factor in the prohibition, the authentic French text of the same provision uses the phrase of the 1899 Regulations ("propres à causer"), suggesting that the drafters did not intend to alter the scope of the prohibition. Indeed, Art. 35 (2) of AP/I reverts to the "of a nature to cause" text, a formula repeated in the Preamble of both the CCW and the 1997 Ottawa Convention respectively, as well as in Art. 8 (2) (b) (xx) of the Rome Statute of the ICC.[115] This Manual employs the phrase "calculated, or of a nature, to cause" to make clear that weapons falling into either category are prohibited. That is to say, it does not necessarily matter whether the weapon was intended (calculated) to cause the unnecessary suffering and superfluous injury; it will be equally sufficient if the weapon by nature has that consequence.

4. The prohibition of weapons calculated, or of a nature to cause, superfluous injury or unnecessary suffering acknowledges that necessary suffering to combatants is lawful, and may include severe injury or death. The prohibition is violated when the weapon in question will, when employed for its intended purpose and with reasonable foresight, cause injuries that serve no military purpose. Beyond that, there is no agreed upon objective standard for superfluous injury or unnecessary suffering. Usually, a weapon will be deemed to violate the prohibition only

conflict to choose methods or means of warfare is not unlimited, on the principle that prohibits the employment in armed conflicts of weapons, projectiles and materials and methods of warfare of a nature to cause superfluous injury or unnecessary suffering and on the principle that a distinction must be made between civilians and combatants."

115 Art. 8 (2) (b) (xx) of the Rome Statute of the ICC renders the following a war crime, in an international armed conflict: "Employing weapons, projectiles and material and methods of warfare which are of a nature to cause superfluous injury or unnecessary suffering or which are inherently indiscriminate in violation of the international law of armed conflict, provided that such weapons, projectiles and material and methods of warfare are the subject of a comprehensive prohibition and are included in an annex to this Statute, by an amendment in accordance with the relevant provisions set forth in articles 121 and 123."

if it inevitably (in its normal use) causes a specific type of injury, i.e., causing unnecessary suffering or superfluous injury to combatants in light of the availability of comparable lawful weapons that cause less suffering or injury. In other words, a weapon's effects must be considered in light of other weapons currently in use that can achieve an equivalent military purpose. Reduced to basics, two questions permeate the assessment: (i) is a less injurious alternative weapon available?; and (ii) is the alternative sufficiently effective in achieving the intended military purpose?[116]

5. Superfluous injury and unnecessary suffering are determined as regards a specific weapon or munition. This has to be done – if the weapon is already in use – by assessing the effects of the weapon as used in actual State practice but in any case through the pre-fielding review of the design of the weapon (see Rule 9).

6. Although the purpose and object of Rule 5 (b) is the protection of combatants, it nevertheless also applies when using weapons against civilians directly participating in hostilities. Naturally, when collateral damage is expected to be caused to civilians, it is impossible to ignore the impact on them on weapons calculated, or of a nature, to cause superfluous injury or unnecessary suffering.

6. Specific weapons are prohibited in air or missile combat operations. These include:

1. The specific weapons listed in this Rule are prohibited on a number of grounds (either jointly or separately), i.e., breach of the principle of distinction (see Rule 5 (a) and Rule 10 (a)) due to the indiscriminate character of the weapon (see Rule 5 (a)); or breach of the prohibition of unnecessary suffering or superfluous injury (see Rule 5 (b)). However, considering their explicit prohibition in the law of international armed conflict, there is no need to debate whether or not they comply with any of these principles.

[116] The ICRC contested that the key criterion for application of the Rule is the absence of any less injurious alternative weapon available to achieve the same military purpose. For the ICRC, the assessment of the legality of a weapon in light of Rule 5 (b) involves weighing the relevant health effects caused by a weapon against the intended military purpose or expected military advantage. The correct questions, according to the ICRC, are: (i) What is the design-dependant nature of the foreseeable injury?; and (ii) Is this more than is necessary to render a combatant *hors de combat*?

2. There is a growing trend, manifested in the 2001 Amendment to Article 1 of the CCW,[117] to apply rules prohibiting specific weapons in international armed conflict to non-international armed conflict as well.[118]

(a) Biological, including bacteriological, weapons.

1. Biological weapons refer to weapons that employ pathogens or toxins. The pathogens include bacteria (hence, bacteriological weapon), viruses or other biological disease producing agents.

2. The "use of bacteriological methods of warfare" was first prohibited by the first operative paragraph of the 1925 Gas Protocol. The prohibition was confirmed in the BWC, which requires (Art. I) States Party to undertake "never in any circumstances to develop, produce, stockpile of otherwise acquire or retain: (1) microbial or other biological agents, or toxins whatever their origin or method of production, of types and in quantities that have no justification for prophylactic, protective or other peaceful purposes; (2) weapons, equipment or means of delivery designed to use such agents or toxins for hostile purposes or in armed conflict". Although not expressly referencing use, the prohibition on possession necessarily includes use.[119] The prohibition on the use of biological and bacteriological weapons undoubtedly reflects customary international law.

3. Since possession of biological weapons is prohibited, their use in non-international armed conflicts is excluded as much as in international armed conflicts.

[117] Art. 1 (1) and Art. 1 (2) of the 2001 Amendment to the CCW, see fn. 3.

[118] For the trend in general, see Prosecutor v. Dusko Tadic, Case IT-94-I, Decision on the Defence Motion for Interlocutory Appeal on Jurisdiction, Decision of 2 October 1995, in which the ICTY Appeals Chamber asserted (Para. 119) that "We shall now briefly show how the gradual extension to internal armed conflict of rules and principles concerning international wars has also occurred as regards means and methods of warfare." In Para. 127, the Appeals Chamber concluded: Notwithstanding these limitations [dealt with in Para. 126 of the Decision], it cannot be denied that customary rules have developed to govern internal strife. These rules... cover such areas as... prohibition of means of warfare proscribed in international armed conflicts and ban of certain methods of conducting hostilities."

[119] In 1996, at the Fourth Review Conference of the 1972 Biological Weapons Convention States Parties reaffirmed in the third preambular paragraph of their Final Declaration "that under any circumstances the use, development, production and stockpiling of bacteriological (biological) and toxin weapons is effectively prohibited under Article I of the Convention." (see <www.un.org/Depts/ddar/bwc/bwc.htm>)

(b) Chemical weapons.

1. The CWC includes a detailed definition of "chemical weapons" in Art. II (1);[120] of "toxic chemicals" in Art. II (2);[121] and of "precursors" in Art. II (3).[122]

2. Chemical weapons were widely used by both sides during WWI, notwithstanding the 1899 Hague Declaration (IV,2) Concerning Asphyxiating Gases, which prohibited gas attacks by projectile.[123] Once circumvented by Germany through use of ground systems dispensing chlorine gas at Ypres in 1915, retaliation, counter-retaliation and escalation followed swiftly. Although the 1925 Gas Protocol attempted to remedy the problem by banning the use of "asphyxiating, poisonous or other gases, and of all analogous liquids, materials or devices . . . ", it did not prohibit possession of chemical weapons, and was widely interpreted as only prohibiting first use. Italy employed air-delivered mustard gas in Ethiopia beginning in December 1935. The fact that Allies and Axis States did not use chemical weapons on the battlefield during WWII may have resulted as much from mutual deterrence as from treaty law. Seeking broader restrictions, the CWC prohibits development, production, acquisition, stockpiling and use (or assist others to do so) of chemical weapons, and imposes a robust verification mechanism.[124] There is no question that the

[120] Art. II (1) of the CWC: "'Chemical Weapons' means the following, together or separately: (a) Toxic chemicals and their precursors, except where intended for purposes not prohibited under this Convention, as long as the types and quantities are consistent with such purposes; (b) Munitions and devices, specifically designed to cause death or other harm through the toxic properties of those toxic chemicals specified in subparagraph (a), which would be released as a result of the employment of such munitions and devices; (c) Any equipment specifically designed for use directly in connection with the employment of munitions and devices specified in subparagraph (b)."

[121] Art. II (2) of the CWC defines "toxic chemicals" as "any chemical which through its chemical action on life processes can cause death, temporary incapacitation or permanent harm to humans or animals. This includes all such chemicals, regardless of their origin or of their method of production, and regardless of whether they are produced in facilities, in munitions or elsewhere."

[122] Art. II (3) of the CWC defines "precursors" as "[a]ny chemical reactant which takes part at any stage in the production by whatever method of a toxic chemical. This includes any key component of a binary or multicomponent chemical system."

[123] First operative paragraph of the 1899 Hague Declaration (IV, 2): "The contracting Powers agree to abstain from the use of projectiles the sole object of which is the diffusion of asphyxiating or deleterious gases."

[124] Art. I (1) of the CWC: "Each State Party to this Convention undertakes never under any circumstances: (a) To develop, produce, otherwise acquire, stockpile or retain chemical weapons, or transfer, directly or indirectly, chemical weapons to anyone; (b) To use

use of chemical weapons is prohibited by customary international law in armed conflicts.[125]

3. Two issues regarding chemical weapons deserve mention. The first involves the use of riot control agents (see paragraph 4 of the Commentary on Rule 1 (v) and paragraph 9 of the Commentary on Rule 2 (a)), such as tear gas. These chemicals (Art. II (7) of the CWC) "can produce rapidly in humans sensory irritation or disabling physical effects which disappear within a short time following termination of exposure." The CWC proscribes[126] the use of "riot control agents as a method of warfare" for Contracting Parties, but fails to address some specific issues. It is generally agreed that the CWC does not limit the use of such chemicals for the purpose of riot control during civil disturbances. It is also maintained by certain States that controlling rioting prisoners in a POW-camp is not a method of warfare. However, controversy exists over certain other types of operations.[127]

4. The second issue relates to herbicides, which are chemicals used to defoliate trees, bushes, shrubs and other vegetation that might be used to shield enemy movements. For instance, US aircraft delivered herbicides

chemical weapons; (c) To engage in any military preparations to use chemical weapons; (d) To assist, encourage or induce, in any way, anyone to engage in any activity prohibited to a State Party under this Convention."

125 Art. 8 (2) (b) (xviii) of the Rome Statue of the ICC, qualifying as a war crime in international armed conflict: "Employing asphyxiating, poisonous or other gases, and all analogous liquids, materials or devices".

126 Art. I (5) of the CWC, see fn. 51.

127 Para. 10.3.2.1 of NWP ("Riot Control Agents in Armed Conflict"): "Under Executive Order 11850, Renunciation of certain uses in war of chemical herbicides and riot control agents, the United States renounced the first use of riot control agents in armed conflict except in defensive military modes to save lives, in situations such as (1) Riot control situations in areas under effective U.S. military control, to include control of rioting prisoners of war; (2) Situations in which civilians are used to mask or screen attacks and civilian casualties can be reduced or avoided; (3) Rescue missions involving downed aircrews or escaping prisoners of war; (4) Protection of military supply depots, military convoys, and other military activities in rear echelon areas from civil disturbances, terrorist activities, or paramilitary operations.

Such employment of riot control agents by U.S. forces in armed conflict requires presidential approval. The United States consider that the prohibition on the use of [riot control agents] as a "method of warfare" applies in international and internal armed conflict, but that it does not apply in normal peacekeeping operations, law enforcement operations, humanitarian and disaster relief operations, counterterrorist and hostage rescue operations, noncombatant rescue operations, and any other operations not considered international or internal armed conflict."

during the Viet Nam conflict to deny cover to enemy lawful targets, a practice challenged by some other States. The sole reference to herbicides in the CWC is a Preambular assertion that their use is forbidden as a method of warfare.[128] The US has formally renounced the first use of herbicides, except "for control of vegetation within U.S. bases and installations or around their immediate defensive perimeters".[129]

5. Since use as well as possession of chemical weapons is prohibited, their use in non-international armed conflicts is excluded as much as in international armed conflicts.

(c) **Laser weapons specifically designed, as their sole combat function or as one of their combat functions, to cause permanent blindness to unenhanced vision, that is to the naked eye or to the eye with corrective eyesight devices.**

1. This Rule is based on the 1995 Protocol IV to the CCW.[130]

2. Protocol IV to the CCW prohibits use of laser weapons specifically designed as a "combat function" to cause permanent blindness, even when wearing corrective eyesight devices such as eyeglasses or contact lenses. It is widely accepted that this prohibition constitutes customary international law. It is noteworthy that there is no prohibition on the use of laser during hostilities for other purposes, such as range-finding and target acquisition, even if their employment may risk causing permanent blindness to those in the vicinity of such use.

3. As with all weapons, employment of weapons systems incorporating laser technology is subject to the requirement to take feasible precautions in attack (see Section G). For Contracting Parties to Protocol IV

[128] Seventh paragraph of the Preamble to the CWC: "Recognizing the prohibition, embodied in the pertinent agreements and relevant principles of international law, of the use of herbicides as a method of warfare."

[129] Para. 10.3.3 of NWP ("Herbicidal Agents"): "The United States considers that use of herbicidal agents in wartime is not prohibited by either the 1925 Gas Protocol or the 1993 Chemical Weapons Convention but has formally renounced the first use of herbicides in time of armed conflict except for control of vegetation within U.S. bases and installations or around their immediate defensive perimeters. Use of herbicidal agents during armed conflict requires presidential approval."

[130] Art. 1 of the 1995 Protocol IV to the CCW: "It is prohibited to employ laser weapons specifically designed, as their sole combat function or as one of their combat functions, to cause permanent blindness to unenhanced vision, that is to the naked eye or to the eye with corrective eyesight devices. The High Contracting Parties shall not transfer such weapons to any State or non-State entity."

to the CCW, Art. 2 thereof augments this obligation for non-blinding laser weapons by providing that Contracting Parties "[i]n the employment of laser systems... shall take all feasible precautions to avoid the incidence of permanent blindness to unenhanced vision. Such precautions shall include training of their armed forces and other practical measures".

4. For Contracting Parties to the 2001 Amendment to the CCW,[131] the applicability of Protocol (IV) to the CCW is extended to non-international armed conflict.

(d) Poison, poisoned substances and poisoned weapons.

1. The prohibition of poison and poisoned weapons predates the modern codification of the law of international armed conflict in Art. 23 (a) of the 1907 Hague Regulations.[132] It undoubtedly enjoys customary international law status.

2. No definition of poison exists in the law of international armed conflict. However, as generally understood, poisons are all substances that can harm humans or animals through a chemical reaction on or in the body. They include chemicals with this effect, as well as toxins (biologically produced substances). It is noteworthy that otherwise harmless substances can become poisoned and thereby prohibited for use as a poison. For instance, it is unlawful to place the cadaver of an animal into a water source in order to poison it and make it unusable.

3. The prohibition has both humanitarian and military underpinnings. For instance, from a military perspective, the poisoning of wells came to be regarded not only as unnecessary destruction, but also as a liability because a retreating commander might subsequently depend on those same wells for water supplies if the course of the battle changes. Similarly, and from a humanitarian perspective, the poisoning of a weapon which is already capable of rendering combatants *hors de combat* serves no military purpose by uselessly aggravating wounds.

131 Art. 1 (1) and Art. 1 (2) of the 2001 Amendment to the CCW, see fn. 3.

132 Art. 23 of the 1907 Hague Regulations: "In addition to the prohibitions provided by special Conventions, it is especially forbidden: (a) To employ poison or poisoned weapons." A similar provision (related to the employment of "poison or poisoned arms") was already contained in Art. 23 (a) of the 1899 Hague Regulations.

See also Art. 8 (2) (b) (xvii) of the Rome Statute of the ICC, declaring it a war crime in an international armed conflict: "[e]mploying poison or poisoned weapons".

4. Certain uses of poisons may also fall within the prohibitions imposed in relation to biological, bacteriological, and chemical weapons (see, respectively, Rule 6 (a) and Rule 6 (b)).

5. The customary prohibition of the use of poison has developed to include non-international armed conflicts.

(e) Small arms projectiles calculated, or of a nature, to cause explosion on impact with or within the human body.

1. The 1868 St. Petersburg Declaration prohibited the use of exploding or inflammable projectiles with a weight under 400 grammes on the basis that their use would uselessly aggravate injuries.[133] This is in line with the contemporary prohibition of causing superfluous injury or unnecessary suffering (see Rule 5 (b)).

2. 400 grammes was the weight of the smallest artillery shell at the time of the adoption of the 1868 St. Petersburg Declaration. The rule of the St. Petersburg Declaration has no application to the use of missiles, since all missiles exceed the weight limitation.

3. State practice has particularly affected application of the norm in air warfare. During WWI (and armed conflicts since then) exploding anti-aircraft bullets were used by both sides. This practice was confirmed in Art. 18 of the HRAW, which provided that the "use of tracer, incendiary or explosive projectiles by or against aircraft is not prohibited".[134] Although the HRAW were never accepted as legally binding by any government, Art. 18 is now considered reflective of customary law. Modern state practice has modified the prohibition of the 1868 St. Petersburg Declaration, and this in line with Art. 18 of the HRAW.[135]

[133] First operative paragraph of the 1868 St. Petersburg Declaration: "The Contracting Parties engage mutually to renounce, in case of war among themselves, the employment by their military or naval troops of any projectile of a weight below 400 grammes, which is either explosive or charged with fulminating or inflammable substances."

[134] Art. 18 of the HRAW: "The use of tracer, incendiary or explosive projectiles by or against aircraft is not prohibited. This provision applies equally to states which are parties to the Declaration of St. Petersburg, 1868, and to those which are not."

[135] This evolution of State practice has been recognised by the ICRC. See ICRC Customary IHL Study, Rule 78, Explanation thereto, at pages 272–273: "Practice since the adoption of the St. Petersburg Declaration has modified this prohibition, as exploding anti-aircraft bullets were introduced in the First World War. Furthermore, lighter grenades and exploding anti-material bullets have been introduced since. These developments have occurred without any objection. The military manuals or statements of several States

4. The rationale of the Commission of Jurists that drew up the Art. 18 of the HRAW was "the impracticability for an airman while in flight to change the ammunition which he is using in the machine-gun in his aircraft".[136] State practice since 1923 is consistent with Art. 18 of the HRAW. However, some modern aircraft (e.g., helicopters) may be capable of transporting personnel who could change ammunition in mid-air. If so, it is arguable that the original provision of the 1868 St. Petersburg Declaration ought to remain intact.

5. The prohibition included in Rule 5 (e) relates only to the use of projectiles calculated, or of a nature to explode on impact with or within the human body. That is to say the prohibition does not affect the use of projectiles against inanimate objects, including aircraft.

6. Since the 1868 St. Petersburg Declaration, it has been widely accepted that exploding projectiles must not be used against personnel. The prohibition is equally applicable in international and non-international armed conflicts,[137] and this subject to the qualification in Art. 18 of the HRAW.

(f) Weapons the primary effect of which is to injure by fragments which in the human body escape detection by x-ray.

1. Incorporating fragments (such as glass) into weapons for the purpose of avoiding detection during medical treatment does not contribute to rendering a combatant *hors de combat*, but does needlessly jeopardize his or her treatment or recovery. This prohibition is based on the 1980

consider only the anti-personnel use of such projectiles to be prohibited or only if they are designed to explode upon impact with the human body. Some military manuals and legislation, nevertheless, continue to refer back to the wording of the prohibition contained in the St. Petersburg Declaration, even though practice has since modified this prohibition." The ICRC now considers that the anti-personnel use of bullets which explode within the human body is prohibited.

[136] Commentary on the HRAW, at pages 20–21: "In the form in which the proposal was first brought forward its provisions were limited to a stipulation that the use of tracer bullets against aircraft generally was not prohibited. Various criticisms were, however, made about the proposed text, chiefly founded on the impracticability for an airman while in flight to change the ammunition which he is using in the machine-gun in his aircraft. He cannot employ different bullets in accordance with the target at which he is aiming, one sort of ammunition for other aircraft and another sort for land forces by whom he may be attacked. The Commission, therefore, came to the conclusion that the most satisfactory solution of the problem would be to state specifically that the use of tracer, incendiary or explosive projectiles by or against aircraft is not prohibited."

[137] NIAC Manual to SRM/ACS at page 35.

Protocol I to the CCW.[138] Portions of many munitions, such as the casing or timing mechanism, may be made of non-metallic parts or other substances not detectable by x-ray to reduce weight, manufacturing cost, and for similar reasons not related to the wounding as such of enemy combatants. Such parts are not prohibited because any injuries they cause are incidental to the primary effect of the weapon.

2. For Contracting Parties to the 2001 Amendment to the CCW,[139] the applicability of Rule 6 (f) is extended to non-international armed conflict.

7. The use of any weapon not expressly mentioned under this Section of the Manual is subject to the general Rules and principles of customary and treaty law of international armed conflict (in particular the principle of distinction and the prohibition of unnecessary suffering), as well as to any other treaty law applicable for Contracting Parties.

1. The use of any weapon is subject to the Rules set forth in this Manual, in particular Sections D on attacks and Section G on feasible precautions in attack. The weapons listed in the Commentary on this Rule are of particular relevance to air and missile warfare. Furthermore, numerous treaties set forth restrictions on the use of some of the following weapons or weapons systems, or ban their use altogether for Contracting Parties. These treaty regimes will be discussed below, it being understood that they are applicable only to Contracting Parties.

2. The following weapons, listed hereafter in alphabetical order, deserve notice: (a) Air- Delivered Land Mines; (b) Air-Delivered Naval Mines; (c) Beyond Visual Range Weapons Systems; (d) Blast Weapons; (e) Cluster Munitions; (f) Delayed-Action Munitions; (g) Depleted Uranium Munitions; (h) Fragmenting Munitions; (i) Incendiary Weapons; (j) Non-lethal weapons; (k) Nuclear Weapons; (l) Small-Calibre Projectiles.

(a) Air-Delivered Land Mines

1. There is no customary international law prohibition on the use of land mines.

[138] 1980 Protocol I to the CCW: "It is prohibited to use any weapon the primary effect of which is to injure by fragments which in the human body escape detection by X-rays." According to the ICRC, this rule has become customary international law. See Rule 79 of the ICRC Customary IHL Study, at page 275: "The use of weapons the primary effect of which is to injure by fragments which are not detectable by X-rays in the human body is prohibited."

[139] Art. 1 (1) and 1 (2) of the 2001 Amendment to the CCW, see fn. 3.

2. For Contracting Parties to the 1997 Ottawa Convention, the use of all anti-personnel land mines – including those that are air-delivered – is prohibited.[140] However, the 1997 Ottawa Convention does not cover command-detonated weapons or anti-tank/vehicle mines.

3. The 1996 Amended Protocol II to the CCW – while prohibiting certain types of booby traps[141] – does not ban the use of anti-personnel mines, but restricts their use (and the use of anti-vehicle mines) for Contracting Parties to this instrument. In particular, air-delivered mines dropped from an aircraft or otherwise qualify as "remotely delivered mines"[142] to which (Art. 6 of the 1996 Amended Protocol II to the CWC)[143]

[140] Art. 1 (1) of the 1997 Ottawa Convention: "Each State Party undertakes never under any circumstances: (a) To use anti-personnel mines; (b) To develop, produce, otherwise acquire, stockpile, retain or transfer to anyone, directly or indirectly, anti-personnel mines; (c) To assist, encourage or induce, in any way, anyone to engage in any activity prohibited to a State Party under this Convention."
The concept "anti-personnel mine" is defined in Art. 2 (1) of the 1997 Ottawa Convention.

[141] Art. 7 (1) and Art. 7 (2) of the 1996 Amended Protocol II to the CCW ("Prohibitions on the use of booby-traps and other devices"): "(1) Without prejudice to the rules of international law applicable in armed conflict relating to treachery and perfidy, it is prohibited in all circumstances to use booby-traps and other devices which are in any way attached to or associated with: (a) internationally recognized protective emblems, signs or signals; (b) sick, wounded or dead persons; (c) burial or cremation sites or graves; (d) medical facilities, medical equipment, medical supplies or medical transportation; (e) children's toys or other portable objects or products specially designed for the feeding, health, hygiene, clothing or education of children; (f) food or drink; (g) kitchen utensils or appliances except in military establishments, military locations or military supply depots; (h) objects clearly of a religious nature; (i) historic monuments, works of art or places of worship which constitute the cultural or spiritual heritage of peoples; or (j) animals or their carcasses. (2) It is prohibited to use booby-traps or other devices in the form of apparently harmless portable objects which are specifically designed and constructed to contain explosive material."

[142] Art. 2 (2) of the 1996 Amended Protocol II to the CCW defines "remotely-delivered mines" as mines "not directly emplaced but delivered by artillery, missile, rocket, mortar, or similar means, or dropped from an aircraft. Mines delivered from a land-based system from less than 500 metres are not considered to be "remotely delivered", provided that they are used in accordance with Article 5 and other relevant Articles of this Protocol."

[143] Art. 6 of the 1996 Amended Protocol II to the CCW ("Restrictions on the use of remotely-delivered mines"): "(1) It is prohibited to use remotely-delivered mines unless they are recorded in accordance with sub-paragraph 1 (b) of the Technical Annex. (2) It is prohibited to use remotely-delivered anti-personnel mines which are not in compliance with the provisions on self-destruction and self-deactivation in the Technical Annex. (3) It is prohibited to use remotely-delivered mines other than anti-personnel mines, unless, to the extent feasible, they are equipped with an effective self-destruction or self-neutralization mechanism and have a back-up self-deactivation feature, which is designed so that the mine will no longer function as a mine when the mine no longer serves the military purpose for which it was placed in position. (4) Effective advance

special restrictions regarding self-destruction and self-deactivation apply.

(b) Air-Delivered Naval Mines

The use of air-delivered free-floating (unanchored) naval mines is prohibited unless they are directed against a military objective and become harmless within a reasonable time after being dropped. Art. 1 (1) of the 1907 Hague Convention (VIII)[144] imposes a one-hour time limit, an approach adopted in the Commentary on the SRM/ACS.[145] The laying of either armed mines or the arming of pre-laid mines must be notified, typically through the NOTMAR ("Notice to Mariners") system, as soon as exigencies permit, unless they are designed only to detonate against vessels that qualify as military objectives.

(c) Beyond Visual Range Weapons Systems

1. The term "beyond visual range" refers to situations in which the target cannot be visually identified, for instance because it is too distant ("over the horizon") or where it cannot be seen due to night, weather conditions, terrain, etc.

2. Beyond visual range weapons systems are not treated separately, either in treaty law or in customary international law. Their use is subject to all standard rules applicable to attacks in international armed conflict.[146]

3. Missiles and other projectiles fired from beyond visual range are lawful when their employment permits distinguishing military objectives and combatants from civilians and civilian objects. Such may be accomplished through sensors on the weapon itself, or through external guidance, for instance from the aircraft.

warning shall be given of any delivery or dropping of remotely-delivered mines which may affect the civilian population, unless circumstances do not permit."

144 Art. 1 (1) of the 1907 Hague Convention (VIII): "It is forbidden: (1) To lay unanchored automatic contact mines, except when they are so constructed as to become harmless one hour at most after the person who laid them ceases to control them."

145 Para. 82 of the SRM/ACS: "It is forbidden to use free-floating mines unless: (a) they are directed against a military objective; and (b) they become harmless within an hour after loss of control over them."

146 Para. 78 of the SRM/ACS: "Missiles and projectiles, including those with over-the-horizon capabilities, shall be used in conformity with the principles of target discrimination as set out in paragraphs 38–46."

NWP, Para. 9.10 ("Over-the-horizon weapons systems"): "Missiles and projectiles with OTH or beyond-visual-range capabilities are lawful provided they are equipped with sensors or are employed in conjunction with external sources of targeting data that are sufficient to ensure effective target discrimination."

(d) Blast Weapons

1. Blast weapons create a pressure wave triggered by an explosion in order to damage objects and/or injure enemy combatants. In other words, the destructive force of a blast weapon is the overpressure it causes. For instance, a bomb relying on blast may be used to cause a building to collapse. Blast weapons must be distinguished from fragmentation weapons, such as a hand grenade, causing material destruction or combatant injury through the fragments of the weapon itself, or through items (e.g., nails) contained within the weapon. Blast is an inherent aspect of high explosive munitions, whether they are weapons dependent solely on blast or a combination of blast and fragmentation. For fragmenting munitions, see the Commentary on Rule 7 (h).

2. Damage to or destruction of military objectives and combatant death or injury through blast has been a feature of air-delivered weapons since the beginning of air warfare. No treaty of the law of international armed conflict prohibits blast weapons. Based upon State practice, blast weapons are not regarded as "calculated, or of a nature, to cause unnecessary suffering or superfluous injury to combatants" (see Rule 5 (b)).

3. Some blast weapons may appear to be incendiary weapons because the explosion that causes the blast can cause a fire. However, blast weapons have no greater fire-starting capability than other high-explosive munitions. Nor do blast weapons have a fire-sustaining capability. In view of the definition of incendiary weapon in Protocol III to the CCW[147], blast weapons are not incendiary weapons. For incendiary weapons, see the Commentary on Rule (7) (i).

(e) Cluster Munitions

1. Cluster munitions consist of a canister or delivery body containing multiple, conventional explosive fragmenting submunitions intended to apply force uniformly over an area. Depending on their nature, submunitions can be effective against enemy heavy armour, vehicles with light armour, parked aircraft, similar "soft" material targets, and enemy combatants.

2. The Final Report to the Prosecutor of the ICTY by the Committee Established to Review the NATO Bombing Campaign against the Federal Republic of Yugoslavia reviewed the use of cluster munitions during

[147] For the definition of "incendiary weapons" in Art. 1 (1) of the 1980 Protocol III to the CCW, see fn. 151.

the 1999 Operation Allied Force Campaign.[148] It recommended against prosecution based on the use of cluster munitions because the law of international armed conflict did not specifically address such weapons, although the report did caution (paragraph 27) that "cluster bombs must be used in compliance with the general principles applicable to the use of all weapons". In the years that followed, international concern grew with respect to cluster munitions. In particular, considering that cluster munitions disperse large numbers of explosive submunitions or bomblets over wide areas, they are liable to cause hazard to civilians (especially when they are used in densely populated areas). In addition, submunitions become a long-term hazard to civilians when they fail to detonate. Technological advances in recent years have dramatically decreased the failure rates of newly produced cluster munitions used by some modern armed forces. Nevertheless, concern also exists about the widespread distribution of the submunitions (bomblets) of cluster munitions.

3. In part, the problem was addressed with the adoption of the 2003 Protocol V to the CCW, which focuses on clearance of all forms of explosive remnants of war from the battlefield (not necessarily cluster munitions). Contracting Parties to the 2003 Protocol V to the CCW agree to mark, clear, remove, or destroy explosive remnants of war in territories under their control as soon as feasible after the cessation of active hostilities. Where a user of explosive remnants of war does not control the territory on which the explosive remnants are located, it must, where feasible, provide technical, financial, material or human resources assistance to effect clearance.[149] Although not reflecting customary international law,

[148] Final Report to the Prosecutor by the Committee Established to Review the NATO Bombing Campaign Against the Federal Republic of Yugoslavia, available via <www.icty.org/x/file/About/OTP/otp_report_nato_bombing_en.pdf>

[149] Art. 3 of the 2003 Protocol V to the CCW ("Clearance, Removal or Destruction of Explosive Remnants of War"): "(1) Each High Contracting Party and party to an armed conflict shall bear the responsibilities set out in this Article with respect to all explosive remnants of war in territory under its control. In cases where a user of explosive ordnance which has become explosive remnants of war, does not exercise control of the territory, the user shall, after the cessation of active hostilities, provide where feasible, inter alia technical, financial, material or human resources assistance, bilaterally or through a mutually agreed third party, including inter alia through the United Nations system or other relevant organisations, to facilitate the marking and clearance, removal or destruction of such explosive remnants of war. (2) After the cessation of active hostilities and as soon as feasible, each High Contracting Party and party to an armed conflict shall mark and clear, remove or destroy explosive remnants of war in affected territories under its control. Areas affected by explosive remnants of war which are assessed pursuant to

the explosive remnants of war treaty obligations are not objected to by any State.

4. However, many States felt that the 2003 Protocol V to the CCW would not be sufficient to address, in a comprehensive way, the humanitarian problems caused during and after the use of cluster munitions, in particular because of some of their inherent characteristics. This led to the adoption, in 2008, of the Convention on Cluster Munitions. Art. 1 (1) of the Convention bans, *inter alia*, the use of many cluster munitions.[150] This Convention, which obviously applies only to Contracting Parties, does not address (as per the definition of "cluster munition" contained in Art. 2 (2)), munitions containing submunitions of 20 kilograms or more, containing fewer than 10 submunitions, weighing more than four kilograms, that have self-deactivating and self-destructive features, and containing submunitions designed to detect and engage a single target. At the time of writing, there are thirty States that are Contracting Parties to the Convention and one hundred and four States are signatories. However, the Convention is openly opposed by a number of States.

(f) Delayed-Action Munitions

Delayed-action munitions are high-explosive munitions generally employed in conjunction with standard, instant-detonation munitions. A key purpose of air-delivered delayed-action munitions is to impede damage control of targeted airfields or similar military objectives. While their employment against military objectives is not as such prohibited, their effects in areas where civilians may be present must be weighed in light of Section D, in particular the principle of proportionality (see Rule 14).

paragraph 3 of this Article as posing a serious humanitarian risk shall be accorded priority status for clearance, removal or destruction. (3) After the cessation of active hostilities and as soon as feasible, each High Contracting Party and party to an armed conflict shall take the following measures in affected territories under its control, to reduce the risks posed by explosive remnants of war: (a) survey and assess the threat posed by explosive remnants of war; (b) assess and prioritise needs and practicability in terms of marking and clearance, removal or destruction; (c) mark and clear, remove or destroy explosive remnants of war; (d) take steps to mobilise resources to carry out these activities. . . . "

[150] Art. 1 (1) of the 2008 Convention on Cluster Munitions: "Each State Party undertakes never under any circumstances to: (a) Use cluster munitions; (b) Develop, produce, otherwise acquire, stockpile, retain or transfer to anyone, directly or indirectly, cluster munitions; (c) Assist, encourage or induce anyone to engage in any activity prohibited to a State Party under this Convention."

(g) Depleted Uranium Munitions

Air-delivered penetrating munitions are common. Penetrating munitions are high velocity projectiles containing a heavy penetrator, generally depleted uranium or tungsten, designed to pierce armoured targets. Depleted uranium (DU) is used in some air-delivered penetrating munitions because its density and toughness create a particularly effective penetrating combination to defeat enemy armour at greater range. DU has been the subject of multiple national and international organization health studies. None of these studies has found that DU munitions could be considered an unlawful weapon.

(h) Fragmenting Munitions

1. Fragmenting munitions are anti-personnel and/or anti-materiel munitions that (as suggested by their name) project a large number of projectiles on detonation. They have been a major casualty producer on the battlefield, either through fragmenting artillery shells, "grape shot", hand grenades, or more modern forms of pre-fragmented ground and air-delivered munitions. The purpose of multiple-fragmenting munitions is to increase the probability of wounding enemy combatants within range of its fragments. Air-delivered fragmenting munitions include single bombs in a variety of weights and canister bombs containing smaller bomblets, the latter commonly referred to as cluster munitions (on cluster munitions, see Commentary on Rule 7 (e)).

2. The fragmenting munitions referred to here ought not to be confused with the weapons dealt with under Rule 6 (f) ("weapons the primary effect of which is to injure by fragments which in the human body escape detection by x-ray), because the fragment munitions referred to here contain fragments that can be detected by x-ray.

(i) Incendiary Weapons

1. An incendiary weapon is any weapon which is primarily designed to set fire to objects or to cause burn injury to persons through the action of flame, heat, or combination thereof, produced by a chemical reaction of a substance on the target. Incendiary weapons can take the form of bombs, rockets, shells, and other containers of incendiary substances.[151]

[151] Art. 1 (1) of the 1980 Protocol III to the CCW defines "incendiary weapons" as "any weapon or munition which is primarily designed to set fire to objects or to cause burn

2. Although the 1868 St. Petersburg Declaration prohibited the use of exploding or inflammable projectiles with a weight under 400 grammes on the basis that their employment would uselessly aggravate "the sufferings of disabled men, or render their death inevitable"[152], State practice demonstrates that tracer ammunition is not prohibited. This practice was confirmed in Art. 18 of the HRAW which provided that the "use of tracer, incendiary or explosive projectiles by or against aircraft is not prohibited".[153] State practice validates the provision of Art. 18 of the HRAW. Aircraft often employ a mix of tracers and standard ammunition against combatants for range-finding purposes during darkness. The simultaneous use of such ammunition against a variety of targets, including vehicles and personnel, is not unlawful because it is not exclusively designed for anti-personnel use.

3. Air-delivered incendiary weapons include anti-personnel flame weapons that may start fire, such as napalm, or anti-materiel fire-sustaining weapons using thermite or thermate. The 1980 Protocol III to the CCW restricts use, but does not prohibit incendiary weapons *per se*. With respect to air-delivered incendiary weapons, the 1980 Protocol III to the CCW prohibits "in all circumstances" (Art. 2 (2)), for Contracting Parties, the employment of air-delivered incendiary weapons against military objectives located within a concentration of civilians.[154] All States,

injury to persons through the action of flame, heat, or a combination thereof, produced by a chemical reaction of a substance delivered on the target. (a) Incendiary weapons can take the form of, for example, flame throwers, fougasses, shells, rockets, grenades, mines, bombs and other containers of incendiary substances. (b) Incendiary weapons do not include: (i) Munitions which may have incidental incendiary effects, such as illumuninants, tracers, smoke or signalling systems ; (ii) Munitions designed to combine penetration, blast or fragmentation effects with an additional incendiary effect, such as armour-piercing projectiles, fragmentation shells, explosive bombs and similar combined-effects munitions in which the incendiary effect is not specifically designed to cause burn injury to persons, but to be used against military objectives, such as armoured vehicles, aircraft and installations or facilities."

152 Fourth operative paragraph of the 1868 St. Petersburg Declaration, see fn. 108.

153 Art. 18 of the HRAW, see fn. 134.

154 Art. 2 (2) of the 1980 Protocol III to the CCW: "It is prohibited in all circumstances to make any military objective located within a concentration of civilians the object of attack by air-delivered incendiary weapons."

The expression "concentration of civilians" is defined in Art. 1 (2) of the 1980 Protocol III to the CCW as "any concentration of civilians, be it permanent or temporary, such as in inhabited parts of cities, or inhabited towns or villages, or as in camps or columns of refugees or evacuees, or groups of nomads."

including non-Contracting Parties to the 1980 Protocol III to the CCW, are governed, in particular, by the Rules prohibiting indiscriminate attacks or attacks violating the principle of proportionality and the obligation to take feasible precautions in attack (see, respectively, Rule 13 and Rule 14 as well as Section G).

4. Art. 2 of the 1980 Protocol III to the CCW ("Protection of civilians and civilian objects") restricts use, but does not prohibit the employment of incendiary weapons against combatants.[155]

5. Unless intentionally used for incendiary purposes, munitions which may have incidental incendiary effects, such as illuminants, tracers, smoke or signalling systems (such as white phosphorous) are not considered incendiary weapons.[156] For example, use of the non-pyrophoric compound barium nitrate in a tracer round is to enable a gunner to direct his rounds onto his target. Similarly, munitions can be used which contain fragments of white phosphorous. Such use is usually intended for marking a target or masking friendly force movement. These weapons do not qualify as incendiary weapons if they are used for such purposes. However, because they may incidentally start fires, caution is called for if used in densely populated areas.

6. Smoke is an inherent by-product of battlefield munition use, but is also deployed as a ground and air-delivered munition for screening movement of friendly forces. It is expressly (Art. 1 (b) (i)) excluded from the definition of incendiary weapon in the 1980 Protocol III to the CCW. Smoke is a chemical weapon only if it meets the definition of a chemical weapon in the CWC. Military smoke weapons historically have not.

7. Incendiary weapons are not chemical weapons as defined in the CWC,[157] nor are they blast weapons (see Rule 7 (d)).

[155] However, the ICRC takes the position that "The anti-personnel use of incendiary weapons is prohibited, unless it is not feasible to use a less harmful weapon to render a person *hors de combat.*" (see Rule 85 of the ICRC Customary IHL Study, at page 289).

[156] Art. 1 (b) of the CCW: "Incendiary weapons do not include: (i) Munitions which may have incidental incendiary effects, such as illuminants, tracers, smoke or signalling systems; (ii) Munitions designed to combine penetration, blast or fragmentation effects with an additional incendiary effect, such as armour-piercing projectiles, fragmentation shells, explosive bombs and similar combined-effects munitions in which the incendiary effect is not specifically designed to cause burn injury to persons, but to be used against military objectives, such as armoured vehicles, aircraft and installations or facilities." The latter are often referred to as combined effects munitions.

[157] Art. II (1) of the CWC, see fn. 120.

(j) Non-Lethal Weapons

1. Non-lethal weapons (often labelled less-lethal) are intended to incapacitate or repel personnel or disable equipment without causing death or serious injury. The distinction between non-lethal and lethal weapons is that the former are intentionally designed with non-lethal effects in mind. Nevertheless, in practice, non-lethal weapons may occasionally cause grave injuries or fatalities, whereas lethal weapons may cause only minor wounding. Therefore, some commentators object to the designation of a category of weapons as "non-lethal".

2. No treaty addresses non-lethal weapons, whether air-delivered or not, as a generic category. Still, if the designation of weapons as "non-lethal" is accepted, it must be remembered that all weapons – however labelled – are governed by the law of international armed conflict. Some weapons which could be considered "non-lethal," such as blinding laser weapons (see Rule 6 (c)), have been prohibited for Contracting Parties through treaty law. The use of all weapons, however labelled, is governed by the law of international armed conflict.

(k) Nuclear Weapons

1. Ever since Hiroshima and Nagasaki, the use of nuclear weapons has been the subject of heated debates.

2. The ICJ, in its 1996 Nuclear Weapons Advisory Opinion, held that "[i]n the view of the vast majority of States as well as writers, there can be no doubt as to the applicability of humanitarian law to nuclear weapons."[158] The ICJ stressed in this context the importance of the cardinal principles of distinction and unnecessary suffering,[159] as well as the principle of proportionality and the rules governing the protection of the environment (see Rule 14 as well as Section D and Section M).[160]

3. The ICJ further pronounced, by an eleven to three majority, that "[t]here is in neither customary nor conventional international law any comprehensive and universal prohibition of the threat or use of nuclear weapons as such."[161] This decision of the ICJ was arrived at after reviewing

[158] ICJ, Nuclear Weapons Advisory Opinion, para. 85.
[159] ICJ, Nuclear Weapons Advisory Opinion, para. 78.
[160] ICJ, Nuclear Weapons Advisory Opinion, para. 30.
[161] ICJ, Nuclear Weapons Advisory Opinion, para. 105 (2) B.

a long list of treaties, ranging from reviewing the prohibition of poison, poisoned weapons, poisonous gases, bacteriological weapons, chemical weapons, to those relating to protection of the environment and those establishing nuclear weapon free zones.

4. The ICJ added (by seven votes to seven, with the President's casting vote): "It follows from the above-mentioned requirements that the threat or use of nuclear weapons would generally be contrary to the rules of international law applicable in armed conflict, and in particular the principles and rules of humanitarian law; However, in view of the current state of international law, and of the elements of fact at its disposal, the Court cannot conclude definitively whether the threat or use of nuclear weapons would be lawful or unlawful in an extreme circumstance of self-defence, in which the very survival of a State would be at stake."[162] The last sentence of this part of the Advisory Opinion has been harshly criticized in the legal literature on the ground that it confuses the *jus in bello* with the *jus ad bellum.*

5. As a matter of policy, authority to employ nuclear weapons is generally retained at the highest level of government.

(l) Small-Calibre Projectiles

1. In the late 1970s, proposals were made for a CCW protocol to regulate certain types of military small-calibre projectiles. However, such proposals received little or no support in the CCW review conferences.

2. Small calibre weapons historically have seen widespread use by air forces, although much less so in post-WWII conflicts. Small-caliber weapons retain relevance in modern air warfare for certain aircraft and missions, such as rotary-wing gunships.

At the time of signature of AP/I, the United Kingdom declared that it had signed AP/I on the basis of the understanding that "the rules introduced by the Protocol apply exclusively to conventional weapons without prejudice to any other rules of international law applicable to other types of weapons. In particular, the rules so introduced do not have any effect on and do not regulate or prohibit the use of nuclear weapons." Similarly, the USA (which, while having signed AP/I, has not ratified it), at signature of AP/I, stated that its signature is subject to the understanding that "the rules established by this protocol were not intended to have any effect on and do not regulate or prohibit the use of nuclear weapons."

[162] ICJ, Nuclear Weapons Advisory Opinion, para. 105 (2) E.

8. There is no specific obligation on Belligerent Parties to use precision guided weapons. There may however be situations in which the prohibition of indiscriminate attacks, or the obligation to avoid – or, in any event, minimize – collateral damage, cannot be fulfilled without using precision guided weapons.

1. There is no express obligation in treaty or customary international law to employ precision guided weapons (see definition in Rule 1 (bb)). Commanders and those executing or otherwise controlling an attack must conduct a proportionality analysis to determine whether the risk to civilians or civilian objects is excessive considering the anticipated military advantage (see Rule 14). Therefore, for instance, it is prohibited to conduct air or missile attacks against military objectives located in a densely populated area without using appropriate and reasonably available target identification or weapon guidance technologies to aim the weapon at those objectives. It is possible that the risk of excessive collateral damage to civilians or civilian objects – as a result of an attack against a military objective – can be mitigated by using precision guided weapons. See also paragraph 4 of the Commentary on Rule 42.

2. The availability of precision guided weapons has two different dimensions: there is the question of the potential general availability of these weapons (in the sense that such weapons can be acquired by a Belligerent Party) and there is a separate question of actual availability to a specific commander in specific circumstances. It is necessary to dispel the error that precision guided weapons must be used whenever they are available in both senses. First, there exists no obligation in the law of international armed conflict for States to acquire particular types of weapons. Second, operational concerns may limit the use of precision guided weapons. For instance, if such weapons are scarce, a commander may elect to preserve them for urban combat when they will be more useful, rather than employ them elsewhere. Simply put, recourse to precision guided weapons (if available) is called for in circumstances when an attack is undertaken and resorting to such weapons is necessary to prevent indiscriminate attacks (see Rule 13) and to avoid – or, in any event, minimize – expected excessive collateral damage to civilians or civilian objects as compared to the anticipated military advantage. On the obligation to avoid – or, in any event, minimize – collateral damage, see Section G, in particular Rule 32 (b). But, when the principle of proportionality does not come into play (e.g., when there are no civilians or civilian objects expected to be in the

vicinity of the military objective), the commander is free to choose any lawful weapon that he deems fit. On the principle of proportionality, see Rule 14.

9. States are obligated to assess the legality of weapons before fielding them in order to determine whether their employment would, in some or all circumstances, be prohibited.

1. The obligation of States to determine the legality of weapons (including munitions) before employing them in battle is longstanding.[163] The State employing the weapons does not need to conduct the legal review itself. However, the fact that an assessment has already been performed by the State which developed or provided them – or from which they were acquired – does not relieve the State employing them of its responsibility to field only lawful weapons.

2. For Contracting Parties to AP/I, Art. 36 extends the requirement to a review of new "method[s]" of warfare. Further, the review is required during the "study, development, acquisition or adoption" phases.[164] However, there is little State practice in either regard.

3. Although (as stated in paragraph 1 of the Commentary on the *chapeau* of Section C), the requirement of a review of new weapons is applicable only in international armed conflicts, this does not relieve the State of its responsibility to field only lawful weapons in non-international armed conflicts.

[163] Art. 1 of the 1899 Hague Convention (II): "The High Contracting Parties shall issue instructions to their armed land forces, which shall be in conformity with the "Regulations respecting the laws and customs of war on land" annexed to the present Convention."
The latter Regulations included (Art. 23 (e)) the prohibition to "employ arms, projectiles, or material of a nature to cause superfluous injury" (see fn. 110).
This was repeated, with non-substantive alteration, in Art. 1 of the 1907 Hague Convention (IV): "The Contracting Powers shall issue instructions to their armed land forces which shall be in conformity with the Regulations respecting the laws and customs of war on land, annexed to the present Convention.", with Art. 23 (e) of the 1907 Hague Regulations stating that it was forbidden "to employ arms, projectiles, or material calculated to cause unnecessary suffering." (see fn. 111).

[164] Art. 36 of AP/I states: "In the study, development, acquisition or adoption of a new weapon, means or method of warfare, a High Contracting Party is under an obligation to determine whether its employment would, in some or all circumstances, be prohibited by this Protocol or by any other rule of international law applicable to the High Contracting Party."

Section D

Attacks

I. General rules

10. (a) In accordance with the basic principle of distinction, attacks must be confined to lawful targets.

1. The principle of distinction is the "foundation on which the codification of the laws and customs of war rests".[165] First set forth in the 1868 St. Petersburg Declaration[166], then reaffirmed in Art. 48 of AP/I[167], the principle is intended to protect against direct attack: (a) civilians unless and for such time as they directly participate in hostilities (see Section F); (b) civilian objects as distinct from military objectives (see Rule 1 (y) and Section E). The principle of distinction also underpins such obligations as the prohibition of indiscriminate attack (see Rule 13), compliance with the principle of proportionality (see Rule 14) and the requirement to take feasible precautions in attack (see Section G).

2. In its Advisory Opinion on the Legality of the Threat or Use of Nuclear Weapons, the ICJ has recognized the principle of distinction as one of the two "cardinal" principles of international humanitarian law, the other being the prohibition of unnecessary suffering.[168] The ICJ, in that Advisory Opinion, stated: "States must never make civilians the object of attack and must consequently never use weapons that are incapable of

[165] Para. 1863 of the ICRC Commentary on AP/I, pertaining to the Commentary on Art. 48 of AP/I.

[166] Second paragraph of the Preamble to the 1868 St. Petersburg Declaration: "That the only legitimate object which States should endeavour to accomplish during war is to weaken the military forces of the enemy."

[167] Art. 48 of AP/I: "In order to ensure respect for and protection of the civilian population and civilian objects, the Parties to the conflict shall at all times distinguish between the civilian population and combatants and between civilian objects and military objectives and accordingly shall direct their operations only against military objectives."

[168] ICJ, Nuclear Weapons Advisory Opinion, at Para. 78.

distinguishing between civilian and military targets."[169] The principle of distinction is indisputably a principle of customary international law.

3. Rule 10 (a), by confining attacks to lawful targets, rules out direct or indiscriminate attacks against civilians (unless and for such time as they are directly participating in hostilities, see Section F). Nevertheless, in warfare, civilians and civilian objects are often harmed, despite not being the object of direct or indiscriminate attack. This is principally related to collateral damage, governed by the principle of proportionality (see Rule 14).

4. An attack is unlawful if aimed at other than a lawful target (see Rule 10 (b)), even if it ultimately fails to cause actual harm.

5. Rule 10 (a) applies also in non-international armed conflict.

(b) Lawful targets are:

This Rule applies also in non-international armed conflict, although the term "combatant" is reserved for international armed conflict. Thus, like members of the regular armed forces of the State concerned, members of a non-State organized armed group in a non-international armed conflict are lawful targets.[170]

(i) Combatants;

1. The customary definition of combatants, originating in Art. 1 of the 1907 Hague Regulations,[171] is found in Art. 4 (A) (1) and in Art. 4 (A) (2) of GC/III.[172]

[169] *Ibid.*

[170] According to the ICRC's Interpretive Guidance on the notion of direct participation in hostilities, organized armed groups in a non-international armed conflict consist only of individuals whose continuous function it is to take a direct part in hostilities ("continuous combat function").

[171] Art. 1 of the 1907 Hague Regulations: "The laws, rights, and duties of war apply not only to armies, but also to militia and volunteer corps fulfilling the following conditions: (1) To be commanded by a person responsible for his subordinates; (2) To have a fixed distinctive emblem recognizable at a distance; (3) To carry arms openly; and (4) To conduct their operations in accordance with the laws and customs of war. In countries where militia or volunteer corps constitute the army, or form part of it, they are included under the denomination 'army'."

[172] Art. 4 of GC/III: "(1) Members of the armed forces of a Party to the conflict as well as members of militias or volunteer corps forming part of such armed forces. (2) Members of other militias and members of other volunteer corps, including those of organized resistance movements, belonging to a Party to the conflict and operating in or outside

2. Combatants include all members of the armed forces of a Belligerent Party, except medical or religious personnel. The armed forces include the officially organized military forces, as well as organized armed forces, groups and units under a command responsible to a Party to the conflict and responsible for his subordinates; which wear a distinctive sign (e.g., clothing or other accoutrements) that distinguish them from the civilian population; carry their weapons openly; and which generally conduct their operations in accordance with the laws and customs of warfare.

3. Paramilitary or other armed law-enforcement agencies may be incorporated into the armed forces. When this occurs, the members of such agencies become combatants. In other words, incorporation renders them lawful targets. Art. 43 (3) of AP/I requires such incorporation to be notified to the other Belligerent Party.[173] However, failure to so notify the enemy does not bar their treatment as lawful targets.

4. Disagreement exists as to whether individuals who do not meet the aforementioned criteria, but nevertheless participate directly in the hostilities, are to be characterized as "civilians" or "unprivileged belligerents" (also termed "unlawful combatants") (see paragraph 4 of the Commentary on the *chapeau* to Rule 111 (b). The issue whether they are "unprivileged belligerents" is relevant only to the rules governing their detention (as POW, civilian internees or under some other category). However, it is clear that civilians who participate directly in hostilities can be attacked or captured no matter whether they are characterized as "civilians" or as "unprivileged belligerents" (see Section F).

5. Persons, including combatants, who are *hors de combat* may not be attacked (see Rule 15 (b)).

6. Certain categories of individuals are singled out in the law of international armed conflict as enjoying specific protection because of the functions they serve. Apart from medical and religious personnel (see Section

their own territory, even if this territory is occupied, provided that such militias or volunteer corps, including such organized resistance movements, fulfil the following conditions: (a) that of being commanded by a person responsible for his subordinates; (b) that of having a fixed distinctive sign recognizable at a distance; (c) that of carrying arms openly; (d) that of conducting their operations in accordance with the laws and customs of war."

173 Art. 43 (3) of AP/I: "Whenever a Party to a conflict incorporates a paramilitary or armed law enforcement agency into its armed forces it shall so notify the other Parties to the conflict."

K), this refers to civil defence personnel which may not be attacked unless they commit acts harmful to the enemy (see Section N (I)). It ought to be noted that civil defence functions can be performed by a military unit. The personnel will remain protected, provided that they are permanently assigned and exclusively devoted to the performance of civil defence tasks (see Art. 67 of AP/I).[174] The performance of recognized civil defence functions is in this connection not considered harmful to the enemy, even when amounting to putting out a fire on a military objective, if the fire endangers the life of civilian persons or threatens civilian objects in the vicinity (see paragraph 3 of the Commentary on Rule 1 (k)).

(ii) Military objectives (as defined in Rules 1 (y) and 22);

1. Military objectives, as defined in Rule 1 (y), are classified by nature, location, purpose or use. The criteria of use, location or purpose may turn an otherwise civilian object into a military objective in certain circumstances (see Rule 22).

2. Under Art. 59 (2) of AP/I, a Belligerent Party may declare any inhabited place in or near the contact zone as a non-defended locality (subject to several conditions, such as that all combatants, mobile weapons and mobile military equipment must have been evacuated, that no hostile use will be made of fixed military installations or establishments located therein).[175] The concept goes back to Art. 25 of both the 1899[176] and the 1907[177] Hague Regulations.[178] A declared non-defended locality must not be attacked. However, the entire construct is based on the idea that it is situated in or near the contact zone, thereby allowing the enemy to enter the locality whenever it desires.

[174] Art. 67 of AP/I, see fn. 487.

[175] Art. 59 (2) of AP/I: "The appropriate authorities of a Party to the conflict may declare as a non-defended locality any inhabited place near or in a zone where armed forces are in contact which is open for occupation by an adverse Party. Such a locality shall fulfil the following conditions: (a) all combatants, as well as mobile weapons and mobile military equipment must have been evacuated; (b) no hostile use shall be made of fixed military installations or establishments; (c) no acts of hostility shall be committed by the authorities or by the population; and (d) no activities in support of military operations shall be undertaken."

[176] Art. 25 of the 1899 Hague Regulations: "The attack or bombardment of towns, villages, habitations or buildings which are not defended, is prohibited."

[177] Art. 25 of the 1907 Hague Regulations: "The attack or bombardment, by whatever means, of towns, villages, dwellings, or buildings which are undefended is prohibited."

[178] Art. 59 (1) of AP/I: "It is prohibited for the Parties to the conflict to attack, by any means whatsoever, non-defended localities."

(iii) Civilians directly participating in hostilities (see Section F of this Manual).

Civilians who directly participate in hostilities lose their immunity from attack for such time as they so participate (see Section F). Although they have no combatant rights, they may be directly attacked like combatants. Yet, once they become *hors de combat* they are subject to – and benefit from – the application of Rule 15 (b).

11. Attacks directed against civilians or civilian objects are prohibited.

1. This Rule is based on the 1868 St. Petersburg Declaration,[179] reaffirmed in the first sentence of Art. 51 (2) of AP/I[180] and in Art. 52 (1) of AP/I.[181]

2. It is necessary to distinguish between two modes of attacks against civilians or civilian objects, which are equally prohibited: (i) Rule 11 addresses the issue of attacks directed against civilians or civilian objects; (ii) Rule 13 deals with an "indiscriminate attack", which is not directed against a specific person or object. Such an attack strikes lawful targets without distinction from civilians or civilian objects.

3. Directing attacks against civilians or civilian objects is prohibited regardless of the purpose. Nor is it important whether the attack is successful.

4. In time of armed conflict, attacks against civilians or civilian objects may result from a weapons system's malfunction. For the purposes of Rule 11, this will not qualify as "attacks directed against civilians or civilian objects". Thus, for example, if a guided missile loses its homing capability, i.e., "goes ballistic", this will not qualify as an attack prohibited under Rule 11.

[179] Second operative paragraph of the 1868 St. Petersburg Declaration: "That the only legitimate object which States should endeavour to accomplish during war is to weaken the military forces of the enemy."

[180] First sentence of Art. 51 (2) of AP/I: "The civilian population as such, as well as individual civilians, shall not be the object of attack."

[181] Art. 52 (1) of AP/I: "Civilian objects shall not be the object of attack or of reprisals. Civilian objects are all objects which are not military objectives as defined in paragraph 2."

5. The prohibition of Rule 11 cannot eliminate cases of human error in targeting. The issue of mistake of fact is particularly relevant in case of criminal legal proceedings against the person. See Art. 32 (1) of the Rome Statute of the ICC.[182]

6. For the purpose of Rule 11, a civilian is any person who is not a combatant. However, a civilian loses protection against direct attack if, and for such time as, he directly participates in hostilities (see Section F).

7. Civilian objects, as defined in Rule 1 (j), are all objects that are not military objectives as defined in Rule 1 (y). The protection does not apply to civilian objects that have become military objectives through location, purpose or use (see Rule 22 (b)–(d)).

8. Rule 11 applies also in non-international armed conflict.

12. (a) In case of doubt as to whether a person is a civilian, that person shall be considered a civilian.

1. This Rule is based on Art. 50 (1) of AP/I.[183]

2. All feasible precautions must be taken in order to verify that attacks are directed at lawful targets (see Rule 32 (a) and Rule 35 (a)). Rule 12 (a) applies when, after a verification process, there is still doubt.

3. Indications that a person is a lawful target, either as a combatant or as a civilian taking a direct part in hostilities, will depend on the circumstances. For instance, in some societies, it is normal for males to carry a firearm routinely. In other environments, similar behaviour could be regarded as conclusive evidence of membership in a non-State organized armed group.

4. It is often the case in aerial operations that some uncertainty exists regarding status of a person as a civilian. The degree of doubt necessary to preclude an attack is that which would cause a reasonable attacker in

[182] Art. 32 (1) of the Rome Statute of the ICC: "A mistake of fact shall be a ground for excluding criminal responsibility only if it negates the mental element required by the crime." Art. 30 of the Rome Statute of the ICC further deals with this "mental element".

[183] Second sentence of Art. 50 (1) of AP/I: "In case of doubt whether a person is a civilian, that person shall be considered to be a civilian."

the same or similar circumstances to abstain from ordering or executing an attack.

5. The issue of doubt as to whether a person is a civilian, is of special importance in the context of direct participation in hostilities (see Section F).

6. Rule 12 (a) applies also in non-international armed conflict.

(b) In case of doubt as to whether an object which is ordinarily dedicated to civilian purposes is being used for military purposes, it may only be attacked if, based on all the information reasonably available to the commander at the time, there are reasonable grounds to believe that it has become and remains a military objective.

1. This Rule is based on Art. 52 (3) of AP/I.[184]

2. Rule 12 (b) only relates to the category of military objectives through "use". In other words, the situation involves enemy forces using for military ends an object that is normally dedicated to civilian purposes. Art. 52 (3) of AP/I offers "a place of worship, a house or other dwelling or a school" as examples of objects which are normally dedicated to civilian purposes. These examples are considered to be only illustrative. The buildings that are mentioned do not have any special status compared to other typically civilian buildings or installations. Additional examples are commercial offices, shopping areas and facilities and markets.[185]

3. All feasible precautions must be taken in order to verify that attacks are directed at lawful targets (see Rule 32 (a) and Rule 35 (a)). Rule 12 (b) applies when, after a verification process, there is still doubt.

4. Doubt is often present in situations of armed conflict. Rule 12 (b) clarifies the standard. It is not the existence of any doubt that precludes attack, but rather reasonable doubt. In other words, an attacker must

[184] Art. 52 (3) of AP/I: "In case of doubt whether an object which is normally dedicated to civilian purposes, such as a place of worship, a house or other dwelling or a school, is being used to make an effective contribution to military action, it shall be presumed not to be so used."

[185] Para. 5.4.2 of the UK Manual: "In cases of doubt, objects that are normally used for civilian purposes are to be presumed as not being used for military purposes. Such objects would include churches, dwelling houses, residential flats, commercial offices and factories, shopping precincts and markets, schools, and libraries."

act reasonably in deciding to attack such objects, specifically taking into account, among other factors, the fact that the intended target is normally one used for civilian purposes. The attacker would also have to take into account the reliability of the information that indicates that the object is used for military purposes. If there is reason to doubt the reliability of the information, one cannot reasonably act on that basis.

5. The status of the object believed to be used for military purposes need not be established beyond reasonable doubt. A reasonable conclusion to the effect that an object is being so used will suffice. A military commander always has to deal with situations of doubt when choosing between alternative courses of action, weighing expected benefits against risks. The same holds true when there is an uncertainty as to whether an object which is ordinarily dedicated to civilian purposes is being used for military purposes.

6. In some situations, the enemy will use places of worship for military purposes as a matter of routine, for instance as observation posts or as a snipers' perch. Before an attack is launched, it has to be established that the particular place of worship is used for military purposes. One may also have to take into account that the place of worship could, in the circumstances ruling at the time, be used as a refuge by civilians. On this subject, see *inter alia* Rule 14 on the principle of proportionality; Rule 32 (b) on avoiding – or, in any event, minimizing – collateral damage, as well as Rule 35 (c)); and Rule 45 regarding the prohibition against using civilians as "human shields".

7. "Information" includes military intelligence. The quality and timeliness of the intelligence has to be considered. Other information, such as visual observations on the spot that may corroborate or contradict military intelligence, must also be taken into account.

8. There will often be hindsight information that was not available at the time of the attack. The question is, however, whether there was doubt at the time when the decision was taken, as well as when the attack is actually launched (see paragraph 4 of the Commentary on Rule 1 (q) and paragraph 5 of the Commentary on Rule 14). Provided that all feasible precautions were taken (as per Rule 32 (a) and Rule 35 (a)) to verify that the target was a lawful target (see Rule 10), additional information that turns up at some later point in time (perhaps as a result of the attack) is irrelevant.

9. Objects normally dedicated to civilian purposes that are being used for military purposes by the enemy regain protected status (although they may still be considered military objectives by purpose, see Rule 22 (c)). Under Rule 1 (j), everything that is not a military objective is a civilian object.

10. Rule 12 (b) applies also in non-international armed conflict.

13. (a) Indiscriminate attacks are prohibited.

1. This Rule is based on Art. 51 (4) of AP/I.[186]

2. Whether an attack is indiscriminate is typically a case-specific determination. Relevant factors include, but are not limited to indications of the attacker's indifference; the nature of the weapons employed; and the location and density of civilians or civilian objects relative to military objectives.

3. Rule 13 (a) applies also in non-international armed conflict.

(b) Indiscriminate attacks are those that cannot be or are not directed against lawful targets (as defined in Rule 10 (b)) or the effects of which cannot be limited as required by the law of international armed conflict, and which therefore are of a nature to strike lawful targets and civilians or civilian objects without distinction.

1. This Rule is based on Art. 51 (4) of AP/I.

2. Indiscriminate attacks may result from either the employment of indiscriminate methods (tactics) or means (weapons) of warfare. On the latter, see also Rule 5 (a).

3. Indiscriminate attacks, just like attacks directed against civilians or civilian objects (see Rule 11) need to be distinguished from instances of a weapons system's malfunction or from human error. As long as a

[186] Art. 51 (4) of AP/I: "Indiscriminate attacks are prohibited. Indiscriminate attacks are: (a) those which are not directed at a specific military objective; (b) those which employ a method or means of combat which cannot be directed at a specific military objective; or (c) those which employ a method or means of combat the effects of which cannot be limited as required by this Protocol; and consequently, in each such case, are of a nature to strike military objectives and civilians or civilian objects without distinction."

See also the first sentence of subpara. 2 of Para. 5.3.2 of NWP: "The principle of distinction, combined with the principle of military necessity, prohibits indiscriminate attacks."

weapon was originally aimed at a lawful target, the fact that it or its weapons system malfunctions (e.g., when a missile "goes ballistic") and as a result hits civilians or civilian objects, does not alter the fact that it was "directed" against a lawful target. See also paragraph 4 and paragraph 5 of the Commentary on Rule 11.

4. If enemy defences or countermeasures deflect a weapon (not otherwise indiscriminate) from its intended target, causing it to strike civilians or civilian objects, the attack will not be deemed indiscriminate (on this ground).

5. Even when target identification and weapons guidance systems are used, an attack may become indiscriminate due to inclement weather conditions or similar reasons. Attacks at night may likewise not be possible to execute with sufficient discrimination using available equipment and weapons.

6. The question of whether the effects of an attack against a target in proximity of civilians or civilians objects is indiscriminate, may depend on such factors as the nature of the target, choice of weapons and meteorological conditions. For an example, see the 2007 judgment of the ICTY Trial Chamber in the Martic case. The Tribunal held that firing non-guided rockets with cluster munitions at a densely populated civilian area, from a distance of approximately 50 kilometers, constituted an indiscriminate attack.[187]

7. An aircraft that releases a weapon over an area in which civilians or civilian objects are likely to be present, without regard for where it will hit, will have conducted an indiscriminate attack. This includes an aircraft which chooses to jettison weapons prior to returning to base. However, in extreme circumstances, it is permissible to release the weapons over a sparsely populated area with a few scattered farms or cottages.

8. Attacks using missiles and other projectiles fired from beyond visual range ("over the horizon", see Commentary on Rule 7 pertaining to "beyond visual range weapons systems") are not as such indiscriminate when their employment permits distinguishing military objectives and combatants from civilians and civilian objects. This may be done through sensors on the weapon itself, or through external guidance, for

[187] ICTY, Prosecutor v. Milan Martic, Case No. IT-95-11-T, Judgment by the Trial Chamber of 12 June 2007, at paras. 462–463.

instance from the aircraft. Indeed, the technological systems used to identify a target and prosecute such attacks can be far more reliable than the naked eye.

9. An operation must qualify as an "attack" (see Rule 1 (e)) before being prohibited as "indiscriminate". For instance, a psychological operation directed against the civilian population which does not cause death/injury to civilians, or destruction/damage of civilian objects does not violate the law of international armed conflict (provided that it is not intended to terrorize civilians, see Rule 18). On this issue in particular, see Rule 21.

10. Rule 13 (b) applies also in non-international armed conflict.

(c) **Attacks must not treat as a single lawful target a number of clearly separated and distinct lawful targets located in a city, town, village or area containing a similar concentration of civilians or civilian objects.**

1. This Rule is based on Art. 51 (5) (a) of AP/I.[188] It is also found in other treaties and in military manuals such as in NWP[189] and in the UK Manual.[190]

2. Rule 13 (c) is derived from the acute need to cope with the problem of "target area" bombing that arose in WWII. The text seriously limits the possibilities in which clusters of military objectives may be attacked as if they were a single lawful target. On the other hand, it does not deny the

[188] Art. 51 (5) of AP/I: "Among others, the following types of attacks are to be considered as indiscriminate: (a) an attack by bombardment by any methods or means which treats as a single military objective a number of clearly separated and distinct military objectives located in a city, town, village or other area containing a similar concentration of civilians or civilian objects; and (b) an attack which may be expected to cause incidental loss of civilian life, injury to civilians, damage to civilian objects, or a combination thereof, which would be excessive in relation to the concrete and direct military advantage anticipated."

[189] Second subpara. of Para. 5.3.2 of NWP: "attacks that employ a method or means of combat that cannot be directed at a specific military objective (e.g., declaring an entire city a single military objective and attacking it by bombardment when there are actually several distinct military objectives throughout the city that could be targeted separately)".

[190] Para. 5.23.2 of the UK Manual: "The following are examples of indiscriminate attacks: (a) an attack by bombardment by any methods or means which treats as a single military objective a number of clearly separated and distinct military objectives located in a city, town, village or other area containing a similar concentration of civilians or civilian objects; ... "

possibility that a number of lawful targets, which are not clearly separated and distinct, may be treated as a single lawful target.

3. As the experience of WWII demonstrated, recourse to "target area" bombing may cause devastation on an unprecedented scale because of the location of lawful targets – which are not clearly separated and distinct – within a city, or other residential area. However, it must be borne in mind that, under the current law of international armed conflict, all attacks are subject to the principle of proportionality (see Rule 14) and the requirement to take feasible precautions in attack (see Section G). Hence, the expected collateral damage to civilians and civilian objects must not be excessive compared to the anticipated military advantage.

4. As in other instances when the attacker is facing the risk of a breach of the principle of proportionality, the availability of precision guided weapons may facilitate striking lawful targets in a manner that will avoid – or, in any event, minimize – the expected collateral damage to civilians or civilian objects (see Rule 8).

5. Rule 13 (c) applies also in non-international armed conflict.

14. An attack that may be expected to cause collateral damage which would be excessive in relation to the concrete and direct military advantage anticipated is prohibited.

1. This Rule is based on Art. 51 (5) (b) of AP/I,[191] and is often referred to as the principle of proportionality.

2. "Collateral damage" does not include inconvenience, irritation, stress, fear or other intangible conditions caused to the civilian population. It is limited to death/injury to civilians, or to damage/destruction of objects. For the definition of collateral damage, see Rule 1 (l).

3. In the context of air or missile combat operations, it is often unavoidable that civilians or civilian objects will be harmed during attacks on lawful targets, especially in circumstances in which military objectives are located in proximity to civilians or civilian objects, or when civilians are located within a military objective. In such cases, the attack may proceed so long as the principle of proportionality and the requirements of Section G are complied with. If an attack would not be possible without excessive collateral damage to civilians or civilian objects being expected,

[191] Art. 51 (5) (b) of AP/I, see fn. 188.

as compared to the anticipated military advantage, the attack is prohibited despite being directed against a lawful target. For the definition of "military advantage", see Rule 1 (w).

4. The members of the Group of Experts could not agree as to what extent (if at all) indirect ("reverberating") effects of attacks have to be factored into the proportionality calculation. In any event, there is no dispute that indirect effects cannot be taken into account if they are too remote or cannot be reasonably foreseen. The Group of Experts could identify no conclusive State practice that settles the issue of indirect effects of attacks.

5. The key to the application of Rule 14 lies in the terms "expected" and "anticipated." The principle of proportionality is not dealing with hindsight. What counts is not hindsight, but foresight (see paragraph 4 of the Commentary on Rule 1 (q) and paragraph 4 of the Commentary on Rule 12 (a)). Foresight includes taking feasible precautions (see Section G) and assessing the likely consequences of the attack that is being planned, bearing in mind the anticipated military advantage. The consequences that actually flow from an attack come into play in the course of an *ex post facto* evaluation of whether the attacker ought reasonably to have expected the resulting collateral damage. But the issue is expectations and not results (see also paragraph 8 of the Commentary on Rule 12 (b) with regard to hindsight in case of doubt).

6. The standard is objective in that expectations must be reasonable. If the attacker expected, in light of reliable information available at the time, that the collateral damage to civilians or civilian objects would be excessive relative to the anticipated military advantage, the principle of proportionality will have been violated. "Expected" collateral damage and "anticipated" military advantage, for these purposes, mean that that outcome is probable, i.e., more likely than not. Both terms assume a good-faith assessment by the commander planning or approving the attack, or the combatant executing it. They are "judged in the light of the information reasonably available" at the time.[192] Moreover, it must be acknowledged that mistakes occur due to the "fog of war" or when it turns out reality did not

[192] Para. 5.20.4. of the UK Manual.
See also the UK statement of understanding made on ratification of AP/I: "Military commanders and others responsible for planning, deciding upon, or executing attacks necessarily have to reach decisions on the basis of their assessment of the information from all sources which is reasonably available to them at the relevant time."

match expectations, perhaps due to faulty intelligence. An attack does not violate the principle of proportionality unless such mistakes were unreasonable in the circumstances. See Section G on feasible precautions in attacks.

7. The term "excessive" is often misinterpreted. It is not a matter of counting civilian casualties and comparing them to the number of enemy combatants that have been put out of action. It applies when there is a significant imbalance between the military advantage anticipated, on the one hand, and the expected collateral damage to civilians and civilian objects, on the other.

8. The fact that collateral damage is extensive does not necessarily render it excessive. The concept of excessiveness is not an absolute one. Excessiveness is always measured in light of the military advantage that the attacker anticipates to attain through the attack. If the military advantage anticipated is marginal, the collateral damage expected need not be substantial in order to be excessive. Conversely, extensive collateral damage may be legally justified by the military value of the target struck, because of the high military advantage anticipated by the attack.[193]

9. The term "concrete and direct" refers to military advantage that is clearly identifiable and, in many cases, quantifiable.[194] Of course, not always is the military advantage easy to establish and anticipate. On the other hand, it is clear that for the military advantage to be concrete and direct, it cannot be based merely on hope or speculation.

10. The term "military advantage" must not be too narrowly construed, for instance by restriction to ground gained or weakening the enemy armed forces (see paragraph 3 of the Commentary on Rule 1 (w)). This is

[193] Para. 1980 of the the ICRC Commentary on AP/I, in connection with Art. 51 of AP/I, disagrees with this view: "The idea has also been put forward that even if they are very high, civilian losses and damages may be justified if the military advantage at stake is of great importance. This idea is contrary to the fundamental rules of the Protocol; in particular it conflicts with Art. 48 (Basic rule) and with paragraphs 1 and 2 of the present Art. 51. The Protocol does not provide any justification for attacks which cause extensive civilian losses and damages. Incidental losses and damages should never be extensive." The ICRC interpretation of Art. 51 of AP/I is not, however, found to be customary law.

[194] Para. 2209 of the ICRC Commentary, in connection with to Art. 57 (2) (b) of AP/I states that the expression "concrete and direct military advantage" "was intended to show that the advantage concerned should be substantial and relatively close, and that advantages which are hardly perceptible and those which would only appear in the long term should be disregarded."

especially true in aerial warfare. An attack can for instance be an element in a ruse (see Section Q, in particular Rule 116 (a)). The security of the attacking forces is also a component of military advantage,[195] as would be general disruption of command and control communications. On the other hand, the term "military advantage" must not be interpreted too broadly: it is limited to impact on the enemy's military tactical or operational level. Thus, for instance, even if striking military objectives weakens the morale of the enemy civilian population (see Rule 18), this effect is not in itself a relevant "military advantage" for the purpose of Rule 14.

11. It is generally accepted as a matter of customary international law that "the military advantage anticipated from an attack is intended to refer to the advantage anticipated from the attack considered as a whole and not from isolated or particular parts of the attack"[196], a standard adopted in the Rome Statute of the ICC.[197] This means that it is necessary to consider the military operation in its entirety and not merely the military advantage immediately accruing from the attack at the time that it is conducted. For instance, an attack on a bridge to deny the enemy the capability to cross a river may seemingly be of low military advantage if the enemy is actually not using that bridge. However, if the purpose of the attack on the bridge is to block avenues of retreat which the commander knows will be taken once he launches his planned offensive, the military advantage of destroying the bridge will be high. On this issue, see also paragraph 6 of the Commentary on Rule 1 (w), paragraph 7 of the Commentary on Rule 1 (y) and paragraph 3 of the Commentary on Rule 33.

12. Aerial attacks are often conducted by multiple military aircraft, in which case it would be improper to consider the impact of each single sortie in isolation. It is rather necessary to assess the overall mission. To consider military advantage in light of the "attack as a whole" has also other

[195] The term "military advantage" involves a variety of considerations, including the security of attacking forces, see declarations made by Australia and New Zealand upon ratification of AP/I : "In relation to paragraph 5 (b) of Art. 51 and to paragraph 2 (a) (iii) of Art. 57, [it is our understanding] that . . . the term "military advantage" involves a variety of considerations, including the security of attacking forces. . . . "

[196] The UK has given the following understanding to Art. 57 of AP/I: "In the view of the United Kingdom, the military advantage anticipated from an attack is intended to refer to the advantage anticipated from the attack considered as a whole and not only from isolated or particular parts of the attack." Similar understandings have also been given by, for example, Australia, Canada, Germany and The Netherlands.

[197] Art. 8 (2) (b) (iv) of the Rome Statute of the ICC, see fn. 58.

aspects. One example could be a contemplated series of attacks against a number of bridges across the same river when they are in proximity to each other. Although the first attack on one of these bridges might appear to yield only a limited military advantage, considering that the enemy can still use the remaining bridges, the military advantage will become apparent once subsequent attacks against the other bridges take place.

13. "An attack considered as a whole" ought not to be confused with the entire armed conflict, but could refer to a large air campaign. For example, a series of air attacks may be directed against military objectives in one zone – in anticipation of a military operation in another – as a ruse to deceive the enemy regarding the actual location of the intended operations (see Rule 116 (a)). Although the expected collateral damage to civilians or civilian objects resulting from the attacks might be excessive if viewed solely from the perspective of the advantage gained from individual target destruction, it must instead be considered in terms of the ruse's value relative to the military operations elsewhere.

14. Opinions in the Group of Experts were divided as to whether civilians who are physically within a military objective (e.g., civilian employees working in a munitions factory) count for the purposes of the application of the principle of proportionality. Three views were expressed. Some experts were of the opinion that such civilians do not count because they have chosen to be there and have thereby voluntarily assumed the risk of an attack by the enemy. The majority of the Group of Experts felt that the principle of proportionality applies to such civilians as in all other cases. However, some experts – while belonging to that majority – pointed out that the application of the principle of proportionality will not make a material difference when the target is a high-value asset (such as a munitions factory), referring to the fact that extensive casualties do not necessarily amount to excessive collateral damage.

15. The principle of proportionality applies throughout all stages of an attack, from planning to execution. Anyone with the ability and authority to suspend, abort or cancel an attack, must do so once he reaches the conclusion that the expected collateral damage would be excessive in relation to the anticipated military advantage. For instance, a pilot who has the target in view and unexpectedly observes civilians in the target area – who were not supposed to be there, based on the information provided to him during the briefing preceding the attack – must assess the collateral damage expected to befall them and cancel the attack if he

concludes that the principle of proportionality will be violated. See Rule 32 (b) and Rule 35 (c).

16. National or policy requirements to seek approval of a specified level of command whenever collateral damage reaches a predetermined level are not a substitute for the application of the principle of proportionality in accordance with the law of international armed conflict. A decision by higher echelons to approve a planned attack will not render lawful an attack which violates Rule 14.

17. Rule 14 applies also in non-international armed conflict.

15. (a) It is prohibited to order that there shall be no survivors in combat operations, to threaten an adversary therewith, or to conduct hostilities on that basis.

1. This Rule is based on Art. 40 of AP/I.[198] See also Art. 23 (d) of the 1907 Hague Regulations.[199]

2. There was some debate in the Group of Experts as to whether it was necessary to have Rule 15 (a) in the Manual, considering that the subject of denial of quarter is also covered in Rule 126 in the context of surrender. The majority of the Group of Experts felt, however, that the issue of denial of quarter – and what is equally important, the threat thereof – is wider in scope and must therefore also be incorporated in Section D.

3. The emphasis in Rule 15 (a) is on the fact that a policy of "take no prisoners" is entirely inadmissible, and it cannot be threatened, even in advance of any fighting and, therefore, before the issue of surrender becomes relevant.

4. Persons who surrender or give themselves up for capture no longer pose a threat to the enemy (see Section S, in particular paragraph 3 of the Commentary on Rule 126). It is unlawful to kill or injure such persons regardless of whether they are combatants or civilians taking a direct part in hostilities.

5. Rule 15 (a) applies also in non-international armed conflict.

[198] Art. 40 of AP/I ("Quarter"): "It is prohibited to order that there shall be no survivors, to threaten an adversary therewith or to conduct hostilities on this basis."

[199] Art. 23 of the 1907 Hague Regulations: "In addition to the prohibitions provided by special Conventions, it is especially forbidden:...(d) To declare that no quarter will be given."

(b) Persons who are *hors de combat* – either because they have clearly expressed an intention to surrender or as a result of sickness, wounds or shipwreck – must not be attacked, provided that they abstain from any hostile act and no attempt is made to evade capture.

1. This Rule is derived from Art. 41 of AP/I.[200] See also Art. 23 (c) of the 1907 Hague Regulations.[201]

2. For the specific context of air or missile operations, there are two categories of persons *hors de combat*: (i) those who have clearly expressed an intention to surrender; (ii) those who are incapacitated. The latter category falls into three subsets: sick; wounded; and shipwrecked.

3. Upon due consideration, the majority of the Group of Experts decided not to retain the separate category of Art. 41 (a) of AP/I, i.e., persons "in the power of an adverse Party", in view of the fact that such category is irrelevant in aerial warfare.

4. Although, as a term of art, the expression "*hors de combat*" is reserved for combatants, for the purposes of Rule 15 (b), it covers incapacitation of both combatants and civilians who have directly participated in hostilities.

5. Combatants (or civilians directly participating in hostilities) must communicate clearly their intention to surrender before becoming immune from attack. If a combatant (or a civilian directly participating in hostilities) does not indicate an intention to surrender in a way that the enemy can perceive and understand, this person is still liable to be attacked. For example, the crew of an attacking aircraft conducting a beyond-visual-range attack may be unaware that the forces they are attacking wish to surrender. As long as the lack of knowledge is reasonable in the circumstances, the attack may lawfully be conducted because the desire to surrender has not been effectively communicated to the aircrews (or other forces which could pass that information to the crew in adequate time).

[200] Art. 41 of AP/I ("Safeguard of an enemy *hors de combat*"): "(1) A person who is recognized or who, in the circumstances, should be recognized to be *hors de combat* shall not be made the object of attack. (2) A person is *hors de combat* if: (a) he is in the power of an adverse Party; (b) he clearly expresses an intention to surrender; or (c) he has been rendered unconscious or is otherwise incapacitated by wounds or sickness, and therefore is incapable of defending himself."

[201] Art. 23 of the 1907 Hague Regulations: "In addition to the prohibitions provided by special Conventions, it is especially forbidden: . . . (c) To kill or wound an enemy who, having laid down his arms, or having no longer means of defence, has surrendered at discretion."

6. In aerial warfare, it is often problematic to assess whether a person is *hors de combat*. When a person is in an aircraft in the air, his aircraft is not immune from attack and the person would have to suffer the consequences of an attack as long as the aircraft has not effectively communicated its intention to surrender (see Section S), although he may actually be wounded. When a person is lying on the ground, it is often difficult to determine from the air whether this is due to incapacitating injuries or because he is taking cover from aerial attack. Thus, it is essential to emphasize that the protection extends only to those who are *hors de combat* from the perspective of the reasonable attacker.

7. In the context of aerial warfare, it is possible to communicate an intention to surrender without actually being captured, for instance when a combatant on the ground surrenders to an aircraft (see dissenting view in the next paragraph). The protection against attack commences as soon as the intention to surrender has been clearly communicated to the enemy, for instance by throwing away one's weapons and raising one's arms. The display of a white flag by ground troops, which means a request to parley, is in practice also frequently used as a means of communicating an intention to surrender.

8. Opinions were sharply divided among the members of the Group of Experts as to whether it is possible for personnel on the ground or on board of ships to validly surrender to an aircraft that is not able to accept the surrender by taking prisoners. There were two views. Some members of the Group of Experts were of the opinion that it is irrelevant whether the aircraft can itself capture prisoners: those manifesting an intent to surrender may not be attacked. By contrast, other members of the Group of Experts insisted that an attack need not be aborted merely because someone on the ground is raising his hands or waving a white flag, since this could easily lead to misuse. All members of the Group of Experts agreed, however, that if a large unit surrenders collectively and ground forces can be summoned to take care of the surrendering enemy soldiers, they cannot be attacked. As to surrender, see Section S.

9. The Group of Experts agreed that those who manifest the intention to surrender must do so in good faith. If ground forces of a Belligerent Party repeatedly raise their hands in order to avoid attack from enemy military aircraft knowing that the military aircraft has no possibility to take prisoners, and continue to fight again when the aircraft has left, this could amount to perfidy (see Section Q, in particular Rule 114 (e)). Furthermore, such personnel cannot expect that similar

behaviour on future occasions will be taken seriously as a genuine offer of surrender.

10. A person may be incapacitated (*hors de combat*) by wounds or sickness. The incapacitation does not have to be caused by the conflict. The concept includes persons who have suffered stroke, heart attack or food poisoning, and even mothers who are delivering babies.

11. The notion of incapacitation is contingent on the combatant (or the civilian taking direct part in hostilities) (i) not continuing to commit any act of hostility; and (ii) not trying to escape.[202] Incapacitation ought not to be confused with lack of capability for defense. For instance, during an aerial attack, enemy forces may have no defensive means of warfare within range of the attacking aircraft. This does not render them *hors de combat.* If they wish to be exempt from attack, they must validly communicate an intention to surrender.

12. The terms "wounded", "sick" and "shipwrecked" are defined in Art. 8 of AP/I. "Wounded" and "sick" are military or civilian persons in need of medical care and who refrain from all acts of hostility.[203] "Shipwrecked" are military or civilian persons in a perilous situation at sea or on any other waters following a misfortune and who refrain from all acts of hostility. Under Art 8 (b) of AP/I the concept is expanded to include persons, who are in peril at sea or in other waters (including lakes).[204] The term "shipwreck" means shipwreck from any cause and includes forced landings at sea by or from aircraft (first paragraph of Art. 12 of GC/II).[205]

[202] Para. 1610 of the ICRC Commentary on AP/I, in connection with Art. 41 (2) of AP/I: "In accordance with this paragraph, a person is considered to be rendered 'hors de combat' either if he is "in the power" of an adverse Party, or if he wishes to surrender, or if he is incapacitated. This status continues as long as the person does not commit any act of hostility and does not try to escape."

[203] Art. 8 (a) of AP/I: "'Wounded' and 'sick' mean persons, whether military or civilian, who, because of trauma, disease or other physical or mental disorder or disability, are in need of medical assistance or care and who refrain from any act of hostility. These terms also cover maternity cases, new-born babies and other persons who may be in need of immediate medical assistance or care, such as the infirm or expectant mothers, and who refrain from any act of hostility."

[204] Art. 8 (b) of AP/I: "'Shipwrecked' means persons, whether military or civilian, who are in peril at sea or in other waters as a result of misfortune affecting them or the vessel or aircraft carrying them and who refrain from any act of hostility. These persons, provided that they continue to refrain from any act of hostility, shall continue to be considered shipwrecked during their rescue until they acquire another status under the Conventions or this Protocol."

[205] First paragraph of Art. 12 of GC/II: "Members of the armed forces and other persons mentioned in the following Article, who are at sea and who are wounded, sick or

13. A person descending by parachute from an aircraft in distress is assimilated to persons *hors de combat* and must not be made the object of attack during his descent. Upon landing in a territory controlled by the enemy, the person who descended in distress must be given an opportunity to surrender (for details, see Section T, in particular Rule 132).

14. Rule 15 (b) applies also in non-international armed conflict.

16. (a) At all times, and particularly after an engagement, Belligerent Parties must, without delay, take all possible measures to search for and collect the wounded, sick and shipwrecked, to protect them against pillage and ill-treatment, and to search for the dead and prevent their being despoiled.

1. This Rule is based on numerous provisions of the 1949 Geneva Conventions and of AP/I. The obligation to take all possible measures to search for, collect and protect the wounded, sick, shipwrecked and the dead is included in Art. 15 of GC/I;[206] Art. 18 of GC/II;[207] Art. 16 of GC/IV[208] and Art. 10 of AP/I.[209] Respect for the obligation to search for and collect the dead is a *conditio sine qua non* of respect for other rules of the law

shipwrecked, shall be respected and protected in all circumstances, it being understood that the term "shipwreck" means shipwreck from any cause and includes forced landings at sea by or from aircraft."

206 Art. 15 of GC/I: "At all times, and particularly after an engagement, Parties to the conflict shall, without delay, take all possible measures to search for and collect the wounded and sick, to protect them against pillage and ill-treatment, to ensure their adequate care, and to search for the dead and prevent their being despoiled. Whenever circumstances permit, an armistice or a suspension of fire shall be arranged, or local arrangements made, to permit the removal, exchange and transport of the wounded left on the battlefield. Likewise, local arrangements may be concluded between Parties to the conflict for the removal or exchange of wounded and sick from a besieged or encircled area, and for the passage of medical and religious personnel and equipment on their way to that area."

207 Art. 18 of GC/II: "After each engagement, Parties to the conflict shall, without delay, take all possible measures to search for and collect the shipwrecked, wounded and sick, to protect them against pillage and ill-treatment, to ensure their adequate care, and to search for the dead and prevent their being despoiled. Whenever circumstances permit, the Parties to the conflict shall conclude local arrangements for the removal of the wounded and sick by sea from a besieged or encircled area and for the passage of medical and religious personnel and equipment on their way to that area."

208 Art. 16 of GC/IV: "The wounded and sick, as well as the infirm, and expectant mothers, shall be the object of particular protection and respect. As far as military considerations allow, each Party to the conflict shall facilitate the steps taken to search for the killed and wounded, to assist the shipwrecked and other persons exposed to grave danger, and to protect them against pillage and ill-treatment."

209 Art. 10 of AP/I ("Protection and care"): "(1) All the wounded, sick and shipwrecked, to whichever Party they belong, shall be respected and protected. (2) In all circumstances they shall be treated humanely and shall receive, to the fullest extent practicable and

of international armed conflict concerning, e.g., the return of remains, decent burial and identification of the dead.

2. For the application of Rule 16 (a) in the specific context of air or missile operations, see Rule 19.

3. For the notion of "wounded", "sick" and "shipwrecked", see paragraph 12 of the Commentary on Rule 15 (b).

4. The requirement set forth in Rule 16 (a) applies "at all times". In practice, however, the ability of a Belligerent Party to perform the activities referred to Rule 16 (a) may be determined by such factors as the availability of search and collection capabilities, weather, terrain, and the constraints of any ongoing hostilities.

5. Rule 16 (a) applies also in non-international armed conflict.

(b) The wounded, sick and shipwrecked must receive, to the fullest extent practicable and with the least possible delay, the medical care and attention required by their condition. No distinction may be made among them founded on any grounds other than medical ones.

1. The obligation to provide medical care and attention to the wounded, sick and shipwrecked is based on Art. 12[210] and Art. 15[211] of GC/I;

with the least possible delay, the medical care and attention required by their condition. There shall be no distinction among them founded on any grounds other than medical ones."

210 Art. 12 of GC/I: "Members of the armed forces and other persons mentioned in the following Article, who are wounded or sick, shall be respected and protected in all circumstances. They shall be treated humanely and cared for by the Party to the conflict in whose power they may be, without any adverse distinction founded on sex, race, nationality, religion, political opinions, or any other similar criteria. Any attempts upon their lives, or violence to their persons, shall be strictly prohibited; in particular, they shall not be murdered or exterminated, subjected to torture or to biological experiments; they shall not wilfully be left without medical assistance and care, nor shall conditions exposing them to contagion or infection be created. Only urgent medical reasons will authorize priority in the order of treatment to be administered. Women shall be treated with all consideration due to their sex. The Party to the conflict which is compelled to abandon wounded or sick to the enemy shall, as far as military considerations permit, leave with them a part of its medical personnel and material to assist in their care."

211 Art. 15 of GC/I, see fn. 206.

Art. 12[212] and Art. 18 of GC/II[213]; Art. 16 of GC/IV[214]; and Art. 10 of AP/I.[215]

2. Rule 16 (b) applies to all wounded, sick, shipwrecked, and dead without adverse distinction. That is to say, there must be no prejudice against certain persons or categories of persons. In particular, distinctions founded on race, colour, sex, language, religion or belief, political or other opinion, national or social origin, wealth, birth or other status, are prohibited. See Art. 12 of GC/I;[216] Art. 12 of GC/II[217] and Art. 10 of AP/I.[218]

3. The obligations under Rule 16 (b) are obligations of conduct and not of result. Each Belligerent Party must use its best efforts to implement these obligations, including acceptance of assistance offered by impartial humanitarian organizations when circumstances permit (see Rule 19 (c)).

4. The "wounded", "sick" and "shipwrecked" referred to in Rule 16 (b) encompass not only (i); combatants; and (ii) civilians taking a direct part in hostilities; but also (iii) ordinary civilians.

212 Art. 12 of GC/II: "Members of the armed forces and other persons mentioned in the following Article, who are at sea and who are wounded, sick or shipwrecked, shall be respected and protected in all circumstances, it being understood that the term "shipwreck" means shipwreck from any cause and includes forced landings at sea by or from aircraft. Such persons shall be treated humanely and cared for by the Parties to the conflict in whose power they may be, without any adverse distinction founded on sex, race, nationality, religion, political opinions, or any other similar criteria. Any attempts upon their lives, or violence to their persons, shall be strictly prohibited; in particular, they shall not be murdered or exterminated, subjected to torture or to biological experiments; they shall not wilfully be left without medical assistance and care, nor shall conditions exposing them to contagion or infection be created. Only urgent medical reasons will authorize priority in the order of treatment to be administered. Women shall be treated with all consideration due to their sex."

213 Art. 18 of GC/II, see fn. 207.

214 Art. 16 of GC/IV: "The wounded and sick, as well as the infirm, and expectant mothers, shall be the object of particular protection and respect. As far as military considerations allow, each Party to the conflict shall facilitate the steps taken to search for the killed and wounded, to assist the shipwrecked and other persons exposed to grave danger, and to protect them against pillage and ill-treatment."

215 Art. 10 of AP/I ("Protection and Care"): "1. All the wounded, sick and shipwrecked, to whichever Party they belong, shall be respected and protected. 2. In all circumstances they shall be treated humanely and shall receive, to the fullest extent practicable and with the least possible delay, the medical care and attention required by their condition. There shall be no distinction among them founded on any grounds other than medical ones."

216 Art. 12 of GC/I, see fn. 210.

217 Art. 12 of GC/II, see fn. 212.

218 Art. 10 of AP/I, see fn. 215.

5. Wounded and sick must be exclusively treated on the basis of medical priority rather than any other criterion. Thus, priority as regards air evacuation from a battlefield has to be given to enemy wounded and sick combatants if they are in more urgent need of medical assistance. Urgency of treatment is typically determined through triage.

6. Rule 16 (b) applies also in non-international armed conflict.

II. Specifics of air and missile operations

17. (a) Only military aircraft, including UCAVs, are entitled to engage in attacks.

1. The Rule is based on the Art. 13[219] and Art 16 of the HRAW,[220] and is also found in national military manuals.[221] See also Rule 115 (b).

2. Rule 17 (a) aims to emphasize that only military aircraft are entitled to exercise any belligerent rights. Just like civilian aircraft, State aircraft other than military aircraft are not entitled to engage in attacks, even if they are owned by or under the exclusive control of the armed forces and being used for government non-commercial services.[222] This means that law-enforcement, customs or coast guard[223] aircraft which do not qualify as military aircraft (see Rule 1 (x)) may not engage in hostilities as long as they are not incorporated into the armed forces.

3. UCAVs (see definition in Rule 1 (ee)), whether remotely piloted or acting autonomously, may engage in attacks as long as they qualify as

[219] Art. 13 of the HRAW: "Military aircraft are alone entitled to exercise belligerent rights."

[220] Art. 16 of the HRAW: "No aircraft other than a belligerent military aircraft shall engage in hostilities in any form. The term 'hostilities' includes the transmission during flight of military intelligence for the immediate use of a belligerent. No private aircraft, when outside the jurisdiction of its own country, shall be armed in time of war."

[221] Para. 12.34 of the UK Manual ("Only military aircraft may carry out attacks"): "Only military aircraft may attack military objectives. If it is intended to use civilian aircraft for combat purposes, they must be embodied into the air force and correctly marked. The classification in the Hague Rules 1923 of public and private aircraft has legal implications for the rights of visit, search, and capture."

Para. 1015 of the German ZDv: "The following vessels and units are competent to perform acts of naval warfare: – warships and other units of naval forces; – military aircraft and; – units of land and air forces."

[222] Para. 12.5 of the UK Manual (see fn. 85) uses the term "auxiliary aircraft".

[223] Some States have organized their coast guard as a non-military law enforcement service. For those States that have organized their coast guard as a part of the armed forces, this exception is not relevant.

military aircraft. Autonomous action means that the unmanned aircraft has sensors and an onboard data processing capability to make decisions to attack according to a computer program. The sensors and computer programs must be able to distinguish between military objectives and civilian objects, as well as between civilians and combatants.

4. The prohibition of an exercise of belligerent rights by State aircraft other than military aircraft, as defined in Rule 1 (cc), is limited to the exercise of belligerent rights reserved for military aircraft, such as conducting an attack. State aircraft other than military aircraft may continue to perform their functions, e.g., genuine law-enforcement activities.

5. Law-enforcement organizations may be incorporated into the armed forces (see Art. 43 (3) of AP/I).[224] In such cases, their aircraft qualify as military aircraft. They will then enjoy all the rights accruing to military aircraft, as well as be liable to be attacked. Members of such agencies incorporated in the armed forces become combatants (see Commentary on Rule 10 (b) (i)). The aircraft of such agencies, being State aircraft, have to be converted to military aircraft (see definition of military aircraft in Rule 1 (x)) before they may engage in attacks.

6. Aircraft operated by private security companies or other private contractors not meeting the requirement to qualify as military aircraft, are civilian aircraft. Once a former military aircraft is operated, or commanded, by private companies, it loses its status as a military aircraft and may no longer engage in attacks in international armed conflicts, though it may carry out security functions for the government, as assigned.

7. Rule 17 (a) does not apply in non-international armed conflict. States are more likely to employ law-enforcement and other State aircraft during these conflicts. It is not in contravention with the law of international armed conflict if such aircraft conduct combat functions.

8. On occasion, States have employed the services of private security companies to conduct aerial operations during non-international armed conflicts. Although governments are not obliged to use military aircraft to conduct air combat operations in non-international armed conflict, all such operations are governed by the Rules, as applicable to non-international armed conflict, reflected in this Manual.

[224] Art. 43 (3) of AP/I, see fn. 173.

(b) The same Rule applies to the exercise of other belligerent rights, such as interception.

1. Examples of belligerent rights other than attack are interception, mentioned Rule 17 (b), as well as inspection, diversion and capture as prize (see Section U).

2. These belligerent rights do not exist as a matter of law in non-international armed conflict.

18. Acts or threats of violence in the course of air or missile operations cannot be pursued for the sole or primary purpose of spreading terror among the civilian population.

1. This Rule is based on the second sentence of Art. 51 (2) of AP/I.[225]

2. Rule 18 pertains to both "acts . . . of violence" and "threats of violence". Acts of violence will always come within the definition of attacks (see Rule 1 (e)). As for threats of violence, they can be issued through broadcasts, the dropping of leaflets or in any other fashion. Whether they constitute "acts" or "threats" of violence, such activities cannot be pursued solely or primarily for the purpose of spreading terror among the civilian population.

3. Rule 18 is limited to activities in which the "sole or primary" purpose is that of spreading terror among the civilian population. The term "primary" is found in Art. 51 (2) of AP/I. *A fortiori*, this includes situations in which doing so is the "sole" purpose. The majority of the Group of Experts did not agree with the limitation of the prohibition in NWP to situations where the "sole purpose" of the threat is to terrorize the civilian population.[226]

4. Rule 18 is confined to the concept of "spreading terror among the civilian population". Rule 18 is irrelevant to "shock and awe" operations designed to "spread terror" among combatants.

5. Very frequently, notwithstanding the obligations of passive precautions (see Section H), some military objectives are intermingled with the civilian

[225] Art. 51 (2) of AP/I: "The civilian population as such, as well as individual civilians, shall not be the object of attack. Acts or threats of violence the primary purpose of which is to spread terror among the civilian population are prohibited."

[226] Para. 8.9.1.2 ("Terrorization") of NWP: "Bombardment for the sole purpose of terrorizing the civilian population is prohibited."

population. If the acts or threats of violence pursued relate to lawful targets, the incidental spreading of terror among the civilian population is not prohibited by Rule 18. However, if the presence of lawful targets in the area is used merely as an excuse to conduct the operation, and in fact the "primary" purpose of the act of violence (or the threat thereof) is to terrorize the civilian population, the operation is prohibited under Rule 18.

6. Rule 18 is confined to operations designed to "terrorize" the civilian population. It must be distinguished from operations designed to affect civilian morale without spreading terror among the civilian population. Examples of such operations – often labeled psychological operations or information operations – are calls to the civilian population to overthrow its national government or to otherwise diminish support for their leadership. Such operations do not come within the bounds of the definition of an "attack" (see Rule 1(e)). On this issue, see also Rule 21.

7. Some commentators contend that attacks designed to destroy civilian morale may be permissible should it lead to an early termination of hostilities. The majority of the Group of Experts believed that the prohibition of terrorizing the civilian population is absolute and, therefore, shattering civilian morale is unacceptable even if it can be explained along so-called utilitarian lines.

8. As long as the targets under attack are lawful targets (see Rule 10 (b)), the fact that their destruction incidentally affects civilian morale does not preclude attack. Civilian morale, as well as the enemy's military morale, may indeed be affected as a side effect of an aerial operation that demonstrates the attacker's ability to strike at military objectives with impunity.

9. The civilian population comprises all persons who are civilians.[227]

10. Rule 18 applies also in non-international armed conflict.

[227] Art. 50 (2) AP/I: "The civilian population comprises all persons who are civilians."

19. Belligerent Parties conducting, or subject to, air or missile operations:

(a) **Must take all possible measures to search for and collect the wounded, sick and shipwrecked, ensure their adequate care, permit their removal, exchange and transport, and search for the dead;**

1. This Rule is based on Art. 15 of GC/I[228] which obliges the Belligerent Parties to take all possible measures to search for and collect the wounded and sick, and provides for the possibility to arrange for a suspension of fire to this end. According to Art. 15 of GC/I, local arrangements may also be concluded to permit the removal, exchange and transport of the wounded on the battlefield.

2. Note must be taken of the expression "all possible measures". These measures are obviously affected by the special circumstances of air warfare. Moreover, it is necessary to distinguish between the conduct of air warfare over land and over sea.

3. Rule 19 (a) also applies in non-international armed conflict.

(b) **Must, whenever circumstances permit, arrange cease-fires, if necessary through a neutral intermediary, to facilitate the activities described in paragraph** (a);

1. This Rule is derived from Art. 15 of GC/I.[229]

2. A cease-fire constitutes the temporary suspension of hostilities, and it may be agreed upon by commanders on the spot. Such a local cease-fire is particularly important when the wounded, sick and shipwrecked have to be collected and evacuated.

3. Whereas a cease-fire presupposes agreement by the opposing sides, the duty to take all possible measures to collect the wounded and sick on the battlefield may require – whenever circumstances permit – unilateral suspension of operations. For an analogy, see Rule 103 regarding humanitarian assistance.

[228] See fn. 206.

[229] *Ibid.*

4. The words "whenever circumstances permit" allow a certain latitude to the Belligerent Party conducting the operations. In particular, considerations of military necessity may preclude the suspension of air or missile attacks.

5. Belligerent Parties may find it difficult to negotiate terms for the suspension of air and missile attacks. They may therefore require the services of a neutral intermediary, in order to open communication between them. The neutral intermediary may be a State or an impartial humanitarian organization, such as the ICRC.

6. Rule 19 (b) applies also in non-international armed conflict.

(c) **Ought to accept the assistance of impartial humanitarian organizations and facilitate their work in favour of the wounded and other victims of air or missile attacks.**

1. This Rule is inspired by Art. 81 of AP/I.[230]

2. Rule 19 (c) emphasizes that the obligation regarding search for, collect and care for the wounded, sick and shipwrecked (Rule 19 (a)) implies a possible need to allow impartial humanitarian organizations to assist Belligerent Parties in the accomplishment of these tasks.

3. On the notion of impartial humanitarian organizations, see Rule 100 (b).

[230] Art. 81 of AP/I: "(1) The Parties to the conflict shall grant to the ICRC all facilities within their power so as to enable it to carry out the humanitarian functions assigned to it by the Conventions and this Protocol in order to ensure protection and assistance to the victims of conflicts; the ICRC may also carry out any other humanitarian activities in favour of these victims, subject to the consent of the Parties to the conflict concerned. (2) The Parties to the conflict shall grant to their respective Red Cross (Red Crescent, Red Lion and Sun) organizations the facilities necessary for carrying out their humanitarian activities in favour of the victims of the conflict, in accordance with the Rules of the Conventions and this Protocol and the fundamental principles of the Red Cross as formulated by the International Conferences of the Red Cross. (3) The High Contracting Parties and the Parties to the conflict shall facilitate in every possible way the assistance which Red Cross (Red Crescent, Red Lion and Sun) organizations and the League of Red Cross Societies extend to the victims of conflicts in accordance with the Rules of the Conventions and this Protocol and with the fundamental principles of the Red Cross as formulated by the International Conferences of the Red Cross. (4) The High Contracting Parties and the Parties to the conflict shall, as far as possible, make facilities similar to those mentioned in paragraphs 2 and 3 available to the other humanitarian organizations referred to in the Conventions and this Protocol which are duly authorized by the respective Parties to the conflict and which perform their humanitarian activities in accordance with the provisions of the Conventions and this Protocol."

4. The activities of these impartial humanitarian organizations are subject to the approval of the Belligerent Party on whose territory they operate, but this approval should not be withheld arbitrarily. The phrase "should not" is used here deliberately, since there was disagreement among the Group of Experts as to the latter issue.

5. Rule 19 (c) applies also in non international armed conflict.

20. Air or missile attacks must be conducted in accordance with those feasible precautions required under Section G of this Manual designed to avoid – or, in any event, minimize – collateral damage.

This Rule refers to "feasible precautions", with a view to avoiding – or, in any event, minimizing – collateral damage to civilians or civilian objects where that is possible. For details, see Section G.

21. The application of the general Rules prohibiting attacks directed against civilians or civilian objects, as well as indiscriminate attacks, is confined to air or missile attacks that entail violent effects, namely, acts resulting in death, injury, damage or destruction.

1. Despite the lack of direct authority for this Rule in treaty law, the majority of the Group of Experts concluded that it generally reflects State practice.

2. The emphasis in Rule 21 on "acts resulting in death, injury, damage or destruction" is intended to exclude psychological warfare, whether directed against combatants or civilians, which does not generate violent effects. See paragraph 9 of the Commentary on Rule 13 (b).

3. By the same token, a CNA which interferes with air traffic control but does not cause any "death, injury, damage or destruction" does not qualify as an attack (see Rule 1 (e) and Rule 1 (m)).

4. Rule 21 applies also in non-international armed conflict.

Section E

Military Objectives

1. Section E applies in its entirety to both international and non-international armed conflicts.

2. Lawful targets can be attacked, subject to the applicable rules of the law of international armed conflict (such as the rules of proportionality and the requirement to take feasible precautions in attack; see respectively Section D, in particular Rule 14, and Section G). Lawful targets are defined in Rule 10 (b) as encompassing combatants; military objectives; and civilians taking a direct part in hostilities.

3. The phrase "military objectives" originated in Art. 24 (1) of the HRAW[231], providing that only military objectives may be attacked through air bombardment. It has been repeated in several treaty texts, pre-eminently in Art. 52 (2) of AP/I, which reiterates that "[a]ttacks shall be limited strictly to military objectives".[232]

4. The foundation of the principle that only lawful targets can be attacked is the principle of distinction, recognized by the ICJ in its Nuclear Weapons Advisory Opinion[233] as an "intransgressible" principle of international law and as one of two "cardinal" principles (the other being unnecessary suffering or superfluous injury) of the law of international armed conflict. The basic requirement of distinction between combatants and military objectives, on the one hand, and civilians and civilian objects, on the other hand, is stressed also in Art. 48 of AP/I.[234] Undoubtedly, it also reflects customary international law. See Rule 10 and Rule 11.

[231] Art. 24 (1) of the HRAW, see fn. 721.
[232] Art. 52 (2) of AP/I, see fn. 73.
[233] ICJ, Nuclear Weapons Advisory Opinion, paras. 78 and 79.
[234] Art. 48 of AP/I, see fn. 167.

I. General rules

22. In the definition of objects as military objectives (see Rule 1 (y)), the following criteria apply:

1. Subject to the other requirements of the definition (see paragraph 3 of the Commentary on the *chapeau* to this Rule), there are four alternative criteria qualifying an object as a military objective: nature, location, purpose or use. These four criteria are the core of the definition of military objective, and they are analyzed in some detail in the four subparagraphs of this Rule.

2. As a practical matter, attacks are most commonly based on an object's nature (generally the enemy's military equipment or installations) or by use by the enemy; qualification by purpose (the enemy's intended future use of an object) or location is less common.

3. The definition of military objective not only requires that an object "make[s] an effective contribution to military action" "by nature, location, purpose or use", but also that its "total or partial destruction, capture, or neutralization, in the circumstances ruling at the time, offers a definite military advantage" (see Rule 1 (y)). As indicated in paragraph 3 of the commentary to Rule 1 (y), compliance with the first criterion will generally result in the advantage required of the second.

(a) The "nature" of an object symbolizes its fundamental character. Examples of military objectives by nature include military aircraft (including military UAV/UCAVs); military vehicles (other than medical transport); missiles and other weapons; military equipment; military fortifications, facilities and depots; warships; ministries of defence and armaments factories.

1. In order to qualify as a military objective by nature, the object in question must have an inherent characteristic or attribute which contributes to military action. Military equipment and facilities most clearly qualify on this basis, as do tanks, military aircraft, military airfields, or military barracks. Even when not in use, such objects always constitute lawful targets during armed conflict.

2. As mentioned in Rule 22 (a), military objectives by nature include Ministries of Defence. This will be the case even if such Ministries are staffed in part by civilians. Of course, to the extent that a Ministry of

Defence has physically separate non-defence departments, as in the case of the Swiss Federal Ministry of Defence, Civil Protection and Sport, its facilities devoted exclusively to such civilian functions are not military objectives by nature.

3. The examples mentioned in Rule 22 (a) are non-exhaustive. Their distinctive feature is that they qualify as military objectives by nature in all circumstances. Other objects could qualify as military objectives by nature as well (see Rule 23).

(b) Application of the "location" criterion can result in specific areas of land such as a mountain pass, a bridgehead or jungle trail becoming military objectives.

"Location" relates to selected areas that have special importance to military operations, such as a particular mountain pass that may offer enemy armed forces a route of retreat in the face of a planned attack. Because of the location of the pass, it is lawful to block it through air attack, irrespective of use. Similarly, an attacker may wish to blind the enemy by depriving it of high ground from which it could observe the attacker's operation. It may also destroy natural cover in the area, to prohibit the enemy from using it as an observation point. In these cases, it is not actual "use" or the enemy's intended future use ("purpose") that matters. The governing criterion is the need to attack a location so as to enhance or safeguard the attacker's operations or to diminish the enemy's options.

(c) The "purpose" of an object – although not military by nature – is concerned with the intended future use of an object.

1. It is essential to distinguish "purpose" from "use" (see Rule 22 (d)). The latter refers to present function of an object, whereas the former focuses on intended future use. The purpose criterion recognizes that an attacker need not wait until an object is actually used for military ends before being allowed to attack it as a military objective.

2. The key issue in determining purpose is the enemy's intent. In many cases, the enemy's intent as to the future use of an object is clear. An example of such clarity is when reliable intelligence or other information indicates that an apartment building is being renovated with a view to serving as a military barracks. The apartment building becomes a military objective by purpose, regardless of its actual or ultimate use.

3. Often, however, the enemy's intent is not clear. In such circumstances, it is necessary to avoid sheer speculation and to rely on hard evidence, based perhaps on intelligence gathering. The dilemma is that intelligence is of varying degrees of reliability. The attacker must always act reasonably, i.e., as would be proper under a similar set of circumstances for any other Belligerent Party. In other words, the attacker must ask itself whether it would be reasonable to conclude that the intelligence was reliable enough to conduct the attack in light of the circumstances ruling at the time.

4. The enemy's intent may be based on specified preconditions prior to actual implementation of any existing plans. In such circumstances, these specified preconditions have to be fulfilled before the civilian object becomes a military objective by purpose. In other words, intelligence or other information has to lead to a reasonable conclusion that plans are in the process of being implemented, or will be implemented in the near future. Two examples can be given: (i) Communication intercepts or other intelligence may reveal that certain civilian airfields have been designated as alternative recovery airfields in the event that a military airfield is unusable. Once the military airfield is unusable, the designated alternative recovery airfields become military objectives by purpose and may be attacked, regardless of their actual or ultimate use; (ii) Overt contingency plans may exist for the use of certain civilian objects (such as civilian transports) for military airlift purposes. As long as no action is taken to activate the civilian transports for these purposes, they remain civilian objects. However, upon activation for military service, the transports in question become military objectives by purpose, regardless of their actual or ultimate use.

(d) The "use" of an object relates to its present function, with the result that a civilian object can become a military objective due to its use by armed forces.

1. This criterion requires actual use by the enemy of a particular object that, on the face of it, is civilian in nature. In other words, the object is not a military objective by nature, but subsequently becomes a lawful target as a result of conversion to military use.

2. For instance, a purely civilian airfield that is subsequently used to launch or recover military aircraft loses its civilian character and becomes a military objective for the duration of its military use. Other examples

would relate to (i) enemy troops billeted in a civilian hotel or school; (ii) enemy use of a civilian broadcast facility for military transmission; or (iii) civilian vehicles being commandeered by enemy forces to transport troops or materiel.

3. In all such instances, the civilian objects become military objectives through use and may be attacked, subject to the principle of proportionality (see Rule 14) and Section G. They may not be attacked prior to such use unless there is sufficient evidence of the enemy's intent to use the object for military ends (thereby qualifying under the purpose criterion, see Rule 22 (c)).

4. Once use for a military purpose ceases, the object ceases to be a lawful target and may no longer be attacked. That said, if there is reliable intelligence that the enemy intends to use the object again in the future, it may remain a military objective, albeit by purpose, rather than by use. However, the mere fact that an object was used once as a military objective does not suffice, in and of itself, to establish purpose for future use.

5. Any civilian object may become a military objective through use, including those entitled to specific protection but abused by a Belligerent Party through military use (see Sections K-N). Even objects entitled to specific protection, such as medical units (see Section K) or cultural property (see Section N (II)) can become military objectives if so used. In such a case, see Rule 32 (a) as well as Rule 35 (a) and Rule 35 (b).

6. In case of doubt as to whether an object which is ordinarily dedicated to civilian purposes is being used for military purposes, it may only be attacked if, based on all the information reasonably available to the commander at the time, there are reasonable grounds to believe that it has become and remains a military objective (see Rule 12 (b)).

7. Any military use of a civilian object renders it a military objective. However, the fact that it has become a military objective by use does not exclude the possibility of simultaneous civilian use. Such objects are commonly referred to as "dual-use" objects. Despite the fact that they have become a military objective, the decision whether or not they can be attacked depends by and large on the application of the principle of proportionality (see Rule 14). The classic example in the context of air or missile operations is an airport used both by military and civilian aircraft.

23. Objects which may qualify as military objectives through the definition in Rules 1 (y) and 22 (a) include, but are not limited to, factories, lines and means of communications (such as airfields, railway lines, roads, bridges and tunnels); energy producing facilities; oil storage depots; transmission facilities and equipment.

1. The Group of Experts hesitated whether this additional list of military objectives by nature is required in light of the already existing Rule 22 (a). There were three views in the Group of Experts. One view was that all objects listed here belong in Rule 22 (a) because they are military objectives by nature at all times. The opposite view was that the objects listed in Rule 23 are not necessarily military objectives by nature, but, if at all, by use, purpose or location.[235] The majority of the Group of Experts accepted the present Rule as a compromise third view, by which military objectives by nature were to be divided into two subsets. The first, reflected in Rule 22 (a), consists of military objectives by nature at all times. By contrast, the second subset – reflected in Rule 23 – consists of objects which become military objectives by nature only in light of the circumstances ruling at the time.

2. The reference to Rule 1 (y) in its totality is designed to stress the fact that the objects listed by way of example may not be attacked unless the criteria of Rule 1 (y) are met. However, it must be borne in mind that the list is given in the context of military objectives by nature. The focus, therefore, is on the cross-reference to Rule 22 (a). That is to say, the present Rule does not refer to Rule 22 (b)–(d). The objects listed in Rule 23, while

[235] According to the ICRC, there are no subsets of military objectives by nature. In its view, it has no foundation in the existing law of international armed conflict. The Commentary to Rule 22 (a) clearly indicates that an object is a military objective by nature only if it has an "inherent characteristic or attribute which contributes to military action". An "inherent characteristic or attribute" cannot be conceived of on a merely temporary basis. By definition it has to be permanent. In the opinion of the ICRC, Rule 23 – for illustration purposes – includes categories of objects which, depending on the circumstances, may qualify as military objectives through use, purpose or location. In other words, every object falling into the categories mentioned in Rule 22 (a) is a military objective by nature, whereas the objects falling into the categories cited in Rule 23 may only under certain circumstances qualify as military objectives. For example, a factory producing weapons (see Rule 24 (a)), is a military objective by nature. A factory producing purely civilian goods is not a military objective. However, depending on use or purpose it may become a military objective. The key is that the test for military objectives set forth in Rule 1 (y) must be met before an object may be attacked.

subject to debate and some disagreement, reflect the views of the majority of the Group of Experts.

24. The connection between a military objective and military action may be direct or indirect.

1. As set forth in Rule 1 (y), the definition of military objectives depends in part on their making "an effective contribution to military action". This Rule stresses that the connection between the target and ongoing military operations need not be direct. For instance, it is lawful to attack enemy military storage depots or barracks far from the battlefield because such assets constitute reserves for further military action by the enemy. It is also well-accepted that factories producing munitions and military equipment are lawful targets (see Rule 22 (a)). So too would be a port, railroad, road or airport used in the transport of supplies necessary for the production by the factory of military items (see Rule 23).

2. There is a controversy as to whether "war-sustaining" economic objects qualify as military objectives. A war-sustaining economic object is one which indirectly but effectively supports the enemy's overall war effort.[236] Those who subscribe to the qualification of such objects as military objectives argue that a Belligerent Party's war-sustaining capability is directly connected to its combat operations. For instance, they contend that a Belligerent Party may lawfully attack export oil production intended for Neutrals since the profits finance the war effort. Materials of actual military value to the enemy – such as oil or petrol dedicated to military use – are not related to the argument, inasmuch as they constitute military objectives by nature. The crux of the issue is related to revenues from exports of oil which is not put to military use by the enemy. The majority of the Group of Experts took the position that the connection between revenues from such exports and military action is too remote. Consequently, it rejected the war-sustaining argument (see also paragraph 8 of the Commentary on Rule 1 (y)).

3. The connection between the military objective and "military action" (concept which appears in the definition of military objectives, see Rule

[236] Second subparagraph of Para. 8.2.5 of NWP ("Objects"): "Proper objects of attack also include enemy lines of communication, rail yards, bridges, rolling stock, barges, lighters, industrial installations producing war-fighting products, and power generation plants. Economic objects of the enemy that indirectly but effectively support and sustain the enemy's war-fighting capability may also be attacked."

1 (y)) must be actual and discernible, not merely hypothetical or speculative. For instance, the destruction of a civilian airfield incapable of launching military aircraft cannot be justified on the basis that the enemy might one day possess the means of launching and recovering in that airfield. Of course, if the enemy has a clear-cut intent to transform the civilian airfield into one usable for military purposes, the purpose criterion of Rule 22 (c) may turn it into a military objective by purpose.

4. Further, the action in question must be military in nature and not, for instance, political, financial, economic or social. As an example, striking otherwise civilian targets in order to create the impression that the enemy civilian leadership is weak would not constitute an attack against a military objective which contributes to the enemy's military action.

II. Specifics of air and missile operations

25. Aircraft may be the object of attack only if they constitute military objectives.

1. This Rule flows from the general rule restricting attacks to lawful targets (see Rule 10).

2. The primary purpose of Rule 25 is to emphasize that attacks against civilian aircraft, civilian airliners, State aircraft that do not qualify as military aircraft, medical aircraft and cartel aircraft are forbidden, unless protection is lost as explained in Rule 27 (for enemy aircraft, other than military aircraft, except enemy civilian airliners); Rule 63 (for civilian airliners, enemy or neutral) and Rule 174 (for neutral civilian aircraft, except neutral civilian airliners), or the aircraft otherwise constitutes a military objective.

3. As for military aircraft, see Rule 22 (a) and Rule 26.

4. State aircraft, such as law-enforcement aircraft, may be armed for purposes other than military operations. They nevertheless do not constitute military objectives unless used for military purposes or incorporated into the armed forces of a belligerent (for details, see Rule 27). That said, they are subject to treatment as booty of war or to capture as prize (for details, see Section U, in particular Rule 136 (a)).

5. Rule 25 is not limited to enemy aircraft. In particular circumstances, neutral aircraft can also become military objectives (see Rule 174

pertaining to neutral civilian aircraft, and paragraph 1 of the Commentary on the *chapeau* of Rule 174 pertaining to neutral State aircraft).

6. In a non-international armed conflict, non-State organized armed groups may have aircraft at their disposal. However, such aircraft do not constitute military aircraft (see Rule 1(x)). They are civilian aircraft, but they may be attacked because of their use for military purposes. See paragraph 8 of the Commentary on Rule 1 (x) and paragraph 7 of the Commentary on Rule 17 (a).

26. All enemy military aircraft constitute military objectives, unless protected under Section L of this Manual, or as otherwise agreed by the Belligerent Parties under Section N (V).

1. The language of this Rule, which is based on customary international law, is derived from Para. 12.39 of the UK Manual.[237]

2. The term "military aircraft" is defined in Rule 1 (x). Military aircraft must be marked as such. The failure to mark properly an aircraft precludes qualification as a "military aircraft" and, therefore, such aircraft may not exercise belligerent rights. However, if used for military purposes, any aircraft would nevertheless qualify as a military objective through use (see Rule 22 (d)).

3. All military aircraft, as defined in Rule 1(x), constitute military objectives by nature at all times (see Rule 22 (a)). Military aircraft need not be armed. They can be used as tanker aircraft and they may even be dedicated to transporting civilian officials, monitoring weather, or performing scientific research. All these aircraft are military objectives by nature, irrespective of use.

4. Because military aircraft can travel great distances in a short period of time, they are generally available for use throughout a theatre of operations. As a result, their destruction, damage or neutralization will always offer a military advantage to an attacker because it deprives the enemy of their subsequent use, and they will therefore constitute military objectives by nature at all times (see Rule 22 (a)).

5. Military aircraft which have clearly communicated an intention to surrender may not be attacked (see Section S).

[237] Para. 12.39 of the UK Manual: "Unless they are exempt from attack under paragraphs 13.33 or 12.29, enemy warships and military aircraft and enemy auxiliary vessels and aircraft are military objectives."

6. Military aircraft may be granted safe conduct as cartel aircraft (see definition in Rule 1 (g) and substantive Rules in Section J (II) and J (III)).

7. Military aircraft may constitute medical aircraft, which are subject to a different legal regime. See the definition of medical aircraft in Rule 1 (u) and Section L.

8. During non-international armed conflicts, similarly to international armed conflicts, it is a violation of the law of armed conflict for either side to attack aircraft that do not qualify as military objectives. Law-enforcement agencies may use State aircraft for purposes unrelated to the conflict. In such cases, an attack on them would violate the law of armed conflict. However, if such aircraft fulfil the criteria that render them a military objective and are being used for purposes related to the armed conflict, an attack on them by the non-State organized armed group does not violate the law of armed conflict, although it will violate the domestic law of the State in which the conflict is occurring.

27. Without prejudice to Sections I, J and L of this Manual, the following activities may render any other enemy aircraft a military objective:

1. This Rule is based on the SRM/ACS.[238] See also Para. 8.8 of NWP[239](*See footnote 239 on next page*) and Paras. 12.36 and 12.37 of the UK Manual.[240](*See footnote 240 on next page*)

[238] Para. 63 of the SRM/ACS: "The following activities may render enemy civil aircraft military objectives: (a) engaging in acts of war on behalf of the enemy, e.g., laying mines, minesweeping, laying or monitoring acoustic sensors, engaging in electronic warfare, intercepting or attacking other civil aircraft, or providing targeting information to enemy forces; (b) acting as an auxiliary aircraft to an enemy's armed forces, e.g., transporting troops or military cargo, or refuelling military aircraft; (c) being incorporated into or assisting the enemy's intelligence-gathering system, e.g., engaging in reconnaissance, early warning, surveillance, or command, control and communications missions; (d) flying under the protection of accompanying enemy warships or military aircraft; (e) refusing an order to identify itself, divert from its track, or proceed for visit and search to a belligerent airfield that is safe for the type of aircraft involved and reasonably accessible, or operating fire control equipment that could reasonably be construed to be part of an aircraft weapon system, or on being intercepted clearly manoeuvring to attack the intercepting belligerent military aircraft; (f) being armed with air-to-air or air-to-surface weapons; or (g) otherwise making an effective contribution to military action."

2. The crux of Rule 27 is qualification as a military objective. In this regard, it is not necessary that the aircraft in question be conducting an attack (see Rule 1 (e)). Instead, it need only be making an effective contribution to the enemy's military action and its destruction, capture or neutralization would yield a definite military advantage in the circumstances ruling at the time (see Rule 1 (y)). For instance, a State aircraft – not qualifying as a military aircraft – passively gathering intelligence or conducting electronic warfare that merely interferes with enemy communications is not "attacking" but its actions still render it a military objective.

3. Any attack on such aircraft must comply with all elements of Section D (see especially Rule 14) and Section G, in particular Section G (III) pertaining to specifics of attacks directed against aircraft in the air.

4. While all enemy aircraft other than enemy military aircraft may lose their protection, it needs to be stressed that civilian aircraft, medical aircraft, civilian airliners and aircraft granted safe conduct do not lose

[239] Para. 8.8 of NWP ("Air Warfare at Sea"): "Enemy merchant vessels and civil aircraft may be attacked and destroyed by military aircraft only under the following circumstances: 1. When persistently refusing to comply with directions from the intercepting aircraft; 2. When sailing under convoy of enemy warships or military aircraft; 3. When armed with systems or weapons beyond that required for self-defense against terrorism, piracy, or like threats; 4. When incorporated into or assisting in any way the enemy's military intelligence system; 5. When acting in any capacity as a naval or military auxiliary to an enemy's armed forces; 6. When otherwise integrated into the enemy's war-fighting or war-sustaining effort."

[240] Para. 12.36 of the UK Manual: "Enemy civil aircraft may only be attacked if they meet the definition of a military objective in paragraph 5.4.1."

Para. 12.37 of the UK Manual: "The following activities may render enemy civil aircraft military objectives: (a) engaging in acts of war on behalf of the enemy, e.g., laying mines, minesweeping, laying or monitoring sensors, engaging in electronic warfare, intercepting or attacking other civil aircraft, or providing targeting information to enemy forces; (b) acting as an auxiliary aircraft to an enemy's armed forces, e.g., transporting troops or military cargo, or refuelling military aircraft; (c) being incorporated into or assisting the enemy's intelligence gathering system, e.g., engaging in reconnaissance, early warning, surveillance, or command, control, and communication missions; (d) flying under the protection of accompanying enemy warships or military aircraft; (e) refusing an order to identify itself, divert from its track, or proceed for visit and search to a belligerent aircraft that is safe for the type of aircraft involved and reasonably accessible, or operating fire control equipment that could reasonably be construed to be part of an aircraft weapon system, or on being intercepted clearly manoeuvring to attack the intercepting belligerent military aircraft; (f) being armed with air-to-air or air-to-surface weapons; or (g) otherwise making an effective contribution to military action."

their protection unless certain conditions are met. These conditions are set out, respectively, in Section I, Section L, and Section J.

5. The following activities relate both to intended future use ("purpose") and to "use", and are therefore subject to the application of Rule 22 (c) and 22 (d).

6. Rule 27 does not apply to civilian airliners, which are dealt with in Rule 63.

7. For enemy civilian aircraft, see also Rule 50.

8. Rule 27 applies only to enemy aircraft. Neutral civilian aircraft are dealt with in Rule 174.

(a) Engaging in hostile actions in support of the enemy, e.g., intercepting or attacking other aircraft; attacking persons or objects on land or sea; being used as a means of attack; engaging in electronic warfare; or providing targeting information to enemy forces.

1. Rule 27 (a) sets forth the most definitive example of aircraft becoming military objectives through purpose or use (see Rule 22 (c) and on 22 (d)).

2. The phrase "hostile actions" refers to actions that typically are conducted by military aircraft during, and in connection with, hostilities. Such activities are not limited to attacks, but would also include, for instance, intelligence gathering, surveillance and reconnaissance activities.

3. "Hostile actions" need not be directed against the military forces or assets. As long as there is a nexus to the armed conflict, such acts are liable to be committed against civilians, the civilian population or even objects within one's own territory, regardless of whether the object is of a military or civilian nature or whether the action is lawful or not.

4. The phrase "in support of the enemy" is included to emphasize that there must be a nexus with the conflict, in other words, that the act in question must be intended to benefit the enemy. This criterion would distinguish a hostile action from a purely criminal act.

5. "Targeting information" is any information that enables an attack to be conducted. Examples include information pertaining to the location of the target, target area defences, description of the target area, and

identification of reference points that identify the target. The acquisition and transmission of targeting information may be carried out by civilian aircraft with sensors used for civilian purposes (such as search-and-rescue aircraft equipped with infrared sensors) or may simply involve passing information as to what the aircrews observe. Such activities will constitute a hostile action in support of the enemy.

6. It is not necessary that the enemy directed or even invited or endorsed the act in question to occur. What counts is the intent of the actor engaging in it, together with the fact that the act is of a nature to support the enemy, which determines whether a nexus to the armed conflict is present.

7. The reference to aircraft "used as a means of attack" is specifically included to cover a situation where a civilian aircraft is flown into the intended target. In such cases, the aircraft effectively becomes a means of warfare, that is, a weapon. Military aircraft used for this purpose, such as those employed in the Japanese Kamikaze attacks of WWII, already qualify as military objectives by nature. As for (hijacked) civilian airliners, see Rule 63.

8. The use of any aircraft other than a military aircraft as a means of attack is prohibited at all times, see Rule 115 (b).

9. State aircraft that are not military aircraft are not entitled to exercise belligerent rights (such as conducting attacks) (see Rule 17) and, as a rule, are not military objectives by nature. However, when under the exclusive control of the armed forces and being used for military purposes, such aircraft qualify as military objectives under Rule 27 (a) or under Rule (b). Hence, they may be attacked for so long as they are so used.

10. Rule 27 (a) applies also in non-international armed conflict.

(b) Facilitating the military actions of the enemy's armed forces, e.g., transporting troops, carrying military materials, or refuelling military aircraft.

1. The examples set forth in Rule 27 (b) are merely illustrative. For instance, being armed with air-to-air or air-to-surface missiles exposes any aircraft to attack because there are no civilian purposes attendant to such arming. In every case, the essential inquiry is whether the aircraft in question has become a military objective through use or purpose.

2. Rule 27 (b) is included to make clear that aircraft need not be engaging in "attacks" to qualify as a military objective. The requirement is that their

actions make an effective contribution to the enemy's military actions. The phrase "military actions" has been intentionally employed to exclude activities that are more general in character, e.g., general support to the enemy's war effort. An example of facilitation of military action will be the carrying of ammunition for use by military units. The key is that a clear nexus exists between the flight and military actions of the enemy.

3. Rule 27 (b) applies also in non-international armed conflict.

> **(c) Being incorporated into or assisting the enemy's intelligence gathering system, e.g., engaging in reconnaissance, early warning, surveillance or command, control and communications missions.**

1. Rule 27 (c) is based on the second sentence of Art. 16 of the HRAW.[241]

2. "Incorporat[ion]" means that the aircraft is an integrated part of the enemy's intelligence gathering system. This could for instance occur if an aircraft the primary function of which is environmental monitoring of the EEZ, routinely reports the presence of foreign warships, thus relieving the workload of military maritime patrol aircraft. The essence of incorporation is that the activity in question is regular or systematic and the enemy relies on the information provided in calculating its actions, thereby relieving it of the need to gather such information itself. "Assisting" means providing assistance to the enemy without necessarily being an integrated part of its intelligence gathering-system.

3. Rule 27 (c) differs from that set forth in Rule 27 (a) regarding the provision of targeting information. In Rule 27 (c), the intent is to address activities that are integrated into the enemy's intelligence gathering system (incorporation) or in which the armed forces obtain assistance for a particular operation (assistance), as distinct from those in which the aircraft merely happens to acquire information that it then passes on to the military which uses it for targeting purposes. In other words, Rule 27 (a) refers to incidental provision of such information, whereas Rule 27 (c) addresses planned activities.

4. The characterization of an activity as intelligence gathering must be made carefully. Information acquired in the course of normal flights operated by other than military aircraft may be of value to enemy forces.

[241] Art. 16 of the HRAW, see fn. 220.

For instance, information regarding weather, the proximity of other aircraft, and communications with other aircraft or ground control may all be militarily useful. However, reporting such information through normal aviation channels, even if it ends up in the hands of the military, does not constitute intelligence gathering. Intelligence gathering is limited to the intentional collection of information for military purposes.

5. Rule 27 (c) applies also in non-international armed conflict.

(d) Refusing to comply with the orders of military authorities, including instructions for landing, inspection and possible capture, or clearly resisting interception.

1. Rule 27 (d) is reflective of Para. 62 (e) of the SRM/ACS.[242] It addresses the situation where military forces encounter an enemy aircraft other than a military aircraft that is not clearly engaging in activities qualifying it as a military objective. When this situation occurs, the military forces are entitled to order that aircraft to identify itself and its activities. If necessary, the aircraft can be ordered to land for inspection (see Rule 134). In certain situations (see Section U (I)), the aircraft may be captured as prize. It may also be diverted from the area of military operations. Refusal to comply with orders to land or clearly resisting interception may render the aircraft a military objective.

2. When an enemy aircraft other than a military aircraft is "escorted" by enemy military aircraft or warships, in either international airspace or the airspace of Belligerent Parties, they will be presumed to refuse to comply with the orders of military authorities.[243] The presumption is rebuttable because the attendant circumstances may indicate to an attacker that the

[242] Para. 62 (e) of SRM/ACS: "Enemy civil aircraft may only be attacked if they meet the definition of a military objective in paragraph 40:... (e) refusing an order to identify itself, divert from its track, or proceed for visit and search to a belligerent airfield that is safe for the type of aircraft involved and reasonably accessible, or operating fire control equipment that could reasonably be construed to be part of an aircraft weapon system, or on being intercepted clearly manoeuvring to attack the intercepting belligerent military aircraft."

[243] Para. 63.3 of the Commentary on the SRM/ACS: "Subparagraph (d) is similar to paragraph 60 (d) which includes sailing under convoy of enemy warships or military aircraft, an activity that may render an enemy merchant vessel a military objective. An enemy civil aircraft that flies under the protection of accompanying enemy warships or military aircraft places itself at risk in the immediate area of hostilities since the enemy warships or military aircraft are military objectives. Belligerent forces might assume that the protected enemy civil aircraft is acting as an auxiliary aircraft to the enemy's armed forces, or, in pressing an attack, belligerent forces may misidentify the enemy civil aircraft."

escorted aircraft will in fact comply. For instance, the flight commander may communicate to an intercepting aircraft his intention to comply. Of course, the escorting military aircraft or warships are military objectives by nature.

(e) Otherwise making an effective contribution to military action.

1. This is a "catch-all" provision designed to emphasize that the activities which render an enemy aircraft other than a military aircraft subject to attack are not necessarily limited to the examples given in Rule 27 (a)–(d).

2. The key is (intending to) engaging in any activity that would meet the criteria set forth for a military objective, i.e., (i) making an effective contribution to the enemy's military action; and (ii) its destruction, capture or neutralization would yield a definite military advantage for the attacker in the circumstances ruling at the time (see Rule 1 (y) and Rule 22).

Section F

Direct Participation in Hostilities

1. According to customary and treaty law applicable in both international and non-international armed conflict, civilians benefit from protection against direct (Rule 11) and indiscriminate (Rule 13) attacks unless and for such time as they take a direct part in hostilities.[244] Thus, for the duration of their direct participation in hostilities, civilians are lawful targets (see Rule 10 (b) (iii)).

2. Despite the serious legal consequences involved, treaty law does not provide a definition of direct participation in hostilities. The notion must therefore be interpreted in good faith in accordance with the ordinary meaning to be given to its constituent terms in their context and in light of the object and purpose of the law of international armed conflict.[245]

3. In essence, the notion comprises two components, namely that of "hostilities" and that of "direct participation" therein. While the concept of "hostilities" refers to the collective resort by the Belligerent Parties to means and methods of injuring the enemy,[246] "participation" in hostilities

[244] Art. 51 (3) of AP/I: "Civilians shall enjoy the protection afforded by this Section, unless and for such time as they take a direct part in hostilities."
Art. 13 (3) of AP/II: "Civilians shall enjoy the protection afforded by this Part, unless and for such time as they take a direct part in hostilities."

[245] Art. 31 (1) of the Vienna Convention on the Law of Treaties (23 May 1969, 1155 *U.N.T.S.* 331): "A treaty shall be interpreted in good faith in accordance with the ordinary meaning to be given to the terms of the treaty in their context and in the light of its object and purpose."

[246] See the 1907 Hague Regulations, Section II of which is entitled "Hostilities". Treaty law does not establish uniform terminology for the conduct of hostilities but refers, apart from "hostilities", also to concepts such as:
- "warfare", used in the title of Part III of AP/I ("Methods and Means of Warfare . . . ") as well as in the title of Section I of Part III of AP/I ("Methods and Means of Warfare"). Expression also used in Art. 35 (1) of AP/I, see fn. 105;
- "military operations", for example used in Art. 53 of GC/IV: "Any destruction by the Occupying Power of real or personal property belonging individually or collectively to

refers to the individual involvement of a person in these "hostilities".[247] Depending on the quality and degree of such involvement, individual participation in hostilities may be described as "direct" or "indirect". Indirect participation in hostilities does not lead to a loss of protection against direct attacks. The term "hostilities" is a generic term which corresponds to the sum total of all hostile acts carried out in an armed conflict.[248] The notion is wider than the notion of "attack".

4. Section F applies in its entirety also to non-international armed conflict, it being understood that there is no substantive difference between the adjective "active" – appearing in common Art. 3 of the Geneva Conventions[249] – and the more commonly used adjective "direct".[250]

private persons, or to the State, or to other public authorities, or to social or cooperative organizations, is prohibited, except where such destruction is rendered absolutely necessary by military operations.";

The expression "military operations" is also used in Art. 51 (1) of AP/I: "1. The civilian population and individual civilians shall enjoy general protection against dangers arising from military operations. To give effect to this protection, the following rules, which are additional to other applicable rules of international law, shall be observed in all circumstances."; and Art. 13 (1) AP/II ("The civilian population and individual civilians shall enjoy general protection against the dangers arising from military operations. . . . ");

– or simply "operations", as used for example in Art. 48 of AP/I (see fn. 167).

247 Art. 43 (2) of AP/I: "Members of the armed forces of a Party to a conflict (other than medical personnel and chaplains covered by Article 33 of the Third Convention) are combatants, that is to say, they have the right to participate directly in hostilities."

Art. 45 (1) of AP/I ("Protection of persons who have taken part in hostilities"): "A person who takes part in hostilities and falls into the power of an adverse Party . . . "

Art. 45 (3) of AP/I: "Any person who has taken part in hostilities, who is not entitled to prisoner-of-war status . . . "

Art. 51 (3) of AP/I, see fn. 244.

Art. 67 (1) (e) of AP/I, see fn. 487.

Art. 13 (3) AP/II, see fn. 244.

248 Some treaty provisions also the use of the term "hostile act". See, e.g., Art. 41 (2) of AP/I (see fn. 200) and Art. 42 (2) of AP/I (see fn. 653).

249 For the text of Common Art. 3 to the Geneva Conventions, see fn. 92. The expression of "persons taking no active part in the hostilities" appears in (1) of the said Common Article 3.

250 The terms "active" (Common Art. 3 to the Geneva Conventions) and "direct" (Art. 51 (3) of AP/I; Art. 43 (2) of AP/I; Art. 67 (1) (e) of AP/I and Art. 13 (3) AP/II) refer to the same quality and degree of individual participation in hostilities. See also: ICTR, The Prosecutor v. Jean-Paul Akayesu, Case No. ICTR-96-4-T, Judgment of 2 September 1998, Para. 629 ("The class of victims"): " . . . the Indictment reads: 'The victims referred to in this Indictment were, at all relevant times, persons not taking an active part in the hostilities'. This is a material averment for charges involving Art. 4 inasmuch as Common

28. Civilians lose their protection from attack if and for such time as they take a direct part in hostilities.

1. Rule 28 is exclusively concerned with the "protection of civilians from attack" and has no bearing on other protections accorded to civilians, such as those which apply during detention.

2. The phrase "for such time" is not in dispute as a reflection of customary international law. What it means is that, ordinarily, once direct participation in hostilities is over, the civilian concerned can no longer be attacked. However, three major controversial issues have emerged.

3. The first issue concerns the exact moment in time at which direct participation in hostilities begins and, similarly, the exact moment when it ends. On this, opinions are divided. One view – reflected in the ICRC Interpretive Guidance[251] – takes the position that only concrete preparatory measures and deployment constitute the earliest point of direct participation, and withdrawal from the particular engagement terminates it.[252] The opposing view is that one could go "downstream" and "upstream" as far as the causal connection would stretch. For example, an individual acquiring materials in anticipation of building an improvised explosive device would qualify as a direct participant in hostilities from the moment of doing so.

4. The second issue relates to the question of individuals who are members in non-State organized armed groups. Civilians who directly participate in hostilities may act entirely on an individual *ad hoc* basis. Often, however, non-State organized armed groups emerge which are joined by multiple individual civilians. Such groups, while organized and while participating in hostilities on behalf of one Belligerent Party and against another, do not necessarily "belong" to the Party which they generally support.[253] Of course, if they belong to a Belligerent Party they become

Art. 3 is for the protection of 'persons taking no active part in the hostilities' (Common Art. 3(1)), and Art. 4 of Additional Protocol II is for the protection of, "all persons who do not take a direct part or who have ceased to take part in hostilities". These phrases are so similar that, for the Chamber's purposes, they may be treated as synonymous."

251 ICRC Interpretive Guidance, at pages 65–68.

252 In accordance with this view, general preparation and capacity building (such as civilian factory workers producing weapons, ammunition and military equipment) may contribute to the general war effort but traditionally is not regarded as direct participation in hostilities.

253 However, according to the ICRC, directly participating in hostilities "on behalf" of a party means nothing else than "belonging to" that party.

part of its armed forces and are no longer civilians, i.e., they are combatants. There is no question that, if such organized armed groups belong to a Belligerent Party, the members are susceptible to attack at all times. The bone of contention relates to non-State organized armed groups in an international armed conflict which do not belong to a Belligerent Party. One view is that if an individual is a member of such a group, that person (at least when in a combat role) is continuously to be regarded as a civilian taking a direct part in hostilities, irrespective of any specific military action against the enemy. The other view, reflected in the ICRC Interpretive Guidance,[254] is that members of an organized armed group not belonging to a Party to the international armed conflict must either be regarded as organized criminals retaining their civilian status or, if the violence reaches the required thresholds of intensity and organization, may qualify as a Party to a separate non-international armed conflict. In the latter case, the organized armed group qualifies as the armed forces of that Party and the individuals concerned lose their civilian status.

5. The third issue relates to the question of the so-called "revolving door" phenomenon, whereby a person directly participates in hostilities on a recurrent basis (in the mode of "farmer by day, fighter by night"). According to one view, the issue of membership in a non-State organized armed group does not exhaust the possibilities of the revolving door phenomenon and anyone who is attempting to be a "farmer by day, fighter by night" is to be considered as directly participating in hostilities at all times, meaning that he can be attacked in between military operations. According to the other view, absent membership in an organized armed group, each specific act of direct participation in hostilities must be considered in isolation from the others. Hence, the fact that the same individual is recurrently participating in hostilities, does not mean that he can be attacked in between these specific acts.

6. Loss of protection against attack does not mean that the individuals concerned fall outside the protection of the law. The force used against civilians directly participating in hostilities must fully comply with the law of international armed conflict.

7. Finally, it ought to be noted that organized armed violence failing to qualify as an international or non-international armed conflict remains an issue of law-enforcement.

[254] ICRC Interpretive Guidance, at page 24.

29. Subject to the circumstances ruling at the time, the following activities are examples of what may constitute taking a direct part in hostilities:

1. According to the ICRC Interpretive Guidance,[255] a specific act amounting to direct participation in hostilities must meet three cumulative requirements: (i) a threshold regarding the harm likely to result from the act; (ii) a relationship of direct causation between the act and the expected harm; and (iii) a belligerent nexus between the act and the hostilities conducted between the Belligerent Parties. Applied in conjunction, these three requirements permit a reliable distinction between activities amounting to direct participation in hostilities and activities which, although occurring in the context of an armed conflict, are not part of the hostilities and, therefore, do not entail loss of protection against direct attack.

2. In the ICRC Interpretive Guidance, the "threshold of harm"[256] requirement is explained as follows. For a specific act to qualify as direct participation in hostilities, the harm likely to result from it must attain a certain threshold. This threshold is reached, most notably, by adversely affecting the military operations or military capacity of a Belligerent Party (e.g., use of weapons against the armed forces, interrupting their deployments). Alternatively, the threshold can also be reached by inflicting death, injury, or destruction on persons or objects protected against direct attack (e.g., shelling or bombardment of residential areas, sniping against individual civilians). Direct participation in hostilities does not require the materialization of harm reaching the threshold but merely the objective likelihood that the conduct in question will result in such harm. Therefore, the relevant threshold determination must be based on "likely" harm, that is to say, harm which may reasonably be expected to result from an act in the prevailing circumstances.

3. The "direct causation"[257] requirement is explained in the ICRC Interpretive Guidance in the following manner. The civilian population has always contributed to the general war effort, whether through the production and provision of arms, equipment, food, and shelter, or through

[255] ICRC Interpretive Guidance, "Direct Participation in Hostilities as a Specific Act", at pages 43–45 and "Constitutive Elements of Direct Participation in Hostilities", at pages 46–64.

[256] ICRC Interpretive Guidance, at pages 47–50.

[257] ICRC Interpretive Guidance, at pages 51–58.

economic, administrative, and political support. In order to qualify as "direct" rather than "indirect" participation in hostilities, however, there must be a direct causal relation between the act in question and the resulting harm. In this context, direct causation means that the harm is brought about in one causal step. Therefore, acts that merely build or maintain the capacity of a Belligerent Party to harm its adversary in unspecified future operations do not amount to "direct" participation in hostilities, even if they are connected to the resulting harm through an uninterrupted chain of events or are indispensable to its causation (e.g., production of weapons and ammunition, general recruiting and training of personnel). Nonetheless, the notion of direct participation in hostilities can include acts which cause harm only in conjunction with other acts (e.g., providing targeting information as part of a specific combat operation), most notably where the act in question is an integral part of a coordinated tactical operation that directly causes the required threshold of harm.

4. The "belligerent nexus"[258] requirement is explained in the ICRC Interpretive Guidance as being an act amounting to direct participation in hostilities must not only be objectively likely to inflict harm meeting the first two criteria, but it must also be specifically designed to do so in support of a Belligerent Party and to the detriment of another. Belligerent nexus relates to the objective purpose and design of an act or operation as part of the conduct of hostilities and does not depend on the subjective mindset or intent of every participating individual. Armed violence which is not designed to harm a Belligerent Party, or which is not designed to do so in support of another Party, cannot amount to "participation" in hostilities taking place between these Parties. Thus, as a general rule, harm would remain of non-belligerent nature if it is caused: (a) in exercise of authority over persons or territory having fallen into the power of a party to the conflict (e.g., lawful and unlawful use of force against prisoners); (b) as part of civil unrest against such authority (e.g., violent demonstrations or riots); (c) in individual self-defence against violence prohibited by the law of international armed conflict (e.g., civilians forcibly defending themselves against marauding soldiers); (d) during inter-civilian violence (e.g., uncontrolled looting due to breakdown of law and order); or (e) for reasons otherwise unrelated to the conduct of hostilities (e.g., murder or arson for private motives).

5. It must be noted that the three criteria established by the ICRC Interpretive Guidance – as summarized in paras. 2–4 of the Commentary on

[258] ICRC Interpretive Guidance, at pages 58–64.

this Rule – were not unanimously accepted by the Group of Experts. It was maintained by a number of members of the Group of Experts that these criteria are not part of existing law and impose inappropriate constraints on the scope of direct participation in hostilities.

6. It is important to stress that the activities listed in Rule 29 are "examples" which may only amount to a direct participation in hostilities "[s]ubject to the circumstances ruling at the time". According to the ICRC, these examples can amount to direct participation in hostilities only if they meet the three cumulative requirements of threshold of harm, direct causation and belligerent nexus set out in its Interpretive Guidance.

(i) Defending of military objectives against enemy attacks.

1. The conduct of hostilities comprises not only offensive, but also defensive acts of violence against the enemy. In principle, therefore, the defence of military objectives against enemy attacks is a clear case of direct participation in hostilities. On the definition of "attacks", see Rule 1 (e). On the definition of military objectives, see Rule 1 (y) and Rule 22.

2. Particularly where Belligerent Parties resort to the use of private contractors, it may not always be easy to determine the precise nature of their activities. For example, when they are assigned to defend certain persons or objects, the line between such defence against enemy attacks (amounting to direct participation in hostilities) and against crime or violence unrelated to the hostilities (qualifying as law-enforcement, defence of self or others) may be thin.

(ii) Issuing orders and directives to forces engaged in hostilities; making decisions on operational/tactical deployments; and participating in targeting decision-making.

Rule 29 (ii) shows that direct participation in hostilities includes acts which are likely to directly harm the enemy (e.g., tactical and operational planning to do harm), even though the person planning does not actually carry out the plan and may be geographically remote from where the plan is carried out.

(iii) Engaging in electronic warfare or computer network attacks targeting military objectives, combatants or civilians directly participating in hostilities, or which is intended to cause death or injury to civilians or damage to or destruction of civilian objects.

1. On the definition of CNAs, see Rule 1(m). On the definition of electronic warfare, see Rule 1 (p).

2. Depending on the precise nature of CNA, they may directly cause death, injury or destruction, or system malfunctions adversely affecting the military capacity or military operations of the enemy. When such operations do so, they may amount to direct participation in hostilities. However, mere hacking into the intranet of a military base will not automatically fall under Rule 29 (iii).

(iv) Participation in target acquisition.

"Target acquisition" covers the identification and localization of targets for engagement. It encompasses providing detailed intelligence data about enemy forces and locating them with sufficient accuracy to permit continued monitoring or target designation and engagement.

(v) Engaging in mission planning of an air or missile attack.

Planning as well as preparation of a mission involving air or missile attacks can amount to direct participation in hostilities, whereas involvement in the planning of the war effort in general is insufficiently specific to meet the requirements of direct participation in hostilities.

(vi) Operating or controlling weapon systems or weapons in air or missile combat operations, including remote control of UAVs and UCAVs.

The use of weapons systems during combat operations will almost invariably qualify as direct participation in hostilities. It bears clarifying, however, that no temporal or geographic proximity is necessarily required. While the use of delayed (e.g., mines, booby-traps or timer-controlled devices), or remote-controlled (e.g., missiles, UAV/UCAV) weapons-systems may be temporally or geographically remote from the resulting harm, such activities may qualify as direct participation in hostilities.

(vii) Employing military communications networks and facilities to support specific air or missile combat operations.

1. To the extent that the use of communications networks and facilities supports specific air or missile combat operations – e.g., through the transmission of orders, intelligence, or other tactical data – such activities qualify as direct participation in hostilities.

2. Rule 29 (vii) applies only to the use of military communications networks and facilities. Whether the use of civilian networks and facilities constitutes direct participation in hostilities will depend on the special circumstances of such use.

(viii) Refueling, be it on the ground or in the air, of a military aircraft which is about to engage in, or which is engaged in, air or missile combat operations.

1. The refuelling of military aircraft engaged in, or about to engage in, air or missile combat operations amounts to direct participation in hostilities because it constitutes either a part of an ongoing hostile act or, respectively, a measure preparatory to such an act.

2. Conversely, the refuelling of military aircraft that are neither engaged in, nor about to engage in air or missile combat operations does not necessarily qualify as direct participation in hostilities.

3. "[A]bout to" means that the engagement of the aircraft in a specific air or missile combat operation is imminent.

(ix) Loading ordnance or mission-essential equipment onto a military aircraft which is about to engage in, or which is engaged in, air or missile combat operations.

1. The loading of ordnance or equipment onto military aircraft engaged in, or about to engage in, air or missile combat operations constitute either a part of an ongoing hostile act or, respectively, a measure preparatory to such an act and, therefore, amounts to direct participation in hostilities.

2. Conversely, the loading of ordnance or equipment onto military aircraft that are neither engaged in, nor about to engage in, combat operations does not qualify as direct participation in hostilities.

3. On the expression "about to", see paragraph 3 of the Commentary on Rule 29 (viii).

(x) Servicing or repairing of a military aircraft which is about to engage in, or which is engaged in, air or missile combat operations.

1. The servicing and repairing of military aircraft engaged in, or about to engage in, air or missile combat operations constitute either a part of an ongoing hostile act or, respectively, a measure preparatory to such an act and, therefore, amounts to direct participation in hostilities.

2. Conversely, the servicing and repairing of military aircraft that are neither engaged in, nor about to engage in, combat operations, may maintain or build the military capacity of a party to the conflict, but does not qualify as direct participation in hostilities (e.g., regular maintenance).

3. On the expression "about to", see paragraph 3 of the Commentary on Rule 29 (viii).

(xi) Loading mission control data to military aircraft/missile software systems.

1. The loading of mission control data to software systems of military aircraft/missiles always amounts to direct participation in hostilities.

2. The term "mission" means that the loading of data is part of an air or missile operation.

3. "Mission control data" refers to data for a specific sortie.

4. Rule 29 (xi) does not apply to the loading of mission control data for medical aircraft.

(xii) Combat training of aircrews, air technicians and others for specific requirements of a particular air or missile combat operation.

1. The preparation and training of aircrews, air technicians and others with a view to the execution of a predetermined air or missile combat operation constitutes a measure preparatory to a specific hostile act and, therefore, amounts to direct participation in hostilities. This follows from the fact that the training needs to be for "specific requirements of a particular air or missile combat operation".

2. Conversely, general preparation and training of aircrews, air technicians and others for unspecified military operations to be executed in the future may maintain or enhance the military capacity of a party to the conflict, but does not qualify as direct participation in hostilities.

Section G

Precautions in Attacks

1. This Section deals with "active precautions", which are those precautions that are to be taken by an attacking Belligerent Party to protect civilians and civilian objects. The efficacy of achieving the overall objective of protecting the civilian population and civilian objects is also dependent upon the obligation of the Belligerent Party subject to an attack to take "passive precautions" (see Section H). As to the relationship between "active precautions" and "passive precautions", see Rule 46.

2. With the exception of Rule 41 (but see paragraphs 7 and 8 of the Commentary on Rule 41), Section G applies in its entirety also in non-international armed conflict.

I. General rules

30. Constant care must be taken to spare the civilian population, civilians and civilian objects.

1. This Rule is based on Art. 57 (1) to (4) of AP/I.[259] See also Para. 8.1. of NWP.[260] *(See footnote on next page)*

[259] Art. 57 of AP/I ("Precautions in attack"): "(1) In the conduct of military operations, constant care shall be taken to spare the civilian population, civilians and civilian objects. (2) With respect to attacks, the following precautions shall be taken: (a) those who plan or decide upon an attack shall: (i) do everything feasible to verify that the objectives to be attacked are neither civilians nor civilian objects and are not subject to special protection but are military objectives within the meaning of paragraph of Article 52 and that it is not prohibited by the provisions of this Protocol to attack them; (ii) take all feasible precautions in the choice of means and methods of attack with a view to avoiding, and in any event to minimizing, incidental loss or civilian life, injury to civilians and damage to civilian objects; (iii) refrain from deciding to launch any attack which may be expected to cause incidental loss of civilian life, injury to civilians, damage to civilian objects, or a combination thereof, which would be excessive in relation to the concrete and direct military

2. Rule 30 makes no distinction between military operations in warfare on land, at sea or in the air. As a general principle, the same norms apply equally in all domains of warfare. It is true that Art. 49 (3) of AP/I[261] and Art. 57 (4) of AP/I[262] imply some form of distinction between the conduct of military operations at sea or in the air compared to land. However, the Group of Experts reached the conclusion that, as a general principle, the same legal regime applies equally in all domains of warfare (land, sea or air).

3. "Constant care" means that there are no exceptions from the duty to seek to spare the civilian population, civilians and civilian objects.

4. The Group of Experts noted that there are some objects which, although not civilian objects in the strict sense of the term, are nevertheless subject to the application of Rule 30. A prominent example is that of POW-camps, which are evidently military installations. The Group of Experts could not see any good reason why in practice there ought to be a distinction between them and civilian objects as regards the application of constant care.

advantage anticipated; (b) an attack shall be cancelled or suspended if it becomes apparent that the objective is not a military one or is subject to special protection or that the attack may be expected to cause incidental loss of civilian life, injury to civilians, damage to civilian objects, or a combination thereof, which would be excessive in relation to the concrete and direct military advantage anticipated; (c) effective advance warning shall be given of attacks which may affect the civilian population, unless circumstances do not permit. (3) When a choice is possible between several military objectives for obtaining a similar military advantage, the objective to be selected shall be that the attack on which may be expected to cause the least danger to civilian lives and to civilian objects. (4) In the conduct of military operations at sea or in the air, each Party to the conflict shall, in conformity with its rights and duties under the rules of international law applicable in armed conflict, take all reasonable precautions to avoid losses of civilian lives and damage to civilian objects."

260 Para. 8.1 of NWP ("Principles of lawful targeting"): "The law of targeting . . . requires that all reasonable precautions must be taken to ensure that only military objectives are targeted so that noncombatants, civilians, and civilian objects are spared as much as possible from the ravages of war."

261 Art. 49 (3) of AP/I: "The provisions of this section apply to any land, air or sea warfare which may affect the civilian population, individual civilians or civilian objects on land. They further apply to all attacks from the sea or from the air against objectives on land but do not otherwise affect the rules of international law applicable in armed conflict at sea or in the air."

262 Art. 57 (4) of AP/I, see fn. 259.

31. All feasible precautions must be taken to spare all persons and objects entitled to specific protection under Sections K, L, M and N of this Manual.

1. The reference to feasible precautions in this Rule is based on Art. 57 (2) (a) (i) of AP/I.[263]

2. The term "feasible" is defined in Rule 1 (q). The expression "feasible precautions", referred to in Rule 31, embraces precautions relating to (i) the general protection to which all civilian objects are entitled; and (ii) the specific protection as detailed in Sections K, L, M and N.

3. All civilian objects enjoy general protection. Specific protection means that the law of international armed conflict provides for specific safeguards for the protection of particular objects. These safeguards come in addition to the general protection these objects enjoy as civilian objects.

32. Constant care includes in particular the following precautions:

1. This Rule is based on Art. 57 (2) (a) of AP/I.[264] See also Para. 8.1[265] and Para. 8.3.1[266] of NWP.

2. The purpose of feasible precautions is to avoid attacks being directed at civilians, civilian objects or objects entitled to specific protection and, when attacking military objectives, to avoid – or, in any event, minimize – collateral damage (see Rule 14).

(a) Doing everything feasible to verify, based on information reasonably available, that a target is a lawful target and does not benefit from specific protection;

[263] Art. 57 (2) (a) (i) of AP/I, see fn. 259.
[264] Art. 57 (2) (a) of AP/I, see fn. 259.
[265] Para. 8.1 of NWP, see fn. 260.
[266] Third, fourth and fifth sentences of Para. 8.3.1 of NWP ("Incidental Injury and Collateral Damage"): "Naval commanders must take all reasonable precautions, taking into account military and humanitarian considerations, to keep civilian casualties and damage to the minimum consistent with mission accomplishment. In each instance, the commander must determine whether the anticipated incidental injuries and collateral damage would be excessive, on the basis of an honest and reasonable estimate of the facts available to him. Similarly, the commander must decide, in light of all the facts known or reasonably available to him, including the need to conserve resources and complete the mission successfully, whether to adopt an alternative method of attack, if reasonably available, to reduce civilian casualties and damage."

1. To facilitate verification that a target is a lawful target and does not benefit from specific protection, command echelons must utilize all technical assets (such as intelligence, reconnaissance and surveillance systems) at their disposal, to the extent that these assets are reasonably available, and utilizing them is militarily sound in the context of the overall air campaign.

2. Verification must be based on sources of information that are sufficiently up-to-date and reliable, according to sound military practice. "Information" includes military intelligence. The quality and timeliness of the intelligence has to be considered. It must be taken into account that the enemy may attempt to provide disinformation (see Rule 116 (b)) or otherwise frustrate target intelligence activity. Other information, such as "on the spot" visual observations that may corroborate or contradict military intelligence, must also be taken into account (see, in this respect, Rule 35). All information gathered has to be evaluated on the basis of the circumstances prevailing at the time.

3. All feasible efforts must be undertaken to obtain reliable information, which may affect the application of the "constant care" rule. Any person planning, ordering or executing an attack can only act on information that is available in the sense that it can be obtained by reasonable efforts. Several States (e.g., Austria) have made statements upon ratification of AP/I, pertaining to Art. 57 (2) thereof, that the latter provision will be applied on the understanding that, "with respect to any decision taken by a military commander, the information actually available at the time of the decision is determinative".

4. The feasibility of applying the precautions requirement for the purposes on the "constant care" rule depends on the level of command and on the availability of information. The information available to the aviator on the scene may be different from the information on which command echelons at a distance from the scene are basing their decisions. The aviator may perform real-time observations that negate the information on which the decision to attack was based. The commander may, on the other hand, know more about the overall objectives of the attack than the aviator does and have access to information from sources that are not immediately available to the aviator, such as satellites or human intelligence sources. Therefore, the question for the aviator is whether the commander's determination is evidently faulty in view of what is visible on site. In this respect, see Rule 35.

5. In order to exercise constant care, a Belligerent Party ought to retain a command and control system capable of collecting, processing relevant information, making the necessary evaluation and directing its combat units accordingly.

6. For the specifics of attacks directed at aircraft in the air, see Rule 40.

(b) Doing everything feasible to choose means and methods of warfare with a view to avoiding – or, in any event, minimizing – collateral damage; and

1. This Rule is derived from the general principle of proportionality, which is dealt with in Rule 14.

2. Means and methods of warfare include weapons, weapons systems and munitions, as well as tactics (such as timing, angle and altitude of attack). The term "means of warfare" is defined in Rule 1 (t). The term "methods of warfare" is defined in Rule 1 (v). The term "weapon" is defined in Rule 1 (ff). "Collateral damage" is defined in Rule 1 (l).

3. Rule 32 (b) imposes a requirement to consider alternative weapons and tactics to avoid – or, in any event, to minimize – collateral damage. For instance, an attacker ought to choose a weapon with greater precision or lesser explosive force if doing so would minimize the likelihood of collateral damage, assuming the selection is militarily feasible (for the definition of feasible, see Rule 1 (q)). Rule 32 (b) also raises the question as to whether the attacker must choose the most precise weapons available. For a discussion thereof, see Rule 8.

4. Similarly, angle of attack is one of the factors that determine where a bomb may land if it falls short of, or beyond, the target. Thus, to spare a building located, e.g., to the west of a target, it may be advisable to attack from the north or the south.

5. Rule 32 (b) further entails that it would be prohibited to conduct air or missile attacks against military objectives without using appropriate and available target identification or weapon guidance technologies to aim the weapon at those objectives when such assets are available and their use is militarily feasible.[267] If such assets are not available, and the

[267] Para. 5.32.5 of the UK Manual ("Factors to be considered"): "In considering the means or methods of attack to be used, a commander should have regard to the following factors: (a) the importance of the target and the urgency of the situation; (b) intelligence about the proposed target – what it is being, or will be, used for and when; (c) the characteristics

attacker for this reason is not able to comply with the prohibition against indiscriminate attacks (Rule 13), the attack has to be cancelled (see Rule 35). This general rule is particularly relevant if the military objectives are located in a densely populated area.

6. "Dual-use" objects – such as airports being used by both civilian and military aircraft – are of particular relevance when it comes to applying Rule 32 (b). Assuming that it is sufficient to put an airfield out of use temporarily, the attacker ought to consider the option of cratering the runway instead of attacking the permanent facilities. This will ensure collateral damage to civilians or civilian objects is avoided, or any event minimized.

(c) Doing everything feasible to determine whether the collateral damage to be expected from the attack will be excessive in relation to the concrete and direct military advantage anticipated.

1. The commander is expected to make an honest assessment of the collateral damage to be expected from the attack, taking into account factors such as known effects of the weapons that are to be used; the vulnerability of any civilian buildings in the target area; the number of civilians that are likely to be present in the target area at the particular time; and whether they have any possibility to take cover before the attack takes place.

2. As indicated in the Commentary on Rule 32 (a), the reality on the ground may appear to an aviator to be different from the one received during the pre-mission briefing. In this respect, see Rule 35 (c).

3. As for "dual-use" objects, and the need to avoid – or, in any event, minimize – expected collateral damage that is excessive compared to the military advantage anticipated, see paragraph 5 of the Commentary on Rule 32 (b).

of the target itself, for example, whether it houses dangerous forces; (d) what weapons are available, their range, accuracy and radius of effect; (e) conditions affecting the accuracy of targeting, such as terrain, weather, and time of day; (f) factors affecting incidental loss or damage, such as the proximity of civilians or civilian objects in the vicinity of the target or other protected objects or zones and whether they are inhabited, or the possible release of hazardous substances as a result of the attack; (g) the risks to his own troops of the various options open to him."

4. The notion of excessive collateral damage is explained in the Commentary on Rule 1 (l) and in the Commentary on Rule 14.

33. When a choice is possible between several military objectives for obtaining a similar military advantage, the objective to be selected must be the one where the attack may be expected to cause the least danger to civilian lives and to civilian objects, or to other protected persons and objects.

1. This Rule is based on Art. 57 (3) of AP/I.[268] The term "military advantage" is defined in Rule 1 (w).

2. Rule 33 deals with choice between targets. A useful scenario would involve two rivers across which a road used by the enemy passes. In this scenario, destroying a bridge spanning either of the rivers will effectively cut the road and deny its use to the enemy. If the two bridges are considered to provide equal military advantage, the bridge selected for attack must be that likely to result in the least danger to civilian lives and to civilian objects, or to other protected persons and objects. Similarly, it may be militarily feasible to attack facilities providing power to a military objective rather than the military objective itself. Assuming that the military advantage is equal, this option must be chosen if less danger to civilian lives and to civilian objects, or other protected persons and objects, is expected.

3. "Similar military advantage" must be understood in terms of the military advantage anticipated from the attack considered as a whole and not only from isolated or particular parts of the attack. The emphasis is on the fact that two or more military objectives can alternatively be attacked. The military advantage anticipated from each alternative attack must be considered as a whole, and not in isolation. Thus, when several parallel bridges have to be destroyed in order to break an axis of communications – and the military advantage that can be achieved depends on the destruction of all the bridges – destruction of only one of them will serve little or no practical purpose. See also paragraph 6 of the Commentary on Rule 1 (w), paragraph 7 of the Commentary on Rule 1 (y) and paragraph 11 of the Commentary on Rule 14.

[268] Art. 57 (3) of AP/I, see fn. 259.

4. For the sake of analysis, it may be a hypothesis that there is a terrain which includes a river barrier and behind it a high mountain, the river being crossed by three bridges and the mountain traversed through a tunnel. If, insofar as the river is concerned, the only practical option is to destroy all three bridges – inasmuch as destroying only one or two of them will leave the river passable – it ought to be considered whether it is feasible, instead, to block the tunnel. The latter option will deny the enemy the use of the axis of communication without any practical need to destroy any of the bridges. It is posited that the bridges and the tunnels are "dual-use" targets, because civilians (especially refugees) use them at the same time as enemy armed forces. If so, the expected collateral damage to be assessed is that resulting from an attack on all three bridges versus the collateral damage expected from the attack on that single tunnel.

5. Another example would be an intended attack against a power generating facility located in the vicinity of civilians or civilian objects, which provides essential power to the civilian population. If the sole objective is to temporarily disrupt power to enemy forces, it might be possible in the circumstances to conduct the attack against the transformers or substations serving the power generating facility. If the attack against the transformers or substations "may be expected to cause the least danger to civilian lives and to civilian objects", then this is the attack that needs to be preferred over an attack against the power generating facility itself.

6. It is to be understood that, for Rule 33 to apply, a choice has to be possible between several military objectives for obtaining a similar military advantage. There is no requirement to select among several objectives if doing so would be militarily unreasonable. As an example, if a choice has to be made between two alternative military objectives – one of which is more densely defended than the other – the attacker is not required to select the latter when heavy casualties are anticipated to the attacking force.[269]

[269] NIAC Manual to SRM/ACS, page 28, Para. 9: " . . . there is no requirement to select an objective if doing so would be militarily 'unreasonable'. As an example, one of the possible objectives may be so much more heavily defended than the others, that it would be unreasonable to select it as the target. Risk to the attacker is a relevant factor. Munitions availability is another. Aside from the fact that certain systems may be unavailable, the attacker will need to take into account future requirements and replenishment. For instance, when the number of precision-guided munitions is limited, it would be imprudent for the attacker to expend them early in the conflict without considering possible future needs and capabilities."

II. Specifics of air and missile operations

34. Constant care must be taken by all those involved in planning, ordering and executing air or missile combat operations to spare the civilian population, civilians and civilian objects.

1. This Rule is an application of Rules 31–33 of this Manual to the specifics of air or missile combat operations (see Rule 1 (c)). See also Para. 5.32.9. of the UK Manual.[270]

2. "Planning" includes all elements necessary to the issuance of an operations order, such as preparation of targeting decisions, recommendations on means of warfare and means of delivery, flight path, suppression of enemy defences and ancillary activities such as warnings.

3. "Ordering" means deciding on the implementation of a particular plan and the issuance of instructions such as an air tasking order to those involved in the execution.

4. "Executing" is not limited to the actual use of means of warfare, but extends to those who provide running directions or information from control units in the air or on the surface, provide targeting data by coordinates, laser designation or other means, or otherwise participate directly in ensuring that the operations order is carried out. This could for instance be an AWACS or a joint terminal attack controller (JTAC) on the ground.

35. In carrying out air or missile combat operations, an attack must be cancelled or suspended if it becomes apparent:

1. The three conditions of this Rule are derived from Art. 57 (2) of AP/I.[271] See also para. 46 (d) of the SRM/ACS.[272]

[270] Para. 5.32.9 of the UK Manual ("Level of responsibility"): "The level at which the legal responsibility to take precautions in attack rests is not specified in Additional Protocol I. Those who plan or decide upon attacks are the planners and commanders and they have a duty to verify targets, take precautions to reduce incidental damage, and refrain from attacks that offend the proportionality principle. Whether a person will have this responsibility will depend on whether he has any discretion in the way the attack is carried out and so the responsibility will range from commanders-in-chief and their planning staff to single soldiers opening fire on their own initiative. Those who do not have this discretion but merely carry out orders for an attack also have a responsibility: to cancel or suspend the attack if it turns out that the object to be attacked is going to be such that the proportionality rule would be breached."

[271] Art. 57 (2) of AP/I, see fn. 259.

[272] Support can also be found in Para. 46 (d) of the SRM/ACS: "With respect to attacks, the following precautions shall be taken:... (d) an attack shall not be launched if it may be expected to cause collateral casualties or damage which would be excessive in relation

2. The three conditions set out in Rule 35 apply the more general norms of Rule 32 to the specific context of air or missile warfare. Rule 35 (a) applies Rule 32 (a); Rule 35 (b) applies Rule 31; and Rule 35 (c) applies Rule 14.

3. Rule 35 applies not only to command echelons planning or ordering an attack. It also applies to aircrews (or operators of UCAVs) executing it when it becomes apparent to them that conditions of Rule 35 (a), Rule 35 (b), or Rule 35 (c), or a combination thereof, applies.

4. Even though Rule 35 is phrased in mandatory language ("must"), it has to be reasonably interpreted. That is to say, the presupposition is that aircrews are in a position to actually cancel or suspend an attack.

5. It must be borne in mind that aircrews may have more or less information than others involved in the planning or execution of attacks, depending on the circumstances of the case. See paragraph 4 of the Commentary on Rule 32 (a). If on-site information makes it clear to the aircrews that any one of the three conditions of this Rule applies, they have to cancel or suspend the attack on their own initiative.

6. The requirement of cancellation of missile attacks is relevant not only to externally controlled and guided missiles, but also to the launching of successive waves of ballistic missiles.

7. For the specifics of attacks directed against aircraft in the air, see Rule 40.

8. Rule 35 applies also in non-international armed conflict.

(a) That the target is not a lawful target; or

For the list of lawful targets, see Rule 10 (b).

(b) That the target is and remains entitled to specific protection in accordance with Sections K, L, M and N of this Manual; or

The Sections referred to deal with medical units and medical transports; medical aircraft; the natural environment and other protected persons and objects.

to the concrete and direct military advantage anticipated from the attack as a whole; an attack shall be cancelled or suspended as soon as it becomes apparent that the collateral casualties or damage would be excessive."

(c) **That the expected collateral damage is excessive in relation to the concrete and direct military advantage anticipated.**

This is the principle of proportionality (see Rule 14).

36. In order to avoid the release of dangerous forces and consequent severe losses among the civilian population, particular care must be taken if works and installations containing dangerous forces, namely dams, dykes and nuclear electrical generating stations (as well as installations located in their vicinity) are attacked.

1. This Rule is confined to dams, dykes and nuclear electrical generating stations (as well as to installations located in their vicinity). It does not apply to any other work or installation containing dangerous forces. Thus, e.g., facilities such as petrochemical industry plants are not covered by Rule 36. For an attack on the latter, Rules 30–33 apply. Under general customary international law, feasible precautions have to be taken when the latter are being attacked, in order to avoid – or, in any event, minimize – collateral damage which may be caused, e.g., by the release of harmful agents.

2. Art. 56 of AP/I[273] provides that the works and installations referred to in Rule 36 cannot be attacked, even when they are military objectives,

[273] Art. 56 of AP/I ("Protection of works and installations containing dangerous forces): "(1) Works or installations containing dangerous forces, namely dams, dykes and nuclear electrical generating stations, shall not be made the object of attack, even where these objects are military objectives, if such attack may cause the release of dangerous forces and consequent severe losses among the civilian population. Other military objectives located at or in the vicinity of these works or installations shall not be made the object of attack if such attack may cause the release of dangerous forces from the works or installations and consequent severe losses among the civilian population. (2) The special protection against attack provided by paragraph 1 shall cease: (a) for a dam or a dyke only if it is used for other than its normal function and in regular, significant and direct support of military operations and if such attack is the only feasible way to terminate such support; (b) for a nuclear electrical generating station only if it provides electric power in regular, significant and direct support of military operations and if such attack is the only feasible way to terminate such support; (c) for other military objectives located at or in the vicinity of these works or installations only if they are used in regular, significant and direct support of military operations and if such attack is the only feasible way to terminate such support. (3) In all cases, the civilian population and individual civilians shall remain entitled to all the protection accorded them by international law, including the protection of the precautionary measures provided for in Article 57. If the

if such attack may cause the release of dangerous forces and consequent severe losses among the civilian population. There is general agreement that Art. 56 of AP/I does not constitute customary law,[274] and it follows that Contracting Parties to AP/I are therefore bound by a higher level of protection than that required under customary law.

3. However, non-Contracting Parties to AP/I acknowledge[275] that the civilian population enjoys protection against excessive collateral damage expected from attacks on dams, dykes and nuclear electrical generating stations, as laid down in Rule 14. In any event, as Rule 36 clarifies, particular care must be taken in order to avoid the release of dangerous forces resulting in severe losses among the civilian population.

4. Under Art 56 (2) and (3) of AP/I, there is a possibility of loss of protection for such installations. However, this is subject to specific restrictions.

protection Ceases and any of the works, installations or military objectives mentioned in paragraph 1 is attacked, all practical precautions shall be taken to avoid the release of the dangerous forces. (4) It is prohibited to make any of the works, installations or military objectives mentioned in paragraph 1 the object of reprisals. (5) The Parties to the conflict shall endeavour to avoid locating any military objectives in the vicinity of the works or installations mentioned in paragraph 1. Nevertheless, installations erected for the sole purpose of defending the protected works or installations from attack are permissible and shall not themselves be made the object of attack, provided that they are not used in hostilities except for defensive actions necessary to respond to attacks against the protected works or installations and that their armament is limited to weapons capable only of repelling hostile action against the protected works or installations. (6) The High Contracting Parties and the Parties to the conflict are urged to conclude further agreements among themselves to provide additional protection for objects containing dangerous forces. (7) In order to facilitate the identification of the objects protected by this article, the Parties to the conflict may mark them with a special sign consisting of a group of three bright orange circles placed on the same axis, as specified in Article 16 of Annex I to this Protocol [Article 17 of Amended Annex]. The absence of such marking in no way relieves any Party to the conflict of its obligations under this Article."

274 See ICRC Customary IHL Study, Rule 42 and the discussion at pages 139–141.

275 Para. 8.9.1.7 of NWP: "Dams, dikes, levees, and other installations, which if breached or destroyed would release flood waters or other forces dangerous to the civilian population, should not be bombarded if the anticipated harm to civilians would be excessive in relation to the anticipated military advantage to be gained by bombardment. Conversely, installations containing such dangerous forces that are used by belligerents to shield or support military activities are not so protected. (See paragraph 8.5.1.2.)."

37. When the attack of a lawful target by air or missile combat operations may result in death or injury to civilians, effective advance warnings must be issued to the civilian population, unless circumstances do not permit. This may be done, for instance, through dropping leaflets or broadcasting the warnings. Such warnings ought to be as specific as circumstances permit.

1. This Rule is based on Art. 57 (2) (c) of AP/I,[276] as well as on Art. 26 of the 1907 Hague Regulations.[277] See also Art. 6 (4) of the 1996 Amended Protocol II to the CCW.[278]

2. Considering that it is based on the 1907 Hague Regulations, the warning obligation can be considered customary law.

3. Art. 57 (2) (c) of AP/I uses the term "may affect the civilian population". So does Art. 6 (4) of the 1996 Amended Protocol II to the CCW. However, Rule 37 of this Manual applies only to air or missile combat operations that "may result in death or injury to civilians".

4. Rule 37 does not come into play when a particular air or missile combat operations may result only in damage to, or destruction of, civilian objects. Neither does it come into play in case the attack results in mere inconveniences to civilians caused by, e.g., electrical blackouts or reduced mobility due to broken lines of communications.

5. There was disagreement among members of the Group of Experts as to whether the duty to issue warnings is limited to civilians located in close proximity to the target.[279]

6. The term "unless circumstances do not permit" is meant to reflect principally the fact that issuance of an advance warning to the civilian population would deprive the attacker of the element of surprise and may allow the defender to enhance target area defences. If a military

[276] Art. 57 (2) (c) of AP/I, see fn. 259.

[277] Art. 26 of the 1907 Hague Regulations: "The officer in command of an attacking force must, before commencing a bombardment, except in cases of assault, do all in his power to warn the authorities."

[278] Art. 6 (4) of the 1996 Amended Protocol II to the CCW, see fn. 143.

[279] Para. 8.9.2 of NWP ("Warning before Bombardment"): "Where the military situation permits, commanders should make every reasonable effort to warn the civilian population located in close proximity to a military objective targeted for bombardment. Warnings may be general rather than specific lest the bombarding force or the success of its mission be placed in jeopardy."

combat operation is predicated on the element of surprise, no warning is obligatory in relation to that attack.

7. The term "as specific as circumstances permit" indicates that the degree of specificity of the warning may depend on further factors such as (i) the length of time prior to the attack in relation to which the warning is issued; and (ii) the most effective mode in which the effective warning can be issued to civilians.

8. The Group of Experts could not determine (i) the level of the commander who is supposed to issue the warning; or (ii) the geographic extent to which the warning must apply. There was unanimity among the members of the Group of Experts, however, that irrespective of the level of the commander and the geographic extent of the warning, it must be "effective" by reaching the civilians likely to suffer death or injury from the attack.

9. In this context, the mode of warning issued to the civilian population may depend on available equipment and other factors affecting its feasibility, such as enemy defences that make the dropping of leaflets from the air impracticable. It is also necessary to consider factors bearing on the effectiveness of the warning. As for timing, an imprecise warning issued well in advance of the attack may be more effective than a precise warning immediately preceding it. Similarly, a warning issued well in advance of the attack – reaching only a certain part of the civilian population – may be more effective than one reaching the entire civilian population, which is issued just prior to the attack.

10. Warnings ought not be vague but be as specific as circumstances permit to allow the civilian population to take relevant protective measures, like seeking shelter or staying away from particular locations.

11. In some situations the only feasible method of warning may be to fire warning shots using tracer ammunition, thus inducing people to take cover before the attack.

12 Warnings have to be made in a language that is understood by the local population.

13. "[B]roadcasting" means not only radio broadcasts but also telecasting and other means such as internet announcements.

14. Warnings must not be abused as a means of spreading terror among the civilian population. See Rule 18 that prohibits acts or threats of

violence in the course of air or missile operations pursued for the sole or primary purpose of spreading terror among the civilian population.

15. Warnings need not be formal in nature. They may be issued either verbally or in writing, or through any other means that can reasonably be expected to be effective under the circumstances.

16. An effective warning does not make an unlawful attack lawful, nor does it divest the attacker from its other obligations to take feasible precautionary measures.

38. Effective advance warnings must also be given before attacking persons and objects entitled to specific protection under Section K, L and N (I and II), as provided for in these Sections, as well as under Section J.

1. This Rule is based on Art. 21 of GC/I (medical units).[280] See also the first paragraph of Art. 34 of GC/II (hospital ships),[281] Art. 19 of GC/IV (civilian hospitals),[282] Art. 13 of AP/I (civilian medical units), and Art. 65 (1) of AP/I (civil defence),[283] as well as Art. 11 (1) of the 1954 Hague Convention (cultural property).[284]

280 Art. 21 of GC/I, see fn. 388.

281 First paragraph of Art. 34 of GC/II: "The protection to which hospital ships and sick-bays are entitled shall not cease unless they are used to commit, outside their humanitarian duties, acts harmful to the enemy. Protection may, however, cease only after due warning has been given, naming in all appropriate cases a reasonable time limit, and after such warning has remained unheeded."

282 Art. 19 of GC/IV: "The protection to which civilian hospitals are entitled shall not cease unless they are used to commit, outside their humanitarian duties, acts harmful to the enemy. Protection may, however, cease only after due warning has been given, naming, in all appropriate cases, a reasonable time limit and after such warning has remained unheeded. The fact that sick or wounded members of the armed forces are nursed in these hospitals, or the presence of small arms and ammunition taken from such combatants and not yet handed to the proper service, shall not be considered to be acts harmful to the enemy."

283 Art. 65 (1) of AP/I, see fn. 504.

284 Art. 11 (1) of the 1954 Hague Convention: "If one of the High Contracting Parties commits, in respect of any item of cultural property under special protection, a violation of the obligations under Art. 9, the opposing Party shall, so long as this violation persists, be released from the obligation to ensure the immunity of the property concerned. Nevertheless, whenever possible, the latter Party shall first request the cessation of such violation within a reasonable time."

2. The relevant Rules in the Sections referred to are: (i) Rule 70 in Section J; (ii) Rule 74 in Section K; (b); (iii) Rule 83 in Section L; (iv) Rule 92 in Section N (I); (v) Rule 96 in Section N (II).

3. The reference in Rule 38 to Sections J, K, L and N (I) and N (II) subjects the general norms to the specific nuances of the warning requirement, as reflected in each specific Section. For example, note has to be taken of the less than settled nature of the obligation to issue advance warning once cultural property has become a military objective (see Rule 96).

4. Advance warnings before attacks in cases of "misuse" of objects entitled to specific protection differ from warnings according to Rule 37 in that the purpose of warnings under the Rule 38 would be to put an end to the misuse, so that the attack would not be necessary and could be cancelled. By contrast, warnings according to Rule 37 have no such purpose and only convey the information that an attack will take place in the near future, with a view to avoiding – or, in any event, minimizing – collateral damage to the civilian population or to civilian objects.

5. Warnings that are intended to put an end to misuse should include a time limit to redress the situation, to the extent that circumstances permit.

6. Warnings need not be formal in nature. See paragraph 15 of the Commentary on Rule 37.

39. The obligation to take feasible precautions in attack applies equally to UAV/UCAV operations.

1. The law of international armed conflict has no provisions that are specific to UAV/UCAV. Therefore, the general requirements to take feasible precautions apply. The fact that a UAV/UCAV is unmanned does not relieve an attacker of taking such precautions. For the definition of UAV, see Rule 1 (dd). For the definition of UCAV, see Rule 1 (ee).

2. UAVs can be a useful asset in complying with the obligation to take feasible precautions in attack. UAVs with on-board sensors will contribute to verification that an intended target is a lawful target (see Rule 32 (a) and Rule 35 (a)). Hence, if available and when their use is feasible, UAVs ought to be employed in order to enhance reliability of collateral damage estimates (especially when this can be done in real-time).

3. With regard to remotely piloted UCAVs, UCAV operators must employ on-board and/or other reasonably available sensors and sources of

intelligence, to the extent feasible, to verify the target and assess expected collateral damage (see Rule 32 (c) and Rule 35 (c)). The fact that the UCAV is unmanned does not necessarily detract from the reliability of information on which the decision to attack is based. Indeed, such assessments by remote operators may be more reliable than those of aircrews on the scene facing enemy defences and other distractions.

4. In case of autonomous systems, the UCAV must only be programmed to engage potential targets based on reliable information that they are lawful targets. The performance of the sensors and the program identifying lawful targets must be comparable to that of manned aircraft or to that of remotely piloted (i.e. non-autonomous) UCAVs.

5. The standards set forth in Rule 12 regarding doubt apply equally to UCAV attacks, whether autonomous or manned.

6. When feasible, the options of using UCAVs in lieu of manned aircraft or other weapon systems, or vice versa, ought to be considered in determining how best to attack a target while avoiding – or, in any event, minimizing – collateral damage. For instance, use of a UCAV in circumstances in which visual identification of the target is necessary – either to reliably verify the target or to avoid excessive collateral damage – may be called for if defensive actions by the defending forces would likely impede visual identification by aircrews. Alternatively, a manned aircraft rather than a UCAV may be called for when its sensors are superior to those of a UCAV or where the visual identification by aircrews would be more reliable than images transmitted from the UCAV's sensors to its operator.

III. Specifics of attacks directed at aircraft in the air

1. Aircraft in the air are given a special treatment in this Manual for two reasons. The first reason is their greater vulnerability when they are airborne, since a successful attack has a high likelihood of killing every person onboard, in particular passengers who will normally have no possibility to escape. The second reason is that the speed of modern aircraft is likely to require rapid decision-making relating to identification of their nature as a lawful target that can be attacked in compliance with the law of international armed conflict. These two elements make it necessary to establish, in air and missile warfare, proper procedures designed to implement the law of international armed conflict. In other words, it is not the law that is different, but rather how it plays out in these situations.

2. With regard to references to ICAO Rules such as the ICAO Manual Concerning Interception of Civil Aircraft,[285] it ought to be borne in mind that these have not been designed for wartime. The ICAO provisions are not a part of the law of international armed conflict proper, but ought to be regarded as valuable guidelines to be adhered to as far as military considerations permit.

3. The requirement to take all feasible precautions to verify that an aircraft to be attacked is a military objective (see Rule 32 (a) and Rule 35 (a) and, in this subsection, see Rule 40), also applies when a UAV is the intended target of an attack. There is a complementary requirement for Belligerent Parties and Neutrals operating civilian UAVs to take all practicable measures to clearly indicate their civilian status.

4. Some members of the Group of Experts believed that consideration must also be given to the possibility that aircraft that are shot down in the air may cause collateral damage on the ground (see Rule 14; see also the paragraph 3 of the Commentary on Rule 68 (d)). The majority of the Group of Experts rejected this assertion, based upon the general impracticality of factoring in such eventual collateral damage during an air-to-air engagement. However, the majority of the Group of Experts conceded that there may be exceptional circumstances in some rare instances of air supremacy. In these circumstances, when a military aircraft intends to shoot down an aircraft – other than an armed military aircraft – over densely populated areas, the attack ought to be delayed in order to avoid – or, in any event, to minimize – collateral damage.

40. Before an aircraft is attacked in the air, all feasible precautions must be taken to verify that it constitutes a military objective. Verification ought to use the best means available under the prevailing circumstances, having regard to the immediacy of any potential threat. Factors relevant to verification may include:

1. The feasibility of taking precautions often depends on the degree of threat presented by an unidentified aircraft, or by other factors. A potential threat can be more or less immediate. A potentially hostile aircraft that is approaching rapidly represents a greater threat than one traveling in another direction. Considerations of force protection suggest that greater

[285] Manual Concerning Interception of Civil Aircraft, Consolidation of Current ICAO Provisions and Special Recommendations, 1990, ICAO, Doc 9433–AN/926.

precautions ought to be taken to verify that the aircraft constitutes a military objective when more time is reasonably available before a decision to engage it.

2. An attacker must bear in mind that verification can be complicated by camouflage, stealth or deception designed to conceal the presence or military status of an enemy aircraft. Certain forms of deception would, however, amount to unlawful perfidy, see Section Q.

3. Rule 40 applies to any type of aircraft, provided that it constitutes a military objective. As to civilian airliners, they are entitled to particular care in terms of precautions, see Section J (I) and J (III).

4. The factors listed are provided by way of illustration, and their specific relevance depends on the factual background. There may be other factors relevant to verification, such as information based upon intelligence gathering. As well, it ought to be borne in mind that medical aircraft have specific means of identification, such as a flashing blue light and radio message (see Commentary on Rule 76 (b)).

(a) Visual identification.

Visual identification means that an aircraft is identified as a military objective by the use of eyesight, including the use of binoculars or similar sight-enhancing devices. This is typically achieved through interception of the aircraft (see the *chapeau* of the Commentary on Section U).

(b) Responses to oral warnings over radio.

An unidentified aircraft ought to be raised on radio and asked to identify itself and state its intentions. The "response" can be either explicit or implicit, in which case it may be demonstrated by conduct such as change of course or any other manoeuvres. The response, or absence thereof, may strengthen or weaken conclusions as to the aircraft's nature.

(c) Infra-red signature.

Infra-red signature means the appearance of the aircraft to infra-red sensors. It depends on several factors, including the temperature of the aircraft and the waveband of the detecting sensor.

(d) Radar signature.

Radar signature means (i) the detailed waveform of a radar echo from the aircraft; and (ii) the detailed characteristics of a radar transmission, i.e., an indication of what kind of radar the aircraft is using. The radar echo can give indications about the size, shape and movements of an aircraft, including moving parts such as the rotor of a helicopter.

(e) Electronic signature.

Electronic signature means the detailed characteristics of the electronic emissions from the aircraft, which may reveal, e.g., the type of radio communication equipment used by the aircraft. The second definition of radar signature, as set forth in Rule 40 (d), may also be regarded as a form of electronic signature.

(f) Identification modes and codes.

Identification modes and codes refer to systems whereby an aircraft that is detected on radar is interrogated by an electronic signal (also called secondary surveillance radar (SSR)) and gives an automatic response by using a transponder. The response ought to be used to identify the aircraft to both an intercepting aircraft and to airspace managers, whether military or civilian. Civilian systems are designed to assist the management of air traffic, while the purpose of military systems (also called Identification, Friend or Foe (IFF)) is to avoid the direction of attacks against friendly forces ("blue-on-blue") or civilian aircraft. The fact that an aircraft identifies itself as either a friendly military aircraft or as a civilian aircraft is not necessarily conclusive evidence of its character.

(g) Number and formation of aircraft.

Civilian aircraft will usually fly alone, while military aircraft may fly in formation depending on their mission. However, civilian aircraft are sometimes "escorted" by military aircraft in which case they may become a military objective (see paragraph 3 of the Commentary on Rule 27 (d)).

(h) Altitude, speed, track, profile and other flight characteristics.

1. Military aircraft on attack missions can make manoeuvres that civilian aircraft are not likely to do, such as approaching the target at low altitude in order to avoid or postpone detection by radar and thereafter making a sharp climb before launching weapons that require a minimum altitude.

2. A steady course by an aircraft originating from one exclusively civilian airport and heading towards another, may suggest that it is a civilian aircraft.

(i) Pre-flight and in-flight air traffic control information regarding possible flights.

1. In some areas, civilian air traffic (including civilian airliners) may be frequent, whereas in other areas such traffic may be light. These factors must be taken into account when determining the nature of an aircraft.

2. Information received from air traffic control services as to whether scheduled or non-scheduled flights can be expected around a particular location at a particular time ought to be taken into account, although the possibility that an aircraft is off schedule or off course ought to be considered.

41. Belligerent Parties and Neutrals providing air traffic control service ought to establish procedures whereby military commanders – including commanders of military aircraft – are informed on a continuous basis of designated routes assigned to, and flight plans filed by, civilian aircraft in the area of hostilities (including information on communication channels, identification modes and codes, destination, passengers and cargo).

1. This Rule is based on Para. 74 of the SRM/ACS.[286]

2. Rule 41 deals with general precautions whose purpose is to promote a clearer understanding of the situation in the air in a general sense, so that confusion and the likelihood of mistakes can be minimized. The feasible precautions mentioned in Rule 40 are specifically directed at clarifying the status of a particular flight.

The extent to which Rule 41 can be applied in practice depends on the circumstances, especially the degree of air control exercised over the relevant airspace.

4. States providing air traffic control services in their region bear a special responsibility for the safety of civilian air traffic.

5. Neutrals providing air traffic control service ought to cooperate in establishing the necessary procedures, in the interest of the safety of

[286] Para. 74 of SRM/ACS: "Belligerents and neutral States concerned, and authorities providing air traffic services, should establish procedures whereby commanders of warships and military aircraft are aware on a continuous basis of designated routes assigned to or flight plans filed by civil aircraft in the area of military operations, including information on communication channels, identification modes and codes, destination, passengers and cargo."

civilian air traffic. However, under the law of neutrality, Neutrals must not appear to support military operations by Belligerent Parties (see Section X).

6. If air traffic control services are operated by a private firm, all concerned parties ought to cooperate with the firm, as far as military requirements permit, in the interest of the safety of civilian aviation.

7. In non-international armed conflicts, there is no such thing as neutrality in the legal sense, and Rule 41 is therefore not applicable. However, (i) the central government providing air traffic control services ought to behave in accordance with Rule 41; and (ii) when a foreign State conducts air traffic control services in an area subject to a non-international armed conflict, it ought to make its best efforts to contribute to the safety of civilian aviation in that area.

8. In non-international armed conflicts, a national air traffic control service can hardly be expected to open channels of communication "on a continuous basis" with the commanders of non-State organized armed groups. All bodies providing air traffic control services, however, ought to do everything feasible to ensure that military commanders – including commanders of military aircraft – are made aware (to the maximum extent possible) of designated routes assigned to, or flight plans filed by, civilian aircraft in the area of military operations (including information on communication channels, identification modes and codes, destination, passengers and cargo).

Section H

Precautions by the Belligerent Party Subject to Attack

This Section applies in its entirety to non-international armed conflicts.[287] See, however, paragraph 6 of the Commentary on Rule 42.

42. Belligerent Parties subject to air or missile attacks must, to the maximum extent feasible, avoid locating military objectives within or near densely populated areas, hospitals, cultural property, places of worship, prisoner of war camps, and other facilities which are entitled to specific protection as per Sections K, L and N (II).

1. The Rule is based on Art. 58 (b) of AP/I.[288] See also the second paragraph of Art. 19 of GC/I[289] as well as Art. 83 of GC/IV.[290]

2. Although it does not follow directly from the text, the spirit of Art. 23 of GC/III[291] entails that similar considerations must apply to POW-camps

[287] NIAC Manual to SRM/NIAC, at page 44.

[288] Art. 58 (b) of AP/I: "The Parties to the conflict shall, to the maximum extent feasible: . . . (b) avoid locating military objectives within or near densely populated areas."

[289] Second paragraph of Art. 19 of GC/I: "The responsible authorities shall ensure that the said medical establishments and units are, as far as possible, situated in such a manner that attacks against military objectives cannot imperil their safety."

[290] Art. 83 of GC/IV: "The Detaining Power shall not set up places of internment in areas particularly exposed to the dangers of war. The Detaining Power shall give the enemy Powers, through the intermediary of the Protecting Powers, all useful information regarding the geographical location of places of internment. Whenever military considerations permit, internment camps shall be indicated by the letters IC, placed so as to be clearly visible in the daytime from the air. The Powers concerned may, however, agree upon any other system of marking. No place other than an internment camp shall be marked as such."

[291] Art. 23 of GC/III: "No prisoner of war may at any time be sent to, or detained in areas where he may be exposed to the fire of the combat zone, nor may his presence be used to render certain points or areas immune from military operations. Prisoners of war

as to densely populated areas and hospitals. The Group of Experts could not see any good reason why in practice there ought to be a distinction between POW-camps and civilian objects.

3. According to Art. 23 of GC/III and Art. 83 of GC/IV, POW-camps and internment camps must – whenever military considerations permit – be indicated by the letters PW/PG and IC respectively, placed so as to be clearly visible in the daytime from the air. The Powers concerned may, however, agree upon any other system of marking. In modern air and missile warfare it may prove necessary to consider other methods than marking in order to bring protected locations to the notice of the enemy.

4. Rule 42 is the general Rule. It must, however, be acknowledged that military objectives are sometimes located in urban areas due to practical or military reasons. Thus, Ministries of Defence and other military objectives have long been located in urban areas and cannot be removed. In such cases, the obligation remains on the attacking party to ensure that the attack is not expected to cause excessive collateral damage (see Rule 14). Under the circumstances, one way of achieving this end may be through the use of precision guided weapons (see Rule 8).

5. The existence of military objectives in urban areas does not preclude the possibility that the locality will become a non-defended place. As to the issue of declared non-defended localities, see the Commentary on Rule 10 (b) (ii).

6. Rule 42 applies also in non-international armed conflict.[292] However, since there is no entitlement to POW-status in non-international armed conflict, there are no POW-camps to consider.

shall have shelters against air bombardment and other hazards of war, to the same extent as the local civilian population. With the exception of those engaged in the protection of their quarters against the aforesaid hazards, they may enter such shelters as soon as possible after the giving of the alarm. Any other protective measure taken in favour of the population shall also apply to them. Detaining Powers shall give the Powers concerned, through the intermediary of the Protecting Powers, all useful information regarding the geographical location of prisoner of war camps. Whenever military considerations permit, prisoner of war camps shall be indicated in the day-time by the letters PW or PG, placed so as to be clearly visible from the air. The Powers concerned may, however, agree upon any other system of marking. Only prisoner of war camps shall be marked as such."

292 See NIAC Manual to SRM/ACS, at page 44.

43. Belligerent Parties subject to air or missile attacks must, to the maximum extent feasible, endeavour to remove the civilian population, individual civilians and other protected persons and objects under their control from the vicinity of military objectives.

1. This Rule is based on Art. 58 (a) of AP/I[293] and on Para. 8.3.2. of NWP.[294]

2. A typical measure would be to evacuate areas close to, e.g., the contact zone, military airports and munitions factories. In some situations one would move particularly vulnerable parts of the civilian population (such as children and expectant mothers) from affected areas. The first paragraph of Art. 14 of GC/IV[295] suggests that hospital and safety zones and localities can be established for such purposes. Art. 15 of GC/IV has corresponding provisions for neutralized zones in the regions where fighting is taking place.[296]

3. Rule 43 is without prejudice to Art. 49 of GC/IV,[297] which limits an Occupying Power's right to undertake transfers of protected persons.

[293] Art. 58 (a) of AP/I: "The Parties to the conflict shall, to the maximum extent feasible: (a) without prejudice to Art. 49 of the Fourth Convention, endeavour to remove the civilian population, individual civilians and civilian objects under their control from the vicinity of military objectives."

[294] First sentence of Para. 8.3.2 of NWP: "A party to an armed conflict has an affirmative duty to remove civilians under its control (as well as the wounded, sick, shipwrecked, and prisoners of war) from the vicinity of objects of likely enemy attack."

[295] First paragraph of Art. 14 of GC/IV: "In time of peace, the High Contracting Parties and, after the outbreak of hostilities, the Parties thereto, may establish in their own territory and, if the need arises, in occupied areas, hospital and safety zones and localities so organized as to protect from the effects of war, wounded, sick and aged persons, children under fifteen, expectant mothers and mothers of children under seven."

[296] Art. 15 of GC/IV: "Any Party to the conflict may, either direct or through a neutral State or some humanitarian organization, propose to the adverse Party to establish, in the regions where fighting is taking place, neutralized zones intended to shelter from the effects of war the following persons, without distinction: (a) wounded and sick combatants or non-combatants; (b) civilian persons who take no part in hostilities, and who, while they reside in the zones, perform no work of a military character. When the Parties concerned have agreed upon the geographical position, administration, food supply and supervision of the proposed neutralized zone, a written agreement shall be concluded and signed by the representatives of the Parties to the conflict. The agreement shall fix the beginning and the duration of the neutralization of the zone."

[297] Art. 49 of GC/IV: "Individual or mass forcible transfers, as well as deportations of protected persons from occupied territory to the territory of the Occupying Power or

Under Art. 49 of GC/IV, the Occupying Powers may totally or partially evacuate a given area if the security of the population or imperative military reasons so demand. Persons thus evacuated must be transferred back to their homes as soon as hostilities in the area in question have ceased. Permanent deportation from occupied territory is prohibited.

4. A Belligerent Party must neither encourage nor tolerate "voluntary human shields" who, therefore, ought to be removed from military objectives (see Rule 45).

5. The expression "other protected persons and objects" means POWs, mobile cultural property, etc.

44. Belligerent Parties subject to air or missile attacks must, to the maximum extent feasible, take necessary precautions to protect the civilian population, individual civilians and civilian objects under their control against the dangers resulting from military operations.

1. This Rule is based on Art. 58 (c) of AP/I.[298]

to that of any other country, occupied or not, are prohibited, regardless of their motive. Nevertheless, the Occupying Power may undertake total or partial evacuation of a given area if the security of the population or imperative military reasons so demand. Such evacuations may not involve the displacement of protected persons outside the bounds of the occupied territory except when for material reasons it is impossible to avoid such displacement. Persons thus evacuated shall be transferred back to their homes as soon as hostilities in the area in question have ceased. The Occupying Power undertaking such transfers or evacuations shall ensure, to the greatest practicable extent, that proper accommodation is provided to receive the protected persons, that the removals are effected in satisfactory conditions of hygiene, health, safety and nutrition, and that members of the same family are not separated. The Protecting Power shall be informed of any transfers and evacuations as soon as they have taken place. The Occupying Power shall not detain protected persons in an area particularly exposed to the dangers of war unless the security of the population or imperative military reasons so demand. The Occupying Power shall not deport or transfer parts of its own civilian population into the territory it occupies."

[298] Art. 58 of AP/I: "The Parties to the conflict shall, to the maximum extent feasible:... (c) take the other necessary precautions to protect the civilian population, individual civilians and civilian objects under their control against the dangers resulting from military operations."

2. The "necessary precautions" contemplated here include, e.g., air warning systems, air raid shelters, etc.

3. The obligations of Belligerent Parties subject to attack to take feasible precautions to protect the civilian population, individual civilians and civilian objects extends to attacks conducted by UCAVs.

4. The availability of UCAVs to the enemy may fundamentally change the nature of the threat to civilians and civilian objects. The smaller visual, radar and noise signatures of UCAVs may allow them greater penetrability than manned aircraft. Thus, UCAVs may be used even when effective air defenses make attacks by manned aircraft highly risky to the aircraft and its crew. When a Belligerent Party subject to missile attacks is aware of the availability of UCAVs to the enemy, its obligation to do everything feasible to protect the civilian population, individual civilians and civilian objects under its control, from the dangers resulting from military operations, is therefore enhanced.

5. As far as dams, dykes or nuclear electrical generating stations are concerned, based upon Art. 56 of AP/I,[299] Belligerent Parties may mark such objects with the international sign provided in Art. 56 (7) of AP/I (consisting of a group of three bright orange circles placed on the same axis). Furthermore (subject to further conditions laid down in Art. 56 (5) of AP/I), they must endeavour to avoid locating any military objectives in the vicinity of such works or installations, with the exception of installations erected for the sole purpose of defending the protected works or installations from attack. Finally (Art. 56 (6) of AP/I), they are urged to conclude further agreements among themselves to provide additional protection for objects containing dangerous forces. The markings specified in AP/I (and any other markings applied pursuant to agreement) are meant to facilitate identification only, and they do not provide protection in and of themselves.

[299] Art. 56 of AP/I, see fn. 273.

45. Belligerent Parties actually or potentially subject to air or missile operations must not use the presence or movements of the civilian population or individual civilians to render certain points or areas immune from air or missile operations, in particular they must not attempt to shield lawful targets from attacks or to shield, favour or impede military operations. Belligerent Parties must not direct the movement of the civilian population or individual civilians in order to attempt to shield lawful targets from attacks or to shield military operations.

1. This Rule is based on Art. 51 (7) of AP/I[300] and on Para. 8.3.2 of NWP.[301]

2. The prohibition entails that a Belligerent Party which is actually or potentially subject to air or missile operations will not take advantage of the presence or movements of civilians at or near a lawful target.

3. In urban warfare, civilians are likely to be present at, or close to, lawful targets. Although such presence may be unavoidable, the Belligerent Party actually or potentially subject to attack is prohibited from deliberately taking advantage of this and must therefore keep their forces separated from the civilian population as far as circumstances permit. This entails that they must – to the maximum extent feasible – keep civilians at sufficient distance from obvious lawful targets and avoid locating military positions close to schools, market-places and other locations where civilians are likely to concentrate.

4. Combat operations are likely to induce large-scale movements of refugees. Combatants are not allowed to mix in the stream of refugees in

[300] Art. 51 (7) of AP/I: "The presence or movements of the civilian population or individual civilians shall not be used to render certain points or areas immune from military operations, in particular in attempts to shield military objectives from attacks or to shield, favour or impede military operations. The Parties to the conflict shall not direct the movement of the civilian population or individual civilians in order to attempt to shield military objectives from attacks or to shield military operations."

[301] Second sentence and following of Para. 8.3.2 of NWP: "Deliberate use of civilians to shield military objectives from enemy attack is prohibited. Although the principle of proportionality underlying the concept of collateral damage continues to apply in such cases, the presence of civilians within or adjacent to a legitimate military objective does not preclude attack of it. Such military objectives may be lawfully targeted and destroyed as needed for mission accomplishment. In such cases, responsibility for the injury and/or death or such civilians, if any, falls on the belligerent so employing them."

order to conceal their presence or discourage the enemy from attacking.[302] Such mixing is in breach of the prohibition of "human shields". Belligerent Parties are likewise prohibited from intentionally directing a stream of refugees towards points where their presence is likely to hamper the movements of the enemy.

5. "Human shields" may be "voluntary" or "involuntary". By "voluntary human shields" is usually meant those who take up position at a lawful target as an act of defiance vis-à-vis the attacking Belligerent Party or as an act of solidarity with the Belligerent Party subject to attack.

6. There were three divergent views within the Group of Experts about the status of "voluntary human shields". One view was that voluntary human shields are not counted in the calculation of collateral damage because they are directly participating in hostilities. A second view held that voluntary human shields do not qualify as civilians directly participating in hostilities. Hence, they remain protected civilians who count fully under the proportionality analysis.[303] Finally, the third view agreed with the second view as to the status of voluntary human shields, but asserted that the principle of proportionality will apply to them in a modified (more relaxed) way, since they have deliberately put themselves in harm's way in order to affect military operations.

7. "Involuntary human shields" include both those who have been compelled to stay at or in the vicinity of a lawful target, and those who do not know or lack the capacity to understand their situation, such as school children. There was no dispute among the Group of Experts that "involuntary human shields" count as civilians in a proportionality analysis. There was, however, disagreement as to whether the principle of proportionality will be applied to such a situation in the usual form, or whether it can be applied in the circumstances in a modified (more relaxed) way because the enemy has caused the situation by bringing the civilians in harm's way.

8. It is often unclear from the circumstances whether human shields are voluntary or not. In such cases, the presumption is that they are

[302] Art. 50 (3) of AP/I: "The presence within the civilian population of individuals who do not come within the definition of civilians does not deprive the population of its civilian character."

[303] For all details of the ICRC position on voluntary human shields, see ICRC Interpretive Guidance at pages 56–57.

involuntary. It is the attacker that bears the burden of proof of establishing that the individuals involved are acting voluntarily.

46. Both the Belligerent Party launching an air or missile attack and the Belligerent Party subject to such an attack have obligations to take precautions. Nevertheless, the latter's failure to take precautionary measures does not relieve the Belligerent Party launching an air or missile attack of its obligation to take feasible precautions.

1. This Rule is based on Art. 51 (8) of AP/I.[304]

2. Rule 46 deals with the interaction between "active precautions" (see Section G) and "passive precautions" (see Rules 42 through 45). The thrust of Rule 46 is that, if a Belligerent Party subject to attack has failed to take the required measures for the protection of its own civilian population, such as providing air raid shelters or evacuating particularly affected areas, an attacker is still obliged to take feasible precautions as indicated in Section G.

3. The Group of Experts disagreed as to whether the situation is different if the Belligerent Party subject to attack has placed, encouraged or tolerated "human shields" at a military objective or its vicinity. This situation is discussed under Rule 45.

[304] Art. 51 of AP/I: "(8) Any violation of these prohibitions shall not release the Parties to the conflict from their legal obligations with respect to the civilian population and civilians, including the obligation to take the precautionary measures provided for in Art. 57."

Section I

Protection of Civilian Aircraft

1. According to Rule 1 (h), "civilian aircraft" means "any aircraft other than military or other State aircraft". Accordingly, all aircraft not owned or used by a State, serving exclusively non-commercial government functions, qualify as civilian aircraft.

2. The object and purpose of this Section is to underline that all civilian aircraft, regardless of their nationality, are civilian objects. Accordingly, an attack on civilian aircraft is lawful only in exceptional cases, i.e., if by their location, purpose or use they effectively contribute to the enemy's military action, and their destruction, capture or neutralization offers – in the circumstances ruling at the time – a definite military advantage, thereby becoming a military objective.

3. Accordingly, this Manual deviates from the approach underlying the HRAW. According to Art. 33[305] and Art. 34 of the HRAW,[306] enemy civilian aircraft "are liable to be fired upon" if any of the conditions laid down in those provisions are met. The same holds true, under Art. 35 of the HRAW,[307] for neutral aircraft which do not "make the nearest available landing" when "flying within the jurisdiction of a belligerent, and warned of the approach of military aircraft of the opposing belligerent". In view of the customary character of the definition of military objectives (see Rule 1 (y) and Rule 22), the Group of Experts took the position that those

[305] Art. 33 of the HRAW: "Belligerent non-military aircraft, whether public or private, flying within the jurisdiction of their own state, are liable to be fired upon unless they make the nearest available landing on the approach of enemy military aircraft."

[306] Art. 34 of the HRAW: "Belligerent non-military aircraft, whether public or private, are liable to be fired upon, if they fly (1) within the jurisdiction of the enemy, or (2) in the immediate vicinity thereof and outside the jurisdiction of their own state, or (3) in the immediate vicinity of the military operations of the enemy by land or sea."

[307] Art. 35 of the HRAW: "Neutral aircraft flying within the jurisdiction of a belligerent, and warning of the approach of military aircraft of the opposing belligerent, must make the nearest available landing. Failure to do so exposes them to the risk of being fired upon."

provisions of the HRAW are no longer valid. Hence, civilian aircraft, enemy or neutral, may be attacked only if they meet the requirements of the definition of military objectives. See, respectively, Rule 27 (enemy aircraft other than enemy military aircraft) and Rule 174 (neutral civilian aircraft). For the circumstances in which civilian airliners constitute a military objective, see Rule 63.

4. Section I is without prejudice to the right of Belligerent Parties to intercept and inspect civilian aircraft and to capture them under the law of prize (see Section U).

I. General rules

47. (a) Civilian aircraft, whether enemy or neutral, are civilian objects and as such are entitled to protection from attack.

1. This Rule emphasizes that, in principle, civilian aircraft are civilian objects that may not be attacked (see Rule 11 and Rule 13).

2. Civilian aircraft, whether enemy or neutral in character, are not military objectives by nature. In case of doubt as to whether a civilian aircraft is being used for military purposes, it may only be attacked if – based on all the information reasonably available to the commander at the time – there are reasonable grounds to believe that it has become and remains a military objective (see Rule 12 (b)).

3. For the determination of enemy or neutral character of an aircraft, see respectively Rules 144–146 and Rule 175.

4. Rule 47 (a), with the exception of the reference to neutral civilian aircraft, applies also in non-international armed conflict.

(b) Civilian aircraft can be the object of attack only if they constitute military objectives.

1. As to the specific circumstances in which an enemy civilian aircraft may become a military objective, see Rule 27. As to neutral civilian aircraft, see Rule 174.

2. As to the circumstances in which a civilian airliner (enemy or neutral) constitutes a military objective, see Rule 63. If a civilian airliner constitutes

a military objective under Rule 63, it may be attacked only if the conditions laid down in Rule 68 are met.

3. Rule 47 (b) applies also in non-international armed conflict.

48. (a) All enemy civilian and State aircraft other than military aircraft may be intercepted, inspected or diverted in accordance with Section U.

1. Rule 48 (a) only deals with enemy aircraft, both enemy civilian aircraft and enemy State aircraft other than military aircraft. As to neutral civilian aircraft, see Rule 48 (b).

2. While enemy civilian aircraft are protected against attack (unless they constitute military objectives, see Rule 47 (b)), they are not protected against other forms of interference by the enemy Belligerent Party. Under customary international law (see Rule 134), enemy civilian aircraft may be captured as prize on the ground or – when flying outside neutral airspace – be intercepted. Moreover, enemy civilian aircraft exempt from capture as prize (e.g., cartel aircraft) may be subjected to inspection if there are reasonable grounds for suspicion that they are not complying with the conditions rendering them immune from capture (see Rule 67).

3. As for State aircraft, it is necessary to recall (see Rule 1 (cc)) that they include not only military aircraft, but also law-enforcement and customs aircraft, as well as aircraft employed for other non-commercial government functions. All State aircraft which are not military aircraft come within the scope of Rule 48 (a).

4. As military objectives by nature (see Rule 22 (a)), enemy military aircraft can be fired upon. *A fortiori*, enemy military aircraft may be subjected to other belligerent rights, which do not entail their destruction.

5. Although State aircraft usually enjoy sovereign immunity, this is irrelevant in the relations between Belligerent Parties

6. As to inspection of civilian airliners, see Rule 61.

7. In non-international armed conflicts, only the government will have military aircraft and State aircraft.

(b) Neutral civilian aircraft may be intercepted, inspected or diverted in accordance with Section U.

1. Rule 48 (b) is meant to preserve the well-established right of Belligerent Parties of intercepting and inspecting civilian aircraft under Art. 49 of the HRAW,[308] which applies equally to neutral civilian aircraft. For the exercise of those rights, see Section U (II).

2. It is to be noticed that unlike Rule 48 (a)), Rule 48 (b) does not specifically mention State aircraft. The reason is that neutral State aircraft, in contrast to neutral civilian aircraft, may not be interfered with by Belligerent Parties unless they constitute military objectives (see paragraph 5 of the Commentary on Rule 54 and paragraph 1 of the Commentary on Rule 174). In other words, the belligerent right of interception, inspecting or diverting – which applies to neutral civilian aircraft – does not apply to neutral State aircraft. Such aircraft enjoy sovereign immunity that must be respected by the Belligerent Parties.

3. Rule 48 (b) does not apply to non-international armed conflict.

II. Enemy civilian aircraft

49. Enemy civilian aircraft are liable to capture as prize in accordance with Rule 134.

1. This Rule recognizes the well-established belligerent right to capture enemy civilian aircraft as prize. Enemy civilian aircraft are liable to capture as prize even if they are not engaged in activities rendering them a military objectives (see Rule 27). As to the capture of enemy civilian airliners as prize, see Rule 62.

2. Capture as prize must be distinguished from capture under the definition of military objectives (see Rule 1 (y) and Rule 22).

3. For capture as prize of enemy civilian airliners, see Rule 62.

4. Rule 49 is not applicable in non-international armed conflict, since there is no concept of prize law in non-international armed conflict.

[308] Art. 49 of the HRAW: "Private aircraft are liable to visit and search and to capture by belligerent military aircraft."

50. Subject to the specific protection of Sections K and L of this Manual, enemy civilian aircraft are liable to attack if engaged in any of the activities set forth in Rule 27.

1. This Rule is meant to emphasize that enemy civilian aircraft are protected from attack (see Rule 47).

2. Enemy civilian aircraft employed as medical aircraft enjoy specific protection from attack under Section L. This specific protection of attack may be lost if the medical aircraft is engaged in acts harmful to the enemy (see Rule 83). The expression "acts harmful to the enemy" is dealt with in Rule 74, part of Section K.

3. Civilian airliners may be attacked only if they constitute military objectives under Rule 63 and if the conditions laid down in Rule 68 are fulfilled.

4. Rule 50 applies also in non-international armed conflict.

III. Neutral civilian aircraft

51. Neutral civilian aircraft are liable to capture as prize if engaged in any of the activities enumerated in Rule 140 and if the requirements of Rule 142 are met.

1. See the Commentary on Rule 140 and on Rule 142.

2. Rule 51 does not apply to non-international armed conflict, since there is no neutrality in non-international armed conflict.

52. Neutral civilian aircraft may not be attacked unless they are engaged in any of the activities enumerated in Rule 174.

1. See the Commentary on Rule 174.

2. Rule 52 does not apply to non-international armed conflict, since there is no neutrality in non-international armed conflict.

IV. Safety in flight

1. With the exception of (i) Rule 53 (a); (ii) the second sentence of Rule 54; and (iii) Rule 56, all the Rules laid down in Section I (IV) –

rather than reflecting obligations under customary international law – are recommendatory in character. Their object and purpose is to enhance the safety of civilian aircraft in flight.

2. Section I (IV) applies in its entirety both to enemy civilian aircraft and to neutral civilian aircraft. Unless otherwise indicated, Subsection I (IV) also applies to neutral State aircraft other than military aircraft.

53. (a) In order to enhance their safety whenever in the vicinity of hostilities, civilian aircraft must file with the relevant air traffic control service required flight plans, which will include information as regards, e.g., registration, destination, passengers, cargo, identification codes and modes (including updates en route).

1. This Rule is derived from Para. 76 of the SRM/ACS.[309] The main difference is that filing required flight plans with the relevant air traffic control service is obligatory during armed conflict. Filing such flight plans will enhance the safety of the aircraft by reducing the risk that it will be attacked by mistake.

2. As to the right of Belligerent Parties to take measures to control civil aviation in the immediate vicinity of hostilities, see Rule 106.

3. It is particularly important that advance information on the flight plans of civilian aircraft, emergency communication channels and identification modes and codes for civilian aircraft associated with the Secondary Surveillance Radar system (as specified in Annex 10 ["Aeronautical Communications"] to the Chicago Convention) be made available to military forces by the relevant air traffic control service.

4. Rule 53 (a) applies also in non-international armed conflict.

[309] Para. 76 of SRM/ACS: "Civil aircraft should file the required flight plan with the cognisant Air Traffic Service, complete with information as to registration, destination, passengers, cargo, emergency communication channels, identification modes and codes, updates en route and carry certificates as to registration, airworthiness, passengers and cargo. They should not deviate from a designated Air Traffic Service route or flight plan without Air Traffic Control clearance unless unforeseen conditions arise, e.g., safety or distress, in which case appropriate notification should be made immediately."

(b) **Civilian aircraft ought not to deviate from a designated air traffic service route or flight plan without air traffic control clearance unless unforeseen conditions arise, e.g., safety or distress, in which case appropriate notification ought to be made immediately.**

1. If a civilian aircraft deviates without clearance from designated air traffic service routes or from a flight plan that has been appropriately filed, it runs an increased risk of being fired upon by mistake when it is in the vicinity of hostilities.

2. Information about any such deviation ought to be provided immediately through the appropriate channels in order to reduce the risk of being fired upon by mistake. This applies also to delays.

3. Rule 53 (b) applies also in non-international armed conflict.

54. Civilian aircraft ought to avoid areas of potentially hazardous military operations. In the vicinity of hostilities, civilian aircraft must comply with instructions from the military forces regarding their heading and altitude.

1. The first sentence of this Rule is based on Para. 72 of the SRM/ACS.[310] The second sentence is based on the principle contained in Para. 73 of the SRM/ACS.[311]

2. If a civilian aircraft, flying in the vicinity of hostilities, disregards instructions emanating from the military forces concerning their heading and altitude, it places itself at risk of being fired upon because it may be perceived as a threat.

3. A civilian aircraft ought to maintain a constant listening watch on frequencies identified for that purpose by relevant NOTAMs (see Rule 55 (a)).

4. As far as civilian airliners are concerned, see Rule 60.

5. Rule 54 deals with civilian aircraft. As far as neutral State aircraft are concerned, they enjoy sovereign immunity that must be respected by Belligerent Parties (see Para. 3 of the Commentary on Rule 48 (b)

[310] Para. 72 of SRM/ACS: "Civil aircraft should avoid areas of potentially hazardous military activity."

[311] Para. 73 of SRM/ACS: "In the immediate vicinity of naval operations, civil aircraft shall comply with instructions from the belligerents regarding their heading and altitude."

and paragraph 1 of the Commentary on Rule 174). Sovereign immunity, however, does not imply permission for a neutral State aircraft to enter the airspace of a Belligerent Party without consent. Even in international airspace, although clearly entitled to sovereign immunity, neutral State aircraft cannot ignore the hazards of military operations by Belligerent Parties in wartime. Hence, if they do not comply with instructions from the military forces of a Belligerent Party – where military operations are underway – they expose themselves to a greater risk of being attacked.

6. The second sentence of Rule 54 applies to "the vicinity of hostilities". When a civilian or other protected aircraft enters an area of potentially hazardous military activity, it must comply with a relevant NOTAM (see Rule 56).

7. In non-international armed conflict, Rule 54 applies to civilian aircraft and to State aircraft other than military aircraft. Aircraft operated by non-State organized armed groups are civilian aircraft. They are not protected against attack when they are being used for military purposes (see Rule 27).

8. In non-international armed conflict, a non-State organized armed group cannot issue legally binding instructions to civilian aircraft. An aircraft that fails to comply with instructions from military forces (either government forces or non-State organized armed groups) in an area of military operations is, however, clearly placing itself at greater risk and therefore the commander of the aircraft would be well advised to comply with even those instructions that might come from a non-State organized armed group.

55. Whenever feasible, a Notice to Airmen (NOTAM) ought to be issued by Belligerent Parties, providing information on military operations hazardous to civilian or other protected aircraft and which are taking place in given areas including on the activation of temporary airspace restrictions. A NOTAM ought to include information on the following:

1. This Rule is derived from Para. 75 of the SRM/ACS.[312]

[312] Para. 75 of SRM/ACS: "Belligerent and neutral States should ensure that a Notice to Airmen (NOTAM) is issued providing information on military activities in areas potentially hazardous to civil aircraft, including activation of danger areas or temporary airspace restrictions. This NOTAM should include information on: (a) frequencies upon which the aircraft should maintain a continuous listening watch; (b) continuous operation of

2. The procedures set forth in Rule 55 are largely based on Section 3 of the ICAO Manual concerning Interception of Civil Aircraft.[313] The construct of Notice to Airmen (NOTAM) is based on ICAO procedures, as established in Annex 15 to the Convention.[314] State practice confirms the use of NOTAMs in recent armed conflicts.

3. For the purpose of Rule 55, the term "military operations" includes training exercises, practice firings or testing of weapons (see Para. 75.1 of the Commentary on the SRM/ACS).[315]

4. The issuance of a NOTAM by a Belligerent Party does not relieve it of the obligation to comply with the requirement to take feasible precautions in attack. In this regard, see also Rule 57.

5. The category of "other protected aircraft" is meant to encompass all aircraft – be they enemy or neutral – which do not constitute military objectives.

6. In a non-international armed conflict, a State retains responsibility for issuing NOTAMs also with regard to hazardous activities of which it is aware in territory under the control of non-State organized armed groups. The feasibility of providing detailed NOTAMs in such cases may however be impaired by the constraints of the situation.

civil weather-avoidance radar and identification modes and codes; (c) altitude, course and speed restrictions; (d) procedures to respond to radio contact by the military forces and to establish two-way communications; and (e) possible action by the military forces if the NOTAM is not complied with and the civil aircraft is perceived by those military forces to be a threat."

313 Manual concerning Interception of Civil Aircraft (Consolidation of Current ICAO Provisions and Special Recommendations), Second Edition, 1990, Doc 9433-AN/926.

314 ICAO, Aeronautical Information Services, Annex 15 to the Chicago Convention on International Civil Aviation.

315 Para. 75.1 of the Commentary on the SRM/ACS: "This paragraph obliges belligerents and neutrals to issue a Notice to Airmen (NOTAM) providing detailed information on military activities in areas potentially hazardous to civil aircraft. These activities could include training exercises, practice firings or testing of weapons in addition to armed conflict at sea. This NOTAM procedure follows the long-standing practice by the military forces of belligerents and neutrals. The NOTAM issued during naval operations in the Adriatic Sea and the Gulf are recent examples. NOTAMs are also prescribed in the ICAO procedures for planning and co-ordinating military activities potentially hazardous to civil aircraft. Subparagraph (e) warns civil aircraft that if the NOTAMs are not adhered to and the civil aircraft flies in a manner perceived to be threatening by naval forces, such as flying an attack profile, the civil aircraft could be fired upon in self-defence by the naval forces."

7. In a non-international armed conflict, a non-State organized armed group is not in a position to issue formal NOTAMs. Analogous warning procedures ought, however, to be provided when it is within the capabilities of that group to do so, in particular when the latter is able to exercise a measure of physical control over a portion of airspace.

(a) Frequencies upon which the aircraft ought to maintain a continuous listening watch.

1. Belligerent Parties are entitled to give instructions to civilian aircraft flying in the vicinity of hostilities (see Rule 54). They may also interrogate an aircraft in order to identify it and, if necessary, to direct warnings to it.

2. Experience shows that civilian aircraft have been shot down due to misidentification. It is therefore of paramount importance that a constant listening watch be maintained to avoid such incidents.

(b) Continuous operation of civilian weather-avoidance radar and identification modes and codes.

Civilian identification modes and codes are useful means of identifying civilian aircraft (see Rule 40 (f)). Their correct use is conducive to reducing the risk of civilian aircraft being shot down due to misidentification in the vicinity of military operations.

(c) Altitude, course and speed restrictions.

Flight profile is one of the factors that may indicate that an unidentified aircraft could pose a threat. For this reason, it is important that civilian aircraft behave in a manner that is not perceived as threatening by military forces in the vicinity. Altitude, course and speed restrictions may be given, with a view to avoid any misunderstandings in this respect.

(d) Procedures to respond to radio contact by the military forces and to establish two-way communications.

As communication between military forces and civilian aircraft in the vicinity of military operations is essential to ensure the safety of flight, NOTAMs ought to set forth precise procedures by which the military forces and civilian aircraft can communicate with each other. In particular, the radio channel which is being monitored by military forces for this purpose has to be included.

(e) **Possible action by the military forces if the NOTAM is not complied with and if the civilian or other protected aircraft is perceived by those military forces to be a threat.**

Rule 55 (e) emphasizes that if a NOTAM is not adhered to, and the civilian or other protected aircraft flies in a manner perceived as threatening by military forces – e.g., by flying in an attack profile or by approaching militarily sensitive facilities without permission – it puts its safety in peril (see also Rule 27 (d)).

56. If a civilian or other protected aircraft enters an area of potentially hazardous military activity, it must comply with a relevant NOTAM.

1. This Rule is derived from the first sentence of Para. 77 of the SRM/ACS.[316] However, the Group of Experts inferred from State practice that compliance by a civilian or other protected aircraft with a relevant NOTAM in an area of potentially hazardous military activity is obligatory and not – as presented in the SRM/ACS – optional. See also the second sentence of Rule 54.

2. As to the meaning of "other protected aircraft", see paragraph 5 of the Commentary on the *chapeau* of Rule 55.

3. As to civilian airliners, see Rule 60.

4. Although a non-State organized armed group is not in a position to issue formal NOTAMs that are legally binding, an aircraft that fails to comply with instructions from a rebel group clearly places itself at risk.

[316] Para. 77 of SRM/ACS: "If a civil aircraft enters an area of potentially hazardous military activity, it should comply with relevant NOTAMs. Military forces should use all available means to identify and warn the civil aircraft, by using, *inter alia*, secondary surveillance radar modes and codes, communications, correlation with flight plan information, interception by military aircraft, and, when possible, contacting the appropriate Air Traffic Control facility."

57. In the absence of a NOTAM (and, whenever feasible, in case of non-compliance with a NOTAM) military forces concerned ought to use all available means to warn the civilian or other protected aircraft – through radio communication or any other established procedures – before taking any action against it.

1. This Rule is based on the second sentence of Para. 77 of the SRM/ACS.[317]

2. Regardless of the existence of a NOTAM, or even in case of non-compliance with an existing NOTAM, Belligerent Parties remain obligated to take all feasible precautions in attack (see Section G). Moreover, they ought to attempt to establish communications with an incoming aircraft, with a view to warning it of measures about to be taken (attack, inspection, etc.).

3. The expression "taking any action against it" is meant to encompass not only attacks, but also belligerent measures like interception or diversion. Firing at a civilian or other protected aircraft may only take place when it fulfills the conditions rendering it a military objective. The military forces concerned ought to make every effort to warn an approaching civilian or other protected aircraft before taking any action against at.

4. Even when no NOTAM or analogous warning has been issued, all feasible precautions must be taken to verify that incoming aircraft are military objectives (see Rule 40), in order to tell them apart from civilian or other protected aircraft that have strayed into the area (see Rule 41).

5. It must be borne in mind that non-compliance with a NOTAM does not necessarily imply any hostile intent on the part of a civil or other protected aircraft. Non-compliance may have several innocent explanations such as language difficulties or navigational error. This is the reason why warnings to an incoming civilian or other protected aircraft have to be issued prior to taking action against it.

6. The expression "military forces concerned" was preferred by the Group of Experts over the alternative phrase "military forces on the spot", in order to convey the notion that the available means may also be used by forces that are at some distance from the scene of action.

7. As to the meaning of "other protected aircraft", see paragraph 5 of the Commentary on the *chapeau* to Rule 55.

8. Rule 57 applies also in non-international armed conflict.

[317] Para. 77 of SRM/ACS, see fn. 316.

Section J

Protection of Particular Types of Aircraft

Section J is subdivided into three Subsections. Subsection I deals with civilian airliners (be they enemy or neutral), which are entitled to particular care in terms of precautions. Subsection II deals with aircraft granted safe conduct, entitled to specific protection. Subsection III includes provisions that applicable to both categories of aircraft.

I. Civilian airliners

58. Civilian airliners are civilian objects which are entitled to particular care in terms of precautions.

1. Civilian airliners are defined in Rule 1 (i).

2. Rule 58 is based on Para. 53 of the SRM/ACS[318] and on Para. 12.28 of the UK Manual.[319] Unlike Para. 53 of the SRM/ACS, Rule 58 of this Manual refers to "civilian airliners" in general and not only to "classes of enemy aircraft". Therefore, according to Rule 58, both enemy and neutral civilian airliners are entitled to protection as civilian objects.[320]

3. As indicated in paragraph 2 of the Commentary on Rule 1 (i), the Group of Experts was divided on the question as to whether civilian

[318] Para. 53 of SRM/ACS: "The following classes of enemy aircraft are exempt from attack: (a) medical aircraft; (b) aircraft granted safe conduct by agreement between the parties to the conflicts; and (c) civil airliners."

[319] Para. 12.28 of the UK Manual: "The following classes of enemy aircraft are exempt from attack: (a) medical aircraft; (b) aircraft granted safe conduct by agreement between the parties to the conflict; and (c) civil airliners."

[320] The provisions of the SRM/ACS do not explicitly state that neutral civil airliners are equally entitled to special protection from attack. This point is only implicitly acknowledged in Para. 70.1 of the Commentary on the SRM/ACS: "Neutral civil aircraft may not be attacked unless they engage in specific activities as listed. Even then paragraph 71 governs. The neutral civil aircraft addressed in paragraphs 70 and 71 are civil aircraft other than medical aircraft, aircraft granted safe conduct and civil airliners which are exempt from attack."

airliners are entitled to specific protection beyond the application of the principle of distinction in general. The principle of distinction is undisputed as a general norm of customary international law (see Rule 10 (a)).

4. The key phrase "particular care in terms of precautions" also relates to the duty to avoid – or, in any event, to minimize – civilian casualties. The purpose of Rule 58 is to ensure that Belligerent Parties will at all times be aware of the vulnerability of civilian airliners and, therefore, must exercise particular care in terms of precautions in order to prevent situations that might lead to the accidental downing of a civilian airliner.

5. The compromise adopted by the Group of Experts resulted from the following views: one part of the Group of Experts argued that civilian airliners are included in the category of civilian aircraft (as defined in Rule 1 (h)) and ought not to legally benefit from an additional (specific) protection. Another part of the Group of Experts – taking into consideration the importance of this category of aircraft because of the vulnerability of civilian airliners, which may have large numbers of civilian passengers on board who are at risk – supported the opposite view.

6. As a compromise, the Group of Experts agreed that civilian airliners are entitled to the general protection under the principle of distinction, but that they are also entitled to "particular care in terms of precautions". This means especially that the general obligation to take every feasible step – in order to ascertain that the target to be attacked is a lawful target – must be meticulously observed. See Rule 32 (a). See also Rule 35 (a) and Rule 35 (c).

7. The protection of civilian airliners is also laid down in the Chicago Convention. The Convention's Art. 3 *bis*, subparagraph (a), provides that the "contracting States recognize that every State must refrain from resorting to the use of weapons against civil aircraft in flight".[321] While the Chicago Convention refers to civil aircraft (including civilian airliners) "in flight" only, this Manual posits that civilian airliners are also protected while on the ground (see Rule 59). Although the Chicago Convention does not apply in armed conflict,[322] this Manual shares the premise that civilian airliners are entitled to particular care in terms of precautions.

[321] Art 3 *bis* (a) of the Chicago Convention, see fn. 20.

[322] Art. 89 of the Chicago Convention ("War and Emergency Conditions"): "In case of war, the provisions of this Convention shall not affect the freedom of action of any of

8. Rule 58 in no way diminishes the general protection to which civilian aircraft are entitled (see Section I).

9. As the protection of civilian airliners can be effective only insofar as Belligerent Parties are able to identify them, Art. 20 of the Chicago Convention provides that "every aircraft engaged in international air navigation shall bear its appropriate nationality and registration marks". Annex 7 of the Chicago Convention further sets out the procedures and rules for selection by ICAO Contracting States of nationality and registration marks.[323] Additionally, civilian airliners can be identified through using Secondary Surveillance Radar (SSR) modes and codes for civil aircraft as specified in Annex 10 to the Chicago Convention.[324]

10. Given the events of 9/11, it is impossible to ignore the danger that civilian airliners can be hijacked (and then used as means of attack) or otherwise be employed in ways harmful to the enemy. Hence, it is important to emphasize that, in certain circumstances, protection of civilian airliners is liable to be lost (see Rule 63). However, even if a civilian airliner loses its protection, certain conditions must still be met before attacking it (see Subsection III of Section J (III)). In ordinary circumstances, the presence on board a civilian airliner of a civilian crew and a large number of civilian passengers underscores the need to avoid collateral damage which, in most circumstances, will be excessive in relation to the military advantage anticipated (see Rule 68 (d)).

11. Rule 58 applies also in non-international armed conflict.

59. In case of doubt, civilian airliners – either in flight or on the ground in a civilian airport – are presumed not to be making an effective contribution to military action.

1. The purpose of this Rule is to affirm the protection of civilian airliners by including a presumption that they are not making an effective contribution to military action. "[M]aking an effective contribution to

the contracting States affected, whether as belligerents or as neutrals. The same principle shall apply in the case of any contracting state which declares a state of national emergency and notifies the fact to the Council."

323 ICAO, Aircraft Nationality and Registration Marks, Annex 7 to the Chicago Convention on International Civil Aviation.

324 ICAO, Aeronautical Telecommunications, Annex 10 to the Chicago Convention on International Civil Aviation.

military action" is one of the activities which may render a civilian airliner a military objective (see Rule 63 (f)).

2. The presumption applies both when civilian airliners are in flight and when they are parked on the ground, provided that they are on the ground in a civilian airport, i.e., an airport that does not constitute a military objective by nature (see Rule 22 (a)).

3. The presumption is rebuttable, since the airliner may actually be used to carry combatants or otherwise make an effective contribution to military action. Once the presumption is rebutted, the airliner loses its protection (see Rule 63 (f)). Hence, if a Belligerent Party is able to establish that the civilian airliner is making an effective contribution to military action, the civilian airliner constitutes a military objective and may be treated as such. However, see Section G and Section J (III).

4. Rule 59 applies also in non-international armed conflict.

60. While civilian airliners (whether enemy or neutral) ought to avoid entering a no-fly or an "exclusion zone", or the immediate vicinity of hostilities, they do not lose their protection merely because they enter such areas.

1. This Rule is partly based on Para. 72 of the SRM/ACS.[325] No-fly zones and "exclusion zones" are dealt with in Section P.

2. Rule 60 is designed to ensure that civilian airliners avoid zones or areas where they may be fired upon inadvertently. It includes not only "exclusion zones" and no-fly zones, as discussed in Section P, but also any other area in the immediate vicinity of hostilities.

3. Rule 60 does not establish an obligation to avoid entering an "exclusion zone" or a no-fly zone or any other area in the immediate vicinity of hostilities, but is merely a recommendation to that effect. The terminology used ("civilian airliners ought to avoid") clarifies that Rule 60 does not reflect a legal obligation.

4. Para. 72.1 of the Commentary on the SRM/ACS states that Para. 72 of the SRM/AC "places an obligation on all States, air traffic services and civil aircraft captains to take action so that civil aircraft will avoid areas of potentially hazardous military activity." The use of the word "and" suggests that each entity (namely States, air traffic services and civil

[325] Para. 72 of the SRM/ACS, see fn. 310.

aircraft pilots) ought to contribute to the safety of civilian airliners by ensuring that civilian airliners avoid entering such zones or areas.

5. The fact that civilian aircraft (including civilian airliners) ought to avoid areas of potentially hazardous military operations was already incorporated in Rule 54. Rule 60 serves the purpose of emphasizing that civilian airliners entering a no-fly zone or an "exclusion zone", or the immediate vicinity of hostilities, do not lose their protection on the sole ground of entering the zone or area.

6. If a civilian or other protected aircraft enters an area of potentially hazardous military activity, it must comply with a relevant NOTAM (see Rule 56).

7. Rule 60 applies in non-international armed conflict only in the context of no-fly zones, and in areas in the immediate vicinity of hostilities. "Exclusion zones" are inapplicable in non-international armed conflict and therefore Rule 60 does not apply in that context (see paragraph 4 of the Commentary in the *chapeau* to Section P).

61. Any civilian airliner suspected on reasonable grounds of carrying contraband or otherwise being engaged in activities inconsistent with its status is subject to inspection by a Belligerent Party in an airfield that is safe for this type of aircraft and reasonably accessible.

1. This Rule applies to civilian airliners in international airspace or in the national airspace of a Belligerent Party. In such areas, a Belligerent Party is entitled to inspect a civilian airliner if it is reasonably suspected of carrying contraband or otherwise being engaged in activities inconsistent with its status. This is in line with the general provision of Rule 48 where a Belligerent Party is entitled to intercept, inspect or divert all civilian aircraft (be they enemy or neutral). However, like Para. 125 of the SRM/ACS,[326]

[326] Para. 125 of SRM/ACS: "In exercising their legal rights in an international armed conflict at sea, belligerent military aircraft have a right to intercept civil aircraft outside neutral airspace where there are reasonable grounds for suspecting they are subject to capture. If, after interception, reasonable grounds for suspecting that a civil aircraft is subject to capture still exist, belligerent military aircraft have the right to order the civil aircraft to proceed for visit and search to a belligerent airfield that is safe for the type of aircraft involved and reasonably accessible. If there is no belligerent airfield that is safe and reasonably accessible for visit and search, a civil aircraft may be diverted from its declared destination."

Rule 61 adds the requirement of conducting the inspection in an airfield that is safe for a civilian airliner and reasonably accessible.

2. A Belligerent Party must have reasonable grounds to suspect that the civilian airliner is carrying contraband or engaging in activities inconsistent with its status. The phrase "reasonable grounds" denotes that the Belligerent Party may only act on the basis of reasonable information. In other words, an inspection may only be conducted if there is reliable information suggesting that the aircraft is carrying contraband or otherwise engaged in activities inconsistent with its status. For the definition of contraband, see Rule 1 (n).

3. Examples of activities inconsistent with the status of a civilian airliner can be found in Rule 63.

4. Unlike Para. 125 of the SRM/ACS, the present Rule does not refer to interception as a necessary stage preceding inspection. It is believed that, with a civilian airliner, instructions to land for inspection ought to be communicated without interception being required.

5. In order to obviate the necessity for inspection of neutral civilian airliners, and in order to decrease inconvenience and financial loss, Neutrals are encouraged to enforce reasonable control measures and certification procedures, such as the use of an "aircert", to ensure that their civilian airliners are not carrying contraband (see Rule 138).[327]

6. "Contraband" is a concept of prize law that does not apply in non-international armed conflict. This is made clear by the terms "susceptible for use in international armed conflict" in the definition of contraband (see Rule 1 (n)).

7. As far as engagement of a civilian airliner in activities inconsistent with its status is concerned, the central government may inspect it during a non-international armed conflict. Non-State organized armed groups have no right to do so.

[327] Para. 134 of SRM/ACS: "In order to obviate the necessity for visit and search, neutral States are encouraged to enforce reasonable control measures and certification procedures to ensure that their civil aircraft are not carrying contraband."

In parallel, Para. 132 of SRM/ACS: "In order to avoid the necessity of visit and search, belligerent States may establish reasonable measures for the inspection of the cargo of neutral civil aircraft and certification that an aircraft is not carrying contraband."

62. Enemy civilian airliners may be captured as prize but only on condition that all passengers and crews are safely deplaned and the papers of the aircraft are preserved.

1. Rule 134 of the Manual acknowledges that enemy civilian aircraft are liable to capture as prize. According to Rule 62, enemy civilian airliners are also liable to such capture. As to the conditions under which capture as prize may take place, see Section U.

2. Rule 62 only covers enemy civilian airliners. The Manual deliberately leaves open the issue of capture as prize of neutral civilian airliners. There is no State practice at all indicating that a legitimate neutral civilian airliner can be captured as prize. However, in the exceptional circumstances in which a neutral civilian airliner is engaging in "hostile actions in support of the enemy" (e.g., by carrying enemy combatants or military supplies) (see Rule 63 (b) and Rule 63 (c)), the neutral civilian airliner may surely be assimilated to an enemy civilian airliner. In any event, it ought to be recalled that a neutral civilian airliner with no civilian passengers on board at all no longer fits the definition of a civilian airliner (see para. 5 of the commentary on Rule 1 (i)). It would then constitute an ordinary neutral civilian aircraft, in which case Art. 140 will apply.

3. Rule 62 further makes this right subject to the condition that all passengers and crews are safely deplaned. It thereby recalls a Belligerent Party's obligation to ensure the safety of passengers and crew as per Rule 143 (see also Para. 145 of SRM/ACS).[328] The personal effects of the crew and passengers have to be safeguarded (see Para. 158 of SRM/ACS).[329]

4. If an enemy civilian airliner is inspected and enemy combatants are found on board among the passengers, they may be detained. However, they must be treated as POWs.

5. The treatment of enemy civilian airliners and passengers landing in neutral territory must be in accordance with the law of neutrality. Members of the armed forces of a Belligerent Party must therefore be interned for the duration of the armed conflict. See the second sentence of Rule 170 (c).

[328] Para. 145 of the SRM/ACS: "If capture is exercised, the safety of passengers and crew and their personal effects must be provided for. The documents and papers relating to the prize must be safeguarded."

[329] Para. 158 of SRM/ACS, see fn. 701.

6. Rule 62 does not apply in non-international armed conflicts, because (i) prize law does not apply in such armed conflicts; and (ii) non-State organized armed groups do not have a right to capture civilian airliners.

63. Subject to Rule 68, activities such as any of the following may render a civilian airliner a military objective:

1. Rule 63 is partially based on Para. 56 of the SRM/ACS[330] and on Para. 12.31 of the UK Manual.[331]

2. Rule 63 sets out the circumstances under which a civilian airliner may constitute a military objective. The term "may" indicates that, even in the circumstances described in Rule 63 (a)—(f), a civilian airliner does not automatically become a military objective. On the other hand, Rule 63 (a)—(f) does not provide an exhaustive list of the activities that may render a civilian airliner a military objective. This is indicated by the words "such as" in the *chapeau* of Rule 63, as well as by the open-ended nature of Rule 63 (f).

3. Rule 63 (a)–(f) is merely meant to give guidance as to how to apply the definition of military objectives (see Rule 1 (y) and Section E, especially Rule 22) to civilian airliners. The activities enumerated in Rule 63 (a)–(f) relate only to "use" and "purpose" (i.e., "intended future use"), and are subject to the application of Rule 22 (c) or Rule 22 (d).

4. Even if a civilian airliner has become a military objective, this does not automatically mean that it may be attacked. In addition to a civilian airliner having become a military objective, the conditions in Rule 68 must be met too before it may be attacked. Moreover, a civilian airliner which has become a military objective regains its civilian status once it ceases to make an effective contribution to military action.

5. Rule 63 must be read against the background of Rule 27 pertaining to attacks against enemy aircraft other than military aircraft. Rule 63 (b)–(f) are textually identical to Rule 27 (a)–(e). It is only Rule 63 (a) which is specific to civilian airliners.

[330] Para. 56 of the SRM/ACS: "Civil airliners are exempt from attack only if they: (a) are innocently employed in their normal role; and (b) do not intentionally hamper the movements of combatants."

[331] Para. 12.31 of the UK Manual is identical to Para. 56 of the SRM/ACS.

6. The use of any aircraft other than a military aircraft as means of attack is prohibited at all times (see Rule 115 (b)).

7. The main conditions precedent to an attack against a civilian airliner that has lost its protection are enumerated in Rule 68. It must be recalled, however, that there are also ancillary conditions in Rule 69 and 70.

8. Rule 63 applies also in non-international armed conflict.

(a) Being on the ground in a military airfield of the enemy in circumstances which make that aircraft a military objective.

1. Rule 63 (a) applies only to civilian airliners parked "on the ground in a military airfield of the enemy". If a civilian airliner is parked on the ground in a civilian airport, Rule 59 applies.

2. A civilian airliner parked "on the ground in a military airfield of the enemy" does not automatically become a military objective. In order for it to become a military objective, a civilian airliner must by its nature, location, purpose or use make an effective contribution to military action and its total or partial destruction, capture or neutralization, in the circumstances ruling at the time, must offer a definite military advantage (See Rule 1 (y) and Rule 22).

3. The presence of a civilian airliner may not be abused by the enemy in order to render a military airfield immune from attack (see Rule 45). A civilian airliner present in a military airfield runs the risk of being destroyed as collateral damage, in case of a lawful attack against the airfield.

4. In case that a civilian airliner (carrying civilian passengers, see the definition in Rule 1 (i)) is landing in distress in a military airfield, the prevailing view among the Group of Expert was that (i) efforts must be made to alert the enemy to the situation; and (ii) the pilot must take every measure available to him to show that the airliner is in fact in distress (open slides, etc.).

5. If a civilian airliner is being diverted to a military airfield, the Belligerent Party responsible for the diversion has an obligation to remove the civilian airliner from its military airfield as soon as possible, in order not to endanger it unnecessarily.

(b) Engaging in hostile actions in support of the enemy, e.g., intercepting or attacking other aircraft; attacking persons or objects on land or sea; being used as a means of attack; engaging in electronic warfare; or providing targeting information to enemy forces.

Rule 63 (b) specifically includes the situation where a civilian airliner is hijacked and is flown into a target. In such cases, the civilian airliner effectively becomes a means of attack, that is, a weapon (see also Commentary on Rule 27 (a)).

(c) Facilitating the military actions of the enemy's armed forces, e.g., transporting troops, carrying military materials, or refuelling military aircraft.

See Commentary on Rule 27 (b).

(d) Being incorporated into or assisting the enemy's intelligence gathering system, e.g., engaging in reconnaissance, early warning, surveillance or command, control and communications missions.

See Commentary on Rule 27(c).

(e) Refusing to comply with the orders of military authorities, including instructions for landing, inspection and possible capture, or clearly resisting interception.

See Commentary on Rule 27 (d).

(f) Otherwise making an effective contribution to military action.

See Commentary on Rule 27 (e). In case of doubt as to whether a civilian airliner is making an effective contribution to military action, Rule 59 provides for a rebuttable presumption that this is not the case.

II. Aircraft granted safe conduct

64. Aircraft granted safe conduct by agreement between the Belligerent Parties – such as cartel aircraft – are entitled to specific protection from attack.

1. Rule 64 is based on Para. 53 (b) of the SRM/ACS.[332]

[332] Para. 53 (b) of SRM/ACS, see fn. 318.

2. Although the category of "aircraft granted safe conduct" relates principally to cartel aircraft (defined in Rule 1(g)), there is no limitation on the type of aircraft (military or other State aircraft, civilian aircraft or medical aircraft), or on the activities carried out, to which safe conduct may be granted by agreement.[333] A safe conduct may be granted for purposes exceeding the role of cartel aircraft, e.g., carrying consignments of humanitarian aid (see Section O).

3. All aircraft granted safe conduct enjoy specific protection from attack contingent on respect for the conditions enumerated in Rule 65. On the notion of specific protection, see paragraph 3 of the Commentary in the *chapeau* on Section K.

4. The specific protection of aircraft granted safe conduct is contingent on the agreement whereby they operate. To the extent that these are civilian or medical aircraft, they also benefit from the protection due to them as such (see, respectively, Section I and Section L).

5. Aircraft granted safe conduct are entitled to specific protection from attack not only when they are performing their assigned mission, such as transporting POWs or parlementaires, but also on their way to collecting such individuals and on their way back after having transported them.[334]

6. The agreement reached by the Belligerent Parties ought to contain details about the flight and activities carried out by the aircraft granted safe conduct. Such details are indispensable in the absence of any special method of identification foreseen for such aircraft.

7. Aircraft granted safe conduct may be identified through the filing of a detailed flight plan pursuant to Rule 53 (a) of this Manual and through the use of Secondary Surveillance Radar (SSR) modes and codes for civilian aircraft.[335] However, it may not use medical aircraft identification. ICRC

[333] See Para. 55.1 of the Commentary on the SRM/ACS: "Belligerents would expect that aircraft granted safe conduct would comply with the conditions in this paragraph. There is no limitation on what the agreed role could be. Aircraft granted safe conduct could be *inter alia* transporting prisoners of war, conducting relief missions, transporting cultural property, or protecting the environment. . . . "

[334] See Para. 47.22 of the Commentary on the SRM/ACS: "Cartel vessels are exempt from capture and attack, not only when they are carrying the prisoners of war or communications, but also on the journeys to collect the prisoners or communications and on their way back after having transported them." This explanation concerning cartel vessels ought to apply by analogy to aircraft granted safe conduct.

[335] See the final sentence of Para. 55.1 of the Commentary to the SRM/ACS: "Other safe conduct aircraft may not use medical aircraft identification, but at present must rely on

aircraft – one type of aircraft that may be granted safe conduct – constitute an exception in this respect: ICRC aircraft may use the same means of identification as medical aircraft, even though they operate under a safe conduct granted by Belligerent Parties.[336]

65. (a) Aircraft granted safe conduct lose their specific protection from attack in any one of the following instances:

1. Rule 65 (a) is based on Para. 55 of the SRM/ACS[337] and on Para. 12.30 of the UK Manual.[338]

2. Aircraft granted safe conduct are entitled to specific protection from attack. This specific protection will be lost in case of any breach of the terms of the special agreement underlying the operation. See also subsection J (III).

3. Loss of specific protection by an aircraft granted safe conduct means that it reverts to the original category to which it belonged. It has to be recalled that such aircraft may include any type of aircraft (military or other State aircraft, civilian aircraft or medical aircraft, see Para. 2 of the Commentary on Rule 64).

4. Notwithstanding the loss of specific protection, attack against such aircraft strictly depends on the application of Section J (III).

5. The two conditions enumerated in Rule 65 (a) (i) and Rule 65 (a) (ii) are alternative and not cumulative.

6. Rule 65 (a) applies also in non-international armed conflict.

(i) They do not comply with the details of the agreement, including availability for inspection and identification.

1. Rule 65 (a) (i) is based on Para. 55 (c) of the SRM/ACS.[339]

filing a detailed flight plan (paragraph 76) and using Secondary Surveillance Radar (SSR) modes and codes for civil aircraft."

336 Penultimate sentence of Para. 55.1 of the Commentary to the SRM/ACS: "With regard to the identification of [aircraft granted safe conduct], aircraft chartered by the ICRC have the same status as medical aircraft and may use the same methods of identification (paragraph 175)."

337 Para. 55 of SRM/ACS: "Aircraft granted safe conduct are exempt from attack only if they: (a) are innocently employed in their agreed role; (b) do not intentionally hamper the movements of combatants; and (c) comply with the details of the agreement, including availability for inspection."

338 Para. 12.30 of the UK Manual is identical to Para. 55 of the SRM/ACS.

339 Para. 55 (c) of SRM/ACS, see fn. 337.

2. Since the agreement reached between the Belligerent Parties is the sole reason for the specific protection of this category of aircraft, the aircraft is obliged to comply with the terms of such agreement in order to retain that specific protection (although it may enjoy some other protection as explained in paragraph 2 of the Commentary on Rule 64).

3. Aircraft granted safe conduct are obliged to submit to inspection on the ground, in order to allow the opposing Belligerent Party to verify that it adheres to the terms of the agreement. Such inspection ought preferably to occur at an airfield or airport before the beginning of the flight (see Para. 55.1 of the Commentary on the SRM/ACS).

4. Aircraft granted safe conduct are also obliged to comply with an order to identify themselves. Such identification will usually occur in flight (*inter alia*, through interception), and will not require inspection on the ground.

(ii) They intentionally hamper the movements of combatants and are not innocently employed in their agreed upon role.

1. Rule 65 (a) (ii) is a combination of Para. 55 (a) and Para. 55 (b) of the SRM/ACS.[340]

2. The conjunction "and" indicates that both conditions listed in Rule 65 (a) (ii) must be fulfilled cumulatively, i.e., the aircraft granted safe conduct must intentionally hamper the movement of combatants and it is not innocently employed in the agreed upon role.

3. The adverb "intentionally" indicates that aircraft granted safe conduct will not lose their specific protection in case that the improper activity happened accidentally.

4. As long as the aircraft granted safe conduct is innocently employed in its agreed upon role, the fact that it actually (but unintentionally) hampers the movement of combatants cannot be held against it.

5. Aircraft granted safe conduct do not lose their specific protection from attack due to their carrying purely defensive weapons (for example, chaff) and individual light weapons for the defence of the crew, unless this runs counter to the basic agreement governing their mission.

[340] Para. 55 (a) and Para. 55 (b) of SRM/ACS, see fn. 337.

(b) Loss of specific protection will only take place if the circumstances of non-compliance are sufficiently grave that the aircraft has become or may reasonably be assumed to be a military objective.

1. Rule 65 (b) is based on Para. 57 (c) of the SRM/ACS.[341]

2. "Sufficiently grave" means that the circumstances of non-compliance cannot be regarded as a trivial matter. This is a *de minimis* clause.

3. Rule 65 (b) applies also in non-international armed conflict.

66. In case of doubt whether an aircraft granted safe conduct qualifies as a military objective as per Rule 27, it will be presumed not to qualify as such.

1. This Rule is based on Art. 52 (3) of AP/I,[342] as well as on Para. 58 of the SRM/ACS.[343] The purpose is to affirm the protection of aircraft granted safe conduct by acknowledging a (rebuttable) presumption in their favour in case of doubt as to their use.

2. The presumption contained in Rule 66 is the counterpart to Rule 59. An aircraft granted safe conduct must not be considered a military objective if doubt remains whether this is indeed the case. See Commentary on Rule 59 *mutatis mutandis.*

3. Rule 66 applies also in non-international armed conflict.

67. Aircraft granted safe conduct are exempt from capture as prize, provided that they:

1. This Rule is based on Para. 142[344] and on Para. 143 of the SRM/ACS.[345]

[341] Para. 57 (c) of SRM/ACS, see fn. 346.

[342] Art. 52 (3) of AP/I, see fn. 184.

[343] Para. 58 of SRM/ACS: "In case of doubt whether a vessel or aircraft exempt from attack is being used to make an effective contribution to military action, it shall be presumed not to be so used".

[344] Para. 142 of SRM/ACS: "The following aircraft are exempt from capture: (a) medical aircraft; and (b) aircraft granted safe conduct by agreement between the parties to the conflict."

[345] Para. 143: Aircraft listed in paragraph 142 are exempt from capture only if they: (a) are innocently employed in their normal role; (b) do not commit acts harmful to the enemy; (c) immediately submit to interception and identification when required; (d) do not intentionally hamper the movement of combatants and obey orders to divert from their track when required; and (e) are not in breach of a prior agreement."

2. The status of aircraft granted safe conduct is different from that of enemy civilian airliners, which do not benefit from exemption from capture (see Rule 62). However, it is clear that aircraft granted safe conduct must abide by the terms of their mission. The four conditions listed in Rule 67 (a) – (d) are cumulative. As the term "provided that" indicates, it suffices that one of the conditions of Rule 67 (a) – (d) is breached for an aircraft granted safe conduct to be liable to capture as prize.

3. Rule 67 applies also in non-international armed conflict.

(a) Are innocently employed in their normal role;

Concerning the expression "innocently employed", see Commentary on Rule 65 (a) (ii). The expression "normal role" means that the aircraft does not perform any activity which is inconsistent with its execution of the mission for which safe conduct was granted.

(b) Immediately submit to interception and identification when required;

1. A Belligerent Party has the right to ensure that the aircraft granted safe conduct is being used only for the purposes agreed upon. Therefore, an aircraft conducting a safe conduct mission is susceptible to being intercepted.

2. As for interception in general (including procedures required for carrying it out) see Section U. Interception is usually conducted for purposes of later inspection on the ground (see Rule 134). As for identification, it can be conducted either in flight or on the ground during inspection. When interception is carried out, the aircraft granted safe conduct is required to cooperate with the intercepting aircraft.

(c) Do not intentionally hamper the movement of combatants and obey orders to divert from their track when required; and

1. The adverb "intentionally" indicates that aircraft granted safe conduct will not lose their specific protection in case that the activity happened accidentally (see Commentary on Rule 65 (a) (ii)).

2. "Orders to divert from their track" may be issued when the flight of the aircraft granted safe conduct interferes with military operations or otherwise poses a security risk. Orders to divert may not be issued capriciously; they must have a military reason.

(d) Are not acting in breach of a prior agreement.

Prior agreement means primarily the agreement under which the safe conduct is provided. However, there may be a supplementary agreement. For instance, the Belligerent Parties may conclude first a general agreement and then an *ad hoc* agreement relating to the specific flight.

III. Provisions common to civilian airliners and aircraft granted safe conduct

68. Civilian airliners and aircraft granted safe conduct may only be attacked if they have lost their protection as per Rules 63 and 65 and if the following cumulative conditions are fulfilled:

1. This Rule is partially based on Para. 57 of the SRM/ACS[346] and on Para. 12.32 of the UK Manual.[347]

2. The purpose of Rule 68 is to specify the conditions that have to be fulfilled before either a civilian airliner or an aircraft granted safe conduct which has lost its protection (because it engages in any of the activities set out in respectively Rule 63 or Rule 65 (a)) may be attacked.

3. A civilian airliner or an aircraft granted safe conduct may only be attacked if all the conditions of Rule 68 (a) to Rule 68 (d) are met.

4. The application of this Rule is subject to the general conditions in Sections D, E and G (especially subsection (III) of Section G), and to the ancillary conditions in Rule 69 and 70.

5. Rule 68 applies also in non-international armed conflict.

(a) Diversion for landing, inspection, and possible capture, is not feasible;

1. This condition is derived from Para. 57 (a) of the SRM/ACS.[348]

[346] Para. 57 of SRM/ACS ("Loss of exemption"): "If aircraft exempt from attack breach any of the applicable conditions of their exemption as set forth in paragraphs 54–56, they may be attacked only if: (a) diversion for landing, visit and search, and possible capture, is not feasible; (b) no other method is available for exercising military control; (c) the circumstances of non-compliance are sufficiently grave that the aircraft has become, or may be reasonably assumed to be, a military objective; and (d) the collateral casualties or damage will not be disproportionate to the military advantage gained or anticipated."

[347] Para. 12.32 of the UK Manual is identical to Para. 57 of the SRM, the cross-reference in the UK Manual being to paragraphs 12.29 to 12.31 of the UK Manual.

[348] Para. 57 (a) of SRM/ACS, see fn. 346.

2. The rules relating to diversion for landing, inspection, and capture are contained in Section U.

3. The reference in Rule 68 (a) to "diversion for landing, inspection, and possible capture", which constitutes a *conditio sine quo non* to attack, does not preclude the possibility of a different type of diversion away from the area of operations in lieu of an attack. Diversion away from the area does not entail landing, inspection, and capture. Such diversion, however, may not be sufficient in the view of the intercepting force. For example, the aircraft may be believed to be transporting combatants or military equipment, and this in breach of the safe conduct agreement. In such a case, there may be no alternative to diversion for purposes of landing, inspection and possible capture.

(b) No other method is available for exercising military control;

1. This condition is virtually identical to Para. 57 (b) of the SRM/ACS.[349]

2. Belligerent military forces must first exhaust all feasible means to exercise control of the aircraft, with a view to the cessation of activities that had brought about the loss of protection in accordance with Rule 63 or Rule 65.

3. When an order to land or to divert is issued, it must be reasonable in the circumstances. The aircraft ordered to land or divert must be afforded a reasonable opportunity to comply with it in terms of both time and practicability.

(c) The circumstances leading to the loss of protection are sufficiently grave to justify an attack; and

1. This condition is based on Para. 57 (c) of the SRM/ACS.[350]

2. "Sufficiently grave" means that the circumstances of non-compliance cannot be regarded as a trivial matter. This is a *de minimis* clause. See also the Commentary on Rule 65 (b).

(d) The expected collateral damage will not be excessive in relation to the military advantage anticipated and all feasible precautions have been taken (see Section G of this Manual).

1. This condition is based on Rule 14. See also Para. 57 (d) of the SRM/ACS.[351]

[349] Para. 57 (b) of SRM/ACS, see fn. 346.
[350] Para. 57 (c) of SRM/ACS, see fn. 346.
[351] Para. 57 (d) of SRM/ACS, see fn. 346.

2. This general requirement is included here explicitly with a view to underscoring, in the specific context of civilian airliners and aircraft granted safe conduct, the general principle of proportionality (Rule 14) and the requirement of taking feasible precautions (Rule 32 (c) and Rule 35 (c)). Civilian airliners are entitled to particular care in terms of precautions.

3. The Group of Experts did not agree as to whether the expected collateral damage is confined to the civilian losses on board the civilian airliner or the aircraft granted safe conduct, or whether it also extends to any further civilian losses on the ground (see paragraph 4 of the chapeau of the Commentary on Section G (III)).

69. Any decision to attack a civilian airliner or an aircraft granted safe conduct pursuant to Rule 68 ought to be taken by an appropriate level of command.

1. The phrase "an appropriate level of command" is relative in its essence. This is due to the fact that States have different military structures and command levels. Since the decision to attack a civilian airliner or an aircraft granted safe conduct is of grave nature, it must be taken by a sufficiently high level of command.

2. As a possible analogy, it is noteworthy that under Art. 13 (2) (c) (i) of the Second Protocol to the 1954 Hague Convention, cultural property under enhanced protection may only be the object of attack if ordered "at the highest operational level of command".[352]

70. In case of loss of protection pursuant to this Section, a warning must be issued – whenever circumstances permit – to the civilian airliner or the aircraft granted safe conduct in flight before any action is taken against it.

1. Rule 70 reiterates an obligation already appearing in Rule 38. However, Rule 38 is confined to objects entitled to specific protection (including aircraft granted safe conduct) but here it is extended also to civilian airliners, which are only entitled to particular care in terms of precautions.

2. A warning must be issued "whenever circumstances permit". In particular, there may be circumstances in which a hostile act by an aircraft is

[352] Art. 13 (2) (c) (i) of the Second Protocol to the 1954 Hague Convention, see fn. 532.

imminent and in which no time is available to issue the warning. In such a situation, a Belligerent Party cannot be expected to give a warning.

3. A warning to a civilian airliner or to an aircraft granted safe conduct in flight may be issued either through radio communication or, where required through the exercise of the acceptable modes of interception detailed in the Commentary on the *chapeau* to Section U. If necessary, warning shots may be fired.

4. For further details concerning this obligation to warn, see Commentary on Rule 37 and on Rule 38.

Section K

Specific Protection of Medical and Religious Personnel, Medical Units and Transports

1. Section K – like Sections L, M and N, as well as Section J (II) – deals with the specific protection afforded to selected objects and persons. Of course, all objects and persons who are exempt from attack are entitled to protection under the law of international armed conflict. However, the notion of "specific protection" is designed to highlight this protection and, in certain cases, to enhance it through the use of a distinctive emblem and other ways as specified in this Manual. These safeguards come in addition to the general protection these objects enjoy as civilian objects. The use of the adjective "specific" was deemed preferable to that of the word "special", inasmuch as the protection involved is not radically different from that accorded to all civilians and civilian objects. Moreover, the term "specific" was chosen in order to avoid any confusion with respect to the notion of "special protection" granted to cultural property under Chapter II of the 1954 Hague Convention.

2. Sections K and L are complementary. While Section K addresses the specific protection granted to medical units and transports, Section L is devoted to the specific protection afforded to medical aircraft, singled out due to their particular relevance and importance in the context of air and missile warfare. In other words, Section L supplements Section K in regard to medical aircraft.

3. Section K does not contain an exhaustive list of the rules that apply to the protection of medical and religious personnel, medical units and transports. It simply contains the most relevant rules with regard to air and missile warfare. Certain rules, e.g., regarding respect and protection of hospital ships or small craft used for coastal rescue operations, were deemed too specific for inclusion in this Manual.

4. This Section applies in both international and non-international armed conflict (see, e.g., Art. 11 (1) of AP/II[353]).

[353] Art. 11 (1) of AP/II: "Medical units and transports shall be respected and protected at all times and shall not be the object of attack."

71. Subject to Rule 74, medical and religious personnel, fixed or mobile medical units (including hospitals) and medical transports by air, land, at sea or on other waters must be respected and protected at all times, and must not be the object of attack.

1. Rule 71 is an introductory provision to Section K reiterating, in simple terms, the general obligation to respect and protect at all times medical and religious personnel, medical units and medical transports. This general obligation encompasses subsidiary protection granted to ensure that wounded and sick receive medical care.

2. The obligation to respect and to protect military medical and religious personnel (who are members of the armed forces) is based on Art. 24[354] and Art. 25 of GC/I;[355] Art. 36 of GC/II[356] and on the first paragraph of Art. 20 of GC/IV.[357] Art. 15 of AP/I extended the scope of the protection to cover civilian medical and religious personnel.[358]

[354] Art. 24 of GC/I: "Medical personnel exclusively engaged in the search for, or the collection, transport or treatment of the wounded or sick, or in the prevention of disease, staff exclusively engaged in the administration of medical units and establishments, as well as chaplains attached to the armed forces, shall be respected and protected in all circumstances."

[355] Art. 25 of GC/I: "Members of the armed forces specially trained for employment, should the need arise, as hospital orderlies, nurses or auxiliary stretcher-bearers, in the search for or the collection, transport or treatment of the wounded and sick shall likewise be respected and protected if they are carrying out these duties at the time when they come into contact with the enemy or fall into his hands."

[356] Art. 36 of GC/II: "The religious, medical and hospital personnel of hospital ships and their crews shall be respected and protected; they may not be captured during the time they are in the service of the hospital ship, whether or not there are wounded and sick on board."

[357] First paragraph of Art. 20 of GC/IV: "Persons regularly and solely engaged in the operation and administration of civilian hospitals, including the personnel engaged in the search for, removal and transporting of and caring for wounded and sick civilians, the infirm and maternity cases shall be respected and protected."

[358] Art. 15 of AP/I ("Protection of civilian medical and religious personnel"): "(1) Civilian medical personnel shall be respected and protected. (2) If needed, all available help shall be afforded to civilian medical personnel in an area where civilian medical services are disrupted by reason of combat activity. (3) The Occupying Power shall afford civilian medical personnel in occupied territories every assistance to enable them to perform, to the best of their ability, their humanitarian functions. The Occupying Power may not require that, in the performance of those functions, such personnel shall give priority to the treatment of any person except on medical grounds. They shall not be compelled to carry out tasks which are not compatible with their humanitarian mission. (4) Civilian medical personnel shall have access to any place where their services are essential, subject to such supervisory and safety measures as the relevant Party to the conflict may deem necessary. (5) Civilian religious personnel shall be respected and protected. The provisions

3. The obligation to respect and to protect medical units and medical means of transport is based on Art. 19[359] and Art. 35 of GC/I;[360] Art. 18[361] and Art. 21 of GC/IV;[362] as well as on Art. 12 (1),[363] Art. 21,[364] and Art. 24 of AP/I.[365]

4. A breach of Rule 71 may qualify as a war crime under the Rome Statute of the ICC in both international[366] and in non-international armed conflict.[367]

5. The term "medical personnel" covers persons assigned exclusively to medical purposes by a Belligerent Party. In this context, the notion of "medical purposes" includes the search for, collection, transportation, diagnosis or treatment (including first-aid treatment) of the wounded, sick and shipwrecked, or the prevention of disease. The personnel assigned by a Belligerent Party to the administration of medical units or to the operation or administration of medical transports are also included under

of the Conventions and of this Protocol concerning the protection and identification of medical personnel shall apply equally to such persons."

359 First sentence of Art. 19 of GC/I: "Fixed establishments and mobile medical units of the Medical Service may in no circumstances be attacked, but shall at all times be respected and protected by the Parties to the conflict."

360 First sentence of Art. 35 of GC/I: "Transports of wounded and sick or of medical equipment shall be respected and protected in the same way as mobile medical units."

361 First sentence of Art. 18 of GC/IV: "Civilian hospitals organized to give care to the wounded and sick, the infirm and maternity cases, may in no circumstances be the object of attack but shall at all times be respected and protected by the Parties to the conflict."

362 First sentence of Art. 21 of GC/IV: "Convoys of vehicles or hospital trains on land or specially provided vessels on sea, conveying wounded and sick civilians, the infirm and maternity cases, shall be respected and protected in the same manner as the hospitals provided for in Art. 18."

363 Art. 12 (1) of AP/I: "Medical units shall be respected and protected at all times and shall not be the object of attack."

364 Art. 21 of AP/I: "Medical vehicles shall be respected and protected in the same way as mobile medical units under the Convention and this Protocol." See also Art. 22 of AP/I pertaining to "Hospital ships and coastal rescue craft."

365 Art. 24 of AP/I, see fn. 407.

366 Art. 8 (2) (b) (ix) of the Rome Statute of the ICC: "Intentionally directing attacks against . . . hospitals and places where the sick and wounded are collected, provided they are not military objectives."

Art. 8 (2) (b) (xxiv): "Intentionally directing attacks against buildings, material, medical units and transports, and personnel using the distinctive emblem of the Geneva Conventions in conformity with international law."

367 Art. 8 (2) (e) (ii): "Intentionally directing attacks against buildings, material, medical units and transports, and personnel using the distinctive emblem of the Geneva Conventions in conformity with international law."

Art. 8 (2) (e) (iv): "Intentionally directing attacks against . . . hospitals and places where the sick and wounded are collected, provided they are not military objectives."

the definition of "medical personnel". For the purposes of this definition, administrative staff includes office staff, ambulance drivers, janitors, cooks, etc.

6. The term "medical personnel" encompasses: (i) medical personnel of a Belligerent Party, whether military or civilian, including those assigned to civil defence organizations; (ii) medical personnel of National Red Cross, Red Crescent, or Red Crystal Societies and other national voluntary aid societies duly recognized and authorized by a Belligerent Party; (iii) medical personnel made available to a Belligerent Party for humanitarian purposes by a Neutral – or a recognized and authorized aid society of such a Neutral – or by an impartial humanitarian organization such as the ICRC. The term "medical personnel" has been defined in Art. 8 (c) of AP/I.[368]

7. "Religious personnel" means military or civilian persons exclusively engaged in the work of their ministry and attached: (i) to the armed forces of a Belligerent Party; (ii) to medical units or medical transports of a Belligerent Party; (iii) to civil defence organizations of a Belligerent Party; or (iv) to medical units or medical transports made available to a Belligerent Party for humanitarian purpose by a Neutral – or a recognized and authorized aid society of a Neutral – or by an impartial humanitarian organization. The specific attachment of religious personnel to one of the four categories listed above presumes the agreement of the Belligerent Party. The term "religious personnel" has been defined in Art. 8 (d) of AP/I.[369]

8. "Medical personnel" and "religious personnel" have to be exclusively assigned to medical or religious duties in order to enjoy respect and

[368] Art. 8 (c) of AP/I: "'Medical personnel' means those persons assigned, by a Party to the conflict, exclusively to the medical purposes enumerated under (e) or to the administration of medical units or to the operation or administration of medical transports. Such assignments may be either permanent or temporary. The term includes (i) medical personnel of a Party to the conflict, whether military or civilian, including those described in the First and Second Conventions, and those assigned to civil defence organizations; (ii) medical personnel of national Red Cross (Red Crescent, Red Lion and Sun) Societies and other national voluntary aid societies duly recognized and authorized by a Party to the conflict; (iii) medical personnel or medical units or medical transports described in Article 9, paragraph 2."

[369] Art. 8 (d) of AP/I: "'Religious personnel' means military or civilian persons, such as chaplains, who are exclusively engaged in the work of their ministry and attached: (i) to the armed forces of a Party to the conflict; (ii) to medical units or medical transports of a Party to the conflict; (iii) to medical units or medical transports described in Article 9, paragraph 2; or (iv) to civil defence organizations of a Party to the conflict. The attachment of religious personnel may be either permanent or temporary, and the relevant provisions mentioned under k) apply to them."

protection under Rule 71. Their exclusive assignment to medical or religious duties may be either permanent or temporary. If the assignment is permanent, respect and protection are due at all times; if the assignment is only temporary, respect and protection are only due during the time of that assignment.

9. Persons performing medical or religious duties without assignment (or agreement) to such functions by a Belligerent Party do not qualify as medical or religious personnel respectively. While they benefit from the general protection granted to civilians (see Rule 11), they are not entitled to display a distinctive emblem (see Rule 72 (a)).

10. "Medical units" are defined as establishments and other units organized for medical purposes. For the expression "medical purposes", see paragraph 5 of the Commentary on Rule 71. Medical units enjoy specific protection regardless of whether they are military or civilian, permanent or temporary, fixed or mobile. Examples of medical units are hospitals and other similar units, blood transfusion centres, preventive medicine centres and institutes, in particular vaccination centres, casualty collection points and triage facilities, rehabilitation centres providing medical treatment, medical depots, and the medical and pharmaceutical stores of such units. The expression "medical units" has been defined in Art. 8 (e) of AP/I.[370]

11. "Medical transports" are defined as any means of transportation – placed under the control of a competent authority of a Belligerent Party – exclusively assigned to medical transportation. They can be military or civilian, permanent or temporary. The expression "medical transports" has been defined in Art. 8 (g) of AP/I.[371]

12. The obligation "to respect" medical and religious personnel as well as medical units and transports entails not only a prohibition against attacking or harming such persons and objects in any way, but also prohibits

[370] Art. 8 (e) of AP/I: "'Medical units' means establishments and other units, whether military or civilian, organized for medical purposes, namely the search for, collection, transportation, diagnosis or treatment – including first-aid treatment – of the wounded, sick and shipwrecked, or for the prevention of disease. The term includes for example, hospitals and other similar units, blood transfusion centres, preventive medicine centres and institutes, medical depots and the medical and pharmaceutical stores of such units. Medical units may be fixed or mobile, permanent or temporary."

[371] Art. 8 (g) of AP/I, see fn. 47.

unnecessarily preventing them from discharging their functions (e.g., by blocking medical supplies for medical units or transports).

13. The obligation "to protect" refers to the duty to take appropriate precautions to ensure respect by non-State actors for medical and religious personnel, medical units and transports (e.g., in order to prevent looting by marauders or rioting mobs).

14. Rule 71 emphasizes that respect and protection is due to medical units, medical transports and medical or religious personnel "at all times". Nevertheless, protection may be lost in certain circumstances. See Rule 74. As to the loss of protection of medical aircraft, see Rule 83.

72. (a) Medical and religious personnel ought to wear a water-resistant armlet bearing a distinctive emblem provided by the law of international armed conflict (the Red Cross, Red Crescent or the Red Crystal). Medical units and medical transports ought to be clearly marked with the same emblem to indicate their status as such; when appropriate, other means of identification may be employed.

1. Rule 72 (a) lays down the principle of marking with a distinctive emblem of medical and religious personnel, medical units and medical transports. This principle is based, as far as international armed conflicts are concerned, on Art. 39,[372] Art. 40,[373] Art. 41[374] *(See footnote on next page)*

[372] Art. 39 of GC/I: "Under the direction of the competent military authority, the emblem shall be displayed on the flags, armlets and on all equipment employed in the Medical Service."

[373] Art. 40 of GC/I: "The personnel designated in Article 24 and in Articles 26 and 27 shall wear, affixed to the left arm, a water-resistant armlet bearing the distinctive emblem, issued and stamped by the military authority. Such personnel, in addition to wearing the identity disc mentioned in Article 16, shall also carry a special identity card bearing the distinctive emblem. This card shall be water-resistant and of such size that it can be carried in the pocket. It shall be worded in the national language, shall mention at least the surname and first names, the date of birth, the rank and the service number of the bearer, and shall state in what capacity he is entitled to the protection of the present Convention. The card shall bear the photograph of the owner and also either his signature or his finger-prints or both. It shall be embossed with the stamp of the military authority. The identity card shall be uniform throughout the same armed forces and, as far as possible, of a similar type in the armed forces of the High Contracting Parties. The Parties to the conflict may be guided by the model which is annexed, by way of example, to the present Convention. They shall inform each other, at the outbreak of hostilities, of the model they are using. Identity cards should be made out, if possible, at least in duplicate, one copy being kept by the home country. In no circumstances may the said

and Art. 42 of GC/I;[375] as well as on Art. 18 (4) of AP/I. [376] As far as non-international armed conflict is concerned, it is based on Art. 12 of AP/II.[377]

2. The Red Cross and the Red Crescent (as well as the Red Lion and Sun, now in disuse),[378] have been recognized as distinctive emblems for a long time. AP/III, which entered into force on 14 January 2007, established the Red Crystal as an additional distinctive emblem with equal status.

3. In the great majority of cases, it will be in the interest of Belligerent Parties to mark medical and religious personnel, medical units and transports in order to facilitate their identification as such by the enemy. However, Belligerent Parties may desist from marking where the distinctive emblem could be detrimental to military exigencies, for example when the localization of an identified medical unit or medical transport may call the enemy's attention to troop deployment (see Rule 72 (c) and Rule 72 (d)).

personnel be deprived of their insignia or identity cards nor of the right to wear the armlet. In case of loss, they shall be entitled to receive duplicates of the cards and to have the insignia replaced."

[374] Art. 41 of GC/I: "The personnel designated in Article 25 shall wear, but only while carrying out medical duties, a white armlet bearing in its centre the distinctive sign in miniature; the armlet shall be issued and stamped by the military authority. Military identity documents to be carried by this type of personnel shall specify what special training they have received, the temporary character of the duties they are engaged upon, and their authority for wearing the armlet."

[375] Art. 42 of GC/I: "The distinctive flag of the Convention shall be hoisted only over such medical units and establishments as are entitled to be respected under the Convention, and only with the consent of the military authorities. In mobile units, as in fixed establishments, it may be accompanied by the national flag of the Party to the conflict to which the unit or establishment belongs. Nevertheless, medical units which have fallen into the hands of the enemy shall not fly any flag other than that of the Convention. Parties to the conflict shall take the necessary steps, insofar as military considerations permit, to make the distinctive emblems indicating medical units and establishments clearly visible to the enemy land, air or naval forces, in order to obviate the possibility of any hostile action."

[376] Art. 18 (4) of AP/I: "With the consent of the competent authority, medical units and transports shall be marked by the distinctive emblem. The ships and craft referred to in Article 22 of this Protocol shall be marked in accordance with the provisions of the Second Convention."

[377] Art. 12 of AP/II: "Under the direction of the competent military authority concerned, the distinctive emblem of the red cross, red crescent or red lion and sun on a white ground shall be displayed by medical and religious personnel and medical units, and on medical transports. It shall be respected in all circumstances. It shall not be used improperly."

[378] No State has used the emblem of the Red Lion and Sun since 1980 when the government of the Islamic Republic of Iran declared that henceforth it would use the Red Crescent as its distinctive emblem.

4. In this respect, specific Rules apply to medical aircraft as contained in Section L, see Rule 76.

5. The use of the distinctive emblem by medical and religious personnel, medical units and medical transports requires the consent, and is subject to control of, the competent authority of the Belligerent Party to which they belong.[379] This authority cannot permit a unit or transport which is not recognized as medical to be marked in this way. Belligerent Parties must take all necessary measures for the prevention and repression, at all times, of any misuse of the distinctive emblems and their designations, including the perfidious use and the use of any sign or designation constituting an imitation. On perfidy, see Section Q, in particular Rule 112 (a).

6. It is recommended that medical and religious personnel wear, affixed to the left arm, a "water-resistant armlet" in order to keep it in good condition. Clearly, religious and medical personnel wearing an armlet that is not waterproof and/or on their right arm must nevertheless be protected.

7. Medical units and medical transports ought to be "clearly" marked as specified in Annex I to AP/I, which emphasizes the visibility of the distinctive emblem. The ideal size of the armlet is not specified but it ought to be wide and the red cross on it as large as appropriate under the circumstances. It has, whenever feasible, to be displayed in a way that it is visible from as many directions and from as far away as possible, and in particular from the air. At night or when visibility is reduced, the distinctive emblem may be lit or illuminated.[380]

8. The second sentence of Rule 72 (a) points to the possibility to use additional means to facilitate identification besides the use of the distinctive emblem.[381] This development arose from concerns that solely having

[379] For that matter, note that the Party to which they belong may also be an enemy, particularly in the case of occupied territory. A similar condition is posed by Art. 12 of AP/II in the context of non-international armed conflict: "Under the direction of the competent authority concerned, the distinctive emblem of the red cross, red crescent or red lion and sun on a white ground shall be displayed by medical and religious personnel and medical units, and on medical transports. It shall be respected in all circumstances. It shall not be used improperly."

[380] Annex I to AP/I (Regulations concerning identification), Arts. 4 and 5. For the latter, see fn. 382.

[381] The possibility of adding to the distinctive emblem other means of identification dates back to the second paragraph of Art. 36 of GC/I which allowed Belligerent Parties to enter

the distinctive emblem displayed on a medical unit or medical transport could prove insufficient for correct identification in circumstances of modern warfare that enable long-range or reduced visibility targeting. The additional means of identification referred to are set out in Annex I of AP/I (as amended in 1993). This includes, for example, a distinctive radio signal earmarked for all medical transports which can be used by digital selective calling systems, transponders or ship borne automatic identification systems. In this respect, see the Commentary on Rule 76 (b) concerning the additional means of identification of medical aircraft.

9. Since a different legal regime applies to States that are and those that are not Contracting Parties to AP/I, the text refers to the use of additional means of identification "when appropriate". However, the use of additional means of identification is certainly to be encouraged.

10. Additional means of identification ought only to be used to supplement the distinctive emblem, which remains the basic element. An exception is laid down concerning temporary medical aircraft which cannot, either for lack of time or because of their characteristics, be marked with the distinctive emblem (see Rule 76 (c)).

(b) As far as possible, the distinctive emblem ought to be made of materials which make it recognizable by technical means of detection used in air or missile operations.

1. Rule 72 (b) is based on Art. 5 of Annex I to AP/I (as amended in 1993).[382]

into ad hoc agreements upon the outbreak or during the course of hostilities: "[Medical aircraft] shall bear, clearly marked, the distinctive emblem prescribed in Article 38, together with their national colours, on their lower, upper and lateral surfaces. They shall be provided with any other markings or means of identification that may be agreed upon between the belligerents upon the outbreak or during the course of hostilities."

At that time of GC/I it was limited to medical aircraft. Since then, Art. 18 (5) of AP/I has explicitly authorized the use of additional means of identification for any type of medical transport or unit: "In addition to the distinctive emblem, a Party to the conflict may, as provided in Chapter III of Annex I to this Protocol, authorize the use of distinctive signals to identify medical units and transports. Exceptionally, in the special cases covered in that Chapter, medical transports may use distinctive signals without displaying the distinctive emblem."

382 Art. 5 of Annex I to AP/I: "(1) The distinctive emblem shall, whenever possible, be displayed on a flat surface, on flags or in any other way appropriate to the lay of the land, so that it is visible from as many directions and from as far away as possible, and in particular from the air. (2) At night or when visibility is reduced, the distinctive emblem may be lighted or illuminated. (3) The distinctive emblem may be made of materials

2. In air or missile operations, some technical means of detection which are used – such as infra-red cameras or radars – are incapable of recognizing the forms and colours of the distinctive emblem. Therefore, it is convenient to use special material to render the distinctive emblem recognizable by such means of detection. Thus, e.g., adhesive tapes with a high thermal reflection coefficient can make the distinctive emblem visible to thermal imaging cameras.

3. As with any technical means of detection, the obligation set forth in Rule 72 (b) is not absolute but only applies "as far as possible". The phrase "as far as possible" recognizes that there may be limitations upon a Belligerent Party's ability to adopt such technical means. In this respect, the ICRC Commentary on AP/I indicates: "[t]he reason that the obligation is not absolute is also because some means of identification are very expensive or highly technical, and it is not possible to impose these on Parties to the conflict which do not have the financial or technical means to employ them."[383] However, to the extent that Belligerent Parties can field such technologies, they ought to do so.

(c) The distinctive emblem and other means of identification are intended only to facilitate identification and do not, of themselves, confer protected status.

1. Protection is granted to medical units, medical transports, as well as medical and religious personnel, because of their functions. The practical value of the distinctive emblem and additional means of identification is to facilitate protection by increasing the likelihood that medical and religious personnel, medical units and transports will be identified as such.

2. Rule 72 (c) reiterates the general principle of the law of international armed conflict that the distinctive emblem and other means of identification do not confer protection as such, but are merely facilitating recognition of the medical status of personnel, units or transports. This

which make it recognizable by technical means of detecting. The red part should be painted on top of black primer paint in order to facilitate its identification, in particular by infrared instruments. (4) Medical and religious personnel carrying out their duties in the battle area shall, as far as possible, wear headgear and clothing bearing the distinctive emblem."

[383] Para. 747 of the ICRC Commentary on AP/I, pertaining to Art. 18 (1) of AP/I.

principle was emphasized in Art. 1 of Annex I of AP/I (as amended in 1993)[384] and in paragraph 4 of the Preamble to AP/III.[385]

(d) The failure of medical and religious personnel, medical units and medical transports to display the distinctive emblem does not deprive them of their protected status.

1. Rule 72 (d) is the corollary of Rule 72 (c). Since protected status is not derived from the distinctive emblem *per se*, medical and religious personnel are protected regardless of whether they wear the emblem.

2. Medical units and transports, as well as medical and religious personnel, enjoy a protected status from the moment they have been identified as such, and shortcomings in the means of identification cannot be used as a pretext for failing to protect their status.

73. A Belligerent Party may inform the enemy of the position of its medical units. The absence of such notification does not exempt any of the Belligerent Parties from the obligations contained in Rule 71.

1. This Rule is based on Art. 12 (3) of AP/I, which invites Belligerent Parties to notify each other of the position of their fixed medical units.[386]

2. Contrary to Art. 12 (3) of AP/I, the scope of application of Rule 73 is not limited to fixed medical units. Many battlefield hospitals are mobile

[384] Art. 1 of Annex I to AP/I: "(1) The regulations concerning identification in this Annex implement the relevant provisions of the Geneva Conventions and the Protocol; they are intended to facilitate the identification of personnel, material, units, transports and installations protected under the Geneva Conventions and the Protocol. (2) These rules do not in and of themselves establish the right to protection. This right is governed by the relevant articles in the Conventions and the Protocol. (3) The competent authorities may, subject to the relevant provisions of the Geneva Conventions and the Protocol, at all times regulate the use, display, illumination and detectability of the distinctive emblems and signals. (4) The High Contracting Parties and in particular the Parties to the conflict are invited at all times to agree upon additional or other signals, means or systems which enhance the possibility of identification and take full advantage of technological developments in this field."

[385] Paragraph 4 of the Preamble to AP/III: "Recalling that the obligation to respect persons and objects protected by the Geneva Conventions and the Protocols additional thereto derives from their protected status under international law and is not dependent on use of the distinctive emblems, signs or signals."

[386] Art. 12 (3) of AP/I: "The Parties to the conflict are invited to notify each other of the location of their fixed medical units. The absence of such notification shall not exempt any of the Parties from the obligation to comply with the provisions of paragraph 1."

in the sense of being deployable, and the Group of Experts considered that Rule 73 ought to be applicable to these hospitals as well. However, when notification of the future location of a mobile medical unit is given to the enemy, it does not have to include the route taken by the unit to reach its destination (although providing such details might enhance the protection of the unit).

3. Rule 73 does not apply to medical transports. It would be unrealistic to expect a Belligerent Party to keep the enemy informed of their constant movement. However, nothing prevents a Belligerent Party from informing the enemy of the major movements of medical transports when doing so may enhance their protection (e.g., in the case of a hospital ship or medical aircraft in circumstances where no consent is required).

4. Rule 73 entails a mere recommendation to Belligerent Parties aimed at reinforcing the security of their medical units. It is up to each Belligerent Party to decide – depending on the particular circumstances of each case – whether it wants to make the position of its medical units known to the enemy. In certain circumstances, informing the enemy could be detrimental to military operations. Mobile medical units, for instance, often operate near firing positions. Indicating their position in such circumstances may invite attacks against the military units in the vicinity of the medical units.

5. Under Rule 73, notification to the enemy requires no special formalities.[387] The position of the medical units may be transmitted through any reliable and efficient means of communication with the enemy.

6. The second sentence of Rule 73 reinforces the principle that the absence of notification does not create an exemption from protection. The obligations contained in Rule 71 exist irrespective of notification (which is optional). Failure to notify increases the risk of collateral damage to the medical units during an attack on military objectives (see Rule 14), but in no way impairs the obligations contained in Rule 71 when these units have been identified. Nor does failure of notification impact upon the obligation of feasible precautions required under the law of international armed conflict (see Section G, in particular Rule 32 and Rule 35).

[387] The notification envisaged in Rule 73 is totally different from the notification in Section V ("Aerial Blockade") of this Manual (see Rule 148 (a) and Rule 149 (a)).

74. (a) The protection to which medical and religious personnel, medical units or medical transports are entitled does not cease unless they commit or are used to commit, outside their humanitarian function, acts harmful to the enemy.

1. This Rule is, as far as international armed conflicts are concerned, based on Art. 21 of GC/I;[388] Art. 34 GC/II;[389] Art. 19 of GC/IV;[390] Art. 13 (1)[391] and Art. 21 of AP/I;[392] and, as far as non-international armed conflicts are concerned, on Art. 11 (2) of AP/II.[393]

2. Rule 74 (a) states that the specific protection conferred on medical and religious personnel, as well as medical units or medical transports, does not cease except when they commit or are used to commit acts harmful to the enemy. Hence, no other reason can give rise to the termination of the obligations contained in Rule 71.

3. The notion of "acts harmful to the enemy" encompasses acts whose purpose or effect is to harm the enemy by facilitating or impeding military operations.[394] Therefore, it does not only include acts inflicting harm on the enemy by direct attack, but also attempts at hindering its military operations in any way whatsoever (e.g., positioning a medical unit in a way that would impede a military attack or using a medical transport as a shelter for able-bodied combatants). "Acts harmful to the enemy" may include intelligence gathering.

[388] Art. 21 of GC/I: "The protection to which fixed establishments and mobile medical units of the Medical Service are entitled shall not cease unless they are used to commit, outside their humanitarian duties, acts harmful to the enemy. Protection may, however, cease only after a due warning has been given, naming, in all appropriate cases, a reasonable time limit and after such warning has remained unheeded."

[389] Art. 34 of GC/II, see fn. 281.

[390] Art. 19 of GC/IV, see fn. 282.

[391] Art. 13 (1) of AP/I ("Discontinuance of protection of civilian medical units"): "The protection to which civilian medical units are entitled shall not cease unless they are used to commit, outside their humanitarian function, acts harmful to the enemy. Protection may, however, cease only after a warning has been given setting, whenever appropriate, a reasonable time-limit, and after such warning has remained unheeded."

[392] Art. 21 of AP/I, see fn. 374.

[393] Art. 11 (2) of AP/II: "The protection to which medical units and transports are entitled shall not cease unless they are used to commit hostile acts, outside their humanitarian function. Protection may, however, cease only after a warning has been given setting, whenever appropriate, a reasonable time-limit, and after such warning has remained unheeded."

[394] Para. 550 of the ICRC Commentary on AP/I, pertaining to Art. 13 of AP/I.

4. To lead to a loss of specific protection, acts harmful to the enemy must be "committed outside of the humanitarian function" of the medical and religious personnel, medical units or medical transports. This implies that certain acts harmful to the enemy may be compatible with the humanitarian function of the medical and religious personnel, medical units or transports. As such, such acts may be accomplished without entailing a loss of specific protection (e.g., the use of electronic equipment at a field hospital may interfere with the enemy's communication system).

5. As to what must not be considered "acts harmful to the enemy", see Rule 74 (c).

6. For the loss of the specific protection of medical aircraft, see Rule 83.

(b) For medical units or medical transports, protection may cease only after a warning has been given setting a reasonable time-limit, and after such warning has remained unheeded.

1. Rule 74 (b) has to be read against the background of Rule 38. The requirement to issue a warning as per Rule 74 (b) is an absolute one, unlike warnings mentioned, e.g., in Rule 37, which must be issued unless circumstances do not permit.

2. Even if there is a valid reason for discontinuing the specific protection of medical units or medical transports, a warning must be issued first. The warning may take various forms. In many instances, it can simply consist of an order to cease the harmful act within a specified period.

3. The time-limit must be reasonable in order to give an opportunity for the unlawful acts to be stopped, or to allow removal to a place of safety of the wounded and sick within the medical units or medical transports, prior to any attack.

4. In some cases, it may be "reasonable" to insist on immediate compliance with a warning. However, even in these cases the principle of proportionality and the requirement to take feasible precautions in attack have to be observed (see Section D and Section G).

(c) The following must not be considered as acts harmful to the enemy:

1. This Rule is a corollary to Rule 74 (a), which hinges on the construct of "acts harmful to the enemy". A list of acts that must not be considered

as harmful to the enemy is also given in Arts. 22 of GC/I[395] and Art. 13 (2) of AP/I[396] on which Rule 74 (c) is based.

2. The fact that acts enumerated in Rule 74 (c) are not to be considered as harmful to the enemy, does not negate the possibility that there would be other acts of that kind, depending on the circumstances. Hence, the following list of a non-exhaustive nature.

(i) that the personnel of a medical unit are equipped with light individual weapons for their own defence or for that of the wounded, sick or shipwrecked in their charge.

1. Rule 74 (c) (i) is based on Art. 22 (1) of AP/I[397] and on Art. 13 (2) (a) of AP/I.[398]

2. The personnel of medical units (as defined in the Commentary on Rule 71) are allowed to carry light individual weapons to prevent themselves or the wounded and sick in their charge from becoming the victims of violence. The term "defence" has to be interpreted restrictively as meaning

[395] Art. 22 of GC/I: "The following conditions shall not be considered as depriving a medical unit or establishment of the protection guaranteed by Article 19: (1) That the personnel of the unit or establishment are armed, and that they use the arms in their own defence, or in that of the wounded and sick in their charge. (2) That in the absence of armed orderlies, the unit or establishment is protected by a picket or by sentries or by an escort. (3) That small arms and ammunition taken from the wounded and sick and not yet handed to the proper service, are found in the unit or establishment. (4) That personnel and material of the veterinary service are found in the unit or establishment, without forming an integral part thereof. (5) That the humanitarian activities of medical units and establishments or of their personnel extend to the care of civilian wounded or sick."

[396] Art. 13 (2) of AP/I: "The following shall not be considered as acts harmful to the enemy: (a) that the personnel of the unit are equipped with light individual weapons for their own defence or for that of the wounded and sick in their charge; (b) that the unit is guarded by a picket or by sentries or by an escort; (c) that small arms and ammunition taken from the wounded and sick, and not yet handed to the proper service, are found in the units; (d) that members of the armed forces or other combatants are in the unit for medical reasons."

[397] Art. 22 (1) of AP/I: "1. The provisions of the Conventions relating to: (a) vessels described in Articles 22, 24, 25 and 27 of the Second Convention, (b) their lifeboats and small craft, (c) their personnel and crews, and (d) the wounded, sick and shipwrecked on board, shall also apply where these vessels carry civilian wounded, sick and shipwrecked who do not belong to any of the categories mentioned in Article 13 of the Second Convention. Such civilians shall not, however, be subject to surrender to any Party which is not their own, or to capture at sea. If they find themselves in the power of a Party to the conflict other than their own they shall be covered by the Fourth Convention and by this Protocol."

[398] Art. 13 (2) (a) of AP/I, see fn. 396.

defence against, e.g., attacks by marauders, rioting mob or looters, or with regard to maintaining order amongst unruly patients (the wounded and sick). But such personnel may only resort to arms when strictly necessary for purely defensive purposes. They cannot use force to try and prevent enemy combatants from capturing the medical unit, without losing their protection.[399]

3. The expression "light individual weapons" refers to weapons, which are generally carried and used by a single individual. Pistols, rifles and submachine guns are permitted. If the personnel of medical units are equipped with machine guns or any other heavy arms, which cannot be easily transported by a single individual and have to be operated by a number of people, this could be considered as an act harmful to the enemy.

4. Rule 74 (c) (i) does not prevent the medical unit from possessing other purely defensive systems (such as flares, jammers or similar protective devices). Such systems must only be used for the defence of the medical personnel or medical unit. Their nature or display must not be such as to lead the enemy to believe that the medical unit is equipped with offensive weaponry.

(ii) that a medical unit is guarded by sentries or by an escort.

1. Rule 74 (c) (ii) contains the same idea as in Art. 22 (2) of GC/I[400] and as in Art. 13 (2) (b) of AP/I.[401] Sentries or an escort may be necessary to guard a medical unit in order either to prevent looting and violence or to prevent the possible escape of enemy combatants treated within the medical unit. Sentries or an escort must not attempt to oppose the capture or control of the medical unit by the enemy.

[399] See also the second subparagraph of Para. 8.6.3 of NWP: "Traditionally, hospital ships could not be armed, although crew members could carry light individual weapons for the maintenance of order, for their own defense and that of the wounded, sick, and shipwrecked. However, due to the changing threat environment in which the red cross symbol is not recognized by various hostile groups and actors as indicating protected status, the United States views the manning of hospital ships with defensive weapons systems, such as anti-missile defense systems or crew-served weapons to defend against small boat threats as prudent AT/TP measures, analogous to armed crew members with small arms, and consistent with the humanitarian purpose of hospital ships and duty to safeguard the wounded and sick."

[400] Art. 22 (2) of GC/I, see fn. 395.

[401] Art. 13 (2) (b) of AP/I, see fn. 396.

2. If the sentries or escort are members of the armed forces, they keep their combatant status, although the mere fact of their presence within a medical unit will usually – as a practical matter – shelter them from attack. In case of capture they will be accorded POW-status.

3. Sentries or escort may include civilian employees of a private security company or law-enforcement officials.[402]

(iii) that portable arms and ammunition taken from the wounded and sick, and not yet handed to the proper service, are found in the medical unit.

1. Rule 74 (c) (iii) is based on Arts. 22 (3) of GC/I[403] and on Art. 13 (2) (c) of AP/I.[404]

2. The arms and ammunition taken from the wounded and sick must be handed over to the proper service as soon as possible. In the meantime, the fact that these arms are kept in the medical unit does not result in a loss of protection.

3. The "portable arms and ammunition taken from the wounded and sick" are not limited to light individual weapons as specified in Rule 74 (c) (i). Arms covered by Rule 74 (c) (iii) may be heavier, provided that they are portable, i.e., that they can be carried by men, even if it requires two or three soldiers (e.g., surface-to-air missile or anti-tank devices).

(iv) that members of the armed forces or other combatants are in the medical unit for medical or other authorized reasons, consistent with the mission of the medical unit.

1. Rule 74 (c) (iv) is based on Art. 13 (2) (d) of AP/I.[405]

2. The fact that combatants are present within a medical unit for medical reasons cannot be considered as an act harmful to the enemy. Thus, it would be unlawful to invoke the presence of military wounded and sick in a medical unit as a reason to terminate the protection to which this unit is entitled.

[402] Montreux Document on Pertinent International Legal Obligations and Good Practices for States related to Operations of Private Military and Security Companies during Armed Conflict, 17 September 2008, available via <www.eda.admin.ch/eda/en/home/topics/intla/humlaw/pse/psechi.html>

[403] Art. 22 (3) of GC/I, see fn. 395.

[404] Art. 13 (2) (c) of AP/I, see fn. 396.

[405] Art. 13 (2) (d) of AP/I, see fn. 396.

3. In that respect, the notion of medical reasons is broader than that of medical treatment. It also encompasses cases where members of the armed forces are in the facility or unit for medical reasons without receiving treatment, e.g., for medical examination or vaccination.

4. The Group of Experts departed from the wording of Art. 13 (2) (d) of AP/I on one point: according to Rule 74 (c) (iv), members of the armed forces may be authorized to visit a medical unit for reasons other than medical ones. Even if the presence of a member of the armed forces or of a combatant within the medical unit is not for medical reasons, it may not necessarily be regarded as an act harmful to the enemy. For instance: delivery of mail to patients or visiting them is not inconsistent with the mission of the medical unit.

(d) Medical units must not be used to shield lawful targets from attack.

1. Rule 74 (d) is based on the first sentence of Art. 12 (4) of AP/I[406] and relates to precautions by the Belligerent Party subject to attack (see Section H, especially Rule 45).

2. Rule 74 (d) – a corollary to the obligations contained in Rule 71 – implies certain obligations for Belligerent Parties with regard to their own medical units and those that have fallen into their hands.

3. In particular, Belligerent Parties must ensure that medical units are sited in a way that they do not shield lawful targets from attacks. For practical reasons, medical units must sometimes be located near firefighting zones and military objectives, with a view to providing urgent medical care to the wounded and sick. Nevertheless, it is not permissible for a Belligerent Party to intentionally place such units in those locations in order to impede enemy attacks against lawful targets, e.g., in the hope that the enemy would hesitate to attack these lawful targets in order to prevent collateral damage. Along the same lines, it is prohibited to locate lawful targets (such as combatants) within or in the vicinity of a medical unit in order to shield them from attack.

[406] Art. 12 (4) of AP/I: "Under no circumstances shall medical units be used in an attempt to shield military objectives from attack. Whenever, possible, the Parties to the conflict shall ensure that medical units are so sited that attacks against military objectives do not imperil their safety."

4. Using medical units to shield lawful targets from attack cannot be justified under any circumstances (see Art. 12 (4) of AP/I).

5. Even if medical units lose protection because they are used to shield lawful targets, the enemy is not relieved from its obligation to respect the principle of proportionality (but see the discussion in paragraph 6 of the Commentary on Rule 45) or from taking feasible precautionary measures (see Section G, as well as Rule 46). In particular, an attack may take place only after a warning has been given requiring the enemy to desist from using the medical unit as a shield and after such warning has remained unheeded (see Rule 74 (b)). This is especially important given that the intention of locating the medical units in the vicinity of military objectives in an attempt to shield the latter from attacks is rarely easy to establish. After all, medical units may be located near the troops simply because this will facilitate and accelerate the provision of care.

Section L

Specific Protection of Medical Aircraft

1. This Section deals with the specific protection of medical aircraft, as defined in Rule 1 (u).

2. Medical aircraft – especially helicopters – are an extremely efficient means of transporting wounded and sick, shipwrecked, medical and religious personnel, as well as medical equipment and supplies. By these means, persons in need of medical care may be quickly accessed and evacuated.

3. Given the potential of all aircraft – including medical aircraft – to participate in military operations (e.g., the collection of intelligence), differentiation between medical aircraft and military aircraft may be difficult, and it may require rapid decision-making on the part of a Belligerent Party responding to a potential attack. It flows naturally that detailed rules are essential to facilitate the proper identification of medical aircraft. Medical aircraft flying over an area covered in Rule 78 (a) may be ordered to land in order to permit inspection (see Rule 80).

75. A medical aircraft is entitled to specific protection from attack, subject to the Rules of this Section of the Manual.

1. This Rule is based on Art. 24 of AP/I.[407] The text differs in that the wording used in Rule 75 is that a medical aircraft "is entitled to specific protection", whereas in AP/I the phrase employed is "shall be respected and protected". The reason for this difference is the desire to highlight the specific protection of medical aircraft (see the *chapeau* of the Commentary on Section K). Of course, Rule 75 does not lessen the obligation to respect

[407] Art. 24 of AP/I: "Medical aircraft shall be respected and protected, subject to the Rules of this Part."

See also Para. 174 of the SRM/ACS: "Medical aircraft shall be protected and respected as specified in the provisions of this document."

and protect medical aircraft: on the contrary, its intention is to strengthen the obligation.

2. The provisions applicable to the protection of medical aircraft will differ depending on the location of the aircraft. The Commentary on Rules 77, 78 and 80 distinguishes between two different situations: (a) medical aircraft operating in and over land areas physically controlled by friendly forces or in and over sea areas not physically controlled by the enemy; (b) medical aircraft operating in and over areas physically controlled by the enemy, as well as in and over those parts of the contact zone which are physically controlled by friendly forces or the physical control of which is not clearly established. This explains why Rule 75 indicates that specific protection from attack is "subject to the Rules of this Section of the Manual".

3. Rule 75 applies also in non-international armed conflict.

76. (a) A medical aircraft must be clearly marked with a distinctive emblem as provided by the law of international armed conflict, i.e., the Red Cross, the Red Crescent or the Red Crystal, together with its national colours, on its lower, upper and lateral surfaces.

1. Unlike the second sentence of Rule 72 (a), which applies to medical transports in general and which says that they "ought to be clearly marked" with the distinctive emblem, Rule 76 (a) – applicable only to medical aircraft – reflects an outright obligation to have such markings. The obligation is based on the second paragraph of Art. 36 of GC/I[408] and on Art. 18 (4) of AP/I,[409] both of which use the expression "shall".

[408] Second para. of Art. 36 of GC/I: "They shall bear, clearly marked, the distinctive emblem prescribed in Article 38, together with their national colours on their lower, upper and lateral surfaces. They shall be provided with any other markings or means of identification that may be agreed upon between the belligerents upon the outbreak or during the course of hostilities."

[409] Art. 18 (4) AP/I: "With the consent of the competent authority, medical units and transports shall be marked by the distinctive emblem. The ships and craft referred to in Article 22 of this Protocol shall be marked in accordance with the provisions of the Second Convention."

This obligation is also found in Para. 175 of the SRM/ACS: "Medical aircraft shall be clearly marked with the emblem of the red cross or red crescent, together with their national colours, on their lower, upper and lateral surfaces. Medical aircraft are encouraged to implement the other means of identification set out in Annex I of Additional Protocol I of 1977 at all times. Aircraft chartered by the International Committee of the Red Cross may use the same means of identification as medical aircraft. Temporary

A special dispensation is created in Rule 76 (c) for temporary medical aircraft which cannot be marked with the distinctive emblem.

2. The 1929 Geneva Convention[410] originally required that medical aircraft be painted white, an obligation that was neither reproduced in the 1949 text of GC/I nor in AP/I of 1977. In addition, the 1929 Geneva Convention required that the identification appear "side by side" rather than "together with" the national colours on the aircraft's lower and upper surfaces. In 1949, GC/I also added the requirement that the medical aircraft be marked on its lateral surfaces.

3. Concerning the Red Cross, Red Crescent and Red Crystal distinctive emblems, see Commentary on Rule 72.

4. Rule 76 (a) applies also in non-international armed conflict.

(b) A medical aircraft ought to use additional means of identification where appropriate.

1. The possibility of adding to the distinctive emblem other means of identification dates back to the second paragraph of Art. 36 of GC/I,[411] which allowed the Parties to enter into *ad hoc* agreements on this issue.

2. Art. 18 (5) of AP/I[412] authorizes the use of several additional means of identification, besides the use of the distinctive emblem. The additional means of identification referred to are set out in Annex I of AP/I. These include a flashing blue light that no other aircraft is allowed to use; a radio message preceded by a distinctive priority (urgency) signal earmarked for all medical transports. This development arose from concerns that solely having the distinctive emblem painted on an aircraft would provide it with insufficient protection in circumstances of modern warfare that enable "beyond visual range" targeting.

medical aircraft which cannot, either for lack of time or because of their characteristics, be marked with the distinctive emblem should use the most effective means of identification available."

410 The second paragraph of Art. 18 of the 1929 Geneva Convention for the Amelioration of the Condition of the Wounded and Sick in Armies in the Field: "They shall be painted white and shall bear, clearly marked, the distinctive emblem prescribed in Article 19, side by side with their national colours, on their lower and upper surfaces."

411 Second paragraph of Art. 36 of GC/I, see fn. 408.

412 Art. 18 (5) of AP/I: "In addition to the distinctive emblem, a Party to the conflict may, as provided in Chapter III of Annex I to this Protocol, authorize the use of distinctive signals to identify medical units and transports. Exceptionally, in the special cases covered in that Chapter, medical transports may use distinctive signals without displaying the distinctive emblem."

3. It is envisaged that, in the future, an automatic radio identification system will be developed using a transponder with digital selective calling techniques, and a Secondary Surveillance Radar (SSR) system identifying and following the course of medical aircraft.

4. Belligerents Parties, by special agreement among them, may also establish for their use complementary light, radio, and electronic means of identification of medical aircraft.

5. Rule 76 (b) applies also in non-international armed conflict.

> (c) **A temporary medical aircraft which cannot – either for lack of time or because of its characteristics – be marked with the distinctive emblem, ought to use the most effective means of identification available.**

1. This Rule restates the substance of the last sentence of Para. 175 of the SRM/ACS.[413] Both Rule 76 (c) and Para. 175 of the SRM/ACS are based to a large degree on Art. 6 (4) of Annex I to AP/I (as amended in 1993).[414]

2. Rule 76 (c) takes account of the fact that some States cannot afford aircraft to be assigned exclusively for medical missions on a permanent basis.[415] Another reason why temporary aircraft are resorted to lies in the fact that a permanent medical aircraft may not be available the moment it is needed.

3. Irrespective of marking, a medical aircraft assigned temporarily to medical tasks must always serve these tasks exclusively (see Rule 1 (u) and, in particular, paragraphs 7–9 of the Commentary on Rule 1 (u)).

4. The phrase "because of its characteristics" refers to configurations which may preclude proper marking of a temporary medical aircraft with a distinctive emblem, e.g., a glass bubble or other structures of a helicopter that do not offer a suitable surface for the markings.

5. According to Rule 76 (c), a temporary medical aircraft which cannot be marked with the distinctive emblem ought to use "the most

[413] Para. 175 of the SRM/ACS, see fn. 409.

[414] Art. 6 (4) of Annex I (to the Protocol I): "Temporary medical aircraft which cannot, either for lack of time or because of their characteristics, be marked with the distinctive emblem, may use the distinctive signals authorized in this Chapter."

[415] Para. 175.1 of the Commentary to the SRM/ACS: "The provision authorising the assignment of aircraft temporarily to medical missions was inserted to assist States who cannot procure aircraft, particularly helicopters, exclusively for medical tasks. However, aircraft temporarily assigned to medical missions must comply with all the provisions pertaining to medical aircraft while performing that mission."

effective means of identification available". For means of identification to be effective, however, the enemy may have to be familiarized with them in advance.

6. Rule 76 (c) applies also in non-international armed conflict.

(d) Means of identification are intended only to facilitate identification and do not, of themselves, confer protected status.

1. Specific protection is conferred on a medical aircraft because of its status as such, and not because of any distinctive emblem with which it is marked. The distinctive emblem is intended only to facilitate recognition of the medical aircraft for what it is. Specific protection must be conferred on a medical aircraft as soon as it is identified as such, even if the medical aircraft does not display the distinctive emblem and employs no additional means of identification. In this respect, see Rule 72 (c) and Rule 72 (d).

2. Specific protection must be granted not only to medical aircraft used by Belligerent Parties, but also to those used by the ICRC.[416] The latter may use the same means of identification.

3. The improper use of the Red Cross, the Red Crescent or the Red Crystal on any aircraft is prohibited at all times (see Rule 112 (a)).

4. Rule 76 (d) applies also in non-international armed conflict.

77. In and over areas controlled by friendly forces, the specific protection of medical aircraft of a Belligerent Party is not dependent on the consent of the enemy.

1. The first paragraph of Art. 18 of the 1929 Geneva Convention[417] provided for the protection of medical aircraft, but the third paragraph of the same provision cautioned that "[i]n the absence of special and express permission, flying over the firing line, and over the zone situated in front of clearing or dressing stations, and generally over all enemy territory or territory occupied by the enemy, is prohibited." Thus, any overflight across these areas was subject to a special and express permission. The formulation used in 1949 in the first paragraph of Art. 36 of GC/I[418] is

[416] Para. 175 of the SRM/ACS, see fn. 409.

[417] First paragraph of Art. 18 of the 1929 Convention for the Amelioration of the Condition of the Wounded and Sick in Armies in the Field: "Aircraft used as means of medical transport shall enjoy the protection of the Convention during the period in which they are reserved exclusively for the evacuation of wounded and sick and the transport of medical personnel and material."

[418] First paragraph of Art. 36 of GC/I: "Medical aircraft, that is to say, aircraft exclusively employed for the removal of wounded and sick and for the transport of medical personnel

less liberal – making any activity of a medical aircraft (irrespective of the zone of operation) dependent on an agreement between the Belligerent Parties.

2. AP/I introduced different legal regimes of protection depending on the location of the medical aircraft and set out three different zones: (i) Art. 25 of AP/I[419] deals with medical aircraft in and over land areas under the physical control of friendly forces and areas not controlled by the enemy; (ii) Art. 26 of AP/I[420] deals with medical aircraft in and over those parts of the contact zone controlled by friendly forces or where control is not clearly established; and (iii) Art. 27 of AP/I[421] deals with medical aircraft over areas controlled by the enemy. The language of Rule 77 is similar to that of Art. 25 of AP/I.

and equipment, shall not be attacked, but shall be respected by the belligerents, while flying at heights, times and on routes specifically agreed upon between the belligerents concerned".

419 Art. 25 of AP/I ("Medical aircraft in areas not controlled by an adverse Party"): "In and over land areas physically controlled by friendly forces, or in and over sea areas not physically controlled by an adverse Party, the respect and protection of medical aircraft of a Party to the conflict is not dependent on any agreement with an adverse Party. For greater safety, however, a Party to the conflict operating its medical aircraft in these areas may notify the adverse Party, as provided in Article 29, in particular when such aircraft are making flights bringing them within range of surface-to-air weapons systems of the adverse Party."

420 Art. 26 of AP/I ("Medical aircraft in contact or similar zones"): "(1) In and over those parts of the contact zone which are physically controlled by friendly forces and in and over those areas the physical control of which is not clearly established, protection for medical aircraft can be fully effective only by prior agreement between the competent military authorities of the Parties to the conflict, as provided for in Article 29. Although, in the absence of such an agreement, medical aircraft operate at their own risk, they shall nevertheless be respected after they have been recognized as such. (2) 'Contact zone' means any area on land where the forward elements of opposing forces are in contact with each other, especially where they are exposed to direct fire from the ground."

421 Art. 27 of AP/I ("Medical aircraft in areas controlled by an adverse Party"): "(1) The medical aircraft of a Party to the conflict shall continue to be protected while flying over land or sea areas physically controlled by an adverse Party, provided that prior agreement to such flights has been obtained from the competent authority of that adverse Party. (2) A medical aircraft which flies over an area physically controlled by an adverse Party without, or in deviation from the terms of, an agreement provided for in paragraph 1, either through navigational error or because of an emergency affecting the safety of the flight, shall make every effort to identify itself and to inform the adverse Party of the circumstances. As soon as such medical aircraft has been recognized by the adverse Party, that Party shall make all reasonable efforts to give the order to land or to alight on water, referred to in Article 30, paragraph 1, or to take other measures to safeguard its own interests, and, in either case, to allow the aircraft time for compliance, before resorting to an attack against the aircraft."

3. The protection of medical aircraft under Rule 77 is wholly independent of the consent of the enemy. This is different from areas covered by Rule 78 (a), where medical aircraft not obtaining prior consent fly at their own risk.

4. Belligerent Parties are nevertheless encouraged to notify each other of medical flights.[422] When given, notification ought to be accompanied by a detailed flight plan (see the second sentence of Rule 78 (b)).

5. The phrase "in and over areas" indicates that the specific protection of medical aircraft exists both while they are in flight and on the ground. Although in Rule 77 only "areas controlled by friendly forces" are mentioned explicitly, it applies also in and over sea areas not physically controlled by the enemy.

6. The notion of control in this context does not refer to the sovereignty of a Belligerent Party over a territory, but rather to its actual domination; in other words, the fact that presence of its armed forces on the territory makes it possible to ensure the safety of the medical aircraft.

7. The term "friendly forces" covers the armed forces of both the Belligerent Party and its co-belligerents.

8. Rule 77 applies also in non-international armed conflict.

78. (a) In and over areas physically controlled by the enemy, as well as in and over those parts of the contact zone which are physically controlled by friendly forces or the physical control of which is not clearly established, the protection of medical aircraft can be fully effective only by virtue of prior consent obtained from the enemy. Although, in the absence of such consent, medical aircraft in the contact zone operate at their own risk, they must nevertheless be respected once they have been identified as such.

1. This Rule was engendered by discussions by the Group of Experts concerning the scope and application of Art. 26 (1)[423] and Art. 27 (1)

[422] Second sentence of Art. 25 of AP/I, see fn. 419.

See also Para. 177 of the SRM/ACS: "Parties to the conflict are encouraged to notify medical flights and conclude agreements at all times, especially in areas where control by any party to the conflict is not clearly established. When such an agreement is concluded, it shall specify the altitudes, times and routes for safe operation and should include means of identification and communications."

[423] Art. 26 (1) of AP/I, see fn. 420.

of AP/I.[424] Rule 78 (a), as a practical matter, applies the same principle in and over areas physically controlled by the enemy as well as in and over the contact zone, whereas both Art. 26 (1) of AP/I and Art. 27 (1) of AP/I distinguish between these two categories. However, the distinction between areas physically controlled by the enemy and the contact zone may be blurred by the pace of ground and air operations. A majority of the Group of Experts considered that Belligerent Parties must take this factor into consideration when contemplating operation of medical aircraft over such areas in order to assist in their protection.

2. The purpose of Rule 78 (a) is to clarify that Belligerent Parties may not be blamed if a medical aircraft – not identified as such and flying without prior agreement in these defined areas – is attacked by mistake. It ought to be emphasized, however, that medical aircraft operating in and over these areas without consent do not lose their specific protection, but rather risk being shot down if they are not identified as medical aircraft.

3. A medical aircraft which – either through navigational error or because of an emergency affecting the safety of the flight – enters an area defined in Rule 78 (a) without (or in deviation from the terms of) an agreement, must make every effort to identify itself, to inform the enemy of the circumstances, and to indicate its submission to the enemy air traffic instructions. Once a medical aircraft has been identified as such, the enemy must not attack it, although it is entitled to order the aircraft to divert, to proceed along a specific route, or to land for inspection. Non-compliance with the order may subject the aircraft to attack. However, sufficient time must be allowed to enable the aircraft to comply with the order before it is attacked (see Art. 27 (2) of AP/I).[425]

4. The contact zone, as defined in Art. 26 (2) of AP/I,[426] means any area on land where the forward elements of opposing forces are in contact with each other, especially where they are exposed to direct fire from the ground. The phrase direct fire from the ground excludes fire coming from aircraft.

5. Rule 78 (a) applies to "those parts of the contact zone which are physically controlled by friendly forces or the physical control of which

[424] Art. 27 (1) of AP/I, see fn. 421.
[425] Art. 27 (2) of AP/I, see fn. 421.
[426] Art. 26 (2) of AP/I, see fn. 420.

is not clearly established". Control over the contact zone is not clearly established where, e.g., the opposing forces may be entangled as a result of a series of assaults and repulses.

6. As explained in paragraph 5 of the Commentary on Rule 77, the phrase "in and over areas" indicates that the special protection of medical aircraft exists both while they are in flight and on the ground.

7. Rule 78 (a) applies also in non-international armed conflict.

> **(b) The consent of the enemy as per paragraph (a) has to be sought in advance (or immediately prior to the commencement of the operation of a medical aircraft) by a Belligerent Party employing a medical aircraft. The request for consent ought to be accompanied by a detailed flight plan (as set forth in the International Civil Aviation Organization Flight Plan form).**

1. The requirement that the enemy's consent has to be sought in advance is implicit in the reference to "prior agreement" which is made in Art. 29 (1) of AP/I.[427] The reference to the ICAO flight plan is derived from Art. 13 of Annex I to AP/I (as amended in 1993).[428]

2. The consequence of a failure to obtain the enemy's consent is that the medical aircraft would fly at its own risk for as long as it is not identified as such.

3. The ICAO Flight Plan form includes fields on aircraft identification, markings, routes and other parameters.[429] It was therefore felt sufficient to require here the submission of a detailed ICAO Flight Plan, without adding other details (as is done in Art. 29 (1) of AP/I). No doubt, the Flight Plan filed ought to be as precise as possible, and it ought to include

[427] Art. 29 (1) of AP/I ("Notifications and agreements concerning medical aircraft"): "Notifications under Article 25, or requests for prior agreement under Articles 26, 27, 28 (paragraph 4), or 31 shall state the proposed number of medical aircraft, their flight plans and means of identification, and shall be understood to mean that every flight will be carried out in compliance with Article 28."

[428] Art. 13 of Annex I to AP/I ("Flight plans"): "The agreements and notifications relating to flight plans provided for in Article 29 of the Protocol shall as far as possible be formulated in accordance with procedures laid down by the International Civil Aviation Organization."

[429] ICAO, Rules of the Air, Annex 2 to the Chicago Convention on International Civil Aviation, Chapter 3.3 on "flight plans".

departure and arrival times, flight path, and altitude. Other elements may be added.

4. Rule 78 (b) applies also in non-international armed conflict.

(c) **When given, consent must be express. Consent for activities consistent with the aircraft's medical status, e.g., evacuation of the wounded, sick or shipwrecked, and transportation of medical personnel or material, ought not to be refused, unless on reasonable grounds.**

1. The Belligerent Party receiving a request for consent ought to respond as quickly as possible. It may give a positive or negative response. It may also propose alternative and/or additional conditions.

2. Rule 78 (c) makes it clear that Belligerent Parties may not refuse consent except on reasonable grounds. This is due to the paramount role that medical aircraft play in rescuing the wounded and sick, and the considerable risk that they would run by operating without consent. In this context, reasonable grounds for refusal of consent ought to be interpreted as imperative reasons, particularly of a security nature, preventing a medical flight over an area.

3. The notion of "activities consistent with the aircraft's medical status" means normal medical functions. Apart from "acts harmful to the enemy" (see Rule 83), these normal functions exclude searching for the wounded and sick as well as combat search-and-rescue operations (see Rule 86).

4. Rule 78 (c) applies also in non-international armed conflict.

79. Any conditions of consent obtained from the enemy for the protection of a medical aircraft must be adhered to strictly.

1. The obligation to adhere to conditions of consent is a logical corollary to Rule 78. Rule 79 is intended to provide the clarity necessary for a well-functioning regime of protection.

2. Any medical aircraft departing from the conditions of consent obtained from the enemy flies at its own risk as long as it has not been identified as a medical aircraft (second sentence of Rule 78 (a)).

3. The obligation to comply with the conditions of consent set by the enemy is far wider than the prohibition imposed on medical aircraft not to engage in acts harmful to the enemy (see Rule 83). The enemy's consent

may be contingent on technical matters such as a specific route or altitude. Even such technical conditions must be strictly adhered to.

4. Rule 79 applies also in non-international armed conflict.

80. (a) While flying over an area covered in Rule 78 (a), medical aircraft may be ordered to land or to alight on water to permit inspection. Medical aircraft must obey any such order.

1. This Rule is based on Art. 30 (1) AP/I[430] and on Para. 180 of the SRM/ACS[431], except that – as noted in the Commentary on Rule 78 (a) – this Manual applies the same legal regime to flights by medical aircraft over areas physically controlled by the enemy as well as those over parts of the contact zone which are physically controlled by friendly forces or the physical control of which is not clearly established.

2. A medical aircraft may be ordered to land, even if the flight has the consent of the enemy (and, *a fortiori*, if it does not). An order to land must be obeyed. Otherwise, it can result in the medical aircraft being forced to land and, as a last resort, being attacked.

3. When ordered to land, all steps must be taken to ensure that the medical aircraft can land under adequate safety conditions. "Alight[ing] on water" refers only to hydroplanes, amphibious aircraft, or other fixed or rotary-winged aircraft capable of a water landing.

4. Medical aircraft may only be ordered to land or alight on water for the clearly specified reason of permitting inspection. The inspection has to be commenced without delay and be conducted expeditiously. This obligation to proceed quickly is due to the fact that the state of health of the wounded and sick aboard the aircraft must not be adversely affected by the inspection. For the same reason, the inspecting Belligerent Party must not remove the wounded and sick from the aircraft unless this is

[430] Art. 30 (1) of AP/I: "Medical aircraft flying over areas which are physically controlled by an adverse Party, or over areas the physical control of which is not clearly established, may be ordered to land or to alight on water, as appropriate, to permit inspection in accordance with the following paragraphs. Medical aircraft shall obey any such order."

[431] Para. 180 of the SRM/ACS: "Medical aircraft flying over areas which are physically controlled by the opposing belligerent, or over areas the physical control of which is not clearly established, may be ordered to land to permit inspection. Medical aircraft shall obey any such order."

essential for the inspection.[432] Shipwrecked who are not wounded or sick may be removed from the aircraft. If they are combatants, they can be detained as POWs.

5. Rule 80 (a) applies also in non-international armed conflict.

(b) If inspection reveals that the medical aircraft has been engaged in activities consistent with its medical status, it must be authorized to continue its flight without delay.

1. This Rule is derived from Art. 30 (3) of AP/I.[433]

2. On the notion of "activities consistent with the aircraft's medical status", see paragraph 3 of the Commentary on Rule 78 (c).

3. Rule 80 (b) applies also in non-international armed conflict.

(c) However, if the medical aircraft has engaged in activities inconsistent with its medical status, or if it has flown without or in breach of a prior agreement, then it may be seized. Its occupants must then be treated in accordance with the relevant rules of the law of international armed conflict.

1. Rule 80 (c) is derived from Art. 30 (4) of AP/I.[434]

2. The decision to seize a medical aircraft ought to be taken with due consideration of the reasons for the aircraft's divergence from activities

[432] Art. 30 (2) of AP/I: "If such an aircraft lands or alights on water, whether ordered to do so or for other reasons, it may be subjected to inspection solely to determine the matters referred to in paragraphs 3 and 4. Any such inspection shall be commenced without delay and shall be conducted expeditiously. The inspecting Party shall not require the wounded and sick to be removed from the aircraft unless their removal is essential for the inspection. That Party shall in any event ensure that the condition of the wounded and sick is not adversely affected by the inspection or by the removal."

[433] Art. 30 (3) of AP/I: "If the inspection discloses that the aircraft: (a) is a medical aircraft within the meaning of Article 8, sub-paragraph (j), (b) is not in violation of the conditions prescribed in Article 28, and (c) has not flown without or in breach of a prior agreement where such agreement is required, the aircraft and those of its occupants who belong to the adverse Party or to a neutral or other State not a Party to the conflict shall be authorized to continue the flight without delay."

[434] Art. 30 (4) of AP/I: "If the inspection discloses that the aircraft: (a) is not a medical aircraft within the meaning of Article 8, sub-paragraph (j), (b) is in violation of the conditions prescribed in Article 28, or (c) has flown without or in breach of a prior agreement where such agreement is required, the aircraft may be seized. Its occupants shall be treated in conformity with the relevant provisions of the Conventions and of this Protocol. Any aircraft seized which had been assigned as a permanent medical aircraft may be used thereafter only as a medical aircraft."

consistent with its medical status or of the reasons why the aircraft was flying without or in breach of a prior agreement where such agreement is required. For example, a Belligerent Party ought to carefully consider authorizing a medical aircraft to continue its flight if it has not wilfully committed a breach, but was the victim of damage, technical problems or adverse weather conditions.

3. If seizure of medical aircraft takes place, the occupants (a term that is broad enough to cover different categories of persons) must be treated in accordance with the law of international armed conflict. Thus, the wounded and sick must get proper medical treatment, and medical personnel cannot be detained as POWs. Such medical personnel may be, however, retained (see paragraph 4 of the Commentary on Rule 87).[435] However, if a Belligerent Party is unable to ensure medical treatment as required by the condition of the wounded and sick on board a medical aircraft, it may have to allow the medical aircraft to continue on its way.

[435] Art. 33 of GC/III: "Members of the medical personnel and chaplains while retained by the Detaining Power with a view to assisting prisoners of war, shall not be considered as prisoners of war. They shall, however, receive as a minimum the benefits and protection of the present Convention, and shall also be granted all facilities necessary to provide for the medical care of, and religious ministration to prisoners of war. They shall continue to exercise their medical and spiritual functions for the benefit of prisoners of war, preferably those belonging to the armed forces upon which they depend, within the scope of the military laws and regulations of the Detaining Power and under the control of its competent services, in accordance with their professional etiquette. They shall also benefit by the following facilities in the exercise of their medical or spiritual functions: (a) They shall be authorized to visit periodically prisoners of war situated in working detachments or in hospitals outside the camp. For this purpose, the Detaining Power shall place at their disposal the necessary means of transport. (b) The senior medical officer in each camp shall be responsible to the camp military authorities for everything connected with the activities of retained medical personnel. For this purpose, Parties to the conflict shall agree at the outbreak of hostilities on the subject of the corresponding ranks of the medical personnel, including that of societies mentioned in Article 26 of the Geneva Convention for the Amelioration of the Condition of the Wounded and Sick in Armed Forces in the Field of August 12, 1949. This senior medical officer, as well as chaplains, shall have the right to deal with the competent authorities of the camp on all questions relating to their duties. Such authorities shall afford them all necessary facilities for correspondence relating to these questions. (c) Although they shall be subject to the internal discipline of the camp in which they are retained, such personnel may not be compelled to carry out any work other than that concerned with their medical or religious duties. During hostilities, the Parties to the conflict shall agree concerning the possible relief of retained personnel and shall settle the procedure to be followed. None of the preceding provisions shall relieve the Detaining Power of its obligations with regard to prisoners of war from the medical or spiritual point of view."

4. There is no State practice concerning any requirement of prize proceedings with respect to seized medical aircraft.

5. Rule 80 (c) applies also in non-international armed conflict, except that – for the purposes of this Manual – "seizure" is a construct of the law of international armed conflict. In a non-international armed conflict, the fate of the medical aircraft engaged in activities inconsistent with its medical status, will be based on the domestic legal system.

(d) Any aircraft seized which had been assigned as a permanent medical aircraft may be used thereafter only as a medical aircraft.

1. This Rule is based on Art. 30 (4) of AP/I.[436]

2. If a permanent medical aircraft is seized by the enemy, it may not be used for purposes other than medical ones. This prohibition lasts until the end of the armed conflict.

3. If the inspection discloses that the aircraft is only a temporary medical aircraft, it may then be used for other purposes provided that any distinctive emblem is removed and any additional means of identification is no longer used.

4. Rule 80 (d) does not apply in non-international armed conflict (but see paragraph 5 of the Commentary on Rule 80 (c)).

81. A medical aircraft must not possess or employ equipment to collect or transmit intelligence harmful to the enemy. It may, however, be equipped with encrypted communications equipment intended solely for navigation, identification and communication consistent with the execution of its humanitarian mission.

1. This Rule is partly based on Art. 28 (2) of AP/I, which stipulates that medical aircraft must not be used to collect or transmit intelligence data and must not carry any equipment intended for such purposes.[437]

2. Rule 81 prohibits both the possession and the use of equipment to collect or transmit intelligence harmful to the enemy ("possess or employ").

[436] Art. 30 (4) of AP/I, see fn. 434.

[437] Art. 28 (2) of AP/I: "Medical aircraft shall not be used to collect or transmit intelligence data and shall not carry any equipment intended for such purposes. They are prohibited from carrying any persons or cargo not included within the definition in Article 8, sub-paragraph (f). The carrying on board of the personal effects of the occupants or of equipment intended solely to facilitate navigation, communication or identification shall not be considered as prohibited."

The mere possession of equipment for the purpose of collecting or transmitting intelligence harmful to the enemy is prohibited because it is difficult to prove in practice that an aircraft actually collected or transmitted such information.

3. Several declarations made upon ratification of AP/I by Contracting Parties (e.g., Ireland and the United Kingdom) were to the effect that Art. 28 (2) of AP/I does not preclude the presence on board of communications equipment and encryption materials or the use thereof solely to facilitate navigation, identification or communication in support of medical transportation.[438]

4. Furthermore, the UK Manual expressly mentions (Para. 12.120.1) that the presence of encryption equipment in a medical aircraft is not prohibited: "The *presence* of communications and encryption equipment in an aircraft operating as a medical aircraft is not precluded. Nor is the *use* of such equipment wholly to facilitate navigation, identification, and communication in support of the operation of medical aircraft. Neither such presence nor such use negates the protection to which the medical aircraft is entitled." A majority of the Group of Experts held that this permission is in conformity with contemporary State practice. Of course, the encryption equipment must not be used in any circumstances to transmit intelligence data harmful to the enemy.

5. Rule 81 applies also in non-international armed conflict.

82. A medical aircraft may be equipped with deflective means of defence (such as chaff or flares) and carry light individual weapons necessary to protect the aircraft, the medical personnel and the wounded, sick or shipwrecked on board. Carrying of the individual weapons of the wounded, sick or shipwrecked during their evacuation does not entail loss of protection.

1. The text of Rule 82 is largely consistent with the language of Art. 28 (3) of AP/I.[439] A notable point of divergence is that – in addition to

[438] E.g., statement made by the UK upon ratification of AP/I in respect of Art. 28 (2) of AP/I: "Given the practical need to make use of non-dedicated aircraft for medical evacuation purposes, the UK does not interpret this paragraph as precluding the presence on board of communications equipment and encryption materials or the use thereof solely to facilitate navigation, identification or communication in support of medical transportation as defined in Art. 8 (f)." Ireland made an identical declaration.

[439] Art. 28 (3) of AP/I: "Medical aircraft shall not carry any armament except small arms and ammunition taken from the wounded, sick and shipwrecked on board and not yet handed to the proper service, and such light individual weapons as may be necessary to

permitting light individual weapons – Rule 82 allows medical aircraft to carry deflective means of defence. This authorization of deflective means of defence was included in Para. 170 of the SRM/ACS regulating hospital ships.[440] Even though there is no similar provision in the SRM/ACS regarding medical aircraft, a majority of the Group of Experts believed that it was a logical step to apply by analogy the same regime to medical aircraft, since there are no significant differences between hospital ships and medical aircraft in this context.

2. When the enemy's consent for the flight of a medical aircraft is required (see Rule 78), the enemy ought to be informed of the presence on board of deflective means of defence.

3. Medical aircraft may carry light individual weapons collected from the wounded, sick and shipwrecked, and not yet handed over to the proper service authority. It is also authorized to carry light individual weapons necessary to enable medical personnel on the medical aircraft to defend themselves and the wounded, sick and shipwrecked in their charge.

4. For the meaning of the expression "light individual weapons", see Commentary on Rule 74 (c) (i).

5. Rule 82 ought to be understood as prohibiting medical aircraft from carrying any other armaments. A medical aircraft carrying machine guns or any other heavy weaponry, which may not easily be transported by an individual, forfeits the protection as a medical aircraft and loses the right to display the distinctive emblem. Independently of legal considerations, a machine gun protruding from a helicopter and clearly visible from the ground would cancel out the protection that is sought from the use of the distinctive emblem because it may be perceived as an offensive aircraft. In fact, the display of an offensive weapon alongside the protective emblem might weaken the protective effect of the distinctive emblem generally in the entire zone of the conflict.

6. Rule 82 applies also in non-international armed conflict.

enable the medical personnel on board to defend themselves and the wounded, sick and shipwrecked in their charge."

[440] Para. 170 of the SRM/ACS: "Hospital ships may be equipped with purely deflective means of defence, such as chaff and flares. The presence of such equipment should be notified."

83. Subject to Rule 74, a medical aircraft loses its specific protection from attack if it is engaged in acts harmful to the enemy.

1. This Rule is based on Para. 178 of the SRM/ACS.[441] It is a summary of the restrictions posed on operations of medical aircraft by Art. 28 (1) of AP/I.[442]

2. Rule 83 subjects itself to Rule 74, which details the conditions under which medical transports – which include medical aircraft – lose their specific protection from attack. Reference must be especially made to the use of the phrase "acts harmful to the enemy" (see Rule 74 (a)), and to the obligation of issuing warnings (see Rule 74 (b)).

3. Rule 83 applies also in non-international armed conflict.

84. Except by prior agreement with a Neutral, a belligerent medical aircraft must not fly over or land in the territory of that Neutral, unless it is exercising the right of transit passage through straits used for international navigation or the right of archipelagic sea lanes passage.

1. This Rule is based on Art. 31 (1) of AP/I[443] and on Para. 181 of the SRM/ACS.[444] The principle[445] is that prior agreement is required

[441] Para. 178 of the SRM/ACS: "Medical aircraft shall not be used to commit acts harmful to the enemy. They shall not carry any equipment intended for the collection or transmission of intelligence data. They shall not be armed, except for small arms for self-defence, and shall only carry medical personnel and equipment."

[442] Art. 28 (1) of AP/I: "The Parties to the conflict are prohibited from using their medical aircraft to attempt to acquire any military advantage over an adverse Party. The presence of medical aircraft shall not be used in an attempt to render military objectives immune from attack."

[443] Art. 31 (1) of AP/I: "Except by prior agreement, medical aircraft shall not fly over or land in the territory of a neutral or other State not a Party to the conflict. However, with such an agreement, they shall be respected throughout their flight and also for the duration of any calls in the territory. Nevertheless they shall obey any summons to land or to alight on water, as appropriate."

[444] Para. 181 of the SRM/ACS: "Belligerent medical aircraft shall not enter neutral airspace except by prior agreement. When within neutral airspace pursuant to agreement, medical aircraft shall comply with the terms of the agreement. The terms of the agreement may require the aircraft to land for inspection at a designated airport within the neutral State. Should the agreement so require, the inspection and follow-on action shall be conducted in accordance with paragraphs 182–183."

[445] It ought to be noted, however, that Art. 37 of GC/I gave Belligerent Parties the right to let their medical aircraft fly over neutral territory without agreement. The Neutral could only impose conditions on the passage.

for the protection of belligerent medical aircraft in and over neutral territory. There are two exceptions: (i) the right of transit passage over straits used for international navigation (including the approach thereto); and (ii) the right of archipelagic sea lanes passage. These two are found respectively in Art. 38 (1) of UNCLOS[446] and by Art. 53 (1)–(3) of UNCLOS.[447]

2. The agreement referred to in Rule 84 is between one or more Belligerent Party(ies), on the one hand, and the Neutral, on the other, even without the enemy's participation to the agreement.

3. When operating within neutral airspace pursuant to an agreement, belligerent medical aircraft must comply with the terms of the agreement. These terms may require the aircraft to land for inspection at a designated airport within the Neutral.

4. Rule 84 does not apply in non-international armed conflict as the law of neutrality only applies in international armed conflicts.

Paragraph 1 and 2 of Art. 37 of GC/I: "Subject to the provisions of the second paragraph, medical aircraft of Parties to the conflict may fly over the territory of neutral Powers, land on it in case of necessity, or use it as a port of call. They shall give the neutral Powers previous notice of their passage over the said territory and obey all summons to alight, on land or water. They will be immune from attack only when flying on routes, at heights and at times specifically agreed upon between the Parties to the conflict and the neutral Power concerned. The neutral Powers may, however, place conditions or restrictions on the passage or landing of medical aircraft on their territory. Such possible conditions or restrictions shall be applied equally to all Parties to the conflict. . . . "

446 Art. 38 (1) of UNCLOS ("Right of transit passage"): "In straits referred to in article 37, all ships and aircraft enjoy the right of transit passage, which shall not be impeded; except that, if the strait is formed by an island of a State bordering the strait and its mainland, transit passage shall not apply if there exists seaward of the island a route through the high seas or through an exclusive economic zone of similar convenience with respect to navigational and hydrographical characteristics."

447 Art. 53. (1)–3 of UNCLOS ("Right of archipelagic sea lanes passage): "(1) An archipelagic State may designate sea lanes and air routes thereabove, suitable for the continuous and expeditious passage of foreign ships and aircraft through or over its archipelagic waters and the adjacent territorial sea. (2) All ships and aircraft enjoy the right of archipelagic sea lanes passage in such sea lanes and air routes. (3) Archipelagic sea lanes passage means the exercise in accordance with this Convention of the rights of navigation and overflight in the normal mode solely for the purpose of continuous, expeditious and unobstructed transit between one part of the high seas or an exclusive economic zone and another part of the high seas or an exclusive economic zone."

85. (a) Should a belligerent medical aircraft, in the absence of a prior agreement with the Neutral or in deviation from the terms of an agreement, enter the neutral airspace, either through navigational error or because of an emergency affecting the safety of the flight, it must make every effort to give notice and to identify itself. Once the aircraft is recognized as a medical aircraft by the Neutral, it must not be attacked but may be required to land for inspection. Once it has been inspected, and if it is determined in fact to be a medical aircraft, it must be allowed to resume its flight.

1. This Rule summarizes the substance of Art. 31 (2) and Art. 31 (3) of AP/I[448] and is an almost *verbatim* restatement of Para. 182 of the SRM/ACS.[449] It takes due note of the fact that there may be circumstances

[448] Art. 31 of AP/I: "(2) Should a medical aircraft, in the absence of an agreement or in deviation from the terms of an agreement, fly over the territory of a neutral or other State not a Party to the conflict, either through navigational error or because of an emergency affecting the safety of the flight, it shall make every effort to give notice of the flight and to identify itself. As soon as such medical aircraft is recognized, that State shall make all reasonable efforts to give the order to land or to alight on water referred to in Article 30, paragraph 1, or to take other measures to safeguard its own interests, and, in either case, to allow the aircraft time for compliance, before resorting to an attack against the aircraft. (3) If a medical aircraft, either by agreement or in the circumstances mentioned in paragraph 2, lands or alights on water in the territory of a neutral or other State not Party to the conflict, whether ordered to do so or for other reasons, the aircraft shall be subject to inspection for the purposes of determining whether it is in fact a medical aircraft. The inspection shall be commenced without delay and shall be conducted expeditiously. The inspecting Party shall not require the wounded and sick of the Party operating the aircraft to be removed from it unless their removal is essential for the inspection. The inspecting Party shall in any event ensure that the condition of the wounded and sick is not adversely affected by the inspection or the removal. If the inspection discloses that the aircraft is in fact a medical aircraft, the aircraft with its occupants, other than those who must be detained in accordance with the rules of international law applicable in armed conflict, shall be allowed to resume its flight, and reasonable facilities shall be given for the continuation of the flight. If the inspection discloses that the aircraft is not a medical aircraft, it shall be seized and the occupants treated in accordance with paragraph 4."

[449] Para. 182 of the SRM/ACS: "Should a medical aircraft, in the absence of an agreement or in deviation from the terms of an agreement, enter neutral airspace, either through navigational error or because of an emergency affecting the safety of the flight, it shall make every effort to give notice and to identify itself. Once the aircraft is recognized as a medical aircraft by the neutral State, it shall not be attacked but may be required to land for inspection. Once it has been inspected, and if it is determined in fact to be a medical aircraft, it shall be allowed to resume its flight."

where a Belligerent Party did not conclude an agreement with a Neutral, because its medical aircraft was never intended to enter the neutral airspace. There are, however, only two possible ways of unexpected entry which bring Rule 85 (a) into application: (i) navigational error; or (ii) an emergency affecting the safety of the flight.

2. In case the Neutral intercepts or diverts the belligerent medical aircraft, it ought – as far as military considerations permit – to observe the guidance in the Manual Concerning Interception of Civil Aircraft issued by ICAO.[450]

3. Art. 31 (3) of AP/I provides that "inspection shall be commenced without delay and shall be conducted expeditiously. The inspecting Party shall not require the wounded and sick of the Party operating the aircraft to be removed from it unless their removal is essential for the inspection. The inspecting Party shall in any event ensure that the condition of the wounded and sick is not adversely affected by the inspection or the removal."

4. The determination of whether or not an aircraft is in fact a medical aircraft needs to be based on Rule 1 (u), i.e., the aircraft needs to be exclusively assigned to "aerial transportation or treatment of wounded, sick, or shipwrecked persons, and/or the transport of medical personnel and medical equipment or supplies."

5. If it turns out on inspection that the aircraft is a belligerent medical aircraft, the resumption of the flight must be permitted and reasonable facilities must be given for the continuation of the flight. All the occupants of medical aircraft are entitled to resume their flight including wounded, sick, and shipwrecked military personnel. See Art. 40 of GC/II[451] and Art.

[450] Para. 182.1 of the Commentary on the SRM/ACS: "Interception and diversion for landing should follow ICAO procedures."

[451] Art. 40 of GC/II ("Medical transports"): "Subject to the provisions of the second paragraph, medical aircraft of Parties to the conflict may fly over the territory of neutral Powers, land thereon in case of necessity, or use it as a port of call. They shall give neutral Powers prior notice of their passage over the said territory, and obey every summons to alight, on land or water. They will be immune from attack only when flying on routes, at heights and at times specifically agreed upon between the Parties to the conflict and the neutral Power concerned.

The neutral Powers may, however, place conditions or restrictions on the passage or landing of medical aircraft on their territory. Such possible conditions or restrictions shall be applied equally to all Parties to the conflict.

Unless otherwise agreed between the neutral Powers and the Parties to the conflict, the wounded, sick or shipwrecked who are disembarked with the consent of the local authorities on neutral territory by medical aircraft shall be detained by the neutral Power,

31 (3) of AP/I[452] (both GC/II and AP/I for shipwrecked, wounded, and sick).

6. If wounded, sick, or shipwrecked combatants are left behind – e.g., because the captain of the medical aircraft considers the continuation of the flight detrimental to their health – the Neutral must intern them until the end of hostilities, unless otherwise agreed between the Neutral and the Belligerent Parties (that is to say, including the enemy). See the third paragraph of Art. 37 of GC/I[453] (for wounded and sick); the third paragraph of Art. 40 of GC/II;[454] and Art. 31 (4) of AP/I.[455]

7. Rule 85 (a) does not apply in non-international armed conflict since the law of neutrality only applies in international armed conflict.

> **(b) If the inspection reveals that the aircraft is not a medical aircraft, it may be seized. Any combatants on board will be interned by the Neutral in accordance with Rule 170 (c).**

1. This Rule is to a large extent based on the substance of Art. 31 (3)[456] and Art. 31 (4) of AP/I,[457] as well as on Para. 183 of the SRM/ACS.[458]

where so required by international law, in such a manner that they cannot again take part in operations of war. The cost of their accommodation and internment shall be borne by the Power on which they depend."

452 Art. 31 (3) of AP/I, see fn. 448.

453 Third paragraph of Art. 37 of GC/I: "Unless agreed otherwise between the neutral Power and the Parties to the conflict, the wounded and sick who are disembarked, with the consent of the local authorities, on neutral territory by medical aircraft, shall be detained by the neutral Power, where so required by international law, in such a manner that they cannot again take part in operations of war. The cost of their accommodation and internment shall be borne by the Power on which they depend."

454 Third paragraph of Art. 40 of GC/II: "Unless otherwise agreed between the neutral Powers and the Parties to the conflict, the wounded, sick or shipwrecked who are disembarked with the consent of the local authorities on neutral territory by medical aircraft shall be detained by the neutral Power, where so required by international law, in such a manner that they cannot again take part in operations of war. The cost of their accommodation and interment shall be borne by the Power on which they depend. "

455 Art. 31 (4) of AP/I: "The wounded, sick and shipwrecked disembarked, otherwise than temporarily, from a medical aircraft with the consent of the local authorities in the territory of a neutral or other State not a Party to the conflict shall, unless agreed otherwise between that State and the Parties to the conflict, be detained by that State where so required by the rules of international law applicable in armed conflict, in such a manner that they cannot again take part in the hostilities. The cost of hospital treatment and internment shall be borne by the State to which those persons belong."

456 Art. 31 (3) of AP/I, see fn. 448.

457 Art. 31 (4) of AP/I, see fn. 455.

458 Para. 183 of the SRM/ACS: "If the inspection reveals that the aircraft is not a medical aircraft, it may be captured, and the occupants shall, unless agreed otherwise between

2. When an inspection reveals that the aircraft is not a medical aircraft, two separate issues arise: (i) whether the aircraft is to be seized by the Neutral; and (ii) whether any combatants on board are to be interned by the Neutral.

3. The issue of the seizure of such an aircraft by the Neutral is contingent on whether the Neutral and the Belligerent Parties[459] are or are not Contracting Parties to AP/I (see, respectively, paragraph 4 and paragraph 5 of the Commentary on this Rule).

4. If the Neutral and the Belligerent Parties are bound by AP/I, the Neutral must seize the aircraft pursuant to Art. 31 (3) of AP/I, if it is in fact not a medical aircraft.

5. If the Neutral or one of the Belligerent Parties are not bound by AP/I, the Neutral "may" according to Rule 85 (b) seize an aircraft. In case the Neutral is not a Contracting Party to AP/I, and the aircraft turns out to be a belligerent military aircraft, Rule 170 (c) applies. If the aircraft turns out to be a civilian aircraft, a Neutral which is not a Contracting Party to AP/I is at liberty to let it resume its flight.

6. Irrespective of the question whether or not the aircraft is to be seized by the Neutral, there still remains the separate issue as to whether the Neutral is obliged to intern the occupants of an aircraft, which is in fact not a belligerent medical aircraft. Whether or not the aircraft is seized, the Neutral must intern all combatants on board who are not wounded, sick or shipwrecked. This applies primarily to combatants who are capable of engaging in hostilities as soon as they are released.[460] However, wounded, sick, and shipwrecked combatants must also be interned, unless otherwise agreed between the Neutral and the Belligerent Parties.

the neutral State and the parties to the conflict, be detained in the neutral State where so required by the rules of international law applicable in armed conflict, in such a manner that they cannot again take part in the hostilities."

459 Third paragraph of Art. 2 common to the Geneva Conventions: "Although one of the Powers in conflict may not be a party to the present Convention, the Powers who are parties thereto shall remain bound by it in their mutual relations. They shall furthermore be bound by the Convention in relation to the said Power, if the latter accepts and applies the provisions thereof."

460 Art. 11 of the 1907 Hague Convention (V): "A neutral Power which receives on its territory troops belonging to the belligerent armies shall intern them, as far as possible, at a distance from the theatre of war. It may keep them in camps and even confine them in fortresses or in places set apart for this purpose. It shall decide whether officers can be left at liberty on giving their parole not to leave the neutral territory without permission."

7. As far as wounded, sick and shipwrecked combatants are concerned, they must also be interned, unless otherwise agreed between the Neutral and the Belligerent Parties (including the enemy).[461] See the third paragraph of Art. 37 of GC/I[462] and the third paragraph of Art. 40 of GC/II,[463] as well as Art. 31 (4) of AP/I.[464]

8. Rule 85 (b) does not apply in non-international armed conflict, as the law of neutrality only applies in international armed conflict.

86. (a) Search-and-rescue aircraft used to recover military personnel, even if they are not military aircraft, are not entitled to protection.

1. Members of a commando operation or long-range reconnaissance patrols in enemy-held territory, surrounded infantryman, stragglers or aircrews who have been "downed" on territory under the control of the enemy and who have not manifested a wish to surrender are lawful targets. Under the law of international armed conflict, the use of military means to recover and rescue them is a combat activity. The enemy is therefore allowed to attack the rescuers or to impede or prevent their rescue.

2. Search-and-rescue aircraft used to recover military personnel are not entitled to any protection. It is possible that the Belligerent Party launching the search-and-rescue is conducting that operation impartially, i.e., saving also enemy personnel. This does not lend the operation immunity from attack.

461 Art. 14 of the 1907 Hague Convention (V): "A neutral Power may authorize the passage over its territory of the sick and wounded belonging to the belligerent armies, on condition that the trains bringing them shall carry neither personnel nor war material. In such a case, the neutral Power is bound to take whatever measures of safety and control are necessary for the purpose. The sick or wounded brought under these conditions into neutral territory by one of the belligerents, and belonging to the hostile party, must be guarded by the neutral Power so as to ensure their not taking part again in the military operations. The same duty shall devolve on the neutral State with regard to wounded or sick of the other army who may be committed to its care."

Whereas Art. 14 of the 1907 Hague Convention (V) was limited to the wounded and sick, this has now been extended to the shipwrecked. See the third paragraph of Art. 37 of GC/I (see fn. 453); the third paragraph of Art. 40 of GC/II (see fn. 454) and Art. 31 (4) of AP/I (see fn. 456).

462 Third paragraph of Art. 37 of GC/I, see fn. 453.

463 Third paragraph of Art. 40 of GC/II, see fn. 454.

464 Art. 31 (4) of AP/I, see fn. 455.

3. Civilian aircraft used for search-and-rescue operations of civilians (e.g., skiers or mariners), while not enjoying specific protection, are civilian aircraft and therefore enjoy general protection.

4. With regard to wounded, sick and shipwrecked, Belligerent Parties must take all possible measures to search, and collect them (see Rule 16 (a)). However, see also Rule 86 (b).

(b) Medical aircraft must not be used to search for the wounded, sick and shipwrecked within areas of combat operations, unless pursuant to prior consent of the enemy. If medical aircraft nevertheless operate for such purposes they do so at their own risk.

1. This Rule is based on Art. 28 (4) of AP/I.[465]

2. Medical aircraft may be used to search for the wounded, sick and shipwrecked over areas controlled by friendly forces (see Rule 77). During such operations, and as long as they are above such areas, they continue to enjoy the specific protection to which medical aircraft are entitled.

3. The term "areas of combat operations" relates to all areas which are not controlled by friendly forces (see Rule 78 (a)).

4. In such areas, medical aircraft may not be used to search for wounded, sick and shipwrecked, except with the prior consent of the enemy.

5. If medical aircraft are nevertheless used to search for wounded or sick within areas of combat operations without prior agreement with the enemy, they operate at their own risk. In order to avoid this – and taking into account the obligation to search for and collect the wounded, sick or shipwrecked (see Rule 16 (a)) – Belligerent Parties ought to do all they can to reach such agreements.

6. Of course, an agreement to operate medical aircraft in a search-and-rescue operation will be more readily achieved following a specific engagement when search-and- rescue is considered necessary. A speculative search-and-rescue operation, conducted when there are no known casualties, is more likely to be construed as a reconnaissance exercise and an agreement is thus less likely to be achieved.

7. Rule 86 (b) applies also in non-international armed conflict.

[465] Art. 28 (4) of AP/I: "While carrying out the flights referred to in Articles 26 and 27, medical aircraft shall not, except by prior agreement with the adverse Party, be used to search for the wounded, sick and shipwrecked."

87. Without prejudice to the status of medical personnel under the relevant provisions of the law of international armed conflict, members of the crew of medical aircraft must not be captured by the enemy and must be allowed to carry out their mission.

1. Rule 87 is based on the fourth paragraph of Art. 39 of GC/II[466] and on the fifth paragraph of Art. 22 of GC/IV.[467] It is a logical consequence of the obligation to respect and to protect medical personnel and to allow them to carry out their mission (see Rule 70).

2. According to Rule 80 (a), medical aircraft flying over areas physically controlled by the enemy or over the contact zone may be ordered to land or to alight on water to permit inspection. Medical aircraft must obey any such order. However, following inspection, the aircraft may continue its flight with its occupants, if its purely medical nature is confirmed. According to Rule 87, it is prohibited in such circumstances to capture medical personnel which includes crew members, even though the latter do not carry out medical activities.

3. In the case of medical aircraft, the reason why members of the aircrews are covered by the definition of "medical personnel" is even more glaring than in the instance of personnel involved in other medical transports, and this in view of the fact that the medical aircraft's activities are entirely dependent on the operation of professional aviators to move it around. For the definition of medical personnel, see Commentary on Rule 71.

4. Under certain circumstances described in Rule 80 (c), a medical aircraft may be seized. In these circumstances, its occupants must be treated in conformity with the relevant rules of the law of international armed conflict. As a consequence, medical personnel cannot be captured but may be retained insofar as the state of health and the number of POWs require.[468] See also paragraph 3 of the Commentary on Rule 80 (c).

5. The special status of medical personnel insofar as capture is concerned is not applicable in non-international armed conflicts.

466 Fourth paragraph of Art. 39 of GC/II: "Medical aircraft shall obey every summons to alight on land or water. In the event of having thus to alight, the aircraft with its occupants may continue its flight after examination, if any."

467 Fifth paragraph of Art. 22 of GC/IV: "Such aircraft shall obey every summons to land. In the event of a landing thus imposed, the aircraft with its occupants may continue its flight after examination, if any."

468 Art. 33 of GC/III, see fn. 435.

Section M

Specific Protection of the Natural Environment

1. The two principal treaties relevant to this Section are (i) Art. 35 (3) of AP/I and Art. 55 of AP/I; and (ii) the ENMOD Convention.

2. Art. 35 (3) of AP/I reads: "It is prohibited to employ methods or means of warfare which are intended, or may be expected, to cause widespread, long-term and severe damage to the natural environment."

3. Art. 55 of AP/I ("Protection of the natural environment") reads: "1. Care shall be taken in warfare to protect the natural environment against widespread, long-term and severe damage. This protection includes a prohibition of the use of methods or means of warfare which are intended or may be expected to cause such damage to the natural environment and thereby to prejudice the health or survival of the population. 2. Attacks against the natural environment by way of reprisals are prohibited."

4. The ENMOD Convention prohibits the deliberate modification of the natural environment for hostile purposes. In short, it prohibits the use of the modified natural environment itself as a weapon (as opposed to damage to the environment, dealt with in AP/I). According to Art. I (1) of the ENMOD Convention, each Contracting Party "undertakes not to engage in military or any other hostile use of environmental modification techniques having widespread, long-lasting or severe effects as the means of destruction, damage or injury to any other State Party."[469]

[469] See Understanding regarding the terms widespread, long-lasting and severe in the Annex attached to the ENMOD Convention: "It is the understanding of the Committee that, for the purposes of this Convention, the terms 'widespread', 'long-lasting' and 'severe' shall be interpreted as follows: (a) 'widespread': encompassing an area on the scale of several hundred square kilometres; (b) long-lasting: lasting for a period of months, or approximately a season; (c) 'severe': involving serious or significant disruption or harm to human life, natural and economic resources or other assets. It is further understood that the interpretation set forth above is intended exclusively for this Convention and is not intended to prejudice the interpretation of the same or similar terms if used in connexion with any other international agreement."

The term "environmental modification technique" refers to any technique for changing – through the deliberate manipulation of natural processes – the dynamics, composition or structure of the Earth (Art. II of the ENMOD Convention).[470] Phenomena that could be caused by "environmental modification techniques" include earthquakes, tidal waves (tsunamis) or changes in weather patterns.[471] For example, the natural environment could be modified by dropping a powerful bomb into the crater of a volcano or into fragile tectonic plates. The result could be the outbreak of the volcano or an earthquake. A tsunami could be initiated by a powerful explosion below sea level.

5. The Group of Experts was divided whether Art. 35 (3) of AP/I and Art. 55 of AP/I, as well as the ENMOD Convention, are declaratory of customary international law.[472] The majority of the Group of Experts expressed doubts as to whether the treaty provisions on the protection of the natural environment have become part of customary international law.

6. There is no general consensus as to the exact meaning and scope of the term "natural environment". Some scholars prefer a comprehensive approach and tend to equate the natural environment with an "ecosystem". Accordingly, components of the natural environment, such as flora, fauna, the lithosphere or the atmosphere, would only be covered by the term if they interact in a way that they may be considered parts of an interdependent and mutually influencing system of diverse components of the natural environment. By contrast, other scholars are prepared to consider components of the natural environment to be protected by the law of international armed conflict, irrespective of their interdependence with

[470] Art. II of the ENMOD Convention: "As used in Art. I, 'environmental modification techniques' refers to any technique for changing – through the deliberate manipulation of natural processes – the dynamics, composition or structure of the Earth, including its biota, lithosphere, hydrosphere and atmosphere, or of outer space."

[471] See illustrative list of examples in the Annex attached to the ENMOD Convention, containing the Understanding pertaining to Art. II thereof: "earthquakes; tsunamis; an upset in the ecological balance of a region; changes in weather patterns (clouds, precipitation, cyclones of various types, and tornadic storms); changes in climate patterns; changes in ocean currents; changes in the state of the ozone layer; and changes in the state of the ionosphere."

This same list is also explicitly included in Para. 5.28.1. of the UK Manual.

[472] According to the ICRC Customary IHL Study, these provisions of AP/I reflect customary international law (see Rule 45 of the ICRC Customary IHL Study, and the summary of state practice on page 151).

other components. There are, however, common denominators between the two schools of thought. First, there is agreement that the term "natural environment" does not cover man-made components of the environment. Second, according to both positions, an ecosystem, like the Amazon River Basin, always qualifies as "natural environment".

7. Art. 2 (4) of the 1980 Protocol III to the CCW[473] does not protect the "natural environment" as such. That provision merely provides that "it is prohibited to make forests or other kind of plant cover the object of attack by incendiary weapons". In none of these instruments, the phrase "natural environment" is defined, nor is it explained in the travaux préparatoires.

8. In view of the lack of a general consensus on the content and scope of the term "natural environment", the Group of Experts felt unable to provide a definition without running the risk of going beyond its mandate of identifying existing international law.

9. Wanton destruction of the natural environment is clearly prohibited (see Rule 88). What this means is that the natural environment is a civilian object unless and until portions of it constitute a military objective. Thus, if a forest comes under deliberate attack, this must be because, e.g., it conceals an armoured division, and therefore qualifies as a military objective by use. If the same forest is deliberately attacked for no such reason, the attack will be categorized as directed against a civilian object, and hence prohibited as per Rule 11. Similarly, when a military objective is attacked, and expected collateral damage is assessed compared to the anticipated military advantage, the proportionality analysis also needs to take into account the expected collateral damage to the natural environment (see Rule 14).

10. In planning, ordering and executing attacks, Belligerent Parties are under an obligation to take constant care for the natural environment as a civilian object (Rule 30). Especially, they must take all feasible precautions in accordance with Rules 31–35.

11. For the meaning of "specific protection" see the Commentary in the *chapeau* of Section K.

[473] Art. 2 (4) of the 1980 Protocol III to the CCW: "It is prohibited to make forests or other kinds of plant cover the object of attack by incendiary weapons except when such natural elements are used to cover, conceal or camouflage combatants or other military objectives, or are themselves military objectives."

I. General rule

88. The destruction of the natural environment carried out wantonly is prohibited.

1. Despite the lack of a generally recognized definition of the term "natural environment", there is evidence in State practice of the customary character of the prohibition laid down in this Rule.[474] Moreover, the prohibition of wanton destruction of enemy property has been affirmed by Art. 23 (g) of the 1907 Hague Regulations[475] and by Art. 147 of GC/IV.[476] See also Art. 8 (2) (a) (iv) of the Rome Statute of the ICC[477] for international armed conflicts and Art. 8 (2) (e) (xii) of the Rome Statute of the ICC[478] for non-international armed conflicts.

2. "Wanton" means that the destruction is the consequence of a deliberate action taken maliciously. In other words, it is an action that cannot be justified by considerations of imperative military necessity. As an outstanding example, the destruction of an entire ecosystem, like the Amazon River Basin, the Baltic Sea, or the Black Forest, will constitute a violation of Rule 88.

3. The prohibition of wanton attacks against the natural environment ought not to imply that other direct attacks against the natural environment (being a civilian object) are permissible, nor ought it to be inferred

[474] Second sentence of Para. 44 of the SRM/ACS: "Damage to or destruction of the natural environment not justified by military necessity and carried out wantonly is prohibited."
Para. 8.4 of NWP: "Destruction of the natural environment not necessitated by mission accomplishment and carried out wantonly is prohibited."
Para. 12.26 of the UK Manual: "In the conduct of attacks against targets on land, the following rules are of importance: . . . (f) the natural environment is specially protected: see paragraph 5.29."

[475] Art. 23 of 1907 Hague Regulations: "In addition to the prohibitions provided by special Conventions, it is especially forbidden . . . (g) To destroy or seize the enemy's property, unless such destruction or seizure be imperatively demanded by the necessities of war."

[476] Art. 147 of GC/IV includes into the list of grave breaches the "extensive destruction and appropriation of property, not justified by military necessity and carried out unlawfully and wantonly."

[477] Art. 8 (2) (a) (iv) of the Rome Statute of the ICC: "Extensive destruction and appropriation of property not justified by military necessity and carried out unlawfully and wantonly." Similarly, see Art. 8 (2) (b) (xiii).

[478] Art. 8 (2) (e) (xii) of the Rome Statute of the ICC: "Destroying or seizing the property of an adversary unless such destruction or seizure be imperatively demanded by the necessities of the conflict."

that attacks against military objectives expected to cause excessive collateral damage to the natural environment, as compared to the anticipated military advantage, are acceptable. For international armed conflicts, see also Art. 8 (2) (b) (iv) of the Rome Statute of the ICC.[479]

4. It is necessary to distinguish "wanton destruction" from a "scorched earth" strategy. Under AP/I, the latter is lawful only if carried out by a Belligerent Party in defence of its national territory against invasion, within territory under its own control, where required by imperative military necessity (see Art. 54 (5) of AP/I).[480]

5. Rule 88 applies also in non-international armed conflict.

II. Specifics of air or missile operations

89. When planning and conducting air or missile operations, due regard ought to be given to the natural environment.

1. The broad dimensions of the natural environment – as referred to in paragraph 6 of the *chapeau* to this Section – imply that almost any air or missile operation may have some adverse effects on it. Consequently, those who plan and conduct air or missile operations must keep that in mind during targeting analysis.[481] They must give the natural environment due regard and constant care (see paragraph 10 of the Commentary on the *chapeau* of this Section).[482]

2. Rule 89 does not require a prior assessment of all possible environmental impacts of air and missile attacks. Those who plan an attack are

[479] Art. 8 (2) (b) (iv) of the Rome Statute of the ICC, see fn. 58.

[480] Art. 54 (5) of AP/I: "In recognition of the vital requirements of any Party to the conflict in the defence of its national territory against invasion, derogation from the prohibitions contained in paragraph 2 may be made by a Party to the conflict within such territory under its own control where required by imperative military necessity."

[481] This is confirmed by, *inter alia*, the following sentence in Para. 8.4 of NWP ("Environmental considerations"): "Therefore, a commander should consider the environmental damage that will result from an attack on a legitimate military objective as one of the factors during targeting analysis."

[482] In that respect, see Rule 44 of the ICRC Customary IHL Study: "Methods and means of warfare must be employed with due regard to the protection and preservation of the natural environment." In addition, Rule 44 equally asserts that "In the conduct of military operations, all feasible precautions must be taken to avoid, and in any event to minimise, incidental damage to the environment. Lack of scientific certainty as to the effects on the environment of certain military operations does not absolve a party to the conflict from taking such precautions."

obliged to take into account that information on the natural environment that is reasonably available to them at the relevant time of planning. In the present context, the pilot is not usually expected to make such decisions on his own.

3. Some members of the Group of Experts were strongly of the opinion that the protection of the natural environment "must" be taken into account when planning and conducting air or missile attacks. In their view, expected collateral damage to the environment, if excessive, requires that any air or missile attack against lawful targets be aborted. The majority of the Group of Experts reached the conclusion that such a high bar is not mandated by customary international law and that the "due regard" criterion adequately reflects the state of the law of international armed conflict today. Needless to say, the disagreement has far-reaching consequences as far as the use of nuclear weapons is concerned (see the Commentary on Rule 7).

4. Rule 89 applies also in non-international armed conflict.

Section N

Specific Protection of Other Persons and Objects

1. Section N complements Sections K and L dealing with the specific protection granted, respectively, to medical and religious personnel as well as to medical units and transports, on the one hand, and to medical aircraft, on the other. It also complements Section M regarding the specific protection of the natural environment. Section N addresses the specific protection of the following "other persons and objects": civil defence, cultural property, objects indispensable to the survival of the civilian population, and UN personnel, as well as protection by special agreement.

2. Section N does not provide an exhaustive list of provisions applicable to the protection of persons and objects covered, but merely restates the most relevant provisions in the context of air and missile warfare.

3. Works and installations containing dangerous forces also benefit from a specific protection under Art. 56 of AP/I.[483] Consequently, some members of the Group of Experts argued for the inclusion, in Section N, of precise Black-letter Rules concerning the protection of dams, dykes and nuclear electrical generating stations. However, this proposal was rejected by a majority of the Group of Experts, which contested the customary nature of Art. 56 of AP/I and asserted that this provision would only be binding on Contracting Parties to AP/I. As a compromise, Rule 36 was included in Section G ("Precautions in attack"), requiring that "particular care" be taken if works and installations containing dangerous forces (as well as installations located in their vicinity) are attacked. In addition, Rule 99 was incorporated in Section N affirming the possibility of protecting, by special agreement, persons or objects not otherwise covered by this Manual.

[483] Art. 56 of AP/I, see fn. 273.

4. As to the meaning of the term "specific protection", see the Commentary in the *chapeau* on Section K.

I. Civil defence

1. Civil defence is defined in Rule 1 (k).

2. Rules 90 through 92 apply to civil defence operations, not only in combat areas but also in the hinterland and in occupied territories. However, precise Black-letter Rules regulating civil defence in occupied territories were deemed inappropriate for inclusion in this Manual.

3. Along the same lines, Rules 90 through 92 apply to civilian civil defence organizations of Neutrals when they perform civil defence tasks in the territory of a Belligerent Party.[484] This Manual does not elaborate on the conditions for foreign assistance to civil defence.

4. Treaties applicable in non-international armed conflict contain no special provisions for civil defence. However, civilian civil defence organizations and their personnel, the building and materiel used for civil defence purposes, and shelters provided for the civilian population benefit from the generic protection granted to civilians and to civilian objects. They must not be directly attacked unless they lose their civilian protection in accordance with the general rules as specified in Sections D; E and F.

5. Military personnel discharging civil defence duties must also be protected in non-international armed conflict, provided that they do not directly participate in hostilities (see Art. 67 (1) (e) of AP/I).[485] Consequently, the basics of Rule 90 apply in non-international armed conflict.

6. It would be useful for civilian civil defence organizations, their personnel, as well as objects used for civil defence purposes, to use the

[484] Art. 64 (1) of AP/I: "Articles 62, 63, 65 and 66 shall also apply to the personnel and 'matériel' of civilian civil defence organizations of neutral or other States not Parties to the conflict which perform civil defence tasks mentioned in Article 61 in the territory of a Party to the conflict, with the consent and under the control of that Party. Notification of such assistance shall be given as soon as possible to any adverse Party concerned. In no circumstances shall this activity be deemed to be an interference in the conflict. This activity should, however, be performed with due regard to the security interests of the Parties to the conflict concerned."

[485] Art. 67 (1) (e) of AP/I, see fn. 487.

international distinctive sign also in non-international armed conflict, in order to ensure clear identification. Military personnel discharging civil defence duties must distinguish themselves from other combatants (see paragraph 4 of the Commentary on Rule 91).

90. (a) Specific protection must be provided to civil defence organizations and their personnel, whether civilian or military. They must be entitled to perform their civil defence tasks except in the case of imperative military necessity.

1. Rule 90 (a) pertains to the specific protection of civil defence organizations and their personnel; in particular, the obligation to respect and protect such organizations and their personnel. It is based on two different provisions of AP/I, namely, Art. 62 (1) of AP/I[486] concerning civilian civil defence organizations and their personnel, and Art. 67 (1) of AP/I[487] concerning members of the armed forces and military units assigned to civil defence organizations. Although Rule 90 covers both civilian and military civil defence organizations and personnel, some disparities exist in the legal regime applicable to civilian or military civil defence. These will be dealt with below.

2. For the purpose of this Manual, the term "civil defence organizations" comprises those establishments and other units which are organized or

[486] Art. 62 (1) of AP/I ("General Protection"): "Civilian civil defence organizations and their personnel shall be respected and protected, subject to the Rules of this Protocol, particularly the Rules of this Section. They shall be entitled to perform their civil defence tasks except in case of imperative military necessity."

[487] Art. 67 (1) of AP/I ("Members of the armed forces and military units assigned to civil defence organizations."): "1. Members of the armed forces and military units assigned to civil defence organizations shall be respected and protected, provided that:(a) such personnel and such units are permanently assigned and exclusively devoted to the performance of any of the tasks mentioned in Article 61; (b) if so assigned, such personnel do not perform any other military duties during the conflict; (c) such personnel are clearly distinguishable from the other members of the armed forces by prominently displaying the international distinctive sign of civil defence, which shall be as large as appropriate, and such personnel are provided with the identity card referred to in Chapter V of Annex I to this Protocol certifying their status; (d) such personnel and such units are equipped only with light individual weapons for the purpose of maintaining order or for self-defence. The provisions of Article 65, paragraph 3 shall also apply in this case; (e) such personnel do not participate directly in hostilities, and do not commit, or are not used to commit, outside their civil defence tasks, acts harmful to the adverse Party; (f) such personnel and such units perform their civil defence tasks only within the national territory of their Party. The non-observance of the conditions stated in (e) above by any member of the armed forces who is bound by the conditions prescribed in (a) and (b) above is prohibited."

authorized by the competent authorities of a Belligerent Party to perform any civil defence tasks, and which are assigned and devoted exclusively to such tasks.[488] The notion of "organizations" does not imply a large organizational set up. These organizations may be rather small establishments.

3. For the purpose of this Manual, the "personnel" of civil defence organizations means those persons exclusively assigned by a Belligerent Party to the performance of civil defence tasks. This definition encompasses, in particular, individuals formally embodied in a unit corresponding to the definition of a civil defence organization.

4. Rule 90 (a) ought not to be interpreted as restricting the specific protection to civil defence organizations and their personnel. Accordingly, civilians responding to an appeal from – and acting under the control of – the authorities of a Belligerent Party must equally be provided specific protection while performing civil defence tasks, even if they are not members of a civil defence organization.[489]

5. Medical and religious personnel assigned to civil defence organizations retain their protection as medical or religious personnel.[490] On the protection of medical and religious personnel, see Section K, in particular Rule 71.

6. Assignment to civil defence tasks for a limited and even relatively short period is possible, provided that it is exclusive throughout that period. The fact that a civil defence assignment provides specific protection only when a person is exclusively so assigned does not detract from the general protection as a civilian this person enjoys before and after the assignment. During the assignment, and as long as the civilian exclusively performs civil defence tasks, he is entitled to specific protection beyond the general protection enjoyed as a civilian, as described in this Section of the Manual.

[488] Art. 61 (b) of AP/I: "For the purposes of this Protocol: . . . 'civil defence organizations' means those establishments and other units which are organized or authorized by the competent authorities of a Party to the conflict to perform any of the tasks mentioned under sub-paragraph (a), and which are assigned and devoted exclusively to such tasks."

[489] Art. 62 (2) of AP/I: "The provisions of paragraph 1 shall also apply to civilians who, although not members of civilian civil defence organizations, respond to an appeal from the competent authorities and perform civil defence tasks under their control."

[490] Art. 8 (c) of AP/I, see fn. 368.
See also Art. 8 (d) (iv) of AP/I concerning religious personnel assigned to civil defence organizations, see fn. 369.

7. The flexible system admitting a switch to and from civil defence assignments does not apply to military units of civil defence. These military units only benefit from specific protection if a number of cumulative conditions are fulfilled, including those of being permanently assigned and exclusively devoted to the performance of civil defence tasks and of not performing any other military duties during the conflict.[491] Once such personnel or units have been assigned to civil defence, they are forbidden – for the whole duration of the armed conflict – to perform any other military duty, in particular combat or combat support duty.[492]

8. The obligation to respect and to protect civil defence organizations and their personnel implies that they may not be deliberately attacked and that they may not be unnecessarily prevented from carrying out their tasks. This latter element – expressly spelled out in the second sentence of Rule 90 – is subject to one exception: the right to perform civil defence functions is suspended in case of "imperative military necessity". This limitation implies that military operations cannot be hindered by the activities of civil defence: a Belligerent Party is not compelled to change major operational military plans in order to avoid affecting civil defence activities.

(b) Specific protection must also be provided to buildings and materiel used for civil defence purposes and to shelters provided for the civilian population. Objects used for civil defence purposes may not be destroyed or diverted from their proper use except by the Belligerent Party to which they belong.

1. Rule 90 (b) extends the specific protection to buildings and materiel used for civil defence purposes and to shelters provided for the civilian population. Buildings used for civil defence purposes include those accommodating civil defence organizations. Examples include buildings for administrative purposes, stations for personnel of civil defence organizations on guard duty for civilian purposes, facilities used for storing of materiel, garages housing vehicles etc.[493]

[491] Art. 67 (1) of AP/I, see fn. 487.
[492] Art. 67 (1) (a) and (b) of AP/I, see fn. 487.
[493] Para. 2454 of the ICRC Commentary on AP/I, pertaining to Art. 62 of AP/I: "The buildings concerned are those accommodating civil defence organizations, i.e., primarily their administrative services, but also the locations for personnel on guard duty, stores for 'matériel,' garages housing vehicles intended for civil defence etc."

2. "Civil defence materiel" comprises equipment and supplies, as well as means of transport of civil defence organizations (on land, water or in the air).[494]

3. Civil defence organizations may use aircraft for purposes such as rescuing or evacuating civilians from a zone of danger, extinguishing fires or transporting civil defence materiel. There is no explicit regulation of civil defence air transportation. However, the specific protection due to civil defence aircraft may be envisaged by analogy with that granted to medical aircraft. In other words, civil defence aircraft benefit from specific protection – even without the consent of the enemy – when operating in and over land areas physically controlled by friendly forces or in and over sea areas not physically controlled by the enemy. In and over areas controlled by the enemy, as well as in and over those parts of the contact zone which are physically controlled by friendly forces or the physical control of which is not clearly established, the protection of civil defence aircraft can be fully effective only by prior consent obtained from the enemy. In the absence of such consent, civil defence aircraft operate at their own risk. They must nevertheless be respected once they have been identified as such (see Rule 77 and Rule 78).

4. Objects used for civil defence purposes may not be directly attacked. They may, however, suffer from collateral damage caused by an attack on a lawful target (see Rule 14). To a large extent, their vulnerability to becoming collateral damage depends on their separation from lawful targets. By comparison to other civilian objects, objects used for civil defence purposes can be marked with a distinctive sign (see Art. 66 of AP/I),[495] thereby enhancing the likelihood that they will be identified as civilian objects entitled to specific protection (see Rule 91).

5. The right to destroy objects used for civil defence purposes or to divert them from their proper use is granted only to "the Party to which they belong".[496]

[494] Art. 61 (d) of AP/I: "For the purposes of this Protocol: . . . (d) 'Matériel' of civil defence organizations means equipment, supplies and transports used by these organizations for the performance of the tasks mentioned under sub-paragraph (a)."

[495] Art. 66 of AP/I, see fn. 497.

[496] Art. 62 (3) of AP/I: "Buildings and 'matériel' used for civil defence purposes and shelters provided for the civilian population are covered by Article 52. Objects used for civil defence purposes may not be destroyed or diverted from their proper use except by the Party to which they belong."

91. Belligerent Parties have to endeavour to ensure that – while exclusively devoted to the performance of civil defence tasks – their civil defence organizations, personnel, buildings and materials, as well as shelters provided to the civilian population, are identified as such by the recognized international distinctive sign for civil defence and any other appropriate means of identification.

1. Rule 91 is derived from Art. 66 of AP/I;[497] as well as from Art. 67 (1) of AP/I[498] and Art. 67 (3) of AP/I[499] dealing with identification of civil defence organizations, personnel, buildings and materials.

2. The international distinctive sign of civil defence is an "equilateral blue triangle on an orange ground".[500]

3. Specific protection is granted to civilian civil defence organizations, personnel, buildings and materials because of their functions. The practical value of the recognized international distinctive sign (and any other

[497] Art. 66 of AP/I: "(1) Each Party to the conflict shall endeavour to ensure that its civil defence organizations, their personnel, buildings and matériel are identifiable while they are exclusively devoted to the performance of civil defence tasks. Shelters provided for the civilian population should be similarly identifiable. (2) Each Party to the conflict shall also endeavour to adopt and implement methods and procedures which will make it possible to recognize civilian shelters as well as civil defence personnel, buildings and matériel on which the international distinctive sign of civil defence is displayed. (3) In occupied territories and in areas where fighting is taking place or is likely to take place, civilian civil defence personnel should be recognizable by the international distinctive sign of civil defence and by an identity card certifying their status. (4) The international distinctive sign of civil defence is an equilateral blue triangle on an orange ground when used for the protection of civil defence organizations, their personnel, buildings and matériel and for civilian shelters. (5) In addition to the distinctive sign, Parties to the conflict may agree upon the use of distinctive signals for civil defence identification purposes. (6) The application of the provisions of paragraphs 1 to 4 is governed by Chapter V of Annex I to this Protocol. (7) In time of peace, the sign described in paragraph 4 may, with the consent of the competent national authorities, be used for civil defence identification purposes. (8) The High Contracting Parties and the Parties to the conflict shall take the measures necessary to supervise the display of the international distinctive sign of civil defence and to prevent and repress any misuse thereof. (9) The identification of civil defence medical and religious personnel, medical units and medical transports is also governed by Art. 18."

[498] Art. 67 (1) of AP/I, see fn. 487.

[499] Art. 67 (3) of AP/I: "The buildings and major items of equipment and transports of military units assigned to civil defence organizations shall be clearly marked with the international distinctive sign of civil defence. This distinctive sign shall be as large as appropriate."

[500] Art. 16 of Annex I to AP/I.

appropriate means of identification) is to facilitate protection by increasing the likelihood that protected persons and objects will be identified as such. In fact, it would be complicated – under armed conflict conditions – to ensure effective protection of civil defence personnel and objects if there was no practical way of recognizing them. However, protection of civilian civil defence organizations, personnel, buildings and materiel is not dependent on their being marked with the international distinctive sign of civil defence; they are to be respected and protected from the moment they have been identified as such, even if they do not display the international distinctive sign. By analogy, see Rule 72 (c)–(d), as well as Rule 76 (d).

4. Military, as distinct from civilian, civil defence personnel benefit from specific protection only if they clearly distinguish themselves from combat personnel (see Art. 67 (1) (c) of AP/I).[501]

5. Civil defence organizations, personnel, buildings and materiel must not display the distinctive sign if they are not exclusively devoted to civil defence tasks.

6. Belligerent Parties have an obligation to supervise the use of the distinctive sign and to prevent and repress possible misuse (see Art. 66 (8) of AP/I).[502] It would be a misuse of the emblem to display it as a civil defence protective sign on organizations, personnel, buildings or materiel which do not exclusively serve a civil defence purpose. In other words, even if a facility serves civil defence purposes, it may not use the emblem if the facility is also used for purposes inconsistent with its civil defence status. The defending Belligerent Party has an important role in ensuring the protection of these facilities by preventing misuse and thus promoting confidence in the right of the facilities to protection (see Section H).

7. Belligerent Parties may agree upon the use of signals for identification purposes in addition to the distinctive sign (see Art. 66 (5) of AP/I).[503] This may be particularly important in the context of civil defence air transportation, where the distinctive emblem may provide insufficient protection due to "beyond visual range" targeting capabilities.

[501] Art. 67 (1) (c) of AP/I, see fn. 487.
[502] Art. 66 (8) of AP/I, see fn. 497.
[503] Art. 66 (5) of AP/I, see fn. 497.

92. The protection to which civilian civil defence organizations, their personnel, buildings, shelters and materiel are entitled does not cease unless they commit or are used to commit, outside their proper tasks, acts harmful to the enemy. Protection may, however, cease only after a warning has been given setting, whenever appropriate, a reasonable time-limit, and after such warning has remained unheeded.

1. Rule 92 restates almost *verbatim* Art. 65 (1) of AP/I.[504] It applies only to "civilian" civil defence organizations, their personnel, buildings, shelters and materiel in situations where there is valid reason for discontinuing the protection because they commit, or are used to commit, outside their proper tasks, acts harmful to the enemy. It ought to be noted that an act may be "harmful" without necessarily being "hostile", i.e., acts without hostile intent may also lead to a loss of specific protection.[505]

2. Art. 65 (2) of AP/I[506] provides for acts which are not considered as harmful to the enemy. These include the possibility that civil defence and military personnel cooperate in the performance of civil defence tasks or that civil defence tasks are carried out under the direction or control of military authorities. If the performance of civil defence tasks incidentally benefits military victims (particularly, those who are *hors de combat*), it cannot be considered as harmful to the enemy.

3. According to Art. 65 (3) of AP/I,[507] civilian civil defence personnel are permitted to bear weapons without thereby losing their specific

[504] Art. 65 (1) of AP/I: "The protection to which civilian civil defence organizations, their personnel, buildings, shelters and 'matériel' are entitled shall not cease unless they commit or are used to commit, outside their proper tasks, acts harmful to the enemy. Protection may, however, cease only after a warning has been given setting, whenever appropriate, a reasonable time-limit, and after such warning has remained unheeded."

[505] Para. 2588 of the ICRC Commentary on AP/I, pertaining to Art. 65 (1) of AP/I: "This expression [acts harmful to the enemy] was contested by some who would have preferred the term "hostile", because of its "more specific" character. It is true that a harmful act can be committed unintentionally and the word "hostile" would have had the advantage of indicating intent to harm.... "

[506] Art. 65 (2) of AP/I: "The following shall not be considered as acts harmful to the enemy: (a) that civil defence tasks are carried out under the direction or control of military authorities; (b) that civilian civil defence personnel co-operate with military personnel in the performance of civil defence tasks, or that some military personnel are attached to civilian civil defence organizations; (c) that the performance of civil defence tasks may incidentally benefit military victims, particularly those who are *hors de combat*."

[507] Art. 65 (3) of AP/I: "It shall also not be considered as an act harmful to the enemy that civilian civil defence personnel bear light individual weapons for the purpose of maintaining order of for self-defence. However, in areas where land fighting is taking

protection. However, this permission is subject to strict conditions. First, civil defence personnel are only entitled to bear light individual weapons (on the definition of this expression, see paragraph 3 of the Commentary on Rule 74 (c) (i)). In the combat zone, the weapons must be limited to handguns – an even narrower concept than light individual weapons (see Rule 74 (c) (i) and Rule 82). Second, these weapons must only be used for the purpose of maintaining law and order in a stricken area or for self-defense against marauders or armed assailants, but not against the enemy. These provisions are modelled on those applicable to medical and religious personnel.

4. Rule 92 needs to be read against the background of Rule 38. The requirement to issue a warning as per Rule 92 is an absolute one. This is to be differentiated from warnings mentioned, e.g., in Rule 37, which must be issued "unless circumstances do not permit".

5. Before protection ceases, a warning setting a reasonable time-limit must have been issued and ignored. The time-limit, however, need only be set "whenever appropriate". There are situations in which it is impracticable to set a time-limit (see Commentary on Rule 74 (b)).

6. The period must furthermore be "reasonable", i.e., either (i) long enough to allow the acts harmful to the enemy to be stopped; or (ii) long enough for the wounded and sick who are within the medical units or medical transports to be removed to a place of safety. In some cases, it may be reasonable to require immediate compliance with a warning to desist from the acts harmful to the enemy or to remove the wounded and sick to a place of safety.

7. The termination of specific protection to which civilian civil defence organizations, their personnel, buildings, shelter and matériel are entitled, does not necessarily mean that they can be attacked as such. It must be borne in mind that they may then benefit from the generic protection of civilians and civilian objects. An attack is contingent on the person or object qualifying as a lawful target (see Sections D; E; F and G).

place or is likely to take place, the Parties to the conflict shall undertake the appropriate measures to limit these weapons to handguns, such as pistols or revolvers, in order to assist in distinguishing between civil defence personnel and combatants. Although civil defence personnel bear other light individual weapons in such areas, they shall nevertheless be respected and protected as soon as they have been recognized as such."

II. Cultural property

1. The specific protection of cultural property is based on AP/I and AP/II, the 1954 Hague Convention, as well as the Protocol and the Second Protocol to the 1954 Hague Convention.[508] These various treaties establish complementary systems of protection: (i) a general protection applicable to all cultural property, as respectively defined in 1977 AP/I and II and in the 1954 Hague Convention; (ii) a "special protection" for cultural property of very great importance to the cultural heritage of every people (in the 1954 Hague Convention); and (iii) a system of "enhanced protection" for cultural heritage of the greatest importance for humanity (in the Second Protocol to the 1954 Hague Convention).

2. The Group of Experts considered it unnecessary to reiterate – in a Manual on International Law Applicable to Air and Missile Warfare – all the nuances of the legal regimes ensuring protection to cultural property.

3. For the definition of cultural property, see Rule 1 (o).

(i) Use of Cultural Property

1. The majority of the Group of Experts reached the conclusion that the decision to use cultural property or its immediate surroundings for military purposes has to be taken by an officer commanding a force the size of a battalion or larger. Commanders of smaller forces may only make this decision where circumstances do not permit otherwise.[509]

2. Equally, the majority of the Group of Experts arrived at the conclusion that, whenever circumstances permit, the enemy must be notified, a reasonable time in advance, of the decision to use cultural property or its immediate surroundings for military purposes.[510]

[508] The 1907 Hague Regulations also contain two relevant provisions: (i) Art. 27, see fn. 35; and (ii) Art. 56 (applicable in occupied territory): "The property of municipalities, that of institutions dedicated to religion, charity and education, the arts and sciences, even when State property, shall be treated as private property. All seizure of, destruction or wilful damage done to institutions of this character, historic monuments, works of art and science, is forbidden, and should be made the subject of legal proceedings."

[509] Art. 6 (c) of the Second Protocol to the 1954 Hague Convention: "the decision to invoke imperative military necessity shall only be taken by an officer commanding a force the equivalent of a battalion in size or larger, or a force smaller in size where circumstances do not permit otherwise."

[510] Art. 6 (d) of the Second Protocol to the 1954 Hague Convention: "in case of an attack based on a decision taken in accordance with sub-paragraph (a), an effective advance warning shall be given whenever circumstances permit."

93. (a) Belligerent Parties must refrain from any use of cultural property and its immediate surroundings, or of the appliances in use for its protection, for purposes which are likely to expose it to destruction or damage.

1. This Rule is based on Art. 4 (1) of the 1954 Hague Convention.[511] It obliges Belligerent Parties to refrain from using not only cultural property, but also its immediate surroundings and the appliances in use for its protection for purposes likely to expose it to destruction or damage.

2. The formulation of Rule 93 (a) does not only prohibit the use of cultural property (or its surroundings) "for military purposes" (*cf.* Art. 9 of the 1954 Hague Convention)[512] or "in support of the military effort" (*cf.* Art. 53 (b) of AP/I),[513] but more broadly its use for any "purposes which are likely to expose it to destruction or damage".

3. As emphasized in Art. 4 (1) of the 1954 Hague Convention,[514] Rule 93 (a) applies to cultural property situated within a Belligerent Party's own territory, as well as to cultural property situated within the territory of other High Contracting Parties. This includes occupied territory (Art. 5 of the 1954 Hague Convention).

4. As regards non-international armed conflict, see Art. 19 of the 1954 Hague Convention.[515]

[511] Art. 4 (1) of the 1954 Hague Convention: "The High Contracting Parties undertake to respect cultural property situated within their own territory as well as within the territory of other High Contracting Parties by refraining from any use of the property and its immediate surroundings or of the appliances in use for its protection for purposes which are likely to expose it to destruction or damage in the event of armed conflict; and by refraining from any act of hostility directed against such property."

[512] Art. 9 of the 1954 Hague Convention: "The High Contracting Parties undertake to ensure the immunity of cultural property under special protection by refraining, from the time of entry in the International Register, from any act of hostility directed against such property and, except for the cases provided for in paragraph 5 of Article 8, from any use of such property or its surroundings for military purposes."

[513] Art. 53 of AP/I: "Without prejudice to the provisions of the Hague Convention for the Protection of Cultural Property in the Event of Armed Conflict of 14 May 1954, and of other relevant international instruments, it is prohibited: (a) to commit any acts of hostility directed against the historic monuments, works of art or places of worship which constitute the cultural or spiritual heritage of peoples; (b) to use such objects in support of the military effort; (c) to make such objects the object of reprisals."

[514] Art. 4 (1) of the 1954 Hague Convention, see fn. 511.

[515] Art. 19 of the 1954 Hague Convention ("Conflicts not of an international character"): "(1) In the event of an armed conflict not of an international character occurring within the territory of one of the High Contracting Parties, each party to the conflict shall be

(b) Cultural property or its immediate surroundings may only be used for military purposes in cases where military necessity imperatively so requires. Such decision can only be implemented after the emblems identifying the object in question as cultural property have been removed.

1. The first sentence of Rule 93 (b) is based on Art. 4 (2) of the 1954 Hague Convention.[516]

2. Rule 93 (b) sets out an exception to the prohibition contained in Rule 93 (a), envisioning the rare cases where military necessity imperatively requires the use of cultural property or its immediate surroundings for military purposes (e.g., if an historic bridge is the only available means to cross a river). According to the majority of the Group of Experts, imperative military necessity may only be invoked when and for as long as there is no other feasible method for obtaining a similar military advantage.[517]

3. Naturally, if a Belligerent Party decides – for reasons of imperative military necessity – to use cultural property, or its immediate surroundings, for military purposes, it must no longer display the distinctive emblem, assuming that such emblem is being used (see Rule 94).

4. Rule 93 (b) applies also in non-international armed conflict. Its applicability is derived from Art. 19 (1) of the 1954 Hague Convention.[518]

bound to apply, as a minimum, the provisions of the present Convention which relate to respect for cultural property. (2) The parties to the Conflict shall endeavour to bring into force, by means of special agreements, all or part of the other provisions of the present Convention. (3) The United Nations Educational, Scientific and Cultural Organization may offer its services to the parties to the conflict. (4) The application of the preceding provisions shall not affect the legal status of the parties to the conflict."

516 Art. 4 (2) of the 1954 Hague Convention: "The obligations mentioned in paragraph 1 of the present Article may be waived only in cases where military necessity imperatively requires such a waiver."

517 Art. 6 (b) of the Second Protocol to the 1954 Hague Convention: "With the goal of ensuring respect for cultural property in accordance with Article 4 of the Convention: . . . (b) a waiver on the basis of imperative military necessity pursuant to Article 4 paragraph 2 of the Convention may only be invoked to use cultural property for purposes which are likely to expose it to destruction or damage when and for as long as no choice is possible between such use of the cultural property and another feasible method for obtaining a similar military advantage."

518 Art. 19 of the 1954 Hague Convention, see fn. 515.

94. Belligerent Parties ought to facilitate the identification and protection of cultural property under their control, by marking it with the internationally recognized emblem and by providing the enemy with timely and adequate information about its location. However, the absence of such measures does not deprive cultural property of its protection under the law of international armed conflict.

1. Rule 94 is partially based on Art. 6[519] and Art. 17 (1) – (2)[520] of the 1954 Hague Convention. The option to mark cultural property and to inform the enemy about its location is designed to enhance protection by making such property distinct from other objects in the vicinity.

2. The distinctive emblem is the so-called "blue-and-white shield". This emblem takes (Art. 16 of the 1954 Hague Convention) the form of a shield, pointed below, per saltire blue and white (a shield consisting of a royal-blue square, one of the angles of which forms the point of the shield, and of a royal-blue triangle above the square, the space on either side being taken up by a white triangle).

3. As highlighted by the words "under their control", Rule 94 applies to cultural property situated either within a Belligerent Party's own territory, or in occupied territory.

4. The absence of the distinctive emblem does not deprive cultural property of its protection, which is derived from the law of international armed conflict, and does not depend on the emblem. The emblem is merely provided to facilitate identification (*cf.* Rule 72 (d)).

5. Rule 94 applies also in non-international armed conflict.

[519] Art. 6 of the 1954 Hague Convention ("Distinctive marking of cultural property"): "In accordance with the provisions of Article 16, cultural property may bear a distinctive emblem so as to facilitate its recognition."

[520] Art. 17 (1) and (2) of the 1954 Hague Convention ("Use of the emblem"): "(1) The distinctive emblem repeated three times may be used only as a means of identification of: (a) immovable cultural property under special protection; (b) the transport of cultural property under the conditions provided for in Articles 12 and 13; (c) improvised refuges, under the conditions provided for in the Regulations for the execution of the Convention. (2) The distinctive emblem may be used alone only as a means of identification of: (a) cultural property not under special protection; (b) the persons responsible for the duties of control in accordance with the Regulations for the execution of the Convention; (c) the personnel engaged in the protection of cultural property; (d) the identity cards mentioned in the Regulations for the execution of the Convention."

(ii) Attacks against Cultural Property

95. (a) Subject to paragraph (b) and to Rule 96, Belligerent Parties must refrain from any act of hostility directed against cultural property.

1. Rule 95 (a) is subject to Rule 95 (b) and to Rule 96. That is to say that both Rule 95(b) and Rule 96 must be complied with when the circumstances for their application are met.

2. The prohibition of directing acts of hostility against cultural property is derived from Art. 27 of the 1907 Hague Regulations,[521] Art. 53 of AP/I,[522] and Art. 4 (1),[523] as well as Art. 9[524] of the 1954 Hague Convention.

3. The protection is against all acts of hostilities and not just attacks. For the definition of "attack", see Rule 1 (e).

4. The prohibition in Rule 95 (a) of "any act of hostility" does not diminish from the obligation to protect cultural property against theft, pillage, misappropriation or vandalism.[525]

5. Rule 95 (a) applies also in non-international armed conflict.

(b) Cultural property, or its immediate surroundings, may only be attacked in cases where military necessity imperatively so requires.

1. Unlike Rule 95 (a), which deals with "acts of hostility", Rule 95 (b) – as well as Rule 95 (c) – deals with "attacks". For the definition of attack, see Rule 1 (e).

2. Rule 95 (b) is partially derived from Art. 4 (2)[526] and Art. 11 (2)[527] of the 1954 Hague Convention. Rule 95 (b) is, however, broader than

[521] Art. 27 of the 1907 Hague Regulations, see fn. 35.
[522] Art. 53 of AP/I, see fn. 513.
[523] Art. 4 (1) of the 1954 Hague Convention, see fn. 511.
[524] Art. 9 of the 1954 Hague Convention, see fn. 512.
[525] Art. 4 (3) of the 1954 Hague Convention: "The High Contracting Parties further undertake to prohibit, prevent and, if necessary, put a stop to any form of theft, pillage or misappropriation of, and any acts of vandalism directed against, cultural property. They shall, refrain from requisitioning movable cultural property situated in the territory of another High Contracting Party."
[526] Art. 4 (2) of the 1954 Hague Convention, see fn. 516.
[527] Art. 11 of the 1954 Hague Convention: "(1) If one of the High Contracting Parties commits, in respect of any item of cultural property under special protection, a violation of the obligations under Article 9, the opposing Party shall, so long as this violation persists, be released from the obligation to ensure the immunity of the property concerned.

those treaty provisions in requiring the existence of "imperative military necessity" in attacking not only the cultural property itself, but also in attacking its immediate surroundings.

3. See the Commentary on Rule 93 (b) for an explanation of the expression "imperative military necessity".

4. The condition of "imperative military necessity", which is derived from the 1954 Hague Convention, is regarded by many as inconsistent with the modern requirement that an object can only be attacked if it meets the definition of military objectives (see Rule 1 (y) and Rule 22). The two concepts have been reconciled for cultural property in Art. 6 (a) (i)[528] and in Art. 13 (1) (b)[529] of the Second Protocol to the 1954 Hague Convention. Although not every State is a Contracting Party to that instrument, the majority of the Group of Experts proceeded from the assumption that no attack can be launched against cultural property unless it constitutes a military objective (see Rule 96).

5. Rule 95 (b) applies also in non-international armed conflict.

(c) **In attacking, through air or missile attacks, military objectives in the immediate surroundings of cultural property, the Belligerent Parties must take feasible precautions to avoid damage to the cultural property (see Section G of this Manual).**

1. Rule 95 (c) is complementary to Rule 95 (b). Whereas Rule 95 (b) deals with attacks against cultural property or its immediate surroundings, Rule 95 (c) deals with attacks against military objectives in close proximity to cultural property. In attacking such military objectives, Belligerent Parties must take all feasible precautionary measures to limit collateral damage to the cultural property (see Rule 14 and Section G).

Nevertheless, whenever possible, the latter Party shall first request the cessation of such violation within a reasonable time. (2) Apart from the case provided for in paragraph 1 of the present Article, immunity shall be withdrawn from cultural property under special protection only in exceptional cases of unavoidable military necessity, and only for such time as that necessity continues. Such necessity can be established only by the officer commanding a force the equivalent of a division in size or larger. Whenever circumstances permit, the opposing Party shall be notified, a reasonable time in advance, of the decision to withdraw immunity. (3) The Party withdrawing immunity shall, as soon as possible, so inform the Commissioner-General for cultural property provided for in the Regulations for the execution of the Convention, in writing, stating the reasons."

[528] Art. 6 (a) (i) of the Second Protocol to the 1954 Hague Convention, see fn. 531.

[529] Art. 13 (1) (b) of the Second Protocol to the 1954 Hague Convention, see fn. 532.

2. Unlike the general protection of civilian objects from collateral damage which is "excessive" (see Rule 14), in the case of cultural property, Belligerent Parties must take feasible precautions to avoid collateral damage to them, even when it is not excessive. This obligation is limited, however, to the taking of "feasible" precautions, rather than to be applicable in an absolute manner.

3. For Contracting Parties to the 1999 Second Protocol to the 1954 Hague Convention, Art. 7 of that Protocol applies.[530]

4. Rule 95 (c) applies also in non-international armed conflict.

96. Whenever cultural property has become a military objective, the decision to attack the object must be taken by an appropriate level of command, and with due consideration of its special character as cultural property. An effective advance warning should be given whenever circumstances permit and an attack should only be conducted if the warning remains unheeded.

1. Rule 96 is derived from Art. 6[531] and Art. 13[532] (*See footnote 532 on next page*) of the Second Protocol to the 1954 Hague Convention.

[530] Art. 7 of the Second Protocol to the 1954 Hague Convention ("Precautions in attack"): "Without prejudice to other precautions required by international humanitarian law in the conduct of military operations, each Party to the conflict shall: (a) do everything feasible to verify that the objectives to be attacked are not cultural property protected under Article 4 of the Convention; (b) take all feasible precautions in the choice of means and methods of attack with a view to avoiding, and in any event to minimizing, incidental damage to cultural property protected under Article 4 of the Convention; (c) refrain from deciding to launch any attack which may be expected to cause incidental damage to cultural property protected under Article 4 of the Convention which would be excessive in relation to the concrete and direct military advantage anticipated; and (d) cancel or suspend an attack if it becomes apparent: (i) that the objective is cultural property protected under Article 4 of the Convention; (ii) that the attack may be expected to cause incidental damage to cultural property protected under Article 4 of the Convention which would be excessive in relation to the concrete and direct military advantage anticipated."

[531] Art. 6 of the Second Protocol to the 1954 Hague Convention: "With the goal of ensuring respect for cultural property in accordance with Article 4 of the Convention: (a) a waiver on the basis of imperative military necessity pursuant to Article 4 paragraph 2 of the Convention may only be invoked to direct an act of hostility against cultural property when and for as long as: (i) that cultural property has, by its function, been made into a military objective; and (ii) there is no feasible alternative available to obtain a similar military advantage to that offered by directing an act of hostility against that objective; (b) a waiver on the basis of imperative military necessity pursuant to Article 4 paragraph 2 of the Convention may only be invoked to use cultural property for purposes which are likely to expose it to destruction or damage when and for as long as no choice is possible between such use of the cultural property and another feasible method for obtaining a similar military advantage; (c) the decision to invoke imperative military necessity shall

2. Rule 96 is based on the assumption that cultural property meets the requirement of a military objective (see paragraph 4 of the Commentary on Rule 95 (b)).

3. Rule 96 has to be read against the background of the general requirement of warning in Rule 38. The phrase used in the text includes the word "should", thus reflecting the disagreement among the Group of Experts as regards the question whether there is such an obligation in customary international law. In any event, Contracting Parties to the Second Protocol to the 1954 Hague Convention must (pursuant to its Art. 6 (d))[533] give such warning "whenever the circumstances permit".

4. Once a warning – when issued – is heeded, any attack against the cultural property will be unlawful.

5. The decision to attack cultural property can only be taken by an "appropriate level of command". In the opinion of the majority of the Group of Experts, that means a commander of an air squadron or a higher echelon, i.e., the equivalent of a battalion commander, as referenced in Art. 6 (c)[534] of the Second Protocol to the 1954 Hague Convention.

6. The decision to attack cultural property must be taken with due consideration of its special character. In other words, the decision cannot be taken lightly and plans of attack ought to seek to minimize the risk to cultural property.

7. Rule 96 applies also in non-international armed conflict.

only be taken by an officer commanding a force the equivalent of a battalion in size or larger, or a force smaller in size where circumstances do not permit otherwise; (d) in case of an attack based on a decision taken in accordance with subparagraph (a), an effective advance warning shall be given whenever circumstances permit."

532 Art. 13 of the Second Protocol to the 1954 Hague Convention ("Loss of enhanced protection"): "(1) Cultural property under enhanced protection shall only lose such protection: (a) if such protection is suspended or cancelled in accordance with Article 14; or (b) if, and for as long as, the property has, by its use, become a military objective. (2) In the circumstances of sub-paragraph 1(b), such property may only be the object of attack if: (a) the attack is the only feasible means of terminating the use of the property referred to in sub-paragraph 1(b); (b) all feasible precautions are taken in the choice of means and methods of attack, with a view to terminating such use and avoiding, or in any event minimising, damage to the cultural property; (c) unless circumstances do not permit, due to requirements of immediate self-defence: (i) the attack is ordered at the highest operational level of command; (ii) effective advance warning is issued to the opposing forces requiring the termination of the use referred to in sub-paragraph 1(b); and (iii) reasonable time is given to the opposing forces to redress the situation."

533 Art. 6 (d) of the Second Protocol to the 1954 Hague Convention, see fn. 531.

534 Art. 6 (c) of the Second Protocol to the 1954 Hague Convention, see fn. 531.

III. Objects indispensable to the survival of the civilian population

97. (a) Starvation of civilians as a method of warfare is prohibited.

1. Rule 97 (a) is based on Art. 54 (1) of AP/I.[535] See also, for international armed conflicts, Art. 8 (2) (b) (xxv) of Rome Statute of the ICC.[536]

2. The prohibition of starvation of civilians as a method of warfare means annihilating or weakening the civilian population by deliberately depriving it of its sources of food, drinking water or of other essential supplies, thereby causing it to suffer hunger or otherwise affecting its subsistence.

3. The prohibition of starvation as a method of warfare does not comprise a prohibition of attacking supplies intended primarily for the sustenance of the enemy's military forces, i.e., starvation of combatants is a permissible method of warfare.

4. It follows that there is no prohibition of siege warfare, provided that the purpose is military in nature and not solely or primarily to starve the civilian population. In such circumstances, if the civilian population is suffering from starvation, the besieging Belligerent Party must provide for the free passage of humanitarian relief supply. On humanitarian aid, see Section O. As for the situation in case of an aerial blockade, see Rule 157–159.

5. Rule 97 (a) applies in occupied as well as in non-occupied territory.

6. Rule 97 (a) applies also in non-international armed conflict.

(b) It is prohibited to attack, destroy, remove, or render useless objects indispensable to the survival of the civilian population, such as foodstuffs, agricultural areas for the production of foodstuffs, crops, livestock, drinking water installations and supplies and irrigation works, for the specific purpose of denying the civilian population their use.

[535] Art. 54 (1) of AP/I: "Starvation of civilians as a method of warfare is prohibited."

[536] Art. 8 (2) (b) (xxv) of the Rome Statute of the International Criminal Court: "Intentionally using starvation of civilians as a method of warfare by depriving them of objects indispensable to their survival, including wilfully impeding relief supplies as provided for under the Geneva Conventions."

1. The prohibition to attack, destroy, remove, or render useless objects indispensable to the survival of the civilian population is a corollary to the prohibition of starvation of civilians as a method of warfare. It is based on Art. 54 (2) of AP/I[537] and on Art. 14 of AP/II.[538]

2. This prohibition only applies if the "specific purpose" of the Belligerent Party is to deny the civilian population the use of objects indispensable to the survival of the civilian population. Rule 97 (b) does not deal with incidental distress of civilians resulting from otherwise lawful military operations. For example, it would not necessarily be unlawful to attack an airport falling under the definition of a military objective (see Rule 1 (y) and Rule 22) even if it is also used for transporting food needed to supply the civilian population. However, such an attack is unlawful if it is committed with the "specific purpose" of destroying, removing, or rendering useless objects indispensable to the survival of the civilian population, e.g., large warehouses of foodstuffs, or storages of drinking water, for the benefit of the civilian population.

3. As highlighted by the term "such as", the list of objects indispensable to the survival of the civilian population given in Rule 97 (b) is not exhaustive. Depending on weather conditions or other circumstances, objects such as shelter or clothing could also become indispensable to survival.

4. The broad formulation of Rule 97 (b) is meant to include a prohibition on any means or methods of warfare that might be used to attack, destroy, remove or render useless objects indispensable to the survival of the civilian population, including pollution of water reservoirs or destruction of crops by chemical or other agents.[539]

5. Rule 97 (b) applies also in non-international armed conflict.

[537] Art. 54 (2) of AP/I: "It is prohibited to attack, destroy, remove or render useless objects indispensable to the survival of the civilian population, such as foodstuffs, agricultural areas for the production of foodstuffs, crops, livestock, drinking water installations and supplies and irrigation works, for the specific purpose of denying them for their sustenance value to the civilian population or to the adverse Party, whatever the motive, whether in order to starve out civilians, to cause them to move away, or for any other motive."

[538] Art. 14 of AP/II: "Starvation of civilians as a method of combat is prohibited."

[539] Para. 2101 of the ICRC Commentary on AP/I, pertaining to Art. 54 of AP/I: "It should be noted that the verbs 'attack', 'destroy', 'remove' and 'render useless' are used in order to cover all possibilities, including pollution, by chemical or other agents, of water reservoirs, or destruction of crops by defoliants . . . "

(c) The prohibitions in paragraph (b) do not apply to such of the objects covered by it as are used by the enemy:

1. Rule 97 (c) provides for two exceptions to the prohibition under Rule 97 (b). It is based on Art. 54 (3) of AP/I.[540]

2. It is doubtful whether rule 97 (c) applies to non-international armed conflict, because Art. 14 of AP/II does not provide for it and no practice supporting it could be found.[541]

(i) as sustenance solely for the members of its armed forces; or

The first exception pertains to objects used by a Belligerent Party exclusively for the sustenance of its armed forces. It could apply, e.g., to foodstuff or livestock exclusively reserved for the armed forces. Another example would be the besieging of a military unit, when no civilians are involved.

(ii) if not as sustenance, then in direct support of military action, provided, however, that in no event can actions against these objects be taken which may be expected to leave the civilian population with such inadequate food or water as to cause its starvation or force its movement.

The second exception relates to objects used in direct support of military action. For example, a food-producing area may be attacked in order to prevent the enemy from advancing, or a food-storage barn may be destroyed if it is being used by the enemy for cover or as an arms depot. However, even if used in direct support of military action, these objects may only be attacked, destroyed, removed, or rendered useless provided that the consequence will not be to leave the civilian population with such inadequate food or water as to cause its starvation or force its movement.

[540] Art. 54 (3) of AP/I: "The prohibitions in paragraph 2 shall not apply to such of the objects covered by it as are used by an adverse Party: (a) as sustenance solely for the members of its armed forces; or (b) if not as sustenance, then in direct support of military action, provided, however, that in no event shall actions against these objects be taken which may be expected to leave the civilian population with such inadequate food or water as to cause its starvation or force its movement."

[541] See the Commentary on Rule 54 of the ICRC Customary IHL Study, at page 192.

IV. UN personnel

98. (a) UN personnel must be respected and protected.

1. The obligation to respect and to protect UN personnel (as well as UN materiel, installations, units and vehicles) is based *inter alia* on the UN Safety Convention. Art. 7 (1) of the latter Convention stipulates that UN personnel, their equipment and premises "shall not be made the object of attack" and that Contracting Parties have a duty to ensure the safety and security of UN personnel.[542]

2. In attacking UN personnel (as well as materiel, installations, units and vehicles) which have become a lawful target, a Belligerent Party is bound to respect Sections D, E and G.

3. UN personnel (as well as materiel, installations, units and vehicles) may display the emblem of the UN in accordance with a Code issued by the UN Secretary-General on December 17, 1949 (amended on November 11, 1952).[543] It is prohibited to use the distinctive emblem of the UN except as authorized by that organization (see Rule 112 (e)). When UN personnel and materiel lose the protection given to civilian persons and objects under the law of international armed conflict, the UN emblem cannot be construed as a protective emblem.

4. According to the UN Safety Convention, the expression "United Nations personnel" covers (Art. 1 (a)) "(i) Persons engaged or deployed by the Secretary-General of the United Nations as members of the military, police or civilian components of a United Nations operation; (ii) Other officials and experts on mission for the UN or its specialized agencies or the International Atomic Energy Agency who are present in an official capacity in the area where a United Nations operation is being conducted."

5. In the UN Safety Convention (Art. 1 (c)), the expression "United Nations operation" is defined as "an operation established by the competent organ of the United Nations in accordance with the Charter of the

[542] Art. 7 (1) of the UN Safety Convention ("Duty to ensure the safety and security of United Nations and associated personnel"): "(1) United Nations and associated personnel, their equipment and premises shall not be made the object of attack or of any action that prevents them from discharging their mandate."

[543] The United Nations Flag Code and Regulations, ST/SGB/132.

United Nations and conducted under United Nations authority and control: (i) Where the operation is for the purpose of maintaining or restoring international peace and security; or (ii) Where the Security Council or the General Assembly has declared, for the purposes of this Convention, that there exists an exceptional risk to the safety of the personnel participating in the operation."

6. The Optional Protocol to the UN Safety Convention expands (Art. II) the expression "United Nations operation" to include, in addition to those operations already covered under Art. 1 (c) of the UN Safety Convention: "all other United Nations operations established by a competent organ of the United Nations in accordance with the Charter of the United Nations and conducted under United Nations authority and control for the purpose of: (a) delivering humanitarian, political or development assistance in peacebuilding; (b) delivering emergency humanitarian assistance."

7. The obligation to respect UN personnel enshrined in Rule 98 (a) means (i) that it is prohibited to attack or to harm them in any way; and (ii) that there ought be no adverse interference with the accomplishment of their mandate. The obligation to protect implies the duty to ensure that these persons are to be respected.

8. Rule 98 (b) specifies that UN personnel only enjoy such protection "as long as they are entitled to the protection given to civilians".[544] As stated in Art. 1.2 of the Secretary-General's Bulletin on the Observance by United Nations Forces of International Humanitarian Law: "The promulgation of this bulletin does not affect the protected status of members of peacekeeping operations under the 1994 Convention on the Safety of United Nations and Associated Personnel or their status as non-combatants, as long as they are entitled to the protection given to civilians under the international law of armed conflict."

9. Rule 98 (a) applies also in non-international armed conflict.

[544] Art. 8 (2) (b) (iii) of the Rome Statute of the ICC declares the following to be a war crime in an international armed conflict: "Intentionally directing attacks against personnel, installations, material, units or vehicles involved in a humanitarian assistance or peacekeeping mission in accordance with the Charter of the United Nations, as long as they are entitled to the protection given to civilians or civilian objects under the international law of armed conflict." An identical provision (Art. 8 (2) (e) (iii)) exists also for armed conflicts not of an international character.

(b) Directing attacks against UN personnel is prohibited, as long as they are entitled to the protection given to civilians.

1. Attacks against UN personnel are prohibited only (i) as long as the UN is not a Party to the armed conflict; or (ii) its forces do not take a direct part in hostilities.

2. When the UN is a Party to the armed conflict, its military personnel may be regarded as combatants and they may be attacked accordingly.

3. Non-military UN personnel will be regarded as civilians in all circumstances, unless and for such time as they directly participate in hostilities (see Section F).

4. When the UN is not a Party to the armed conflict, resort to force in "self-defence" or in implementation of a robust mandate by UN personnel will not necessarily vest them with a combatant role. Any act of self-defence not overstepping the threshold of armed conflict or not amounting to an act of direct participation in hostilities will not result in the loss of the protection afforded to civilians under the law of international armed conflict.

5. The fact that UN military personnel are engaged in an armed conflict as a Party thereto does not imply that the entirety of the personnel engaged in the UN mission lose their protection against direct attack. While UN armed forces and UN personnel taking a direct part in hostilities lose their protection and are lawful targets, the remainder of the UN personnel – e.g., those participating in relief actions – remain protected.

6. Rule 98 (b) applies also in non-international armed conflict.

(c) Directing attacks against material, installations, units and vehicles of the UN is prohibited, unless they constitute military objectives.

1. UN materiel, installations, units and vehicles are protected only as long as they are entitled to the protection given to civilian objects under the law of international armed conflict (see Rule 1 (j)). They constitute lawful targets if they are military objectives as defined in Rule 1 (y) and in Section E of this Manual.

2. The prohibition of directing attacks against UN vehicles extends to UN aircraft and UAVs or UCAVs, unless they constitute military objectives. UN forces may use UAVs for a variety of purposes, ranging from providing

information useful for their deployment and subsequent movements to acquiring information valuable in force protection. They may also be used to accomplish the UN Security Council mandate. For instance, UAVs may be useful in monitoring the need for humanitarian relief, determining how best to deliver such relief, and monitoring the location and activities of military forces, as during an agreed cease-fire. UCAVs may be used to provide protection for UN forces – or civilians under their protection – pursuant to the UN Security Council mandate. In these and other cases of employment by UN forces, the UCAV/UCAVs retain their immunity from attack as long as (i) the UN is not a Party to the armed conflict; or (ii) its forces do not take a direct part in hostilities.

3. Rule 98 (c) also applies in non-international armed conflict.

V. Protection by special agreement

99. Belligerent Parties may agree at any time to protect persons or objects not otherwise covered by this Manual.

1. The main thrust of Rule 99 is extending specific protection to persons or objects not otherwise enjoying such protection under this Manual.

2. As a general rule, special agreements may only be concluded with a view to enhancing, and not adversely affecting, protection. See also common Art. 6 to the Geneva Conventions.[545]

3. For example, Belligerent Parties not bound by AP/I may conclude a special agreement conferring specific protection on works and installations containing dangerous forces. Along the same lines, a special agreement may be concluded to protect oil production installations, oil rigs, petroleum storage facilities, oil refineries or chemical production facilities.

4. Special agreements under Rule 99 may be concluded without resort to the usual formalities of signature and ratification. Under certain circumstances, they may even be oral. In every case, the exact terms of the agreement must be clear.

[545] Common Art. 6 to the Geneva Conventions: "the High Contracting Parties may conclude other special agreements for all matters concerning which they may deem it suitable to make separate provision. No special agreement shall adversely affect the situation of the wounded and sick, of members of the medical personnel or of chaplains, as defined by the present Convention, nor restrict the rights which it confers upon them."

5. An impartial humanitarian body, such as the ICRC, can facilitate the conclusion of such special agreements.

6. Rule 99 applies also in non-international armed conflict. It is noteworthy that the penultimate paragraph of common Art. 3 to the Geneva Conventions states that "[t]he Parties to the conflict should further endeavour to bring into force, by means of special agreements, all or part of the other provisions of the present Convention".[546]

[546] Common Art. 3 of the 1949 Geneva Conventions, see fn. 92.

Section O

Humanitarian Aid

1. Section O deals with humanitarian aid, i.e., relief operations aiming to ease the plight of victims by ensuring that consequences of the armed conflict – such as disease, injury, hunger, or exposure to the elements – do not jeopardize their lives and health.

2. For the purposes of this Manual, the expressions "humanitarian aid", "humanitarian assistance" and "humanitarian relief" are synonymous.

3. Humanitarian aid is not limited to situations of armed conflict but is also relevant in case of, e.g., natural disaster. However, outside a situation of armed conflict, the law of international armed conflict does not apply and humanitarian assistance is regulated by other legal regimes.

4. Specific provisions concerning the supply of items essential for the survival of the civilian population in the context of aerial blockade are located in Section V (see Rules 157–158).

I. General rules

100. (a) If the civilian population of any territory under the control of a Belligerent Party is not adequately provided with food, medical supplies, clothing, bedding, means of shelter or other supplies essential to its survival, relief actions which are humanitarian and impartial in character – and conducted without adverse distinction – should be undertaken, subject to agreement of the Parties concerned. Such agreement cannot be withheld in occupied territories.

1. Rule 100 (a) is based on Art. 23,[547] Art. 55[548] and Art. 59 of GC/IV[549] as well as on Art. 69[550] and Art. 70 (1) of AP/I.[551] See also Rule 19 (c).

2. The expression "any territory under the control of a Belligerent Party" covers primarily the national territory of a State involved in an international armed conflict, but also those territories under the effective control

547 Art. 23 of GC/IV, see fn. 735.

548 Art. 55 of GC/IV: "To the fullest extent of the means available to it, the Occupying Power has the duty of ensuring the food and medical supplies of the population; it should, in particular, bring in the necessary foodstuffs, medical stores and other Arts. if the resources of the occupied territory are inadequate."

549 Art. 59 of GC/IV: "If the whole or part of the population of an occupied territory is inadequately supplied, the Occupying Power shall agree to relief schemes on behalf of the said population, and shall facilitate them by all the means at its disposal. Such schemes, which may be undertaken either by States or by impartial humanitarian organizations such as the ICRC, shall consist, in particular, of the Rule of consignments of foodstuffs, medical supplies and clothing. All Contracting Parties shall permit the free passage of these consignments and shall guarantee their protection."

550 Art. 69 of AP/I: "(1) In addition to the duties specified in Article 55 of the Fourth Convention concerning food and medical supplies, the Occupying Power shall, to the fullest extent of the means available to it and without any adverse distinction, also ensure the Rule of clothing, bedding, means of shelter, other supplies essential to the survival of the civilian population of the occupied territory and objects necessary for religious worship. (2) Relief actions for the benefit of the civilian population of occupied territories are governed by Articles 59, 60, 61, 62, 108, 109, 110 and 111 of the Fourth Convention, and by Article 71 of this Protocol, and shall be implemented without delay."

551 Art. 70 (1) of AP/I: "If the civilian population of any territory under the control of a Party to the conflict, other than occupied territory, is not adequately provided with the supplies mentioned in Art. 69, relief actions which are humanitarian and impartial in character and conducted without any adverse distinction shall be undertaken, subject to the agreement of the Parties concerned in such relief actions. Offers of such relief shall not be regarded as interference in the armed conflict or as unfriendly acts. In the distribution of relief consignments, priority shall be given to those persons, such as children, expectant mothers, maternity cases and nursing mothers, who, under the Fourth Convention or under this Protocol, are to be accorded privileged treatment or special protection."

or authority of a Belligerent Party. Rule 100 (a) thereby covers relief actions intended both for occupied territories and for other territories.[552]

3. The list of items essential for the survival of the civilian population ("food, medical supplies, clothing, bedding, means of shelter") in Rule 100 (a) is based on the first paragraph of Art. 55[553] of GC/IV and on Art. 69 (1) of AP/I.[554] However, the list is not exhaustive (note the words: "or other supplies essential to survival"). It all depends on the circumstances: heating oil, e.g., may be an essential item in a cold region. Among other essential items may be objects necessary for religious worship, mentioned specifically in Art. 69 (1) of AP/I.

4. In occupied territories, there is an affirmative obligation on the Occupying Power to accept relief actions if it is not in a position to ensure the adequate provision of supplies essential to the survival of the civilian population itself (see Art. 59 of GC/IV).[555]

5. In non-occupied territories, humanitarian relief actions are "subject to the agreement of the Parties concerned". The insistence on agreement indicates that consent by the relevant Belligerent Party is essential. Opinions in the Group of Experts were divided as to whether the absence of agreement implies that there is no obligation to enable humanitarian aid from the outside to proceed. Hence, the use of the term "should" in the text. The majority of the Group of Experts were of the opinion that agreement by a Belligerent Party ought not to be withheld except for valid reasons (e.g., objective security risks for relief personnel or reasonable grounds to suspect that the aid is not humanitarian or impartial in character) and as an exceptional measure. Therefore, there may be extreme circumstances of privation in which agreement by a Belligerent Part to humanitarian aid from abroad cannot be withheld in view of the prohibition of starvation of civilians as a method of warfare.[556]

6. Rule 100 (a) covers all "Parties concerned". These Parties include not only the Belligerent Parties, but also Neutrals from which relief is sent or through whose territory the relief consignments pass.

552 The difference between occupied territories and non-occupied territories is based on the first paragraph of Art. 59 of GC/IV, see fn. 549.

553 First paragraph of Art. 55 of GC/IV, see fn. 548.

554 Art. 69 (1) of AP/I, see fn. 550.

555 Art. 59 of GC/IV, see fn. 549.

556 Para. 47.26 of the Commentary on the SRM/ACS: "[i]t is likely that it would be unlawful to withhold agreement in the case of shipments of objects indispensable for the survival of the population."

7. The operation of relief personnel "shall be subject to the approval of the Party in whose territory they will carry out their duties" (see Art. 71 (1) of AP/I).[557]

8. Rule 100 (a) refers to "relief consignments" which are (i) essential to the survival of the civilian population; (ii) humanitarian and impartial in character; and (iii) conducted without adverse distinction.

9. Humanitarian relief actions must be aimed at bringing relief to victims, i.e., the civilian population lacking essential supplies. They must also be impartial in character and conducted without adverse distinction. Individuals must be assisted according to their needs only (on the basis of the urgency and severity of the case). At the same time, particularly vulnerable segments of the civilian population (such as children, expectant mothers and persons with disabilities) may get a preferential treatment.

10. Rule 100 (a) applies also in non-international armed conflict.[558] As the concept of occupation does not exist in non-international armed conflict, the final sentence of Rule 100 (a), however, does not apply. As in international armed conflict, the agreement for such humanitarian relief may not be withheld on arbitrary grounds (see paragraph 5 of the Commentary on Rule 100 (a)).

(b) Relief actions may be undertaken either by States or by impartial humanitarian organizations such as the International Committee of the Red Cross.

1. Rule 100 (b) is based on the second paragraph of Art. 59 of GC/IV.[559]

[557] Art. 71 (1) of AP/I: "Where necessary, relief personnel may form part of the assistance provided in any relief action, in particular for the transportation and distribution of relief consignments; the participation of such personnel shall be subject to the approval of the Party in whose territory they will carry out their duties."

[558] Art. 18 (2) of AP/II: "If the civilian population is suffering undue hardship owing to a lack of the supplies essential for its survival, such as foodstuffs and medical supplies, relief actions for the civilian population which are of an exclusively humanitarian and impartial nature and which are conducted without any adverse distinction shall be undertaken subject to the consent of the High Contracting Party concerned."

[559] Second Para. of Art. 59 of GC/IV: "Such schemes, which may be undertaken either by States or by impartial humanitarian organizations such as the International Committee of the Red Cross, shall consist, in particular, of the provision of consignments of foodstuffs, medical supplies and clothing."

As regards the expression "relief actions which are humanitarian and impartial in character", used in Art. 70 (1) of AP/I, Para. 2804 of the ICRC Commentary on AP/I, states: "obviously all this also applies to actions undertaken by impartial humanitarian organizations, such as the ICRC."

2. Whereas all States may, in principle, undertake relief actions, only Neutrals will in practice be capable of providing the essential guarantees of impartiality.

3. Only impartial humanitarian organizations qualify for the purposes of Rule 100 (b). The ICRC is mentioned due to its special qualifications and as an example of an impartial humanitarian organization.[560]

4. Rule 100 (b) applies also in non-international armed conflict.

101. The Parties concerned must allow and facilitate rapid and unimpeded passage of relief consignments, equipment and personnel in accordance with Rule 100, subject to technical arrangements including search.

1. Rule 101 relates to the passage of relief consignments. It is based on Art. 70 (2) – (4) of AP/I.[561] The reference to Rule 100 implies that an agreement is required in non-occupied territories. In occupied territories, an Occupying Power which cannot ensure the adequate provision of supplies essential to the survival of the civilian population is under an affirmative obligation to facilitate passage of relief consignments (see paragraph 4 of the Commentary on Rule 100 (a)).

2. As to the meaning of the expression "Parties concerned", see paragraph 6 of the Commentary on Rule 100 (a).

[560] ICRC Commentary on GC/IV, pertaining to the second paragraph of Art. 59 at page 321: "This form of words ["impartial humanitarian organization"] . . . is general enough to cover any institutions or organizations capable of acting effectively and worthy of trust. The International Committee is mentioned both on account of its own special qualifications and as an example of a humanitarian organization whose impartiality is assured."

[561] Art. 70 (2)–(4) of AP/I: "(2) The Parties to the conflict and each High Contracting Party shall allow and facilitate rapid and unimpeded passage of all relief consignments, equipment and personnel provided in accordance with this Section, even if such assistance is destined for the civilian population of the adverse Party. (3) The Parties to the conflict and each High Contracting Party which allows the passage of relief consignments, equipment and personnel in accordance with paragraph 2: (a) shall have the right to prescribe the technical arrangements, including search, under which such passage is permitted; (b) may make such permission conditional on the distribution of this assistance being made under the local supervision of a Protecting Power; (c) shall, in no way whatsoever, divert relief consignments from the purpose for which they are intended nor delay their forwarding, except in cases of urgent necessity in the interest of the civilian population concerned. (4) The Parties to the conflict shall protect relief consignments and facilitate their rapid distribution."

3. The Parties concerned must allow and facilitate the rapid and unimpeded passage of relief consignments (meeting the conditions spelled out in paragraph 9 of the Commentary on Rule 100 (a)).

4. Rule 101 emphasizes that the requirement to "allow and facilitate" relates not only to relief consignments, but also to the relief personnel and their equipment.

5. The passage of relief consignments must be rapid and unimpeded, that is, subject to no harassment or undue delays and with as little formalities as possible.

6. The Parties concerned may demand that certain technical arrangements (including search) be undertaken, but these arrangements must not infringe the overall obligation to facilitate the passage of relief consignments.

7. Rule 101 applies also in non-international armed conflict. Its applicability may be derived from Art. 18 (2) AP/II.[562]

102. (a) Humanitarian relief personnel, acting within the prescribed parameters of their mission, must be respected and protected. The protection extends to humanitarian transports, installations and goods.

1. Rule 102 (a) is based on Art. 71 (1) and (2) of AP/I.[563]

2. Humanitarian relief personnel may be working, e.g., for one of the Belligerent Parties or a Neutral, a national relief Society, an international non-governmental organization or an international organization. The notion of humanitarian relief personnel includes, *inter alia*, medical and para-medical personnel, experts in hygiene and nutrition, and those engaged in transportation, distribution and administration.

562 Art. 18 (2) of AP/II: "If the civilian population is suffering undue hardship owing to a lack of the supplies essential for its survival, such as foodstuffs and medical supplies, relief actions for the civilian population which are of an exclusively humanitarian and impartial nature and which are conducted without any adverse distinction shall be undertaken subject to the consent of the High Contracting Party concerned."

563 Art. 71 (1)–(2): "(1) Where necessary, relief personnel may form part of the assistance provided in any relief action, in particular for the transportation and distribution of relief consignments; the participation of such personnel shall be subject to the approval of the Party in whose territory they will carry out their duties. (2) Such personnel shall be respected and protected."

3. The phrase "prescribed parameters" ought to be understood to mean especially (i) humanitarian mission, impartial in character and conducted without adverse distinction; (ii) consent of the Party in whose territory they will carry out their duties; (iii) non-commission of acts harmful to a Belligerent Party; and (iv) compliance with the technical requirements which the authorities could impose (route, schedule, curfew, etc.) (see Art. 71 (4) of AP/I).[564]

4. In the event that the prescribed parameters are not observed, the humanitarian mission may be terminated.

5. The phrase "transports, installations and goods" is deliberately broader than the expression "equipment" used in Rule 101, inasmuch as practice demonstrates that a large-scale relief operation requires protection that goes beyond mere equipment.

6. Relief operations may include the use of aircraft. In addition to delivering aid, aircraft (including UAVs) may also serve, e.g., to assess the conditions of the population or to identify viable routes for the delivery of relief supplies, in particular where ongoing hostilities may endanger the relief effort or where significant damage to the transportation system has occurred due to fighting, natural disaster or other causes. Aircraft exclusively engaged in such activities pursuant to an agreement between the Belligerent Parties are entitled to specific protection from attack (see Rule 64).

7. The protection conferred upon humanitarian relief personnel must not be abused by Belligerent Parties. Hence, the enemy must not be deceived through the use of the logo of a humanitarian organization (such as the ICRC) to transport combatants, to carry weapons, or to invade a particular area. Such acts jeopardize the whole system of protection of humanitarian relief personnel. Some of these acts may amount to prohibited perfidy (see Section Q, in particular Rule 112 (a)).

8. Rule 102 (a) applies also in non-international armed conflict. The protection of humanitarian relief personnel, transports, installations and goods is indispensable for the provision of relief to the civilian populations in need.

[564] Art. 71 (4) of AP/I: "Under no circumstances may relief personnel exceed the terms of their mission under this Protocol. In particular they shall take account of the security requirements of the Party in whose territory they are carrying out their duties. The mission of any of the personnel who do not respect these conditions may be terminated."

(b) **Each Belligerent Party in receipt of relief consignments must, to the fullest extent practicable, assist the relief personnel referred to in Para. (a) in carrying out their relief mission. Only in case of imperative military necessity may the activities of the relief personnel be limited or their movements temporarily restricted.**

1. Rule 102 (b) is based on Art. 71 (3) of AP/I.[565]

2. In addition to its duty to protect relief personnel under Rule 105 (a), each Belligerent Party in receipt of relief consignments has the duty, to the fullest extent practicable, to assist such personnel in carrying out their mission. For example, the receiving Belligerent Party must do its utmost to facilitate the task of relief personnel by simplifying administrative formalities and by offering practical assistance, e.g., in discharging cargo. This obligation may extend, as far as possible, to the repair of air traffic control capability or to the repairs (e.g., filling holes) of an airstrip to allow relief aircraft to safely access the persons in need.

3. The activities or movements of relief personnel may only be temporarily restricted by a Belligerent Party in case of "imperative military necessity". For example, the distribution of relief items to the civilian population may be limited if it is known that relief personnel are passing foodstuffs to the armed forces of the enemy.[566] Before any unilateral decision is taken by the Belligerent Party concerned, any limitation on the activities of relief personnel ought to be discussed with those responsible for the humanitarian relief. At the same time, it must be appreciated that quick decisions may be necessary in light of the developing hostilities.

4. In any event, any limitation imposed by a Belligerent Party on the activities of the relief personnel, must be temporary in nature, and it may not be prolonged beyond what is required by the "imperative military necessity".

5. Rule 102 applies also in non-international armed conflict.

[565] Art. 71 (3) of AP/I: "Each Party in receipt of relief consignments shall, to the fullest extent practicable, assist the relief personnel referred to in paragraph 1 in carrying out their relief mission. Only in case of imperative military necessity may the activities of the relief personnel be limited or their movements temporarily restricted."

[566] Para. 2894 of the ICRC Commentary on AP/I, pertaining to Art. 71 of AP/I.

II. Specifics of air or missile operations

103. Whenever circumstances permit, Belligerent Parties conducting air or missile operations ought to suspend air or missile attacks in order to permit the distribution of humanitarian assistance.

1. In certain circumstances – e.g., when one of the Belligerent Parties is conducting an intense air campaign in inhabited areas, making entry into them very risky – humanitarian organizations can be temporarily barred from delivering humanitarian assistance. Therefore, whenever circumstances permit, Belligerent Parties ought to suspend air or missile operations. This suspension ought then to allow humanitarian relief personnel safe passage to any area in humanitarian need and allow civilians to safely leave their (possible) shelters to receive assistance.

2. The suspension of air attacks may take different forms. Ideally, all Belligerent Parties reach a formal agreement to cease air and missile attacks for a specified period. Alternatively, one Belligerent Party may suspend air and missile attacks unilaterally. In that case, the enemy ought not to make use of that situation to further its military goals. Of course, Belligerent Parties are at liberty to agree on a formal cease-fire, temporarily halting all conduct of hostilities. This ought especially to be considered where air or missile operations threaten the distribution of humanitarian assistance.

3. Belligerent Parties ought to suspend air or missile attacks only "whenever circumstances permit". This qualifier has been inserted because, for reasons of military necessity, it may not be possible to suspend air or missile operations. Similarly, it may also be the case that, while one Belligerent Party has suspended air and missile attacks, the enemy launches a counter-offensive. In that case, it would be unreasonable to expect the Belligerent Party which suspended its air and missile attacks not to resume them. However, in such a scenario, a warning and sufficient time ought to be given to the relief personnel and to the civilians, respectively, to allow them to withdraw from the area or to go into shelters.

4. Rule 103 applies also in non-international armed conflict.

104. "Technical arrangements" as used in Rule 101 may include such matters as:

1. As indicated by the words "may include such matters as", Rule 104 merely sets forth examples of "technical arrangements".

2. Rule 104 applies also in non-international armed conflict.

(a) Establishment of air corridors or air routes.

Whilst the Parties concerned must allow the unimpeded passage of relief consignments (see Rule 101), delivery of such consignments through "air corridors" or "air routes" may be arranged. "Air route" is the more general term of the two. It is simply "the navigable airspace between two points, identified to the extent necessary for the application of flight rules".[567] The term "air corridor" has more specific implications. It means "a restricted air route of travel specified for use by friendly aircraft and established for the purpose of preventing friendly aircraft from being fired on by friendly forces."[568]

(b) Organization of air drops.

Where territory is not otherwise accessible, air drops present an alternative to relief consignments distributed on the ground. Obviously, where air drops are carried out, it is impossible to meet the condition of relief actions being "conducted without adverse distinction" (see Rule 100 (a)). Hence, as soon as it is possible, relief consignments ought to be distributed on the ground evenly and with priority to those most in need.[569]

(c) Agreement on flight details (i.e., timing, route, landing).

The deliverer of relief supplies and the Party concerned may agree on flight details such as timing, route or landing. This is true even of occupied territories (see the fourth paragraph of Art. 59 of GC/IV).[570] However, if an aircraft carrying relief consignments fails to meet a minor condition in an agreement (e.g., the flight is conducted at a slight time variance from the agreed upon schedule), this ought not to be used as a pretext to refuse relief supplies.

567 DoD Dictionary of Military and Associated Terms, at page 24.

568 DoD Dictionary of Military and Associated Terms, at page 13.

569 Art. 70 (1) of AP/I, final sentence, see fn. 551.

570 Fourth Para. of Art. 59 of GC/IV: "A Power granting free passage to consignments on their way to territory occupied by an adverse Party to the conflict shall, however, have the right to search the consignments, to regulate their passage according to prescribed times and routes, and to be reasonably satisfied through the Protecting Power that these consignments are to be used for the relief of the needy population and are not to be used for the benefit of the Occupying Power."

(d) Search of relief supplies.

The Parties concerned may search relief supplies (see Commentary on Rule 101). Evidently, a search ought to be conducted as expeditiously as possible, in order not to delay relief supplies too long. The terms "relief supplies" and "relief consignments" are used interchangeably; they both mean goods delivered for humanitarian ends.

Section P

"Exclusion Zones" and No-Fly Zones

1. The term "zone" is used for various, and often unrelated, operational concepts: safety zones, security zones, protection zones, danger zones, warning zones, air defence identification zones, operational zones, etc.

2. Section P sets out the legal framework of two zones that have become part of State practice: "exclusion zones" and no-fly zones.[571] Other operational concepts are referred to for the purpose of distinction only. Whereas no-fly zones, as the phrase implies, relate merely to aircraft, "exclusion zones" pertain both to flights and to activities by vessels at sea.

3. An "exclusion zone", for the purpose of this Manual, is a three dimensional space beyond the territorial sovereignty of any State in which a Belligerent Party claims to be relieved from certain provisions of the law of international armed conflict, or where that Belligerent Party purports to be entitled to restrict the freedom of aviation (or navigation) of other States.

4. A no-fly zone, for the purposes of this Manual, is a three dimensional airspace by which the Belligerent Party restricts or prohibits aviation in its own or in enemy national territory.

5. "Exclusion zone" is discussed herein only in the context of an international armed conflict. No-fly zones are discussed in the context of both international and non-international armed conflicts.

6. Whereas there is no doubt that State practice confirms proclamation of "exclusion zones", there is no indication that a Belligerent Party may absolve itself of its obligations under the law of international armed

[571] For a distinction between zones in international and zones in national airspace see Para. 12.58 of the UK Manual ("War Zones Restrictions") at Para. 12.58.1: "These zones may exist over the territories and territorial waters of any state involved in the armed conflict and, where military necessity justifies it, may include airspace over the high seas."

conflict within that zone (see Rule 105 (a) and Rule 107 (a)). The value added of the establishment of an "exclusion zone" is therefore unclear at the present juncture, but as a minimum they may warn off neutral aircraft (or vessels) from areas of hostilities and thereby reduce their exposure to collateral damage.[572]

7. Whereas the legality of no-fly zones has not been seriously questioned, the legality of "exclusion zones" has been a matter of dispute in post-WWII State practice. Indeed, the majority of "zones" ("war zones", "barred areas", etc.) established and enforced during international armed conflicts of the past, were in violation of the law of international armed conflict because they resulted in unrestricted warfare. However, since the 1990s, "exclusion zones" have gained increasing acceptance and they have been recognized as a lawful method of warfare, to varying extents, in military manuals and elsewhere.[573] On the basis of recent State practice, the Group of Experts has identified some parameters for the establishment and operation of "exclusion zones". In view of the uncertainties regarding the usefulness and extent of "exclusion zones", the Group of Experts considered it necessary to identify, in a non-exhaustive manner, the limits applicable to such zones.

8. No-fly zones may be enforced by any lawful method or means of warfare. Typically, such zones are enforced by aircraft or missiles (including UAVs and UCAVs). However, at sea, it would not be uncommon for

[572] According to Para. 8.18 of the Australian Book of Reference 5179 Manual of International Law, there are certain operational advantages in declaring an EEZ, such as limiting the geographic spread of the conflict and to warn neutral merchant shipping.

Para. 7.9 of NWP ("Exclusion Zones and War Zones"), second paragraph thereof: "Exclusion or war zones established by belligerents in the context of limited warfare that has characterized post–World War II belligerency at sea, have been justified, at least in part, as reasonable, albeit coercive, measures to contain the geographic area of the conflict or to keep neutral shipping at a safe distance from areas of actual or potential hostilities. To the extent that such zones serve to warn neutral vessels and aircraft away from belligerent activities and thereby reduce their exposure to collateral damage and incidental injury (see paragraph 8.3.1), and to the extent that they do not unreasonably interfere with legitimate neutral commerce, they are undoubtedly lawful."

[573] Para. 13.77 of the UK Manual: "Security zones may be established by belligerents as a defensive measure or to impose some limitation on the geographical extent of the area of conflict. However, a belligerent cannot be absolved of its duties under the law of armed conflict by establishing zones in such a manner that they adversely affect the legitimate uses of defined areas of the sea."

See also Para. 7.9 of NWP, see fn. 572.

warships to serve such purposes. Analogously, air defence weapons could be employed to enforce such zones over land.

9. "Exclusion zones" and no-fly zones must be clearly distinguished from blockades. An aerial blockade, according to Rule 147 of this Manual, "is a belligerent operation to prevent aircraft (including UAVs/UCAVs) from entering or exiting specified airfields or coastal areas belonging to, occupied by, or under the control of the enemy". With blockades, the focus lies on the horizontal line (or "curtain") marking the outer limits of the blockaded area. The area/space within that line is of minor interest. By contrast, the focal point of "exclusion zones" and of no-fly zones is the three dimensional area/space within the declared borderline.

10. "Exclusion zones" and no-fly zones may not be established for the purpose of interfering with enemy exports on board neutral aircraft (or vessels), although the practical effect of the establishment of such zones may be to do so. The only lawful method of warfare for the purpose of preventing enemy exports on board neutral aircraft (or vessels) is an aerial (or naval) blockade.

11. "Exclusion zones" and no-fly zones must be clearly distinguished from the customary belligerent right to control the immediate area of naval operations and neutral communication at sea (see Para. 108 of SRM/ACS[574] and Para. 7.8 of NWP[575]).

12. While civilian airliners (whether enemy or neutral) ought to avoid entering a no-fly zone or an "exclusion zone" (as well as the immediate vicinity of hostilities), they do not lose their protection merely because they enter such areas (see Rule 60).

[574] Para. 108 of SRM/ACS: "Nothing in this Section should be deemed to derogate from the customary belligerent right to control neutral vessels and aircraft in the immediate vicinity of naval operations."

[575] Para. 7.8 of NWP ("Belligerent control of the immediate area of naval operations and neutral communication at sea"): "Within the immediate area or vicinity of naval operations, to ensure proper battle space management and self–defense objectives, a belligerent may establish special restrictions upon the activities of neutral vessels and aircraft and may prohibit altogether such vessels and aircraft from entering the area. The immediate area or vicinity of naval operations is that area within which hostilities are taking place or belligerent forces are actually operating. A belligerent may not, however, purport to deny access to neutral nations, or to close an international strait to neutral shipping, pursuant to this authority unless another route of similar convenience remains open to neutral traffic."

I. General rules

105. (a) A Belligerent Party is not absolved of its obligations under the law of international armed conflict by establishing "exclusion zones" or no-fly zones.

1. Rule 105 (a) emphasizes that, by establishing "exclusion zones" or no-fly zones, Belligerent Parties are not absolved from their obligations under the law of international armed conflict,[576] nor do they acquire additional rights. Laws concerning neutrality (see section X) and targeting (see Section D), in particular, still apply within a zone.

2. Aircraft not qualifying as military objectives may not be attacked for the mere reason of being encountered within an "exclusion zone" or a no-fly zone. While unauthorized presence in a zone may be considered an indicator of hostile intent, the principles of target discrimination as well as the rules on feasible precautions in attack still apply (see Sections D; E and G).[577]

3. "Exclusion zones" or no-fly zones may not be abused for preventing enemy exports on board neutral aircraft (or vessels). The only lawful method for achieving that goal is blockade (for aerial blockade, see Section V).

(b) Zones designated for unrestricted air or missile attacks are prohibited.

1. Rule 105 (b) clearly prohibits any form of unrestricted air and missile attacks, i.e., attacks on sight against all objects and persons encountered within the zone without prior target identification or precautionary measures (see Canadian Joint Doctrine Manual[578] and Para. 7.9 of

[576] Para. 13.78 of the UK Manual: "Should a belligerent, as an exceptional measure, establish such a zone: (a) the same body of law applies both inside and outside the zone."
Para. 7.9 of NWP, in the second Para. thereof: "the establishment of such a zone does not relieve the proclaiming belligerent of the obligation under the law of armed conflict to refrain from attacking vessels and aircraft that do not constitute lawful targets. In short, an otherwise protected platform does not lose that protection by crossing an imaginary line drawn in the ocean by a belligerent."

[577] See also Para. 12.58 of the UK Manual: "The right to fire upon any aircraft disregarding a general prohibition of entry into such a zone must be based on military necessity. That requires an assessment as to whether in all circumstances the aircraft is a military objective and whether an attack upon it can be carried out without disproportionate loss of civilian life or civilian property."

[578] Para. 852 of the Canadian Joint Doctrine Manual: "(1) Parties to naval conflicts have on a number of occasions established different kinds of zones in and over water areas that

NWP[579]).[580] Sometimes, the term "free-fire zone" is used in this context. Since, however, that is not a legal term of art, the Group of Experts preferred the use of the more established term "unrestricted . . . attacks".

2. Aircraft may not be attacked based on mere presence in an "exclusion zone" or in a no-fly zone. Aircraft can only be attacked if they constitute military objectives in accordance with all the criteria discussed in Rule 1 (y) and Section E before being made the object of attack.

3. However, the prohibition of unrestricted warfare is without prejudice to the possibility of a specific area of land being a military objective on the basis of the location criterion (see Rule 1 (y) and Rule 22 (b)).[581]

106. Nothing in this Section of the Manual ought to be deemed as derogating from the right of a Belligerent Party:

(a) to control civil aviation in the immediate vicinity of hostilities; or

1. As indicated in paragraph 11 of the *chapeau* to this Section, "exclusion zones" and no-fly zones must be distinguished from other well-established belligerent rights, such as the right of belligerent control within the immediate area of operations.[582]

deny or restrict access to vessels and aircraft of states that are not parties to the conflict. Vessels or aircraft entering such zones risk being attacked. These zones have been given a variety of names including exclusion zones, military areas, barred areas, war zones and operational zones. (2) A belligerent is not absolved of its duties under International Law by establishing zones that might adversely affect the legitimate uses of defined areas of the sea. In particular, such zones are not "free fire zones."

[579] Para. 7.9 of NWP, third paragraph thereof: "Because exclusion and war zones are not simply free fire zones for the warships of the belligerents, the establishment of such a zone carries with it certain obligations for belligerents with respect to neutral vessels entering the zones."

[580] See also Para. 8.18 of the Australian Book of Reference 5179 Manual of International Law.

[581] See, e.g., the statement made by the UK on ratification of AP/I, pertaining to Art. 52 of AP/I: "It is the understanding of the UK that a specific area of land may be a military objective if, because of its location or other reasons specified in this Article, its total or partial destruction, capture or neutralisation in the circumstances ruling at the time offers definite military advantage."

[582] Para. 12.58 of the UK Manual: "Parties to a conflict may establish zones of immediate operations or exclusion zones within which they intend to pursue or are actively pursuing hostilities."

Para. 7.8 of NWP, see fn. 575.

2. The concept "immediate vicinity of hostilities" includes the contact zone on land and the counterpart area at sea or in the air in which hostilities are taking place or in which belligerent forces are actually operating in support of the hostilities.

3. In order to prevent "civil aviation in the immediate vicinity of hostilities" from jeopardizing the military operations through (i) presence; or (ii) communication with anyone outside that area, a Belligerent Party may prohibit civil aviation from entering that area, or may establish special restrictions upon flights or activities (e.g., by controlling or blocking their communication).[583]

4. Art. 30 of the HRAW provides: "In case a belligerent commanding officer considers that the presence of aircraft is likely to prejudice the success of the operations in which he is engaged at the moment, he may prohibit the passing of neutral aircraft in the immediate vicinity of his forces or may oblige them to follow a particular route. A neutral aircraft which does not conform to such directions, of which it has had a notice issued by the belligerent commanding officer, may be fired upon."

(b) to take appropriate measures of force protection in the form of, e.g., the establishment of warning zones.

1. Rule 106 (b) relates to "force protection", which is a generally recognized belligerent right. Such measures may include the establishment and enforcement of "warning zones" around naval units ("defence bubbles") or around military units stationed on the ground, and other measures the responsible commander considers necessary in view of a given threat.

2. Such "warning zones" merely serve to keep aviation or navigation at a distance from the force subject to protection, and to indicate that – should they enter the zone – they are at increased risk of defensive action. The establishment of a "warning zone" may never result in attacks without prior warning. However, aircraft approaching a "warning zone" may become liable to attack if, after prior warning, they continue on their course and military necessity warrants attack.

Para. 703 of the Canadian Joint Doctrine Manual: "2. Operational Zones. Parties to a conflict may, by appropriate notice, establish areas of immediate air operations where they pursue combat activities. Such zones may exist over the territories and territorial waters of all states involved in the hostilities. All aircraft entering such zones, including the aircraft of neutral states, risk damage from the hostilities."

583 Para. 108 of SRM/ACS, see fn. 574.

II. "Exclusion Zones" in international airspace

This subsection is without prejudice to the rights of proclaiming "Air Defence Identification Zones" (ADIZ) or "Flight Information Regions" (FIR). These rights are enjoyed by every State, in times both of peace and armed conflict. ADIZs are zones established in international airspace adjacent to national airspace by which States establish reasonable conditions of entry into their territory. FIR is an aviation term used to describe airspace with specific dimensions, in which a flight information service and an alerting service are provided. Oceanic airspace is divided into Oceanic Information Regions and delegated to controlling authorities bordering that region. The division of authorities is done by international agreement through ICAO.

107. Should a Belligerent Party establish an "exclusion zone" in international airspace:

1. This Rule specifies the criteria that are constitutive for the legality of an "exclusion zone". The preconditions spelled out in Rule 107 (a) – (e) must be fulfilled cumulatively.

2. The expression "international airspace", as used in Rule 107, has been understood by the Group of Experts not to be applicable to any parts of the airspace above Antarctica, and this notwithstanding paragraph 8 of the Commentary on Rule 1 (a). Although some parts of Antarctica are considered "territory not subject to the sovereignty of any State", there is no right for a Belligerent Party to establish an exclusion zone in the airspace above Antarctica.

(a) The same rules of the law of international armed conflict will apply both inside and outside the "exclusion zone".

1. Rule 107 (a) re-emphasizes the general Rule set out in Rule 105 (a) that a Belligerent Party, by establishing an "exclusion zone", neither acquires additional rights nor becomes absolved from its obligations under the law of international armed conflict. Laws concerning neutrality and targeting, in particular, still apply within an "exclusion zone" (see the Commentary on Rule 105).

2. A Belligerent Party may, as a matter of policy, decide to limit the hostilities to the area covered by the "exclusion zone".

(b) The extent, location and duration of the "exclusion zone" and the measures imposed must not exceed what is reasonably required by military necessity.

1. There are no specific limits on the extent, location and duration of an "exclusion zone" or the measures imposed within it on international aviation. All this will depend upon the circumstances of each case. There must, however, be a reasonable and proportionate nexus between the zone and considerations of military necessity. The weight of the latter must be established in light of the specific purpose pursued with the establishment of the "exclusion zone".

2. Moreover, the nature of the respective area in which the zone is established ought to be taken into consideration. For instance, the location of major civil aviation routes within the zone and subsequent impact on neutral trade may be a factor in assessing what is "reasonably required by military necessity".

(c) The commencement, duration, location and extent of the "exclusion zone", as well as the restrictions imposed, must be appropriately notified to all concerned.

1. Since an "exclusion zone" is established and enforced in international airspace, it necessarily impacts on international civil aviation (and navigation). A Belligerent Party cannot expect international civil aviation (and navigation) to observe the restrictions imposed if neutral aircraft (and vessels) are unaware of the zone, its location, extent and duration.

2. Therefore, based on Rule 107 (c), the Belligerent Party establishing an "exclusion zone" is obliged to publicize these details as well as the restrictive measures it purports to apply within the "exclusion zone". The term "notify" is to be understood in a non-technical manner. It is not necessary to communicate the information via diplomatic channels. In most cases it will be appropriate to make use of a NOTAM.

(d) The establishment of an "exclusion zone" must neither encompass nor completely bar access to the airspace of Neutrals.

1. Neutral territory, including neutral airspace, is inviolable under the law of international armed conflict (see Rule 166). Moreover, the existence of an international armed conflict does not deprive a Neutral of its right to use its national airspace for all lawful purposes, such as egress

from and entry into international airspace, as well as military exercises and operations. Based on Rule 107 (d), Belligerent Parties are under an affirmative obligation to respect these neutral rights.

2. One ought to distinguish between (i) what is impermissible (i.e., the establishment of an "exclusion zone" encompassing neutral airspace within the zone); and (ii) what is permissible (i.e., the establishment of an "exclusion zone" in areas of the high seas, including for this purpose the EEZ, provided that adequate access / exit routes are established). While an "exclusion zone" encompassing neutral airspace within the zone will always be illegal, the mere fact that access to neutral airspace on certain routes is no longer possible, or has become restricted, is not sufficient to render an "exclusion zone" illegal. However, a partial barring of access to neutral airspace may be a violation of the Neutral's rights if other access routes of similar safety and convenience are unavailable.

(e) Due regard must be given to the lawful use by Neutrals of their Exclusive Economic Zones and continental shelf, in particular artificial islands, installations, structures and safety zones.

1. The obligation of Belligerent Parties to pay due regard to the rights of Neutrals is not limited to areas in which Neutrals enjoy territorial sovereignty. According to Rule 107 (e), which is derived from Art. 58[584] and Art. 87 of UNCLOS,[585] Belligerent Parties are obliged to pay due

[584] Art. 58 UNCLOS ("Rights and duties of other states in the exclusive economic zone"): "(1) In the exclusive economic zone, all States, whether coastal or land-locked, enjoy, subject to the relevant provisions of this Convention, the freedoms referred to in Article 87 of navigation and overflight and of the laying of submarine cables and pipelines, and other internationally lawful uses of the sea related to these freedoms, such as those associated with the operation of ships, aircraft and submarine cables and pipelines, and compatible with the other provisions of this Convention. (2) Articles 88 to 115 and other pertinent rules of international law apply to the exclusive economic zone insofar as they are not incompatible with this Part. (3) In exercising their rights and performing their duties under this Convention in the exclusive economic zone, States shall have due regard to the rights and duties of the coastal State and shall comply with the laws and regulations adopted by the coastal State in accordance with the provisions of this Convention and other rules of international law insofar as they are not incompatible with this Part."

[585] Art. 87 UNCLOS ("Freedom of the high seas"): "(1) The high seas are open to all States, whether coastal or land-locked. Freedom of the high seas is exercised under the conditions laid down by this Convention and by other rules of international law. It comprises, *inter alia*, both for coastal and land-locked States: (a) freedom of navigation; (b) freedom of overflight; (c) freedom to lay submarine cables and pipelines, subject to Part VI; (d) freedom to construct artificial islands and other installations permitted under

regard to installations and other structures Neutrals have established in accordance with the respective provisions of the law of the sea.[586] As long as they are paying such due regard to artificial islands, installations, structures and safety zones, Belligerent Parties are free to conduct military activities within the EEZ of Neutrals (see also paragraph 8 of the Commentary on Rule 1 (b)) and the third paragraph of the Commentary on Rule 166).

2. The "due regard" principle is a concept of the law of the sea and therefore established in peacetime international law. In the relations between Belligerent Parties and Neutrals, the law of the sea – to the extent it does not conflict with the law of neutrality – continues to apply. It needs to be stressed that the "due regard" principle imposes no absolute and affirmative obligation. According to that principle, Belligerent Parties are called upon to balance the military advantages anticipated with the negative impact on the Neutral's rights in the respective airspace and sea areas.

3. Members of the Group of Experts disagreed over whether Rule 107 (e) reflects customary international law. Some members of the Group of Experts felt that there was no established State practice with regard to this principle.

III. No-fly zones in Belligerent Airspace

108. A Belligerent Party may establish and enforce a no-fly zone in its own or in enemy national airspace.

The object and purpose of this Rule is to emphasize this belligerent right and to distinguish no-fly zones from "exclusion zones". For the purposes of this Manual, no-fly zones cannot be established in international airspace.

international law, subject to Part VI; (e) freedom of fishing, subject to the conditions laid down in section 2; (f) freedom of scientific research, subject to Parts VI and XIII. (2) These freedoms shall be exercised by all States with due regard for the interests of other States in their exercise of the freedom of the high seas, and also with due regard for the rights under this Convention with respect to activities in the Area."

586 Para. 34 of SRM/ACS: "If hostile actions are conducted within the exclusive economic zone or on the continental shelf of a neutral state, belligerent states shall, in addition to observing the other applicable rules of the law of armed conflict at sea, have due regard for the rights and duties of the coastal state, inter alia, for the exploration and exploitation of the economic resources of the exclusive economic zone and the continental shelf and the protection and preservation of the marine environment. They shall, in particular, have due regard for artificial islands, installations, structures, and safety zones established by neutral states in the exclusive economic zone and on the continental shelf." Similar language is also used in Para. 13.21 of the UK Manual.

109. The commencement, duration, location and extent of the no-fly zones must be appropriately notified to all concerned.

A Belligerent Party establishing and enforcing a no-fly zone is under an obligation to publicize the details laid down in Rule 109 to "all concerned", i.e., to civil aviation – own, enemy or neutral – if the zone will have an impact on such aviation. There is no obligation to inform enemy military aircraft (which are military objectives by nature). As to the means of communicating the details (e.g., by NOTAM), see paragraph 2 of the Commentary on Rule 107 (c).

110. Subject to the Rules set out in Sections D and G of this Manual, aircraft entering a no-fly zone without specific permission are liable to be attacked.

1. Sections D and G deal, respectively, with attacks and precautions in attack.

2. Rule 110 reflects that unauthorized presence in a no-fly zone may be considered an indicator of hostile intent, but in no way implies that mere presence within the zone is sufficient to warrant attack. In other words, such presence by itself does not trigger the application of the criterion of "location" to render it a military objective under Rule 22 (b).

3. As emphasized in the UK Manual, "attacks on ostensibly civil aircraft ought only to be carried out as a last resort when there is reason to believe that it is itself deployed on an attack".[587]

4. Rule 110 does not authorize automatic engagement or a "free-fire zone". As in "exclusion zones", the principles of target discrimination (Sections D and E) and the Rules of Section G still apply.

[587] Para. 12.58.2. of the UK Manual: "The presumption, in Additional Protocol I, of civilian status in cases of doubt does not, strictly speaking, apply in air-to-air combat [see Art. 49 (4) of AP/I] Nevertheless, attacks on ostensibly civil aircraft should only be carried out as a last resort when there is reason to believe that it is itself deployed on an attack. An example might be when, during an armed conflict, an exclusion zone has been established around the United Kingdom and an apparently civilian airliner enters the zone on a course set for a major city, all required notification and other procedures to establish the zone have been meticulously completed, and all attempts to communicate with the aircraft, including buzzing, have failed or been ignored."

Section Q

Deception, Ruses of War and Perfidy

I. General rules

111. (a) It is prohibited to kill or injure an adversary by resort to perfidy. Acts inviting the confidence of an adversary to lead him to believe that he is entitled to, or is obliged to accord, protection under the Rules of the law of international armed conflict, with the intent to betray that confidence, constitute perfidy.

1. This Rule is derived from Art. 37 (1) of AP/I.[588] See also Para. 12.1.2 of NWP.[589]

2. Betrayal of confidence is the nucleus of perfidy. In the past, perfidy used to be called "treachery" (see Art. 23 (b) of the 1907 Hague Regulations).[590] In introducing and defining the term perfidy, Art. 37 (1) of AP/I denotes the same concept.

[588] Art. 37 (1) of AP/I: "(1) It is prohibited to kill, injure or capture an adversary by resort to perfidy. Acts inviting the confidence of an adversary to lead him to believe that he is entitled to, or is obliged to accord, protection under the rules of international law applicable in armed conflict, with intent to betray that confidence, shall constitute perfidy. The following acts are examples of perfidy: (a) the feigning of an intent to negotiate under a flag of truce or of a surrender; (b) the feigning of an incapacitation by wounds or sickness; (c) the feigning of civilian, non-combatant status; and (d) the feigning of protected status by the use of signs, emblems or uniforms of the United Nations or of neutral or other States not Parties to the conflict."

[589] Para. 12.1.2 of NWP ("Prohibited deceptions"): "The use of unlawful deceptions is called "perfidy". Acts of perfidy are deceptions designed to invite the confidence of the enemy to lead him to believe that he is entitled to, or is obliged to accord, protected status under the law of armed conflict, with the intent to betray that confidence. Feigning surrender in order to lure the enemy into a trap is one example of an act of perfidy."

[590] Art. 23 of the 1907 Hague Regulations: "In addition to the prohibitions provided by special Conventions, it is especially forbidden : (b) to kill or wound treacherously individuals belonging to the hostile nation or army."

3. Not all perfidious action (i.e., acts involving a betrayal of confidence) is prohibited. The prohibition in Art. 37 (1) of AP/I covers only those instances in which the adversary, through perfidy, is killed, injured or captured.

4. Art. 8 (2) (b) (xi) of the Rome Statute of the ICC declares the following to be a war crime in international armed conflicts: "[k]illing or wounding treacherously individuals belonging to the hostile nation or army". Art. 8 (2) (e) (ix) of the Rome Statute declares the following to be a war crime in a non-international armed conflict: "[k]illing or wounding treacherously a combatant adversary".

5. The Group of Experts was divided on the question whether, as a matter of customary international law, the prohibition includes "capture" by perfidy. The majority of the Group of Experts reached the conclusion that perfidious capture is not an integral part of customary international law. It is not included in the 1907 Hague Regulations, which only prohibits (Art. 23 (b)) "to kill or wound treacherously". A prohibition against capture by perfidy is also not recognized by several States. On the other hand, perfidious killing or injuring is undeniably considered customary international law.

6. The minority of the Group of Experts relied on the ICRC Customary IHL Study, which reaches the conclusion that capture is included in the customary prohibition.[591] According to this view, the omission of capture from the Rome Statute of the ICC affects the definition of the war crime, but not the scope of the substantive rule of the law of international armed conflict.

7. All members of the Group of Experts agreed that unlawful perfidious action does not go beyond killing, injuring (or capturing). A clear example of perfidious action which is not prohibited as "perfidy" under customary international law or under AP/I, is the destruction of property (which does not entail killing or injuring of – or even capturing – an adversary).

[591] Rule 65 of the ICRC Customary IHL Study, with discussion at pages 221–226: "Killing, injuring or capturing an adversary by resort to perfidy is prohibited." (underlining added), with at page 225: "On the basis of this practice, it can be argued that killing, injuring or capturing by resort to perfidy is illegal under customary international law but that only acts that result in serious bodily injury, namely killing or injuring, would constitute a war crime. This argument is also based on the consideration that the capture of an adversary by resort to perfidy nevertheless undermines a protection provided under international humanitarian law even though the consequences may not be grave enough for it to constitute a war crime."

8. A typical example of perfidy would be to open fire upon an unsuspecting enemy after having displayed the flag of truce, thereby inducing the enemy to lower his guard.

9. It is useful to analyze a scenario in which an ambulance is used by combatants to move from one point to another. This abuse of the ambulance is perfidious, but it does not fall under the prohibition of perfidy according to customary international law or AP/I, unless the combatants – availing themselves of the protective status of the ambulance – do so in order to kill, injure (or capture) the enemy by advancing surreptitiously against enemy forces. Nevertheless, in view of Rule 112 (a), the activity will still be prohibited because of the improper use of the distinctive emblem.

10. Prohibited perfidy must not be confused with espionage. The essence of prohibited perfidy is the killing or injuring (or capturing) of a person. By contrast, espionage focuses on the clandestine gathering of certain useful information of military value, and it does not pertain to killing or injuring (or capturing) of a person. For a definition of espionage, see Rule 118.

11. Rule 111 (a) applies also in non-international armed conflict (see also Art. 8 (2) (e) (ix) of the Rome Statute of the ICC).[592]

(b) The following acts are examples of perfidy as per paragraph (a): feigning of civilian, neutral or other protected status.

1. This Rule is derived from Art. 37 (1) (a) – (d) of AP/I.[593]

2. Rule 111 (b) illustrates the prohibition of perfidy defined in Rule 111 (a) without exhausting the scope of the prohibition.

3. Combatants are obliged to accord protection to civilian, neutral or other protected persons. Feigning such privileged status would therefore be liable to lead a combatant to believe that he is obliged to accord protection. If such an act – which invites the confidence of the enemy – is committed with intent to betray that confidence, the conduct is perfidious. Still, not every perfidious act is unlawful. A perfidious act is prohibited only when it entails killing, injuring (or capturing) an adversary.

[592] Art. 8 (2) (e) (ix) of the Rome Statute of the ICC, see Para. 4, Rule 111 (a), Section Q.
[593] Art. 37 (1) (a)–(d) of AP/I, see fn. 588.

4. The mere fact that a person is fighting in civilian clothing does not constitute perfidy, although the person may thus become an "unprivileged belligerent" (the term "unlawful combatant" is also used, see paragraph 4 of the Commentary on Rule 10 (b) (i); see also the Commentary on Rule 117). "Unprivileged belligerents" do not enjoy combatant privilege and can be prosecuted and punished under the domestic law of the enemy for mere participation in hostilities. As opposed to unlawful perfidy, "unprivileged belligerency" is not in itself a war crime. For unlawful perfidy, there must always be an intention to betray confidence, as in the case of a person who advances to an advantageous position under the cover of being a civilian in order to fire on, and kill or injure, an unsuspecting enemy.

5. "Other protected status" (in addition to civilian and neutral status) includes *inter alia* UN personnel.

6. The applicability of Rule 111 (b) to non-international armed conflicts is multi-layered. Neutrality in the legal sense does not exist in non-international armed conflict. Neither do distinctions between combatant, "unprivileged belligerent" and civilian status, at least not on the side of the non-State organized armed group. It is still, however, prohibited to kill, injure (or capture) an enemy after having intentionally misled him by pretending to be a civilian (who is protected by Common Art. 3[594] of the 1949 Geneva Conventions against acts of violence while not participating actively in the hostilities).

112. Without prejudice to the rules of naval warfare, the following acts are prohibited at all times irrespective of whether or not they are perfidious:

1. Whereas Rule 111 hinges on the perfidious nature of the acts set forth in it, Rule 112 includes absolute prohibitions of certain activities at all times.

2. Special rules apply in the case of naval warfare, see paragraph 3 of the Commentary on Rule 112 (c).

3. The prohibition of perfidy does not cover the whole spectrum of unlawful acts linked to deception. There are specific prohibitions of "improper" conduct, which is prohibited *per se*, irrespective of whether or not the acts concerned constitute prohibited perfidy. Moreover, prohibitions of

[594] Common Art. 3 of the Geneva Conventions, see fn. 92.

"improper conduct" do not require proof of any specific intent to betray the confidence of the enemy. For an example of the interplay between perfidy and "improper" conduct, see the ambulance scenario given in paragraph 9 of the Commentary on Rule 111 (a).

(a) Improper use of the distinctive emblem of the Red Cross, Red Crescent or Red Crystal, or of other protective emblems, signs or signals provided for by the law of international armed conflict.

1. This Rule is based on Art. 38 (1) of AP/I.[595] The principle is also found in Art. 23 (f) of the 1907 Hague Regulations.[596]

2. An example of "improper use" referred to in Rule 112 (a) would be transportation of munitions in an aircraft bearing the distinctive emblem of the Red Cross.

3. Other protective emblems will include *inter alia* the protective sign indicating cultural property (see Rule 94), the protective sign for civil defence (see Rule 91), and the sign for works and installations containing dangerous forces (see paragraph 5 of the Commentary on Rule 44).

4. The prohibition of improper use of protective emblems, signs or signals applies regardless of whether the Belligerent Party is a Contracting Party to the particular treaty that has established the emblem, sign or signal in question.

5. The Rome Statute of the ICC makes "improper use . . . of the distinctive emblems of the Geneva Conventions" punishable when "resulting in death or serious personal injury" (see Art. 8 (2) (b) (vii) of the Rome Statute of the ICC).[597]

6. Rule 112 (a) applies also in non-international armed conflict.

[595] Art. 38 (1) of AP/I: "(1) It is prohibited to make improper use of the distinctive emblem of the red cross, red crescent or red lion and sun or of other emblems, signs or signals provided for by the Conventions or by this Protocol. It is also prohibited to misuse deliberately in an armed conflict other internationally recognized protective emblems, signs or signals, including the flag of truce, and the protective emblem of cultural property." See also Para. 8.5.1.6. of NWP ("Permitted use"): "Protective signs and symbols may be used only to identify personnel, objects, and activities entitled to the protected status that they designate. Any other use is forbidden by international law."

[596] Art. 23 (f) of the 1907 Hague Regulations: "In addition to the prohibitions provided by special Conventions, it is especially forbidden: . . . (f) To make improper use of a flag of truce, of the national flag or of the military insignia and uniform of the enemy, as well as the distinctive badges of the Geneva Convention".

[597] Art. 8 (2) (b) (vii) of the Rome Statute of the ICC, see fn. 601.

(b) Improper use of the flag of truce.

1. This Rule is based on Art. 38 (1) of AP/I[598] and on Art. 23 (f) of the 1907 Hague Regulations.[599]

2. Traditionally, the flag of truce is a white flag.[600]

3. Naturally, aircraft in flight cannot hoist the flag of truce. However, the flag of truce may be improperly used by combatants on the ground who have no intention of negotiating a truce. These can be ground forces seeking to protect themselves from air attacks, or aircrews who are engaged in combat on the ground. It is therefore important to emphasize that any improper use of the flag of truce is prohibited at all times (irrespective of any intent to kill, injure (or capture) an adversary).

4. The Rome Statute of the ICC makes "improper use . . . of a flag of truce" punishable in international armed conflict when "resulting in death or serious personal injury".[601]

5. Rule 112 (b) also applies in non-international armed conflict.

(c) Improper use by a Belligerent Party of the flags or military emblems, insignia or uniforms of the enemy.

1. This Rule is based on Art. 23 (f) of the 1907 Hague Regulations,[602] in which there is a prohibition against "improper use of . . . the military insignia and uniform of the enemy". See also Art. 39 (2) of AP/I.[603] See also Para. 12.5.3 of NWP.[604]

598 Art. 38 (1) of AP/I, see fn. 595.

599 Art. 23 (f) of the 1907 Hague Regulations, see fn. 596.

600 Art. 32 of the 1907 Hague Regulations ("Flags of truce"): "A person is regarded as a parlementaire who has been authorized by one of the belligerents to enter into communication with the other, and who advances bearing a white flag. He has a right to inviolability, as well as the trumpeter, bugler or drummer, the flag-bearer and interpreter who may accompany him."

601 Art. 8 (2) (b) (vii) of the Rome Statute of the ICC, declaring the following to be a war crime: "Making improper use of a flag of truce, of the flag or of the military insignia and uniform of the enemy or of the United Nations, as well as of the distinctive emblems of the Geneva Conventions, resulting in death or serious personal injury."

602 Art. 23 (f) of the 1907 Hague Regulations, see fn. 596.

603 Art. 39 (2) of AP/I: "It is prohibited to make use of the flags or military emblems, insignia or uniforms of adverse Parties while engaging in attacks or in order to shield, favour, protect or impede military operations."

604 Para. 12.5.3 of NWP: "The law of land warfare does not prohibit the use by belligerent land forces of enemy flags, insignia, or uniforms to deceive the enemy

2. The prohibition on the use of enemy uniforms pertains only to "improper use". When such use is not "improper", it would be legal. One example will be the use of overcoats from captured enemy warehouses in order to protect against the weather (provided that all enemy insignia are removed therefrom). This is also true of a POW who attempts to escape, wearing the uniform of the enemy.[605]

3. AP/I contains an exception with regard to the existing generally recognized rules of international law applicable to espionage or to the use of flags during naval warfare.[606] With regard to espionage (see Section R), the exception relates to Rule 122 whereby a member of the armed forces of a Belligerent Party – having been engaged in espionage – rejoins his own forces but is subsequently captured by the enemy, he may no longer be prosecuted for his previous acts. This applies even if he has used a false uniform during his clandestine actions. With regard to the law of naval warfare, it is accepted – or at least tolerated – that a warship displays the enemy flag (or a neutral flag), as long as it displays its true colours prior to an actual armed engagement.[607] This exception does not apply in air warfare.

either before or following an armed engagement. Once an armed engagement begins, a belligerent is prohibited from deceiving an enemy by wearing an enemy uniform, or using enemy flags and insignia; combatants risk severe punishment if they are captured while displaying enemy colors or insignia or wearing enemy uniforms in combat."

605 Para. 1576 of the ICRC Commentary on AP/I, pertaining to Art. 39 of AP/I: "A prisoner of war who escapes may be inclined to put on the uniform of the enemy in order to conceal, facilitate or protect his escape and hinder the search for him. If he is caught before successfully completing his escape, he will be liable to disciplinary punishment (Third Convention, Art. 93, paragraph 2). If he is captured again after successfully escaping, he is not liable to any punishment (Third Convention, Art. 91, paragraph 2). Under the provisions of the Hague Regulations, there is no doubt whatsoever that wearing an enemy uniform is not prohibited in this case."

606 See Art. 39 (3) of AP/I: "Nothing in this Article or in Article 37, paragraph 1 (d), shall affect the existing generally recognized rules of international law applicable to espionage or to the use of flags in the conduct of armed conflict at sea."

607 Para. 12.5.1 of NWP ("Enemy Flags, Insignia, and Uniforms – At Sea"): "Naval surface and subsurface forces may fly enemy colors and display enemy markings to deceive the enemy. Warships must, however, display their true colors prior to an actual armed engagement."

Para. 856 (4) of the Canadian Joint Doctrine Manual: "Certain types of ruses are not permitted. Warships and auxiliary vessels are prohibited from opening fire while flying a false flag. They may, however, display the enemy flag or a neutral flag during pursuit. Such conduct at sea is accepted or at least tolerated, whether the ship in question is pursuing an enemy ship or is trying to escape from it."

4. Opinions among the members of the Group of Experts were divided as to whether the qualifying words appearing in Art. 39 (2) of AP/I – "while engaging in attacks or in order to shield, favour, protected or impede military operations" – fully reflect customary international law. Some members of the Group of Experts took the position that any use of enemy uniform for deception purposes, even before or after an attack, is improper.

5. The Rome Statute of the ICC makes "improper use . . . of the flag or of the military insignia and uniform of the enemy" punishable when resulting in death or serious personal injury.[608]

6. The term "military emblem", as referred to in Rule 112 (c) includes markings of military aircraft (see Rule 1 (x)). The use of "military emblems" of the enemy by a Belligerent Party is "improper" under Rule 112 (c), whether the enemy markings are painted on a military aircraft or on any other type of aircraft.

7. Rule 112 (c) applies also to non-international armed conflict.

(d) Use by a Belligerent Party of the flags or military emblems, insignia or uniforms of Neutrals.

1. This Rule is based on Art. 39 (1) of AP/I.[609] See also Para. 12.3.2. of NWP[610]

2. Rule 112 (d) – unlike Rule 112 (c) – refers not to "improper use" but to "use". The reason is that any use of flags, military emblems, insignia or uniforms of Neutrals (except under conditions of naval warfare, as explained in paragraph 3 of the Commentary on Rule 112 (c)) is unlawful. See also paragraph 5 of the Commentary on Rule 114 (c).

3. Rule 112 (d) does not apply in non-international armed conflict, since there is no neutrality in the legal sense. However, any use of the flags, military emblems, insignia or uniforms of a foreign State not taking part in the hostilities will be regarded as improper.

608 Art. 8 (2) (b) (vii) of the Rome Statute of the ICC, see fn. 601.

609 Art 39 (1) of AP/I: "It is prohibited to make use in an armed conflict of the flags or military emblems, insignia or uniforms of neutral or other States not Parties to the conflict."

610 Para. 12.3.2 of NWP ("Neutral flags, insignia and uniforms – In the Air"): "Use in combat of false or deceptive markings to disguise belligerent military aircraft as being of neutral nationality is prohibited."

(e) Use by a Belligerent Party of the distinctive emblem of the United Nations, except as authorized by that Organization.

1. This Rule is based on Art. 38 (2) of AP/I.[611] See also Para. 12.4 of NWP.[612]

2. The UN flag is not a protective emblem on the same line as the distinctive emblems of the the Red Cross, Red Crescent or Red Crystal but indicates a connection with the UN, in the same way as the flag of a Neutral indicates nationality. When the UN is present in a conflict area in a purely peacekeeping, humanitarian or other impartial function, the UN flag has a protective function. The UN personnel must then be respected and protected as long as they are entitled to the protection given to civilians (see Rule 98).

3. Even when the UN is engaged in an armed conflict as a Party thereto, so that its position is analogous to that of a Belligerent Party, and its personnel are not entitled to the protection of civilians, there must be no improper use of the distinctive emblem of the UN. Such unauthorized use would be similar to the improper use of the military emblems or uniforms of the enemy, prohibited in Rule 112 (c).

4. The Rome Statute of the ICC makes "improper use . . . of the flag . . . of the United Nations" punishable when resulting in death or serious personal injury.[613]

5. Rule 112 (e) applies also in non-international armed conflict.

113. Ruses of war are permitted. Such ruses are acts which are intended to mislead an adversary or to induce him to act recklessly but which infringe no Rule of the law of international armed conflict and which do not meet the definition of perfidy in Rule 111 (a).

1. This Rule is based on Art. 24 of the 1907 Hague Regulations[614] and on Art. 37 (2) of AP/I.[615](See footnote 615 on next page)

[611] Art. 38 (2) of AP/I: "It is prohibited to make use of the distinctive emblem of the United Nations, except as authorized by that Organization."

[612] Para. 12.4 of NWP ("The United Nations Flag and Emblem"): "The flag of the United Nations and the letters "UN" may not be used in armed conflict for any purpose without the authorization of the United Nations."

[613] Art. 8 (2) (b) (vii) of the Rome Statute of the ICC, see fn. 601.

[614] Art. 24 of the 1907 Hague Regulations: "Ruses of war and the employment of measures necessary for obtaining information about the enemy and the country are considered permissible."

2. Belligerent Parties are entitled, under the law of international armed conflict, to make use of any ruses of war they may wish to avail themselves of, as long as the acts do not infringe any rule of that law and do not constitute prohibited perfidy.

3. Ruses of war may result in the death of an adversary. This is not prohibited *per se* as long as such ruses of war do not amount to prohibited perfidy (see Rule 111 (a)) insofar as they do not include the element of betrayal of confidence. In particular, there must be no improper use of civilian, neutral, enemy or other protected status (see Rule 112).

4. Specific examples of lawful ruses of war in air or missile warfare are given in Rule 116 on an illustrative basis.

5. Rule 113 applies also in non-international armed conflict.

II. Specifics of air or missile operations

114. In air or missile combat operations, the following acts are examples of perfidy (subject to the definition in Rule 111 (a)):

1. This Rule highlights acts of perfidy which are particularly apposite to air or missile combat operations. The use of the term "perfidy" is based on the general definition in Rule 111 (a). The main constituent element of perfidy is the intent to betray the confidence of the enemy. Perfidious acts by themselves are not unlawful. Perfidy is only prohibited when linked to the act of killing, injuring (or capturing) an adversary.

2. The acts listed Rule 114 (a)–(e) are merely examples of perfidy. In other words, the list is not exhaustive.

(a) The feigning of the status of a protected medical aircraft, in particular by the use of the distinctive emblem or other means of identification reserved for medical aircraft.

1. Conduct covered by Rule 114 (a) only constitutes prohibited perfidy when used as a means to kill or injure (or capture) an adversary.

[615] Art. 37 (2) of AP/I: "Ruses of war are not prohibited. Such ruses are acts which are intended to mislead an adversary or to induce him to act recklessly but which infringe no rule of international law applicable in armed conflict and which are not perfidious because they do not invite the confidence of an adversary with respect to protection under the law. The following are examples of such ruses: the use of camouflage, decoys, mock operations and misinformation."

2. There are various ways of feigning the status of a medical aircraft (see Section L, in particular Rule 76). One way is when deliberate use is made of signals that, by multilateral treaty – or by a bilateral agreement with the enemy – are reserved for medical aircraft (see Rule 76 (a) or (b)). When an aircraft other than a medical aircraft follows an air route or an air corridor agreed upon between the Belligerent Parties for the exclusive use of medical aircraft, this could also amount to the feigning of the status of a medical aircraft.

3. Signals, such as blue flashing lights, are in many States used by police or fire-fighting services, and could in certain circumstances lead to confusion with medical aircraft. This does not amount to perfidy as long as there is no intent to betray the confidence of the enemy by feigning the status of a medical aircraft.

4. Rule 114 (a) applies also in non-international armed conflict.

(b) The feigning of the status of a civilian aircraft.

1. This Rule is based on Art. 37 (1) (c) of AP/I.[616] See also Para. 109 of the SRM/ACS.[617]

2. Conduct covered by Rule 114 (b) constitutes prohibited perfidy only when used as a means to kill or injure (or capture) an adversary.

3. It is perfidious for a military aircraft to feign the status of a civilian aircraft. This could, for instance, occur if that military aircraft uses a transponder that on interrogation gives a response indicating that it is a civilian aircraft.

4. Feigning of civilian status by painting civilian markings on a military aircraft has a superficial similarity to a combatant feigning civilian status by wearing civilian clothing. There is, however, a big difference in that changing the markings on a military aircraft requires a lot more effort and will necessarily be a deliberate act, while soldiers may appear to be in civilian clothing as a result of wear and tear in uniforms, inadequate supplies, etc.

5. Some air forces employ low-visibility markings for military aircraft, with national colours replaced by a black or grey outline indicating

[616] Art. 37 (1) (c) of AP/I, see fn. 588.

[617] Para. 109 of the SRM/ACS: "Military and auxiliary aircraft are prohibited at all times from feigning exempt, civilian or neutral status."

the national marking. This is done for camouflage purposes. Although recourse to such a system of marking will make it more difficult to ascertain the nationality and the military status of the aircraft by visible means, it is not considered feigning of the status of a civilian aircraft. (see paragraph 11 of the Commentary on Rule 1 (x) as well as the Commentary on Rule 116 (e)).

6. If markings are erased altogether from military aircraft, they are no longer entitled to engage in attacks – or to exercise any other belligerent rights, such as interception (see Rule 17) – in view of the fact that the aircraft no longer meet the definitional requirements of military aircraft (see Rule 1 (x)).

7. UCAVs feigning the status of civilian UAVs to conduct an attack are acting perfidiously, and the act will be unlawful if it results in killing or injuring (or capturing) an adversary.

8. UAVs used by the military but feigning civilian status, although used mainly for intelligence gathering purposes, will be deemed to be acting perfidiously if they are used in close conjunction with attacking military units in order to identify a target, designate it, monitor the engagement, or assess the results in order to determine whether a re-attack is necessary. In all such cases, the UAV can be regarded as part of the attacking force.

9. In non-international armed conflicts, aircraft used by non-State organized armed groups cannot qualify as military aircraft (see paragraph 8 of the Commentary on Rule 1 (x)). Thus, they are technically civilian aircraft. However, if measures are intentionally taken to convince the enemy that they are exclusively dedicated to innocent civilian purposes, an attack by such aircraft will constitute perfidious action and be unlawful if resulting in the killing or injuring (or capturing) of an adversary.

(c) The feigning of the status of a neutral aircraft.

1. The prohibition is based on Art. 37 (1) (d) of AP/I.[618] See also Para. 12.3.2 of NWP[619] and Para. 109 of the SRM/ACS.[620]

2. Conduct covered by Rule 114 (c) constitutes prohibited perfidy only when used as a means to kill or injure (or capture) an adversary.

[618] Art. 37 (1) (d) of AP/I, see fn. 588.
[619] Para. 12.3.2 of NWP, see fn. 610.
[620] Para. 109 of SRM/ACS, see fn. 617.

3. The core of the prohibition is feigning the status of neutral aircraft by painting the markings of a Neutral on the aircraft of a Belligerent Party.

4. Feigning of the status of a neutral aircraft could also be done by employing false electronic signals or deceptive radio transmissions.

5. On the face of it, there is no difference between the feigning of the status of a neutral aircraft and the use of neutral military emblems (see Rule 112 (d)). In actuality, however, there is a difference. Perfidy goes beyond mere use, entailing betrayal of the adversary's confidence.

6. Neutrality in the legal sense does not exist in non-international armed conflict. However, it would be perfidious to feign the status of an aircraft from a foreign State not taking part in the hostilities.

(d) The feigning of another protected status.

1. Another protected status could be that of an aircraft granted safe conduct (such as cartel aircraft, see Section J (II) and Section J (III)), UN,[621] ICRC, etc.

2. Conduct covered by Rule 114 (d) constitutes prohibited perfidy only when used as a means to kill or injure (or capture) an adversary.

3. Rule 114 (d) applies also in non-international armed conflict.

(e) The feigning of surrender.

1. The prohibition is based on Art. 37 (1) (a) of AP/I.[622] See also Para. 12.2 of NWP[623] and Rule 111 (b) of SRM/ACS.[624] Surrender is dealt with extensively in Section S.

2. Aircrews of a military aircraft wishing to surrender may communicate their intention on a common radio channel such as a distress frequency (see Rule 128). Falsely communicating such intention can amount to perfidious conduct.

[621] Second sentence of Para. 111 of SRM/ACS: "Perfidious acts include the launching of an attack while feigning: (a) exempt, civilian, neutral or protected United Nations status; (b) surrender or distress by, e.g., sending a distress signal or by the crew taking to life rafts."

[622] Art. 37 (1) (a) of AP/I, see fn. 588.

[623] Last sentence of Para. 12.2 of NWP: "Similarly, use of the white flag to gain a military advantage over the enemy is unlawful."

[624] Second sentence of Para. 111 of the SRM/ACS, see fn. 621.

3. In view of the fact that signals such as rocking the aircraft's wings or lowering the landing gear are not conclusive evidence of an intent to surrender (see paragraph 3 of the Commentary on Rule 128), it is not clear whether the misuse of such signals constitutes perfidy.

4. Conduct covered by Rule 114 (e) constitutes prohibited perfidy only when used as a means to kill or injure (or capture) an adversary.

5. Rule 114 (e) applies also in non-international armed conflict.

115. Irrespective of whether or not they are perfidious, in air or missile combat operations, the following acts are prohibited at all times:

(a) Improper use by aircraft of distress codes, signals or frequencies.

1. Improper use means any use of distress codes, signals or frequencies (as prescribed by a competent international authority) for other than normal purposes.

2. Improper use of distress signals is in breach of the provisions regulating the use of such signals (see Art. 10 of the 1923 Hague Rules for the Control of Radio Wireless Telegraphy in Time of War).[625] Distress signals must be reserved for their humanitarian purposes.

3. The improper use by aircraft of distress codes must be clearly distinguished from situations in which the aircraft feigns distress through other means. For example, an aircraft may simulate distress by maneuvering in a way that suggests that it has been damaged in order to induce the enemy to discontinue an attack or to gain some other military advantage. As for surrender, see Section S.

4. However, if an aircraft simulates a situation of distress in order to create the false impression that airborne troops descending from it are parachutists from an aircraft in distress (see Section T), this could amount to prohibited perfidy if it leads to killing, injuring (or capturing) an adversary.

[625] Art. 10 of the 1923 Hague Rules for the Control of Radio in Time of War: "The perversion of radio distress signals and distress messages prescribed by international conventions to other than their normal and legitimate purposes constitutes a violation of the laws of war and renders the perpetrator personally responsible under international law."

5. IFF codes are not distress codes. The false use of the enemy's IFF Codes is not prohibited (see Rule 116 (c)).

6. Rule 115 (a) applies also in non-international armed conflict.

(b) Use of any aircraft other than a military aircraft as a means of attack.

1. Under Rule 17 (a), only military aircraft are entitled to engage in attacks. The present Rule refers to the use of an aircraft, other than a military aircraft, as a "means of attack".

2. Using a manned aircraft as a weapon, would usually mean a suicide mission. Whereas suicide attacks by military aircraft are not unlawful *per se*, a suicide attack carried out by an aircraft other than a military aircraft (in particular a hijacked civilian airliner with passengers on board) would be unlawful.

3. On September 11, 2001, terrorists attacked the World Trade Center in New York and other targets using hijacked civilian airliners as weapons. Using as a means of attack a civilian aircraft (or any other protected aircraft) is in breach of the law of international armed conflict.

4. Rule 115 (b) does not apply to non-international armed conflict (see paragraph 7 of the Commentary on Rule 17).

116. In air or missile combat operations, the following are examples of lawful ruses of war:

1. The examples are based on Art. 37 (2) of AP/I.[626] See also Para. 12.1.1. of NWP.[627]

2. Rule 116 applies also in non-international armed conflict.

(a) Mock operations.

1. Mock operations, as lawful ruses of war, are illustrated by feint attacks leading the enemy to believe that a heavy attack would be delivered against a particular target and thereby inducing it to commit its forces to the

[626] Art. 37 (2) of AP/I, see fn. 615.

[627] Para. 12.1.1 of NWP: "Stratagems and ruses of war permitted in armed conflict include such deceptions as camouflage; deceptive lightning; dummy ships and other armament; decoys; simulated forces; feigned attacks and withdrawals; ambushes; false intelligence information; electronic deceptions; and utilization of enemy codes, passwords and countersigns."

defence of that target, while the main blow is delivered at another target which has been left more thinly defended.

2. An example from history is the Allied air attacks on targets in the Pas de Calais area during the weeks preceding D-Day in 1944. The air attacks convinced Nazi Germany that the invasion would come in that area, and not in Normandy.

3. Another example is that of moving an aircraft carrier to a particular area, in order to make the enemy believe that an air strike will be delivered from the air carrier. In fact, the main target of the attack may be located in an area beyond the flight capability of the carrier's aircraft.

4. Simulated attacks may also be used as lawful ruses of war to entice the enemy to activate its air defence systems, thus providing valuable information about those systems that can be used to facilitate a real attack later. While this is different from mock operations in the classic sense, it has a common element in that it presents the enemy with a false appearance of what is actually going on, thereby lawfully gaining a military advantage.

(b) Disinformation.

1. Disinformation consists of information that is either false or which is designed to lead the enemy to draw incorrect conclusions. Misinformation is mentioned in Art. 37 (2) of AP/I[628] as a lawful ruse of war. Misinformation is a wider term, including information that is incorrect objectively, whereas disinformation is confined to the situation where only the person conveying it is aware of the fact that the information is false. Even disinformation, which is obviously based on deception, is a lawful ruse of war.

2. An example of use of disinformation is an attempt to induce the enemy to surrender by creating the false impression that it is surrounded, or that massive air attacks are impending whereas no such attack is planned, or even feasible. An historical example relates to WWII. When Belligerent Parties captured enemy aircraft, they gave them the proper new nationality markings, yet employed them in such a manner that the enemy was misled to consider them friendly military aircraft because of their silhouette. In such cases, the captured aircraft were used to great advantage by mixing them with enemy night bombers returning to base from bombing

[628] Art. 37 (2) of AP/I, see fn. 615.

missions, and attacking the enemy airbases that were lit up in order to receive the returning bombers.

3. False information that suggests civilian, neutral or other protected status is not lawful (see Rule 114).

(c) False military codes and false electronic, optical or acoustic means to deceive the enemy (provided that they do not consist of distress signals, do not include protected codes, and do not convey the wrong impression of surrender).

1. The use of false military codes and false electronic, optical or acoustic means to deceive the enemy can be seen as a special case of lawful disinformation.

2. An example might be the use of the enemy's IFF codes when responding to an IFF interrogation (see Commentary on Rule 40 (f)), thus falsely indicating friendly status as seen from the enemy's perspective. Such false response is not to be equated to wearing enemy uniform (which is prohibited, see Rule 112 (c)). The correct analogy would be that of a patrol (which is a lawful ruse of war) using the enemy's password to avoid being fired upon when summoned by an enemy sentry.

3. Another example of a lawful ruse of war consists of a Belligerent Party's creating false return on enemy radar, giving the impression of a large formation of approaching aircraft, thus confusing enemy defences. This was done during WWII by dropping aluminium strips ("windows"), and is today done by electronic means.

(d) Use of decoys and dummy-construction of aircraft and hangars.

1. Unmanned decoys may be used to simulate manned military aircraft by creating an unusually large radar return or in other ways simulating a larger aircraft.

2. Missile decoys may be used to mislead anti-missile defences. Due to their velocity, they can create destruction when they hit the ground, although they do not contain warheads with explosives.

3. Dummy construction was used during WWII by Belligerents Parties, in order to simulate objects such as military installations, parked military aircraft or tanks.

4. Dummy construction that is intended to attract attacks from the enemy must, to the extent feasible, not be located within or near densely populated areas (see Rule 42).

(e) Use of camouflage.

1. It is permissible to paint military aircraft with camouflage colours, as long as the military markings of the aircraft are there, even though their visibility is impaired (see paragraphs 4 and 5 of the Commentary on Rule 114 (b) as well as paragraph 14 of the Commentary on Rule 11 (x)).

2. Use of camouflage includes the reduction of electronic, acoustic or infrared signature of a military aircraft, in order to make it "invisible" or "inaudible" to other sensors than the human eye.

3. It has not been considered unlawful to camouflage ground installations at military airfields, like hangars and workshops, to look like unspecified civilian buildings.

117. Aircrews conducting combat operations on land or on water – outside their aircraft – must distinguish themselves from the civilian population, as required by the law of international armed conflict.

1. The HRAW required in Art. 15 that crews of military aircraft bear a fixed distinctive emblem.[629] However, State practice clearly shows that aircrews of military aircraft in flight are not required to wear uniform as long as they are in the aircraft, since the necessary markings of the military aircraft are sufficient indication of combatant status, thus distinguishing the military aircraft and its crew from civilian aircraft and civilian personnel.

2. The main thrust of Art. 15 of the HRAW was, however, that the crews must be recognizable at a distance in the event of the crew finding themselves separated from the aircraft. This provision is supported by subsequent State practice. If the aircrews leave their aircraft, they are in no different position from soldiers or sailors operating on land or on water. They must distinguish themselves from civilians as required by the law of international armed conflict, normally by wearing military uniform.

[629] Art. 15 of the HRAW: "Members of the crew of a military aircraft shall wear a fixed distinctive emblem of such character as to be recognizable at a distance in case they become separated from their aircraft."

3. If aircrews do not observe Rule 117, this does not alter their status as combatants but makes it more difficult for the enemy to identify their status and increases the risk that they may be misidentified as spies (see Section R and Rule 120). It is also possible that a Belligerent Party might consider them to be "unprivileged belligerents" (or "unlawful combatants", see paragraph 4 of the Commentary on Rule 10 (b) (i) and paragraph 4 of the Commentary on the *chapeau* to Rule 111 (b)).

4. There is no State practice indicating how Rule 117 is applied, if at all, in a non-international armed conflict.

Section R

Espionage

The Rules set forth in this Section apply only in international armed conflict, for the legal concept of espionage applies only to activities conducted by one State, or its agents, (including non-military personnel) against another.

I. General rules

118. Espionage consists of activities by spies. A spy is any person who, acting clandestinely or on false pretences, obtains or endeavours to obtain information of military value in territory controlled by the enemy, with the intention of communicating it to the opposing Party.

1. The term "clandestine" has been repeated consistently since it first appeared in Art. 29 of the 1899 Hague Regulations,[630] and therefore, is included in Rule 118 for purposes of consistency. Nevertheless, in State practice, a change in terminology has occurred. At the present time, it is common to distinguish between "clandestine" and "covert" operations. "Clandestine operations" are those which are conducted in a fashion intended to assure secrecy or concealment. For instance, an aircraft may fly at night or below radar coverage to conceal the fact that a flight has even occurred. By contrast, "covert operations" are designed to conceal

[630] Art. 29 of 1899 Hague Regulations: "An individual can only be considered a spy if, acting clandestinely, or on false pretences, he obtains, or seeks to obtain information in the zone of operations of a belligerent, with the intention of communicating it to the hostile party. Thus, soldiers not in disguise who have penetrated into the zone of operations of a hostile army to obtain information are not considered spies. Similarly, the following are not considered spies: soldiers or civilians, carrying out their mission openly, charged with the delivery of despatches destined either for their own army or for that of the enemy. To this class belong likewise individuals sent in balloons to deliver despatches, and generally to maintain communication between the various parts of an army or a territory." Similar language is found in Art. 29 of the 1907 Hague Regulations.

the identity of the individual or equipment conducting the operation, and sometimes even the identity of the State sponsoring it. As an example, an aircraft which is falsely marked would be engaging in a covert operation. Thus, whereas clandestine activities are designed to mask the fact of the operation, covert operations aim to conceal the identity of the actors. Consequently, in modern terminology, the term "clandestinely" in Rule 118 ought to be understood as "covertly." The essence of Rule 118 is that the individual is acting covertly or otherwise under false pretences.

2. Although Art. 29 of the 1899/1907 Hague Regulations restricts the scope of the definition of espionage to the "zone of operations of a belligerent", the phrase has been interpreted in State practice as including the entire territory of the Belligerent Party. It also includes territory occupied or otherwise under control of the enemy.

3. To qualify as espionage, the information sought must be of military value. For instance, in the context of the law of international armed conflict, gathering information of political or economic value does not amount to espionage.

4. As noted in Art. 24 of the 1907 Hague Regulations "obtaining information about the enemy" is "considered permissible".[631] The mere act of gathering information about the enemy does not by itself constitute espionage. On the contrary, military forces dedicate significant resources to information gathering. Such activities include intelligence gathering, surveillance and reconnaissance, as well as CNAs designed to exploit data resident in enemy computer networks.

5. Intelligence refers generally to any information concerning enemy forces and activities, as well as information necessary to facilitate one's own operations, such as information about terrain features or the layout of a city. It includes, *inter alia*, communications intelligence; electronic intelligence; electro-optical intelligence; signals intelligence; human intelligence; imagery intelligence; photographic intelligence; radar intelligence; and radiation intelligence.[632]

6. Surveillance refers to the systematic observation of areas, places, persons, or things, by visual, aural, electronic, photographic, or other

[631] Art. 24 of the 1907 Hague Regulations: "Ruses of war and the employment of measures necessary for obtaining information about the enemy and the country are considered permissible."

[632] DoD Dictionary of Military Terms, at 267–268.

means.[633] Reconnaissance is a single mission undertaken to obtain – by visual observation or other detection methods – specific information about the activities and resources of an enemy.[634] None of these activities constitutes espionage unless conducted covertly ("clandestinely") in territory controlled by the enemy. CNAs designed to acquire access to computer data by concealing the identity of the intruder do not amount to espionage unless the attack is launched from within or over enemy-controlled territory. Typically, this will not be the case, as connectivity to the target network can be achieved from other than enemy controlled territory.

7. The definition of espionage is not limited to members of the armed forces. It includes civilians who engage in acts of espionage. Depending on the circumstances, acts of espionage may well constitute direct participation in hostilities (see Section F). Several Black-letter Rules of this Section, however, are restricted to "members of the armed forces", as indicated in the respective Black-letter Rules.

8. Art. 29 of the 1907 Hague Regulations implies that the delivery of despatches, when carried out clandestinely, is included in the definition of espionage. This element has been deleted from Rule 118 in view of the fact that, at the present time, the transmission of despatches across enemy lines will generally not require the use of human messengers.

119. Acts of espionage are not prohibited under the law of international armed conflict.

1. Espionage is the activity of a spy as defined in Rule 118, that is, collecting information covertly ("clandestinely") or under false pretences in enemy controlled territory.

2. Espionage must be distinguished from perfidy (see Section Q), which is feigning protected status with the intent of betraying the confidence of an adversary. As well, unlike prohibited perfidy, espionage does not entail killing or injuring (or capturing) of an adversary, in that it is confined to the gathering of information of military value.

3. Espionage is not unlawful *per se* under the law of international armed conflict, and *a fortiori* it is not a war crime under international law. Spies (whether members of the armed forces or civilians) may be prosecuted

[633] DoD Dictionary of Military Terms, at 528.
[634] DoD Dictionary of Military Terms, at 453.

for their acts only on the basis of the domestic law of the Belligerent Party (see Rule 121).

4. Art. 24 of the Hague Regulations acknowledges that "the employment of measures necessary for obtaining information about the enemy and the country are considered permissible". More to the point, the act of espionage requires the spy to act covertly ("clandestinely") or under false pretences.

120. A member of the armed forces of a Belligerent Party who gathers or attempts to gather information in a territory controlled by the enemy is not considered a spy if, while so acting, he is in the uniform of his armed forces.

1. This Rule is based on Art. 46 (2) of AP/I.[635]

2. Aerial warfare presents unique circumstances as regards espionage (see Rule 123 and Rule 124). Generally, it is the marking of the aircraft, or other characteristics (such as the electronic signals transmitted by the aircraft), which determine whether the operation is covert ("clandestine"), or is carried out under false pretences. The wearing of civilian clothing by military members of the aircrews in no way affects the nature of the flight. Thus, members of military aircrews wearing civilian clothing in properly marked military aircraft are not spies (see the Commentary on Rule 117). However, if captured, the non-wear of the uniform may put them at risk of not being accorded POW status (see Rule 117).

3. By the same token, wearing a military uniform in an aircraft engaged in covert ("clandestine") operations does not shield aircrews from being treated as a spy because the uniform worn in no way diminishes the covert ("clandestine") nature of the operation.

121. A member of the armed forces of a Belligerent Party who falls into the power of the enemy while engaging in espionage does not have the right to prisoner of war status and may be prosecuted for his acts before domestic courts.

1. This Rule is based on Art. 46 (1) of AP/I, which provides that "any member of the armed forces of a Party to the conflict who falls into the

[635] Art. 46 (2) of AP/I: "A member of the armed forces of a Party to the conflict who, on behalf of that Party and in territory controlled by an adverse Party, gathers or attempts to gather information shall not be considered as engaging in espionage if, while so acting, he is in the uniform of his armed forces."

power of an adverse Party while engaging in espionage shall not have the right to the status of prisoner of war and may be treated as a spy". Art. 46 (1) of AP/I reflects customary international law.[636]

2. Although spies are not entitled to POW status, they remain entitled to the protections that detainees who do not qualify as POWs are entitled to under customary international law. Such customary law protection is reflected in Common Art. 3 to the Geneva Conventions. See also Art. 75 of AP/I.

3. As noted, espionage does not constitute a war crime under international law (see paragraph 3 of the Commentary on Rule 119). However, it usually violates the domestic law of the country which is being spied on, and that country is entitled to prosecute the person for espionage under its domestic law.[637] In conformity with customary international law, as reflected in Art. 30 of the Hague Regulations, "a spy taken in the act shall not be punished without previous trial".

4. In addition to domestic law, a spy may also be tried for actions that violate the security legislation enacted by an Occupying Power.

5. Although espionage by itself is not a war crime under international law, a spy may still commit a war crime while engaged in a mission of espionage. In such a case, he may be prosecuted and punished for the war crime independently of the act of espionage. For instance, if the spy intentionally kills civilians during the act of espionage, as far as international law is concerned, the spy may be tried for the war crime, although not for espionage (see Rule 119).

[636] Para. 12.9 of NWP: "Spying during armed conflict is not a violation of international law. Captured spies are not, however, entitled to prisoner-of-war status. The captor nation may try and punish spies in accordance with its national law."

[637] Para. 4.9.3 of the UK Manual: "The Hague Regulations formally sanctioned the employment of measures necessary for the obtaining of intelligence in enemy-held territory. The collection of such information openly by combatants wearing uniform is a recognized branch of the art of warfare. The obtaining of such information by secret methods is governed by different rules. Thus, it is lawful to employ spies and secret agents but the fact that these methods are lawful under international law does not prevent the punishment under domestic or occupation law of individuals who are engaged in procuring intelligence in other than an open manner."

See also Para. 4.9.7 of the UK Manual: "Spies are usually tried by civilian courts under the domestic legislation of the territory in which they are captured."

122. A member of the armed forces of a Belligerent Party who, having been engaged in espionage rejoins his own forces but is subsequently captured by the enemy, may no longer be prosecuted for his previous acts of espionage.

1. This Rule is based on Art. 31 of the 1907 Hague Regulations,[638] as well as on Art. 46 (4) of AP/I.[639] See also Para. 12.9 of NWP.[640]

2. Under Rule 122, a member of the armed forces who has engaged in espionage achieves immunity for such acts if this person manages to rejoin his own armed forces. Upon subsequent capture, the individual can no longer be prosecuted for his previous acts (although he may be prosecuted for a new act of espionage committed after having rejoined his own armed forces).

3. Rule 122 does not apply to civilians who have engaged in espionage and managed to return to friendly territory, but were later captured; they remain subject to prosecution under domestic law for all acts of espionage.

II. Specifics of air or missile operations

123. Military aircraft on missions to gather, intercept or otherwise gain information are not to be regarded as carrying out acts of espionage.

1. The definition of espionage (see Rule 118) excludes from its scope military aircraft on overt missions of information gathering.

2. Military aircraft that do not enter the airspace above enemy-controlled territory can never be regarded as engaged in espionage because they do not come within the bounds of the definition in Rule 118, which requires

638 Art. 31 of the 1907 Hague Regulations: "A spy who, after rejoining the army to which he belongs, is subsequently captured by the enemy, is treated as a prisoner of war, and incurs no responsibility for his previous acts of espionage."

639 Art. 46 (4) of AP/I: "A member of the armed forces of a Party to the conflict who is not a resident of territory occupied by an adverse Party and who has engaged in espionage in that territory shall not lose his right to the status of prisoner of war and may not be treated as a spy unless he is captured before he has rejoined the armed forces to which he belongs."

640 Para. 12.9 of NWP, third and fourth sentence: "Should a spy succeed in eluding capture and return to friendly territory, he is immune from punishment for his past espionage activities. If subsequently captured during some other military operation, the former spy cannot be tried or punished for the earlier act of espionage."

that the information be obtained "in territory controlled by the enemy". This is so even if they indulge in intelligence gathering when they fly adjacent to enemy airspace.

3. When military aircraft engaged in intelligence gathering enter the airspace above enemy-controlled territory, they can be regarded as engaged in espionage only if they are "acting clandestinely or on false pretences", in other words, they are acting covertly ("clandestinely").

4. The nature of the information gathered, so long as it is of military value, is irrelevant. For instance, military aircraft may intercept electronic signals, listen into phone and other communications, take photos, observe heat signature, etc.

5. Operations such as air refuelling for special operations involving infiltration, exfiltration, or airdrops, do not as such amount to espionage, because they have nothing to do with intelligence gathering.

6. When a military aircraft does not qualify as being engaged in espionage, neither do the aircrews in it. This is so even if the aircrews are not wearing uniform while on board, because the wearing of the uniform is generally not apparent to the enemy, and because the military aircraft's marking allows sufficient identification. See, however, Rule 117.

7. Even when not engaged in espionage, military aircraft constitute military objectives by nature (see Rule 1 (y) and Rule 22 (a)).

8. Rule 123 deals only with military aircraft. For other categories of aircraft, see Rule 124.

124. The use of civilian aircraft and State aircraft other than military aircraft of a Belligerent Party, flying outside the airspace of or controlled by the enemy – in order to gather, intercept or otherwise gain information – is not to be regarded as espionage, although the aircraft may be attacked at such time as it is carrying out its information-gathering mission.

1. Civilian and State aircraft other than military aircraft of a Belligerent Party may be used to gather information of military value from outside the airspace of, or the airspace controlled by, the enemy. Nevertheless, such aircraft, when engaged in such activities, constitute military objectives (see Rule 27 (a) and Rule 27 (c)).

2. Of course, this Rule is without prejudice to the provision of Rule 171 (b), which does not allow use of neutral airspace for "intelligence purposes".

3. However, when civilian and State aircraft other than military aircraft gather information of military value within enemy controlled airspace, the acts concerned constitute espionage because they create the false pretences of being entitled to protection from attack.

4. The use of weather aircraft – equipped and employed to monitor, collate and report data concerning weather conditions – does not amount to espionage, regardless of where the mission is conducted, because the information gathered is not military in nature (although aircraft conducting such missions for military purposes, or which will provide data to the military, may qualify as a military objective (see Rule 27, especially Rule 27 (a) and Rule 27 (c)).

5. The expression "airspace of or controlled by the enemy" includes occupied territory. Information gathering missions over occupied territory are treated as if they were conducted over enemy territory.

6. Rule 124 covers State aircraft other than military aircraft. As for military aircraft, see Rule 123.

Section S

Surrender

I. General rules

125. Enemy personnel may offer to surrender themselves (and the military equipment under their control) to a Belligerent Party.

1. Surrendering enemy personnel are automatically *hors de combat*, even when they are not incapacitated, and the enemy is not entitled to deny quarter to them (see Rule 126).

2. "Enemy personnel" include combatants and non-combatants who are eligible for POW status (for full details, see Art. 4 of GC/III).[641]

3. Medical and religious personnel are subject to a special regime (see Art. 33 of GC/III).[642]

4. A Belligerent Party may under its own legislation prohibit personnel under its jurisdiction to offer surrender. However, this does not impact on the law of international armed conflict and has no bearing upon the validity of the surrender under international law.

5. Enemy personnel who surrender will normally be taken into the custody – and placed under the protection – of the detaining Belligerent Party. However, this is not always feasible. If the military unit, in whose custody the surrendering personnel are, is incapable (because of unusual combat conditions) to escort them to a POW-camp, they must be released without harm (see Art. 41 (3) of AP/I).[643] Thus, the obligation on the part of the Belligerent Party is not necessarily to detain surrendering enemy

[641] Art. 4 of GC/III, see fn. 172.

[642] Art. 33 of GC/III, see fn. 435.

[643] Art 41 (3) of AP/I: "When persons entitled to protection as prisoners of war have fallen into the power of an adverse Party under unusual conditions of combat which prevent their evacuation as provided for in Part III, Section 1, of the Third Convention, they shall be released and all feasible precautions shall be taken to ensure their safety."

personnel, but to desist from further attack on persons complying with the conditions set out in Rule 127.

6. In a non-international armed conflict, "surrender" with the rights and duties as provided in GC/III is irrelevant. Nevertheless, members of armed forces and of non-State organized armed groups may give themselves up for "capture".

126. It is prohibited to deny quarter to those manifesting the intent to surrender.

1. This Rule is based on Art. 23 (d) of the 1907 Hague Regulations[644] and on Art. 40 of AP/I.[645] See also Para. 6.2.6. of NWP.[646]

2. To give quarter to an enemy means to desist from further attack.

3. Persons who surrender (or give themselves up for capture, see paragraph 6 of the Commentary on Rule 125) no longer pose a threat to the enemy. It is unlawful to kill or injure such persons regardless of whether they have combatant status or not.

4. On the face of it, there may seem to be an inconsistency between Rule 126 and Rule 15 (a), inasmuch as Rule 15 (a) refers explicitly not only to the denial of quarter but also to the threat of following such a policy. However, the Group of Experts felt that Rule 126 deals only with post-surrender situations, and therefore there was no need to reiterate the prohibition of the threat of a "no quarter"-policy.

5. If an individual soldier manifests the intent to surrender while his comrades continue to fight, difficult situations may arise. The following considerations must be borne in mind: (i) in battle it may be impossible to distinguish between the individual who has surrendered and his comrades who continue the fight; and (ii) the soldier purporting to surrender may

[644] Art. 23 of the 1907 Hague Regulations: "In addition to the prohibitions provided by special Conventions, it is especially forbidden: . . . (d) to declare that no quarter will be given."

[645] Art. 40 of AP/I: "It is prohibited to order that there shall be no survivors, to threaten an adversary therewith or to conduct hostilities on this basis."

[646] Subpara. 3 of Para 6.2.6 of NWP: "The following acts, if committed intentionally, are examples of war crimes that could be considered grave breaches: . . . (4) Denial of quarter (i.e., killing or wounding an enemy unable to fight due to sickness or wounds or one who is making a genuine offer of surrender) and offenses against combatants who have laid down their arms and surrendered."

be conspiring with his comrades, acting perfidiously in order to lure the enemy into a trap. Hence, the importance of Rule 127.

6. As indicated in paragraph 6 of the Commentary on Rule 125, Rule 126 applies both to surrender in international armed conflict, and to capture in non-international armed conflict.

127. Surrender is contingent on three cumulative conditions:

(a) The intention to surrender is communicated in a clear manner to the enemy.

1. This Rule is based on Para. 8.2.3.3 of NWP[647] and on Para. 5.6. of the UK Manual.[648]

2. This condition is of a practical, not a legal nature. If the forces of a Belligerent Party are reasonably unaware of the intention to surrender, they cannot be expected to desist from further attacks.

3. If a person makes an attempt to communicate an intention to surrender in a manner that is not clear, the condition is not met. However, if circumstances permit, the enemy ought to seek clarification.

4. It ought to be noted that retreat is not surrender, even if the retreating troops have thrown away their weapons.

[647] Para. 8.2.3.3 of NWP ("Surrender"): "Combatants, whether lawful or unlawful, cease to be subject to attack when they have individually laid down their arms and indicate clearly their wish to surrender. The law of armed conflict does not precisely define when surrender takes effect or how it may be accomplished in practical terms. Surrender involves an offer by the surrendering party (a unit or individual combatant) and an ability to accept on the part of the opponent. The latter may not refuse an offer of surrender when communicated, but that communication must be made at a time when it can be received and properly acted upon – an attempt to surrender in the midst of an ongoing battle is neither easily communicated nor received. The issue is one of reasonableness. The mere fact that a combatant or enemy force is retreating or fleeing the battlefield, without some other positive indication of intent, does not constitute an attempt to surrender, even if such combatant or force has abandoned his or its arms or equipment."

[648] Para. 5.6 of the UK Manual: "A person who is recognized or who, in the circumstances, should be recognized to be *hors de combat* shall not be made the object of attack. A person is *hors de combat* if: (a) 'he is in the power of an adverse Party'; (b) 'he clearly expresses an intention to surrender'; or (c) 'he has been rendered unconscious or is otherwise incapacitated by wounds or sickness, and therefore is incapable of defending himself'; 'provided that in any of these cases he abstains from any hostile act and does not attempt to escape'."

5. In land warfare, classical ways of communicating intention to surrender are to throw one's weapons and to raise one's arms. The display of a white flag,[649] which once meant only a request to parley, is nowadays in practice also used as a means of communicating an intention to surrender.

6. In naval warfare, the traditional signal of surrender is to strike the flag.

7. Rule 127 (a) applies *mutatis mutandis* to capture in non-international armed conflict (see paragraph 6 of the Commentary on Rule 125).

(b) Those offering to surrender must not engage in any further hostile acts.

1. As long as a person engages in hostile acts, he is not regarded as having laid down his arms in the legal sense.

2. Hostile acts may include acts like transmitting intelligence to the enemy. Such acts are not compatible with surrender.

3. Killing or injuring (or capturing) an adversary while feigning surrender amounts to unlawful perfidy (see Rule 114 (e)).

4. Rule 127 (b) applies *mutatis mutandis* to capture in non-international armed conflict. (see paragraph 6 of the Commentary on Rule 125).

(c) No attempt is made to evade capture.

1. A person who tries to evade capture has not laid down his arms in the legal sense, and is thereby not *hors de combat.* He can therefore be attacked (see Rule 15 (b)).

2. A combatant on the ground or at sea who surrenders to an aircraft must stay visible to the aircraft and obey any instructions given, until he can be taken into custody by any aircraft, vessel or ground forces called to the scene by the capturing aircraft. He may not be attacked, even if it is not feasible to take him into custody (see paragraph 5 of the Commentary on Rule 125).

3. Those who manifest the intention to surrender must do so in good faith. If ground forces of a Belligerent Party repeatedly raise their hands in order to avoid attack from enemy military aircraft – knowing that the

[649] Art. 32 of the 1907 Hague Regulations, see fn. 600.

aircraft has no possibility to take prisoners – and continue to fight again when the military aircraft has left, they cannot expect similar behaviour on future occasions to be taken seriously as a genuine offer of surrender.

4. Rule 127 (c) applies *mutatis mutandis* to capture in non-international armed conflict. (see paragraph 6 of the Commentary on Rule 125).

II. Specifics of air or missile operations

128. Aircrews of a military aircraft wishing to surrender ought to do everything feasible to express clearly their intention to do so. In particular, they ought to communicate their intention on a common radio channel such as a distress frequency.

1. The law of international armed conflict does not precisely define when surrender of a military aircraft takes effect or how it may be accomplished in practical terms.

2. Unlike land or naval warfare (see paragraphs 5 and 6 of the Commentary on Rule 127 (a)), the practice of air warfare does not reveal any commonly accepted indication of an aircrew's wish to surrender.

3. Rocking the aircraft's wings, lowering the landing gear and other signals (such as flashing of navigational lights or jettisoning of weapons) are sometimes cited as indications of an intent to surrender, but they cannot be regarded as conclusive evidence, since there may be other reasons for the activity in question. Moreover, when air and missile combat is conducted beyond visual range, as frequently happens in modern warfare, such gestures are futile. Consequently, only an appropriate radio communication – duly transmitted to the enemy, preferably on an ICAO distress frequency – may be deemed an effective message of surrender in over-the-horizon aerial encounters.

4. The ICAO distress frequency must not be disrupted by any Belligerent Party (see paragraph 2 of the Commentary on Rule 115). Continuous watch ought to be kept on this frequency at the appropriate command centres.

5. Rule 128 applies *mutatis mutandis* to capture in non-international armed conflict (see paragraph 6 of the Commentary on Rule 125).

129. A Belligerent Party may insist on the surrender by an enemy military aircraft being effected in a prescribed mode, reasonable in the circumstances. Failure to follow any such instructions may render the aircraft and the aircrews liable to attack.

1. In the absence of generally prescribed modes of surrender in air warfare, there may be no alternative to such modes being set *ad hoc* by a Belligerent Party in light of the prevailing circumstances. However, any prescribed mode established in such fashion must be reasonable.

2. A "prescribed mode" – established under Rule 129 – could include flying a particular course, at a fixed altitude and at a given airspeed, as well as landing at a pre-arranged location.

3. Once a prescribed mode of surrender is established in conformity with Rule 129, any deviation from its terms may expose the aircraft to an attack.

4. Rule 129 applies *mutatis mutandis* to capture in non-international armed conflict (see paragraph 6 of the Commentary on Rule 125).

130. Aircrews of military aircraft wishing to surrender may, in certain circumstances, have to parachute from the aircraft in order to communicate their intentions. The provisions of this Section of the Manual are without prejudice to the issue of surrender of aircrews having descended by parachute from an aircraft in distress (see Section T of this Manual).

1. Since there is no generally prescribed mode indicating surrender of an aircraft and its crew, and since radio communications may fail, aircrews of military aircraft may have no alternative but to resort to parachuting from their aircraft if they want to surrender.

2. Aircrews of military aircraft may descend by parachute from their aircraft because of distress, irrespective of any intention to surrender (see Section T). Whether or not they wish to surrender, they must not be attacked during the descent, and must be given an opportunity to surrender upon reaching enemy-controlled territory (see Rule 132 (b)). Only airborne troops may be attacked during their descent.

3. Rule 129 applies *mutatis mutandis* to capture in non-international armed conflict (see paragraph 6 of the Commentary on Rule 125).

131. Subject to Rule 87, surrendering combatants, as well as captured civilians accompanying the armed forces (such as civilian members of military aircraft crews) and crews of civilian aircraft of the Belligerent Parties who do not benefit from a more favorable treatment, are entitled to prisoner of war status.

1. This Rule is based on Art. 4 (A) (4)–(5) of GC/III,[650] which deals with persons who accompany the armed forces without actually being members thereof, such as civilian members of military aircraft crews. It also includes crews of civilian aircraft of the Belligerent Parties. Such civilians are entitled to POW-status if they are captured.

2. Civilians who are entitled to POW-status under GC/III must be differentiated in this respect from ordinary civilians who are covered by GC/IV.

3. Generally speaking, aircrews and passengers of State aircraft (other than military aircraft) will be civilians. However, some passengers transported by a State aircraft other than a military aircraft, may be members of the armed forces. In that case, they may be taken as POW upon capture of the aircraft.

4. Medical or religious personnel cannot be taken as POW and must be allowed to carry out their mission (see Rule 71 and 87).

5. The status of POW does not exist as a legal category in non-international armed conflict. Nevertheless, those who have given themselves up for capture (see paragraph 6 of the Commentary on Rule 125) enjoy certain protections under Common Art. 3 of the Geneva Conventions[651] and under customary international law.

[650] Art. 4 (A) (4) and (5) of GC/III: "(4) Persons who accompany the armed forces without actually being members thereof, such as civilian members of military aircraft crews, war correspondents, supply contractors, members of labour units or of services responsible for the welfare of the armed forces, provided that they have received authorization from the armed forces which they accompany, who shall provide them for that purpose with an identity card similar to the annexed model. (5) Members of crews, including masters, pilots and apprentices, of the merchant marine and the crews of civil aircraft of the Parties to the conflict, who do not benefit by more favourable treatment under any other provisions of international law."

[651] Common Art. 3 of the Geneva Conventions, see fn. 92.

Section T

Parachutists from an Aircraft in Distress

132. (a) No person descending by parachute from an aircraft in distress may be made the object of attack during his descent.

1. This Rule is based on Art. 42 (1) of AP/I.[652]

2. Rule 132 (a) covers both aircrews and passengers, although not airborne troops (see Rule 133).

3. Rule 132 (a) is absolute and applicable even if it appears that aircrews parachuting from an aircraft in distress will reach – or be rescued by – friendly forces and live to fight another day.

4. Rule 132 (a) covers aircrews and passengers parachuting from an aircraft in distress not only over land but also over sea areas. Once they alight on sea, they become shipwrecked.

5. If survivors at sea who are members of the armed forces of a Belligerent Party are picked up by neutral vessels, they must be interned for the duration of the international armed conflict (see Rule 172 (b)).

6. Rule 132 (a) applies also in non-international armed conflict.

(b) Upon landing in a territory controlled by the enemy, a person who descended by parachute from an aircraft in distress is entitled to be given an opportunity to surrender prior to being made the object of attack, unless it is apparent that he is engaging in a hostile act.

[652] Art. 42 (1) of AP/I: "No person parachuting from an aircraft in distress shall be made the object of attack during his descent."

1. This Rule is based on Art. 42 (2) of AP/I.[653] See also Para. 8.2.3.1 of NWP.[654]

2. The thrust of Rule 132 (b) is that, upon the completion of the descent from an aircraft in distress and once landing in territory controlled by the enemy is effected, an opportunity must be given to the parachutist to surrender.

3. For his part, the parachutist who has descended must not try to evade capture by the enemy. An attempt to evade capture denotes that the person concerned has not laid down his arms in the legal sense (see Rule 15 (b) and Rule 127).

4. It has happened that parachuting airmen have been attacked by a mob of local civilians with the intention of lynching. Such an act constitutes a war crime. In this case, the parachuting airman is entitled to attempt to escape the mob without losing his *hors de combat* status.

5. Rule 132 (b) presupposes that the parachutists lands in "territory controlled by the enemy". If, for whatever reason (e.g., due to wind currents), the parachutists lands in neutral territory, he must be interned by the Neutral (see Commentary on Rule 170 (c)).

6. Rule 132 (b) applies also in non-international armed conflict.

133. This Section does not apply to airborne troops.

1. This Rule is based on Art. 42 (3) of AP/I.[655] See also Para. 8.2.3.1 of NWP.[656]

[653] Art. 42 (2) of AP/I: "Upon reaching the ground in territory controlled by an adverse Party, a person who has parachuted from an aircraft in distress shall be given an opportunity to surrender before being made the object of attack, unless it is apparent that he is engaging in a hostile act."

[654] Para. 8.2.3.1. of NWP ("Airborne Forces versus Parachutists in Distress"), first sentence: "Parachutists descending from disabled aircraft may not be attacked while in the air unless they engage in combatant acts while descending. Upon reaching the ground, such parachutists must be provided an opportunity to surrender."

[655] Art. 42 (3) of AP/I: "Airborne troops are not protected by this Article."

[656] NWP, Para. 8.2.3.1, third and fourth sentences: "Airborne troops, special warfare infiltrators, and intelligence agents parachuting into combat areas or behind enemy lines are not so protected and may be attacked in the air as well as on the ground. Such personnel may not be attacked, however, if they clearly indicate in a timely manner their intention to surrender."

2. Although the phrase "airborne troops" is used in the plural, Rule 133 applies also to one individual person. The term must, furthermore, be understood comprehensively: it includes paratroopers, special forces, commando units, etc.

3. The real difference between "airborne troops" and "parachut[ists] from an aircraft in distress" relates to their status during the descent from the aircraft. Airborne troops may be lawfully attacked during their descent. However, upon landing, they may surrender (see Rule 125). Should they surrender, they are no different from any other combatant. Therefore, all conditions of Rule 127 must be complied with.

4. Rule 133 applies also in non-international armed conflict.

Section U

Contraband, Interception, Inspection and Capture

1. Section U recognizes the right of a Belligerent Party to interfere with enemy aircraft as well as with neutral civilian aircraft, if the latter engage in the activities referred to in Rule 140 (for neutral civilian aircraft) and in Rule 141 (for goods on board neutral civilian aircraft). The issues arising in this Section have traditionally been dealt with in the context of prize law, i.e., visit and search, capture and condemnation of civilian aircraft and of goods on board such aircraft.

2. Despite the use of the concept "visit and search" in the HRAW[657] and elsewhere,[658] the Group of Experts decided to use the term "inspection" and to add "interception", in order to clearly distinguish between the aerial and the naval contexts. In naval warfare, visit and search of a merchant vessel can be exercised at sea. By contrast, a civilian aircraft can be inspected only if it is on the ground. This presupposes that it has been intercepted and ordered to land.

3. For the purposes of this Section, interception means an operation by which military aircraft make visual, radio or electronic contact with another aircraft, with a view to (i) verifying its identity, destination, character, or function; (ii) to force that aircraft to land for inspection, or (iii) to divert it from its destination.

[657] Chapter VII of the HRAW, entitled "Visit and Search, Capture and Condemnation".

[658] UK Manual, paras. 12.74 to 12.103 as part of "F. Measures Short of Attack: Interception, Visit, Search, Diversion, and Capture". See also Para. 13.91 of the UK Manual on "Visit and search of merchant vessels".

See also SRM/ACS, Part V entitled "Measures short of attack: interception, visit, search, diversion and capture.", corresponding to Para. 112 until Para. 158. More in particular, see, e.g., Paras. 125 to 134 of SRM/ACS, all under the heading "Interception, Visit and Search of Civil Aircraft."

See also Paras. 12.81 to 12.103 of the UK Manual – under the same heading – and Para. 13.91 of the UK Manual on "visit and search of merchant vessels".

4. Based upon Rule 17 (a) "[o]nly military aircraft, including UCAVs, are entitled to engage in attacks" and, based upon Rule 17 (b), [t]he same Rule applies to the exercise of other belligerent rights, such as interception". Thus, interception of – enemy or neutral – civilian aircraft is a right enjoyed exclusively by belligerent military aircraft. Other State aircraft are not allowed to take prize measures.

5. All enemy civilian aircraft may be captured with enemy goods on board, and condemned as prize, irrespective of whether they carry contraband. Capture and condemnation of enemy civilian aircraft and goods on board must not be confused with attacks directed against enemy civilian aircraft because they constitute a military objective (see Rule 27).

6. In contradistinction to enemy civilian aircraft, neutral civilian aircraft (and goods on board) can neither be attacked nor captured, unless the goods on board constitute contraband, or unless they engage in activities spelled out in Rule 140 or in Rule 141. Capture of such aircraft and goods is always subject to condemnation as prize. Prize proceedings follow interception and inspection. In exceptional circumstances, listed in Rule 174, neutral civilian aircraft may even be attacked as military objectives.

7. The belligerent rights dealt with in this Section exclusively apply in situations of international armed conflict. There is no concept of prize law in non-international armed conflict.

I. Enemy aircraft and goods on board such aircraft

Rule 134 and Rule 135 apply to enemy civilian aircraft (except enemy civilian airliners, dealt with in Rule 62). Rule 136 applies to enemy military, law-enforcement and customs aircraft.

134. Enemy civilian aircraft and goods on board may be captured as prize on the ground or – when flying outside neutral airspace – be intercepted and ordered to proceed to a reasonably accessible belligerent airfield that is safe for the type of aircraft involved. Prior exercise of inspection is not required.

1. Interception is a stage preliminary to inspection and possible capture. As a rule, interception will be necessary for the purpose of verification of the aircraft's identity. However, if the enemy character of the civilian aircraft has been established by other means, interception may not be

necessary. Nor is it necessary in such circumstances to inspect goods on board.

2. Rule 134 reflects customary international law (see also Rule 49), according to which enemy civilian aircraft "are liable to capture in all circumstances",[659] unless they come within special categories that are exempt from capture under the law of international armed conflict (see Section K on medical aircraft and Rule 67 on aircraft granted safe conduct).

3. In this respect, air warfare is like sea warfare and not like land warfare. Whereas in land warfare Belligerent Parties are – other than in exceptional circumstances – not allowed to interfere with private property, in sea warfare enemy civilian vessels can be captured as prize with a view to interfering with the enemy's trade and lines of commercial communication. The same applies in air warfare, where a civilian aircraft is liable to capture as prize solely on account of its enemy character.

4. The right of capture applies to enemy civilian aircraft and goods wherever they are on the ground – i.e., if they are encountered on the territory of the captor State, a co-belligerent or the enemy – as long as they are not within neutral territory. Capture is exercised by taking physical control over the aircraft and its cargo.

5. If encountered in the air, capture of an aircraft is impossible. Therefore, the aircraft must be intercepted and ordered to land in an airfield where capture can be exercised. Rule 134 refers to a "belligerent airfield", meaning any airfield which is controlled either by the Belligerent Party that effected the capture or by a co-belligerent thereof.

6. The airfield that the intercepted aircraft is ordered to land in must be "reasonably accessible" and "safe for the type of aircraft involved". Accordingly, an enemy civilian aircraft may not be ordered or forced to land in an airfield if the aircraft, its crew or its passengers are exposed to any undue risks. This is a logical consequence of the fact that the enemy aircraft does not qualify as a military objective (unless one of the conditions of Rule 27 has been met) but it is merely liable to capture.

[659] Art. 52 of the HRAW: "Enemy private aircraft are liable to capture in all circumstances." See also Para. 141 of the SRM/ACS: "Subject to the provisions of paragraph 142, enemy civil aircraft and goods on board such aircraft may be captured outside neutral airspace. Prior exercise of visit and search is not required."

7. Contrary to what is the case for neutral civilian aircraft (see paragraph 2 of the Commentary on Rule 137 (c)), consent is not required to divert an enemy civilian aircraft from its declared destination.

8. Interception of enemy civilian aircraft for the purpose of the exercise of the right of capture is permissible outside neutral airspace only. Interception of aircraft in neutral airspace is a violation of the Neutral's territorial sovereignty and is a violation of the prohibition to conduct hostile actions in neutral territory as laid down in Rule 171 (c).

9. The aircrews of captured enemy civilian aircraft are entitled to POW status under GC/III.[660] Civilian passengers may be detained only if they pose a security threat in accordance with Art. 42[661] and Art. 43 of GC/IV.[662] Otherwise, they must be promptly released.

10. Capture of enemy civilian aircraft and goods on board is subject to adjudication by a prize court "in order that any neutral claim may be duly heard and determined".[663]

11. The prize court is a domestic court of the captor Belligerent Party (usually an admiralty court). An attempt in 1907 to establish an International Prize Court failed.[664]

[660] Art. 4 (A) (5) of GC/III, see fn. 650.

[661] Art. 42 of GC/IV: "The internment or placing in assigned residence of protected persons may be ordered only if the security of the Detaining Power makes it absolutely necessary. If any person, acting through the representatives of the Protecting Power, voluntarily demands internment, and if his situation renders this step necessary, he shall be interned by the Power in whose hands he may be."

[662] Art. 43 of GC/IV: "Any protected person who has been interned or placed in assigned residence shall be entitled to have such action reconsidered as soon as possible by an appropriate court or administrative board designated by the Detaining Power for that purpose. If the internment or placing in assigned residence is maintained, the court or administrative board shall periodically, and at least twice yearly, give consideration to his or her case, with a view to the favourable amendment of the initial decision, if circumstances permit. Unless the protected persons concerned object, the Detaining Power shall, as rapidly as possible, give the Protecting Power the names of any protected persons who have been interned or subjected to assigned residence, or who have been released from internment or assigned residence. The decisions of the courts or boards mentioned in the first paragraph of the present Article shall also, subject to the same conditions, be notified as rapidly as possible to the Protecting Power."

[663] Art. 55 of the HRAW: "Capture of an aircraft or of goods on board an aircraft shall be made the subject of prize proceedings, in order that any neutral claim may be duly heard and determined."

[664] 1907 Hague Convention (XII) relative to the Creation of an International Prize Court, which never entered into force due to insufficient ratifications.

135. As an exceptional measure, captured enemy civilian aircraft and goods on board may be destroyed when military circumstances preclude taking the aircraft for prize adjudication, provided that all persons on board have first been placed in safety and documents relating to the prize have been preserved.

1. According to customary international law, Belligerent Parties are entitled to destroy captured prizes "if sending them in for adjudication would be impossible or would imperil the safety of the belligerent aircraft or the success of the operations in which it is engaged."[665] Hence, considerations of military necessity may justify the destruction of a captured enemy civilian aircraft and of goods on board such aircraft. However, destruction of this type is only recognized as an exceptional measure and must be clearly distinguished from destruction under the definition of military objectives (see Rule 11 (y) and Section E).

2. Destruction is permissible only if passengers and crew "have first been placed in safety". Whether a place is sufficiently safe for those persons is a question of fact and will depend upon the circumstances of each case. Since capture presupposes physical control over the aircraft, it will be exercised on the ground. Therefore, the airfield where the aircraft is captured will not qualify as a sufficiently safe place if it is located within the combat zone or if it is under continuous attacks by the enemy.

3. If a captured enemy civilian aircraft is destroyed, the captor "must bring the capture before a prize court".[666] The obligation of preserving the aircraft's documents is meant to enable the prize court to render its

[665] Art. 58 of the HRAW: "Private aircraft which are found upon visit and search to be neutral aircraft liable to condemnation upon the ground of unneutral service, or upon the ground that they have no external marks or are bearing false marks, may be destroyed, if sending them in for adjudication would be impossible or would imperil the safety of the belligerent aircraft or the success of the operations in which it is engaged. Apart from the cases mentioned above, a neutral private aircraft must not be destroyed except in the gravest military emergency, which would not justify the officer in command in releasing it or sending it in for adjudication."

[666] Art. 59 of the HRAW: "Before a neutral private aircraft is destroyed, all persons on board must be placed in safety, and all the papers of the aircraft must be preserved. A captor who has destroyed a neutral private aircraft must bring the capture before the prize court, and must first establish that he was justified in destroying it under Article 58. If he fails to do this, parties interested in the aircraft or its cargo are entitled to compensation. If the capture is held to be invalid, though the act of destruction is held to have been justifiable, compensation must be paid to the parties interested in place of the restitution to which they would have been entitled."

decision on the legality of the capture, as well as the destruction, and on possible neutral claims.

4. If the prize court rules that capture or destruction was illegal, the neutral owners of the cargo on board the enemy civilian aircraft are entitled to compensation.

136. (a) Enemy military, law-enforcement and customs aircraft are booty of war. Prize procedures do not apply to captured enemy military aircraft and other State aircraft, inasmuch as their ownership immediately passes to the captor government by virtue of capture.

1. This Rule is based on Art. 32 of the HRAW.[667] In the case of enemy civilian aircraft, the property does not pass to the captor until the prize has been condemned by a prize court. For their part, enemy military aircraft captured on the ground, are no different from other enemy governmental property. All captured enemy governmental property which is movable becomes automatically the property of the captor Belligerent Party as booty of war.

2. In view of the nature of enemy military aircraft, it is immaterial whether they have been captured after a military engagement or whether they have been forced, by whatever means, to land on the territory of a Belligerent Party. Capture is effected by securing possession of the aircraft. The effect of capture of an enemy military aircraft is the immediate and final transfer of property to the captor Belligerent Party, who is then entitled to deal with the military aircraft as it wishes. Use of the captured aircraft as a military aircraft by the captor Belligerent Party presupposes of course that the aircraft in question meets the requirements laid down in Rule 1 (x).

3. As regards State aircraft other than military aircraft, it must be recalled (see Commentary on Rule 1 (c)) that there is a distinction between those aircraft which are used for law-enforcement (including police) and customs purposes, on the one hand, and other State aircraft, on the other. According to Art. 5 of the HRAW,[668] State aircraft other than police and customs aircraft are treated on the same footing as "private" (namely civilian) aircraft and, according to Art. 32 of the HRAW, are not subject to

[667] Art. 32 of the HRAW: "Enemy public aircraft, other than those treated on the same footing as private aircraft, shall be subject to confiscation without prize proceedings."

[668] Art. 5 of the HRAW, see fn. 84.

confiscation without prize proceedings, i.e., they do not constitute booty of war. The expression in Rule 136 (a) of "other State aircraft" ought to be interpreted as State aircraft other than law-enforcement and customs aircraft. There is no question that the distinction for the purposes of booty of war and prize, made in Art. 5 and in Art. 32 of the HRAW, is still valid today.

4. Rule 136 (a) uses the somewhat broader term "law-enforcement" in preference to the term "police" (used in Art. 4 of the HRAW).[669]

(b) If a military aircraft becomes disabled or experiences technical problems that require it to land in enemy territory, the aircraft may be seized and destroyed or converted for use by the enemy.

The fact that a military aircraft is forced to land in enemy territory, because it has become disabled or because of technical problems, does not alter that aircraft's nature as booty of war (see Rule 136 (a)).

(c) Captured aircrews of military aircraft covered under this Rule are prisoners of war.

The military aircrews of military aircraft are combatants and, as such, entitled to POW status. It needs to be observed that, according to Art. 4 A (4) of GC/III,[670] "civilian members of military aircraft crews" are also entitled to POW-status.

II. Neutral civilian aircraft

137. (a) Belligerent Parties are entitled to intercept neutral civilian aircraft outside neutral airspace, provided that due regard is given to the safety of civil aviation.

1. It is a well-established rule of customary international law that neutral civilian aircraft are liable to interception,[671] in order to enable Belligerent Parties to verify their true character or whether they are employed in their innocent role. In most cases, interception of neutral civilian aircraft will be sufficient to establish whether they in fact have neutral character and are not employed in any of the activities referred to in Rules 140–141.

[669] Art. 4 of the HRAW, see fn. 83.

[670] Art. 4 (A) (4) of GC/III, see fn. 650.

[671] Art. 49 of the HRAW: "Private aircraft are liable to visit and search and to capture by belligerent military aircraft."

Following interception, the neutral civilian aircraft may be ordered to land for inspection. Inspection can also be carried out when the neutral civilian aircraft is encountered on the ground.

2. Neutral State aircraft, including neutral military aircraft, enjoy sovereign immunity and may not be interfered with, unless they are engaged in activities in support of the enemy's military actions (see paragraph 6 of the Commentary on Rule 1 (cc)).

3. Interception of neutral civilian aircraft must always be conducted with due regard to their safety. ICAO has published a Manual on the interception of civil aircraft[672] that may be considered as reflecting customary international peacetime law. While the recommendations given and the procedures described in the ICAO Manual do not necessarily apply in times of armed conflict,[673] they ought to serve as a useful guidance for interception of civilian aircraft even by Belligerent Parties.

4. In any event, under the law of international armed conflict: "Belligerent States should promulgate and adhere to safe procedures for intercepting civil aircraft as issued by the competent international organization." See Para. 128 of the SRM/ACS[674] and Para. 12.84 of the UK Manual.[675] Furthermore, as an additional example, see the detailed interception procedures issued by the US Federal Aviation Administration.[676]

[672] International Civil Aviation Organization, Manual concerning Interception of Civil Aircraft (2nd ed. 1990), ICAO Doc. 9433-AN/926.

[673] This especially holds true for Principle 2.5 lit. a) of the ICAO Manual concerning Interception of Civil Aircraft, which states at 2-1: "interception of civil aircraft will be undertaken only as a last resort."

[674] Para. 128 of the SRM/ACS: "Belligerent States should promulgate and adhere to safe procedures for intercepting civil aircraft as issued by the competent international organisation."

[675] Para. 12.84 of the UK Manual: "Belligerent states should promulgate and adhere to safe procedures for intercepting civil aircraft as issued by the competent international organization."

[676] US Federal Aviation Administration, Aeronautical Administration Manual, Official Guide to Basic Flight Information and ATC procedures, Chapter 5 ("Air Traffic Procedures"), Section 6 ("National Security and Interception Procedures", available via <www.faa.gov/air_traffic/publications/ATpubs/AIM/chap5toc.htm> Interception procedures are dealt with in Section 5.6.2.:

"5.1 In phase 1 – approach phase – the aircraft to be intercepted will be approached from the stern by two intercepting military aircraft. At night or in Instrument Meteorological Conditions (e.g. fog), a radar trail tactic will be used.

5.2 In phase 2 – identification phase – the intercepted aircraft ought to expect to visually acquire the lead interceptor and possibly the wingman. The wingman will assume a surveillance position while the flight leader approaches the intercepted aircraft.

5. As per Rule 17 (b), only military aircraft are entitled to intercept neutral civilian aircraft.

(b) If, after interception, reasonable grounds for suspecting that a neutral civilian aircraft is subject to capture exist, it may be ordered to proceed for inspection at a reasonably accessible belligerent airfield that is safe for the type of aircraft involved.

1. If the information acquired during interception is unsatisfactory, and if the grounds for suspicion continue to exist or have been reinforced, the neutral civilian aircraft may be ordered to proceed to a sufficiently safe airfield under the control of the intercepting Belligerent Party or its co-belligerents.

2. On the ground, the aircraft may be inspected. Inspection is limited to such measures that are necessary to verify whether the neutral civilian aircraft is engaged in activities rendering it liable to capture. Hence, a physical inspection of the aircraft will be the exception rather than the rule. In most cases, an inspection of the aircraft's documents will be sufficient to verify that it is not engaged in activities rendering it liable to capture under Rule 140.

3. Notwithstanding the position taken by Art. 58[677] and Art. 59[678] of the HRAW, the Group of Experts has reached the conclusion that – unlike captured enemy civilian aircraft (see Rule 135) – captured neutral civilian aircraft may not be destroyed, even as an exceptional measure.

(c) As an alternative to capture as prize, a neutral civilian aircraft may consent to be diverted from its declared destination.

1. In some situations, the intercepting Belligerent Party may prefer to divert the aircraft from its declared destination, instead of exercising the right of inspection. Similarly, the crew of the neutral civilian aircraft may prefer to proceed to a new destination rather than go to a belligerent

5.3 In phase 3 – post intercept phase – after identification of the aircraft by type, nationality, etc., the flight leader will turn away from the intercepted aircraft. The wingman will remain well clear and accomplish a rejoin with the leader."

677 Art. 58 of the HRAW, see fn. 665.

678 Art. 59 of the HRAW, see fn. 666.

airfield and be subjected to inspection. Accordingly, Rule 137 (c) provides for an alternative to capture by diverting the aircraft from its destination.[679]

2. However, since neutral civilian aircraft are not under an obligation to comply with a diversion order, the consent of the neutral civilian aircraft is required. It may be recalled in this context that consent is not required to divert an enemy civilian aircraft from its declared destination (see Rule 134).

138. In order to avoid the need for interception, Belligerent Parties are allowed to establish reasonable measures for the inspection of the cargo of neutral civilian aircraft and the certification that an aircraft is not carrying contraband.

1. This Rule is based on Para. 132 of the SRM/ACS.[680]

2. Interception, inspection or diversion of neutral civilian aircraft may entail considerable financial losses for the operators of the affected aircraft, as well as for the owners of the cargo on board. Such measures will also tie up belligerent forces that could be used elsewhere. Additionally, they can place such forces at risk. These problems were partially solved by Great Britain and its allies in WWI and WWII through introduction of the "navicert" system.[681]

[679] Para. 126 of the SRM/ACS: "As an alternative to visit and search: (a) an enemy civil aircraft may be diverted from its declared destination; (b) a neutral civil aircraft may be diverted from its declared destination with its consent."

[680] Para. 132 of the SRM/ACS: "In order to avoid the necessity of visit and search, belligerent States may establish reasonable measures for the inspection of cargo of neutral civil aircraft and certification that an aircraft is not carrying contraband."

Para. 12.88 of the UK Manual contains an identical provision.

[681] Para. 7.4.2 of NWP ("Certificate of Noncontraband carriage"): "A certificate of noncontraband carriage is a document issued by a belligerent consular or other designated official to a neutral vessel (navicert) or neutral aircraft (aircert) certifying that the cargo being carried has been examined, usually at the initial place of departure, and has been found to be free of contraband. The purpose of such a navicert or aircert is to facilitate belligerent control of contraband goods with minimal interference and delay of neutral commerce. The certificate is not a guarantee that the vessel or aircraft will not be subject to visit and search or that cargo will not be seized. (Changed circumstances, such as a change in status of the neutral vessel, between the time of issuance of the certificate and the time of interception at sea may cause it to be invalidated.) Conversely, absence of a navicert or aircert is not, in itself, a valid ground for seizure of cargo. Navicerts and aircerts issued by one belligerent have no effect on the visit and search rights of a belligerent of the opposing side. The acceptance of a navicert or aircert by a neutral ship or aircraft does not constitute 'unneutral service.'"

3. Today, the right to issue such certificates is widely recognized and is considered to also apply to neutral civilian aircraft. Accordingly, a Belligerent Party is entitled to issue "aircerts" certifying, after inspection in neutral territory, that the aircraft is not carrying contraband.

4. Notwithstanding the previous issuance of an "aircert", a Belligerent Party remains entitled to insist on further inspection of the neutral civilian aircraft in light of new developments or new information.

139. The fact that a neutral civilian aircraft has submitted to such measures of supervision as the inspection of its cargo and grant of certificates of non-contraband cargo by one Belligerent Party is not an act of unneutral service with regard to the opposing Belligerent Party.

1. This Rule is based on Para. 133 of the SRM/ACS.[682]

2. Because of the doubts raised – especially during WWII – as to the consequences of carrying a navicert issued by a Belligerent Party, the Group of Experts considered it necessary to stress that the mere carrying of an "aircert" does not render the neutral civilian aircraft liable to capture by the enemy.

3. The expression "unneutral service" is long-standing in the law of international armed conflict, and is defined in detail in Chapter III of the 1909 London Declaration.[683] The thrust of the definition is that the neutral

Para. 13.97 of the UK Manual: "In order to obviate the necessity for visit and search, neutral states are encouraged to enforce reasonable control measures and certification procedures to ensure that their merchant vessels are not carrying contraband."

682 Para. 133 of the SRM/ACS: "The fact that a neutral civil aircraft has submitted to such measures of supervision as the inspection of its cargo and grant of certificates of non-contraband cargo by one belligerent is not an act of unneutral service with regard to an opposing belligerent."

Para. 12.89 of the UK Manual contains an identical provision.

683 Chapter III of the London Declaration is entitled "Unneutral Service". See, in particular, Art. 45 of the 1909 London Declaration: "A neutral vessel will be condemned and will, in a general way, receive the same treatment as a neutral vessel liable to condemnation for carriage of contraband: (1) If she is on a voyage especially undertaken with a view to the transport of individual passengers who are embodied in the armed forces of the enemy, or with a view to the transmission of intelligence in the interest of the enemy. (2) If, to the knowledge of either the owner, the charterer, or the master, she is transporting a military detachment of the enemy, or one or more persons who, in the course of the voyage, directly assist the operations of the enemy. In the cases specified under the above heads, goods belonging to the owner of the vessel are likewise liable to condemnation. The provisions of the present Article do not apply if the vessel is encountered at sea while unaware of

vessel (in this case: aircraft) engages in activities that are inconsistent with its neutral character.

140. Neutral civilian aircraft are subject to capture as prize outside neutral airspace, if it is determined as a result of inspection or by other means that any one of the following conditions is fulfilled:

1. Capture as prize is a belligerent act and may therefore not be exercised within neutral territory. It is made clear in Rule 140 that the determination that a neutral civilian aircraft is liable to capture need not be based on the results of an inspection. The captor Belligerent Party may rely on intelligence or other information to determine that a neutral civilian aircraft is liable to capture as prize. As long as the information thus gained is sufficient to establish one of the conditions laid down in Rule 140 (a)–(f), there is no need for a prior exercise of inspection. If, however, the source of the information cannot be disclosed, the aircraft ought to be inspected in order to enable the prize court to adjudicate on the legality of capture.

2. The conditions rendering a neutral civilian aircraft liable to capture are generally recognized as reflecting customary international law (see Art. 53 of the HRAW[684] and Para. 153 of the SRM/ACS).[685] (*See footnote 685 on next page*)

the outbreak of hostilities, or if the master, after becoming aware of the outbreak of hostilities, has had no opportunity of disembarking the passengers. The vessel is deemed to be aware of the existence of a state of war if she left an enemy port subsequently to the outbreak of hostilities, or a neutral port subsequently to the notification of the outbreak of hostilities to the Power to which such port belongs, provided that such notification was made in sufficient time."

684 Art. 53 of the HRAW: "A neutral private aircraft is liable to capture if it: (a) Resists the legitimate exercise of belligerent rights; (b) Violates a prohibition of which it has had notice issued by a belligerent commanding officer under Article 30; (c) Is engaged in unneutral service; (d) Is armed in time of war when outside the jurisdiction of its own country; (e) Has no external marks or uses false marks; (f) Has no papers or insufficient or irregular papers; (g) Is manifestly out of the line between the point of departure and the point of destination indicated in its papers and after such enquiries as the belligerent may deem necessary, no good cause is shown for the deviation. The aircraft, together with its crew and passengers, if any, may be detained by the belligerent, pending such inquiries; (h) Carries, or itself constitutes, contraband of war; (i) Is engaged in breach of a blockade duly established and effectively maintained; (k) [sic] Has been transferred from belligerent to neutral nationality at a date and in circumstances indicating an intention of evading the consequences in which an enemy aircraft, as such, is exposed. Provided that in each case (except (k)) the ground for capture shall be an act carried out in the flight in which the neutral aircraft came into belligerent hands, i.e., since it left its point of departure and before it reached its point of destination."

(a) They are carrying contraband.

1. This Rule is based on Art. 53 (h) of the HRAW[686] and on Para. 153 (a) of the SRM/ACS.[687]

2. Neutral civilian aircraft continue to enjoy the rights of pursuing their commercial activities, even when an international armed conflict is going in. These rights include the transportation of goods, regardless of whether they are neutral or enemy in character. However, neutral civilian aircraft are not free to transport contraband.

3. According to Rule 1 (n), "contraband means goods which are ultimately destined for territory under the control of an enemy Belligerent Party and which are susceptible for use in international armed conflict". Hence, ownership – be it enemy or neutral – is irrelevant.

4. Rule 140 (a) reflects State practice that has lead to an abolition of the traditional distinction between "absolute" and "relative" contraband (see Commentary on Rule 1 (n)). Moreover, it is not necessary that the goods considered contraband are contained in a contraband list. It is sufficient to establish that the goods are susceptible to belligerent use and that they are ultimately destined for territory under the control of an enemy Belligerent Party. However, for reasons of legal clarity, Belligerent Parties ought to publish contraband lists prior to the exercise of prize measures.[688]

5. The fact that the goods in question must be "ultimately destined for territory under the control" of the enemy confirms the validity of the "doctrine of continuous voyage". According to the aircraft's papers, the goods may appear to be destined for neutral territory. Nevertheless, the captor Belligerent Party may possess information according to which the

685 Para. 153 of the SRM/ACS: "Neutral civil aircraft are subject to capture outside neutral airspace if they are engaged in any of the activities in paragraph 70 or if it is determined as a result of visit and search or by any other means, that they: (a) are carrying contraband; (b) are on a flight especially undertaken with a view to the transport of individual passengers who are embodied in the armed forces of the enemy; (c) are operating directly under enemy control, orders, charter, employment or direction; (d) present irregular or fraudulent documents, lack necessary documents, or destroy, deface or conceal documents; (e) are violating regulations established by a belligerent within the immediate area of naval operations; or (f) are engaged in a breach of blockade."

686 Art. 53 (h) of the HRAW, see fn. 684.

687 Para. 153 (a) of SRM/ACS, see fn. 685.

688 Para. 149 of SRM/ACS: "In order to exercise the right of capture . . . , the belligerent must have published contraband lists. The precise nature of a belligerent's contraband list may vary according to the particular circumstances of the armed conflict. Contraband lists shall be reasonably specific."

goods will eventually be transported from neutral to enemy controlled territory. In such cases, the initial destination is irrelevant. The legality of the capture will eventually be determined by a prize court.

6. The concept of contraband is limited to goods destined for territory under the control of the enemy and it does not apply to exports from enemy territory. Goods exported from enemy territory do not qualify as contraband. The only lawful way of interfering with enemy exports aboard neutral civilian aircraft is by establishing and enforcing a blockade (for aerial blockade, see Section V).

7. It is immaterial whether the pilot, the aircrew, the owner or the operator of the aircraft knows that the cargo is contraband.

(b) They are on a flight especially undertaken to transport individual passengers who are members of the enemy's armed forces.

1. Rule 140 (b) is based on Para. 153 (b) of the SRM/ACS.[689] See also Art. 45 (1) of the 1909 London Declaration.[690]

2. It is a well-established belligerent right to prevent neutral civilian aircraft from transporting enemy troops. It must be stressed, however, that the incidental presence on board of some enemy nationals who are members of the armed forces or who are going to enlist does not justify capture as prize. Therefore, the flight must be undertaken "especially" for that purpose.

(c) They are operating directly under enemy control, orders, charter, employment or direction.

1. Rule 140 (c) is based on Art. 46 (2) of the 1909 London Declaration.[691]

[689] Para. 153 (b) of SRM/ACS, see fn. 685.

[690] Art. 45 (1) of the 1909 London Declaration, see fn. 683.

[691] Art. 46 of the 1909 London Declaration: "A neutral vessel will be condemned and, in a general way, receive the same treatment as would be applicable to her if she were an enemy merchant vessel: (1) if she takes a direct part in the hostilities; (2) if she is under the orders or control of an agent placed on board by the enemy Government; (3) if she is in the exclusive employment of the enemy Government; (4) if she is exclusively engaged at the time either in the transport of enemy troops or in the transmission of intelligence in the interest of the enemy. In the cases covered by the present Article, goods belonging to the owner of the vessel are likewise liable to condemnation."

2. Neutral civilian aircraft "operating directly under enemy control, orders, charter, employment or direction" lose their neutral character. Then, they may be assimilated to enemy civilian aircraft that, according to Rule 134, are always liable to capture as prize.

(d) They present irregular or fraudulent documents, lack necessary documents, or destroy, deface or conceal documents.

1. According to Art. 53 (f) of HRAW,[692] a neutral civilian aircraft is liable to capture as prize if it "has no papers or insufficient or irregular papers".

2. Para. 153 of the SRM/ACS states that [n]eutral civil aircraft are subject to capture outside neutral airspace if they are engaged in any of the activities in Para. 70 or if it is determined as a result of visit and search or by any other means, that they ... (d) present irregular or fraudulent documents, lack necessary documents, or destroy, deface or conceal documents."

3. The lack of papers or the presentation of irregular or fraudulent papers is sufficient ground for suspicion that the aircraft has in fact enemy character and that it is, thus, subject to capture as prize.

4. According to Art. 54 of the HRAW, the "papers of a private aircraft will be regarded as insufficient or irregular if they do not establish the nationality of the aircraft and indicate the names and nationality of the crew and passengers, the points of departure and destination of the flight, together with the particulars of the cargo and the conditions under which it is transported. The logs must also be included."

(e) They are violating regulations established by a Belligerent Party within the immediate area of military operations.

1. This Rule is based on Art. 53 (b) of the HRAW[693] and on Para. 153 (e) of the SRM/ACS.[694]

2. In the immediate area of military operations (see Rule 106 (a)), Belligerent Parties enjoy the right to prevent the passing of neutral civilian aircraft if their presence is "likely to prejudice the success of the

692 Art. 53 (h) of HRAW, see fn. 684.
693 Art. 53 (b) of HRAW, see fn. 684.
694 Para. 153 (e) of SRM/ACS, see fn. 685.

operations".[695] Not complying with such belligerent orders, renders the neutral civilian aircraft liable to capture as prize.

(f) They are engaged in breach of an aerial blockade (see Section V of this Manual).

1. According to Art. 53 (i) of the HRAW,[696] a neutral civilian aircraft is liable to capture as prize if it "is engaged in breach of a blockade duly established and effectively maintained". See also Para. 153 (f) of the SRM/ACS.[697]

2. If a Belligerent Party has established an aerial blockade, and if that aerial blockade meets the requirement of effectiveness, that Belligerent Party is entitled (and, in fact, expected) to prevent all aircraft from entering or leaving the blockaded area (see Rule 151 and Rule 154).

141. Goods on board neutral civilian aircraft outside neutral airspace are subject to capture as prize in any one of the following cases:

Rule 141 reaffirms the traditional principle "free ship – free goods"[698] (which is also applicable to aircraft) from which one can deduce that cargos on board neutral civilian aircraft are exempt from capture as prize. However, there are two exceptions to this principle. These two exceptions are listed in Rule 141 (a) and in Rule 141 (b).[699]

(a) They constitute contraband.

1. When the goods on board a neutral civilian aircraft constitute contraband, they may be captured as prize. This is the legal position,

[695] Art. 30 of the HRAW: "In case a belligerent commanding officer considers that the presence of aircraft is likely to prejudice the success of the operations in which he is engaged at the moment, he may prohibit the passing of neutral aircraft in the immediate vicinity of his forces or may oblige them to follow a particular route. A neutral aircraft which does not conform to such directions, of which he has had notice issued by the belligerent commanding officer, may be fired upon."

[696] Art. 53 (i) of HRAW, see fn. 684.

[697] Para. 153 (f) of SRM/ACS, see fn. 685.

[698] Para. 2 and Para. 3 of the 1856 Paris Declaration: "(2) The neutral flag covers enemy's goods, with the exception of contraband of war. (3) Neutral goods, with the exception of contraband of war, are not liable to capture under enemy's flag."

[699] Para. 154 of the SRM/ACS: "Goods on board neutral civil aircraft are subject to capture only if they are contraband."

notwithstanding the fact that the aircraft – being neutral – must be released after inspection.

2. Traditionally, if contraband goods on board a vessel (and, presumably, also an aircraft) form more than half the cargo,[700] the neutral vessel (and aircraft) may itself be captured as prize.

(b) The neutral civilian aircraft is engaged in activities rendering it a military objective under Rule 174.

1. According to Section E and Rule 174, a neutral civilian aircraft becomes a military objective and thus liable to attack, if it engages in activities making an effective contribution to the enemy's military action.

2. In such cases, the cargo shares the legal status of the aircraft. If the aircraft is not attacked but merely captured (see Rule 140), its cargo may be captured as well, and this irrespective of its standing as contraband.

142. The capture of neutral civilian aircraft and of goods on board can be exercised only in the cases provided for in Rules 140 and 141 and is subject to prize adjudication.

1. Any interference with neutral civilian aircraft and goods on board can only take place outside neutral territory.

2. The capture as prize of neutral civilian aircraft can only take place in accordance with Rule 140.

3. The capture as prize of goods on board neutral civilian aircraft can only take place in accordance with Rule 141.

4. In all cases, the validity of capture as prize must be adjudicated by a prize court.

5. It follows from Rule 142 that, if no prize court exists, there is no way for a Belligerent Party to enforce its entitlements under Rule 140 and Rule 141. Hence, if it wishes to condemn neutral civilian aircraft and goods on board, it has no choice but to set up such courts.

[700] Art. 40 of the 1909 London Declaration: "A vessel carrying contraband may be condemned if the contraband, reckoned either by value, weight, volume, or freight, forms more than half the cargo."

III. Safeguards

143. In all circumstances of capture of a civilian aircraft – whether neutral or enemy – the safety of passengers and crew on board must be provided for. Documents and papers relating to the aircraft must be safeguarded.

1. This Rule is based on Para. 158 of the SRM/ACS.[701]

2. Rule 143 obliges Belligerent Parties to take all necessary measures to provide for the safety of all persons on board captured civilian aircraft. As long as they are under the control of the captor Belligerent Party, such persons must be provided for with all the means necessary to guarantee their well-being.

3. The obligation to safeguard all documents and papers relating to the aircraft is a necessary corollary to the need to submit all capture as prize to adjudication by a prize court.

IV. Determination of enemy character

144. The fact that a civilian aircraft bears the marks of an enemy Belligerent Party is conclusive evidence of its enemy character. Enemy character of a civilian aircraft can also be determined by registration, ownership, charter or other appropriate criteria.

1. A civilian aircraft bearing the marks of the enemy is incontestably of enemy character, and may be dealt with accordingly. *Prima facie*, goods on board such aircraft share the aircraft's legal status.

2. The bearing of enemy marks is not the only criterion for establishing the enemy character of a civilian aircraft. Registration, ownership, charter, etc., are relevant considerations as well. While the commander on the spot will regularly not be in a position to inquire into these criteria, the information may be made available through intelligence sources.

3. As regards ownership, it is an unsettled issue whether the owner's enemy character is to be determined according to nationality or domicile. If the aircraft is owned by a corporation, it is unclear whether its enemy

[701] Para. 158 of the SRM/ACS: "If capture is exercised, the safety of passengers and crew and their personal effects must be provided for. The documents and papers relating to the prize must be safeguarded."

character may be determined by reference to the place of incorporation, the seat, the nationality or domicile of the majority of shareholders.

4. As for civilian aircraft bearing the marks of a Neutral, see Rule 175.

145. For the purposes of capture and prize, a civilian aircraft bearing no marks is presumed to have enemy character.

In case a civilian aircraft bears no marks identifying its true nationality, there is a presumption that it is endeavouring to escape capture. Hence, according to Art. 53 (e) of the HRAW,[702] a civilian aircraft that "has no external marks or uses false marks" is liable to capture and, according to the first paragraph of Art. 56 of the HRAW, is liable to condemnation.[703]

146. (a) If the commander of a military aircraft suspects that a civilian aircraft with neutral marks in fact has enemy character, the commander is entitled to exercise the right of interception and, if circumstances require, the right to divert for the purpose of inspection.

1. While the bearing of neutral marks is *prima facie* evidence of the neutral character of a civilian aircraft (see Rule 175), the true character of the aircraft – according to Rule 144 – may be determined by "other appropriate criteria". Hence, the commander who has information at his disposal justifying reasonable grounds of suspicion that the aircraft is in fact of enemy character, may take all measures necessary to determine the aircraft's true character. Hence, the aircraft may be summoned and interrogated.

2. If the information given is insufficient to rule out doubts as to its true character, the civilian aircraft may be ordered to a belligerent airfield for the purpose of inspection. If inspection reveals its enemy character, the civilian aircraft may be captured as prize (see Rule 134).

(b) If it is established, after inspection, that the civilian aircraft with neutral marks does not have enemy character, it must be allowed to proceed without delay.

[702] Art. 53 (e) of HRAW, see fn. 684.

[703] First Para. of Art. 56 of the HRAW: "A private aircraft captured upon the ground that it has no external marks or is using false marks, or that it is armed in time of war outside the jurisdiction of its own country, is liable to condemnation."

1. If it is established that a civilian aircraft has in fact neutral character, it must be released promptly, unless inspection reveals that it has been engaged in activities rendering it liable to capture as prize (see Rule 140).

2. Although diversion as well as inspection may result in financial losses for the owner or operator, there is no right for compensation as long as the reasons justifying doubts as to the true character of the aircraft have been "reasonable".[704] This is the case if the responsible commander acted on the basis of information available to him, justifying the conclusion that the aircraft is in fact owned by enemy nationals or operating under charter by an enemy national. If, however, no such information existed at the time of diversion, the owner or those having a legal interest in the aircraft are entitled to compensation. This applies *a fortiori* if the diversion was arbitrary.

[704] For a similar approach see UNCLOS, Art. 106 ("Liability for seizure without adequate grounds"): "Where the seizure of a ship or aircraft on suspicion of piracy has been effected without adequate grounds, the State making the seizure shall be liable to the State the nationality of which is possessed by the ship or aircraft for any loss or damage caused by the seizure."

Section V

Aerial Blockade

1. The law of blockade has traditionally evolved in the naval context.[705] Naval blockade was historically understood as involving enforcement by warships against vessels. However, with the advent of aviation, naval blockades – i.e., blockades designed to prevent entry or exit by vessels – have become relevant also to aircraft.

2. This Manual does not deal with naval blockades, even when they are enforced by military aircraft. The thrust of this Section is aerial blockade. Today, there is widespread agreement that an aerial blockade is enforced against aircraft, either by military aircraft (including UCAVs) or by other means (including warships).

3. An aerial blockade is a belligerent operation to prevent aircraft from entering or exiting specified airfields or coastal areas belonging to, occupied by, or under the control of the enemy (see Rule 147).

4. The primary purpose of establishing an aerial blockade is to deny the enemy the use of neutral aircraft to transport personnel and goods to or from the blockaded area. However, an aerial blockade must be enforced against all aircraft, even when they are not actually transporting anything or anyone.

5. An aerial blockade must equally be enforced against UAVs and UCAVs (otherwise the aerial blockade will not be regarded as "effective", see Rule 151 and Rule 154).

6. An aerial blockade cannot preclude consignments for the civilian population from going through in accordance with Rule 158 and Rule 159. Ingress and egress by medical aircraft (see Section L) and aircraft granted safe conduct (see Section J (II) and Section J (III)) depends on consent

[705] 1856 Paris Declaration and 1909 London Declaration. The 1909 London Declaration never entered into force but is in most parts considered as reflective of customary international law.

given by the Blockading Party to their flights to or from the blockaded area. As for aircraft in distress, see Rule 153 (b).

7. Aerial blockade is a method of warfare exclusively applicable in international armed conflicts. Nevertheless, in a non-international armed conflict, the central government can always impose restrictions on entry into and exit from areas formally subject to the territorial sovereignty of the State but *de facto* under the control of non-State organized armed groups opposing it. The central government, however, cannot exceed its sovereign rights and may not impose any restrictions relating to areas beyond the territory of the State.

8. If, in the course of a non-international armed conflict, non-State organized armed groups bar access to airfields or coastal areas held by government forces or by opposing organized armed groups, such conduct has no *de jure* consequences for foreign States.

9. The fact that such measures are taken by non-State organized armed groups does not relieve the respective State from its obligation to give appropriate publicity to any danger to overflights over international straits or archipelagic sea lanes.[706]

147. An aerial blockade is a belligerent operation to prevent aircraft (including UAVs/UCAVs) from entering or exiting specified airfields or coastal areas belonging to, occupied by, or under the control of the enemy.

1. The primary purpose of establishing an aerial blockade is to deny the enemy the benefit of the use of neutral aircraft to transport personnel and goods to or from enemy controlled territory. That purpose may be achieved by the use of a variety of lawful means of warfare.

2. As explained in the *chapeau* of the Commentary on this Section, a naval blockade is enforced against vessels, whereas an aerial blockade is enforced against – even empty – aircraft (including UAVs / UCAVs). The means of enforcement are irrelevant, i.e., both types of blockade can be

[706] Art. 44 of UNCLOS ("Duties of States bordering straits"): "States bordering straits shall not hamper transit passage and shall give appropriate publicity to any danger to navigation or overflight within or over the strait of which they have knowledge. There shall be no suspension of transit passage."

Art. 54 of UNCLOS declares Art. 44 of UNCLOS (among other provisions) to be equally applicable to archipelagic sea lanes passage.

enforced by either warships or by military aircraft (see Rule 153 (a) and Rule 154).

3. An aerial blockade against "coastal areas" can be imposed irrespective of the existence of any airfield within the area affected.

4. A blockade, whether aerial or naval, is the only method of warfare entitling a Belligerent Party to lawfully interfere with enemy exports on board neutral civilian aircraft (or vessels). If no blockade is established and enforced, goods on board neutral civilian aircraft (and vessels) may be captured as prize only when they constitute contraband (see Rules 141 (a)).

148. (a) An aerial blockade must be declared by a Belligerent Party and notified to all States.

1. This Rule is based on Art. 8 of the 1909 London Declaration,[707] according to which a naval blockade, in order to be binding for neutral navigation must be declared. The same obligation applies to neutral civil aviation in case of an aerial blockade.

2. An aerial blockade can either be strategic or local. The declaration of a strategic blockade is reserved to the Blockading Party's government. A local aerial blockade may be imposed by a competent commander and is of limited extent and duration (e.g., in preparation of a military operation).

3. Every aerial blockade must always be notified to all Neutrals. In the case of a strategic aerial blockade, notification must also be given to the enemy government. However, in the case of a local aerial blockade, notification may be addressed to the authorities of the blockaded area.

(b) The declaration must specify the commencement, duration, location, and extent of the aerial blockade and the period in which neutral aircraft may leave the blockaded area.

1. The declaration of an aerial blockade must be as specific as possible, in order to enable neutral aviation to avoid the blockaded area or to leave it before enforcement measures take effect. A lack of specificity may render

[707] Art. 8 of the 1909 London Declaration: "A blockade, in order to be binding, must be declared in accordance with Article 9, and notified in accordance with Articles 11 and 16."

the declaration void.[708] Moreover, all measures taken by the Blockading Party must conform to the particulars of the declaration.

2. In principle, the declaration must provide for a period of grace during which neutral aircraft are allowed to leave the blockaded area. There is no absolute rule as to the duration of such a period.[709] However, in most cases 24 hours are considered reasonable. A period of grace must be granted only if, in fact, neutral aircraft are present in the blockaded area.

(c) Whenever feasible, a Notice to Airmen (NOTAM) about the establishment of the aerial blockade ought to be issued by the Blockading Party in accordance with Rule 55.

1. The notification of an aerial blockade must be communicated to all States and not merely to those in the region where the aerial blockade has been established. The reason is that, according to Rule 155, an aerial blockade must be enforced against all aircraft regardless of their nationality or origin.

2. While Art. 11 of the 1909 London Declaration provides that the notification to Neutrals must be made "by means of a communication addressed to the Governments direct, or to their representatives accredited to it",[710] today there is no longer a need for such a formal way of making the establishment of an aerial blockade known to the international community.

3. Ordinarily, the Blockading Party will fulfil its obligation by making use of the usual channels established for international aviation. Therefore, a NOTAM will in most cases be sufficient as a most effective and timely means of conveying the information necessary. In other words, a notification through diplomatic channels will be necessary in exceptional circumstances only.

[708] Art. 10 of the London Declaration: "If the operations of the blockading Power, or of the naval authorities acting in its name, do not tally with the particulars, which, in accordance with Article 9 (1) and (2), must be inserted in the declaration of blockade, the declaration is void, and a new declaration is necessary in order to make the blockade operative."

[709] Art. 9 of the London Declaration: "A declaration of blockade is made either by the blockading Power or by the naval authorities acting in its name. It specifies: ... (3) the period within which neutral vessels may come out."

[710] Art. 11 of the London Declaration: "A declaration of blockade is notified (1) To neutral Powers, by the blockading Power, by means of a communication addressed to the Governments direct, or to their representatives accredited to it; (2) To the local authorities, by the officer commanding the blockading force. The local authorities will, in turn, inform the foreign consular officers at the port or on the coastline under blockade as soon as possible."

4. If, notwithstanding the use of the usual channels available for international aviation, the local authorities in the blockaded area cannot be made aware of the establishment of the aerial blockade, the Blockading Party (or the competent commander) will have to inform them separately by whatever means of communication considered adequate.

149. (a) The cessation, temporary lifting, re-establishment, extension or other alteration of an aerial blockade must be declared and notified to all States.

1. This Rule is based on Art. 12[711] and on Art. 13[712] of the 1909 London Declaration and is self-explanatory. As to the content of the declaration and the manner of notification see the Commentary on Rule 148 (a) – (b). Again, if feasible, a NOTAM ought to be issued (see Commentary on Rule 148 (c)).

2. The obligation under Rule 149 (a) does not apply in cases where, due to stress of weather, the Blockading force has been temporarily withdrawn.[713] This especially holds true if the weather conditions as such prevent any aviation.

3. If the Blockading force is withdrawn for any other reason, and the blockade is to be re-established, the same formalities must be observed as if it were established for the first time.

4. The mere fact that military aircraft enforcing the aerial blockade are not in the air may not be considered a cessation or temporary lifting. The airspace may be monitored by long-range electronic surveillance (e.g., AWACS), which would enable the Blockading force to immediately respond to any attempt of breaching the aerial blockade. See also paragraph 3 of the Commentary on Rule 151, as well as Rule 154.

(b) Whenever feasible, a Notice to Airmen (NOTAM) about any changes under paragraph (a) ought to be issued by the Blockading Party in accordance with Rule 55.

As to the use of a NOTAM, see the Commentary on Rule 148 (c) and on Rule 55.

711 Art. 12 of the London Declaration: "The rules as to declaration and notification of blockade apply to cases where the limits of a blockade are extended, or where a blockade is re-established after having been raised."

712 Art. 13 of the London Declaration: "The voluntary raising of a blockade, as also any restriction in the limits of a blockade, must be notified in the manner prescribed by Article 11."

713 Art. 4 of the London Declaration: "A blockade is not regarded as raised if the blockading force is temporarily withdrawn on account of stress of weather."

150. An aerial blockade must not bar access to the airspace of Neutrals.

1. This Rule is based on Art. 18 of the 1909 London Declaration[714] that, in view of the inviolability of neutral territory and neutral airspace, is declaratory of customary international law.

2. Since aerial blockade is a method of warfare directed against the enemy, it may not have the effect of preventing access to and egress from neutral airspace. Hence, the Blockading Party is under an obligation to provide free passage to and from neutral airspace if the aerial blockade is established and maintained in the vicinity of the territory of a Neutral.

3. In the airspace above straits used for international navigation or above archipelagic sea lanes, leading to a Neutral's airspace, neutral aviation may not be prevented from using the airspace above these straits or lanes. See Art. 37,[715] Art. 38 (1),[716] Art. 44[717] and Art. 54[718] of UNCLOS.

151. An aerial blockade must be effective. The question whether such a blockade is effective is a question of fact.

1. This Rule is based on Principle 4 of the 1856 Paris Declaration[719] and on Art. 2[720] and Art. 3[721] of the 1909 London Declaration. Its object and purpose is to rule out so-called "paper blockades", i.e., aerial blockades

714 Art. 18 of the 1909 London Declaration: "The blockading forces must not bar access to neutral ports or coasts."

715 Art. 37 ("Scope of this Section" on "Transit Passage") of UNCLOS: "This section applies to straits which are used for international navigation between one part of the high seas or an exclusive economic zone and another part of the high seas or an exclusive economic zone."

716 Art. 38 (1) of UNCLOS: "In straits referred to in article 37, all ships and aircraft enjoy the right of transit passage, which shall not be impeded; except that, if the strait is formed by an island of a State bordering the strait and its mainland, transit passage shall not apply if there exists seaward of the island a route through the high seas or through an exclusive economic zone of similar convenience with respect to navigational and hydrographical characteristics."

717 Art. 44 of UNCLOS, see fn. 706.

718 Art. 54 of UNCLOS, see fn. 706.

719 Principle 4 of the 1856 Paris Declaration: "Blockades, in order to be binding, must be effective, that is to say, maintained by a force sufficient really to prevent access to the coast of the enemy."

720 Art. 2 of the 1909 London Declaration: "In accordance with the Declaration of Paris of 1856, a blockade, in order to be binding, must be effective – that is to say, it must be maintained by a force sufficient really to prevent access to the enemy coastline."

721 Art. 3 of the 1909 London Declaration: "The question whether a blockade is effective is a question of fact."

which have been merely declared and which are enforced randomly or not at all.

2. No absolute rule can be laid down as to the strength or position of the Blockading force. All depends on matters of fact and geographical circumstances. Hence, effectiveness is to be judged on the merits of each case. Based on the provisions of the 1856 Paris Declaration and on Art. 2 of the 1909 London Declaration, an aerial blockade would be effective only if it is "maintained by a force sufficient really to prevent access to the coast of the enemy". This does not mean that every single aircraft must in fact be prevented from either entering or leaving the blockaded area. It is sufficient if the Blockading force is of such a strength or nature that there is a high probability that ingress to and egress from the blockaded area will be detected and prevented by the Blockading Party. In other words, an aerial blockade is to be considered effective if any attempt to leave or enter the blockaded area proves to be a hazardous undertaking.

3. For an aerial blockade to be effective, it is not necessary that military aircraft are in the air on a permanent basis. The area may thus be monitored by electronic means of surveillance and/or by UAVs. If the Blockading Party is in a position to immediately respond to an attempted breach of the aerial blockade, the aerial blockade remains effective. See also paragraph 3 of the Commentary on Rule 149 (a).

152. The force maintaining the aerial blockade may be deployed at a distance determined by military requirements.

1. There has always been general agreement that, when judging the effectiveness of an aerial blockade (whether naval or aerial), technological developments are to be taken into account. In view of the evolution of modern weapons, surveillance and communications technology, it is no longer necessary for the Blockading force to be deployed in close vicinity to the blockaded area. The traditional concept of "close blockade" has been replaced by the concept of "long-distance blockade". Therefore, the Blockading force may be deployed at a distance beyond the range of the enemy's coastal or other defence systems.

2. If the aerial blockade is enforced by military aircraft, the aircraft in question will usually be deployed at some distance (e.g., on aircraft carriers, or on the ground in a safe area). This is not necessarily prejudicial to the effectiveness of the aerial blockade, provided that the conditions of Rule 151 and Rule 154 are complied with. The test of an effective aerial blockade is not the distance of the Blockading force from the blockaded

area, but whether there is a reasonable risk that access to and exit from the blockaded area will in fact be prevented. This will be the case if the Blockading Party is in a position to detect an attempted breach of the aerial blockade (e.g., by long-range surveillance, including UAVs) and to react by communicating the relevant information (in real time) to the forces entrusted with the enforcement of the aerial blockade which, for their part, must be capable of reaching the aircraft engaged in a breach in due time. Hence, even long-distance aerial blockades covering a considerable area will remain effective if the Blockading force disposes of the necessary means of surveillance, communication and force projection.

153. (a) An aerial blockade may be enforced and maintained by a combination of lawful means of warfare, provided that this combination does not result in acts inconsistent with the law of international armed conflict.

1. An aerial blockade may be maintained by the Blockading Party through the use of any means of warfare not prohibited under the law of international armed conflict. Therefore, an aerial blockade may be maintained and enforced by military aircraft (including UAVs and UCAVs), missiles, warships, or by a combination thereof.

2. No category of aircraft other than military aircraft is allowed to participate in maintaining and enforcing an aerial blockade (see Rule 17 (b)).

(b) Aircraft in distress must be allowed to enter the blockaded area when necessary.

1. Rule 153 (b) is based on Art. 7 of the 1909 London Declaration[722] and on the customary norm – as reflected in UNCLOS[723] – that assistance must be rendered to those who are in distress in the air or at sea.

[722] Art. 7 of the London Declaration: "In circumstances of distress, acknowledged by an officer of the blockading force, a neutral vessel may enter a place under blockade and subsequently leave it, provided that she has neither discharged nor shipped any cargo there."

[723] There is an affirmative obligation under both customary and treaty law to render assistance to those who are in distress in the high seas, as affirmed in Art. 98 (1) of UNCLOS ("Duty to render assistance"): "(1) Every State shall require the master of a ship flying its flag, insofar as he can do so without serious danger to the ship, the crew or the passengers: (a) to render assistance to any person found at sea in danger of being lost; (b) to proceed with all possible speed to the rescue of persons in distress, if informed of their need of

2. As indicated by the words "when necessary", Rule 153 (b) is not absolute in character. For instance, access to the blockaded area may be denied if there exist equally safe and timely alternatives for the aircraft in distress to land.

154. To the extent that an aerial blockade is maintained and enforced exclusively by military aircraft, the condition of effectiveness (Rule 151) requires a sufficient degree of air superiority.

1. Rule 154 exclusively applies to aerial blockades maintained and enforced by military aircraft. It does not apply to cases in which an aerial blockade is maintained and enforced by other lawful means of warfare (such as missiles or warships). If these other means of warfare are sufficient to deny the enemy the airspace affected by the aerial blockade, there is no necessity for an additional element of effectiveness, such as air superiority.

2. The Group of Experts was in agreement that an aerial blockade, in order to be binding, must comply with the requirements of the principle of effectiveness (see Rule 151). However, there was a division of views on how to determine effectiveness of an aerial blockade by military aircraft. Some members of the Group of Experts took the position that there were no criteria that would make possible an abstract determination of the effectiveness of all aerial blockades. Accordingly, these members preferred to defer to the general and abstract Rule 151. However, the majority of the Group of Experts pointed at the fact that, in case an aerial blockade is maintained and enforced exclusively by military aircraft, such aircraft would be exposed to a considerable risk of attack unless the Blockading force in fact controls the airspace affected by the aerial blockade. Otherwise, interception operations would become unlikely and the aerial blockade would, thus, lose its effectiveness.

3. While the majority of the Group of Experts rejected the concept of "air domination" or of "air supremacy" in the context of aerial blockade, it was decided to adopt the term "air superiority".[724] The Group of Experts was

assistance, insofar as such action may reasonably be expected of him; (c) after a collision, to render assistance to the other ship, its crew and its passengers and, where possible, to inform the other ship of the name of his own ship, its port of registry and the nearest port at which it will call."

[724] NATO Glossary of Terms and Definitions, at 2-A-11 defines "air superiority" as "that degree of dominance in the air battle of one force over another which permits the conduct of operations by the former and its related land, sea and air forces at a given time and place

aware that "air superiority" was an operational term of art. Still, it decided in favour of using the expression in this context, not as a legal concept but as a criterion for determining the effectiveness of the aerial blockade. Air superiority can be gained by a combination of lawful methods and means of warfare, including the use of radar and AWACS aircraft.

4. The Blockading force does not need to have gained full air superiority in the operational sense. This is made clear by the formulation "sufficient degree of air superiority". The adjective "sufficient" relates to the purpose of an aerial blockade, i.e., preventing access to and exit from the blockaded area. The degree of air superiority does not need to remain on the same level for the entire duration of the aerial blockade. The determination of the necessary degree of air superiority, as in the case of effectiveness in general, is dependent on the circumstances of each case. Hence, a lesser degree will suffice if the aerial blockade is maintained not exclusively by military aircraft, but also by other means of warfare (such as missiles or warships). The temporal element of "air superiority" is to be determined in light of international air traffic in the region concerned.

155. An aerial blockade must be enforced impartially as regards the aircraft of all States.

1. This Rule is based on the long-standing principle of impartiality, as laid down in Art. 5 of the 1909 London Declaration.[725] This is a necessary corollary to the principle of effectiveness and to the very object and purpose of an aerial blockade. If an aerial blockade is to effectively prevent access to and exit from the blockaded area by aircraft, that purpose would not be achieved if the Blockading Party distinguishes between aircraft of different nationalities.

2. Accordingly, an aerial blockade must be enforced as regards all aircraft of any nationality, including civilian aircraft bearing the marks of the Blockading Party or of its co-belligerents. This means that, in principle, neutral military or other neutral State aircraft must be prevented from entering or leaving the blockaded area as well. Neutral military or other State aircraft – despite their sovereign immunity – enjoy no positive right

without prohibitive interference by the opposing force." The notion "air superiority" is to be distinguished from "air supremacy", which is defined in the same document (also at 2-A-11) as "that degree of air superiority wherein the opposing air force is incapable of effective interference."

[725] Art. 5 of the 1909 London Declaration: "A blockade must be applied impartially to the ships of all nations."

of access to blockaded areas. However, as an exceptional measure, the Blockading Party, or the local commander, may authorize – subject to conditions or restrictions – entry or exit of an individual neutral military aircraft. This exceptional measure is based on Art. 6 of the 1909 London Declaration[726] and on Para. 7.7.3 of NWP.[727]

3. Rule 155 does not detract from the validity of Rule 153 (b) relating to the entrance of aircraft in distress in the blockaded area.

156. For an aerial blockade to be considered effective under Rule 151, it is required that civilian aircraft believed on reasonable grounds to be breaching, or attempting to breach, an aerial blockade, be forced to land, inspected, captured or diverted. If civilian aircraft clearly resist interception, an order to land and capture, they are at risk of attack after prior warning. As for civilian airliners, Section J applies.

1. It follows from the reference to Rule 151 in the introductory sentence of Rule 156 that a Blockading Party must take action with a view to preventing access to, or exit from, the blockaded area. If the Blockading force decides to remain inactive, the aerial blockade is no longer effective and becomes invalid.

2. The wording of the first sentence of Rule 156 does not necessarily imply that interception is mandatory. The important factor is that a civilian aircraft suspected of breaching an aerial blockade, will be "forced to land, inspected, captured, or diverted". This may be done without prior interception.

[726] Art. 6 of the 1909 London Declaration: "The commander of a blockading force may give permission to a warship to enter, and subsequently to leave, a blockaded port."

[727] Para. 7.7.3 ("Special Entry and Exit Authorization") of NWP: "Although neutral warships and military aircraft enjoy no positive right of access to blockaded areas, the belligerent imposing the blockade may authorize their entry and exit. Such special authorization may be made subject to such conditions as the blockading force considers to be necessary and expedient. Neutral vessels and aircraft in evident distress should be authorized entry into a blockaded area, and subsequently authorized to depart, under conditions prescribed by the officer in command of the blockading force or responsible for maintenance of the blockading instrumentality (e.g., mines). Similarly, neutral vessels and aircraft engaged in the carriage of qualifying relief supplies for the civilian population and the sick and wounded should be authorized to pass through the blockade cordon, subject to the right of the blockading force to prescribe the technical arrangements, including search, under which passage is permitted."

3. Since neutral civilian aircraft are obliged to respect an aerial blockade that conforms to the legal requirements of publicity and effectiveness, they become liable to inspection, capture or diversion. A breach of an aerial blockade – inbound or outbound – occurs at the moment an aircraft crosses the outer limit of the blockaded area as defined in the respective declaration (see Rule 148).

4. An attempt to breach an aerial blockade only occurs in either of the following two sets of circumstances: (i) if an aircraft takes off in the blockaded area with a course evidently set in the direction of the outer limit of the blockaded area; or (ii) if it is in international airspace and clearly on a route destined for the blockaded area.

5. Reasonable grounds for concluding that a breach, or attempt to breach, of an aerial blockade has occurred exist if a neutral civilian aircraft that has been summoned (i) gives false information as to its cargo or destination; or (ii) it lingers in the vicinity of the blockaded area, thus leading to reasonable grounds to suspect that it intends to cross the blockade line as soon as the patrol aircraft have left the respective airspace.

6. Liability to capture presupposes knowledge of the existence of the aerial blockade. That knowledge may be actual or presumptive.[728] The Blockading Party may rely on an assumption that neutral aviation has acquired the knowledge from a NOTAM, if issued (see Rule 148 (in particular Rule 148 (c)) and Rule 149).

7. If a neutral aircraft approaches the blockaded area in ignorance of the aerial blockade (in particular when no NOTAM has been issued), the aircraft must be informed individually about the existence of the aerial blockade by an officer of the Blockading Party (see Art. 16 of the 1909 London Declaration).[729] This can be done through establishing radio communication with the aircraft concerned.

[728] Art. 14 of the 1909 London Declaration: "The liability of a neutral vessel to capture for breach of blockade is contingent on her knowledge, actual or presumptive, of the blockade."

Art. 15 of the 1909 London Declaration: "Failing proof to the contrary, knowledge of the blockade is presumed if the vessel left a neutral port subsequently to the notification of the blockade to the Power to which such port belongs, provided that such notification was made in sufficient time."

[729] Art. 16 of the 1909 London Declaration: "If a vessel approaching a blockaded port has no knowledge, actual or presumptive, of the blockade, the notification must be made to the vessel itself by an officer of one of the ships of the blockading force. This notification

8. If civilian aircraft "clearly resist" interception, they become military objectives and are at risk of attack after prior warning (an attack against a civilian aircraft under such circumstances may offer a definite military advantage, since this may be the only means of preserving the effectiveness of the aerial blockade). As for enemy civilian aircraft, see Rule 27 (d). As for neutral civilian aircraft, see Rule 174 (e). As for civilian airliners (be they enemy or neutral), see Rule 63 (e).

9. If a civilian aircraft is trying to escape, the escaping aircraft may be pursued by the intercepting military aircraft. As long as the pursuit is not abandoned ("hot pursuit"), it remains at risk of attack. The pursuit will be sufficiently "hot" if the escaping aircraft is continuously tracked by the military aircraft of the Blockading force, such as an AWACS that is an integral part of the Blockading Party. Pursuit must be abandoned as soon as the neutral civilian aircraft enters neutral airspace.

10. Since capture is but a means to effectively enforce an aerial blockade, punitive aims may not be pursued. Hence, a civilian aircraft which has successfully escaped capture may not be captured later for the sole reason of having breached, or attempted to breach, an aerial blockade in the past.

11. As regards capture of, and attacks on, civilian airliners, see Section J (I) and Section J (III).

157. The establishment or maintenance of an aerial blockade is prohibited in any one of the following cases:

Rule 157 (a) and Rule 157 (b) are limited to the effects of an aerial blockade on the civilian population. They are irrelevant to any similar effects on combatants or on civilians directly participating in hostilities.

(a) Its sole or primary purpose is to starve the civilian population or to deny that population other objects essential for its survival.

1. Under customary international law, starvation of civilians as a method of warfare is prohibited (see Rule 97).

should be entered in the vessel's logbook, and must state the day and hour, and the geographical position of the vessel at the time. If through the negligence of the officer commanding the blockading force no declaration of blockade has been notified to the local authorities, or, if in the declaration, as notified, no period has been mentioned within which neutral vessels may come out, a neutral vessel coming out of the blockaded port must be allowed to pass free."

2. Para. 7.7.2.5 of NWP states as its final sentence that "[a] blockade is prohibited if the sole purpose is to starve the civilian population or to deny it other objects essential for its survival." The majority of the Group of Experts took the position that an aerial blockade is also prohibited if the "primary purpose" is to either starve the civilian population or to deny it objects essential for its survival. Hence, an aerial blockade may be unlawful even if it serves a secondary and minor military purpose.

3. An aerial blockade will regularly affect the civilian population of the blockaded area, which will be under an increasing risk of being deprived of objects essential for its survival and, ultimately, of starvation. Still, the blockade would, in such cases, not become of itself illegal under Rule 157 (a). It is made clear by the wording ("sole or primary purpose") that a blockade remains legal if denying the population objects essential for its survival is but a mere side-effect pursued by the Blockading Party. Therefore, a blockade is not illegal *per se* if it primarily serves a lawful military purpose. In that case, however, the obligations set out in Rule 157 (b) and in Rule 158 may be applicable.

(b) The suffering of the civilian population is, or may be expected to be, excessive in relation to the concrete and direct military advantage anticipated from the aerial blockade.

1. The expression "suffering", as it appears in Rule 157 (b), does not relate to mere inconveniences to the civilian population. The main thrust of Rule 157 (b) is to preclude a "hunger blockade" which causes severe suffering of the civilian population.

2. The "suffering of the civilian population" is not confined to extreme instances of a "hunger blockade". Where a "hunger blockade" is not the issue, the suffering of the civilian population will be unlawful only if it is, or may be expected to be, excessive in relation to the concrete and direct military advantage anticipated.

3. It is necessary to distinguish between the establishment and the maintenance of an aerial blockade. The suffering of the civilian population may not originally be expected to be excessive in relation to the concrete and direct military advantage anticipated. However, later on, there may be empirical evidence to the effect that such excessive suffering is actually taking place. In these circumstances, the aerial blockade has to be lifted, or free passage of foodstuffs and essential supplies is to be allowed in accordance with Rule 158.

158. Subject to Rule 100, if the civilian population of the blockaded area is inadequately provided with food or other objects essential for its survival, the Blockading Party must provide for free passage of such foodstuffs or other essential supplies, for example by establishing a humanitarian air corridor, subject to the following conditions:

1. This Rule is a corollary to Rule 157 and it reemphasizes the general obligation under Rule 100.

2. Under the existing law of international armed conflict, when the civilian population in a blockaded area is not provided with food or other objects essential to its survival, the Blockading Party must allow free passage of foodstuffs or essential supplies, in order to avoid that the aerial blockade will become a "hunger blockade".

3. For the purpose of securing the safe passage of relief consignments, the Blockading Party may designate a specified route – "humanitarian corridor"– through which aircraft or other means of transport can enter and leave the blockaded area.

4. Rule 158 is "subject to Rule 100" with respect to humanitarian aid. For relief actions from the outside to be undertaken, agreement in non-occupied territory is required of the parties concerned, i.e., in this instance from the Blockading Party. However, agreement by the Blockading Party may not be withheld if it results in starvation of the civilian population as a method of warfare.

(a) The Blockading Party retains the right to prescribe the technical arrangements, including inspection, under which such passage is permitted.

1. Irrespective of the issue of agreement, the Blockading Party has a right to insist on "technical arrangements", which include inspection. This is designed to ensure that relief consignments will not be abused for military or other purposes harmful to the Blockading Party.

2. Moreover, the Blockading Party may limit the transport of relief consignments to certain quantities, times, routes or means of transport, in order to prevent both infringements of the aerial blockade's effectiveness and diversion of the relief consignments to enemy armed forces.

(b) The distribution of such supplies may be made subject to the condition that it will be carried out under the local supervision of a Protecting Power or a humanitarian organization which offers guarantees of impartiality, such as the International Committee of the Red Cross.

1. Rule 158 (b) is intended to safeguard the minimal concerns of the Blockading Party in that it is allowed to insist on the distribution of supplies being carried out under supervision. The supervision may be entrusted either to a Protecting Power (assuming that there is a Protecting Power) or alternatively to an impartial humanitarian organization (such as the ICRC).

2. The institution of the "Protecting Powers" (i.e., a State appointed by consent in order to safeguard the interests of a Belligerent Party)[730] has been introduced in the realm of the law of international armed conflict in the Geneva Conventions of 1929,[731] reiterated in the Geneva Conventions of 1949,[732] and reinforced in AP/I.[733] In practice, the consent to the

[730] Art. 5 (1) of AP/I, see fn. 733.

[731] 1929 Geneva Convention relative to the Treatment of Prisoners of War, where "protecting Powers" are referred to in Arts. 39, 42, 43, 77, 86 and 87.

[732] See, e.g., Art. 9 of GC/IV: "The present Convention shall be applied with the cooperation and under the scrutiny of the Protecting Powers whose duty it is to safeguard the interests of the Parties to the conflict. For this purpose, the Protecting Powers may appoint, apart from their diplomatic or consular staff, delegates from amongst their own nationals or the nationals of other neutral Powers. The said delegates shall be subject to the approval of the Power with which they are to carry out their duties. The Parties to the conflict shall facilitate to the greatest extent possible the task of the representatives or delegates of the Protecting Powers. The representatives or delegates of the Protecting Powers shall not in any case exceed their mission under the present Convention. They shall, in particular, take account of the imperative necessities of security of the State wherein they carry out their duties."

[733] Art. 5 of AP/I ("Appointment of Protecting Powers and of their substitute"): "(1) It is the duty of the Parties to a conflict from the beginning of that conflict to secure the supervision and implementation of the Conventions and of this Protocol by the application of the system of Protecting Powers, including inter alia the designation and acceptance of those Powers, in accordance with the following paragraphs. Protecting Powers shall have the duty of safeguarding the interests of the Parties to the conflict. (2) From the beginning of a situation referred to in Article 1, each Party to the conflict shall without delay designate a Protecting Power for the purpose of applying the Conventions and this Protocol and shall, likewise without delay and for the same purpose, permit the activities or a Protecting Power which has been accepted by it as such after designation by the adverse Party. (3) If a Protecting Power has not been designated or accepted from the beginning of a situation referred to in Article 1, the International Committee of the Red Cross, without prejudice to the right of any other impartial humanitarian organization to do likewise, shall offer

operation of a Protecting Power is only rarely secured. Hence the need for other options, especially performance of the humanitarian functions of a Protecting Power by international humanitarian organizations, such as the ICRC.

159. The Blockading Party must allow the passage of medical supplies for the civilian population or for the wounded and sick members of armed forces, subject to the right to prescribe technical arrangements, including inspection, under which such passage is permitted.

1. This Rule is based on Para. 104 of the SRM.[734] See also Art. 23 of GC/IV.[735]

its good offices to the Parties to the conflict with a view to the designation without delay of a Protecting Power to which the Parties to the conflict consent. For that purpose it may inter alia ask each Party to provide it with a list of at least five States which that Party considers acceptable to act as Protecting Power on its behalf in relation to an adverse Party and ask each adverse Party to provide a list or at least five States which it would accept as the Protecting Power of the first Party; these lists shall be communicated to the Committee within two weeks after the receipt or the request; it shall compare them and seek the agreement of any proposed State named on both lists. (4) If, despite the foregoing, there is no Protecting Power, the Parties to the conflict shall accept without delay an offer which may be made by the International Committee of the Red Cross or by any other organization which offers all guarantees of impartiality and efficacy, after due consultations with the said Parties and taking into account the result of these consultations, to act as a substitute. The functioning of such a substitute is subject to the consent of the Parties to the conflict; every effort shall be made by the Parties to the conflict to facilitate the operations of the substitute in the performance of its tasks under the Conventions and this Protocol. (5) In accordance with Article 4, the designation and acceptance of Protecting Powers for the purpose of applying the Conventions and this Protocol shall not affect the legal status of the Parties to the conflict or of any territory, including occupied territory. (6) The maintenance of diplomatic relations between Parties to the conflict or the entrusting of the protection of a Party's interests and those of its nationals to a third State in accordance with the rules of international law relating to diplomatic relations is no obstacle to the designation of Protecting Powers for the purpose of applying the Conventions and this Protocol. (7) Any subsequent mention in this Protocol of a Protecting Power includes also a substitute."

734 Para. 104 of the SRM/ACS: "The blockading belligerent shall allow the passage of medical supplies for the civilian population or for the wounded and sick members of armed forces, subject to the right to prescribe technical arrangements, including search, under which such passage is permitted."

735 Art. 23 of GC/IV: "Each High Contracting Party shall allow the free passage of all consignments of medical and hospital stores and objects necessary for religious worship intended only for civilians of another High Contracting Party, even if the latter is its adversary. It shall likewise permit the free passage of all consignments of essential foodstuffs, clothing and tonics intended for children under fifteen, expectant mothers and maternity cases. The obligation of a High Contracting Party to allow the free passage of

2. Rule 159 is complementary to Rule 158, except that the element of consent implied in the subjection of Rule 158 to Rule 100 (see paragraph 4 of the Commentary on the *chapeau* to Rule 158) is not included in Rule 159. Allowing the passage of medical supplies for the civilian population or for the wounded and sick members of armed forces (as well as POWs who may be held in custody in the blockaded area) is, therefore, an absolute requirement.

3. Although the agreement of the Blockading Party is not required for the operation of Rule 159, the Blockading Party remains entitled to prescribe technical arrangements – including inspection – to ensure that there is no abuse.

the consignments indicated in the preceding paragraph is subject to the condition that this Party is satisfied that there are no serious reasons for fearing: (a) that the consignments may be diverted from their destination, (b) that the control may not be effective, or (c) that a definite advantage may accrue to the military efforts or economy of the enemy through the substitution of the above-mentioned consignments for goods which would otherwise be provided or produced by the enemy or through the release of such material, services or facilities as would otherwise be required for the production of such goods. The Power which allows the passage of the consignments indicated in the first paragraph of this Article may make such permission conditional on the distribution to the persons benefited thereby being made under the local supervision of the Protecting Powers. Such consignments shall be forwarded as rapidly as possible, and the Power which permits their free passage shall have the right to prescribe the technical arrangements under which such passage is allowed."

Section W

Combined Operations

1. The need for this Section is principally derived from Rule 3 (a) and Rule 3 (b) as regards the scope of application of this Manual, which encompasses United Nations forces and the forces of other – global or regional – international governmental organizations.

2. This Manual also applies to combined operations between the armed forces of two or more States taking place outside any institutional framework. Thus, this Section deals with multinational operations conducted against a common enemy. It does not matter whether the combined operation is carried out as part of a permanent alliance (such as NATO) or whether the coalition is formed on an *ad hoc* basis for a particular international armed conflict.

3. Section W applies only to combined operations involving the armed forces of two or more States; it has no bearing on any coalition between different non-State organized armed groups.

4. Section W applies exclusively to international armed conflicts. The Group of Experts felt unable to come to any conclusion as to whether the *lex lata* allows the Rules reflected in this Section to apply to non-international armed conflicts, and the question was therefore left open.

5. Section W focuses on how legal rights and obligations of a State are affected by the activities of the armed forces of its co-belligerent.

6. The purpose of Section W is not to deal with State responsibility or responsibility of international organizations. Instead, the purpose of this Section is to identify the applicable law in combined operations – where there is more than one State involved on the same side of the armed conflict – addressing the problems that arise when different legal obligations exist among the partners in a combined operation.

160. A combined operation is an operation in which two or more States participate on the same side of an international armed conflict, either as members of a permanent alliance or an *ad hoc* coalition.

Rule 160 clarifies that combined operations relate to the integration and alignment of the forces of two or more States that are partners in a combined operation, fighting a common enemy in an international armed conflict. It is not important whether this alignment reflects an *ad hoc* coalition or a permanent alliance (such as NATO). Moreover, Rule 160 applies equally to forces that are integrated – fighting under unified command – and to forces which merely operate in some degree of cooperation against a common enemy.

161. A State may not invoke its participation in combined operations as justification for its failure to perform its obligations under the law of international armed conflict.

1. Rule 161 refers mainly to non-universal treaties which apply to different sets of Contracting Parties and therefore create different legal regimes. Customary international law is in principle the same for all States (with the exception of a persistent objector), but account must be taken of the fact that the interpretation of specific norms of customary international law may also be subject to divergent views.

2. States occasionally undertake, by treaty, obligations that are not binding upon their partners in a combined operation, since the latter have not signed, ratified, or adhered to the same treaty. Absent a *si omnes* condition in the treaty (i.e., a treaty stipulation that its application is contingent on the condition that all Belligerent Parties are Contracting Parties), a treaty remains binding on Contracting Parties irrespective of whether co-belligerents are also Contracting Parties.

162. The legal obligations of a State participating in combined operations do not change when its armed forces are operating in a multinational force under the command or control of a military commander of a different nationality.

1. The obligations of any State under international law are based on customary law and on any treaties to which it is a Contracting Party. These obligations do not change when the State participates in a combined

operation with States that have different obligations. This is the case even when the commanding officer of the combined operation comes from a State that has different treaty obligations.

2. The problem transcends the issue of different treaty obligations undertaken by partners in a combined operation (see Commentary on Rule 161). It is a common phenomenon for States which are Contracting Parties to the same treaty to interpret certain clauses of that treaty in a different way, just as States often differ in their interpretation of customary international law. This would be an issue of legal interoperability (see Rule 164). A good example of the latter phenomenon involves the divergent approaches to the application of the principles pertaining to military objectives (see Section E, especially paragraph 2 of the Commentary on Rule 24). Specifically, two or more partners to a combined operation may have different interpretations of the law of international armed conflict as regards targeting in a manner affecting their respective assessment of the legality of a particular bombing mission. The result may be that one partner in the combined operation may be willing to undertake the mission, whereas another may not. The question that arises is whether the latter State may nevertheless provide the former with escort fighter aircraft, while the bombing itself is conducted by a bomber of the former State.

3. One way of resolving such issues is by using common Rules of Engagement as a tool. A State may agree to Rules of Engagement that are more restrictive than its obligations under the law of international armed conflict (as it interprets it), in order to be in harmony with the conduct of partners in the combined operation or for other reasons.

4. Another way is to permit partners in the combined operation to insert "caveats" if they find common Rules of Engagement to be too "robust". This is done before an operation commences or when the common Rules of Engagement of an ongoing combined operation are to be reconsidered. Such caveats may be based on legal, as well as political or other reasons. A partner in the combined operation may find it necessary to put certain restrictions on the operations of its troops, in order to maintain sufficient domestic political support for its participation in the combined operation. Caveats may also be based on reasons that have a technical basis, such as when one partner in the combined operation has less accurate weaponry at its disposal than other partners in the combined operation,

and therefore finds it necessary to apply stricter Rules of Engagement for its forces in order to keep the risk of collateral damage at a sufficiently low level.

5. Such caveats will give other partners in the combined operation advance notice of a partner's inability or unwillingness to undertake certain tasks, thus enabling the force commander of the combined operation to adapt plans accordingly. This is typically done by applying a "troops to task" solution, which means that particular tasks are assigned to troops that are not barred from executing them by caveats. In combined operations with many partners and a substantial number of caveats, the commander may use a matrix that shows which troops can be assigned which tasks.

6. For reasons of operational efficiency, and in order to keep planning simple and reduce the potential for misunderstandings, force commanders would prefer to have the least possible number of caveats to the common Rules of Engagements from the partners in the combined operation. However, the legal and political constraints may be such that this becomes unavoidable.

7. It is up to the partners in a combined operation to decide how to organize the decision-making process. One solution may be to have a collective body, typically with representatives from all partners in the combined operation, undertaking analyses of proportionality and other requirements of the law of international armed conflict and deciding on targeting issues. When such a collective procedure is adopted, each partner to the combined operation may have the power to impose a veto barring any particular attack. The imposition of veto is called "red card" procedure. If a partner in the combined operation "shows the red card" with regard to a particular attack that is being planned, the attack will have to be cancelled.

8. Another way to organize the decision-making process may be to vest the authority to make targeting decisions not with the operational commander alone, but allowing partners in the combined operation the use of a "red card" to preclude assignment of particular missions to their respective forces, in accordance with their caveats (see paragraphs 4–6 of the Commentary on this Rule) or for other reasons. Under this arrangement, the operational commander may still be able to carry out his plan, but only if he has at his disposal forces that are able and willing to execute it.

163. A State's obligations under the law of international armed conflict do not change when its air or missile forces are operating from the territory of a co-belligerent, including when its air or missile forces are operating from the territory of a co-belligerent that has different obligations under the law of international armed conflict.

1. The basis for this Rule is the same as for Rule 162.

2. The principle is obvious when an operation takes place in enemy territory, but applies also when the combined operation is conducted in or from a co-belligerent's territory.

3. It must be emphasized that Rule 163 only applies to the "territory of a co-belligerent". Thus, it is without prejudice to the obligations arising under Section X.

4. The specifics of the use of the territory of one co-belligerent by another will depend on an agreement between the two States. This agreement may be either general or *ad hoc* in character.

5. Required consent to operate in or from the territory of a co-belligerent may be subject to restrictions on the visiting force – imposed by the host State – based on the host State's legal obligations or on other considerations. It depends on the nature of the host State's legal obligations whether it must insist on particular restrictions affecting the activities of a partner in a combined operation launched from bases in its territory.

164. A State may participate in combined operations with States that do not share its obligations under the law of international armed conflict although those other States might engage in activities prohibited for the first State.

1. This Rule deals with the issue usually known as "legal interoperability", and it is based on the general practice of States as it has developed in the past two decades.

2. So far, the only treaty law is Art. 21 (3) of the 2008 Convention on Cluster Munitions: "Notwithstanding the Rules of Article 1 of this Convention and in accordance with international law, States parties, their military personnel or nationals, may engage in military cooperation and operations with States not party to this Convention that might engage in

activities prohibited to a State Party."[736] Art. 21 (3) of the 2008 Convention on Cluster Munitions is in accordance with understandings expressed by several Contracting Parties to the 1997 Ottawa Convention.[737]

3. When one co-belligerent has carried out an operation, it is not prohibited for another co-belligerent to exploit the situation that has arisen, although it would have been illegal for the latter to carry out the operation. If, e.g., a minefield has been laid by one partner to a combined operation that is not bound by a treaty provision on the matter, another co-belligerent who is a Contracting Party to the respective treaty may nevertheless deploy its troops taking into consideration the existence of the minefield.

[736] Art. 1 ("General Obligations and Scope of Application") of the 2008 Convention on Cluster Munitions reads: "1. Each State Party undertakes never under any circumstances to (a) Use cluster munitions; (b) Develop, produce, otherwise acquire, stockpile, retain or transfer to anyone, directly or indirectly, cluster munitions; (c) Assist, encourage or induce anyone to engage in any activity prohibited to a State Party under this Convention. (2) Paragraph 1 of this Article applies, mutatis mutandis, to explosive bomblets that are specifically designed to be dispersed or released from dispensers affixed to aircraft. (3) This Convention does not apply to mines."

[737] Australia, for example, made the following declaration of understanding upon ratification of the 1997 Ottawa Convention: "It is the understanding of Australia that, in the context of operations, exercises or other military activity authorised by the UN or otherwise conducted in accordance with international law, the participation by the Australian Defence Force, or individual Australian citizens or residents, in such operations, exercises or other military activity conducted in combination with the armed forces of States not party to the Convention which engage in activity prohibited under the Convention would not, by itself, be considered to be in violation of the Convention." A similar declaration of understanding was made by Canada and the United Kingdom.

Section X

Neutrality

1. According to Rule 1 (aa) of this Manual, "Neutral" means "a State not a Belligerent Party in an international armed conflict". Accordingly, the status of a State as "Neutral" does not depend upon a declaration of neutrality, nor is it to be judged in light of the various positions taken by States on the traditional law of neutrality.[738]

2. The Group of Experts was guided by the object and purpose of the rules and principles of customary international law governing the relations between Belligerent Parties and States not taking part in the armed hostilities, as they have consolidated in post-1945 State practice. While the international armed conflicts that occurred after the end of WWII cast doubts on the continued applicability of the traditional law of neutrality, they give sufficient evidence of some core rules and principles recognized as applicable to every international armed conflict.[739]

3. Those rules and principles can be summarized as serving a double protective purpose. On the one hand, they are to protect Neutrals and their nationals against the harmful effects of the ongoing hostilities. On the other hand, they aim at the protection of interests of any Belligerent Party against interference by Neutrals and their nationals to the benefit of the enemy. Thus, these rules and principles aim to prevent an escalation of

[738] Some States claim the law of neutrality to apply in case of a formally declared war only. Others take the position the law of neutrality applies with the outbreak of an armed conflict of considerable size. Again, others maintain that the law of neutrality becomes binding on States not parties to an international armed conflict only if they have formally declared their neutral status.

[739] Accordingly, the same approach underlies the SRM/ACS, where Para. 13 (d) defines "neutral" as "any State not party to the conflict". See Para. 13.11 and 13.11 of the Commentary on the SRM/ACS: "13.11 This definition corresponds to the definition of neutrality traditionally used in international law. The question has been raised whether it still applies in present-day international law. . . . 13.13 The controversy referred to does not affect the Manual. All the rules on neutrals contained in it apply to all States not party to the conflict, even to those who may consider themselves authorized to depart from certain rules of neutrality."

an ongoing international armed conflict. Accordingly, Belligerent Parties are obliged to respect the inviolability of Neutrals. For their part, Neutrals are under an obligation of strict impartiality and of defending their neutral status.

4. There is no prohibition to continuing neutral aviation and navigation during armed conflict, subject to the Rules listed in this Section, as well as to the Rules listed in Section U.

5. The law of neutrality exclusively applies to Belligerent Parties, on the one side, and to Neutrals, on the other. Accordingly, Section X does not apply to non-international armed conflicts.

I. Scope of application

165. Where the Security Council takes binding preventive or enforcement measures under Chapter VII of the Charter of the United Nations – including the authorization of the use of force by a particular State or group of States – no State may rely upon the law of neutrality to justify conduct which would be incompatible with its obligations under the Charter of the United Nations.

1. This Rule deals with the situation in which the Security Council, acting under Chapter VII ("Action With Respect to Threats to the Peace, Breaches of the Peace, and Acts of Aggression") of the UN Charter, has determined that a threat to the peace, breach of the peace or an act of aggression exists under Art. 39,[740] and has taken preventive or enforcement measures. When this occurs, States not Belligerent Parties to the international armed conflict in question are no longer allowed to rely upon the law of neutrality. According to Art. 25 of the UN Charter,[741] decisions of the Security Council, as distinguished from recommendations, are binding on Member States. Moreover, treaties, such as the 1907 Hague Convention V and the 1907 Hague Convention XIII, become inapplicable because Art. 103 of the UN Charter provides that "[i]n the event of a conflict

[740] Art. 39 of the UN Charter: "The Security Council shall determine the existence of any threat to the peace, breach of the peace, or act of aggression and shall make recommendations, or decide what measures shall be taken in accordance with Articles 41 and 42, to maintain or restore international peace and security."

[741] Art. 25 of the UN Charter: "The Members of the United Nations agree to accept and carry out the decisions of the Security Council in accordance with the present Charter."

between the obligations of the Members of the United Nations under the present Charter and their obligations under any other international agreement, their obligations under the present Charter shall prevail".

2. It is generally recognized that a binding decision by the UN Security Council on the use of force (including an authorization of the use of force under Chapter VIII) not only serves as a legal basis for the resort to force under the authority of the UN Security Council, but also imposes obligations on States not participating in the enforcement or preventive action. This has been demonstrated by State practice. States not participating in the hostilities may not hamper or impede measures taken in accordance with a binding decision of the UN Security Council. They are not entitled to rely upon the impartiality of Neutrals or to intern members of the armed forces that are acting on the basis of the UN Security Council decision.

3. The UN Security Council may decide on either enforcement or on preventive measures. The former are taken with a view to responding to a breach of the peace or an act of aggression. The latter are taken in the face of a threat to peace.

4. Needless to say perhaps, Rule 165 applies only when the UN Security Council adopts binding decisions under Chapter VII of the UN Charter. Rule 165 is inapplicable in other situations, where the UN Security Council abstains from doing so, for whatever reason.

II. General rules

166. Hostilities between Belligerent Parties must not be conducted within neutral territory.

1. The prohibition of conducting hostilities within neutral territory is reflected in Art. 1 of the 1907 Hague Convention (V)[742] and in Art. 1 of the 1907 Hague Convention (XIII).[743] It was reaffirmed by Art. 39[744] and

[742] Art. 1 of 1907 Hague Convention (V): "The territory of neutral Powers is inviolable."

[743] Art. 1 of 1907 Hague Convention (XIII): "Belligerents are bound to respect the sovereign rights of neutral Powers and to abstain, in neutral territory or neutral waters, from any act which would, if knowingly permitted by any Power, constitute a violation of neutrality."

[744] Art. 39 of the HRAW: "Belligerent aircraft are bound to respect the rights of neutral Powers and to abstain within the jurisdiction of a neutral state from the commission of any act which it is the duty of that state to prevent."

Art. 40 of the HRAW,[745] and is today considered to be part of customary international law.[746] In view of the object and purpose of the law of neutrality, to prevent an escalation of an international armed conflict, Belligerent Parties are under a strict obligation to respect the territorial sovereignty of Neutrals.

2. The term "neutral territory" comprises the land territory of Neutrals as well as sea areas which are under the territorial sovereignty of the neutral coastal State, i.e., internal waters, territorial sea and, where applicable, archipelagic waters, and the airspace above those areas. It needs to be emphasized that the prohibition of conducting hostilities within neutral territory is without prejudice to the passage rights Belligerent Parties continue to enjoy in and over international straits and archipelagic sea lanes.

3. Although States have certain sovereign rights in the EEZ, they do not enjoy territorial sovereignty therein (see paragraph 8 of the Commentary on Rule 1 (b)). Accordingly, it is not prohibited to conduct hostilities in the EEZ of a Neutral or in international airspace above that EEZ (see Para. 34[747] and Para. 35[748] of the SRM/ACS). This, however, does not mean that Belligerent Parties are entitled to disregard altogether the sovereign

[745] Art. 40 of the HRAW: "Belligerent military aircraft are forbidden to enter the jurisdiction of a neutral state."

[746] See, e.g., Para. 7.3. of NWP: "As a general rule of international law, all acts of hostility in neutral territory, including neutral lands, neutral waters, and neutral airspace, are prohibited. A neutral nation has the duty to prevent the use of its territory as a place of sanctuary or a base of operations by belligerent forces of any side. If the neutral nation is unable or unwilling to enforce effectively its right of inviolability, an aggrieved belligerent may take such acts as are necessary in neutral territory to counter the activities of enemy forces, including warships and military aircraft, making unlawful use of that territory. Belligerents are also authorized to act in self-defense when attacked or threatened with attack while in neutral territory or when attacked or threatened from neutral territory."

[747] Para. 34 of SRM/ACS: "If hostile actions are conducted within the exclusive economic zone or on the continental shelf of a neutral State, belligerent States shall, in addition to observing the other applicable rules of the law of armed conflict at sea, have due regard for the rights and duties of the coastal State, inter alia, for the exploration and exploitation of the economic resources of the exclusive economic zone and the continental shelf and the protection and preservation of the marine environment. They shall, in particular, have due regard for artificial islands, installations, structures and safety zones established by neutral States in the exclusive economic zone and on the continental shelf."

[748] Para. 35 of SRM/ACS: "If a belligerent considers it necessary to lay mines in the exclusive economic zone or the continental shelf of a neutral State, the belligerent shall notify that State, and shall ensure, inter alia, that the size of the minefield and the type of mines used do not endanger artificial islands, installations and structures, nor interfere with access thereto, and shall avoid so far as practicable interference with the exploration

rights of the neutral coastal State. Belligerent Parties are obliged to pay "due regard" to the rights and duties of neutral coastal States, *inter alia*, for the exploration and exploitation of the economic resources of the EEZ and the protection and preservation of the marine environment. This obligation especially applies with respect to safety zones established around artificial islands, installations and structures in the EEZ of Neutrals (see also Rule 107 (e)).[749] The "due regard" principle imposes no absolute obligation. Instead, Belligerent Parties are supposed to balance the military advantages anticipated as against any negative impact on the rights of Neutrals.

167. (a) Belligerent Parties are prohibited in neutral territory to conduct any hostile actions, establish bases of operations or use such territory as a sanctuary. Furthermore, neutral territory must not be used by Belligerent Parties for the movement of troops or supplies, including overflights by military aircraft or missiles, or for operation of military communication systems.

1. This Rule specifies the general prohibition of conducting hostilities in neutral territory. It is based on Art. 2[750] and Art. 3[751] of the 1907 Hague Convention V; Art. 2[752] and Art. 5[753] of the 1907 Hague Convention

or exploitation of the zone by the neutral State. Due regard shall also be given to the protection and preservation of the marine environment."

[749] Art. 60 (4) and (6) of UNCLOS ("Artificial islands, installations and structures in the exclusive economic zone"): "(4) The coastal State may, where necessary, establish reasonable safety zones around such artificial islands, installations and structures in which it may take appropriate measures to ensure the safety both of navigation and of the artificial islands, installations and structures... (6) "All ships must respect these safety zones and shall comply with generally accepted international standards regarding navigation in the vicinity of artificial islands, installations, structures and safety zones."

[750] Art. 2 of the 1907 Hague Convention (V): "Belligerents are forbidden to move troops or convoys of either munitions of war or supplies across the territory of a neutral Power."

[751] Art. 3 of the 1907 Hague Convention (V): "Belligerents are likewise forbidden to: (a) Erect on the territory of a neutral Power a wireless telegraphy station or other apparatus for the purpose of communicating with belligerent forces on land or sea; (b) Use any installation of this kind established by them before the war on the territory of a neutral Power for purely military purposes, and which has not been opened for the service of public messages."

[752] Art. 2 of the 1907 Hague Convention (XIII): "Any act of hostility, including capture and the exercise of the right of search, committed by belligerent war-ships in the territorial waters of a neutral Power, constitutes a violation of neutrality and is strictly forbidden."

[753] Art. 5 of the 1907 Hague Convention (XIII): "Belligerents are forbidden to use neutral ports and waters as a base of naval operations against their adversaries, and in particular

XIII; Art. 39,[754] Art. 40,[755] Art. 42,[756] and Art. 47 of the HRAW,[757] and corresponding customary international law.[758]

2. The activities referred to in Rule 167 (a) are prohibited in an absolute manner. The Neutral is not entitled to give its consent to such activities. Should it nevertheless do so, this will be in breach of the law of neutrality.

3. The provisions of UNCLOS concerning maritime regimes continue to apply. Accordingly, belligerent warships may still exercise the right of innocent passage in neutral territorial sea. However, innocent passage is strictly defined in UNCLOS. Thus, Belligerent Parties may not engage in activities such as "launching, landing, or taking on board of any aircraft" or of "any military device".[759]

(b) However, when Belligerent Parties use for military purposes a public, internationally and openly accessible network such as the Internet, the fact that part of this infrastructure is situated within the jurisdiction of a Neutral does not constitute a violation of neutrality.

1. The Group of Experts could not identify either express treaty law or customary international law to substantiate Rule 167 (b). However,

to erect wireless telegraphy stations or any apparatus for the purpose of communicating with the belligerent forces on land or sea."

754 Art. 39 of the HRAW, see fn. 744.

755 Art. 40 of the HRAW, see fn. 745.

756 Art 42 of the HRAW: "A neutral government must use the means at its disposal to prevent the entry within its jurisdiction of belligerent military aircraft and to compel them to alight if they have entered such jurisdiction. A neutral government shall use the means at its disposal to intern any belligerent military aircraft which is within its jurisdiction after having alighted for any reason whatsoever, together with its crew and the passengers, if any."

757 Art. 47 of the HRAW: "A neutral state is bound to take such steps as the means at its disposal permit to prevent within its jurisdiction aerial observation of the movements, operations or defenses of one belligerent, with the intention of informing the other belligerent."

758 Para. 7.3 of NWP, see fn. 767.

759 Art. 19 (2) of UNCLOS ("Meaning of Innocent Passage"): "Passage of a foreign ship shall be considered to be prejudicial to the peace, good order or security of the coastal State if in the territorial sea it engages in any of the following activities: (a) any threat or use of force against the sovereignty, territorial integrity or political independence of the coastal State, or in any other manner in violation of the principles of international law embodied in the Charter of the United Nations; (b) any exercise or practice with weapons of any kind; (c) any act aimed at collecting information to the prejudice of the defence or security of the coastal State; (d) any act of propaganda aimed at affecting the defence or security of the coastal State; (e) the launching, landing or taking on board of any aircraft; . . . "

according to Art. 8 of the 1907 Hague Convention (V), a "neutral Power is not called upon to forbid or restrict the use on behalf of the belligerents of telegraph or telephone cables or of wireless telegraphy apparatus belonging to it or to companies or private individuals". The Group of Experts was convinced that a similar Rule could be extrapolated to the Internet.

2. Given the complexity and interdependence of an openly accessible network such as the Internet, it is impossible for any State to effectively control or interfere with communications over such a network. After all, most Internet communications are not traceable, since they are transmitted over lines of communications and routers passing through various States before reaching their ultimate destination. Therefore, the mere fact that military communications, including CNAs, have been transmitted via a router situated in the territory of a Neutral is not to be considered a violation of neutrality.

168. (a) A Neutral must not allow any of the acts referred to in Rule 167 (a) to occur within its territory and must use all the means available to it to prevent or terminate them.

1. Rule 168 (a) reemphasizes that any military use of neutral territory or airspace will constitute a violation of the law of neutrality under Section X. If a Neutral desires to remain protected by the law of neutrality, it is not allowed to consent to an abuse of its territory. The Neutral's obligation to "not allow any of the acts referred to in Rule 167 (a) to occur within its territory" is based on Art. 5 of the 1907 Hague Convention (V),[760] and on Art. 42 of the HRAW.[761] It also reflects customary international law.[762]

[760] Art. 5 of the 1907 Hague Convention (V): "A neutral Power must not allow any of the acts referred to in Articles 2 to 4 to occur on its territory. It is not called upon to punish acts in violation of its neutrality unless the said acts have been committed on its own territory."

[761] Art. 42 of the HRAW, see fn. 779.

[762] Para. 22 of the SRM/ACS: "Should a belligerent State be in violation of the regime of neutral waters, as set out in this document, the neutral State is under an obligation to take the measures necessary to terminate the violation. If the neutral State fails to terminate the violation of its neutral waters by a belligerent, the opposing belligerent must so notify the neutral State and give that neutral State a reasonable time to terminate the violation by the belligerent. If the violation of the neutrality of the State by the belligerent constitutes a serious and immediate threat to the security of the opposing belligerent and the violation is not terminated, then that belligerent may, in the absence of any feasible and timely alternative, use such force as is strictly necessary to respond to the threat posed by the violation."

2. Moreover, a Neutral whose territory is abused by one of the Belligerent Parties is under an affirmative obligation to use the means at its disposal to prevent any breaches of its neutral status under Section X. This part of Rule 168 (a) is based on Art. 8 of the 1907 Hague Convention (XIII),[763] as well as on Art. 42[764] and Art. 47 of the HRAW.[765] It also reflects customary international law.[766]

3. Depending on the circumstances, the means to be used by a Neutral whose territory is abused by one of the Belligerent Parties may range from diplomatic steps up to the use of force (see also Rule 170).

(b) If the use of the neutral territory or airspace by a Belligerent Party constitutes a serious violation, the opposing Belligerent Party may, in the absence of any feasible and timely alternative, use such force as is necessary to terminate the violation of neutrality.

1. If a Neutral is either unwilling or unable to prevent or terminate a violation of its neutral status by a Belligerent Party, the aggrieved Belligerent Party is entitled to take the measures necessary to terminate that

[763] Art. 8 of the 1907 Hague Convention (XIII): "A neutral Government is bound to employ the means at its disposal to prevent the fitting out or arming of any vessel within its jurisdiction which it has reason to believe is intended to cruise, or engage in hostile operations, against a Power with which that Government is at peace. It is also bound to display the same vigilance to prevent the departure from its jurisdiction of any vessel intended to cruise, or engage in hostile operations, which had been adapted entirely or partly within the said jurisdiction for use in war."

[764] Art. 42 of the HRAW, see fn. 779.

[765] Art. 47 of the HRAW, see fn. 780.

[766] Para. 7.3 of NWP, see fn. 767.

Para. 15 of SRM/ACS: "Within and over neutral waters, including neutral waters comprising an international strait and waters in which the right of archipelagic sea lanes passage may be exercised, hostile actions by belligerent forces are forbidden. A neutral State must take such measures as are consistent with Section II of this Part, including the exercise of surveillance, as the means at its disposal allow, to prevent the violation of its neutrality by belligerent forces."

Also, see Para. 18 of the SRM/ACS: "Belligerent military and auxillary aircraft may not enter neutral airspace. Should they do so, the neutral State shall use the means at its disposal to require the aircraft to land within its territory and shall intern the aircraft and its crew for the duration of the armed conflict. Should the aircraft fail to follow the instructions to land, it may be attacked, subject to the special rules relating to medical aircraft as specified in paragraphs 181–183."

Finally, see also Para. 22 of SRM/ACS, see fn. 762.

violation, including – where necessary – the use of force.[767] It follows that, in these exceptional situations, the inviolability of neutral territory is not enforced by the respective Neutral but by the aggrieved Belligerent Party. Where feasible, such measures of "substitutional" enforcement of the law of neutrality are subject to a prior warning and a reasonable time given to the Neutral to terminate the violation.[768] If the violation of the neutral status by a Belligerent Party constitutes an immediate threat to the security of the enemy, the latter may, in the absence of any feasible and timely alternative, use such force as is necessary to terminate the violation.[769]

2. Once the conditions spelled out in Rule 168 (b) are met, and a Belligerent Party uses such force as is necessary to terminate a violation of neutrality, its action is not to be regarded by the Neutral as an "armed attack" in the sense of Art. 51 of the UN Charter.[770] Consequently, in these circumstances, the Neutral does not have a right of self-defence against the acting Belligerent Party.

[767] Para. 22 of the SRM/ACS, see fn. 762.
Para. 7.3 of NWP: "As a general rule of international law, all acts of hostility in neutral territory, including neutral lands, neutral waters, and neutral airspace, are prohibited. A neutral nation has the duty to prevent the use of its territory as a place of sanctuary or a base of operations by belligerent forces of any side. If the neutral nation is unable or unwilling to enforce effectively its right of inviolability, an aggrieved belligerent may take such acts as are necessary in neutral territory to counter the activities of enemy forces, including warships and military aircraft, making unlawful use of that territory. Belligerents are also authorized to act in self-defense when attacked or threatened with attack while in neutral territory or when attacked or threatened from neutral territory."

[768] Note that the requirements of warning and time limit are recognized in the UK Manual and in the SRM/ACS but not in NWP.
See Para. 13.9E of the UK Manual: "Should a belligerent State be in violation of the regime of neutral waters, as set out in this manual, the neutral State is under an obligation to take the measures necessary to terminate the violation. If the neutral state fails to terminate the violation of its neutral waters by a belligerent, the opposing belligerent must so notify the neutral State and give that neutral State a reasonable time to terminate the violation by the belligerent. If the violation of the neutral of the State by the belligerent constitutes a serious and immediate threat to the security of the opposing belligerent and the violation is not terminated, then that belligerent may, in the absence of any feasible and timely alternative, use such force as is strictly necessary to respond to the threat posed by the violation."

[769] Para. 22 of SRM/ACS, see fn. 762.

[770] Art. 51 of the UN Charter, see fn. 15.

169. The fact that a Neutral resists, even by force, attempts to violate its neutrality cannot be regarded as a hostile act. However, the use of force by the Neutral must not exceed the degree required to repel the incursion and maintain its neutrality.

1. Rule 169 is based on Art. 10 of the 1907 Hague Convention (V),[771] Art. 26 of the 1907 Hague Convention (XIII),[772] and Art. 48 of the HRAW.[773] It is also considered to reflect customary international law. Measures taken by a Neutral against a Belligerent Party that is acting in violation of its duty to respect neutral territory are not to be considered unlawful. More specifically, if the Neutral resorts to the use of force against the Belligerent Party, the latter cannot consider those acts of the Neutral as an "armed attack" triggering the right of self-defence under *jus ad bellum.*[774] Consequently, the Belligerent Party is under an obligation to either tolerate such enforcement measures or to immediately terminate the violation.

2. While the Neutral may use force in order to terminate a violation, it is obliged to strictly observe the constraints of the situation. If the measures taken by the Neutral exceed what is necessary for terminating the violation of its neutral status, the affected Belligerent Party is entitled to take countermeasures. This requirement is due to the object and purpose of the law of neutrality that, *inter alia*, aims at preventing an escalation of an international armed conflict.

III. Specifics of air or missile operations

170. (a) Any incursion or transit by a belligerent military aircraft (including a UAV/UCAV) or missile into or through neutral airspace is prohibited. This is without prejudice to the right of transit passage through straits used for international navigation or archipelagic sea lanes passage.

1. The first sentence of Rule 170 (a) is based on Art. 40 of the HRAW ("Belligerent military aircraft are forbidden to enter the jurisdiction of

[771] Art. 10 of the 1907 Hague Convention (V): "The fact of a neutral Power resisting, even by force, attempts to violate its neutrality cannot be regarded as a hostile act."

[772] Art. 26 of the 1907 Hague Convention (XIII): "The exercise by a neutral Power of the rights laid down in the present Convention can under no circumstances be considered as an unfriendly act by one or other belligerent who has accepted the Articles relating thereto."

[773] Art. 48 of the HRAW: "The action of a neutral Power in using force or other means at its disposal in the exercise of its rights or duties under these Rules cannot be regarded as a hostile act."

[774] Art. 51 of the UN Charter, see fn. 15.

a neutral state") and reemphasizes the principle of inviolability of neutral airspace. Accordingly, any entry into neutral airspace by belligerent military aircraft or missiles constitutes a violation of the Neutral's inviolability.

2. However, in view of the recent development of international law regarding the rights of transit and archipelagic sea lanes passage, the airspace above neutral international straits and archipelagic sea lanes remains open at all times to belligerent aircraft, including armed military aircraft. Of course, such passage must be continuous and expeditious and must be undertaken in the normal mode of flight of the aircraft involved. Belligerent aircraft must refrain from acts of hostility while in transit, but may engage in activities that are consistent with their security and the security of accompanying surface and subsurface forces. The Neutral is under an obligation not to suspend, hamper or otherwise impede the right of transit passage or the right of archipelagic sea lanes passage (see Para. 7.3.6 of NWP[775] and Para. 7.3.9 of NWP[776]). See also paragraph 8 of the Commentary on Rule 1 (a).

3. UAVs/UCAVs also enjoy the rights of transit or of archipelagic sea lanes passage. Therefore, they may transit the airspace above an international strait or an archipelagic sea lane continuously and expeditiously. They are, however, prohibited to loiter within that airspace for purposes other than transit.

[775] Para. 7.3.6 of NWP ("Neutral international straits"): "Customary international law as reflected in the 1982 LOS Convention provides that belligerent and neutral surface ships, submarines, and aircraft have a right of transit passage through, over, and under all straits used for international navigation. Neutral nations cannot suspend, hamper, or otherwise impede this right of transit passage through international straits. Belligerent forces transiting through international straits overlapped by neutral waters must proceed without delay, must refrain from the threat or use of force against the neutral nation, and must otherwise refrain from acts of hostility and other activities not incident to their transit. Belligerent forces in transit may, however, take defensive measures consistent with their security, including the launching and recovery of military devices, screen formation steaming, and acoustic and electronic surveillance, and may respond in self-defense to a hostile act or hostile intent. Belligerent forces may not use neutral straits as a place of sanctuary or as a base of operations, and belligerent warships may not exercise the belligerent right of visit and search in those waters."

[776] Para. 7.3.9 of NWP ("Neutral airspace and duties"): "(1) Neutral territory extends to the airspace over a neutral nation's lands, internal waters, archipelagic waters (if any), and territorial sea. Belligerent military aircraft are forbidden to enter neutral airspace with the following exceptions: (a) The airspace above neutral international straits and archipelagic sea lanes remains open at all times to belligerent aircraft, including armed

4. Warships exercising the rights of transit passage or of archipelagic sea lanes passage are entitled to launch and to take on board UAVs and UCAVs. If UAVs are a necessary element of a warship's force protection, they may be employed even if they do not transit "continuously and expeditiously", provided that the use of such UAVs is "incidental" to the warship's "normal mode".[777]

5. The prohibition to enter neutral airspace does not apply to belligerent military aircraft in distress (see Rule 172 (a) (i)).

6. For the entry of belligerent medical aircraft into neutral airspace, see Rule 84 and Rule 85.

(b) A Neutral must exercise surveillance, to the extent that the means at its disposal allow, to enable it to prevent the violation of its neutrality by belligerent forces.

The obligation to prevent or to terminate violations of its neutral status implies that the Neutral must be sufficiently aware of what is occurring both within and in the vicinity of its national airspace. This denotes an

military aircraft, engaged in transit or archipelagic sea lanes passage. Such passage must be continuous and expeditious and must be undertaken in the normal mode of flight of the aircraft involved. Belligerent aircraft must refrain from acts of hostility while in transit, but may engage in activities that are consistent with their security and the security of accompanying surface and subsurface forces.... (2) Neutral nations have an affirmative duty to prevent violation of neutral airspace by belligerent military aircraft, to compel offending aircraft to land, and to intern both offending aircraft and crew. Should a neutral nation be unable or unwilling to prevent the unlawful entry or use of its airspace by belligerent military aircraft, belligerent forces of the other side may undertake such self-help enforcement measures as the circumstances may require."

777 Art. 39 (1) and (3) of UNCLOS ("Duties of Ships and Aircraft during Transit Passage"): "(1) Ships and aircraft, while exercising the right of transit passage, shall: (a) proceed without delay through or over the strait; (b) refrain from any threat or use of force against the sovereignty, territorial integrity or political independence of States bordering the strait, or in any other manner in violation of the principles of international law embodied in the Charter of the United Nations; (c) refrain from any activities other than those incident to their normal modes of continuous and expeditious transit unless rendered necessary by *force majeure* or by distress; (d) comply with other relevant provisions of this Part.... (3) Aircraft in transit passage shall: (a) observe the Rules of the Air established by the International Civil Aviation Organization as they apply to civil aircraft; State aircraft will normally comply with such safety measures and will at all times operate with due regard for the safety of navigation; (b) at all times monitor the radio frequency assigned by the competent internationally designated air traffic control authority or the appropriate international distress radio frequency."

Art. 54 of UNCLOS declares Art. 44 to be applicable to archipelagic sea lanes passage, see fn. 706.

obligation to use all available means, including radar and other electronic equipment, with a view to monitoring on a constant basis the national and adjacent airspace.

(c) In the event a belligerent military aircraft enters neutral airspace (other than straits used for international navigation or archipelagic sea lanes), the Neutral must use all the means at its disposal to prevent or terminate that violation. If captured, the aircraft and their crews must be interned for the duration of the armed conflict.

1. A Neutral is bound to use all the means at its disposal to prevent belligerent military aircraft from entering its jurisdiction (see Rule 170 (b)).

2. Rule 170 (c) is derived from Art. 25 of the 1907 Hague Convention (XIII),[778] as well as from Art. 42[779] and Art. 47 of the HRAW.[780]

3. The Neutral whose national airspace has been violated by an intruding belligerent military aircraft is obliged to terminate that violation. If possible, the intruding aircraft ought to be compelled to land. But, if it does not comply, the Neutral is entitled to shoot it down. Should the aircraft land, as required, the Neutral must intern the aircraft and its crew for the duration of the international armed conflict. This obligation derives from Art. 42 of the HRAW[781] and customary international law.[782]

[778] Art. 25 of Hague Convention (XIII): "A neutral Power is bound to exercise such surveillance as the means at its disposal allow to prevent any violation of the provisions of the above Arts. occurring in its ports or roadsteads or in its waters."

[779] Art. 42 of the HRAW: "A neutral government must use the means at its disposal to prevent the entry within its jurisdiction of belligerent military aircraft and to compel them to alight if they have entered such jurisdiction. A neutral government shall use the means at its disposal to intern any belligerent military aircraft which is within its jurisdiction after having alighted for any reason whatsoever, together with its crew and the passengers, if any."

[780] Art. 47 of the HRAW: "A neutral state is bound to take such steps as the means at its disposal permit to prevent within its jurisdiction aerial observation of the movements, operations or defenses of one belligerent, with the intention of informing the other belligerent."

[781] Art. 42 of the HRAW, see fn. 779.

[782] The final sentence of the first subpara. of Para. 7.3.1. of NWP reads: "Belligerent troops that enter neutral territory must be disarmed and interned until the end of the armed conflict."

4. Whenever members of the armed forces of a Belligerent Party enter neutral territory, they have to be interned by the Neutral for the duration of the international armed conflict. This general norm applies irrespective of the circumstances in which aircrews enter the territory of a Neutral. According to Art. 43 of the HRAW "[t]he personnel of a disabled belligerent military aircraft rescued outside neutral waters and brought into the jurisdiction of a neutral state by a neutral military aircraft and there landed shall be interned."

5. Parachutists from an aircraft in distress (see Section T), landing in neutral territory (for whatever reason, e.g., due to wind currents), must also be interned. If such parachutists in distress land in international waters, and are rescued by neutral vessels or aircraft, they must equally be interned for the duration of the international armed conflict.

171. Belligerent Parties must not commit any of the following acts:

Rule 171 specifies, in a non-exhaustive manner, the general prohibition contained in Rule 166 and in Rule 167 (a).

(a) Attack on or capture of persons or objects located in neutral airspace.

The prohibition of Rule 171 (a) is based on Art. 2 of the 1907 Hague Convention (XIII)[783] and on Art. 39 of the HRAW.[784] Attacks on and capture of persons or objects are belligerent acts which, if committed in neutral airspace, constitute a breach of the inviolability of neutral territory. This means that the activities referred to in Section D or in Section U, cannot be exercised in neutral airspace.

(b) Use of neutral territory or airspace as a base of operations – for attack, targeting, or intelligence purposes – against enemy targets in the air, on land or on water outside that territory.

1. Rule 171 (b) is based on Art. 5 of the 1907 Hague Convention (XIII).[785] In contrast to the situation envisioned in Rule 171 (a), Rule 171 (b) posits

[783] Art. 2 of Hague Convention (XIII): "Any act of hostility, including capture and the exercise of the right of search, committed by belligerent warships in the territorial waters of a neutral Power, constitutes a violation of neutrality and is strictly forbidden."

[784] Art. 39 of the HRAW: "Belligerent aircraft are bound to respect the rights of neutral Powers and to abstain within the jurisdiction of a neutral state from the commission of any act which it is the duty of that state to prevent."

[785] Art. 5 of Hague Convention (XIII): "Belligerents are forbidden to use neutral ports and waters as a base of naval operations against their adversaries, and in particular to erect

a deployment of forces in neutral airspace or territory in order to attack enemy targets located outside such airspace or territory.

2. The term "base of operations" in neutral airspace is to be interpreted in broad terms. Thus, for example, a UCAV loitering in neutral airspace before launching a missile against belligerent target is acting in breach of Rule 171 (b).

(c) Conducting interception, inspection, diversion or capture of vessels or aircraft in neutral territory.

1. Rule 171 (c) is based on Art. 2 of the 1907 Hague Convention (XIII),[786] which prohibits the exercise of prize measures (see Section U) within neutral territory.

2. "Neutral territory" as used in Rule 171 (c) encompasses not only neutral airspace but also land territory or sea areas covered by the territorial sovereignty of the Neutral.

3. A Belligerent Party is not allowed to intercept any aircraft within neutral airspace, even with a view to forcing it to land outside the neutral territory

4. Obviously, there is a certain overlap in terms of "capture" between Rule 171 (a) and Rule 171 (c). The reason is that Rule 171 (c) refers not merely to capture of aircraft, but also to capture of vessels. The Group of Experts felt that it was important to ensure that all aspects of capture are covered either in Rule 171 (a) or in Rule 171 (c).

(d) Any other activity involving the use of military force or contributing to the war-fighting effort, including transmission of data or combat search-and-rescue operations in neutral territory.

1. The purpose of Rule 171 (d) is to emphasize that any "use of military force" in neutral territory, as well as any activity "contributing to the war-fighting effort" of the enemy, constitutes a violation of neutral territory even if such use or contribution does not amount to an act prohibited by Rule 171 (a)–(c).

wireless telegraphy stations or any apparatus for the purpose of communicating with the belligerent forces on land or sea."

786 Art. 2 of Hague Convention (XIII), see fn. 783.

2. An illustration of such activity is the transmission of data for targeting or other military purposes, which must be distinguished from the use of neutral airspace or territory as a base of operations prohibited under Rule 171 (b). The transmission of military data from neutral territory by a Belligerent Party must be considered a violation of neutral territory and airspace even if it is not performed for attack, targeting or other purposes.

3. Rule 171 (d) has to be read in conjunction with Rule 167 (b), according to which the "use for military purposes of a public, internationally and openly accessible network, such as the Internet" will not constitute a violation of neutrality if "part of this infrastructure is situated within the jurisdiction of a neutral".

4. Combat search and rescue operations are genuinely military in character (see Rule 86) and, thus, constitute a violation of neutrality. The fact that such operations are aimed at the rescue of combatants who may be wounded, sick or shipwrecked (see Rule 16 (a)) is irrelevant. Combatants present in neutral territory – whatever the reason for their presence – must be interned by the Neutral for the duration of the international armed conflict (see Rule 170 (c), as well as the second paragraph of Art. 42 of the HRAW[787] and Art. 43 of the HRAW[788]).

172. (a) Belligerent military aircraft may not enter the airspace of Neutrals, except that:

Rule 172 (a) is a specification of the general prohibition laid down in the first sentence of Rule 170 (a). The prohibition for belligerent military aircraft to enter neutral airspace is based on Art. 40 of the HRAW,[789] and it is a necessary corollary to the inviolability of neutral territory.

(i) Belligerent military aircraft in distress may be permitted to enter neutral airspace and to land in neutral territory under such safeguards as the Neutral may wish to impose. The Neutral is obligated to require such aircraft to land and to intern the aircraft and their crews.

1. Following the general obligation to render assistance to those who are in distress in the air, a Neutral may allow a belligerent military aircraft in

787 Art. 42 of the HRAW, see fn. 779.
788 Art. 43 of the HRAW, see Para. 4, Rule 170 (c), Section X.
789 Art. 40 of the HRAW, see fn. 745.

distress to land in its territory. Such permission may not be considered a violation of neutrality by the other Belligerent Party.

2. However, the Neutral is not allowed to permit Belligerent Parties the use of its airspace for transit purposes. The Neutral is obliged to require any belligerent military aircraft to land, if necessary by the use of appropriate force. For the duration of the international armed conflict, the belligerent military aircraft and its crew may not leave the Neutral's territory, and the crew must be interned in order to prevent them from re-engaging in the hostilities.

(ii) The airspace above neutral international straits and archipelagic sea lanes remains open at all times to belligerent aircraft, including armed military aircraft engaged in transit or archipelagic sea lanes passage.

Rule 172 (a) (ii) safeguards the customary rights of transit passage and of archipelagic sea lanes passage as recognized in Rule 170 (a).

(iii) The Neutral may permit belligerent military aircraft to enter for purposes of capitulation.

1. Entry by belligerent military aircraft into neutral airspace is not prohibited if the aircrews intend to capitulate to the Neutral. Should that occur, the Neutral is under an obligation to intern the aircrews for the duration of the international armed conflict (see Rule 172 (b)).

2. Rule 172 (a) (iii) deals with the issue of military personnel giving themselves up. The term "capitulation" used here is reserved for such act taking place vis-à-vis a Neutral. When military personnel give themselves up to the enemy, the expression used in this Manual is "surrender" (see Section S). As to the modalities of capitulation, see Rule 172 (b).

(b) Neutrals must use the means at their disposal to require capitulating belligerent military aircraft to land within their territory, and must intern the aircraft and their crews for the duration of the international armed conflict. Should such an aircraft commit hostile acts, or should it fail to follow the instructions to land, it may be attacked without further notice.

1. Capitulation, as required by Rule 172 (a) (iii), must not be abused by turning the Neutral territory into a "base of operations". Hence, the Neutral must insist on the capitulating aircraft landing within its territory

rather than transiting, and must then intern both the aircraft and its crew for the duration of the international armed conflict. The rationale of this Rule is that, if the aircraft or aircrews were allowed to leave the neutral territory, it might re-engage in the hostilities.

2. Any act of resistance or deliberate non-compliance is to be considered a "hostile act" and, therefore, sufficient ground for the Neutral to attack the aircraft. In that case, prior warnings or periods of grace are not required.

173. A Neutral is not bound to prevent the private export or transit on behalf of a Belligerent Party of aircraft, parts of aircraft, or material, supplies or munitions for aircraft. However, a Neutral is bound to use the means at its disposal:

1. The first sentence of Rule 173 is based on Art. 45 of the HRAW,[790] Art. 7 of the 1907 Hague Convention (V),[791] and Art. 7 of the 1907 Hague Convention (XIII).[792]

2. Without prejudice to an embargo decided upon by the UN Security Council, Rule 173 exclusively applies to private activities and not to government activities. Accordingly (see Art. 44 of the HRAW), "[t]he supply in any manner, directly or indirectly, by a neutral government to a belligerent Power of aircraft, parts of aircraft, or material, supplies or munitions required for aircraft is forbidden."

3. The distinction between public and private export and transit activities has been recognized by Art. 6[793], Art. 7[794] and Art. 8[795] of the 1907 Hague

[790] Art. 45 of the HRAW: "Subject to the provisions of Article 46, a neutral Power is not bound to prevent the export or transit on behalf of a belligerent or aircraft, parts or aircraft, or material, supplies or munitions for aircraft."

[791] Art. 7 of the 1907 Hague Convention (V): "A neutral Power is not called upon to prevent the export or transport, on behalf of one or other of the belligerents, of arms, munitions of war, or, in general, of anything which can be of use to an army or a fleet."

[792] Art. 7 of the 1907 Hague Convention (XIII): "A neutral Power is not bound to prevent the export or transit, for the use of either belligerent, of arms, ammunition, or, in general, of anything which could be of use to an army or fleet."

[793] Art. 6 of the 1907 Hague Convention (XIII): "The supply, in any manner, directly or indirectly, by a neutral Power to a belligerent Power, of war-ships, ammunition, or war material of any kind whatever, is forbidden."

[794] Art. 7 of the 1907 Hague Convention (XIII), see fn. 791.

[795] Art. 8 of the 1907 Hague Convention (XIII): "A neutral Government is bound to employ the means at its disposal to prevent the fitting out or arming of any vessel within its

Convention (XIII), as well as by Art. 44,[796] Art. 45[797] and Art. 46 of the HRAW.[798] There has nevertheless been some scepticism as to its continued validity. It has been argued that,[799] in an era when exports of military and "dual-use" goods are subject to State regulation, it is no longer correct to say that Neutrals are at liberty to allow private exports of such goods in an unregulated manner. Still, the majority of the Group of Experts has not been able to confirm on the basis of State practice that a modification of the traditional rule relating to the distinction between public and private exports has occurred. State practice clearly gives evidence of an increasing control of exports of arms and other military equipment by States. However, it gives no evidence that States consider themselves obliged by the law of neutrality to exercise such control. It seems that this is only a policy preference and not an expression of *opinio juris.*

jurisdiction which it has reason to believe is intended to cruise, or engage in hostile operations, against a Power with which that Government is at peace. It is also bound to display the same vigilance to prevent the departure from its jurisdiction of any vessel intended to cruise or engage in hostile operations, which had been adapted entirely or partly within the said jurisdiction for use in war."

796 Art. 44 of the HRAW: "The supply in any manner, directly or indirectly, by a neutral government to a belligerent Power of aircraft, parts of aircraft, or material, supplies or munitions required for aircraft is forbidden."

797 Art. 45 of the HRAW, see fn. 790.

798 Art. 46 of the HRAW: "A neutral government is bound to use the means at its disposal: (1) To prevent the departure from its jurisdiction of an aircraft in a condition to make a hostile attack against a belligerent Power, or carrying or accompanied by appliances or materials the mounting or utilization of which would enable it to make a hostile attack, if there is reason to believe that such aircraft is destined for use against a belligerent Power. (2) To prevent the departure of an aircraft the crew of which includes any member of the combatant forces of a belligerent Power. (3) To prevent work upon an aircraft designed to prepare it to depart in contravention of the purposes of this Article; On the departure by air of any aircraft despatched by persons or companies in neutral jurisdiction to the order of a belligerent Power, the neutral government must prescribe for such aircraft a route avoiding the neighborhood of the military operations of the opposing belligerent, and must exact whatever guarantees may be required to ensure that the aircraft follows the route prescribed."

799 Para. 1112 of the German ZDv: "State practice has modified the former convention rule that a neutral state is not bound to prohibit export and transit of war material by private persons for the benefit of one of the parties to the conflict (Art. 7 HC V). To the extent that arms export is subject to control by the state, the permission of such export is to be considered as a non-neutral service."

(a) To prevent the departure from its jurisdiction of an aircraft in a condition to make a hostile attack against a Belligerent Party, if there is reason to believe that such aircraft is destined for such use.

1. This Rule is based on Art. 46 (1) of the HRAW.[800]

2. Rule 173 (a) is historically an outgrowth of a similar prohibition relating to warships, having its roots in the famous 1872 Arbitral Award in the "Alabama" case.[801]

3. The words "in a condition to make a hostile attack" mean that the aircraft is fuelled, armed and manned, ready for immediate hostile action after departure.

(b) To prevent the departure from its jurisdiction of the crews of military aircraft, as well as passengers and crews of civilian aircraft, who are members of the armed forces of a Belligerent Party.

1. This Rule is based on Art. 46 (2) of the HRAW.[802]

2. Members of the armed forces of a Belligerent Party must be interned by the Neutral for the duration of the international armed conflict (see Rule 170 (c)). It follows that the Neutral must prevent their departure from its jurisdiction.

3. The category "members of the armed forces of a Belligerent Party" is comprehensive. It includes not only crews of military aircraft, but also passengers and crews of civilian aircraft who are members of those armed forces.

174. Without prejudice to Sections J and V of this Manual, the following activities may render a neutral civilian aircraft a military objective:

1. This Rule, when considered in its entirety, applies only to neutral civilian aircraft. Having said that, it must be understood that other neutral

[800] Art. 46 (1) of the HRAW, see fn. 798.
See also Art. 8 of the 1907 Hague Convention (XIII), see fn. 795.

[801] See Alabama Claims Award (1872), 1 History and Digest of the International Arbitrations to which the United States Has Been a Party 653 (J.B. Moore ed., 1898).

[802] Art. 46 (2) of the HRAW, see fn. 798.

aircraft – military or other State aircraft – may not engage in any of the activities enumerated in Rule 174 (b); Rule 174 (c); Rule 174 (d) and in Rule 174 (f). If they do, they become military objectives that may be attacked without prior warning. However, unlike neutral civilian aircraft, both Rule 174 (a) and Rule 174 (e) are inapplicable to neutral military aircraft and to other neutral State aircraft. Such aircraft benefit from the sovereign immunity of the Neutral that must be respected by Belligerent Parties (see also paragraph 2 of the Commentary on Rule 48 (b) and paragraph 5 of the Commentary to Rule 54). Consequently, they cannot be intercepted, diverted, or inspected when suspected of carrying contraband, and they do not have to comply with orders of military authorities of a Belligerent Party (except where aerial blockade is concerned, see Rule 155).

2. Neutral civilian aircraft are protected under the law of neutrality, as long as they are engaged in their normal and innocent role. Nevertheless, if they engage in acts which make an effective contribution to the enemy's military action and if their destruction, capture or neutralization offers a definite military advantage in the circumstances ruling at the time, they lose their protected status and become military objectives.

3. Neutral civilian aircraft, if engaged in one of the activities enumerated in Rule 174, lose their neutral protected status and become liable to attack,[803] subject to Sections D and G.

4. Rule 174 is without prejudice to the right of Belligerent Parties to establish an aerial (or naval) blockade against the enemy (see Section V). According to Rule 156, neutral civilian aircraft believed on reasonable grounds to be breaching, or attempting to breach, an aerial blockade may be intercepted, diverted, forced to land and captured. If they clearly resist

[803] Para. 70 of the SRM/ACS: "Civil aircraft bearing the marks of neutral States may not be attacked unless they: (a) are believed on reasonable grounds to be carrying contraband, and, after prior warning or interception, they intentionally and clearly refuse to divert from their destination, or intentionally and clearly refuse to proceed for visit and search to a belligerent airfield that is safe for the type of aircraft involved and reasonably accessible; (b) engage in belligerent acts on behalf of the enemy; (c) act as auxiliaries to the enemy's armed forces; (d) are incorporated into or assist the enemy's intelligence system; or (e) otherwise make an effective contribution to the enemy's military action, e.g. by carrying military materials, and, after prior warning or interception, they intentionally and clearly refuse to divert from their destination, or intentionally and clearly refuse to proceed for visit and search to a belligerent airfield that is safe for the type of aircraft involved and reasonably accessible."

Similar language can be found in Para. 12.43.1 of the UK Manual.

interception, or fail to comply with an order to land, they are at risk of attack after prior warning.

5. Rule 174 does not apply to any of the categories covered in Section J, i.e., civilian airliners and aircraft granted safe conduct (such as cartel aircraft). For the parallel provision, see Rule 63.

6. Rule 174 must be read against the background of Rule 27 pertaining to attacks against enemy aircraft other than military aircraft. Rule 174 (b)–(f) is textually identical to Rule 27 (a)–(e). It is only Rule 174 (a) which is specific to neutral civilian aircraft.

7. The status of neutral civilian aircraft must always be borne in mind. In addition to their civilian character, there is the extra added dimension of their being neutral. On both grounds, a Belligerent Party must not rush to the conclusion that a neutral civilian aircraft constitutes a military objective.

8. The following activities relate only to use and intended future use, and are therefore subject to the application of Rule 22 (c) and Rule 22 (d).

> **(a) It is believed on reasonable grounds to be carrying contraband, and, after prior warning or interception, it intentionally and clearly refuses to divert from its destination, or intentionally and clearly refuses to proceed for inspection to a belligerent airfield that is safe for the type of aircraft involved and reasonably accessible.**

1. Rule 174 (a) is based on the second sentence of Art. 50 of the HRAW, which provides: "Refusal, after warning, to obey such orders to alight or to proceed for visit and search to such a locality for examination exposes an aircraft to the risk of being fired upon." This corresponds with customary international law (see Para. 70 (a) of the SRM/ACS).[804]

2. Neutral civilian aircraft flying outside neutral airspace and that are carrying contraband on board, may be intercepted, inspected, diverted and / or captured (see Rule 137). If they intentionally and clearly refuse to comply with orders to divert or proceed for inspection, this will render them a military objective.

3. A neutral civilian aircraft does not become a military objective only because it carries contraband. It is the intentional and clear refusal of such

[804] Para. 70 (a) of SRM/ACS, see fn. 803.

an aircraft to divert from its destination or to proceed for inspection that may render it a military objective.

(b) Engaging in hostile actions in support of the enemy, e.g., intercepting or attacking other aircraft; attacking persons or objects on land or sea; being used as a means of attack; engaging in electronic warfare; or providing targeting information to enemy forces.

The language of Rule 174 (b) is identical to that appearing in Rule 27 (a). See the Commentary on the latter as well as Para. 70 (b) of SRM/ACS.[805]

(c) Facilitating the military actions of the enemy's armed forces, e.g., transporting troops, carrying military materials, or refuelling military aircraft.

The language of Rule 174 (c) is identical to that appearing in Rule 27 (b). See the Commentary on the latter and see Para. 70 (c) of SRM/ACS.[806]

(d) Being incorporated into or assisting the enemy's intelligence gathering system, e.g., engaging in reconnaissance, early warning, surveillance or command, control and communications missions.

If neutral civilian aircraft engage – in support of the enemy armed forces – in reconnaissance, early warning, surveillance or command, control and communications mission, they may be considered as having become incorporated into the enemy's intelligence system under Rule 174 (d). The language of Rule 174 (d) is identical to that appearing in Rule 27 (c). See the Commentary on the latter and Para. 70 (d) of SRM/ACS.[807]

(e) Refusing to comply with the orders of military authorities, including instructions for landing, inspection and possible capture, or it clearly resists interception.

Neutral civilian aircraft are under an obligation to comply with the orders of a Belligerent Party. If a neutral civilian aircraft does not comply with such orders, the Belligerent Party is entitled to use such force as is necessary to overcome the resistance. The language of this Rule 174 (e) is identical to that appearing in Rule 27 (d). See the Commentary on the latter.

[805] Para. 70 (b) of SRM/ACS see fn. 803.
[806] Para. 70 (c) of SRM/ACS, see fn. 803.
[807] Para. 70 (d) of SRM/ACS, see fn. 803.

(f) Otherwise making an effective contribution to military action.

Rule 174 (f) is a residual provision in that it covers situations in which a neutral civilian aircraft makes an effective contribution to the enemy' military actions that are not dealt with in Rule 174 (a)–(d). See Para. 70 (e) of SRM/ACS.[808] The language of Rule 170 (f) is identical to that appearing in Rule 27 (e). See the Commentary on the latter.

175. The fact that a civilian aircraft bears the marks of a Neutral is *prima facie* evidence of its neutral character.

1. While the fact that a civilian aircraft bears the marks of an enemy State is conclusive evidence of its enemy character (see Rule 144), bearing the marks of a Neutral does not provide such conclusive evidence. Therefore, Rule 175 merely contains a presumption of the neutral character of civilian aircraft bearing neutral marks.

2. As laid down in the second sentence of Rule 144, enemy character of a civilian aircraft can also be determined by registration, ownership, charter or other appropriate criteria. According to Rule 145, civilian aircraft bearing no marks are presumed to have enemy character for the purposes of capture and prize. If there merely are grounds for suspicion that a civilian aircraft has enemy character, Rule 146 applies.

[808] Para. 70 (e) of SRM/ACS, see fn. 803.

Appendix I

Group of Experts

A. Core Group of Experts[809]

1. **Air Commodore William H. Boothby**
   Position: Legal Advisor
   Organization: UK Royal Air Force, RAF Air Command

2. **Prof. Dr. Michael Bothe**
   Position: Professor Emeritus of International Law
   Organization: Johann Wolfgang Goethe University

3. **Prof. Dr. Ove Bring**
   Position: Professor of International Law
   Organization: Swedish National Defence College

4. **Mr. Claude Bruderlein**
   Position: Director
   Organization: Program on Humanitarian Policy and Conflict Research Harvard University

5. **General (ret.) Arne Willy Dahl**
   Position: Judge Advocate General
   Organization: Office of the Judge Advocate General, Norwegian Ministry of Defence

6. **Rear-Admiral (ret.) Jane G. Dalton, US Navy**
   Position: Attorney-Advisor
   Organization: US Department of State

7. **Prof. Dr. Yoram Dinstein**
   Position: Senior Academic Advisor, HPCR
   Professor Emeritus ofInternational Law, Tel Aviv University
   Organization: Program on Humanitarian Policy and Conflict Research Harvard University

[809] Professional affiliation as in May 2009 (the date of the adoption of the final version of the Black-letter Rules by the Group of Experts).

8. **Mr. Knut Dörmann**
   Position: Head of the Legal Division
   Organization: International Committee of the Red Cross

9. **Major General Charles J. Dunlap, Jr.**
   Position: Deputy Judge Advocate General
   Organization: US Air Force

10. **Colonel (ret.) Charles H.B. Garraway**
    Position: Legal Advisor
    Organization: British Red Cross

11. **Prof. Dr. Wolff Heintschel von Heinegg**
    Position: Dean of the Faculty of Law and Professor of International Law
    Organization: Europa-University Viadrina

12. **Colonel Peter Hostettler**
    Position: Head of International Law of Armed Conflicts Section
    Organization: Swiss Federal Department of Defence, Civil Protection and Sports

13. **Prof. Dr. Frits Kalshoven**
    Position: Professor Emeritus of International Law
    Organization: Leiden University

14. **Colonel (ret.) W. Hays Parks**
    Position: Former Special Assistant to the Judge Advocate General of the Army for Law of War Matters
    Organization: Office of General Counsel US Department of Defense

15. **Mr. Jean-François Queguiner**
    Position: Head of the Unit of the Thematic Legal Advisors Legal Division
    Organization: International Committee of the Red Cross

16. **Prof. Dr. Natalino Ronzitti**
    Position: Professor of International Law
    Organization: LUISS University G. Carli

17. **Dr. Yves Sandoz**
    Position: Lecturer, University of Geneva and University of Fribourg
    Member of the Comité of the International Committee of the Red Cross
    Organizations: International Committee of the Red Cross

18. Prof. Dr. Marco Sassòli
Position: Professor of International Law
Organization: University of Geneva

19. Prof. Michael N. Schmitt
Position: Dean and Professor of International Law
Organization: George C. Marshall Center

20. Captain Dale Stephens
Position: Director of Operations and International Law
Organization: Legal Division, Australian Defence Force

21. Brigadier General Kenneth Watkin
Position: Judge Advocate General
Organization: Canadian Armed Forces

22. Prof. Dr. Zhu Wenqi
Position: Professor of International Law
Organization: Law School, Renmin University of China

23. Prof. Dr. Rüdiger Wolfrum
Position: Professor of International Law, Heidelberg University Director, Max Planck Institute
Organization: Max Planck Institute for Comparative Public Law and International Law

Project Coordinator

24. Mr. Bruno Demeyere
Position: Advisor on International Humanitarian Law
Organization: Program on Humanitarian Policy and Conflict Research Harvard University

B. Government Experts[810]

25. Group Captain Paul Cronan (2008–2009)
Position: Director Military Discipline Law
Organization: Legal Division, Australian Defence Force

26. Major Christian De Cock (2006–2008)
Position: Head of International Law Section
Organization: Belgian Ministry of Defense

[810] Professional affiliation as in May 2009 (the date of the adoption of the final version of the Black-letter Rules by the Group of Experts).

27. **Mr. Peter Dreist**
    Position: Legal Advisor to Chief of Staff of the Air Force
    Organization: German Ministry of Defence

28. **Lieutenant Colonel Geir Anders Fagerheim** (2005–2008)
    Position: Legal Advisor
    Organization: Chief Legal Office, Joint Warfare Centre

29. **Dr. Marie Jacobsson** (2004–2008)
    Position: Principal Legal Adviser on International Law
    Organization: Swedish Ministry of Foreign Affairs

30. **Mr. Daniel Klingele** (2004–2009)
    Position: Head Human Rights and Humanitarian Law Section
    Organization: Directorate of International Law, Swiss Federal Department of Foreign Affairs

31. **Colonel Edward Monahan** (2008)
    Position: Legal Advisor
    Organization: US Air Force

C. Participants in Some Sessions of the Group of Experts[811]

32. **Brigadier General Titus Githiora** (2004)
    Position: Legal Advisor
    Organization: Kenyan Ministry of Defence

33. **Mr. Jean-Philippe Lavoyer** (2004–2006)
    Position: Head of the Legal Division
    Organization: International Committee of the Red Cross

34. **Commander Angela Miller** (2009)
    Position: Legal Advisor
    Organization: US Navy

35. **Professor Emmanuel Roucounas** (2004)
    Position: Professor of International Law
    Organization: University of Athens

36. **Lieutenant Colonel Philip T. Wold** (2004)
    Position: Legal Advisor
    Organization: US Air Force

37. **Ms. Sarah Wolf** (2005–2009)
    Position: Researcher
    Organization: Max Planck Institute for Comparative Public Law and International Law

[811] Titles relate to dates of participation in the work of the Group of Experts.

Appendix II

Sessions of the Group of Experts

First Session of Experts (Plan of Action), January 2004, Cambridge (MA)

Second Session of Experts (Research Papers (I)), September 2004, Luzern (Switzerland)

Third Session of Experts (Research Papers (II)), January 2005, Heidelberg (Germany)[812]

Fourth Session of Experts (Research Papers (III)), September 2005, Oslo (Norway)

Fifth Session of Experts (First Draft of the Manual), March 2006, Brussels (Belgium)

Sixth Session of Experts (Revised Text of the Manual),[813] December 2006, Spiez (Switzerland)

Seventh Session of Experts (Further Review of the Manual), April 2008, Frankfurt (Oder) (Germany)[814]

Eighth Session of Experts (Adoption of the Final Text of the Manual), May 2009, Bern (Switzerland)

Note: Each Session listed above lasted on the average four full working days.

[812] The meeting was hosted by the Max Planck Institute for Comparative Public Law and International Law.

[813] The text of the Draft Manual was revised following comments made during the "Alabama III" meeting in Montreux in May 2006 (see Appendix III).

[814] The meeting was hosted by Europa-University Viadrina Frankfurt (Oder).

Appendix III

List of Informal Meetings with State Representatives

A. Third Informal High Level Expert Meeting on Current Challenges to IHL ("Alabama III"), May 2006, Montreux (Switzerland)

Belgium
Brazil
Canada
Congo, Democratic Republic of
China, People's Republic of
Denmark
Egypt
France
India
Italy
Japan
Jordan
Korea, Republic of
Mexico
Netherlands
Nigeria
Norway
Pakistan
Russian Federation
Saudi Arabia
Spain
Sweden
Switzerland
United Kingdom
United States
European Union
International Committee of the Red Cross
Office for the Coordination of Humanitarian Affairs and Office of Legal Affairs, United Nations

B. Regional Meetings

B.1 Meeting in Australia (Asia-Pacific region)[815]

Australia
Cambodia
China, People's Republic of
Indonesia
Japan
Korea, Republic of
Malaysia
New Zealand
Pakistan
Philippines
Singapore
Thailand

B.2 Meeting in Namibia (African region)[816]

Austria
Belgium
China, People's Republic of
Côte d'Ivoire
Denmark
Finland
France
Germany
Greece
Latvia
Libya
Namibia
Netherlands
Nigeria
Norway
Pakistan
Poland
Romania
Rwanda

[815] This meeting took place in November 2007 in Sydney (Australia) and was hosted by the Asia Pacific Centre for Military Law (APCML).
[816] This meeting took place in March 2008 in Windhoek (Namibia) and was hosted by the International Society for Military Law and the Law of War.

South Africa
Spain
Tanzania
Uganda
Zambia
Zimbabwe

B.3 Meeting in Canada[817]

Argentina
Brazil
Canada
Israel
United States

C. Bilateral Meetings

China, People's Republic of (Beijing), March 2008
France (Paris), June 2008
Russian Federation (Moscow), March 2009
United States (Washington D.C.), June 2007

[817] This meeting took place in September 2008 in Kingston (Canada) and was hosted by the Canadian Forces Office of the Judge Advocate General.

Appendix IV

Drafting Committee: Members & Meetings

A. Members of the Drafting Committee[818]

Arne Willy Dahl
Bruno Demeyere
Yoram Dinstein (Chair)
Wolff Heintschel von Heinegg
Jean-François Queguiner
Michael N. Schmitt

B. Meetings of the Drafting Committee as a Whole

May 2008, Brussels
November 2008, Hamburg[819]
January 2009, Brussels
February 2009, Brussels
August 2009, Oslo
October 2009, Brussels

C. Final Editing

January 2010, Brussels, Yoram Dinstein and Bruno Demeyere

Note: Each Session listed above lasted on the average four full working days

[818] For full references, see Appendix I.

[819] This meeting was hosted by the Max Planck Institute for Comparative Public Law and International Law.

Appendix V

Table of Treaties (Chronological)

1856 Paris Declaration Respecting Maritime Law, *Laws of Armed Conflicts* 1053.

1868 St. Petersburg Declaration Renouncing the Use, in Time of War, of Explosive Projectiles Under 400 Grammes Weight, *Laws of Armed Conflicts* 91.

1899 Hague Convention (II) with Respect to the Laws and Customs of War on Land, *Laws of Armed Conflicts* 55.

1899 Hague Regulations respecting the Laws and Customs of War on Land, Annex to the Convention, *Laws of Armed Conflicts* 66.

1899 Hague Declaration (IV, 2) Concerning Asphyxiating Gases, *Laws of Armed Conflicts* 95.

1907 Hague Convention (IV) Respecting the Laws and Customs of War on Land, *Laws of Armed Conflicts* 55.

1907 Hague Regulations respecting the Laws and Customs of War on Land, Annex to the Convention, *Laws of Armed Conflicts* 66.

1907 Hague Convention (V) Respecting the Rights and Duties of Neutral Powers and Persons in Case of War on Land, *Laws of Armed Conflicts* 1399.

1907 Hague Convention (VIII) relative to the Laying of Automatic Submarine Contact Mines, *Laws of Armed Conflicts* 1071.

1907 Hague Convention (XII) relative to the Creation of an International Prize Court, *Laws of Armed Conflicts* 1093.

1907 Hague Convention (XIII) Concerning the Rights and Duties of Neutral Powers in Naval War, *Laws of Armed Conflicts* 1407.

1909 London Declaration Concerning the Laws of Naval War, *Laws of Armed Conflicts* 1111.

1925 Geneva Protocol for the Prohibition of the Use in War of Asphyxiating, Poisonous or Other Gases, and of Bacteriological Methods of Warfare, 94 *LNTS* 65.

1935 Washington Treaty on the Protection of Artistic and Scientific Institutions and Historic Monuments (Roerich Pact), 67 *LNTS* 290.

1944 Chicago Convention on International Civil Aviation, 15 *UNTS* 295.

1945 Charter of the United Nations, 1 *UNTS* xvi.

1949 Geneva Convention (I) for the Amelioration of the Condition of the Wounded and Sick in Armed Forces in the Field, 75 *UNTS* 31.

1949 Geneva Convention (II) for the Amelioration of the Condition of Wounded, Sick and Shipwrecked Members of Armed Forces at Sea, 75 *UNTS* 85.

1949 Geneva Convention (III) relative to the Treatment of Prisoners of War, 75 *UNTS* 135.

1949 Geneva Convention (IV) relative to the Protection of Civilian Persons in Time of War, 75 *UNTS* 287.

1954 Hague Convention for the Protection of Cultural Property in the Event of Armed Conflict, 249 *UNTS* 240.

- 1954 Protocol to the Convention, 249 *UNTS* 358.
- 1999 Second Protocol to the Convention, 38 *ILM* 769.

1958 Washington Antarctic Treaty, 402 *UNTS* 71.

1972 UN Convention on the Prohibition of Development, Production and Stockpiling of Bacteriological (Biological) and Toxin Weapons and on Their Destruction, 1015 *UNTS* 164.

1976 UN Convention on the Prohibition of Military or Any Other Hostile Use of Environmental Modification Techniques, 1108 *UNTS* 151.

1977 Protocol (I) Additional to the Geneva Conventions of 12 August 1949, and Relating to the Protection of Victims of International Armed Conflicts, 1125 *UNTS* 3.

- 1993 Amendment of Annex I, *Laws of Armed Conflicts* 762.

1977 Protocol (II) Additional to the Geneva Conventions of 12 August 1949, and Relating to the Protection of Victims of Non-International Armed Conflicts, 1125 *UNTS* 609.

1980 UN Convention on Prohibitions or Restrictions on the Use of Certain Conventional Weapons Which May be Deemed to be Excessively Injurious or to Have Indiscriminate Effects, 1342 *UNTS* 137.

- 1980 Protocol on Non-Detectable Fragments (Protocol I), 1342 *UNTS* 168.
- 1980 Protocol on Prohibitions or Restrictions on the Use of Mines, Booby-Traps and Other Devices (Protocol II), 1342 *UNTS* 168.
- 1980 Protocol on Prohibitions or Restrictions on the Use of Incendiary Weapons(Protocol III), 1342 *UNTS* 171.
- 1995 Protocol on Blinding Laser Weapons (Protocol IV), 35 *ILM* 1218.
- 1996 Amendment of Protocol II, 35 *ILM* 1209.
- 2001 Amendment of Article 1, *Laws of Armed Conflicts* 185.

2003 Protocol on Explosive Remnants of War (Protocol V), UN Doc. CCW/MSP/2003/2.

1982 UN Law of the Sea Convention, 1833 *UNTS* 396.

1994 Convention on the Safety of United Nations and Associated Personnel, 34 *ILM* 482.

2005 Optional Protocol to the Convention, UN Doc. A/Res/60/42.

1993 Paris Convention on the Prohibition of the Development, Production, Stockpiling and Use of Chemical Weapons and on Their Destruction, 32 *ILM* 800.

1997 Ottawa Convention on the Prohibition of the Use, Stockpiling, Production and Transfer of Anti-Personnel Mines and on Their Destruction, 36 *ILM* 1507 (the Convention was actually adopted in Oslo).

1998 Rome Statute of the International Criminal Court, 2187 *UNTS* 90.

2005 Protocol (III) Additional to the Geneva Conventions of 12 August 1949, and Relating to the Adoption of an Additional Distinctive Emblem, 45 *ILM* 558.

2008 Convention on Cluster Munitions, 48 *ILM* 357

Appendix VI

Table of Abbreviations

(Full cites of treaties appear in Appendix V)

A

1977 Additional Protocols: AP/I and AP/II.

AP/I: Protocol Additional to the Geneva Conventions of 12 August 1949, and Relating to the Protection of Victims of International Armed Conflicts (Protocol I).

AP/II: Protocol Additional to the Geneva Conventions of 12 August 1949, and Relating to the Protection of Victims of Non-International Armed Conflicts (Protocol II).

AP/III: Protocol Additional to the Geneva Conventions of 12 August 1949, and Relating to the Adoption of an Additional Distinctive Emblem (Protocol III).

Art(s).: Article(s).

AWACS: Airborne Warning and Control System.

B

BWC: UN Convention on the Prohibition of the Development, Production and Stockpiling of Bacteriological (Biological) and Toxin Weapons and on their Destruction.

C

Canadian Joint Doctrine Manual: Law of Armed Conflict at the Operational and Tactical Levels, Joint Doctrine Manual Issued on Authority of the Chief of Defence Staff.[820]

CCW: UN Convention on Prohibitions or Restrictions on the Use of Certain Conventional Weapons Which May be Deemed to be Excessively Injurious or to Have Indiscriminate Effects.

CNA: Computer Network Attack.

[820] B-GJ-005-104/FP-021, 2001.

Commentary on the HRAW: Commission of Jurists to Consider and Report Upon the Review of the Rules of Warfare, General Report.[821]

Commentary on the SRM/ACS: Explanation of the San Remo Manual on International Law Applicable to Armed Conflicts at Sea.[822]

CWC: Paris Convention on the Prohibition of the Development, Production, Stockpiling and Use of Chemical Weapons and on Their Destruction.

D

DoD Dictionary of Military Terms: Department of Defense Dictionary of Military and Associated Terms.[823]

E

EEZ: Exclusive Economic Zone.

ENMOD Convention: UN Convention on the Prohibition of Military or Any Other Hostile Use of Environmental Modification Techniques.

EW: Electronic Warfare.

F

fn.: footnote.

G

1925 Gas Protocol: Geneva Protocol for the Prohibition of the Use in War of Asphyxiating, Poisonous or Other Gases, and of Bacteriological Methods of Warfare.

GC/I: Geneva Convention for the Amelioration of the Condition of the Wounded and Sick in Armed Forces in the Field.

GC/II: Geneva Convention for the Amelioration of the Condition of Wounded, Sick and Shipwrecked Members of Armed Forces at Sea.

GC/III: Geneva Convention relative to the Treatment of Prisoners of War.

GC/IV: Geneva Convention relative to the Protection of Civilian Persons in Time of War.

1949 Geneva Conventions: GC/I, GC/II, GC/III and GC/IV

821 1923, reprinted in 32 American Journal of International Law Supplement 1 (1938).

822 Prepared by International Lawyers and Naval Experts convened by the International Institute of Humanitarian Law, Adopted in June 1994, Cambridge University Press (1995).

823 Joint Publication 1-02, 2001 (As amended through 31 October 2009).

German ZDv: Joint Services Regulations (ZDv) 15/2, German Bundeswehr, 1992.

H

1899 Hague Convention (II): Hague Convention (II) with Respect to the Laws and Customs of War on Land.

1899 Hague Regulations: Hague Regulations respecting the Laws and Customs of War on Land, Annex to 1899 Hague Convention (II).

1899 Hague Declaration (IV, 2): Hague Declaration (IV, 2) Concerning Asphyxiating Gases.

1907 Hague Convention (IV): Hague Convention (IV) Respecting the Laws and Customs of War on Land.

1907 Hague Regulations: Hague Regulations respecting the Laws and Customs of War on Land, Annex to 1907 Hague Convention (IV).

1907 Hague Convention (V): Hague Convention (V) Respecting the Rights and Duties of Neutral Powers and Persons in Case of War on Land.

1907 Hague Convention (VIII): Hague Convention (VIII) relative to the Laying of Automatic Submarine Contact Mines.

1907 Hague Convention (XIII): Hague Convention (XIII) Concerning the Rights and Duties of Neutral Powers in Naval War.

1954 Hague Convention: Hague Convention for the Protection of Cultural Property in the Event of Armed Conflict.

HRAW: Hague Rules of Air Warfare, Drafted by a Commission of Jurists at The Hague, 1923.[824]

I

ICAO: International Civil Aviation Organization.

ICC: International Criminal Court.

ICJ: International Court of Justice.

ICJ Nuclear Weapons Advisory Opinion: International Court of Justice, Advisory Opinion, Legality of the Threat or Use of Nuclear Weapons.[825]

ICRC: International Committee of the Red Cross.

ICRC Commentary on AP/I: Commentary on the Additional Protocols of 8 June 1977 to the Geneva Conventions of 12 August 1949.[826]

ICRC Customary IHL Study: Customary International Humanitarian Law, Volume I: Rules.[827]

824 *Laws of Armed Conflicts* 315.
825 [1996] ICJ Reports 226.
826 Y. Sandoz, Ch. Swinarski and B. Zimmermann (eds.), ICRC, Martinus Nijhoff (1987).
827 ICRC, J-M Henckaerts and L. Doswald-Beck, Cambridge University Press (2005).

ICRC Interpretive Guidance: Interpretive Guidance on the Notion of Direct Participation in Hostilities under International Humanitarian Law.[828]
ICTY: International Criminal Tribunal for the former Yugoslavia.
ICTR: International Criminal Tribunal for Rwanda.
IFF: Identification, Friend or Foe.
***ILM*:** International Legal Materials.

L

***Laws of Armed Conflicts*:** The Laws of Armed Conflicts: A Collection of Conventions, Resolutions and Other Documents.[829]
1909 London Declaration: London Declaration Concerning the Laws of Naval War.
***LNTS*:** League of Nations Treaty Series.

N

NATO: North Atlantic Treaty Organization.
NATO Glossary of Terms and Definitions: NATO Glossary of Terms and Definitions.[830]
NOTAM: Notice to Airmen.
NWP: The Commander's Handbook on the Law of Naval Operations.[831]

O

Optional Protocol to the UN Safety Convention: Optional Protocol to the Convention on the Safety of United Nations and Associated Personnel.
1997 Ottawa Convention: Ottawa Convention on the Prohibition of the Use, Stockpiling,Production and Transfer of Anti-Personnel Mines and on Their Destruction.

P

Para(s).: paragraph(s).
1856 Paris Declaration: Declaration Respecting Maritime Law.
POW: Prisoner of War.

[828] ICRC (2009).
[829] D. Schindler and J. Toman (eds.), 4th edition, Martinus Nijhoff (2004).
[830] Listing terms of military significance and their definitions for use in NATO, North Atlantic Treaty Organization NATO Standardization Agency (NSA), AAP-6 (2009).
[831] NWP 1–14M, U.S. Navy – U.S. Marine Corps – U.S. Coast Guard, July 2007 Edition.

1980 Protocol I to the CCW: Protocol on Non-Detectable Fragments.
1980 Protocol III to the CCW: Protocol on Prohibitions or Restrictions on the Use of Incendiary Weapons.
2003 Protocol V to the CCW: Protocol on Explosive Remnants of War.

R

Roerich Pact: Washington Treaty on the Protection of Artistic and Scientific Institutions and Historic Monuments.
Rome Statute of the ICC: Rome Statute of the International Criminal Court.

S

SAR: Search and Rescue
SEAD: Suppression of Enemy Air Defences.
Second Protocol to the 1954 Hague Convention: Second Protocol to the Hague Convention of 1954 for the Protection of Cultural Property in the Event of Armed Conflict.
SRM/ACS: San Remo Manual on International Law Applicable to Armed Conflicts at Sea.[832]
SRM NIAC Manual: Manual on the Law of Non-International Armed Conflict: With Commentary.[833]
1868 St. Petersburg Declaration: Declaration Renouncing the Use, in Time of War, of Explosive Projectiles Under 400 Grammes Weight.

U

UAV: Unmanned Aerial Vehicle.
UCAV: Unmanned Combat Aerial Vehicle.
UK: United Kingdom.
UK Manual: The Manual of the Law of Armed Conflict. UK Ministry Of Defence.[834]
UN: United Nations.
UN Charter: Charter of the United Nations.
US: United States.
UNCLOS: United Nations Convention on the Law of the Sea.

[832] Prepared by International Lawyers and Naval Experts convened by the International Institute of Humanitarian Law, Cambridge University Press (1995).
[833] International Institute of Humanitarian Law, M. Schmitt, C. Garraway and Y. Dinstein, 36 Israel Yearbook on Human Rights, Special Supplement (2006).
[834] Oxford University Press (2004).

UN Safety Convention: Convention on the Safety of United Nations and Associated Personnel.
UNTS: United Nations Treaty Series.

W

WWI: First World War.
WWII: Second World War.

INDEX

For EU product safety concerns, contact us at Calle de José Abascal, 56–1°, 28003 Madrid, Spain or eugpsr@cambridge.org.

www.ingramcontent.com/pod-product-compliance
Lightning Source LLC
LaVergne TN
LVHW020326220926
848484LV00001BB/243
9781107034198